Fodor's 90 Germany

Fodor's Travel Publications, Inc.
New York and London

ISBN 0-679-01769-0

Fodor's Germany

Editor: Thomas Cussans
Area Editors: Helmut Koenig, Robert Tilley
Editorial Contributors: Charles Barr, Hampton Binden, Sheila Brownlee, Hannah Clements, Michael Cresswell, Birgit Gericke, George Hamilton, Andrew Heritage, Liz Hulme, Anita Peltonen, Tony Peisley, Isabelle Pöhlman, Susan Williams
Art Director: Fabrizio La Rocca
Cartographer: David Lindroth
Illustrator: Karl Tanner
Cover Photograph: Owen Franken

Design: Vignelli Associates

Special Sales

Fodor's Travel Publications are available at special discounts for bulk purchases (100 copies or more) for sales promotions or premiums. Special editions, including personalized covers, excerpts of existing guides, and corporate imprints, can be created in large quantities for special needs. For more information write to Special Marketing, Fodor's Travel Publications, 201 East 50th Street, New York, NY 10022. Inquiries from the United Kingdom should be sent to Fodor's Travel Publications, 30–32 Bedford Square, London WC1B 3SG.

MANUFACTURED IN THE UNITED STATES OF AMERICA
10 9 8 7 6 5 4 3

Contents

Maps

Foreword

This is an exciting time for Fodor's, as we continue our ambitious program to rewrite, reformat, and redesign all 140 of our guides. Here are just a few of the new features:

★ Brand-new computer-generated maps locating all the top attractions, hotels, restaurants, and shops

★ A unique system of numbers and legends to help readers move effortlessly between text and maps

★ A new star rating system for hotels and restaurants

★ Restaurant reviews by major food critics around the world

★ Stamped, self-addressed postcards, bound into every guide, give readers a chance to help evaluate hotels and restaurants

★ Complete page redesign for instant retrieval of information

★ ITINERARIES—The experts help you decide where to go

★ FODOR'S CHOICE—Our favorite museums, beaches, cafés, romantic hideaways, festivals, and more

★ HIGHLIGHTS—An insider's look at the most important developments in tourism during the past year

★ TIME OUT—The best and most convenient lunch stops along exploring routes

★ A Traveler's Menu and Phrase Guide in all major foreign guides

★ Exclusive background essays create a powerful portrait of each destination

★ A mini-journal for travelers to keep track of their own itineraries and addresses

We would like to express our gratitude to Robert Tilley for his patience, enthusiasm, and endless hard work in preparing this new edition.

While every care has been taken to assure the accuracy of the information in this guide, the passage of time will always bring change, and consequently, the publisher cannot accept responsibility for errors that may occur.

All prices and opening times quoted here are based on information available to us at press time. Hours and admission fees may change, however, and the prudent traveler will avoid inconvenience by calling ahead.

Fodor's wants to hear about your travel experiences, both pleasant and unpleasant. When a hotel or restaurant fails to live up to its billing, let us know and we will investigate the complaint and revise our entries where the facts warrant it.

Send your letters to the editors of Fodor's Travel Publications, 201 East 50th Street, New York, NY 10022.

Highlights '90 and Fodor's Choice

Highlights '90

With the possible exception of rail fares, prices in West Germany look set to remain among the most stable in Europe during 1990. The Federal government has a vested interest in keeping inflation below 3%—the lowest in Europe—in a national election year.

The deutschemark should continue to remain strong, so **exchange rates** against major currencies such as the dollar and the British pound are not expected to change to the benefit of overseas visitors. West Germany enjoys one of the highest standards of living in Europe—and one of the costliest. But these costs vary considerably between city and countryside and from region to region. For example, in Bavaria, which has become the playground for Germans who are not vacationing abroad, there is a big gulf in costs between the "poor" north and the more affluent southern half of the state. A meal for two with beer in a pleasant Munich pub/restaurant will cost about DM50 (US$26), while in the picturesque and historic northern Bavarian towns of Bamberg and Bayreuth the same meal might cost DM30 (US$16).

Increasing competition will keep hotel costs in line. Several hotel chains are expanding their operations in 1991, with new luxury hotels opening in West Berlin, Hamburg, Munich, and Frankfurt. The "Castle" hotel group, "Gast im Schloss," has three spectacular additions listed for 1990. Two of them—**Burg Hohenstein** in the Tanus mountains and **Burg Staufenberg**, between Marburg and Giessen—are beautifully restored and modernized medieval castles; the third, **Schloss Wolfsbrunnen**, near the East German border, is a small fin-de-siècle palace.

Rail travel costs will rise, but only marginally, in 1990. The financially strapped German federal railway system, the Deutsche Bundesbohn, is racing into the '90s with an ultra high-speed service, the **ICE (Inter-City Express)**. The first two ICE services, between Hamburg and Munich, will cut travel time from eight hours to five hours, with trains that reach a speed of 150 miles per hour. Hourly services will connect to Hamburg, Frankfurt, Mannheim, Stuttgart, and Wurzburg. The new high-speed trains go into service in May 1990, with the Wurzburg service added in September.

German railways have something new for winter sports fans: **cross-country skis for hire** at more than 50 stations in Bavaria, the Black Forest, and other highland regions. It's an extension of the popular bikes-for-hire service offered by more than 200 railway stations. Travelers will be able virtually to step off the train and onto skis, for a tour along groomed trails that often begin and end right at the station entrance.

For the traveler in a hurry, a new enterprise in Munich is offering an airborne version of the highly successful hitch-hiking service, which acts as an agency between motorists and passengers seeking a lift. For a fee of DM25, the agency will put you in touch with a private-plane pilot heading in the direction you want to go. You pay the pilot 30 pfennigs a kilometer—not much more than a first-class rail ticket. The agency, the **Mitflugzentrale Robinson,** is run by a young woman pilot and has its booking office at St.-Wolfgang-Platz 9g, Munich 80 (tel. 089/4485175). The passenger-car hitch-hiking service, by the way, is based in most West German cities—just look up **Mitfahrzentrale** in the phone book and you're on your way. Don't hesitate if you're not fluent in German; the drivers registered with these agencies want company on the road, and if that includes an English-language lesson they regard it as a bonus.

The major cultural event of 1990 is the **Oberammergau Passion Play,** which is held every 10 years by the villagers of Oberammergau in fulfillment of an ancient vow to give thanks to God for sparing them from the ravages of the plague. Oberammergau today is plagued by nothing more harmful than tourist buses, which clog the alpine village's streets on most weekends and throughout the summer. If you don't like crowds, stay away from Oberammergau in 1990, particularly from May 21 to September 28, when the Passion Play is being performed. It's too late, anyway, to book a seat, as all 100 performances are sold out, although there is a long waiting list of those hoping for a cancellation. The Passion Play is seldom free of controversy, and as 1989 drew to a close trouble again loomed over the mountain village. The latest row centered on a daring break with tradition in the 1990 production. The producer dropped many veteran members of previous casts—recasting some in minor roles—but his most radical move was to cast a 31-year-old mother of two as the Virgin Mary. Local tradition has always demanded that the part be taken by an unmarried woman under the age of 30 (young women have even been known to postpone their weddings in order to qualify for an audition). There have been suggestions that this flap could threaten the 1990 production, but we've heard such talk before, and the odds are that all will be well by showtime.

Munich is again the scene for one of Germany's most exciting festivals of modern music and musical theater, the **Munich Biennale.** Held for the first time in 1988, it was an instant success, introducing some outstanding new works by young and little-known composers and writers. In Hamburg, a new city theater, the **Neue Flora** (on the corner of Stresemannstrasse and Alsenstrasse) will be opening in 1990, with a production of *Phantom of the Opera*.

Visitors to Frankfurt will find a new cultural center, the **Kunstlerhaus Mouson-Turmhoused,** on the eight floors of a former soap-and-perfume factory. In surroundings still redolent of sandalwood and spice, you'll find everything from art galleries to studio theaters.

A series of **classical music concerts** in picturesque settings will take place during July and August in and around Rheingau, near Wiesbaden west of Frankfurt, most notably at the Eberbach monastery, where scenes from the film *The Name of the Rose* were shot.

The trend of the moment in West Germany is **tennis.** Since Boris Becker and Steffi Graf became world champions almost everybody has acquired a tennis racket. Courts have sprung up everywhere and there's been a boom in tennis clothes. That most English of games, **cricket,** has also caught on here in a big way. It's gotten serious enough that a German national cricket federation has been formed to promote the game.

Try not to stare if you should come upon a group of **nude sunbathers** in a park or beside a river, even in the heart of a city. This German penchant for baring the body to nature's elements is increasingly popular, and most Germans think nothing of it.

Talk of one Germany—the **re-unification** of East and West—is more and more on the political agenda, particularly in the wake of the massive flight of thousands of young East Germans to the west via Hungary in late summer 1989. The "Germany Question," along with the economy and the government's performance, is expected to figure in the 1990 federal elections. It's a sensitive topic, but no longer taboo, and in conversation with locals the subject may well turn to re-unification.

Another big issue is the **environment.** Closer to the German heart even than Becker and Graf are the country's forests, many of which are sick from pollution. This concern for the environment is seen not only in the growing political influence of the Green party, but in everyday public tidiness, as well. Though fast-food outlets have become popular in West Germany, the litter fallout from them is most unwelcome. The courteous visitor will take care that litter lands in a trash can, of which there are many.

Fodor's Choice

No two people will agree on what makes a perfect vacation, but it's fun and helpful to know what others think. We hope you'll have a chance to experience some of Fodor's Choices during your visit to Germany. For detailed information about each entry, refer to the appropriate chapters of the book.

Dining

Aubergine, Munich *(Very Expensive)*

Bado La Poêle d'Or, Köln *(Very Expensive)*

Bareiss, Baiersbronn *(Very Expensive)*

Landhaus Scherer, Hamburg *(Very Expensive)*

Peter Lembcke, Hamburg *(Expensive)*

Säumerhof, Grafenau *(Expensive)*

Stahlbad, Baden-Baden *(Expensive)*

Nürnberger Bratwurstglöckl, Munich *(Moderate)*

Perkeo, Heidelberg *(Moderate)*

Ratskeller, Bremen *(Moderate)*

Ratsweinkeller, Hamburg *(Moderate)*

Romantik-Restaurant zum Ritter St. Georg, Heidelberg *(Moderate)*

Lodging

Bayerischer Hof, Munich *(Very Expensive)*

Brenner's Parkhotel, Baden-Baden *(Very Expensive)*

Bristol-Hotel Kempinski, West Berlin *(Very Expensive)*

Dom Hotel, Köln *(Very Expensive)*

Gravenbruch-Kempinski, Frankfurt *(Very Expensive)*

Steigenberger Insel-Hotel, Konstanz *(Very Expensive)*

Vier Jahreszeiten, Hamburg *(Very Expensive)*

Alte Thorsehenke, Cochem *(Expensive)*

Eisenhut, Rothenburg ob der Tauber *(Expensive)*

Castles

Altes Schloss, Meersburg

Burg Eltz, Mosel

Burg Katz, Rhine

Kaiserburg, Nürnberg

Kaiserpfalz, Bad Wimpfen

Heidelberg Schloss

Neuschwanstein, Füssen

Schloss Guttenberg, Neckar

Museums

Ägyptisches Museum, West Berlin

Alte Pinakothek, Munich

Deutsches Museum, Munich

Deutsches Schiffahrtsmuseum, Bremerhaven

Domschatzkammer, Aachen

Gemäldegalerie, West Berlin

Gemäldegalerie Alte Meister, Dresden

Kunsthalle, Hamburg

Museum der Bildenden Kunste, Leipzig

Römisch-Germanisches Museum, Köln

Churches

Asamkirche, Munich

Frauenkirche, Munich

Freiburg, Münster

Kölner Dom, Köln

Kaiserdom, Aachen

Kaiserdom, Speyer

Trier Dom, Trier

Vierzehnheiligen, Franconia

Wieskirce, Upper Bavaria

Towns Where Time Stands Still

Bad Wimpfen

Bernkastel-Kues

Freinsheim

Goslar

Hameln

Lindau

Passau

Rothenburg-ob-der-Tauber

Memorable Sights

Baden-Baden's casino

The Berlin Wall

The confluence of the Inn and Danube rivers at Passau

Hamburg's Reeperbahn

Mardi Gras in Mainz

Munich's Oktoberfest

Opera night in Bayreuth

The Rhine in Flames fireworks

Scharlachrennen Festival, Nördlingen

Wilhelmshöhe, Kassel

Unforgettable Excursions

A boat ride on Bavaria's Königsee

A bus ride into East Berlin

A Hamburg harbor cruise at night

A raft ride on the Isar River from Wolfratshausen to Munich

A Rhine cruise

A round-trip ride from Freiburg on the Black Forest railway

To the summit of Germany's highest mountain, the Zugspitze, by cable car

. . . and to the depths of the country's largest salt mine, at Berchtesgaden

A torch-lit sleigh ride through the Bavarian snow and a nighttime toboggan ride down an Alpine slope

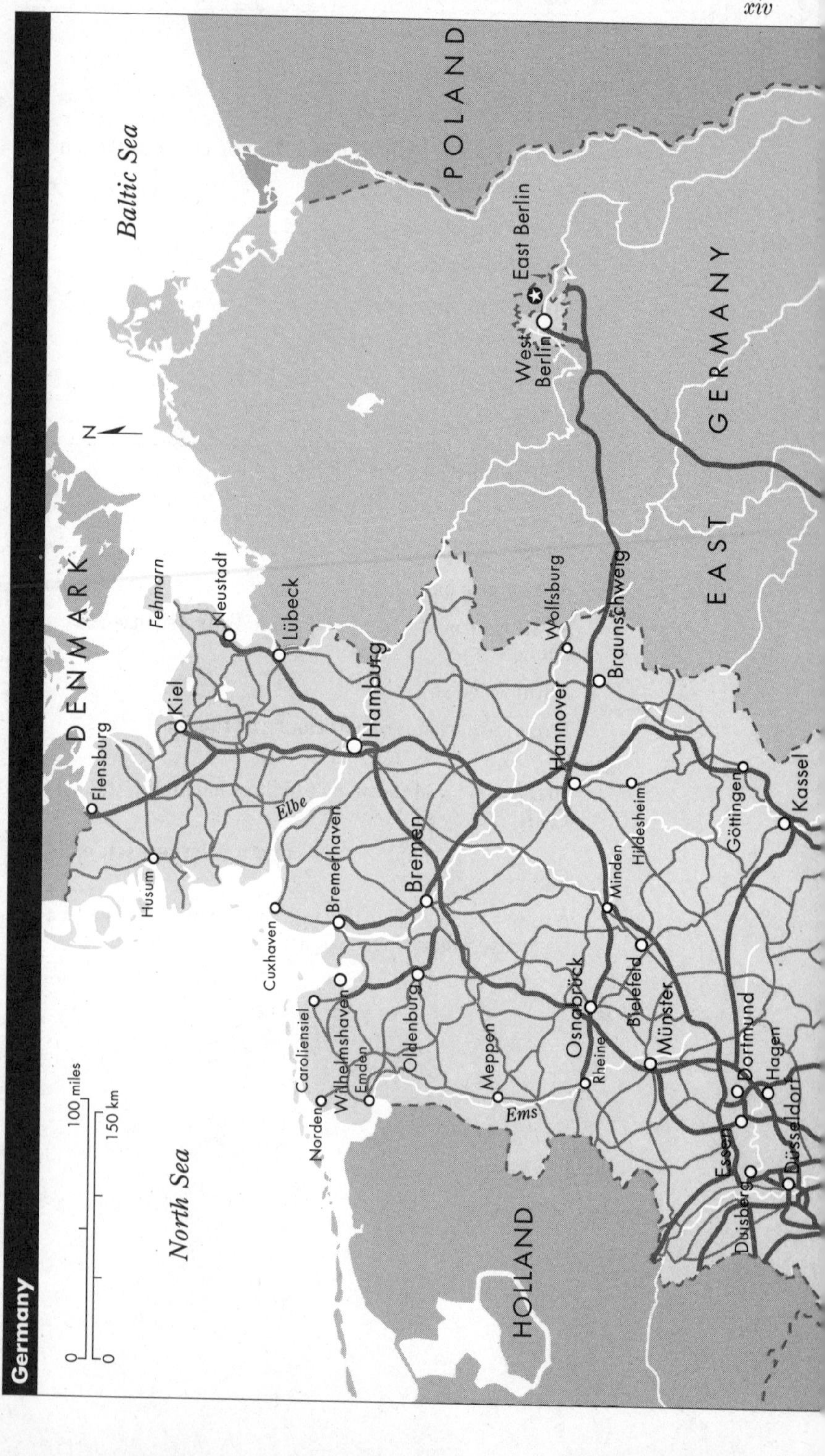
Germany
0 100 miles
0 150 km
N
Baltic Sea
North Sea
DENMARK
POLAND
EAST GERMANY
HOLLAND
Fehmarn
Elbe
Ems
Flensburg
Kiel
Neustadt
Lübeck
Husum
Hamburg
Cuxhaven
Bremerhaven
Bremen
Carolinensiel
Wilhelmshaven
Norden
Emden
Oldenburg
Meppen
Wolfsburg
Braunschweig
Hannover
Hildesheim
Göttingen
Kassel
Minden
Bielefeld
Osnabrück
Rheine
Münster
Dortmund
Hagen
Essen
Düsseldorf
Duisburg
West Berlin
East Berlin

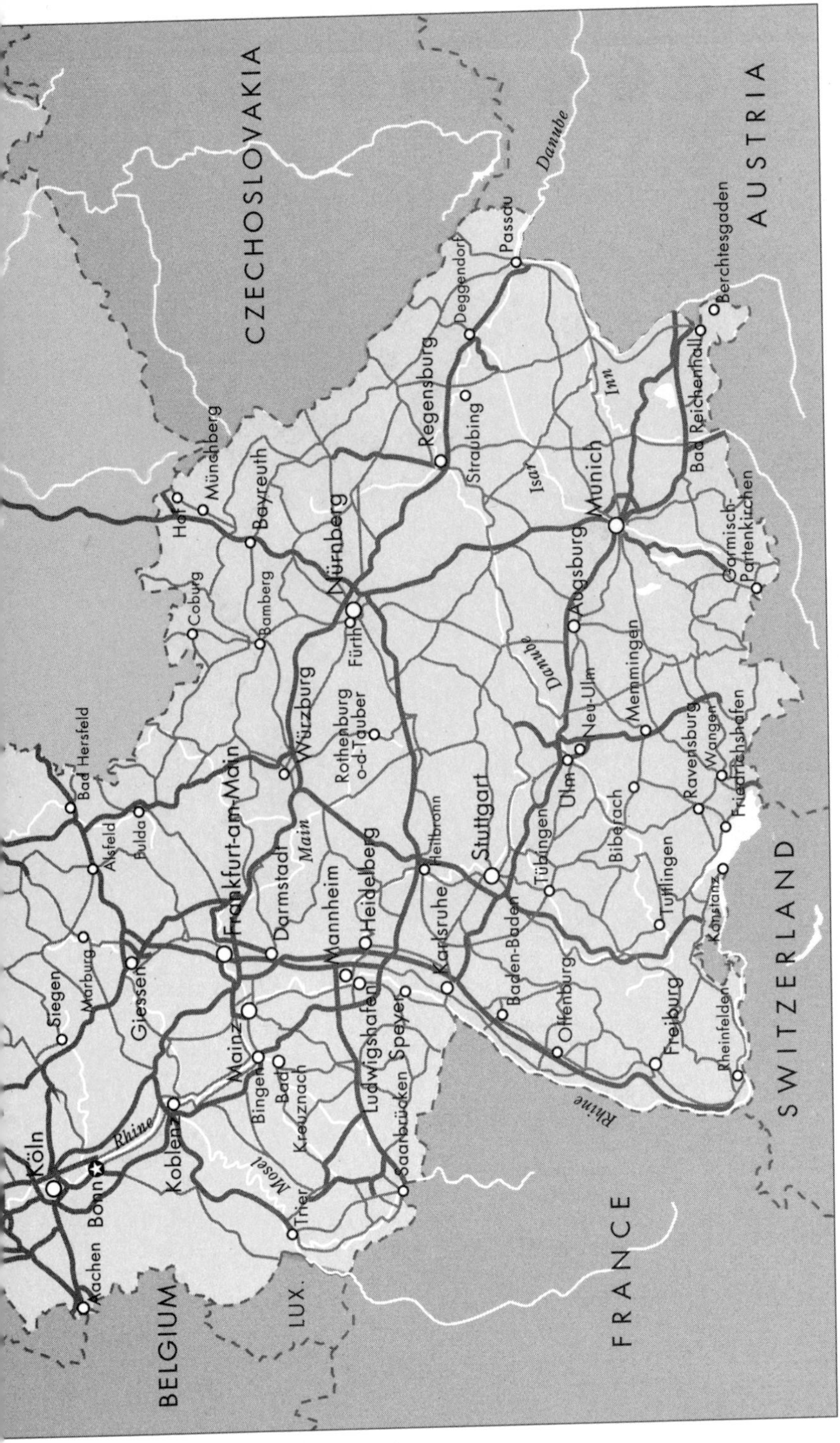
CZECHOSLOVAKIA
AUSTRIA
SWITZERLAND
FRANCE
BELGIUM
LUX.
Danube
Rhine
Main
Mosel
Isar
Inn
Passau
Deggendorf
Berchtesgaden
Bad Reichenhall
Regensburg
Straubing
Münchberg
Hof
Bayreuth
Munich
Garmisch-Partenkirchen
Nürnberg
Fürth
Coburg
Bamberg
Augsburg
Memmingen
Neu-Ulm
Ulm
Würzburg
Rothenburg o-d-Tauber
Bad Hersfeld
Alsfeld
Fulda
Frankfurt-am-Main
Darmstadt
Mannheim
Heidelberg
Heilbronn
Stuttgart
Tübingen
Biberach
Ravensburg
Wangen
Friedrichshafen
Tuttlingen
Konstanz
Karlsruhe
Baden-Baden
Offenburg
Freiburg
Rheinfelden
Marburg
Siegen
Giessen
Mainz
Bingen
Bad Kreuznach
Ludwigshafen
Speyer
Saarbrücken
Koblenz
Trier
Köln
Bonn
Aachen

World Time Zones

Numbers below vertical bands relate each zone to Greenwich Mean Time (0 hrs.).
Local times may differ, as indicated by lightface numbers on the map.

Algiers, **29**
Anchorage, **3**
Athens, **41**
Auckland, **1**
Baghdad, **46**
Bangkok, **50**
Beijing, **54**

Berlin, **34**
Bogotá, **19**
Budapest, **37**
Buenos Aires, **24**
Caracas, **22**
Chicago, **9**
Copenhagen, **33**
Dallas, **10**

Delhi, **48**
Denver, **8**
Djakarta, **53**
Dublin, **26**
Edmonton, **7**
Hong Kong, **56**
Honolulu, **2**

Istanbul, **40**
Jerusalem, **42**
Johannesburg, **44**
Lima, **20**
Lisbon, **28**
London (Greenwich), **27**
Los Angeles, **6**
Madrid, **38**
Manila, **57**

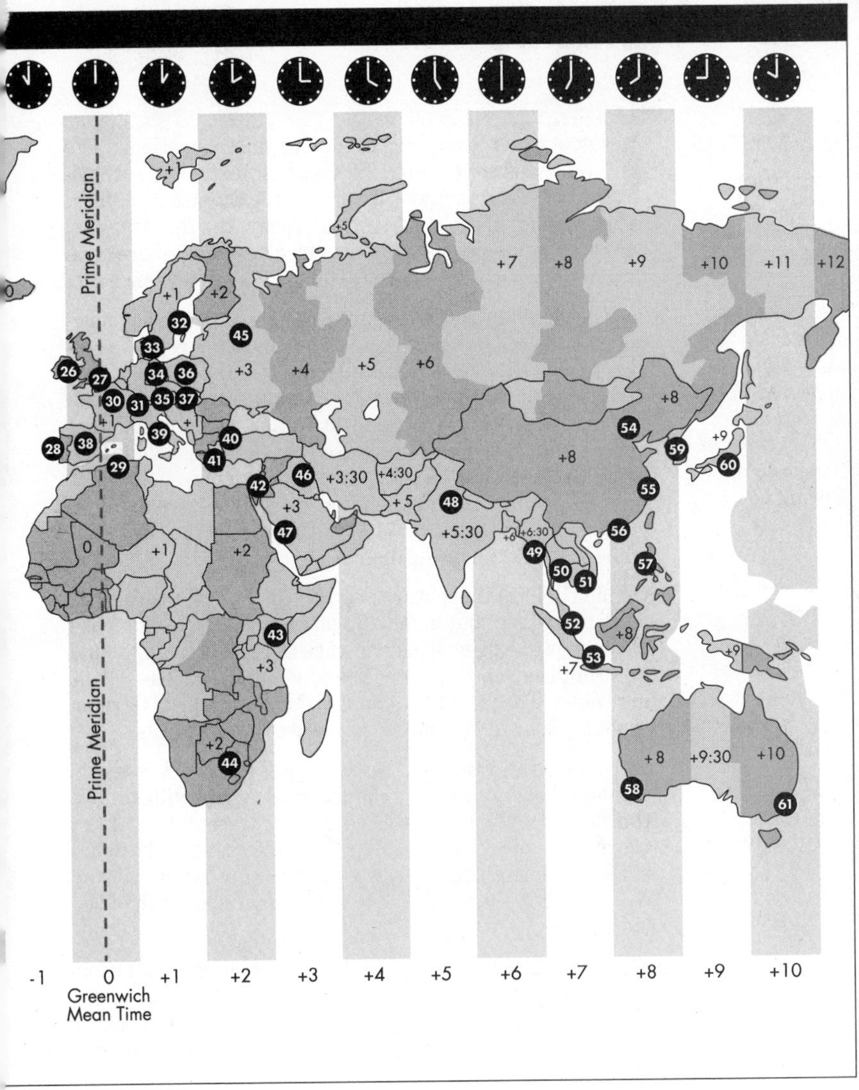

Mecca, **47**
Mexico City, **12**
Miami, **18**
Montreal, **15**
Moscow, **45**
Nairobi, **43**
New Orleans, **11**
New York City, **16**
Ottawa, **14**
Paris, **30**
Perth, **58**
Reykjavík, **25**
Rio de Janeiro, **23**
Rome, **39**
Saigon, **51**
San Francisco, **5**
Santiago, **21**
Seoul, **59**
Shanghai, **55**
Singapore, **52**
Stockholm, **32**
Sydney, **61**
Tokyo, **60**
Toronto, **13**
Vancouver, **4**
Vienna, **35**
Warsaw, **36**
Washington, DC, **17**
Yangon, **49**
Zürich, **31**

Introduction

by Robert Tilley

A longtime resident of Munich, British-born Robert Tilley is a journalist and broadcaster whose work has appeared in numerous publications in Germany and Britain.

Let's sweep away some popular misconceptions: The Germans are not all militaristic, inflexible, or authoritarian, and many of them do have a sense of humor. Why else should the West German Army, the *Bundeswehr*, have recruiting problems? And why else is the cabaret tradition so strong, and political and social satire so trenchant?

Two world wars and an accumulation of superficial comic-book observations of the German people have created a catalogue of prejudices as fictitious as any of the Grimm fairy-tales. An opinion poll recently commissioned in Britain by the mass-circulation German magazine *Stern* found that only 42% of those questioned liked the Germans, while 20% expressed active dislike. The magazine organized a similar poll in the United States, where the results were more favorable for the Germans: 71% said they liked the Germans, while only 7% expressed dislike.

Opinion polls of this nature are often invidious, inaccurate, and misleading; and in moving instinctively to the defense of the maligned Germans one runs the risk of being found guilty of the same prejudices and generalizations—albeit in reverse. The fact of the matter is that the typical German is not typical, and cannot be reduced to stock clichés.

Of course, the beer-swilling Bavarian in *Lederhosen* and climbing boots can be seen in many an Alpine village, but the Berliner would disown him as a representative of the German people. Then, too, the elegant Prussian who dominates the Berlin street scene would be regarded as an envoy from another nation when abroad in any town south of the Main River.

This north-south division is almost as perceptible as the fortified frontier that divides the country into two ideological halves. The rivalry between the English and the Scots is schoolboy stuff compared to the hearty animosity separating the Bavarians and the "Prussians."

Like the English-Scottish rivalry, it is rooted in a shared history scarred by internecine quarrels, although the most traumatic event occurred when Prussians and Bavarians were united in one of their many alliances against Austria. The Prussian commander reputedly manned the front line with untrained Bavarian peasants, many armed only with pitchforks. Thousands are said to have been slaughtered. "It was a massacre," sighed my Munich taxi driver, tracing the roots of Prussian-Bavarian hostility to this one battle.

Certainly, there are other causes, also rooted in history. The Bavarians are proud that their royal dynasty—the Wittelsbachs—is older than the Prussian house of Hohenzollern and, moreover, actually outlasted it. The fact that two of Bavaria's latter-day rulers were insane is smilingly dismissed as a slight deviation in the Wittelsbach line. Indeed, the much celebrated insanity of young King Ludwig II is welcomed as *Gluck im Ungluck* (a prevalent German expression meaning "Fortune in misfortune"), for the eccentric king built a collection of castles that bankrupted the royal purse but that now reap large sums of money in tourist revenues. Similarly, Ludwig's munificent patronage of Wagner cost the Bavarians dearly in terms of hard cash—but what an investment!

But there are other more visible differences that distinguish the Bavarian from his fellow German to the north or, for that matter, the Berliner from the Rhinelander, and both of these from the Saarlander. You've only got to join them at table to sort out one from another. This applies both to the food they eat and—above all—to their liquid refreshment.

The Berliner really does drink, and apparently enjoys, beer sweetened with fruit juice, and the Bavarian really does quaff what he calls his "hop-juice" from oversize, liter mugs. Each regards the drinking habits of the other with amusement and some distaste. The Rhinelander, in contrast, is the country's wine connoisseur, and the humblest Rhineland home often hides a cellar full of the finest vintages. At the modest sitting-room table of a Saarland coal miner's home, I've been served the rarest of *Trockenbeerenauslese* wines, taken from a rack stacked with bottles bearing labels that read like a guide to the best wines of Germany.

But fine as Germany's wine indisputably is, beer is the country's drink and its emblem. Germany has more breweries—1,300—than the rest of Western Europe put together, and the tiniest village is often dominated by a massive brewery producing a beer that is world-class but consumed only by a small circle of lucky initiates who happen to live there. An English colleague of mine spends blissful vacations touring the country breweries of Bavaria on a bicycle. "I won't live long enough to sample them all," he says, recommending his tour to anyone who wants to get to know Germany and the Germans at close hand; which, in this case, means at eye-level over the foaming rim of a full beer glass.

This is the time to put to rest another misconception. The Germans are not the world's greatest beer drinkers. In Europe alone they lag behind the Belgians and the Czechoslovaks, and in fact they consume less beer than coffee. But beer nonetheless occupies a central role in German popular mythology and culture, and, in Bavaria at any rate, it dominates not only social life but working life, too. Crates of beer arrive simultaneously with the bricks at any building site. The employees at my own place of work accumulate enough empty beer bottles to finance a wild annual Christmas party. Doctors prescribe it for hospital patients, Augustinian monks supplement their Lenten diet with it (Munich's *Augustiner* beer is one of Germany's finest), while the award for the best Bavarian brewer recently went to a retiring nun, who produces her excellent brew for her convent!

The beer is not only very good, it is pure, kept that way (in Bavaria at least) by a strict purity code established nearly five centuries ago by Duke William IV. How long the code will stand is questionable, for the Bavarians are fighting a rearguard action against Common Market bureaucrats who want to standardize German beer with that of other community countries. The rot has already set in, the Bavarians complain, with the replacement of wooden barrels by pressurized containers in the beer gardens and even in the hallowed pavilions of the Munich Oktoberfest. "Is nothing sacred?" sighed my neighbor at a table groaning with the burden of many liter mugs of beer, beneath the shade of a chestnut tree in one of Munich's innumerable beer gardens.

These beer gardens are the center of Bavarian life in the summer, which in a good year means the long, balmy span between Easter and the first cold snap of October. This is the time to visit Munich, when the velvety southern German nights draw families out, like moths to a candle, to the lantern-hung, throbbing beer gardens. Baskets bursting with home-baked delicacies are emptied onto rough wooden tables, jostling for room with liter mugs and glasses. Join one of these tables and your glass will still be half full by the time you are drawn into the magic circle and invited to share a *Leberkäs* (spicy meat loaf) or to try a slice of pungent, white radish. This is the Bavarian at home; there's no need to court an invitation to his house.

The Bavarians, of course, have no monopoly on outdoor delights like these. In Frankfurt, on off-duty summer nights, the city's businessmen can be found in the cider pubs of Sachsenhausen; in Berlin, the pavement cafés are an extension of the German living-room; while along the Rhine, the arrival of the first new wine after the grape harvest is party time for all.

It's said that the German takes even his pleasures seriously, and the truth of that observation is clear to anyone who watches the people at play. The loving care and attention with which the picnic basket is packed for the beer garden, the studied jollity with which the beer mugs are lifted and clattered against each other in toasts to good health and long life, the frenetic but indefinably well-ordered abandon of Fasching revelers—all embody an unmistakable seriousness of purpose.

Fasching, the German carnival period that reaches its peak on Shrove Tuesday, the eve of Lent, starts with disciplined precision at the eleventh hour of the eleventh day of the eleventh month. You can't take your pleasures much more seriously than that!

The German carnival has not only a strict calendar but a rigid social framework within which almost anything goes. Staid old hotels open up their ballrooms, which for much of the rest of the year serve as conference centers. On the crowded dance floor, business tycoons dressed as tramps bump elbows with bus drivers passing as princes. At nearby tables, office staff on a night out drop conventions for a few hours, slip into the informal *Du* form of address, and call the boss by his first name. Slipping into the *Du* form, by the way, is by no means as straightforward as it sounds; it usually involves a formal ritual in which the two parties drink to each other while entwining their arms in a contortion well-nigh impossible to perform. Perhaps that's the point of the exercise. The night after the ball, the social code will have been restored, the *Du* form will have been put away for another year, and colleagues of many years standing will be addressing each other again as *Sie, Herr Schmidt* and *Sie, Frau Braun.*

Fasching, with its centuries of tradition, has its own mythology, and for the sake of the uninitiated at least one of these myths should be laid to rest. It used to be said that no German divorce court judge would recognize a dalliance during Fasching as grounds for ending a marriage, and everybody appears to have a neighbor who knows somebody who knows a married couple who go their separate ways at Fasching. The reality of Fasching is usually less uninhibited, and even the titillating promise of the masked balls of the Saarland and Rhineland, when otherwise retiring ladies are allowed to hunt down eligible men in a Leap Year–like splurge, compressed into the evening hours, rarely yields anything more exciting than a stolen kiss or two.

Before we are tempted to smile indulgently at the well-organized excesses of the German carnival, it should be pointed out that the Germans chuckle at the sublimated Fasching celebrated in the English-speaking world: Christmas. Although Germany gave the English-speaking world many yuletide traditions—not least the Christmas tree—it kept for itself its own style of celebrating Christmas.

Christmas in Germany sums up much of the German character and culture, but for the outsider it's difficult to partake of this rite because the Germans celebrate it within a closed circle of family and friends. Those lucky enough to break into this circle cannot fail to be impressed, even moved, by the subdued but perceptible joy that takes hold of a German family on Christmas Eve. German carols are indisputably among the richest and most beautiful of the genre, and to hear them picked out carefully on the keys of a sitting-room piano or sung in a snow-swathed town square is an experience that makes a visit to Germany at this time of year particularly worthwhile.

German folk songs of all kinds are a fascinating guide to what, for want of a better word, must be called the soul of the people. The close identification of the people with the beauty of their homeland is the chief characteristic of the German *Folkslied*, in which can be detected an atavistic fascination with the forests that cover a quarter of the land. The German forest, however, is dying, with one-third of its trees probably irreversibly sick, victims of industrial pollution. It's significant that this pernicious threat to the German forest has mobilized the people like no other postwar force and given Europe's only truly viable ecological political movement, the Greens, a big thrust forward. Walking in the dense, dark forests that wrap themselves around most German cities is a national pastime, which takes on added purpose in the fall when half the population, or so it seems, combs the woodlands for mushrooms. The identification and gathering of mushrooms and their preparation for the table is a very German pursuit, and a delectable one, too, given the fine mushroom recipes that abound in this part of the world.

The German—walking in the woods, hiking in the hills or over the wild, wide heaths—is a very outdoor person. Around 40% of all adult Germans claim to participate actively in one sport or another, and Germany's wide variety of climate and terrain ensures a wide choice. The German tackles his sport, whether it's the weekend round of golf or the daily bout in the gym, with a seriousness of purpose that takes both enjoyment and success for granted.

In summer, biking is the mass sport, for the health-conscious German has rediscovered the freedom of two wheels. Bicycles far outnumber cars in the major cities, although the preponderance of bicycles is not obvious, particularly during the rush hour. Yet official statistics show that 67% of West German homes own at least one bicycle, whereas only 65% have a car. Municipalities throughout the country have reacted to the trend by providing bike paths, a refinement of city planning that can hold unexpected perils for the uninitiated. Many of these paths are demarcations of, or extensions of, pedestrian pavements, and woe betide the unwary who strays from one to the other. The German motorist is notoriously aggressive, but he (or she) pales before the livid anger of a cyclist whose rights have been transgressed.

The Germans love to travel, but there is nothing more sacred to them than their homes. When the German moves into that most precious of possessions, his home, he moves in to stay. The country's housing market is very static, with little mobility. The German develops an attachment to his home that reaches far deeper than its foundations, possibly because he has not only struggled so hard to put together the required cash but has also lent a hand in its actual construction. There are villages and towns, particularly in industrial and relatively poorer regions of Germany, where the majority of homes have been built by their owners, with some help from friends and relatives. My wife carried bricks for her father at an age when she was scarcely able to carry her satchel to school. In those postwar years, when all Germany resembled a building site, the family home rose floor by floor, from the cellar up, with the family moving into each level as it was completed. The ties that now bind that modest house with those who built it are so strong that just the hint that one day it may come under the hammer in public auction is enough to kindle a family quarrel.

It is perhaps significant that the wood most often used by the German householder to furnish his home and panel its walls is oak, that most noble and lasting of forest products. If the real thing is too expensive, veneers and "oak-like" surfaces are acceptable.

Not surprisingly, the average German family is well served by the products of the country's advanced electrical and electronics industries (and those, of course, of Japan, Germany's main competitor in this field). Eight out of 10 West German kitchens have a washing machine and a refrigerator, and a quarter of them have a dishwasher, too. Only 4% of West German homes are without an electric vacuum cleaner, and 12% have no telephone. Color televisions are to be found in nearly three quarters of West German homes, while some 50% of West German families have now succumbed to VCRs.

The increasing accessibility of labor-saving devices in the home and the trend toward 35-hour work weeks are giving the Germans an unprecedented amount of leisure time. Art cinemas, theaters, concert halls, and opera houses consistently play to full houses. The German cinema, whose prewar preeminence was smashed by the Nazis, has enjoyed significant renaissance after the doldrums of the '50s and '60s. Festivals abound, and Munich is now challenging Berlin as the major German film festival city.

So there it is, Germany at work and play. No open-minded German—and I like to think he represents the majority of the nation—will deny the magnitude of the American contribution to postwar German reconstruction, particularly that channeled through the Marshall Plan. Yet no open-minded non-German should be blind to the role played by individual effort and the ingenuity that sprang from necessity. The Germans rebuilt their country as so many of them build their own homes—from the foundations up, with their own hands, and with a lot of help from their friends.

1 Essential Information

Before You Go

Government Tourist Offices

In the U.S. Contact the German National Tourist Office at 747 Third Avenue, New York, NY 10017, tel. 212/308–3300; or 444 South Flower Street, Suite 2230, Los Angeles, CA 90017, tel. 213/688–7332.

In Canada Box 417, 2 Fundy, Place Bonaventure, Montreal H5A 1B8, tel. 514/878–9885.

In the U.K. Nightingale House, 65 Curzon Street, London W1Y 7PE, England, tel. 01/495–3990.

Tour Groups

Package tours are typically the most economical way to visit Germany. Thanks to the volume of passengers tour operators handle, they can wring significantly lower prices out of airlines, hotels, and other travel suppliers than you can get on your own. There are, of course, potential drawbacks—you might find yourself dining with 20 people you don't particularly care for or being forced to march to the beat of someone else's drum. The key to a successful vacation is finding the tour that best suits your personal style, so ask a lot of questions. How many people are in the group? How much free time is there? Is there a special-interest tour I might find appealing?

The tours listed below should give you some idea of the wealth of programs available. Some are good introductory tours, some are more in-depth, others leave you to organize much of your own itinerary. For additional resources, contact your travel agent or the German National Tourist Office.

There are also some important practical considerations to investigate. Be sure to find out exactly what expenses are included (particularly tips, taxes, side trips, additional meals, and entertainment); ratings of all hotels on the itinerary and the facilities they offer; cancellation policies for both you and the tour operator; and, if you are traveling alone, what the single supplement is. Most tour operators request that bookings be made through a travel agent; there is no additional charge for doing so.

General-Interest Tours For a basic but good overview of the country, consider the 15-day "Best of Germany" from **Caravan Tours** (401 N. Michigan Ave., Chicago, IL 60601, tel. 312/321–9800 or 800/621–8338). Caravan's "Gothic Splendor" is a little less hectic, featuring a four-day Rhine cruise. Another good, comprehensive tour is "Romantic Germany" from **Globus Gateway** (150 S. Los Robles Ave., Suite 860, Pasadena, CA 91101, tel. 818/449–0919 or 800/556–5454). **Olson-Travelworld** (5855 Green Valley Circle, Culver City, CA 90230, tel. 213/670–7100 or 800/421–2255) offers "Fairytale Germany" (eight days) and "Storybook Germany" (17 days), both strong on old-world charm. "From Berlin to Leningrad" follows an intriguing itinerary that includes stops in both East and West Berlin and heads east through Poland to Moscow. All three Olson tours include private limousine transportation between your home and local airport. **American Express Vacations** (Box 5014, Atlanta, GA 30302, tel. 800/241–

1700 or 800/282–0800 in Georgia) is a veritable supermarket of tours. You name it, they've either got it packaged or can customize a package for you. The **Cortell Group** (770 Lexington Ave., New York, NY 10021, tel. 212/751–4200 or 800/223–6626) also offers a number of packages.

Special-Interest Tours

Art/Architecture **Esplanade Tours** (581 Boylston St., Boston, MA 02116, tel. 617/266–7465) offers several in-depth art and architecture tours led by noted lecturers.

Barge Cruising Drift in leisure and luxury down the Rhine, Lahn, and Mosel rivers (crossing into France) with **Floating Through Europe** (271 Madison Ave., New York, NY 10016, tel. 212/685–5600).

Health/Fitness **DER Tours** offers spa packages at five classic spas in the Black Forest and Bavaria.

Music **Dailey-Thorp Travel** (315 W. 57th St., New York, NY 10019, tel. 212/307–1555) offers deluxe opera and music tours, including "Musical Heartland of Europe." The tour features operas in both East and West Berlin, as well as performances in Dresden (East Germany) and Prague (Czechoslovakia). Itineraries vary, according to available performances.

Wine/Cuisine **Travel Concepts** (373 Commonwealth Ave., Suite 601, Boston, MA 02115–1815, tel. 617/266–8450) offers the "German Wine Academy." Usually based at Kloster Eberbach, a 12th-century monastery, the program includes tastings and visits to vineyards and wine cellars in seven of Germany's 11 wine-producing regions. **DER Tours** (11933 Wilshire Blvd., Los Angeles, CA 90025, tel. 213/479–4140 or 800/421–4343) offers a tour called "Romantic Rhine and Wine."

Package Deals for Independent Travelers

DER Tours (11933 Wilshire Blvd., Los Angeles, CA 90025, tel. 213/479–4140 or 800/421–4343) specializes in independent packages. Travelers can choose from a variety of air, transportation, and overnight options. The company also offers bed-and-breakfast packages.

Lufthansa German Airlines (750 Lexington Ave., New York, NY 10022, tel. 718/895–1277) offers air/hotel packages throughout the country, as does **American Express** (*see* above for address).

When to Go

The tourist season in Germany runs from May to late October, when the weather is at its best. In addition to many tourist events, this period has hundreds of folk festivals. The winter sports season in the Bavarian Alps runs from Christmas to mid-March. Prices everywhere are generally higher during the summer, so you may find considerable advantages in visiting out of season. Most resorts offer out-of-season (*Zwischensaison)* and "edge-of-season" *(Nebensaison)* rates, and tourist offices can provide lists of hotels offering special low-price inclusive weekly packages *(Pauschalangebote)*. Similarly, many winter resorts offer lower rates for the periods immediately before and after the high season (*Weisse Wochen*, or "white weeks"). The other advantage of out-of-season travel is that crowds are very much less in evidence. The disadvantages of visiting out of season, especially in winter, are that the weather, which is generally good in summer, is often cold and gloomy, and many tourist attractions, especially in rural areas, are closed.

Climate Germany's climate is temperate. Winters can be dull though never particularly cold, except in the Alps, the Harz region of Lower Saxony, and the higher regions of northern Franconia. Summers are usually sunny and warm, though be prepared for a few cloudy and wet days. The south is normally always a few degrees warmer than the north. As you get nearer the Alps, however, the summers get shorter, often not beginning until the end of May. Fall is sometimes spectacular in the south: warm and soothing. The only real exception to the above is the strikingly variable weather in southern Bavaria caused by the *Föhn,* an Alpine wind that gives rise to clear but oppressive conditions in summer and, in winter, can cause snow to disappear overnight.

The following are the average daily maximum and minimum temperatures for Munich.

Jan.	35F	1C	**May**	64F	18C	**Sept.**	67F	20C
	23	−5		45	7		48	9
Feb.	38F	3C	**June**	70F	21C	**Oct.**	56F	14C
	23	−5		51	11		40	4
Mar.	48F	9C	**July**	74F	23C	**Nov.**	44F	7C
	30	−1		55	13		33	0
Apr.	56F	14C	**Aug.**	73F	23C	**Dec.**	36F	2C
	38	3		54	12		26	−4

Festivals and Seasonal Events

Top seasonal events in Germany include carnival festivities throughout the country in January and February, spring festivals (nationwide), Munich's Opera Festival in July, the July Richard Wagner Festival in Bayreuth, horse-racing at Baden-Baden in August, wine festivals throughout Rhineland in September, the Oktoberfest in Munich, the Frankfurt Book Fair in October, and the December Christmas markets (nationwide). Contact the **German National Tourist Office** for exact dates and further information.

January **New Year International Ski Jumping,** among other winter-sports competitions, at Garmisch-Partenkirchen.

Fasching season: Carnival events, including proclamations of carnival princes, street fairs, parades, masked balls, and more, take place in Munich, Köln, Bonn, Düsseldorf, Offenburg, and around the Black Forest. Festivities reach their peak just prior to Ash Wednesday.

International Green Week Agricultural Fair is held in Berlin.

February **International Toy Fair,** with models, hobbies, and handicrafts, takes place in Nürnburg.

International Clock, Watch, Jewelry, Gems, and Silverware Trade Fair is held in Munich.

Frankfurt International Fair is a major consumer goods trade fair.

Black Forest Ski Marathon is a 60-kilometer ski race in Schonach-Hinterzarten.

March **Frankfurt Music Fair and Frankfurt Jazz Festival.**

Spring Fairs. In towns such as Münster, Hamburg, Nürnburg, Stuttgart, and Augsburg, festivities ring in the spring season.
Munich Fashion Week is a popular trade fair of the latest fashions.
International Easter Egg Fair takes place in Köln.

April **Stuttgart Jazz Festival.**
Munich Ballet Days.
German International Tennis Championships are held in Hamburg.
Mannheim May Fair is a traditional spring fair with flower floats and parades.
Walpurgis Festivals. Towns in the Harz Mountains celebrate this night before May Day.

May **International Mime Festival,** in Stuttgart, attracts some of the best in the world.
International May Festival, in Wiesbaden, means a month of artistic celebrations.
Folk Festivals. Hamburg, Frankfurt, and Deidesheim celebrate their folk heritage.
International Theater Week takes place in Erlangen.
Hamburg Summer is a whole season of festivals, concerts, plays, and exhibitions.
Folklore, Jazz, Rock, and Pop Music are featured on weekends of entertainment in Köln's Rheinpark.
Red Wine Festival is held at Assmannshausen in Rüdesheim.
Four Castles Illumination presents fireworks on the heights of Neckarsteinach.

Early June–Aug. **Frankfurt Summertime Festival** features outdoor activities throughout the city.
Franco-German Folk Festival is held in Berlin.
Castle Concerts and musical events are held in several Munich castles.
Mosel Wine Week celebrations take place in Cochem.
Castle Illuminations, with spectacular fireworks, are presented in Heidelberg.
Frankfurt Craft Week.
Weilburg Castle Concerts.
Kiel Week is an international sailing regatta in Kiel.
Würzburg Mozart Festival is held in several Würzburg locations.
Nymphenburg Summer Festival, with concerts at Nymphenburg Palace, is held in Munich.
Munich Film Festival.
International Theater Festival takes place in Freiburg.

July **Folk Festivals.** Outdoor festivities are held in Krov, Wald-Michelbach, Walsdhut-Tiengen, Würzburg, Geisenheim, Speyer, Lübeck, Karlsruhe, Düsseldorf, Oestrich-Winkel, and Paderhorn.
Opera Festival is Munich's major operatic affair.
German-American Folk Festival is Berlin's celebration of two cultures.
Richard Wagner Festival is a major musical event in Bayreuth.
Old Town Festival includes castle illuminations in Neckarsteinach.
Kulmbach Beer Festival.

August **Castle Festival** features open-air theater presentations at the castle in Heidelberg.

Partenkirchen Festival Week is held in Garmisch-Partenkirchen.
Stuttgart European Music Festival.
Wine Festivals break out throughout the Rhineland.
Grand Baden-Baden Week highlights international horse-racing at Iffezheim in Baden-Baden.

September **Oktoberfest** in Munich attracts millions of visitors from throughout Germany, Europe, and abroad.

October **Frankfurt Book Fair** is a famous annual literary event.
Berlin International Marathon.
Bremen Freimarkt is a centuries-old folk festival and procession in Bremen.

November **Six-Day Cycle Race** takes place in Munich.
St. Martin's Festival, with children's lantern processions, is celebrated throughout the Rhineland.
Antiques Fair is held in Berlin.

December **Christmas Markets** are held in Munich, Heidelberg, Hamburg, Nürnberg, Lübeck, Freiberg, Berlin, Essen, and elsewhere.

What to Pack

Pack light—luggage restrictions on international flights are tight. Airlines allow two pieces of check-in luggage and one carry-on piece, per passenger. No piece of check-in luggage can exceed 62 inches (length + width + height) or weigh more than 70 pounds. The carry-on luggage cannot exceed 45 inches (length + width + height) and must fit under the seat or in the overhead luggage compartment.

What you pack depends more on the time of year you visit than on any particular dress code. Winters can be bitterly cold, summers are warm but with days that suddenly turn cool and rainy. In the summer, take a warm jacket or heavy sweater for the Bavarian Alps, where the nights are chilly even during the height of summer.

For the cities, pack as you would for an American city: dressy outfits for formal restaurants and nightclubs, casual clothes elsewhere. Jeans are as popular in Germany as anywhere else, and are perfectly acceptable for sightseeing and informal dining. In the evening, men will probably feel more comfortable wearing a jacket and tie in more expensive restaurants. Many German women are extremely fashion conscious and wear stylish outfits to restaurants and the theater, especially in the larger cities. Women who don't want to join the fashion parade will be perfectly fine in street dresses or slacks outfits.

If you plan to swim in a pool, take a bathing cap. They're obligatory in Germany, for both men and women. For stays in budget hotels, take your own soap. Many do not provide soap or provide only one small bar. You will need an electrical adapter for your hair dryer or other small appliances. The current is 220 volts, 50 cycles.

Taking Money Abroad

Traveler's checks and major U.S. credit cards, particularly Visa, are accepted in large cities and resorts. In smaller towns and rural areas, you'll need cash. Many small restaurants and shops in the cities also tend to operate on a cash basis. You won't get as good an exchange rate at home as abroad, but it's wise to exchange a small amount of money into German Deutschmarks before you go to avoid lines at airport currency exchange booths. Most U.S. banks will exchange your money into Deutschmarks. If your local bank can't provide this service, you can exchange money through **Deak International.** To find the office nearest you, contact them at 630 Fifth Avenue, New York, NY 10011, tel. 212/635–0515.

For safety and convenience, it's always best to take traveler's checks. The most recognized traveler's checks are **American Express, Barclay's, Thomas Cook,** and those issued through such major commercial banks as **Citibank** and **Bank of America.** Some banks will issue the checks free to established customers, but most charge a 1% commission fee. Buy part of the traveler's checks in small denominations to cash toward the end of your trip. This will save your having to cash a large check and ending up with more foreign money than you need. You can also buy traveler's checks in Deutschmarks, a good idea if the dollar is falling and you want to lock into the current rate. Remember to take the addresses of offices where you can get refunds for lost or stolen traveler's checks.

The best places to change money are banks and bank-operated currency exchange booths in airports and railway stations. Hotels and privately run exchange firms will give you a significantly lower rate.

Getting Money from Home

There are at least three ways to get money from home: (1) Have it sent through a large commercial bank with a branch in the town where you're staying. The only drawback is that you must have an account with the bank; if not, you'll have to go through your own bank and the process will be slower and more expensive. (2) Have it sent through American Express. If you are a cardholder, you can cash a personal check or a counter check at an American Express office for up to $1,000; $200 will be in cash and $800 in traveler's checks. There is a 1% commission on the traveler's checks. American Express also offers a service called **American Express MoneyGram,** which allows you to receive up to $5,000 cash. It works this way: You call home and ask someone to go to an American Express office or an American Express MoneyGram agent located in a retail outlet, and fill out an American Express MoneyGram. It can be paid for with cash or any major credit card. The person making the payment is given a reference number and telephones you with that number. The American Express MoneyGram agent calls an 800 number and authorizes the transfer of funds to an American Express office or participating agency in the town where you're staying. In most cases, the money is available immediately on a 24-hour basis. You pick it up by showing identification and giving the reference number. Fees vary according to the amount of money sent. For $300, the fee is $22; for $5,000, $150. For the American Express MoneyGram location nearest your home and to find out where the service is available overseas, call tel. 800/543–4080. You do not have to be a cardholder to use this service. (3) Have it sent through **Western Union,** U.S. telephone number 800/988–4726. If you have a MasterCard or Visa, you can have money sent for any amount up to your credit limit. If not, have someone take cash or a certified cashier's check to a Western Union office. The money will be delivered in two business days to a bank in the city where you're staying. Fees vary with the amount of money sent. For $1,000 the fee is $67; for $500, $57.

German Currency

The units of currency in Germany are the Deutschmark (DM) and the pfennig (pf). The bills are DM 1,000, 500, 50, 20, and 10. Coins are DM 5, 2, and 1; and 50, 10, 5, 2, and 1 pf. At press time (spring '89) the exchange rate was about DM1.98 to the U.S. dollar, DM1.66 to the Canadian dollar, and DM3.96 to the pound sterling.

What It Will Cost

Germany has an admirably high standard of living—perhaps the highest in Europe—which inevitably makes it an expensive country to visit, particularly if you spend time in the cities. Many items—gas, food, hotels, and trains, to name but a few—are often more expensive than in the United States.

You can cut your budget by visiting less-known cities and towns, and avoiding summer and winter resorts. All along the Main and Neckar rivers, for example, you will find small towns as charming as, but significantly less expensive than, the likes of Rothenburg and Heidelberg; similarly, Westphalia offers atmosphere but lower prices than the fabled towns and cities of the Rhine. Wine lovers should explore the Palatinate instead of the classical Rhine-Mosel tour. In north Germany, the East Frisian islands from Emden eastward are less crowded than their more expensive sisters along the North Frisian coast. Ski enthusiasts would do well to investigate the advantages of the Harz and Eifel mountains, the Allgäu, with charming resorts like Kleinwalsertal, the mountains and forests of Swabia, the Black Forest, and most particularly, Oberpfalz and Bayerischer Wald in East Bavaria. Known as the stepchild of German tourism, East Bavaria offers excellent quality at bargain rates.

Passports and Visas

Americans All U.S. citizens require a passport to enter West Germany. Applications for a new passport must be made in person; renewals can be obtained in person or by mail (*see* below). First-time applicants should apply well in advance of their departure date to one of the 13 U.S. Passport Agency offices. In addition, local county courthouses, many state and probate courts, and some post offices accept passport applications. Necessary documents include: (1) a completed passport application (Form DSP-11); (2) proof of citizenship (birth certificate with raised seal or naturalization papers); (3) proof of identity (driver's license, employee ID card, or any other document with your photograph and signature); (4) two recent, identical, 2-inch-square photographs (black-and-white or color); (5) $42 application fee for a 10-year passport (those under 18 pay $27 for a five-year passport). Passports are mailed to you in about 10 working days.

To renew your passport by mail, you'll need a completed Form DSP-82, two recent, identical passport photographs, and a check or money order for $35.

A tourist/business visa is not required for U.S. citizens staying up to three months in West Germany. Check with the West German Embassy in Washington, DC, for longer stays. (For visas for East Germany, *see* Chapter 17, Excursions to East Germany.)

Canadians All Canadian citizens require a passport to enter West Germany. Send your completed application (available at any post office or passport office) to the **Bureau of Passports,** Complexe Guy Favreau, 200 Dorchester West, Montreal, Quebec H2Z 1X4. Include $25, two photographs, a guarantor, and proof of Canadian citizenship. Applications can also be made in person at the regional passport offices in Edmonton, Halifax, Montreal, Toronto, Vancouver, or Winnipeg. Passports are valid for five years and are nonrenewable.

Visas are not required by Canadian citizens to enter West Germany.

Britons All British citizens require a passport to enter West Germany. Application forms are available from travel agencies and main post offices. Send the completed form to a regional passport office or apply in person at a main post office. The application must be countersigned by your bank manager, or by a solicitor, barrister, doctor, clergyman, or justice of the peace who knows you personally. In addition, you'll need two photographs and a £15 fee. The occasional tourist might opt for a British visitors passport. It is valid for one year, costs £7.50 and is nonrenewable. You'll need two passport photographs and identification. Apply at your local post office.

Visas are not required for British citizens to enter West Germany.

Customs and Duties

On Arrival There are three levels of duty-free allowance for visitors to West Germany.

Entering West Germany from a non-European country, the allowances are (1) 400 cigarettes or 100 cigars or 500 grams of tobacco, plus (2) 1 liter of spirits more than 22% proof or 2 liters of spirits less than 22% proof, plus (3) 2 liters of wine, plus (4) 50 grams of perfume and ¼ liter of toilet water, plus (5) other goods to the value of DM 115.

Entering West Germany from a country belonging to the EEC, the allowances are (1) 200 cigarettes (300 if not bought in a duty-free shop) or 75 cigars or 400 grams of tobacco, plus (2) 1 liter of spirits more than 22% proof (1.5 liters if not bought in a duty-free shop) or 3 liters of spirits less than 22% proof, plus (3) 5 liters of wine, plus (4) 75 grams of perfume and ⅓ liter of toilet water, plus (5) other goods to the value of DM 780.

Entering Germany from a European country not belonging to the EEC (Austria or Switzerland, for example), the allowances are (1) 200 cigarettes or 50 cigars or 250 grams of tobacco, plus (2) 1 liter of spirits more than 22% proof or 2 liters of spirits less than 22% proof, plus (3) 2 liters of wine, plus (4) 50 grams of perfume and ¼ liter of toilet water, plus (5) other goods to the value of DM 115.

Tobacco and alcohol allowances are for visitors aged 17 and over. Other items intended for personal use may be imported and exported freely. There are no restrictions on the import and export of West Germany currency.

On Departure **U.S. Customs:** If you are bringing any foreign-made equipment from home, such as cameras, it's wise to carry the original receipt with you or register it with U.S. customs before you leave (Form 4457). Otherwise you may end up paying duty on your return. U.S. residents may bring home duty-free up to $400 worth of foreign goods, as long as they have been out of the country for at least 48 hours. Each member of the family is entitled to the same exemption, regardless of age, and exemptions can be pooled. For the next $1,000 worth of goods, a flat 10% rate is assessed; above $1,400, duties vary with the merchandise. Included for travelers 21 or older are one liter of alcohol, 100 cigars (non-Cuban), and 200 cigarettes. Only one bottle of perfume trademarked in the U.S. may be brought in. However, there is no duty on antiques or art over 100 years old. Anything exceeding these limits will be taxed at the port of entry, and may be taxed additionally in the traveler's home state. Gifts valued at under $50 may be mailed to friends or relatives at home duty-free, but not more than one package per day to any one addressee may be sent, and packages may not include perfumes costing more than $5, tobacco, or liquor.

Canadian Customs: Canadian residents have a $300 exemption and may also bring in duty-free up to 50 cigars, 200 cigarettes, 2 pounds of tobacco, and 40 ounces of liquor, provided these are declared in writing to customs on arrival and accompany the traveler in hand or in checked-through baggage. Personal gifts should be mailed as "Unsolicited Gift—Value under $40." Request the Canadian customs brochure "I Declare" for further details.

British Customs: There are two levels of duty-free allowance for people entering the United Kingdom: (1) for goods bought outside the EEC or for goods bought in a duty-free shop within the EEC and (2) for goods bought in an EEC country but not in a duty-free shop.

In the first category, you may import duty-free (1) 200 cigarettes or 100 cigarillos or 50 cigars or 250 grams of tobacco (*Note:* If you live outside Europe, these allowances are doubled), plus (2) 1 liter of alcoholic drinks over 22% volume or 2 liters of alcoholic drinks not over 22% volume or fortified or sparkling wine, plus (3) 2 liters of still table wine, plus (4) 50 grams of perfume, plus (5) 9 fluid ounces of toilet water, plus other goods to the value of £32.

In the second category, you may import duty-free (1) 300 cigarettes or 150 cigarillos or 75 cigars or 400 grams of tobacco, plus (2) 1.5 liters of alcoholic drinks over 22% volume or 3 liters of alcoholic drinks not over 22% volume or fortified or sparkling wine, plus (3) 4 liters of still table wine, plus (4) 75 grams of perfume, plus (5) 13 fluid ounces of toilet water, plus (6) other goods to the value of £250. (*Note:* Though it is not classified as an alcoholic drink by EEC countries for customs' purposes and is thus considered part of the "other goods" allowance, you may not import more than 50 liters of beer.)

In addition, no animals or pets of any kind may be brought into the United Kingdom. The penalties for doing so are severe and are strictly enforced.

Traveling with Film

If your camera is new, shoot and develop a few rolls before leaving home. Pack some lens tissue and an extra battery for your built-in light meter. Invest about $10 in a skylight filter and screw it onto the front of your lens. It will protect the lens and reduce haze.

Film doesn't like hot weather. If you're driving in summer, don't store film in the glove compartment or on the shelf under the rear window. Put it behind the front seat on the floor, on the side opposite the exhaust pipe.

On a plane trip, never pack unprocessed film in check-in luggage; if your bags get X-rayed, say goodbye to your pictures. Always carry undeveloped film with you through security and ask to have it inspected by hand. (It helps to isolate your film in a plastic bag, ready for quick inspection.) Inspectors at American airports are required by law to honor requests for hand inspection; abroad, you'll have to depend on the kindness of strangers.

The old airport scanning machines—still in use in some Third World countries—use heavy doses of radiation that can turn a family portrait into an early morning fog. The newer models—used in all U.S. and West German airports—are safe for anything from five to 500 scans, depending on the speed of your film. The effects are cumulative; you can put the same roll of film through several scans without worry. After five scans, you're asking for trouble.

If your film gets fogged and you want an explanation, send it to the **National Association of Photographic Manufacturers** (600 Mamaroneck Ave., Harrison, NY 10528). It will try to determine what went wrong. The service is free.

Language

The Germans are great linguists and you will find English spoken in virtually all hotels, restaurants, airports and stations, museums, and other places of interest. However, English is not always widely spoken in rural areas.

If you speak some German, you may find some regional dialects hard to follow, particularly in Bavaria. At the same time, however, all Germans can speak "high," or standard, German; even in the backwoods of Bavaria, the locals can alternate between dialect and standard German at will.

Staying Healthy

German sanitation and health standards are as high as those anywhere in the world, and there are no serious health risks associated with travel to Germany. If you have a health problem that might require purchasing prescription drugs while in Germany, have your doctor write a prescription using the drug's generic name. Brand names vary widely from country to country.

The **International Association for Medical Assistance to Travelers** (IAMAT) is a worldwide association offering a list of approved physicians and clinics whose training meets British and American standards. For a list of German physicians and clinics that are part of this network, contact IAMAT (736 Center St., Lewiston, NY 14092, tel. 716/754–4883; in **Canada,** 188 Nicklin Rd., Guelph, Ontario NIH 7L5; in **Europe,** Gotthardstr. 17, 6300 Zug, Switzerland). Membership is free.

Inoculations are not required for entry to Germany.

Insurance

Travelers may seek insurance coverage in three areas: health and accident, loss of luggage, and trip cancellation. Your first step is to review your existing health and homeowner policies; some health-insurance plans cover health expenses incurred while traveling, some major-medical plans cover emergency transportation, and some homeowner policies cover the theft of luggage.

Health and Accident Several companies offer coverage designed to supplement existing health insurance for travelers:

Carefree Travel Insurance (Box 310, 120 Mineola Blvd., Mineola, NY 11501, tel. 516/294–0220 or 800/645–2424) provides coverage for medical evacuation. It also offers 24-hour medical phone advice.

Health Care Abroad, International Underwriters Group (243 Church St., Vienna, VA 22180, tel. 703/281–9500 or 800/237–6615), offers comprehensive medical coverage, including emergency evacuation, for trips of 10–90 days.

International SOS Insurance (Box 11568, Philadelphia, PA 19116, tel. 215/244–1500 or 800/523–8930) does not offer medical insurance but provides medical-evacuation services to its clients, who are often international corporations.

Travel Guard International, underwritten by Cygna (1100 Centerpoint Dr., Stevens Point, WI 54481, tel. 715/345–0505 or 800/782–5151), offers medical insurance, with coverage for emergency evacuation when Travel Guard's representatives in the United States say it is necessary.

Lost Luggage Luggage loss is usually covered as part of a comprehensive travel-insurance package that includes personal accident, trip cancellation, and sometimes default and bankruptcy insurance. Several companies offer comprehensive policies: **Access America, Inc.,** a subsidiary of Blue Cross–Blue Shield (Box 807, New York, NY 10163, tel. 800/851–2800); **Near, Inc.** (1900 N. MacArthur Blvd., Suite 210, Oklahoma City, OK 73127, tel. 800/654–6700); and **Travel Guard International** (*see* Health and Accident Insurance, above).

Trip Cancellation Flight insurance is often included in the price of a ticket when paid for with American Express, Visa, and other major credit and charge cards. It is usually included in combination travel-insurance packages available from most tour operators, travel agents, and insurance agents.

Renting, Leasing, or Purchasing Cars

Renting If you're flying into a major German city and planning to spend some time there, save money by arranging to pick up your car in the city the day you depart; otherwise, arrange to pick up and return your car at the airport. You'll have to weigh the added expense of renting a car from a major company with an airport office against the savings on a car from a budget company with offices in town. You could waste precious hours trying to locate the budget company in return for only a small financial savings. If you're arriving and departing from different airports, look for a one-way car rental with no return fees. If you're traveling to more than one country, make sure your rental contract permits you to take the car across borders and that the insurance policy covers you in every country you visit. Be prepared to pay more for a car with an automatic transmission. Since they are not as readily available as those with manual transmissions, reserve them in advance.

Rental rates vary widely, depending on size and model, number of days you use the car, insurance coverage, and whether special drop-off fees are imposed. In most cases, rates quoted include unlimited free mileage, and standard liability protection. Not included are collision damage waiver (CDW), which eliminates your deductible payment should you have an accident; personal accident insurance; gasoline; and European value added taxes (VAT). The VAT in Germany is 14%.

Driver's licenses issued in the United States, Canada, and Britain are valid in Germany. You might also take out an international driving permit before you leave, to smooth out difficulties if you have an accident or as an additional identification. Permits are available for a small fee through local offices of the American Automobile Association (AAA) and the Canadian Automobile Association (CAA), or from their main offices (**AAA,** 8111 Gatehouse Rd., Falls Church, VA 22047–0001, tel. 703/AAA,–6000; **CAA,** 2 Carlton St., Toronto, Ontario M5B 1K4, tel. 416/964–3170).

It's best to arrange a car rental before you leave. You won't save money by waiting until you arrive in Germany, and you may find that the type of car you want is not available at the last minute. Rental companies usually charge according to the exchange rate of the dollar at the time the car is returned or when the credit-card payment is processed. Three companies with special programs to help you hedge against the falling dollar, by guaranteeing advertised rates if you pay in advance, are **Budget Rent-a-Car** (3350 Boyington St., Carrollton, TX 75006, tel. 800/527–0700), **Connex Travel International** (983 Main St., Peekskill, NY 10566, tel. 800/333–3949), and **Cortell International** (770 Lexington Ave., New York, NY 10021, tel. 800/223–6626 or 800/442–4481 in NY).

Other budget rental companies serving Germany include **Europe by Car** (1 Rockefeller Plaza, New York, NY 10020, tel. 800/223–1516 or 800/252–9401 in CA), **Auto Europe** (Box 1097 Sharps Wharf, Camden, ME 04843, tel. 800/223–5555, or 800/342–5202 in ME, or 800/237–2465 in Canada) **Foremost Euro-Car** (5430 Van Nuys Blvd., Van Nuys, CA 91404, tel. 800/423–3111), and **Kemwel** (106 Calvert St., Harrison, NY 10528, tel. 800/ 678–0678).

Other companies include **Avis** (tel. 800/331–1212); **Hertz** (tel. 800/223–6472 or 800/522–5568 in NY); and **National** or **Europcar** (tel. 800/CAR–RENT).

Leasing

For trips of 21 days or more, you may save money by leasing a car. Under a leasing arrangement, you are technically buying a car and then selling it back to the manufacturer after you've used it. You receive a factory-new car, tax free, and with international registration and extensive insurance coverage. Rates vary with the make and model of car and length of time used. Car leasing programs are offered by Renault, Citroën, and Peugeot in France, and by Volkswagen, Ford, Audi, and Opel, among others, in Belgium. Delivery to Germany can be arranged for an additional fee. Before you go, compare long-term rental rates with leasing rates. Remember to add taxes and insurance costs to the car rentals, something you don't have to worry about with leasing. Companies that offer leasing arrangements include **Kemwel, Europe by Car,** and **Auto Europe,** all listed above.

Purchasing Given the weakness of the dollar on the international market and the logistical complexities of shipping a car home, the option of purchasing a car in Germany is less appealing today than it was a decade ago. The advantage to buying a car abroad is that you'll get what amounts to a free car rental during your stay in Europe. If you plan to purchase a car in Germany, be certain the prices quoted are for cars built to meet specifications set down by the U.S. Department of Transportation. If not, you will have to go through considerable expense to convert the car before you can drive it legally in the United States. You will also be subject to a U.S. customs duty. For more information, contact **Kemwel** or **Europe by Car,** both listed above, or ask your local car dealer to put you in touch with an importer.

Rail Passes

The **EurailPass,** valid for unlimited first-class train travel through 16 countries, including West Germany, is an excellent value if you plan on traveling around the Continent. The ticket is available for periods of 15 days ($298), 21 days ($370), one month ($470), two months ($650), and three months ($798). For those 26 and under there is the **Eurail Youthpass,** for one or two months' unlimited second-class train travel, at $320 and $420.

For travelers who like to spread out their train journeys, there is the **Eurail Flexipass.** With this pass, travelers get nine days of unlimited first-class train travel, but they do not have to ride for nine consecutive days, as they can use the pass on any nine days in a 21-day period. The Flexipass costs $310.

The EurailPass does not cover Great Britain, and is available only if you live outside Europe or North Africa. The pass must be bought from an authorized agent in the Western Hemisphere or Japan before you leave for Europe. Apply through your travel agent, or **Germanrail** (747 Third Ave., New York, NY 10017, tel. 212/308–3106).

For details of other rail passes, *see* Getting Around, By Train, below.

Student and Youth Travel

The **International Student Identity Card** (ISIC) entitles students to youth rail passes, special fares on local transportation, Intra-European student charter flights, and discounts at museums, theaters, sports events, and many other attractions. If purchased in the United States, the $10 cost of the ISIC also includes $2,000 in emergency medical insurance, plus $100 a day for up to 60 days of hospital coverage. Apply to the **Council on International Student Exchange** (CIEE, 205 E. 42nd St.,

New York, NY 10017, tel. 212/661–1414). In Canada, the ISIC is available for CN $10 from the Association of Student Councils (187 College St., Toronto, Ontario M5T 1P7).

The **Youth International Educational Exchange Card** (YIEE), issued by the **Federation of International Youth Travel Organizations** (FIYTO, 81 Islands Brugge, DK-2300 Copenhagen S, Denmark), provides similar services to nonstudents under the age of 26. In the United States, the card costs $10 and is available from CIEE (address above) or from **ISE** (Europa House, 802 W. Oregon St., Urbana, IL 61801, tel. 217/344–5863). In Canada, the YIEE is available from the Canadian Hostelling Association (CHA, 333 River Rd., Vanier, Ottawa, Ontario K1L 8H9, tel. 613/476–3844).

An **International Youth Hostel Federation** (IYHF) membership card is the key to inexpensive dormitory-style accommodations at thousands of youth hostels around the world. Hostels provide separate sleeping quarters for men and women at rates ranging from $7 to $15 a night per person and are situated in a variety of facilities, including converted farmhouses, villas, and restored castles, as well as specially constructed modern buildings. IYHF membership costs $20 a year and is available in the United States through American Youth Hostels (AYH, Box 37613, Washington, DC 20013, tel. 202/783–6161). AYH also publishes an extensive directory of youth hostels around the world.

Council Travel, a CIEE subsidiary, is the foremost U.S. student travel agency, specializing in low-cost charters and serving as the exclusive U.S. agent for many student airfare bargains and student tours. CIEE's 80-page *Student Travel Catalog* and "Council Charter" brochure are available free from any Council Travel office in the United States (enclose $1 postage if ordering by mail). In addition to the CIEE headquarters (205 E. 42nd St.) and branch office (35 W. 8th St.) in New York City, there are Council Travel offices in Berkeley, La Jolla, Long Beach, Los Angeles, San Diego, and San Francisco, CA; Chicago, IL; Amherst, Boston, and Cambridge, MA; Portland, OR; Providence, RI; Austin and Dallas, TX; and Seattle, WA.

The **Educational Travel Center** (438 N. Frances St., Madison, WI 53703, tel. 608/256–5551) is another student travel specialist worth contacting for information on student tours, bargain fares, and bookings.

Students who would like to work abroad should contact CIEE's **Work Abroad Department** (205 E. 42nd St., New York, NY 10017). The council arranges various types of paid and voluntary work experiences overseas for up to six months. CIEE also sponsors study programs in Europe, Latin America, and Asia, and publishes many books of interest to the student traveler: These include *Work, Study, Travel Abroad: The whole world handbook* ($8.95 plus $1 postage); *Work Your Way Around the World* ($10.95 plus $1 postage); and *Volunteer! The Comprehensive Guide to Voluntary Service in the U.S. and Abroad* ($5.50 plus $1 postage).

The Information Center at the **Institute of International Education** (IIE) has reference books, foreign university catalogs, study-abroad brochures, and other materials, which may be consulted by students and nonstudents alike, free of charge.

The Information Center, 809 UN Plaza, New York, NY 10017, tel. 212/984–5413, is open Mon.–Fri. 10–4 and Wed. until 7. *It is not open on holidays.*

IIE administers a variety of grant and study programs offered by U.S. and foreign organizations, and publishes a well-known annual series of study-abroad guides, including *Academic Year Abroad, Vacation Study Abroad,* and *Study in the United Kingdom and Ireland.* The institute also publishes *Teaching Abroad,* a book of employment and study opportunities overseas for U.S. teachers. For a current list of IIE publications with prices and ordering information, write to Publications Service, (Institute of International Education, 809 UN Plaza, New York, NY 10017). Books must be purchased by mail or in person; telephone orders are not accepted.

General information on IIE programs and services is available from its regional offices in Atlanta, Chicago, Denver, Houston, San Francisco, and Washington, D.C.

Traveling with Children

Publications ***Family Travel Times*** is a newsletter published 10 times a year by **TWYCH** (Travel with Your Children, 80 Eighth Ave., New York, NY 10011, tel. 212/206–0688). Subscription includes access to back issues and twice-weekly opportunities to call in for specific advice.

Young People's Guide to Munich is a free pamphlet available from the German National Tourist Office (747 Third Ave., New York, NY 10017, tel. 212/308–3300).

Hotels A likely choice for families is any one of the Schloss (castle) hotels in Germany; many have parklike grounds. U.S. representatives are **Europa Hotels and Tours** (tel. 800/523–9570 or 206/485–6985 in WA) and **DER Tours Inc.** (tel. 800/421–4343 or 213/479–4411 in CA).

Home Exchange See *Home Exchanging: A Complete Sourcebook for Travelers at Home or Abroad* by James Dearing (Globe Pequot Press, Box Q, Chester, CT 06412, tel. 800/243–0495 or 800/962–0973 in CT).

Getting There On international flights, children under 2 not occupying a seat pay 10% of adult fare. Various discounts apply to children from age 2 to 12. Reserve a seat behind the bulkhead of the plane, which offers more leg room and can usually fit a bassinet (supplied by the airline). At the same time, inquire about special children's meals or snacks, offered by most airlines. (See "TWYCH's Airline Guide," in the February 1988 issue of *Family Travel Times,* for a rundown on children's services offered by 46 airlines.)

Ask the airline in advance if you can bring aboard your child's car seat. For the booklet *Child/Infant Safety Seats Acceptable for Use in Aircraft,* write to the **Community and Consumer Liaison Division** (APA-400 Federal Aviation Administration, Washington, D.C. 20591, tel. 202/267–3479).

Baby-sitting Services First check with the hotel desk for recommended childcare arrangements. Also, most local tourist offices in Germany maintain updated lists of baby-sitters. Munich agencies include **Student Quick Service** (Studentenservis, Martiusstr. 5, tel. 089/39

–5051) and, for the convenience of shoppers, the **Karstadt** department store on Neuhauserstrasse operates a small babysitting service. Also, contact the **Munich American High School** (Cincinnatistr. 61A, Munich, tel. 089/622–98354). The **American Women's Club of Frankfurt** (Abrams Bldg., Frankfurt, West Germany, APO, NY 09757) runs a child-care center at the military base near the Abrams Building (tel. 069/55–3129).

Pen Pals For names of children in Germany to whom your children can write before your trip, send a self-addressed, stamped envelope to the **International Friendship League** (55 Mount Vernon St., Boston, MA 02108, tel. 617/523–4273), or the **Student Letter Exchange** (308 Second St. NW, Austin, MN 55912).

Hints for Disabled Travelers

The **Information Center for Individuals with Disabilities** (20 Park Plaza, Room 330, Boston, MA 02116, tel. 617/727–5540) offers useful problem-solving assistance, including lists of travel agents that specialize in tours for the disabled.

Moss Rehabilitation Hospital Travel Information Service (12th St. and Tabor Rd., Philadelphia, PA 19141, tel. 215/329–5715) provides information on tourist sights, transportation, and accommodations in destinations around the world. The fee is $5 for each destination. Allow one month for delivery.

Mobility International (Box 3551, Eugene, OR 97403, tel. 503/343–1284) has information on accommodations, organized study, and so on around the world.

The **Society for the Advancement of Travel for the Handicapped** (26 Court St., Brooklyn, NY 11242, tel. 718/858–5483) offers access information. Annual membership costs $40, or $25 for senior travelers and students. Send a stamped, self-addressed envelope.

The Itinerary (Box 1084, Bayonne, NJ 07002, tel. 201/858–3400) is a bimonthly travel magazine for the disabled. ***Access to the World: A Travel Guide for the Handicapped,*** by Louise Weiss, is useful but out of date. It is available from Facts on File (460 Park Ave. S., New York, NY 10016, tel. 212/683–2244).

Hints for Older Travelers

The **American Association of Retired Persons** (AARP, 1909 K St. NW, Washington, DC 20049, tel. 202/662–4850) has two programs for independent travelers: (1) the "Purchase Privilege Program," which offers discounts on hotels, airfare, car rentals, and sightseeing; and (2) the "AARP Motoring Plan," which offers emergency aid and trip routing information for an annual fee of $29.95 per couple. The AARP also arranges group tours, including apartment living in Europe, through two companies: **Olson-Travelworld** (5855 Green Valley Circle, Culver City, CA 90230, tel. 800/227–7737) and **RFD, Inc.** (4401 W. 110th St., Overland Park, KS 66211, tel. 800/448–7010). AARP members must be 50 or older. Annual dues are $5 per person or per couple.

When using an AARP or other identification card, ask for a reduced hotel rate at the time you make your reservation, not when you check out. At restaurants, show your card to the maitre d' before you're seated, since discounts may be limited to certain set menus, days, or hours. When renting a car, remember that economy cars, priced at promotional rates, may cost less than cars that are available with your ID card.

Elderhostel (80 Boylston St., Suite 400, Boston, MA 02116, tel. 617/426–7788) is an innovative 14-year-old program for people 60 and older. Participants live in dorms on some 1,200 campuses around the world. Mornings are devoted to lectures and seminars; afternoons, to sightseeing and field trips. The all-inclusive fee for two- to three-week trips, including room, board, tuition, and roundtrip transportation, is from $1,700 to $3,200.

Travel Industry and Disabled Exchange (TIDE, 5435 Donna Ave., Tarzana, CA 91356, tel. 818/343–6339) is an industry-based organization with a $15 per person annual membership fee. Members receive a quarterly newsletter and information on travel agencies and tours.

National Council of Senior Citizens (925 15th St. NW, Washington, DC 20005, tel. 202/347–8800) is a nonprofit advocacy group with some 4,000 local clubs across the country. Annual membership is $10 per person or $14 per couple. Members receive a monthly newspaper with travel information and an ID card for reduced-rate hotels and car rentals.

Mature Outlook (Box 1205, Glenview, IL 60025, tel. 800/336–6330), a subsidiary of Sears Roebuck & Co., is a travel club for people over 50, with hotel and motel discounts and a bimonthly newsletter. Annual membership is $7.50 per couple. Instant membership is available at participating Holiday Inns.

Travel Tips for Senior Citizens (U.S. Dept. of State Publication 8970, revised Sept. 1987) is available for $1 from the Superintendent of Documents, U.S. Government Printing Office, Washington, DC 20402.

Further Reading

Germany is the setting for many good spy novels, including *The Odessa File,* by Frederick Forsyth; John Le Carré's *A Small Town in Germany;* Alistair MacLean's *Where Eagles Dare;* Walter Winward's *The Midas Touch;* and *The Leader and the Damned,* by Colin Forbes.

If you like to travel with an historical novel, look for Christine Bruckner's *Flight of Cranes;* Timothy Findley's *Famous Last Words;* and Fred Uhlman's *Reunion.* Also, Silvia Tennenbaum's *Yesterday's Streets* covers three generations of a wealthy German family.

Other suggested titles include Günter Grass's *The Tin Drum;* Christa Wolf's *No Place on Earth;* and *Buddenbrooks,* by Thomas Mann.

For books about Berlin in the '20s, pick up Vicki Baum's *Grand Hotel.* Leon Uris's *Armageddon: A Novel of Berlin* is set at the end of World War II. Contemporary novels about Berlin include Len Deighton's *Berlin Game* and Peter Schneider's *The Wall Jumper.*

Arriving and Departing

From North America by Plane

Since the air routes between North America and Germany are heavily traveled, the passenger has many airlines and fares to choose from. But fares change with stunning rapidity, so consult your travel agent on what bargains are currently available.

Be certain to distinguish among (1) nonstop flights—no changes, no stops; (2) direct flights—no changes but one or more stops; and (3) connecting flights—two or more planes, two or more stops.

The Airlines The U.S. airlines that serve Germany are **Northwest Airlines** (tel. 800/447–4747), which flies to Frankfurt; **Delta** (tel. 800/241–4141), which flies to Frankfurt, Stuttgart, and Munich; **TWA** (tel. 800/892–4141), which flies to Frankfurt, Stuttgart, Munich, and Berlin; **Pan Am** (tel. 800/221–1111), which flies to Frankfurt, Stuttgart, Munich, Berlin, Hamburg, and Dortmund; and **American Airlines** (tel. 800/433–7300), which flies to Frankfurt, Berlin, Hamburg, Munich, and Nürnberg. **Lufthansa** (tel. 800/645–3880), the West German national airline, flies to Düsseldorf, Frankfurt, Köln/Bonn, Hamburg, Munich, and Stuttgart. It has *no* flights to West Berlin.

Flying Time The flying time to Frankfurt from New York is 7.5 hours; from Chicago, 10 hours; from Los Angeles, 12 hours.

Enjoying the Flight If you're lucky enough to be able to sleep on a plane, it makes sense to fly at night. Many experienced travelers, however, prefer to take a morning flight to Europe and arrive in the evening, just in time for a good night's sleep. Since the air on a plane is dry, it helps to drink a lot of nonalcoholic liquids; drinking alcohol contributes to jet lag. Feet swell at high altitudes, so it's a good idea to remove your shoes while in flight. Sleepers usually prefer window seats to curl up against; those who like to move about the cabin should ask for aisle seats. Bulkhead seats (adjacent to the exit signs) have more leg room, but seat trays are attached to the arms of your seat rather than to the back of the seat in front of you.

Discount Flights The major airlines offer a range of tickets that can increase the price of any given seat by more than 300%, depending on the day of purchase. As a rule, the further in advance you buy the ticket, the less expensive it is and the greater the penalty (up to 100%) for canceling. Check with airlines for details.

The best buy is not necessarily an APEX (advance purchase) ticket on one of the major airlines. APEX tickets carry certain restrictions: They must be bought in advance (usually 21 days); they restrict your travel, usually with a minimum stay of seven days and a maximum of 90; and they also penalize you for changes—voluntary or not—in your travel plans. But if you can work around these drawbacks, they are among the best-value fares available.

Charter flights offer the lowest fares but often depart only on certain days, and seldom on time. Though you may be able to arrive at one city and return from another, you may lose all or most of your money if you cancel your ticket. Travel agents can make bookings, though they won't encourage you, since commissions are lower than on scheduled flights. Checks should, as a rule, be made out to the bank and specific escrow account for your flight. To make sure your payment stays in this account until your departure, don't use credit cards as a method of payment. Don't sign up for a charter flight unless you've checked with a travel agency about the reputation of the packager. It's particularly important to know the packager's policy concerning refunds should a flight be canceled. One of the most popular charter operators is **Council Charter** (tel. 800/223–7402), a division of CIEE (Council on International Education Exchange). Other companies advertise in Sunday travel sections of newspapers.

Somewhat more expensive—but up to 50% below the cost of APEX fares—are tickets purchased through companies known as consolidators, which buy blocks of tickets on scheduled airlines and sell them at wholesale prices. Here again, you may lose all or most of your money if you change plans, but at least you will be on a regularly scheduled flight with less risk of cancellation than on a charter. Once you've made your reservation, call the airline to make sure you're confirmed. Among the best known consolidators are **UniTravel** (tel. 800/325–2222) and **Access International** (250 W. 57th St., Suite 511, New York, NY 10107, tel. 212/333–7280). Others advertise in the Sunday travel section of the newspapers as well.

A third option is to join a travel club that offers special discounts to its members. Three such organizations are **Moments Notice** (40 E. 49th St., New York, NY 10017, tel. 212/486–0503); **Discount Travel International** (114 Forrest Ave., Barberth, PA 19072, tel. 215/668–2182); and **Worldwide Discount Travel Club** (1674 Meridian Ave., Miami Beach, FL 33139, tel. 305/534–2082). These cut-rate tickets should be compared with APEX tickets on the major airlines.

Smoking Regulations

If smoking bothers you, ask for a seat far away from the smoking section. If the airline tells you there are no nonsmoking seats, insist on one: FCC regulations require all U.S. airlines to find seats for all nonsmokers.

From North America by Ship

Although there are no ocean liners that make direct crossings from North America to Germany, several cruise ships use Hamburg as a port of call. These include ships of the Cunard Line and the Royal Viking Line. The *QE2* is the only cruise ship that makes regular transatlantic crossings. Other cruise ships that sail from European ports in the summer and North American ports in the winter make transatlantic, repositioning crossings as one season ends and another begins. Some sail straight across, often at reduced rates to passengers. Others have several ports of call before heading for open sea. Arrangements can be made to cruise one way and fly one way. Since itineraries can change at the last minute, contact the cruise line for the latest information.

Cunard Line (555 5th Ave., New York, NY 10017, tel. 212/661–7777 or 800/221–4770) operates four ships that make transatlantic crossings. The *QE2* makes regular crossings April through December, between Southampton, England, and Baltimore, Boston, and New York City. Arrangements for the *QE2* can include one-way airfare. The *Sea Goddess I* and *Sea God-*

dess II sail to and from Madeira, Portugal, and St. Thomas, in the U.S. Virgin Islands, for their repositioning crossings. The *Vistafjord* sails to and from Marseilles, France, and Fort Lauderdale, Florida, on its repositioning crossings. Cunard Line offers fly/cruise packages and pre- and post-land packages.

Royal Viking Line (750 Battery St., San Francisco, CA 94111, tel. 800/634–8000) has four ships that cruise out of European ports. Two of the ships make repositioning crossings to and from Ft. Lauderdale and Lisbon, Portugal. Fly-cruise packages are available.

From Britain by Plane

British Airways and **Lufthansa** are the main airlines flying from London to Germany. Between them, they serve nine German destinations—10, including Münster, to which Lufthansa's subsidiary airline, **DLT**, flies.

The main gateways to Germany by air are Köln/Bonn, Frankfurt, Munich, and Berlin. British Airways and Lufthansa each have up to two flights a day into Köln, with a flying time of 1¼ hours and a minimum roundtrip fare of £71. British Airways has up to seven flights (including three from Gatwick) and Lufthansa six flights into Frankfurt, with a flying time of 1 hour and 25 minutes and a minimum fare of £88. Both have up to three flights into Munich, with a 1 hour and 40 minute flying time and a minimum fare of £112. British Airways has up to three nonstop and three one-stop flights into Berlin, with a nonstop flying time of 1 hour and 40 minutes and a minimum fare of £124.

The airlines also fly to Bremen, Düsseldorf, Hannover, and Stuttgart, and Lufthansa also has one flight a day into Nürnberg.

Commuter-style airline **Connectair** flies twice a day from Gatwick to Düsseldorf with a £68 cheapest roundtrip fare, and **Air Europe** has recently started flying to Frankfurt as well as Munich from Gatwick. **Air UK** flies weekdays from London's third airport, Stansted, to Frankfurt (1 hour and 55 minutes flying time) and DLT's other Gatwick service is also to Frankfurt.

The only other airline with the rights to fly into Berlin is **Pan Am,** which can also fly you into Frankfurt, Hamburg, and Munich as a continuation of its transatlantic flights into London.

Dan Air operates regular charter flights for German holiday company GTF, with up to four flights a week to Berlin and two to Hamburg, Hannover, Frankfurt, Düsseldorf, Munich, and Stuttgart.

Increasing competition, as airlines such as Air Europe have been allowed to fly scheduled services to Germany, has brought fares down to lower levels than still exist on other European routes from the United Kingdom and further improvement is expected now that British Midland, the U.K. independent airline, flies from Heathrow to Düsseldorf and Frankfurt.

For reservations and information: **British Airways** (tel. 01/897–4000); **Air Europe** (tel. 0345/444737); **Air UK** (tel. 0345/666777); **Lufthansa** (tel. 01/408–0442); **Pan Am** (tel. 01/409–0688); **Connectair** (tel. 0293/862971); **GTF** (tel. 01/229–2474).

From Britain by Train

British Rail operates up to 10 services a day to West Germany under its Rail Europe banner. Eight of the departures are from Victoria (via the Dover–Ostend ferry or jetfoil) with the other two from Liverpool Street (via Harwich–Hook of Holland).

Most of the services stop at Köln, Koblenz, Frankfurt, Osnabruck, Hannover, Hamburg, Stuttgart, and Munich, with the journey time to Köln usually 9 hours via jetfoil, 12 hours via the Dover–Ostend ferry, and 13 hours via the Harwich–Hook route. To Munich the times are 15, 19, and 22 hours, respectively.

West Berlin is reached via Hannover in about 20 hours, with up to four departures a day—two from Victoria, two from Liverpool Street.

Cheapest roundtrip fares to Köln and Munich are £51 and £105 with the ordinary fares set at £80 and £157. These apply to the Victoria departures; Liverpool Street services are more expensive.

A one-way fare to Berlin is £80; roundtrip fare is £160. Book through British Rail travel centers (tel. 01/834–2345).

From Britain by Bus

The fastest service is by **Europabus,** which has up to three departures a day from London's Victoria coach station. The buses cross the Channel on Sealink's Dover–Zeebrugge ferry service and then drive via the Netherlands and Belgium to Köln (14½ hours), Frankfurt (17½ hours), Mannheim (18¾ hours), Stuttgart/Nürnberg (20½ hours), and Munich (22¾ hours). One-way and roundtrip fares are: Köln (£33/£56), Frankfurt (£38/£65), Mannheim (£41/£70), Stuttgart/Nürnberg (£48/£76), and Munich (£48/£82).

Bookings can also be made through **Transline** (tel. 0708/864911), which runs a service to 35 smaller towns in West Germany. There are up to four departures a week, also from Victoria, and the buses cross either via P&O European Ferries' Dover–Ostend or Sally Line's Ramsgate–Dunkerque services. Destinations include Hannover, Dortmund, Essen, and Düsseldorf as well as the smaller towns. Fares range from £32 to £36 one way and £59 to £66 roundtrip.

From Britain by Car

The choice of Channel crossing from the United Kingdom when driving to Germany, and not using the direct Harwich–Hamburg link, will depend on the final destination. If northern Germany is the destination, then ports in the Netherlands are the most convenient. For central and southern Germany, the Belgian entry ports are best.

A sample of the mileages confirm this. For Berlin and Hannover, the Hook of Holland is considerably closer at 476 and 282 miles than Ostend at 520 and 387 miles respectively; for Munich, Ostend is 23 miles closer at 530. For Köln and Frankfurt, the two ports are almost equidistant. Both are considerably closer than the French ports.

For the Hook of Holland, ferries depart from Harwich—the east coast port reached from London via A12 (about 2½ hours drive). **Sealink** operates one ferry daily and one overnight; both sail year-round. It is an eight-hour crossing, and passengers' fares start at £21 (£7 supplement for first-class travel), car rates range from £27 to £54, and a two-berth cabin costs from £6 to £12.

Like Sealink, **Olau Line** operates newer, high-quality ships on its Netherlands route. There is one daily and one overnight departure from the north Kent port of Sheerness (two hours from London via A2/M2) to Vlissingen. Fare is £20; car rates start at £25.

P&O European Ferries operates services from Dover to both Zeebrugge (up to six a day) and to Ostend, 19 miles southwest down the coast. Crossing time to Ostend is four hours, half an hour longer to Zeebrugge. Motorists' fares to both Belgian ports are £12, with car rates from £22 to £71.

All four ports mentioned are between one and two hours' drive of the German border. From the Hook, take A12 to Arnhem and then A1 toward Dortmund, Essen, and so on. From Vlissingen, take A58 and then A67 to Düsseldorf.

Both Zeebrugge and Ostend are a short drive from E5, from which you can turn off onto E3 at Ghent for Düsseldorf and Essen, or stay on and join A61 for Bonn and, farther south, Koblenz, Wiesbaden, Frankfurt, and Mannheim.

P&O also operates a ferry service into Zeebrugge from Felixstowe (another English east coast port just north of Harwich) while **North Sea Ferries** operates from much farther north at Hull to Zeebrugge and Rotterdam Europoort, two miles south of the Hook.

There is a **Motorail** service from Paris to Munich. A distance of 575 miles, the journey takes 10 hours and there is one departure a day.

For ferry reservations: **Sealink,** tel. 01/834–8122; **P&O,** tel. 01/734–4431; **Olau,** tel. 0795/666666; **North Sea Ferries,** tel. 0482/795141; **French Motorail,** tel. 01/409–3518 (information only).

Motorists are recommended to acquire a green card from their insurance companies. This gives comprehensive insurance coverage for driving in Germany. The most comprehensive breakdown insurance and vehicle and personal security coverage is sold by the **Automobile Association** (AA) in its Five Star scheme.

Staying in Germany

Getting Around

By Plane Germany's internal air network is excellent, with frequent flights linking all major cities. Services are operated by **Lufthansa** and by Germany's leading charter company, **LTU,** except for flights to Berlin, which are operated by **British Airways** and **Pan Am.** In addition, three small airlines operate services between a limited number of northern cities and the East and North Frisian islands, though many of these flights operate only in the summer. Details of all internal services are available from travel agents; otherwise, contact Lufthansa at Frankfurt airport (tel. 069/6961).

Lufthansa also runs an excellent train, the "Lufthansa Express," linking Düsseldorf, Köln, Bonn, and Frankfurt airports and acting as a supplement to existing air services. Only passengers holding air tickets may use the train, but there is no extra charge for it. Service is first class. Luggage is automatically transferred to your plane on arrival at the airport. German Railways operates a similar service called "Rail-Fly," and trains on the Köln–Munich line stop at Frankfurt airport instead of at Wiesbaden for connections with flights to and from Frankfurt.

By Train German Federal Railways—or **DB,** meaning Deutsche Bundesbahn, as it is usually referred to—operates one of the most comprehensive rail systems in Europe. Services are reliable, fast, and comfortable.

Major reorganization and improvement of the Intercity network, with increased services and several new inclusive package deals, have been put into effect over the last five years. On mainline services, there are six basic Intercity routes—look for the "IC" logo—and the number of trains traveling the length and breadth of Germany every day has increased from 156 to 219.

On all IC routes there is an hourly service, and all trains have first and second class. However, a supplemental charge of around DM 6 (irrespective of distance traveled or whether a change of trains is required) is payable. The service gives excellent connections between IC trains at the main nodal points—Hannover, Dortmund, Köln, Mannheim, Würzburg, and Frankfurt Airport—and changing trains couldn't be easier. You only have to cross to the other side of the platform, and, if you have reserved your seats, the car you will board will stop exactly opposite the one you have gotten off. Before boarding your train, look at the notice board on the platform: It will show how the train is made up (for example, where the first- and second-class cars and the buffet car are in the train). Then look for the car identification letters (A–E) which hang from the station roof. These show where each pair of cars will come to a halt, and will also correspond with the carriage letters on your reservation. It is possible to check your baggage for Frankfurt Airport from any of 52 stations throughout Germany. Except on weekends, there is guaranteed overnight delivery.

If you buy your ticket in advance, the cost of the seat reservation is included in the IC supplement—so plan ahead, reserve your seat, and save money.

Rail passengers in possession of a valid roundtrip air ticket can buy a "Rail and Fly" ticket for DB trains to major German airports: Hamburg, Bremen, Hannover, Düsseldorf, Köln/Bonn, Saarbrücken, Stuttgart, Nürnberg, and Munich. The price is around DM 90 second class, and DM 140 first class. This includes IC and EC surcharges as well as subway connections.

The IC network is complemented by "FD" trains *(Fernexpresszüge)*, which are long-distance express trains, and "D" trains *(Schnellzüge)*, which are the ordinary fast trains. On both, a small supplement—currently DM 6—must be paid if you are traveling under 50 kilometers (30 miles). No supplements are necessary for traveling on the semi-fast "E" trains *(Eilzuge)* or local services. The moral of the tale is simple: Don't use fast trains for short hops.

Note that in high season you will frequently encounter lines at ticket offices for seat reservations. Unless you are prepared to board the train without a reserved seat, taking the (slender) chance of a seat being available, the only way to avoid these lines is to make an advance reservation by phone. Call the ticket office *(Fahrkarten Schalter)* of the rail station from which you plan to depart. Here again, you will probably have to make several attempts before you get through to the reservations section *(Reservierungen-Platzkarten)*, but you will then be able to collect your seat ticket from a special counter without having to wait in line.

Tourist Rail Cards

Holders of British Rail Senior Citizens' Rail Cards can buy an "add on" **European Senior Citizens' Rail Card** that permits half-price train travel in most European countries, including West Germany. Senior citizens from other countries who intend to stay in Germany for some time should consider buying the DB **Senioren Pass.** This is available in two forms: the Senioren Pass "A" (which costs DM 70) allows half-price travel for distances over 50 kilometers (30 miles) from Monday to Saturday, while the Senioren Pass "B" (which costs around DM 110) permits half-price travel on any day of the week. Both are valid for a year and can be bought before going to Germany.

There is a wide range of special-offer tickets for West Germany, all of which provide substantial savings. First, if you intend to travel widely in Europe as well as Germany, the **EurailPass** is an unbeatable bargain. (*See* Rail Passes, in Before You Go, above). Second, for travel within Germany only, there is the DB **Germanrail** tourist card. This covers the complete German rail network and the Europabus services along the Romantic Road and the Rhine–Mosel line. In addition, the card entitles you to reduced fares for crossing East Germany to visit West Berlin—with a free bus tour of West Berlin thrown in—*and* gives you a reduction on the fares of the K.D. Rhineline steamers on the Rhine River. Costs for Germanrail cards are around $135 for 4 days, $220 for 9 days, and $300 for 16 days in first class; and $100, $150, and $200 in second class; the cards must be purchased in the United States.

Third, there are the DB Regional Rail Rovers (**Tourenkarten**), which cover some 73 areas, including all the main tourist regions. They are excellent value for money. Valid for any 10 days within a 21-day vacation period, they cost around DM 50 for one person, DM 65 for two people traveling together, and DM 80 for a family (one or two parents, plus any number of unmarried children under 26 and grandparents). Unless you are going to Germany on a vacation run by the railways themselves, the Tourenkarte has to be bought when you arrive in Germany. However, there is one catch: To be eligible you must travel at least 250 kilometers (155 miles) on a German train to reach your vacation area and the same distance when you leave. So check distances carefully on your map—it may be worth making a slight detour to qualify.

For further information, contact **Germanrail** (747 Third Ave., New York, NY 10017, tel. 212/308–3106).

By Bus Germany has a good bus network. A large proportion of services are operated by the railways **(Bahnbus)** and are closely integrated with train services, while on less busy rail lines, services are run by buses in off-peak periods—normally midday and weekends. Rail tickets are valid on these services. The railways, in the guise of **Deutsche Touring,** also operate the German sections of the Europabus network. Contact them at Am Römerhof 17,6000-Franfurt/Main 90, for details. Most other local bus services are operated by the German post office.

One of the best services is provided by the Romantic Road bus between Würzburg (with connections to and from Frankfurt and Wiesbaden) and Füssen (with connections to and from Munich, Augsburg, and Garmisch-Partenkirchen). This is an all-reserved-seats bus with a stewardess and one daily service in each direction, leaving in the morning and arriving in the evening. Details and reservations are available from the German National Tourist Office or local tourist offices.

All towns of any size operate their own local buses. For the most part, those link up with local trams (streetcars), electric railways services (S-bahn), and subways (U-bahn). Fares vary according to distance, but a ticket usually allows you to transfer freely between the various forms of transportation. Some cities issue 24-hour tickets at special rates.

By Bike Information on all aspects of cycling in Germany is available from the **Bund Deutscher Radfahrer,** the Association of German Cyclists (Otto-Fleck-Schneise 4,6000 Frankfurt 71). There are no formalities governing the importation of bikes into Germany, and no duty is required. Bikes can also be carried on trains —though *not* on Intercity trains—if you buy a *Fahrradkarte*, or bicycle ticket. These cost DM 6.50 per journey and can be bought at any train station. Those under 26 with a "Tramper Ticket"—a monthly rover that costs DM 234—can take bikes free of charge. Full details are given in the German railway's brochure *Fahrrad am Bahnhof*.

Bicycles are also available to rent at over 270 train stations throughout the country, most of them in southern Germany. Cost is DM 10 per day, DM 5 if you have a valid rail ticket. They can be returned at any other station.

By Boat River and lake trips are among the greatest delights of a vacation in Germany, especially along the Rhine, Germany's longest river. The Rhine may be viewed at a variety of paces: by fast hydrofoil, by express boat, by sedate motorship, or by romantic paddle steamer. For those in a hurry, there is a daily hydrofoil service from Düsseldorf right through to Mainz. It is advisable to book in advance for this. For gentler souls, there is a wide range of more leisurely cruises. German cruise ships also operate on the Upper Rhine as far as Basel, Switzerland; on the Main between Frankfurt and Mainz; on the Danube to Linz and on to Vienna; on the Europe Canal joining the Main and the Danube; on the Elbe and Weser and their estuaries; on the Inn and Ilz; and on the Ammersee, Chiemsee, Königsee, and Bodensee.

EurailPasses are valid on all services of the KD Rhineline and on the Mosel between Trier and Koblenz. (If you use the fast hydrofoil, a supplementary fee has to be paid.) DB Tourist Card holders are given a 50% reduction on KD ships. Regular rail tickets are also accepted, meaning that you can go one way by ship and return by train. All you have to do is pay a small surcharge to KD Rhineline and get the ticket endorsed at one of the landing stage offices. But note that you have to buy the rail ticket first and *then* get it changed.

Ever felt like pampering yourself? KD Rhineline has the package for you. The company offers a program of luxury tours ranging from a five-day cruise along the Rhine from Amsterdam to Basel to a four-day "Four-Country Cruise," which visits Amsterdam, Köln, Strasbourg, and Basel among other cities, and costs from around DM 1,300 first class. The ships cruise slowly to give you time to appreciate the landscape. The tours can be booked either for the cruise only to fit in with your own program, or as a complete vacation. One of the best and most attractive ways of seeing the glories of the Rhine and Mosel is on one of the traditional KD old-time paddle steamers or on one of their large modern motor vessels. During the summer there are good services between Bonn and Koblenz and between Koblenz and Birgen; both trips take around five hours.

KD has several budget deals, too; for example, on Sundays or holidays, children between 4 and 14 accompanied by adults pay only DM 5. Likewise, senior citizens pay only half price on Mondays. If it's your birthday, you travel free. For details of all KD services, contact the company at Frankenwerft 15, 5000-Köln 1, tel. 0221/208–8288.

By Car Entry formalities for motorists are few: All you need is proof of insurance, an international car registration document, and an international driver's license. If you or your car are from an EEC country, or Austria, Norway, Switzerland, Sweden, or Portugal, all you need is your domestic license and proof of insurance. *All* foreign cars must have a country sticker.

German roads are excellent. All larger roads are both well-maintained and fast, while an endless network of smaller roads makes getting off the beaten track both easy and desirable.

There are three principal automobile clubs: **ADAC** (Allegmeiner Deutscher Automobil-Club, Am Westpark, 8000-Munich 70), **AvD** (Lyonerstr. 16, Frankfurt/Niederrad), and **DTC** (Amalienburgstr. 23, Munich 60).

ADAC and AvD operate tow trucks on all Autobahns; they also have emergency telephones every 7½ miles. On minor roads, go to the nearest call box and dial 19211. Ask, in English, for "road service assistance," if you have to use the service. Help is free, but all materials have to be paid for.

Scenic Routes Germany boasts 26 specially designated tourist roads, all covering areas of particular scenic and/or historic interest. The longest is the **Deutsche Ferienstrasse**, the German Holiday Road, which runs from the Baltic to the Alps, a distance of around 1,070 miles. The most famous, however, and also the oldest, is the **Romantische Strasse,** the Romantic Road, which runs from Würzburg in Franconia to Füssen in the Alps, covering around 220 miles and passing some of the most historic cities and towns in Germany. (*See* Chapter 8 for full details).

Among other notable touring routes—all with expressive and descriptive names—are the **Grüne Küstenstrasse** (Green Coast Road), running along the North Sea coast from Denmark to Emden; the **Burgenstrasse** (Castle Road), running from Mannheim to Nürnberg; the **Deutsche Weinstrasse** (German Wine Road), running through the heartland of German wine country; and the **Deutsche Alpenstrasse** (German Alpine Road), running the length of the country's southern border. In addition, there are many other equally delightful, if less well-known, routes, such as the **Märchenstrasse** (the Fairy-tale Road); the **Schwarwald Hochstrasse** (the Black Forest Mountain Road); and the **Deutsche Edelsteinstrasse** (German Gem Road).

Regulations In built-up areas, the speed limit is 50 kph (approximately 30 mph) while on all other roads except Autobahns the limit is 100 kph (approximately 60 mph). There is no speed limit on the Autobahns, a fact that the Germans, among the most aggressive drivers in Europe, take full advantage of. There is, however, a recommended limit of 130 kph (80 mph), though few people seem to take much notice of it.

Note that seat belts must be worn at all times by front- *and* back-seat passengers.

Fuel Gasoline (petrol) costs are around DM 1.10 and DM 1.30 per liter (*see* the conversion charts at the end of this book). West German fuel contains less lead than is customary elsewhere on the Continent. Some older cars may not run especially well on it, but it makes no difference at all to the performance of newer models. German filling stations are highly competitive and bargains are often available if you shop around, but *not* at Autobahn filling stations. Self-service, or *SB-Tanken*, stations are cheapest. Pumps marked *Bleifrei* contain unleaded petrol.

Telephones

Local Calls Local calls cost a minimum of 23 pfennigs. Public phones take 10 pfennigs, 50 pfennigs, and DM 1 coins. If you plan to make an out-of-town call, take along a good supply of DM 1 coins. Most phone booths have instructions in English as well as German; if yours doesn't, simply lift the receiver, put the money in, and dial.

International Calls These can be made from public phones bearing the sign "Inlands and Auslandsgespräche." They take 10 pfennigs, DM 1, and DM 5 coins; a four-minute call to the United States costs DM 15. To avoid weighing yourself down with coins, however, make international calls from post offices; even those in small country towns will have a special booth for international calls. You pay the clerk at the end of your call. Never make international calls from your hotel room; rates will be at least double the regular charge.

Operators and Information The West German telephone system is fully automatic, and it's unlikely that you'll have to employ the services of an operator. If you do, dial 1188, or 00118 for international calls. If the operator doesn't speak English (also unlikely), you'll be passed to one who does.

Mail

Postal Rates Airmail letters to the United States and Canada cost DM 1.40; postcards cost 90 pfennigs. Airmail letters to the United Kingdom cost 80 pfennigs; postcards cost 60 pfennigs.

Receiving Mail You can arrange to have mail sent to you in care of any West German post office; have the envelope marked "Postlagernd."

This service is free. Alternatively, have mail sent to any American Express office in Germany. There's no charge to cardholders, holders of American Express traveler's checks, or anyone who has booked a vacation with American Express. Otherwise, you pay DM 2 per collection (not per item).

Tipping

The service charges on hotel bills suffice for most tips in your hotel, though you should tip bell hops and porters; DM 2 per bag or service is ample. Whether you tip the desk clerk depends on whether he or she has given you any special service.

Service charges are included in all restaurant bills (listed as *Bedienung*), as is tax (listed as *MWST*). Nonetheless, it is customary to round out the bill to the nearest mark or to leave about 5% (give it to the waiter or waitress as you pay the bill; don't leave it on the table).

In taxis, round out the fare to the nearest full mark as a tip. Only give more if you have particularly cumbersome or heavy luggage (though you will be charged 50 pfennigs for each piece of luggage anyway).

Opening and Closing Times

Banks Times vary from state to state and city to city, but banks are generally open weekdays from 8:30 or 9 to 3 or 4 (5 or 6 on Thursday). Branches at airports and main train stations open as early as 6:30 AM and close as late as 10:30 PM.

Museums Most museums are open from Tuesday to Sunday 9–6. Some close for an hour or more at lunch, and some are open on Monday.

Shops Times vary, but are generally Monday to Saturday from 8:30 or 9 until 5:30 or 6; some close at 2 or 2:30 Saturday. On the first Saturday of each month, larger shops and department stores are open until 7:30 or 8.

National Holidays January 1; April 15, 16 (Easter); May 1 (May Day); May 24 (Ascension); June 4 (Pentecost Monday); June 14 (Corpus Christi, southern Germany only); June 17 (German Unity Day); August 15 (Assumption Day, Bavaria and Saarland only); November 1 (All Saints); November 22 (Day of Prayer and Repentance); December 25, 26 (Christmas).

Sports and Outdoor Activities

The Germans are nothing if not sports crazy, and there is practically no sport, however arcane, except perhaps cricket, that cannot easily be arranged almost anywhere in the country. A good number of sports packages—for sailboats, tennis, climbing, walking, horseback riding, to name only a few—are also available. Consult the German National Tourist Office or your travel agent for details. Below, we give details of some of the more popular participant sports. Details of important sporting events are also published every month by regional and local tourist offices.

Fishing Fishing is available at many locations in Germany, but a permit, valid for one year and costing from DM 10 to DM 20, available from local tourist offices, is required, as is a local permit to fish in a particular spot. These last are available from the owner of the stretch of water you plan to fish. Further details are available from local tourist offices or from **Verband der Deutschen Sportfischer** (Bahnhofstr. 37,605 Offenbach).

A number of hotels offer fishing for guests, but you will normally be expected to deliver your catch—if any—to the hotel.

Golf Golf in Germany is rapidly increasing in popularity, and there are growing numbers of courses around the country. Clubs will usually allow nonmembers to play if they are not too busy; charges will be about DM 30 during the week and up to DM 60 on weekends and on public holidays. For information, write the **German Golf Association** (Rheinblickstr. 24, 6202 Wiesbaden Biebrich).

Hiking and Mountaineering Germany's hill and mountain regions have around 82,000 miles of marked hiking and mountain-walking tracks. They are administered by regional hiking clubs and, where appropriate, mountaineering groups, all of which are affiliated with the **Verband Deutscher Gebirgs- und Wandervereine e.V.** (Hospitalstr. 21b, D-7000 Stuttgart 1). It can provide information on routes, hiking paths, overnight accommodations, and mountain huts; addresses of individual clubs are also available from local tourist offices.

For Alpine walking, contact the **Deutsche Alpenverein** (Praterinsel 5, D-8000 Munich 22). It administers over 50 mountain huts and about 9,500 miles of Alpine paths. In addition, it can provide courses in mountaineering and touring suggestions for routes in both winter and summer. Foreign members are admitted.

There are also various mountaineering schools that offer weeklong courses ranging from basic techniques for beginners to advanced mountaineering. Contact the **Verband Deutscher Ski- und Bergführer** (Lindenstr. 16, D-8980 Oberstdorf).

Local tourist offices and sports shops can usually supply details of mountain guides.

Horseback Riding Riding schools and clubs can be found throughout Germany. Rates are generally high, and most schools will insist on a minimum standard of competence before allowing novices out. Alternatively, pony treks are available in many parts of the country. Contact the German National Tourist Office or local tourist offices.

Sailing A wide variety of sailing vacations and opportunities to rent sailboats are available throughout Germany. Most North Sea and Baltic resorts and harbors will have either sailing schools or sailboats of varying types to rent. Lake sailing is equally popular, particularly on Chiemsee in Bavaria and the Bodensee. For details, write **Verband Deutscher Segelschulen** (Graelstr. 45, 44 Münster).

Swimming Almost all larger towns and resorts have open-air and indoor pools, the former frequently heated, the latter often with wave or whirlpool machines. In addition, practically all coastal resorts have indoor seawater pools, as well as good, if bracing, beaches. Similarly, all German spas have thermal or mineral-water indoor pools. Finally, Bavaria's Alpine lakes and large numbers of manmade lakes elsewhere have marked-off swimming and sunbathing areas.

Note that swimming in rivers, especially the larger ones, is not recommended and in some cases is positively forbidden—look for the "Baden Verboten" signs—either because of shipping or pollution, or both.

Bathing caps are obligatory at all indoor and outdoor pools; if you don't have your own, you can rent one. It's hard not to notice that the Germans are keen on nudism. Many pools will have special days for nude bathing only, and on certain beaches nude bathing is also allowed. Signs reading "FKK" mean nudity is allowed.

Tennis Courts are available practically everywhere, summer and winter. Local tourist offices will supply details of where to play, charges, and how to book, the latter being essential in most areas. Charges vary from DM 16 to DM 22 for outdoor courts and DM 25 to DM 35 for indoor courts.

Windsurfing This has become so popular, particularly on the Bavarian lakes, that it has had to be restricted on some beaches as a result of collisions between Windsurfers and swimmers. Nonetheless, there are still many places where you can windsurf and where Windsurfers can easily be rented. Lessons, at around DM 25 per hour, are also generally available. For further information, contact the German National Tourist Office or **VDWS** (Fasserstr. 30, 8120 Weilheim, Oberbayern).

Winter Sports Southern Bavaria is the big winter-sports region, with Garmisch-Partenkirchen the best-known center. There are also winter-sports resorts in the Black Forest, the Harz region, the Bavarian Forest, the Rhön Mountains, the Fichtelgebirge, the Sauerland, and the Swabian mountains. The season generally runs from the middle of December to the end of March, but at higher altitudes, such as the Zugspitze (near Garmisch), you can usually ski from as early as the end of November to as late as the middle of May. There's no need to bring skis with you—you can rent them or buy them on the spot. Look for the special winter off-season rates *(Weisse Wochen)* offered by most winter sports resorts for cross-country and downhill skiing vacations. Prices include seven days' bed and breakfast (or half-board) plus ski lessons.

For cross-country (or *Langlauf*) skiing, which is becoming increasingly popular—the equipment is considerably cheaper than downhill (or *Alpin*) equipment, and there is no waiting at ski-lifts—there are stretches of prepared tracks (or *Loipen*) to be found in the valleys and foothills of most winter-sports centers, as well as in the suburbs of larger towns in southern Bavaria.

Ski-bobbing is on the increase. There are runs and schools at Bayrischzell, Berchtesgaden, Garmisch-Partenkirchen, Füssen, and Oberstdorf in the Alps, as well as at Altglashütten, Bernau, and Felberg in the Black Forest. Ice rinks, many open all year, are prolific.

Dining

The choice of eating places in Germany is extremely varied both in style and price. The most sophisticated spots—and the most expensive—are found principally in cities. Munich and Düsseldorf, for example, boast the only three-star restaurants in Germany, but Köln, Frankfurt, Hamburg, Aachen, Wiesbaden, and Berlin are close on their heels. At the opposite end of the scale, almost every street has its *Gaststätte*, a sort of combination diner and pub, and every village its *Gasthof*, or inn. The emphasis in both is on the characteristic German preference for *gut bürgerliche Küche*, or good home cooking, with simple food, wholesome rather than sophisticated, at reasonable prices. These are also places where people meet in the evening for a chat, a beer, and a game of cards, so you needn't feel compelled to leave as soon as you have eaten. They normally serve hot meals from 11:30 AM to 8:30 or 9 PM, after which cold snacks are usually available. Lunch rather than dinner is the main meal in Germany, a fact reflected in the almost universal appearance of a *Tageskarte*, or suggested menu, every lunchtime. And at a cost of DM 8 to DM 15, in either a Gaststätte or Gasthof, for soup, a main course, and simple dessert (though this is not always offered), it's excellent value. Coffee, however, even in expensive restaurants, is not usually served, and then is often not particularly good. Go to a café after your meal and have your coffee there. Some, though not all, expensive restaurants also offer a table d'hôte (suggested or special) daily menu. Prices will be much higher than in a Gaststätte or Gasthof, but considerably cheaper than à la carte. In fact, as far as à la carte eating in Germany is concerned, there's normally not much difference between lunch and dinner prices.

Regional specialties are given in the Dining sections of individual chapters. For names of German foods and dishes, *see* the Menu Guide at the end of this book.

Budget Eating Tips

Foreign Restaurants Germany has a vast selection of moderately priced Italian, Greek, Chinese, and—largely as a result of the numbers of Yugoslav and Turkish workers in Germany—Balkan restaurants. All are good value, though you may find food in Balkan restaurants spicy. Italian restaurants are about the most popular of all specialty restaurants in Germany—the pizza-to-go is as much a part of the average German's diet as *Bratwürst* or a hamburger. You'll find that Chinese restaurants in particular offer special tourist and lunch menus.

Stand-up Snack Bars Often located in pedestrian zones, *Imbiss* stands can be found in almost every busy shopping street, in parking lots, train stations, and near markets. They serve *Würst* (sausages), grilled, roasted, or boiled, of every shape and size, and rolls filled with cheese, cold meat, or fish, usually accompanied by french fries. Prices range from DM 3 to DM 6 per portion.

Department Stores For lunch, restaurants in local department stores *(Kaufhäuser)* are especially recommended for wholesome, appetizing, and inexpensive food. **Kaufhof, Karstadt, Horton,** and **Hertie** are names to note, as well as the enormous **Kadewe** in Berlin.

Butcher Shops Known as *Metzgerei*, these often have a corner serving warm snacks. The **Vincenz-Murr** chain in Munich and Bavaria have particularly good-value food. Try *Warmer Leberkäs mit Kartoffelsalat*, a typical Bavarian specialty, which is a sort of baked meat loaf with sweet mustard and potato salad. In north Germany, try *Bouletten*, small hamburgers, or *Currywürst*, sausages in piquant curry sauce.

Fast Food A number of fast-food chains exist all over the country. The best are **Wienerwald, McDonald's,** and **Wendy's.** There are also **Nordsee** fish bars, serving hot and cold fish dishes for lunch.

Picnics Buy some wine or beer and some cold cuts and rolls *(Brötchen)* from a department store, supermarket, or delicatessen and turn lunchtimes into picnics. You'll not only save money, but you'll also be able to enjoy Germany's beautiful scenery. Or leave out the beer and take your picnic to a beer garden, sit down at one of the long wood tables, and order a *Mass* (liter) of beer.

Ratings Restaurants in our listings are divided by price into four categories: Very Expensive; Expensive; Moderate; and Inexpensive. *See* Dining in individual chapters for specific prices. All restaurants other than the least expensive display their menus, with prices, outside; all prices shown will include tax and service. Prices for wine also include tax and service.

Lodging

The standard of German hotels—from sophisticated luxury spots (of which the country has more than its fair share) to the humblest pension—is excellent. Rates can be high, though not disproportionately so in comparison to other north European countries. You can nearly always expect courteous and polite service, clean and comfortable rooms, and more than a little atmosphere.

In addition to hotels proper, the country also has numerous Gasthöfe or *Gasthäuser*, which are country inns that serve food and also have rooms; pensions, or *Fremdenheime* (guest houses); and, at the lowest end of the scale, *Zimmer*, meaning simply "rooms," normally in private houses (look for the sign reading *Zimmer frei* or *zu vermieten* on a green background, meaning "to rent"; a red sign reading *besetzt* means that there are no vacancies).

Lists of German hotels are available from the German National Tourist Office and all regional and local tourist offices. (Most hotels have restaurants, but those listed as *Garni* will provide breakfast only.) Tourist offices will also make bookings for you at a nominal fee, but may have difficulty doing so after 4 PM in high season and on weekends, so don't leave it until too late in the day before looking for your accommodations. (If you do get stuck, ask someone who looks local—a postman, policeman, or waitress, for example—for a Zimmer zu vermieten or Gasthof; in rural areas especially you'll find that people are genuinely helpful). A hotel reservation service is also operated by **ADZ** (Beethovenstr. 61, 6000 Frankfurt/Main, tel. 069/740767). It is able to make reservations in many hotels throughout the country for a small fee.

Many major American hotel chains—Hilton, Sheraton, Holiday Inn, Arabella, Canadian Pacific, Ramada, Preferred—have hotels in the larger German cities. Similarly, European chains are well represented.

Romantik Hotels Among the most delightful places to stay—and eat—in Germany are the aptly named Romantik Hotels and Restaurants. The Romantik group now has establishments throughout northern Europe (and even a few in the United States), including around 60 in Germany itself. All are in atmospheric and historic buildings—an essential precondition of membership—and are personally run by the owners, with the emphasis on excellent food and service. Prices vary considerably from Very Expensive to Moderate (*see* Ratings, below), but in general represent good value, particularly the special-weekends and short-holiday rates. A three- or four-day stay, for example, with one main meal, is available at about DM 250 to DM 400 per person.

In addition, German Railways offers a special "Romantik Hotel Rail" program, which, in conjunction with a German Rail Tourist Ticket, gives nine days' unlimited travel. You don't need to plan your route in advance—only your first night's accommodations need to be reserved before you leave. The remaining nights can be reserved as you go. The package also includes sightseeing trips, a Rhine/Mosel cruise, bicycle rentals, and the like.

A detailed brochure listing all Romantik Hotels and Restaurants is available at $7.50 (including mailing) from **Romantik Hotels Reservations** (Box 1278, Woodinville, WA 98072, tel. 206/485–6985; for reservations, tel. 800/826–0015).

Castle Hotels Of comparable interest and value are Germany's castle, or *Schloss*, hotels, all privately owned and run and all long on atmosphere. A number of the simpler ones may lack some amenities, but the majority combine four-star luxury with valuable antique furnishings, four-poster beds, stone passageways, and baronial atmosphere. Some offer full resort facilities, too (tennis, swimming pools, horseback riding, hunting, and fishing. Nearly all are located away from cities and towns.

The German National Tourist Office issues a *Castle Hotels in Germany* brochure. They, and your travel agent, can also advise on a number of packages available for castle hotels, including four- to six-night tours.

Spas Taking the waters in Germany, whether for curing the body or merely beautifying it, has been popular since Roman times. There are about 250 health resorts and mineral springs in the country—the word *Bad* before the name of a place is a sure sign that it's a spa—offering treatments, normally at fairly high prices. Beauty farms, a growth industry if ever there was one, are normally found only in Very Expensive spa hotels.

There are four main groups of spas and health resorts: (1) the mineral and moorland spas, where treatments are based on natural warm-water springs; (2) those by the sea on the Baltic and North Sea coasts; (3) hydropathic spas, which use an invigorating process developed in the 19th century; and (4) climatic health resorts, which depend on their climates—usually mountainous—for their health-giving properties.

The average cost for three weeks of treatment is from DM 800 to DM 2,100; for four weeks, DM 1,300 to DM 3,200. This includes board and lodging, doctor's fees, treatments, and tax. A complete list of spas, giving full details of their springs and treatments, is available from the German National Tourist Office, or from **Deutsche Bäderverband,** the German Health Resort and Spa Association (Schumannstr. 111, 5300 Bonn 1).

Rentals Bungalows or apartments *(Ferienwohungen* or *Ferienapartments)*, usually accommodating two to eight people, can be rented throughout Germany. Rates are low, with reductions for longer stays. Gas and electricity, and sometimes water, are usually charged extra. There is also normally a charge for linen, though you may also bring your own.

Details of rentals in all regions of the country are available from the regional and local tourist offices. In addition, the German Automobile Association also issues listings of family holiday apartments; write **ADAC Reisen** (Am Westpark, 8000 Munich 70).

Farm Vacations *Urlaub auf dem Bauernhof,* or vacations down on the farm, have increased dramatically in popularity throughout Germany over the past five years, and almost every regional tourist office now produces a brochure listing farms in its area offering bed and breakfast, and apartments and whole farmhouses to rent. The German Agricultural Association (DLG) also produces an illustrated brochure listing over 1,500 farms, all inspected and graded, from the Alps to the North Sea, offering accommodations. It costs DM 7.50 (send an international reply coupon if writing from the United States) and is available from **DLG Reisedenst, Agratour** (Rüsterstr. 13, D-6000 Frankfurt/Main 1).

Camping Campsites—some 2,000 in all—are scattered the length and breadth of Germany. The **DCC,** or German Camping Club (Mandlstr. 28, D-8000 Munich 40) produces an annual listing of 1,600 sites; it also details sites where trailers and mobile homes can be rented. Similarly, the German Automobile Association (*see* Rentals, above, for address) publishes a listing of all campsites located at autobahn exits. In addition, the German National Tourist Office publishes a comprehensive and graded listing of campsites.

Sites are generally open from May to September, though about 400 are open year-round for the very rugged. Most sites get crowded during high season, however. Prices range from around DM 10 to DM 15 for a car, trailer, and two adults; less for tents. If you want to camp outside a site, you must get permission from the landowner beforehand; ask the police if you can't track him down. Drivers of mobile homes may park for one night only on roadsides and in Autobahn parking lots areas, but may not set up camping equipment there.

Youth Hostels Germany's youth hostels—*Jugendherbergen*—are probably the most efficient, up-to-date, and proportionally numerous of any country's in the world. There are some 600 in all, many located in castles that add a touch of romance to otherwise utilitarian accommodations. Other than in Bavaria, where there is an age limit of 27, there are no restrictions on age, though those under 20 take preference when space is limited. You'll need an International Youth Hostel card, valid one year, for reduced rates, usually about DM 3.20 to DM 4 for children and DM 10.50 for adults. Rates for families are around DM 20 per night. Cards are available from the **American Youth Hostels Association** (Box 37613, Washington, D.C. 20013) and the **Canadian Hostelling Association** (333 River Rd., Ottawa, Ontario K1L 8H9).

For listings of German youth hostels, contact the **Deutsches Jugendhergerswerk Hauptverband** (26 Bulowstr., D-4930 Detmold, tel. 05231/74010) or the German National Tourist Office.

Ratings Hotels in our listings are divided by price into four categories: Very Expensive; Expensive; Moderate; and Inexpensive. *See*

Lodging in individual chapters for specific prices. Note that there is no official grading system for hotels in Germany. Rates are by no means inflexible, and depend very much on supply and demand. Many resort hotels offer substantial reductions in winter, except in the Alps, where rates often rise in winter. Likewise, many Very Expensive and Expensive hotels in cities offer substantial reductions on weekends and when business is quiet. It's always worth checking to see if reductions are available; the savings can be considerable. Rooms booked after 10 PM are often cheaper, too, on the basis that an occupied room at a reduced rate is better than an empty one. You should be careful about trying to book late in the day at peak times, however. During trade fairs (most seem to be held in the spring and fall), rates in city hotels can rise appreciably. Breakfast is usually but not always included in room rates; be sure to check before you book. Check, too, if your room has a shower or a tub—rooms with neither are rare in Germany—as a room with a shower will be a little less expensive than a room with a tub. Finally, if you don't like the room you're offered, ask to see another.

Credit Cards

The following credit card abbreviations are used: AE, American Express; DC, Diners Club; MC, Mastercard; V, Visa.

Great Itineraries

The Castles of Ludwig II

Munich tour operators offer day trips to the four famous castles of Bavaria's flamboyant King Ludwig II, but for those who want to get to know them without distracting interruptions, there's no alternative but to strike out on your own. The castles are set in magnificent countryside that invites the visitor to linger and complete his stay with a walk or a hike undisturbed by the demands of a tour operator's timetable. If you're relying on public transportation, you'll have to return to Munich to visit the fourth castle, Herrenchiemsee, but arrange your itinerary so you can spend the night outside the city.

Length of Trip 6 to 7 days.

Getting Around **By Car:** From Munich, this is a 210-mile roundtrip drive.

By Public Transportation: Füssen, Ettal (Oberammergau), and the Chiemsee Lake are all easily reached by fast trains from Munich.

The Main Route **Two Nights: Füssen.** Neuschwanstein and Hohenschwangau (Ludwig's childhood home) can both be reached on foot from Füssen. Alternatively, hire bikes from the local station. Allow at least a full day to appreciate Neuschwanstein.

Two Nights: Ettal. Buses run from the picturesque mountain village of Ettal to Linderhof (which some class as the finest product of Ludwig's imagination). Find time to visit the Ettal monastery. Oberammergau is a 10-minute bus-ride away.

Two Nights: Chiemsee. The unfinished Herrenchiemsee palace stands on Herren Island in the Chiemsee. Passenger boats offer regular service to the island (and to the smaller, equally charming Fraueninsel) from the lakeside resorts of Prien and Gstadt. A mainline train service runs from Munich to Prien, and the Munich–Salzburg Autobahn runs alongside the southern shore of Chiemsee.

Further Information: *See* Excursions from Munich, in Chapter 3; Chapter 4; and Chapter 8.

Through Central Germany to the North Sea

The Germans have always waxed romantic about their rivers, and not just about the Rhine and the Danube. At the idyllic point where the rivers Werra and Fulda join to become the Weser there's a granite stone with an inscription in verse that, loosely translated, reads:

Where Werra and Fulda gently kiss
and thereby lose their right to be,
The stately Weser is born by this
Embrace and flows on to the far-off sea.

The Weser is truly stately, one of Germany's most beautiful rivers, bordered by sleepy towns with medieval streets of half-timbered houses running down to the water's edge, and spilling into the North Sea's great German Bight after donating its last services to the shipbuilders of Bremen and Bremerhaven. This is literally fairy-tale country, where the Grimm Brothers lived and worked and soaked up the inspiration for their immortal stories. Our itinerary diverges from theirs, however, beginning on the banks of another great German river, the Main, at Aschaffenburg with its magnificent Renaissance palace, the former seat of the electors of Mainz. Behind Aschaffenburg rise the wild, wooded heights of the Spessart. You'll leave the Spessart at the picturesque little town of Steinau an der Strasse, where the Grimm brothers spent their childhood, and then head into another wild area of central Germany, the Rhön mountains. From here you can look into the eastern, Communist half of the divided country. Here also you'll find the source of the Fulda River, the start of the main itinerary. From there, you continue on to Münden, where the Fulda "embraces" the Werra and travels onward as the Weser to the North Sea.

Length of Trip 7 to 10 days.

Getting Around **By Car:** From Frankfurt, take Autobahn A-3 (direction Würzburg and Munich) to Aschaffenburg, then follow the well-marked "Rhön- und Spessfahrt" route through the Spessart and Rhön to Fulda. From Fulda, follow the Fulda River valley road to Bad Hersfeld, Rotenburg an der Fulda, and Kassel. From Kassel, follow the Wesertal road to Bremen and the sea.

By Public Transportation: All the main points on the route—Aschaffenburg, Fulda, Kassel and Bremen—can be reached by regular Intercity trains from Frankfurt. Bus services connect the smaller centers.

The Main Route **One Night: Aschaffenburg.** Spare a morning or an afternoon to tour the mighty Elector's Palace, the Renaissance-style Johannisburg.

Two Nights: Take your time traveling through the **Spessart,** pulling in to spend the night at bed-and-breakfast farmhouses along the way.

Two Nights: A similarly unhurried tour of the **Rhön** is recommended. Find time for an excursion to the Schwarzes Moor (Black Moor) on the East German frontier.

One Night: Fulda, with an evening stroll through its Baroque quarter.

One Night: Kassel—you'll need an entire day to appreciate fully the beauty of the Wilhelmshöhe park and palace.

Three Nights: You'll find three nights the minimum length of time to travel the **Wesertal** route to Bremen. If you're driving, reserve at least one night in one of the castle hotels in the Reinhardswald. For the rest of the trip, hunt out waterside hotels and guesthouses along the banks of the Weser.

One Night: Bremen—and one day at least to sit back and take stock of the trip. Take a morning or afternoon excursion to the fishing-boat harbor of Bremerhaven.

Further Information: *See* Chapter 14.

The Castle Road

Just outside the city of Heilbronn, amid rich vineyards, are the romantic ruins of the castle of the "Faithful Women." The explanation of its strange name is as romantic as the castle's setting. The German King Konrad III laid siege to the castle in 1140, and in a moment of uncharacteristic weakness allowed the women living within its walls to leave with as many of their possessions as they could carry. He is said to have lost his regal cool when the women of the castle trooped out carrying their menfolk on their shoulders. But he kept his word—and the men of the castle were spared. It's a marvelous yarn, typical of the stories you'll hear throughout this "castle" trail. There are about 50 castles along the 180-mile route between Mannheim and Nürnberg, a greater concentration than in any other part of Germany. Time and other circumstances (some of the castles are in private hands or serve some municipal function, and can't be visited) will prevent you from looking over them all. On the other hand, some are now hotels where you'll be tempted to linger at least for a meal, perhaps to stay the night.

Length of Trip 12 to 14 days.

Getting Around **By Car:** It's 180 miles from Mannheim to Nürnberg. Follow the Neckar Valley road, B-27, from Mannheim to Heilbronn, then take the Burgenstrasse (the Castle Road itself) to Rothenburg ob der Tauber. From Rothenburg, head for Colmberg and Hessbach, joining B-13 for the final stretch to Ansbach and Nürnberg.

By Public Transportation: Mannheim, Heidelberg, Heilbronn, and Nürnberg are all connected by regular express train services, but you'll have to rely on country bus services to reach many of the remoter castles.

The Main Route **One Night: Mannheim.** Take part of the day to visit Mannheim's magnificent 18th-century Elector's Palace, one of the largest Baroque buildings in Europe, and the Reissinsel Park and its walks alongside the Rhine.

Two Nights: Heidelberg. Spend a full day exploring Heidelberg itself, then make an excursion to the Heiligenberg, into the

Odenwald forest or to the castles of Schadeck, Hornberg, Hirschorn (all of them hotels, with excellent restaurants), or to Zwingenberg and Minneburg.

Three Nights: Heilbronn. Plan excursions to the remains of the imperial palace of Bad Wimpfen and to the castles of Horneck, Guttenberg (with its aviary of birds of prey, including some fine eagles), Bad Rappenau, Ehrenberg, Weinsberg (the castle of "Faithful Women"), Neuenstein, and perhaps to the museum of bicycle and motorcycle technology at Neckarsulm.

Two Nights: Rothenburg an der Tauber. You'll want to spend a full day at least exploring Rothenburg, Europe's best-preserved medieval town. After that, make excursions along the Tauber river valley and to the castles of Langenburg, Bartenstein, and Colmberg.

Two Nights: Ansbach. Visit the margraves' palace and to the 12th-century monastery church of Heilsbronn.

Two Nights: Nürnberg.

Further Information: *See* Chapter 8, Chapter 9, and Chapter 11.

Rivers of Wine

The Rhine and Mosel need no introduction, but who knows the attractions of their tributaries—the rivers Saar and Nahe? Or the remote villages that scatter across the Hunsrück range of hills, which is bordered by all four rivers? A tour of the four "rivers of wine" takes you from the crowds and crush of the Rhine of picture-postcard fame to the less dramatic but much more peaceful valley of the Saar. The Hunsrück high road leads you back at your own pace to the point where the well-trodden tourist trail picks up again on the Nahe River. In little more than a week, you'll have skirted (and perhaps visited) Germany's most famous vineyards—and you should have tasted some of the country's finest wines.

Length of Trip 10 to 12 days.

Getting Around **By Car:** It's a 280-mile roundtrip drive from Wiesbaden.

By Public Transportation: The rail journey along the Rhine between Bingen and Koblenz is Germany's most spectacular train ride. River boats also make the journey, and you can stop off at any point on the way. From Koblenz, the rail line hugs the contours of the Mosel River to Trier; alternatively, you can again choose to travel the river by boat. A combination of train and bus will complete the itinerary along the Saar and across the Hunsrück to the Nahe River. Bus tours are offered by travel agencies in Wiesbaden, Bingen, Koblenz, and Trier.

The Main Route **Two Nights:** The **Rheingau** region, between Eltville and Rüdesheim. Visit the vineyards of the Rheingau (they produce Germany's finest wine), and Bingen, at the mouth of the Nahe River.

Four Nights: Along the **Rhine** between Rüdesheim and Koblenz. See the vineyards of Bacharach, Boppard, Brey, Kaub, Lorch, Oberwesel, Spay, and St. Goar, and the castles (or what remains of them) of Ehrenfels, Katz, Reichenstein, Rheinstein, Schönburg, and Sooneck.

Four Nights: Along the **Mosel** between Koblenz and Trier. Take excursions to the Deutsche Eck (where the Mosel and Rhine meet) and to the vineyards of Alken, Bernkastel-Kues, Bremm (Europe's steepest vineyard), Ediger, Kobern-Gondorf, Kröv, Nehren, Neumagen (Germany's oldest wine town, praised by the 4th-century Roman poet Ausonius in his work *Mosella*), Piesport, Traben-Trarbach, Winningen, (its August wine festival is one of Germany's oldest), Zell, and to the castles of Cochem, Ehrenburg, Eltz (a medieval picture-book castle so treasured by the Germans that they've put its image on their DM 500 bank notes), and Thurant.

Two Nights: Trier. Explore Trier and follow the Saar River to Saarburg, Mettlach, and as far as the great "Saar Bend," a spectacular point where the river nearly doubles back on itself.

Two Nights: Idar-Oberstein. Venture into the Hunsrück hills and along the Nahe River to Bad Kreuznach. Take a day tour of the "Precious Stones Route," a well-marked 30-mile itinerary, starting and ending in Idar Oberstein, where precious stones are still mined and polished.

Further Information: *See* Chapter 13.

Through the Black Forest

Many first-time visitors to the Black Forest literally can't see the forest for the trees. There are so many contrasting attractions that the basic, enduring beauty of the area passes them by. So in your tour of the forest, take time to stray from the tourist path and inhale the cool, mysterious air of its darker recesses. Walk or ride through its shadowy corridors or across its open upland; row a canoe and tackle the wild water of the Nagold and Wolf rivers. Then take time out to relax in any of the many spas, order a Baden wine enlivened by a dash of local mineral water, seek out the nearest restaurant that confesses its food is influenced by the cuisine of neighboring France. And, if you have money to spare at the end of your tour, return to Baden-Baden, try your luck on the gaming tables, and celebrate your good fortune or forget ill fate at the bar of the casino's "Equipage" nightclub.

Length of Trip 12 to 14 days.

Getting Around **By Car:** It's a 250-mile roundtrip drive from Stuttgart.

By Public Transportation: Stuttgart, Baden-Baden, and Freiburg are all on Intercity train routes, and local trains and buses link them with most towns and spas of the Black Forest. Bus tours of the Black Forest are offered by travel agencies in Baden-Baden and Freiburg.

Two Nights: Freudenstadt. Take excursions to the Schwarzwald Museum at Lossburg, the Freilicht museum Vogtsbauernhof near Wolfach, the Alpirsbach brewery, and the Glasswald lake near Schapbach.

One Night: Triberg area. See the Triberg waterfall and the clock museums of Triberg and Furtwangen.

Two Nights: Hinterzarten or **Titisee.** Visit the Feldberg, the Black Forest's highest mountain and the Titisee and Schluchsee.

Two Nights: Freiburg. Explore Freiburg, the Schauinsland mountain, the Dr. Faustus town of Staufen, and the vineyards on the slopes of the Kaiserstuhl.

One Night: Offenburg. Visit the surrounding vineyards.

Two Nights: Baden-Baden. Enjoy the sights in and around Baden-Baden and travel to the summit of nearby Merkur Mountain, to Schloss Favorite, and to Windeck Castle.

One Night: Bad Liebenzell. See Calw.

Further Information: *See* Chapter 7.

Toward East Bavaria

There's a corner of Germany that's on the doorstep of the country's most popular tourist area and yet can seem a thousand miles from it. It stretches eastward from Munich to the Austrian border, its southern edge marked by the Salzburg-bound Autobahn, which propels most visitors and tourists to the greater attractions of the Bavarian Alps looming in the hazy distance. It's a gentle, pastoral region of rolling farmland, forgotten villages asserting their presence with hilltop, onion-domed Baroque churches, of reed-fringed lakes and willow-bordered rivers. And what rivers! You'll meet the Inn as it meanders northward in search of the Danube, Salzburg's Salzach River, then the mighty Danube itself as it surges into Austria, and finally the Isar, ice-green and—just as the poet promised—still "rolling rapidly" from its mountain source.

Length of Trip 7 to 8 days.

Getting Around **By Car:** It's a 250-mile roundtrip drive from Munich.

By Public Transportation: The route can be covered entirely by train, beginning with the main-line route from Munich to Wasserburg and then using local services between the remaining towns.

The Main Route **One Night: Wasserburg.** Visit the medieval Amerang castle (in summer, scene of chamber-music concerts) and the farmhouse museum at Amerang.

One Night: Laufen, on the Austrian border. Take excursions to the Waginger See, Germany's warmest lake, and across the Salzach River to the Austrian town of Oberndorf, where the Christmas carol "Silent Night" was composed.

One Night: Burghausen. In Altötting, see the 14th-century "Black Madonna" in an 8th-century chapel chosen by the Wittelsbachs to be the repository of silver urns containing the hearts of the Bavarian rulers.

Two Nights: Passau. Venture into the Bavarian Forest and to the border of Czechoslovakia.

One Night: Straubing. Travel to the Danube towns Deggendorf and Bogen.

Further Information: *See* Chapter 6.

2 Portraits of Germany

Germany at a Glance: A Chronology

c 5000 BC Primitive tribes settle in the Rhine and Danube valleys

c 2000–800 BC Distinctive German Bronze Age culture emerges, with settlements ranging from coastal farms to lakeside villages

c 450–50 BC Salzkammergut people, whose prosperity is based on abundant salt deposits (in the area of upper Austria), trade with Greeks and Etruscans; they spread as far as Belgium and have first contact with the Romans

9 BC–AD 9 Roman attempts to conquer the "Germans"—the tribes of the Cimbri, the Franks, the Goths, and the Vandals—are only partly successful; the Rhine becomes the northeastern border of the Roman Empire (and remains so for 300 years)

212 Roman citizenship is granted to all free inhabitants of the Empire

c 400 Pressed forward by Huns from Asia, German tribes such as the Franks, the Vandals, and the Lombards migrate to Gaul (France), Spain, Italy, and North Africa, scattering the Empire's populace and eventually leading to the disintegration of central Roman authority

486 The Frankish kingdom is founded by Clovis; his court is in Paris

497 The Franks convert to Christianity

---

776 Charlemagne becomes king of the Franks

800 Charlemagne is declared Holy Roman Emperor; he makes Aachen capital of his realm, which stretches from the Bay of Biscay to the Adriatic and from the Mediterranean to the Baltic. Under his enlightened patronage, there is an upsurge in art and architecture—the Carolingian renaissance

843 The Treaty of Verdun divides Charlemagne's empire among his three sons: West Francia becomes France; Lotharingia becomes Lorraine (territory to be disputed by France and Germany into the 20th century); and East Francia takes on, roughly, the shape of modern Germany

911 Five powerful German dukes (of Bavaria, Lorraine, Franconia, Saxony, and Swabia) establish the first German monarchy by electing King Conrad I

962 Otto I is crowned Holy Roman Emperor by the Pope; he establishes Austria—the East Mark. The Ottonian renaissance is marked especially by the development of Romanesque architecture

1024–1125 The Salian Dynasty is characterized by a struggle between emperors and Church that leaves the empire weak and disorganized; the great Romanesque cathedrals of Speyer, Trier, Mainz, and Worms are built

1138–1254 Frederick Barbarossa leads the Hohenstaufen Dynasty; there is temporary re-centralization of power, underpinned by strong trade and Church relations

1158 Munich, capital of Bavaria, is founded by Duke Henry the Lion; Henry is deposed by Emperor Barbarossa, and Munich is presented to the House of Wittelsbach, which rules it until 1919

1241 The Hanseatic League is founded to protect trade; Bremen, Hamburg, Köln, and Lübeck are early members. Agencies soon extend to London, Antwerp, Venice, and the Baltic and North seas; a complex banking and finance system results

mid-1200s The Gothic style, exemplified by the grand Köln Cathedral, flourishes

---

1445 Johannes Gutenberg (1397–1468) prints first book in Europe

1471 The painter Albrecht Dürer (dies 1528) is born into what becomes a time of intellectual and artistic upheaval—the Renaissance. The Humanist philosophy of central Italy and the rediscovery of ancient Greek and Roman learning spread north to Germany at the beginning of the 16th century. The philosopher Erasmus (1466–1536), and the painters Hans Holbein the Younger (1497–1543), Lucas Granach (1472–1553), and Albrecht Altdorfer (1480–1538) help disseminate the new view of the world. Increasing wealth among the merchant classes leads to strong patronage for the revived arts

1517 The Protestant Reformation begins in Germany when Martin Luther (1483–1546) nails his "Ninety-Five Theses" to a church door in Wittenberg, contending that the Roman Church has forfeited divine authority through the corrupt sale of indulgences. Though Luther is outlawed, his revolutionary doctrine splits the Church; much of north Germany embraces Protestantism

1524–25 The (Catholic) Hapsburgs rise to power; their empire spreads throughout Europe (and as far as North Africa, the Americas, and the Philippines). In 1530, Charles V (a Hapsburg) is crowned Holy Roman Emperor; he brutally crushes the Peasants' War, one in a series of populist uprisings in Europe

1545 The Council of Trent marks the beginning of the Counter-Reformation. Through diplomacy and coercion, most Austrians, Bavarians, and Bohemians are won back to Catholicism, but the majority of Germany remains Lutheran; persecution of religious minorities grows

1618–48 Germany is the main theater for combat in the Thirty Years' War. The powerful Catholic Hapsburgs are defeated by Protestant forces, swelled by disgruntled Hapsburg subjects and the armies of King Gustav Adolphus of Sweden. The bloody conflict ends with the Peace of Westphalia (1648); Hapsburg and papal authority are severly diminished

---

1689 Louis XIV of France invades the Rhineland Palatinate and sacks Heidelberg. Elsewhere at the end of the 17th century, Germany consolidates its role as a center of scientific thought; Gottfried Wilhelm Leibniz (1646–1716) helps found the Berlin Academy in 1696

1708 Johann Sebastian Bach (1685–1750) becomes court organist at Weimar and launches his prolific career; he and George Frideric Handel (1685–1759) fortify the great tradition of German music. Baroque and, later, Rococo art and architecture flourish, reaching a peak in the work of the brothers Cosmas

Damian Asam (1686–1739) and Egid Quirin Asam (1692–1750), Dominikus Zimmermann (1685–1766), and Balthasar Neumann (1687–1753)

1740–86 Reign of Frederick the Great of Prussia; his rule sees both the expansion of Prussia (it becomes the dominant military force in Germany) and the growth of Enlightenment thought

c 1790 The great age of European orchestral music is raised to new heights in the work of Joseph Haydn (1732–1809), Wolfgang Amadeus Mozart (1756–1791), and Ludwig van Beethoven (1770–1827)

---

early 1800s The author Johann Wolfgang von Goethe (1749–1832) initiates Romanticism with his publication of the wildly popular *Sorrows of Young Werther* (his most famous work is *Faust*). Other Romantics include the writers Friedrich Schiller (1759–1805) and Henrich Kleist (1777–1811); the composers Robert Schumann (1810–1856), Franz Schubert (1797–1828), Richard Wagner (1813–1883), and Johannes Brahms (1833–1897); and the painter Casper David Friedrich (1774–1840). In architecture, the severe lines of Neoclassicism replace the delicacy of Rococo designs, especially in the Protestant north

1806 Napoléon's armies invade Prussia; it briefly becomes part of the French Empire

1807 The Prussian prime minister Baron vom und zum Stein frees the serfs, creating a new spirit of patriotism; the Prussian army is rebuilt

1813 The Prussians defeat Napoléon at Leipzig

1815 Britain and Prussia defeat Napoléon at Waterloo. At the Congress of Vienna, the German Confederation is created as a loose union of 39 independent states, reduced from more than 300 principalities. The *Bundestag* (national assembly) is established at Frankfurt. Already powerful Prussia increases, gaining the Rhineland, Westphalia, and most of Saxony

1848 The "Year of the Revolutions" is marked by uprisings across the fragmented German Confederation; Prussia uses the opportunity for further expansion. A national parliament is elected; taking the power of the Bundestag to prepare a constitution for a united Germany

1862 Otto von Bismarck (1815–1898) becomes Prime Minister of Prussia; he is determined to wrest German-populated provinces from Austro-Hungarian (Hapsburg) control

1866 Austria-Hungary is defeated by the Prussians at Sadowa; Bismarck sets up the Northern German Confederation in 1867. A key figure in Bismarck's plans is Ludwig II of Bavaria (the Dream King). Ludwig—a political simpleton—lacks successors, making it easy for Prussia to grab his lands

1867 Karl Marx (1818–1883) publishes *Das Kapital;* much of his life is spent in exile

1870–71 The Franco-Prussian War: Prussia lays siege to Paris. Victorious Prussia seizes Alsace-Lorraine but eventually withdraws from all other occupied French territories

1871 The four southern German states agree to join the Northern Confederation; Wilhelm I is proclaimed first Kaiser of the united Empire

1882 Triple Alliance is forged between Germany, Austria-Hungary, and Italy. Germany's industrial revolution blossoms, enabling it to catch up with the other great powers of Europe. Germany establishes colonies in southwest and east Africa and the Pacific

c 1885 Daimler and Benz pioneer the automobile

1890 Kaiser Wilhelm II (rules 1888–1918) dismisses Bismarck and begins a new, more aggressive course of foreign policy; he oversees the expansion of the Navy

1890s First Impressionism, then German Expressionism, come to the fore in the arts, placing the country at the vanguard of European culture; a new school of writers, including Rainer Maria Rilke (1875–1926), emerges. Rilke's *Sonnets to Orpheus* gives German poetry new lyricism

1905 Albert Einstein (1879–1955) announces his theory of relativity

1907 Great Britian, Russia, and France form the Triple Entente which, set against the Triple Alliance, divides Europe into two armed camps

1914–18 Austrian Archduke Franz Ferdinand is assassinated in Serbia. The attempted German invasion of France sparks off World War I; Italy and Russia join the Allies, and four years of pitched battle ensue. By 1918, the Central Powers are encircled and must capitulate

---

1918 Germany is compelled by the Versailles Treaty to give up its overseas colonies and much European territory (including Alsace-Lorraine to France) and to pay huge reparations to the Allies; the tough terms leave the new democracy (the Weimar Republic) shaky

1919 Bauhaus design, the brainchild of Walter Gropius (1883–1969), is born. Thomas Mann (1875–1955) and Hermann Hesse (1877–1962) forge a new style of visionary intellectual writing—until quashed by Nazism

1923 Germany suffers runaway inflation. Adolf Hitler's "Beer Hall Putsch," a rightist revolt, fails; leftist revolts are frequent

1925 Hitler publishes *Mein Kampf* ("My Struggle")

1932 The Nazi Party gains the majority in the Bundestag

1933 Hitler becomes chancellor; the Nazi "revolution" begins

1934 President Paul von Hindenburg dies; Hitler declares himself "Führer" (leader) of the Third Reich (empire). Nazification of all German social institutions begins, spreading a policy that is virulently racist and anti-Communist. Germany recovers industrial might and re-arms

1936 Germany signs anti-Communist agreements with Italy and Japan, forming the Axis; Hitler re-occupies the Rhineland

1938 The *Anschluss* (annexation): Hitler occupies Austria; Germany occupies the Sudetenland in Czechoslovakia

1939–40 In August, Hitler signs a pact with the Soviet Union; in September he invades Poland; war is declared by the Allies. Over the next three years, there are Nazi invasions of Denmark, Norway, the Low Countries, France, Yugoslavia, and Greece. Alliances form between Germany and the Baltic states

1941–45 Hitler launches his anti-Communist crusade against the Soviet Union, reaching Leningrad in the north and Stalingrad and the Caucasus in the south. In 1944, the Allies land in France; their combined might brings the Axis to its knees. In addition to the millions killed in the fighting, over 6 million have died in Hitler's concentration camps. Germany is again in ruins. Hitler kills himself. Berlin (and today's East Germany) is occupied by the Soviet Union

---

1945 At the Yalta Conference, France, the United States, Britain, and the Soviet Union divide Germany into four zones; each country occupies a quarter of Berlin. The Potsdam Agreement expresses the determination to rebuild Germany as a democracy

1948 The Soviet Union tears up the Potsdam Agreement and attempts, by blockade, to exclude the three other Allies from their agreed zones in Berlin. Stalin is frustrated by a massive airlift of supplies to West Berlin

1949 The three Western zones are combined to form the Federal Republic of Germany (FRG); the new West German parliament elects Konrad Adenauer as chancellor. Soviet-held East Germany becomes the Communist German Democratic Republic (GDR)

1950s West Germany, aided by the financial impetus provided by the Marshall Plan, rebuilds its devastated cities and economy—the *Wirtschaftswunder* (economic miracle) gathers pace

1957 The Treaty of Rome hearlds the formation of the European Economic Community (EEC); Germany is a founder member

1961 Communists build the Berlin Wall to stem the outward tide of refugees. The writers Heinrich Böll and Günter Grass emerge; these and other intellectuals grapple with the themes of demoralization and guilt for Nazism

1966–74 Diplomatic Willy Brandt is chancellor

1973 West and East Germany join the United Nations. Externally more secure than ever, Germany is troubled by internally extremist political actitivity, notably by the leftist, nihilist Baader-Meinhoff gang

1975 At the European Security Conference, the Helsinki Agreement is struck; West Germany officially recognizes the GDR and Poland

1980s The German Green Party, whose main concern is the environment, becomes one of Europe's most outspoken minority political parties; West Germany is the leading industrial power in Europe

A Survey of German Architecture

Think of German architecture and what comes to mind? A half-timbered Hansel-and-Gretel cottage with weathered doors, pointed gables, and tiny windows? Or maybe blocks of joyless high rises, the legacy of wartime destruction and a tribute to post-war reconstruction? Either way, it's unlikely that anything suggesting a heritage of major architectural achievement springs to mind. The tourist in search of fine architecture will head for Italy or France. There may be many reasons for visiting Germany but architecture, it seems, isn't one of them.

It's easy to understand why this view has gained currency, but that doesn't make it any less false. Despite wartime bomb damage, Germany remains a treasure house of architectural riches, from the brick churches of Hamburg and the austere Neoclassical monuments of Berlin to the imposing Romanesque cathedrals of the Rhineland and the giddy Rococo palaces of Franconia. Learning about them is fun and will enrich your visit immeasurably—as well as dispel some misconceptions.

Apart from the handful of remains dating from the time when Germany was occupied by the Romans, the oldest buildings standing today are the churches and palaces built during the Carolingian era, named after Charlemagne, who was crowned Holy Roman Emperor in 800. (The reason they remain is that they were the first native German buildings to be built in stone, rather than wood, and they couldn't burn down.) The Holy Roman Empire was the most powerful political entity in the western world at the time, and the Emperor's court, in Aachen, attracted artists, writers, musicians, and architects from far afield. Under Charlemagne, there was a remarkable rebirth of artistic creativity—the Carolingian Renaissance—which marked the end of the so-called Dark Ages.

The builders of the Carolingian period drew inspiration from 6th-century, often octagonal, Byzantine churches such as San Vitale in Ravenna, Italy, and from ancient Roman basilicas (long and rectangular, with side aisles), such as the one in Trier. Charlemagne's palace at Aachen, for instance, had an octagonal chapel and a basilica-shaped Great Hall.

Over the next two centuries, the Roman style gained over the Byzantine and evolved into what is now known as Romanesque, the first major European style of architecture. Though different countries within Europe had their own variations, Romanesque buildings generally had thick walls that were frescoed on the inside, extensive vaulting, small windows placed high up, and round arches. The finest examples of German Romanesque you can see today are the Rhineland cathedrals of Speyer, Mainz, Trier, and Worms.

The basilica form dominated Romanesque church architecture. Typically, it consisted of a central nave between two lower aisles with an apse at one end and a complex of columns, galleries, and steps as well as a baptistrey at the other. Beneath the altar there was usually a crypt where martyrs, bishops, and princes were buried. What was different about a Romanesque church, as distinct from a pure Roman building, was its taller height, its steep-roofed towers, and its molded brick arches and columns (Roman surfaces tended to be of smooth marble). Also, Romanesque column capitals, portal arches, and choir stalls were often sculpted or carved with human figures or abstract designs.

The Middle Ages saw the rise of monastic orders and of the aristocracy; international trade was flourishing; people were traveling more (mostly for religious pilgrimages and the Crusades), and were spreading their culture. By the early 13th century, a new aesthetic, allied to a sophisticated new building technology, had evolved in France and was quickly moving to other parts of Europe. Even though this new style, Gothic, evolved out of Romanesque designs, it could hardly have been more different. Whereas Romanesque was massive, Gothic was light and airy. The new effect was achieved partly through delicate rib-vaulting and partly through the balance of structural forces: The weight of the vault (the roof) was now supported by a network of "flying buttresses" outside the building, making the heavy pillars and arches of Romanesque architecture redundant. Masons had also discovered how to make pointed arches—which are more graceful than rounded ones—and safely install much larger windows. Stained glass bathed the interior of Gothic churches in shimmering pools of multi-colored light. On the outside, too, Gothic churches marked a departure from Romanesque design. Not only were there flying buttresses, there were also forests of vertical, filigree-like elements everywhere you looked, and tall, slender spires that seemed to reach up to the clouds.

An early example of the new architecture is St. George's Cathedral in Limburg, which is Romanesque on the outside, but Gothic inside. St. Elisabeth, in Marburg, and other "hall churches" (with naves and aisles of equal height)—followed. Most famous of all Gothic cathedrals in Germany is Köln, which, especially in its quest for height, is essentially French in style, though its architect was German. It was intended to be far larger than anything then built in France, but only its east end was finished in medieval times (building began in 1248; the church was consecrated in 1322). The rest, notably the two enormous towers, were completed in the 19th century.

French-type Gothic cathedrals continued to be built in the north, principally in the Rhineland, for several centuries. A hallmark of these later Gothic churches was the decoration by master sculptors, such as Tilman Riemenschneider, Michael Pacher, and Veit Stoss, who covered almost every stone with exuberant, witty carvings of people, animals, and plants.

Gothic was mainly an ecclesiastical style, a reflection of the great power and influence of the Church at the time. But it also found expression in military and civic architecture, such as the Teutonic Knights' castle at Marienburg and the town halls of Braunschweig, Lübeck, and Hannover. The Gothic town of Rothenburg-ob-der-Tauber remains virtually intact today.

The 15th and 16th centuries saw an increase in prosperity in Germany, for the bourgeoisie and aristocracy at least, if not for the clergy. Few new churches were built, and cathedrals remained unfinished. The rich burghers would no longer pay for them, preferring to spend their money instead on the new status symbols of comfortable town houses and prestigious civic buildings. Among the best examples are the Leipzig and Rothenburg town halls, the Plassenburg near Kulmbach, and the Pellerhaus in Nürnberg. It was the time of the half-timbered, steeply gabled town halls and patrician houses that make so many German towns look so quintessentially German. It was also a time of constant civil disturbance. The revolutionary ideas of Martin Luther were spreading throughout northern Europe. Peasants, made aware of the injustice of their social system, attacked and destroyed hundreds of castles and monasteries. The conflicts engendered by the Reformation continued into the 17th century, culminating in the appalling devastation of the Thirty Years' War (1618–48).

The Gothic style of architecture lasted longer in Germany than in other parts of Europe. Although it went through several phases of development (now categorized as early, high, and late), it still lagged behind the Renaissance movement, which began in Italy in the late 15th century and came to full flower there in the 16th century. The Humanist ideas and ideals of the Italian Renaissance made the mystical illusionism of Gothic designs out of step with the new, rational view of the world, in which man took a central role for the first time. In architecture, the soaring lines of Gothic buildings gave way to the rediscovered Classical styles of ancient Rome. Proportion and symmetry were the new goals; the vertical was abandoned in favor of the horizontal.

The Renaissance style was slow to travel north; it began to take root in Germany only in the early 17th century. Elias Holl's town hall at Augsburg is the prime example of this new style in Germany. The Thirty Years' War put an end to Germany's Renaissance almost as soon as it began; in the late 17th century, German architecture more or less leapfrogged Renaissance and went straight into Baroque, a development away from Classicism to something more extravagant, dramatic and theatrical. The appeal now was not to the head but to the heart—not to an ideal order, but to the emotional needs of the worshipper.

By the early 18th century, the country's political and economic climate had stabilized sufficently to allow the arts to thrive again, and the first stirrings of an astonishing cultural revival took place. Germany had become a mass of small states, each competing for political and artistic leadership, and each taking its cue from the absolutist court of the French Sun King, Louis XIV. Monasteries, abbeys, convents, and, above all, palaces were built, many deliberately modeled on Versailles, with sprawling, landscaped parks featuring ornamental fountains, canals, terraces, sweeping flights of stairs, tropical greenhouses ("orangeries"), and graceful statues. Political stability may have been a precondition for this upsurge, but it didn't explain it entirely. There could have been no artistic revival without some major artistic figures. Fortunately, 18th-century Germany was blessed with a bumper crop of artists.

In church architecture, the Baroque style (which, being Italian, was generally associated with the Catholic church and was never popular in the Protestant north of Germany) aimed to overwhelm through its illusion of swirling movement and its rich decorative effects, created by a liberal use of gilt and veined marble (or plaster painted to look like veined marble). The onion-dome churches of Bavaria are perfect examples. The basic ground plan of a Baroque church was round, or oval, a shape that was echoed in the concave and convex lines of walls, cornices, and side chapels. Complex illusionistic frescoes spread their way over the ceilings and down the walls. The statues that filled Baroque churches seemed more life-like—even larger than life—than previous sculptures. Their gestures were theatrical; their garments flowed as if the figures were moving.

In the 1720s and '30s, the Baroque style evolved into an even more ornamental, elaborate movement: Rococo. As a result of this style, named after its chief motif, the *rocaille* (an abstract, shell-like form), interiors became lighter, with pastel colors often highlighted by gold and silver. Curve countered curve; mirrors reflected swirl on swirl in rippling rhythms that reflected the music of the day created by Bach, Telemann, and Handel. Stucco (or plaster, to give it its more plebian name) reached astonishing heights of technical sophistication.

Two of the most significant German Rococo architects were the Asam brothers, Egid Quirin (1692–1750) and Cosmas Damian (1686–1739), whose richly decorated gold-and-brown church of St. John Nepomuk in Munich reflects both Italian influences and the brothers' abilities in sculpture and painting. Dominikus Zimmermann (1685–1766) was equally versatile. His masterpiece is the bright Die Wies church in Bavaria, decorated mainly in pinks, blues, and greens, with white painted statues and dream-like frescoes. In north Germany, Georg Wenzeslaus von Knobelsdorff (1699–1753) introduced the Prussians to Rococo with his spectacular Sanssouci palace at Potsdam, built for Frederick the Great. In Dresden you can see the extraordinary Zwinger summer palace, built by Matthaeus Daniel Poppleman (1662–1736) for the powerful Elector of Saxony. The building resembles nothing so much as a gargantuan piece of Meissen porcelain.

The genius of the German Rococo was Balthasar Neumann (1687–1753), who was chiefly responsible for the Würzburg Residenz, with its magnificent ceremonial staircase, later decorated with frescoes by the Italian artist Tiepolo. Of the many churches built by Neumann, that of Vierzehnheiligen, near Bamberg in Bavaria, begun in 1743, is his masterpiece, combining sophisticated spatial effects with exquisite decoration.

In the late 18th century, a reaction against the sumptuousness of Rococo set in, principally in the Protestant north, where architects (and their patrons) caught the French enthusiasm for the clear, symmetrical lines of classical Greek and Roman, and even Italian Renaissance, buildings. Neoclassical architecture was monumental and used "pure" geometrical forms, such as columns, cubes, cylindrical vaults, and rounded arches. Building activity centered on theaters, schools, academies, museums, and such monuments as victory arches and obelisks. Some of the finest examples are the Brandenburger Tor (Gate), Karl Friedrich Schinkel's (1781–1841) Berlin Opera House, Gottfried Semper's (1803–79) Dresden Opera House, and Leo von Klenze's (1784–1864) Walhalla temple near Regensburg. Klenze also created a whole street in Munich, the Ludwigstrasse, between the Siegestor victory arch and the Feldherrnhalle, in rigid neoclassical style.

In a counter-reaction to the austerity of neoclassicism, the architects of the mid- and late 19th century turned to earlier, more decorative styles, creating neo-Gothic, neo-Baroque, and other revival movements. The best-known example is the fantastic mock-medieval Bavarian castle of Neuschwanstein, commissioned by the eccentric King Ludwig II.

Around the turn of the century art nouveau (Jugendstil) grew out of the return to medievalism. It was a movement that started in England, with William Morris's arts and crafts designs, and had simple but stylized plant forms as its basic motif. You can see these free-flowing, asymmetrical buildings all over Germany; occasionally you'll run across entire Jugendstil districts, such as Darmstadt's Mathildenhohe.

Germany was one of the first countries to shake off the succession of pseudo-historical styles and take Europe into the 20th century with the Modern Movement. Peter Behrens's turbine factory in Berlin (1908–9) was a celebration of the machine age, a revolutionary structure of iron, glass, and concrete. In 1919, Behrens's pupil, Walter Gropius, formed the *Bauhaus* (house of building) school of architecture, in which architects, craftsmen, and artists worked together to create functional designs. It seems appropriate that the country that, after the war, had no choice but to adopt modernism—a style that has spanned the globe—to rebuild its shattered cities, should also have seen its birth.

Germany and Beer

by Graham Lees

British-born Graham Lees has lived in Munich since the early '80s and has traveled throughout Germany in search of its beers. He is a member of the British Guild of Beer Writers and a founder member of Britain's Campaign for Real Ale.

No country is more closely associated with beer than Germany. And rightly so, for no other country has so many breweries or so much reverence for the heady brew. The West Germans don't just produce *a* beverage called beer, they brew more than 5,000 varieties in a range of tastes and colors to tempt the palates of almost everyone. You'll find beer served up black, strong, and sweet, or pale, frothy, and bitter. Sometimes it's the color of a copper kettle and has a fruity taste; other times it's sharp and sour and has a slice of lemon floating in it. It may even come to your table with the aroma of smoldering beechwood. If you're in Berlin, don't be surprised if it's tinged red or green and is served in what looks like a fruit bowl (that's Berliner Weisse).

West Germany probably has as many breweries—1,250 at last count—as the rest of the world put together. There, beer is brewed in farmhouse cellars by grandmothers, in backyards by retired soldiers, in push-button factories by young technicians, in monasteries and convents by monks and nuns. Beer is drunk for breakfast (usually Weizenbier, or wheat beer), lunch, and supper. It's drunk on Alpine peaks, in boisterous beer halls, in chic cafés, and during intermission at the opera. It's even dispensed in maternity wards. And in Bavaria, it is legal to sip beer in the office because the drink is officially recognized as a food: "liquid bread."

The quintessential hallmark of West Germany's dedication to beer is the purity law, *das Reinheitsgebot,* which guards the quality of every last quaffable drop from Bremen to Berchtesgaden. The oldest food-protection law in the world, it has remained unchanged since Duke Wilhelm IV introduced it in Bavaria in 1516. The law decrees that only malted barley, hops, yeast, and water may be used to make beer, except for specialty wheat beers (Weizenbier or, in northern Germany, Weisse). In many other countries, it is common practice to substitute barley for cheaper fermentables, such as rice grits, maize, or potato flakes. The Reinheitsgebot prevents the use of any such substitutes, as well as the addition of shelf-life-enhancing adjuncts, which are commonly used elsewhere.

This fastidious attitude toward beer has led West Germans into bitter squabbles with their partners in Europe. Germany's West European neighbors have complained long and loud that the strict brewing law amounts to trade protectionism and prevents foreign brewers from competing to quench the great German thirst. The Bonn government has defended the purity law in the European Court with a petition signed by 2½ million beer drinkers and the telling statistic that beer supplies up to 25% of the daily nutritional needs of the average German man. Alas, the Germans lost their battle to stop less wholesome beers from being imported into their country. Nonetheless, the Reinheitsgebot still strictly applies to all beers brewed within Germany.

Asking for a "beer" in most German hostelries is like going into a cheese shop and asking for cheese. Even the simplest country inn will more than likely have a choice of beers and, in many pubs, there may be available several different draft beers in addition to the selection of bottled beers. To take just one example from hundreds, there's a pub in the Weihenstephan brewery at Freising, in southern Bavaria, that sells up to 11 different in-house brews. (The brewery itself, incidentally, claims to be the oldest in the world, with a history reaching back to the year 1040.)

The type of beer available varies from one part of the country to another. In areas of southern Germany, the choice can also depend on the time of year. Some beers are brewed for a particular season or an event in the religious calendar. For instance, Munich's *Starkbierzeit* (strong-beer season) celebrates spring; the dark, malty, double-strength beers produced for the occasion have their origins in a 17th-century monastery where the monks reputedly fortified themselves with a nourishing but potent ale during the long days of Lent.

In northern Germany, the most popular standard beers are export lagers or the paler, more pungent pilsners. There are countless varieties of pilsner, which takes its name from the Bohemian town of Pilsen in Czechoslovakia, where this bitter, hops-fragrant beer originated in the last century. Popular German varieties of pilsner, now widely available, include Bitburger and Warsteiner, brewed in the north, and Löwenbräu and Fürstenberg in the south.

Should you wander into a watering hole in Köln or Düsseldorf, you will be offered something altogether different. The breweries of these two cities on the Rhine produce "old-fashioned" beers similar to English ales. In Köln, the light, soft-flavored tipple is called Kölsch. It's served flatter and warmer than most Continental beers. In nearby Düsseldorf, the darker Alt (old) beer has a creamy, mild taste. It is served straight from wooden barrels in small, narrow glasses, which a liter-swilling Bavarian would liken to thimbles.

Germany's biggest breweries are in the northern city of Dortmund, which feeds the industrial Ruhr region. But it's in Bavaria where the majority of the country's breweries—and beer traditions—are found. Indeed, while West Germany as a whole is at the head of the international beer-drinking table, the Bavarians and the Saarlanders to the southwest consume more beer per person than any other group in the country.

Many Bavarian breweries are tiny businesses catering, alongside the local butcher and baker, to just one village's needs. A large percentage of the state's 825 breweries are concentrated in the north of the state, where any attempt at sober-minded research is nearly impossible. Some northern Bavarian towns, which are really no more than large villages, maintain three or four breweries each; the beautifully preserved medieval town of Bamberg boasts 10. In that city, you can sample many of the brewing styles of the Franconia region, including what's probably the best example of smoked beer (Rauchbier), which is flavored with the aroma of beechwood smoke. Drink it in the black-beamed Schlenkerla tavern, where sturdy waitresses in black-and-white uniforms serve it from oak casks. Also in Bamberg, the Mahrs brewery tavern will refuse to serve you its delicious pils before 5 PM, when the day's barrel is tapped for homeward-bound workers. It would be sacrilege, they say, to open the barrel earlier, since it loses its freshness if it's not imbibed quickly.

Other, more quaint customs of the pub endure in this region. If someone walks into a room and raps his or her knuckles on each table before taking a seat, don't think you've stumbled across some secret rite: The person is simply using a traditional way to say hello or goodbye. There is one special table in nearly all pubs where strangers should never sit, unless specifically invited to. This is the *Stammtisch* or clan table, where the pub's regulars congregate. It's usually indicated by a sign.

There's no single word to signify the traditional German pub where you can enjoy a beer, a coffee, or something to eat at most times of the day and evening. It can be described by a variety of prefixes, however, including *Gasthof, Wirtschaft, Gaststätte.* The terms *Kneipe* and *Stube* often apply to small bars where the lights are low and the music is loud or seductive. Pubs are often named after an old craft, a creature, or a local landmark, hence: *Gaststätte Hammerschmied*—"The Hammersmith"; *Gasthof Hechten* —"The Pike." Old coach inns always have the word "post" in their names, and always offer accommodations at reasonable prices.

You will inevitably encounter the *Ruhetag,* the day in the week when a pub closes so that the landlord and staff can go fishing or enjoy a quiet beer or two on their own. The Ruhetag system is usually worked so at least one pub in a village or district stays open each day. It can be frustrating, though, to arrive on the Ruhetag in a village with only one pub.

Bavaria holds beer in such reverence that it remains one of the few places in Europe where brewing continues in religious foundations. It is mainly monks who keep up the tradition, but at Mallersdorf, a village 75 miles northeast of Munich, an order of Franciscan nuns produces its own delightful liquid bread. The convent ladies drink much of their tiny brewery's output themselves but, like all religious orders, are happy to share. They run a pub on convent grounds.

Ultimately, all beer routes must lead the traveler to the world's beer-drinking capital: Munich. This is where you'll find the biggest beer halls, the largest beer gardens, the most famous breweries, the biggest and most indulgent beer festival, and the widest selection of brews; even the beer glasses are bigger. It's a measure of how seriously the Germans take their beer that they see no conflict in the fact that one of the most cosmopolitan cities in the country—a place with great art galleries and museums, an opulent opera house, and chic lifestyles—is internationally recognized as the most beer-drenched city on earth. It is an image they are proud to propagate: Letters and postcards dispatched from Munich are framed with the message *Bierstadt München*—"Munich, the Beer City."

First-time visitors to Munich invariably feel they haven't paid their respects to Gambrinus—the patron saint of brewers—unless they go to what has become the most famous of beer halls, the Hofbräuhaus. The fact is, however, that the Hofbrähaus caters to tourists as much as to locals. A far more earthy watering hole is the Mathäser beer hall (near the main train station), which can accommodate more than 5,000 people. Up to 16,000 pints are downed here on a thirsty day.

In beer halls and beer gardens throughout Munich you will be served beer in liter-size (2-pint) glasses, which are called *Mass*. In Bavaria, the standard everyday pale beer is known as *Helles*, a term not used elsewhere; a dark beer is a *Dunkles*.

The appetite for beer in Munich is so great that two new breweries were established in the city in 1988. They are pint-size in comparison to the six brewing giants that stake most of Munich's thirst, but they have unusual attractions. One of them is in a converted train station (Grosshesselohe, on the S-7 line of the S-bahn), where customers can drink their favorite tipple while they watch through a window the next batch being brewed. The other, in Luitpold Park, Schwabing, is run by a prince whose ancestors ruled Bavaria and invented the world's greatest beer festival, the Oktoberfest.

Bavarians are sometimes regarded with disdain by their less-indulgent Prussian brothers to the north. But not even the widest-girthed southerners can be held wholly responsible for the staggering consumption of beer and food at the annual, two-week Oktoberfest. Typically, 10 million pints of beer, as well as 750,000 roasted chickens and 650,000 sausages are put away by revelers. Clearly, visitors must be helping a little.

The Oktoberfest, held during the second half of September, is such an important event in Munich's social calendar that the most senior city and state politicians are expected to participate in the opening ceremonies. Traditionally, the mayor taps the first barrel and gives the first Mass of beer to the Bavarian state government premier. This ritual is watched by a television audience of millions. There was public uproar in 1988 when Premier Franz Josef Strauss declined to attend. He outraged the city by going to a basket-weaving festival instead!

3 Munich

Introduction

Munich, München to the Germans, third-largest city in the Federal Republic and capital of the Free State of Bavaria, is the single most popular tourist destination in Germany. This simple statistic speaks volumes about the enduring appeal of what by any standard is a supremely likable city. Munich is kitsch and class, vulgarity and elegance. It's a city of ravishing Rococo and smoky beer cellars, of soaring Gothic and sparkling shops, of pale stucco buildings and space-age factories, of millionaires and lederhosen-clad farmers.

Germany's favorite city is a place with extraordinary ambience and a vibrant lifestyle all its own, in a splendid setting within view of the towering Alps.

Munich belongs to the relaxed and sunny south. Call it Germany with a southern exposure, although it may be an exaggeration to claim, as some Bavarians do, that Munich is the only Italian city north of the Alps.

Still, there's no mistaking the carefree spirit that infuses the place, a positively un-Teutonic joie de vivre that the Bavarians refer to as *Gemütlichkeit,* which could be loosely translated as conviviality, along with an easygoing approach to life, liberty, and the pursuit of happiness, Bavarian-style.

It may be all too easy to point to the abundance of beer that flows through the city and its numerous beer restaurants, beer cellars, and beer gardens as the most obvious manifestation of this take-life-as-it-comes attitude. Certainly it's hard not to feel something approaching awe at the realization that Munich University has a beer faculty.

What makes Munich so special? How can its secret be explained?

Is it that Munich, despite a population in excess of 1.3 million, retains something of a small-town, almost villagelike atmosphere? Is it in the variety of buildings that dot its center, giving the city, on the one hand, a Baroque grandeur, on the other the semblance of a toy town?

Perhaps you need look no further than Ludwig II, one of the last of the Wittelsbachs, who served as rulers of Bavaria from 1253 to 1918.

While Bismarck was ruthlessly unifying Germany in the 19th century from his power base in Berlin, Ludwig—"Mad" King Ludwig to some, the "Dream King" to others—was building a succession of ever more elaborate and wildly romantic palaces, summer houses, and public buildings in and around Munich.

Though he came close to bankrupting the throne in the process and died under mysterious circumstances in his early forties, having been declared insane by his own government, Ludwig II remains an apt and enigmatic symbol for the touch of fantasy that turns a stay in Munich into such a special experience.

Munich bills itself as *Die Weltstadt mit Herz* (the cosmopolitan city with heart), which it most assuredly is. It is frequently referred to as the "clandestine" capital of Germany. A survey suggests that, given the choice, most Germans would prefer to live in Munich rather than where they currently reside. Such is the attraction for native Germans.

This is not to suggest that all Germans subscribe to the "I Love Munich" concept. Certain buttoned-up types in Hamburg or Düsseldorf, for example, might look down their imperious noses at Munich as being just a mite crass and somewhat tacky, and the Bavarians as only a few rungs up the ladder from the barbarians. So be it.

Munich is obviously Germany's "good-time city," its image indelibly tied to a series of splashy celebrations that have spread the city's fame far and wide. Mention of Munich invariably triggers thoughts of the colorful carnival season that goes by the name *Fasching*, and the equally gaudy spectacle of the 16-day-and-night nonstop beer bust known as *Oktoberfest*. The city has become synonymous with beer, *Wurst* (sausage), and Gemütlichkeit. This triad comes close to the essence of the Munich experience.

The stock concept is that the heart and soul of this joyous overgrown town can be encountered in those cavernous beer halls (such as the Hofbräuhaus) that reverberate to the blast of oompah bands, where oak tables are lined with burly men decked out in lederhosen and funny green hats with feathers, singing along to the music and putting away enormous steins of beer with great aplomb as buxom waitresses in flaring dirndls rush in reinforcements of beer and platters of Wurst and sauerkraut.

True. Munich really is like that—at least in part. This is the Munich promoted on the tourist circuit; this is the city visitors look for (and find). Call it the Munich of cliché and celebration. But there are far more arresting (and satisfying) aspects of the city to be discovered beyond its more obvious facets, a totally different city beyond the Hofbrauhaus and Oktoberfest image. Call it the *other* Munich: a high-style metropolis of elegance, charm, charisma, refinement, and sophistication, to go along with the renowned Gemütlichkeit and *Stimmung* (mood or atmosphere). A city as spacious and impressive as Paris, for example, in its own highly individual way.

Endowed with vast tracts of greenery in the form of parks, gardens, and forests; grand boulevards set with remarkable edifices; fountains and statuary; and rivers spanned by graceful bridges, Munich is easily Germany's most beautiful and interesting city. If the traveler were to visit only one city in Germany, then this would be it. No question about it.

Add the fact that the city has changed dramatically over the past decade or so, and for the traveler who has not been here for a number of years, one might say that a whole new Munich has evolved in the interim. For, quietly and without fanfare, Munich has taken its place as the high-tech capital of Germany, developing into the number-one industrial center in the country and one of the most important in Europe.

The concentration of electronics and computer firms—Siemens, IBM, Apple, and such—in and around the city has turned the area into the Silicon Valley of Europe, or in this case the Isar Valley, after the Isar River, which flows through Munich much as the Seine passes through Paris.

Also based in and around Munich are the BMW factory, branches of the aerospace industry, international technological and chemical corporations, machine-tool works . . . and on and on.

All this has turned Munich into one of Europe's wealthiest cities. And it shows. Here everything is extremely upscale and up-to-date; this is the Yuppie capital of the Federal Republic. For starters, you'll notice the glitz and glamour in refurbished superluxury hotels. Myriad shops display merchandise suggesting an extravagance that exists nowhere else on the Continent to quite the same degree: $150 men's shirts, $1,000 sport jackets, $300 pairs of shoes, and dresses with astronomical price tags all seem the norm, along with gold-plated bathroom fixtures and $700 toilet seats. "If you've got it, flaunt it" serves as the current theme. And the traffic appears to be composed primarily of the latest and largest Audi models, high-number-series BMWs and Mercedes-Benzes, Porsches, and the occasional Jaguar, Ferrari, Lamborghini, and Maserati, all looking as though they had been driven straight from the showroom.

Munich has the highest concentration of Michelin-star restaurants of any German city—*two* three-star attractions feature the finest in haute and nouvelle cuisine in the French style at positively outrageous prices. No dumplings served here.

At times the aura of affluence may become all but overpowering. But that's what Munich is all about these days and nights: A new city superimposed on the old; conspicuous consumption on a scale we can hardly imagine as a way of life; a fresh patina of glitter along with the traditional rustic charms. Such are the dynamics and duality of this fascinating metropolis that remains a joy to explore and get to know.

Essential Information

Important Addresses and Numbers

Tourist Information The **Fremdenverkehrsamt** (central tourist office) is located in the heart of the city (Sendlingerstr. 1, tel. 089/23911), just around the corner from Marienplatz. This office can help with room reservations; if you arrive after hours, call for a recorded message detailing hotel vacancies. (Open Mon.–Thurs. 8:30–3, Fri. 8:30–2.) Longer hours are kept by the city tourist office at the **Hauptsbahnhof** train station (at the entrance on Bayerstr., tel. 089/239–1256; open Mon.–Sat. 8:30 AM–10 PM, Sun. and holidays 1–9:30). There are also tourist offices at **Reim Airport** (tel. 089/907–256; open Mon.–Sat. 9 AM–10 PM, Sun. 11–7), and in the **Rathaus** (city hall), on Marienplatz (open weekdays 9–5).

For information on regions outside Munich, contact the **Fremdenverkehrsverband München-Oberbayern** (Upper Bavarian Regional Tourist Office) on Sonnenstrasse 10 (tel. 089/597–347).

An official monthly listing of upcoming events, the *Monatsprogramm*, is available at most hotels and newsstands and all tourist offices for DM 1.50. Information in English about museums and galleries may be obtained round-the-clock by dialing

089/239–162, and about castles and city sights by dialing 089/239–172.

Consulates **U.S. Consulate General,** Königstrasse 5, tel. 089/23011. **British Consulate General,** Amalienstrasse 62, tel. 089/394–015. **Canadian Consulate,** Maximiliansplatz 9, tel. 089/558–531.

Emergencies **Police:** tel. 089/110. **Fire department:** tel. 089/112. **Ambulance:** tel. 089/19222. **Medical emergencies:** tel. 089/558–661. **Pharmacy emergency service:** tel. 089/594–475. The **Internationale Inter-Apotheke** (corner of Luisenstr. and Elisenstr., tel. 089/595–444), stocks American and British products (open Mon.–Fri. 8–5:30, Sat. 8–1).

English-Language Bookstores The **Anglia English Bookshop** (Schnellstr. 3, tel. 089/283–642) has the largest selection of English-language books in Munich. A library of English-language books is kept in the **Amerika-Haus** (Karolinenpl. 3, tel. 089/595–367).

Travel Agencies **American Express,** Promenadenplatz 6, tel. 089/2199. **ABR,** the official Bavarian travel agency, has outlets all over Munich; call 089/12040 for information.

Lost and Found **Fundstelle der Stadtverwaltung** (city lost-property office), Ruppertstrasse 19, tel. 089/233. **Fundstelle der Bundesbahn,** (railway lost-property office), Hauptbahnhof, Bahnhofplatz 2, tel. 089/128–6664.

Car Rental **Avis:** Airport Riem, tel. 089/9211–8350; Nymphenburgerstrasse 61, tel. 089/1260–0020; Balanstrasse 74, tel. 089/497–301.

Europcar: Airport Riem, tel. 089/908–108; Schwanthalerstrasse 10A, tel. 089/5947–2325.

Hertz: Airport Riem, tel. 089/908–744; Holiday Inn Hotel, Kistlerhofstrasse 142, tel. 089/786–335; Nymphenburgerstrasse 81, tel. 089/129–5001.

Arriving and Departing by Plane

Flughafen Riem, Munich's international airport, is located about 10 kilometers (6 miles) from the city center. Conditions can be chaotic around Christmas and in the summer, and the airport authorities are periodically driven to appeal to visitors for patience. A new, much larger airport is scheduled to open in 1991.

Between the Airport and Downtown Buses to Munich Hauptbahnhof (the main train station) leave Riem every half hour between 6 AM and 8 AM and every 15 minutes between 8 AM and 9 PM; thereafter, they run according to aircraft arrivals. Buses to Riem leave from the north side of the Hauptbahnhof (opposite the hotel Deutscher Kaiser) every 15 minutes between 5 AM and 9 PM. The 30-minute ride costs DM 5 each way. You can also take the S-bahn (electric suburban train) from the airport; take bus 37 from the airport to the Riem S-bahn station, then ride line S-6 directly to the train station. The ride takes about 30 minutes, and one-way tickets cost DM 5. At normal times, a taxi can take you into the city in about 15 minutes; however, in rush hour it could take half an hour. The normal one-way fare is about DM 20. If you're picking up a rental car at the airport, the trip to Munich is easy: Take the main road out of the airport and follow the signs for *Stadtmitte* (downtown).

Arriving and Departing by Train, Bus, and Car

By Train All long-distance rail services arrive at and depart from the main train station; trains to and from destinations in Bavaria use the adjoining Starnbergerbahnhof. For information on train times, call 089/592–991; all railroad staff speak English. For tickets and travel information, go to the station information office or try the ABR travel agency, right by the station on Bahnhofplatz.

By Bus Long-distance buses arrive at and depart from the north side of the main train station. A taxi stand is located right next to it.

By Car From the north (Nürnberg and Frankfurt), leave the autobahn at the Schwabing exit. From Stuttgart and the west, the autobahn ends at Obermenzing. The autobahns from Salzburg and the east, Garmisch and the south, and Lindau and the southwest all join the Mittlere Ring (city beltway). When leaving any autobahn, follow the Stadtmitte signs for downtown Munich.

Getting Around

On Foot Downtown Munich is only a mile square and is easily explored on foot. Almost all of the major sights in the city center are on the interlinking web of pedestrian streets that runs from Karlsplatz by the main train station to Marienplatz and the Viktualienmarkt and extends north around the Frauenkirche and up to Odeonsplatz. The central tourist office issues a free map with suggested walking tours. For sights and attractions away from the city center, make use of the excellent public transportation system.

By Public Transportation Munich has an efficient and well-integrated public transportation system consisting of the **U-bahn** (subway), the **S-bahn** (suburban railway), the **Strassenbahn** (streetcars), and **buses.** Marienplatz forms the heart of the U-bahn and S-bahn network, which operates from around 5 AM to 1 AM. For a clear explanation in English of how the system works, pick up a copy of *Rendezvous mit München,* available free from any tourist office.

Fares are uniform for the entire system. So long as you are traveling in the same direction, you can transfer from one mode of transportation to another on the same ticket. The system used to calculate the fares, however, is complex. In essence, it's based upon the number of zones you cross. A basic **Einzelfahrkarte** (one-way ticket) costs DM 2.40 (DM 2 for children under 15) for a ride in the inner zone; if you plan to take a number of trips around the city, you'll save money buying a **Mehrfahrtenkarten,** or multiple "strip" ticket. A strip of seven red tickets, valid for rides in the inner zone (and for both zones for children under 15) costs DM 6.50. Strips of 10 or 16 blue tickets, valid for rides in the outer zone, cost DM 9.50 and DM 15, respectively. Best value of all is the **24-Stunden** (24-hour) ticket, which provides unlimited travel on all public transportation for any 24-hour period. Costs are DM 7 (DM 2.50 for children under 15) for an inner-zone ticket and DM 12.50 (DM 4.50 for children under 15) for the entire network.

All tickets can be purchased from the blue dispensers at U- and S-bahn stations and at bus and streetcar stops. Bus and streetcar drivers, all tourist offices, and Mehrfahrtenkarten booths

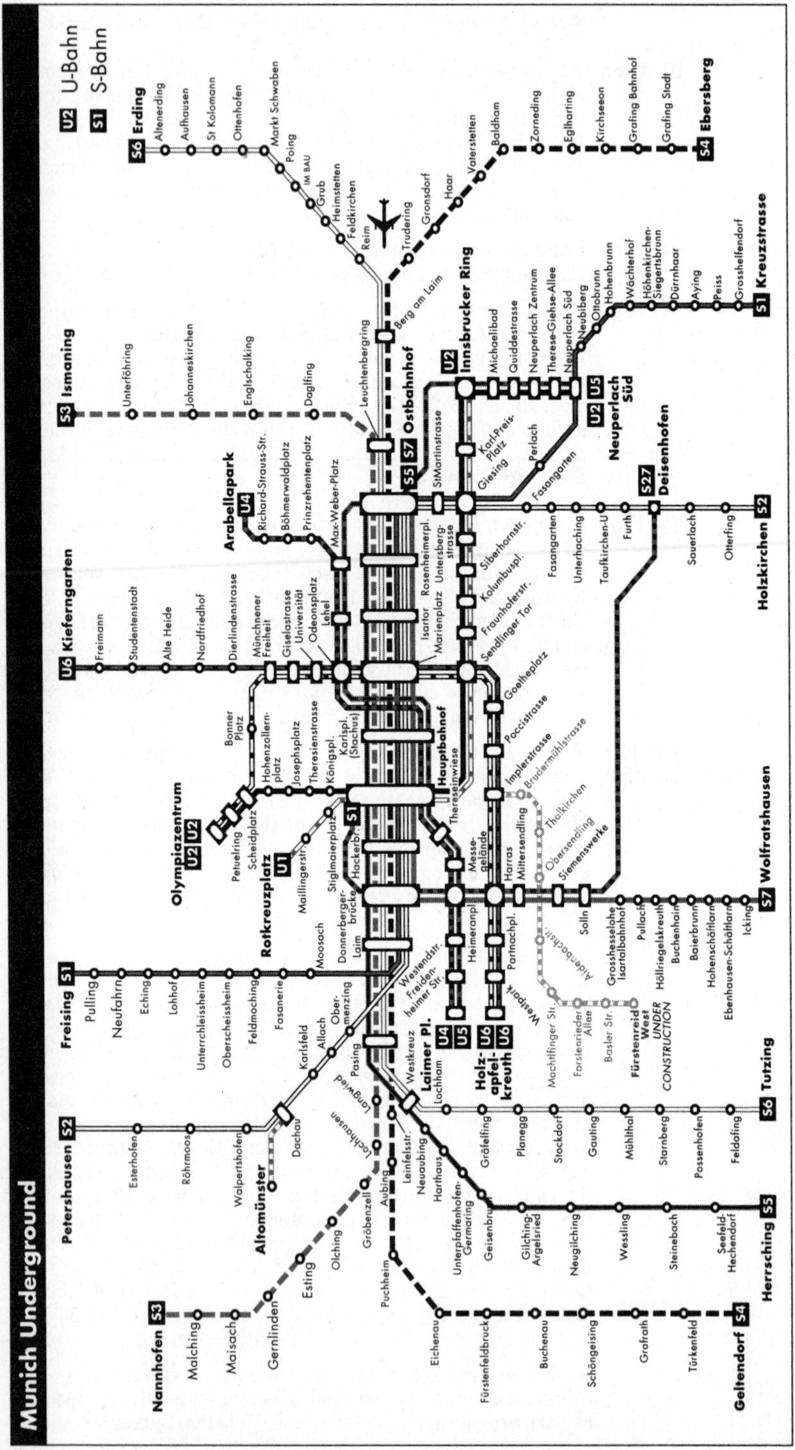
Munich Underground
U2 U-Bahn
S1 S-Bahn
S6 Erding
Altenerding
Aufhausen
St Kolomann
Ottenhofen
Markt Schwaben
Poing
IM BAU
Grub
Heimstetten
Feldkirchen
Reim
Trudering
Gronsdorf
Haar
Vaterstetten
Baldham
Zorneding
Eglharting
Kirchseeon
Grafing Bahnhof
Grafing Stadt
S4 Ebersberg
S3 Ismaning
Unterföhring
Johanneskirchen
Englschalking
Daglfing
Leuchtenbergring
Berg am Laim
S5 S7 Ostbahnhof
U2 Innsbrucker Ring
Michaelibad
Quiddestrasse
Neuperlach Zentrum
Therese-Giehse-Allee
Neuperlach Süd
Neubiberg
Ottobrunn
Hohenbrunn
Wächterhof
Höhenkirchen-Siegertsbrunn
Dürrnhaar
Aying
Peiss
Grosshelfendorf
S1 Kreuzstrasse
U2 U5 Neuperlach Süd
StMartinstrasse
Karl-Preis-Platz
Perlach
Giesing
Fasangarten
S27 Deisenhofen
U6 Kieferngarten
Freimann
Studentenstadt
Alte Heide
Nordfriedhof
Dierlindenstrasse
Münchner Freiheit
Giselastrasse
Universität
Odeonsplatz
Lehel
Arabellapark
U4
Richard-Strauss-Str.
Böhmerwaldplatz
Prinzregentenplatz
Max-Weber-Platz
Rosenheimerpl.
Isartor
Marienplatz
Untersberg-strasse
Silberhornstr.
Kolumbuspl.
Fraunhoferstr.
Sendlinger Tor
Fasangarten
Unterhaching
Taufkirchen-U
Furth
Sauerlach
Otterfing
Holzkirchen S2
Olympiazentrum
U2 U2
Petuelring
Scheidplatz
Bonner Platz
Hohenzollern-platz
Josephsplatz
Theresienstrasse
Königspl.
Karlspl. (Stachus)
Hauptbahnhof
Theresienwiese
Goetheplatz
Poccistrasse
Implerstrasse
Brudermühlstrasse
Thalkirchen
Obersendling
Siemenswerke
Harras
Mittersendling
Messe-gelände
Heimeranpl.
Partnachpl.
Westpark
Aidenbachstr.
Machtlfinger Str.
Forstenrieder Allee
Basler Str.
Fürstenreid West
UNDER CONSTRUCTION
Solln
Grosshesselohe Isartalbahnhof
Pullach
Höllriegelskreuth
Buchenhain
Baierbrunn
Hohenschäftlarn
Ebenhausen-Schäftlarn
Icking
S7 Wolfratshausen
Rotkreuzplatz
U1
Maillingerstr.
Stiglmaierplatz
Hackerbr.
Donnersberger-brücke
S1
Laim
Westendstr.
Friedenheimer Str.
U4 U5 Laimer Pl.
U6 U6 Holz-apfel-kreuth
Freising S1
Pulling
Neufahrn
Eching
Lohhof
Unterschleissheim
Oberschleissheim
Feldmoching
Fasanerie
Moosach
Karlsfeld
Allach
Ober-menzing
Pasing
Westkreuz
Lochham
Gräfelfing
Planegg
Stockdorf
Gauting
Mühlthal
Starnberg
Possenhofen
Feldafing
S6 Tutzing
Petershausen S2
Esterhofen
Röhrmoos
Walpertshofen
Dachau
Altomünster
Langwied
Lochhausen
Gröbenzell
Olching
Esting
Gernlinden
Maisach
Malching
Nannhofen S3
Leinfelsstr.
Aubing
Neuaubing
Harthaus
Puchheim
Unterpfaffenhofen-Germaring
Geisenbrunn
Gilching-Argelsried
Neugilching
Wessling
Steinebach
Seefeld-Hechendorf
Herrsching S5
Eichenau
Fürstenfeldbruck
Buchenau
Schöngeising
Grafrath
Türkenfeld
Geltendorf S4

(which display a white *K* on a green background) also sell tickets. Note that you must cancel your ticket in one of the blue machines at station entrances and on all buses and streetcars before starting your journey. Spot-checks are common and carry an automatic fine of DM 40 if you're caught. One final tip: Holders of a Eurail Pass, a Youth Pass, an Inter-Rail card, or a DB Tourist Card may travel free on all suburban railway trains.

By Taxi Munich's cream-color taxis are numerous. Hail them in the street or telephone 089/2161 (there's an extra charge for the drive to the pickup point). Rates start at DM 2.90 for the first mile. There is an additional charge of 50 pfennig for every piece of luggage. Reckon on paying DM 7 to DM 10 for a short trip within the city.

By Bicycle Munich and its environs can easily be explored on two wheels. The city is threaded with a network of specially designated bike paths. A free map showing all bike trails and suggested biking tours is available at branches of the Bayerische Vereinsbank.

You can rent bicycles at the **Englischer Garten** (corner of Königstr. and Veterinärstr., tel. 089/397–016) for DM 5 per hour or DM 15 for the day (May–Oct., Sat. and Sun. in good weather); **Lothar Borucki** (Hans-Sachs Str. 7, tel. 089/266–506) hires them out for DM 60 per week. Bikes can also be rented from **S-bahn** stations. The cost is DM 5 a day if you've used public transportation to reach the station; otherwise, it's DM 10.

Guided Tours

Orientation Tours A variety of city bus tours is offered by **Münchner Fremden-Rundfahrten** (Arnulfstr. 8, tel. 089/120–4248). The blue buses operate all year round, departing from in front of the Hertie department store on Bahnhofplatz (across from the main entrance to the train station). The Kleine Rundfahrt, a one-hour city tour, leaves daily at 10 AM, 11:30 AM, and 2:30 PM; cost is DM 13. The Olympiagelände-Tour, which lasts about 2½ hours, explores the Olympia Tower and grounds; it departs daily at 10 AM and 2:30 PM, and the cost is DM 23. The Grosse Rundfahrt, or extended city tour, comes in two varieties; each lasts around 2½ hours and costs DM 23. The morning tour includes visits to the Frauenkirche and Alte Pinakothek; the afternoon tour visits Schloss Nymphenburg. They run Tuesday–Sunday, leaving at 10 and 2:30, respectively. The München bei Nacht tour provides five hours of Munich by night and includes dinner and visits to three night spots. It departs Wednesday–Saturday at 7:30 PM; the cost is DM 100.

Walking Tours The Munich tourist office (*see* Tourist Information, above) organizes guided walking tours for groups or individuals on demand, but no regular walking tours are offered. Tours can be tailored to suit individual requirements; costs vary accordingly.

Excursions Bus excursions to the Alps, to Austria, to the royal palaces and castles of Bavaria, or along the Romantic Road can be booked through the tourist office or through **ABR** (Hauptbahnhof, tel. 089/591–315 or 089/59041). **Münchner Fremden-Rundfahrten** (*see* Orientation Tours, above) also organizes bus trips to most leading tourist attractions outside the city; the Royal Castles

Tour, for example, costs DM 62. All tours leave from outside the Hertie department store. Other tours are offered by **Reiseburo Autobus Oberbayern** (Lenbachpl. 1, tel. 089/558–061); offerings include a Late Riser's Excursion, which departs at 10 AM. All tours leave from Elisenstrasse, in front of the Botanischer Garten.

The Upper Bavarian Regional Tourist Office (*see* Tourist Information, above) provides information and brochures for excursions and accommodations outside Munich.

The **S-bahn** can quickly take you to some of the most beautiful places in the countryside around Munich. Line S-6, for example, will whisk you lakeside to Starnberger See in half an hour; line S-4 runs to the depths of the Ebersberger Forest. You can bring along a bicycle on S-bahn trains.

Exploring Munich

Numbers in the margin correspond with points of interest on the Munich map.

Highlights for First-time Visitors

Frauenkirche
Marienplatz
Viktualienmarkt
Asamkirche
Residenztheater
Englischer Garten
Alte Pinakotek
Schloss Nymphenburg
Deutsches Museum
Tierpark Hellabrunn (zoo)

Downtown Munich

1 Begin your tour of the city at the **Hauptbahnhof,** the main train station and site of the city tourist office, which is located on the corner of Bayerstrasse. Pick up a detailed city map here. Cross Bahnhofplatz, the square in front of the station, and make for Schützenstrasse. During the summer you'll see a blue-and-white maypole here—unless, that is, it's been stolen. A vigorous local custom, one that you'll find throughout Bavaria, holds that a neighboring town or city's maypole is fair game, and it will be returned only on payment of a suitable ransom, generally several barrels of beer. Notice the patterns painted on the pole; they represent the trades carried on in the city.

Schützenstrasse marks the start of Munich's pedestrian shopping mall, the Fussgängerzone, a mile and a half of traffic-free streets. Running virtually the length of Schützenstrasse is
2 Munich's largest department store, **Hertie.** At the end of the street you descend via the pedestrian underpass into another shopping empire, a vast underground complex of boutiques and cafés. Above you stretches one of Europe's busiest traffic
3 intersections, **Karlsplatz,** known locally as *Stachus.* You'll emerge at one of Munich's most popular fountains, a circle of water jets that acts as a magnet on hot summer days for city shoppers and office workers seeking a cool corner. The semicircle of yellow-fronted buildings that back the fountain, with

their high windows and delicate cast-iron balconies, gives the area a southern, almost Mediterranean air.

Ahead stands one of the city's oldest gates, the **Karlstor,** first mentioned in local records in 1302. Beyond it lies Munich's main shopping thoroughfare, Neuhauserstrasse and its extension, Kaufingerstrasse. On your left as you enter Neuhauserstrasse is another attractive Munich fountain, a jovial, late-19th-century figure of Bacchus. Neuhauserstrasse and Kaufingerstrasse are a jumble of ancient and modern buildings. This part of town was bombed almost to extinction in World War II and has been extensively rebuilt. Great efforts were made to ensure that these new buildings harmonized with the rest of the old city, though some of the newer structures are little more than functional. Still, even though this may not be one of the architectural high points of the city, there are at least some
4 redeeming features. **Hans Obepollinger,** a department store hiding behind an imposing 19th-century facade, is one. Notice the weather vanes of old merchant ships on its high-gabled roof.

Shopping, however, is not the only attraction on these streets. Worldly department stores rub shoulders with two remarkable churches: Michaelskirche and the Bürgersaal. You come first to
5 the **Bürgersaal,** built in 1710. Beneath its modest roof are two contrasting levels. The upper level—the church proper—consists of a richly decorated Baroque oratory. Its elaborate stucco foliage and paintings of Bavarian places of pilgrimage project a distinctly different ambience from that of the lower level, reached by descending a double staircase. This gloomy, cryptlike chamber contains the tomb of Rupert Mayer, a famous Jesuit priest, renowned for his energetic and outspoken opposition to the Nazis.

A few steps farther on is the restrained Renaissance facade of
6 the 16th-century **Michaelskirche.** It was built by Duke Wilhelm V. Seven years after the start of construction the principal tower collapsed. The duke regarded the disaster as a sign from heaven that the church wasn't big enough, so he ordered a change in the plans—this time without a tower. Seven years later the church was completed, the first Renaissance church of this size in southern Germany. The duke is buried in the crypt, along with 40 members of Bavaria's famous Wittelsbach family (the ruling dynasty for seven centuries), including eccentric King Ludwig II. A severe Neoclassical monument in the north transept contains the tomb of Napoleon's stepson, Eugene de Beauharnais, who married a daughter of Bavaria's King Maximilian I and died in Munich in 1824. You'll find the plain white stucco interior of the church and its slightly barnlike atmosphere soothingly simple after the lavish decoration of the Bürgersaal.

Time Out Across the road beckons the *Jugendstil* (German Art Nouveau) facade of the **Augustiner Gaststätte.** Within its late-19th-century interior a delicious nut-flavored beer is served. Even if you don't stay for a beer, take a look inside for more stunning examples of Bavarian Jugendstil.

The massive building next to Michaelskirche was once one of Munich's oldest churches, built in the late 13th century for Benedictine monks. It was secularized in the early 19th century,

Alte Pinakothek, **25**
Alter Botanischer Garten, **32**
Alter Hof, **15**
Altes Rathaus, **11**
Antikensammlungen, **30**
Asamkirche, **13**
Bürgersaal, **5**
Englischer Garten, **24**
Feldherenhalle, **21**
Frauenkirche, **8**
Glyptothek, **29**
Hauptbahnhof, **1**
Haus Oberpollinger, **4**
Hertie, **2**
Hofgarten, **20**
Hotel Vier Jahreszeiten, **17**
Jagd-und Fishereimuseum, **7**
Karlsplatz, **3**
Karolinenplatz, **27**
Königsplatz, **28**
Marienplatz, **9**
Maximilianstrasse, **16**
Michaelskirche, **6**
Nationaltheater, **18**
Neue Pinakothek, **26**
Neues Rathaus, **10**
Palace of Justice, **33**
Peterskirche, **14**
Residenz, **19**
Siegestor, **22**
Theatinerkirche, **23**
Viktualienmarkt, **12**
Wittelsbacher Fountain, **31**

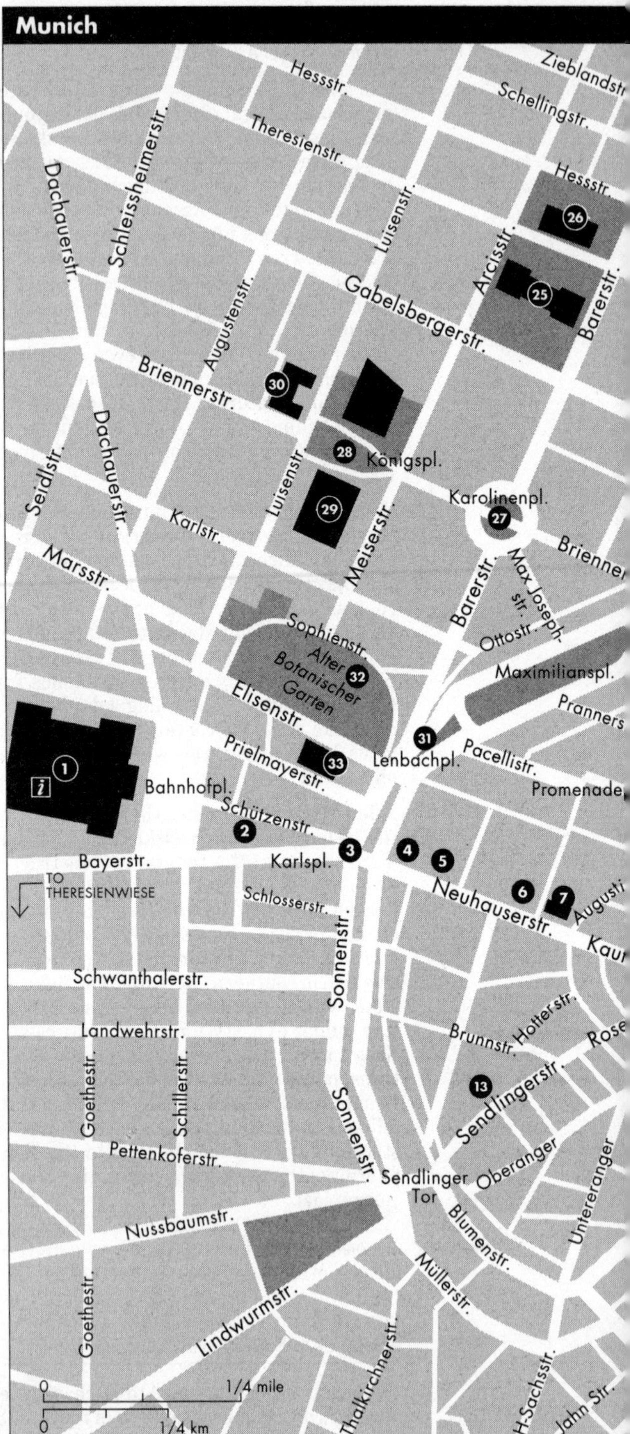

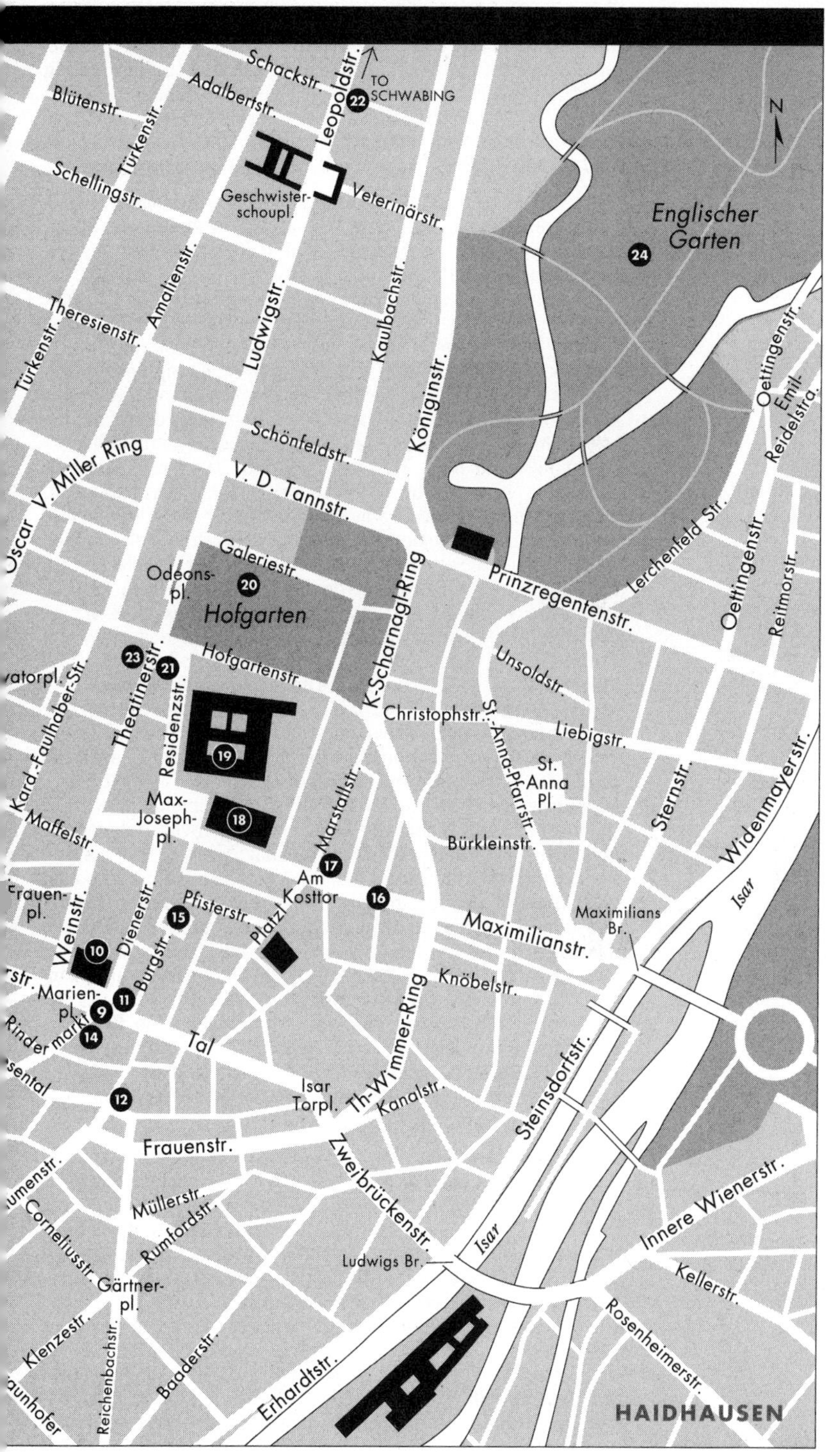

TO SCHWABING
Schackstr.
Adalbertstr.
Blütenstr.
Türkenstr.
Leopoldstr.
Schellingstr.
Geschwister-schoupl.
Veterinärstr.
Englischer Garten
Amalienstr.
Kaulbachstr.
Theresienstr.
Ludwigstr.
Türkenstr.
Königinstr.
Oettingenstr.
Emil-Reidelstra.
Schönfeldstr.
Oscar V. Miller Ring
V. D. Tannstr.
Lerchenfeld Str.
Galeriestr.
Odeons-pl.
Prinzregentenstr.
Oettingenstr.
Reitmorstr.
Hofgarten
K-Scharnagl-Ring
Hofgartenstr.
Unsoldstr.
Theatinerstr.
Residenzstr.
Kard.-Faulhaber-Str.
Christophstr.
St.-Anna-Pfarrstr.
Liebigstr.
St. Anna Pl.
Max-Joseph-pl.
Maffeistr.
Marstallstr.
Sternstr.
Widenmayerstr.
Bürkleinstr.
Am Kosttor
Frauen-pl.
Pfisterstr.
Maximilians Br.
Isar
Weinstr.
Dienerstr.
Platzl
Maximilianstr.
Burgstr.
Knöbelstr.
Marien-pl.
Rinder markt
Tal
Th.-Wimmer-Ring
Steinsdorfstr.
Isar Torpl.
Kanalstr.
Frauenstr.
Zweibrückenstr.
Innere Wienerstr.
Müllerstr.
Rumfordstr.
Corneliusstr.
Isar
Ludwigs Br.
Kellerstr.
Gärtner-pl.
Rosenheimerstr.
Klenzestr.
Reichenbachstr.
Baaderstr.
Erhardtstr.
HAIDHAUSEN

served as a warehouse for some years, and today houses
7 Munich's **Jagd-und Fishereimuseum** (hunting and fishing museum). Lovers of the thrill of the chase will find it a fascinating place. It also contains the world's largest collection of fishhooks. *Neuhauserstr. 53. Admission: DM 3 adults, DM 1.50 children and senior citizens. Open Apr.–Oct., Tues.–Sun. 9:30–5; Nov.–Mar., Tues.–Sun. 9:30–4, Mon. 7 PM–10 PM.*

Turn left on Augustinerstrasse and you will soon arrive in Frauenplatz, a quiet square with a shallow sunken fountain.
8 Towering over it is **Frauenkirche** (Church of Our Lady), Munich's cathedral. It's a distinctive late-Gothic brick structure with two enormous towers. Each is more than 300 feet high, and both are capped by very un-Gothic, onion-shape domes. The towers have become the symbol of Munich's skyline, some say because they look like overflowing beer mugs. The main body of the cathedral was completed in 20 years—a record time in those days—and the building was consecrated in 1494. The towers were added, almost as an afterthought, between 1524 and 1525. Jörg von Halspach, the Frauenkirche's original architect, is buried within the walls of the cathedral. The building suffered severe damage during the Allied bombing of Munich, as a series of photographs taken at the end of the war testifies. They show a gaunt, rubble-filled skeleton of a building. The cathedral was lovingly restored from 1947 to 1957. Today you'll find a church that combines most of von Halspach's original features with a stark, clean modernity and simplicity of line, emphasized by the slender white octagonal pillars that sweep up through the nave to the yellow-traced ceiling far above. There's a striking contrast between the pristine interior and the worn, shrapnel-studded red-brick exterior. As you enter the church, look on the stone floor for the dark imprint of a large footstep—the *Teufelstritt* (Devil's footprint). Local lore has many explanations for the phenomenon. One of the most fanciful is that the Devil challenged von Halspach to build a nave without windows. Von Halspach wagered his soul and accepted the challenge, building a cathedral that is flooded with light from 66-foot-high windows that are invisible to anyone standing at the point marked by the Teufelstritt. Put the legend to the test and stand where the Devil is said to have been led by von Halspach: You'll see only the magnificent east windows in the apse. On your right, in the south aisle, is the elaborate, 15th-century black-marble memorial to Emperor Ludwig the Bavarian, guarded by four 16th-century armored knights. Two modern additions to the cathedral also seize the visitor's attention: the 1957 multicolored pulpit, and the huge 1954 crucifix that hangs over the chancel.

From the cathedral, follow any of the alleys heading east and
9 you'll reach the very heart of Munich, **Marienplatz,** which is surrounded by shops, restaurants, and cafés. The square is named after the gilded statue of the Virgin Mary that has been watching over it for more than three centuries. It was erected in 1638 at the behest of elector Maximilian I as an act of thanksgiving for the survival of the city during the Thirty Years' War, the cataclysmic religious struggle that devastated vast regions of Germany. When the statue, which stands on a marble column, was taken down to be cleaned for a eucharistic world congress in 1960, workmen found a small casket in the base containing a splinter of wood said to come from the cross of Christ.

10 Marienplatz is dominated by the 19th-century **Neues Rathaus** (new town hall), built between 1867 and 1908 in the fussy, turreted, neogothic style so beloved by King Ludwig II. Architectural historians are divided over its merits, though its dramatic scale and lavish detailing are impressive. Perhaps the most serious criticism is that the Dutch and Flemish style of the building seems out of place amid the Baroque and Rococo of 11 so much of the rest of the city. The **Altes Rathaus** (old town hall), a medieval building of assured charm, sits modestly, as if forgotten, in a corner of the square. Its great hall—destroyed in 1944 but now fully restored—was the work of the cathedral's chief architect, Jörg von Halspach.

In 1904, a glockenspiel (a chiming clock with mechanical figures) was added to the tower of the new town hall; it plays daily at 11 AM (also at 5 PM June–Sept.). As the chimes peal out over the square, doors flip open and brightly colored dancers and jousting knights go through their paces. They act out two events from Munich's past: a tournament held on Marienplatz in 1568, and the *Schäfflertanz* (Dance of the Coopers), which commemorated the end of the plague of 1517. When Munich was in ruins after the war, an American soldier contributed some paint to restore the battered figures, and he was rewarded with a ride on one of the jousters' horses, high above the cheering crowds. You can travel up there, too, by elevator. *Admission: DM 2 adults, DM 1 children. May–Oct., Mon.–Fri. 9–4, Sat.–Sun. 10–7; Nov–Apr., Mon.–Fri. 9–4.*

Time Out As the chimes of the glockenspiel fade, duck into the arcades to your left and seek out the smoky welcome of **Donisl** (Weinstr. 1), one of Munich's oldest beer halls. Line up with the locals for pea soup, served in metal bowls, and all the more delicious for that. If you need shelter and sustenance after a night out, Donisl is open until 4 AM.

If you're thinking of lunch after the glockenspiel performance, cross the square, head through the old town hall arcade, turn right, and join the crowds doing their day's shopping at the 12 **Viktualienmarkt**, the city's open-air food market (*Viktualien* is an old German word for food). You'll find a wide range of produce available. German and international food, Bavarian beer, and French wines make the market a feast for the eyes as well as for the stomach. It is also the realm of the garrulous, sturdy market women who run the stalls with dictatorial authority; one of them was lately soundly told off by Munich's leading newspaper for rudely warning an American tourist not to touch the fruit!

Somewhere beneath the tough exterior of the typical Munich market woman a sentimental heart must beat, for each morning fresh flowers are placed in the extended hand of a statue that stands along the edge of the market. The statue is of Munich's famous comedian Karl Valentin and is one of some half-dozen memorial fountains with statues of legendary Bavarian music-hall stars, singers, and comedians from the past that grace the market square.

In summer, take a chair at one of the tables of a lively beer garden set up beneath great chestnut trees to enjoy an alfresco lunch of Bavarian sausage and sauerkraut.

Various *Metzgereien* (butcher shops) in and around the market dispense different types of sausage and will make up sandwiches either to go or to be eaten on the premises.

The small-scale restaurants in the market serve up slightly more elaborate fare, as does *Die Suppen Kuche* (the Soup Kitchen), which offers half a dozen hearty soups every day from mid-morning until near closing, along with all kinds of sandwiches, snacks, beer, wine, and coffee. The Soup Kitchen is a self-serve operation. Get in line, read the blackboard menu, pick up one of the specialties, carry it to the long, communal tables set up under an awning, and join the party.

The market even sports a champagne bar, where high-tone tidbits go along with the bubbly served by the glass.

From the market, follow Rosental into Sendlingerstrasse, one of the city's most interesting shopping streets, and head left toward Sendlinger Tor, a finely restored medieval brick gate. On your right as you head down Sendlingerstrasse is the remarkable 18th-century church of St. Johann Nepomuk, known as the
13 **Asamkirche** because of the two Asam brothers, Cosmas Damian and Egid Quirin, who built it. The exterior fits so snugly into the housefronts of the street (the Asam brothers lived next door) that you might easily overlook the church as you pass; yet the raw rock foundation of the facade, with its gigantic pilasters, announces the presence of something really unusual. Before you go in, have a look above the doorway at the statue of St. Nepomuk, a 14th-century Bohemian monk who drowned in the Danube; you'll see that angels are conducting him to heaven from a rocky riverbank. Inside you'll discover a prime example of true south-German, late-Baroque architecture. Red stucco and rosy marble cover the walls; there is an explosion of frescoes, statuary, and gilding. The little church overwhelms with its opulence and lavish detailing—take a look at the gilt skeletons in the little atrium—and creates a powerfully mystical atmosphere. This is a vision of paradise on earth that those who are more accustomed to the gaunt Gothic cathedrals of northern Europe may find disconcerting. It is a fine example, though, of the Bavarian taste for ornament and, possibly, overkill. Is it vulgar or a great work of architecture? You'll want to decide for yourself.

Return down Sendlingerstrasse toward the city center and turn right into the Rindermarkt (the former cattle market),
14 and you'll be beneath the soaring tower of **Peterskirche,** or Alter Peter (Old Peter), as Munich's oldest and smallest parish church is affectionately known. The church traces its origins to the 11th century and over the years has been restored in a variety of architectural styles. Today you'll find a rich Baroque interior with a magnificent late-Gothic high altar and aisle pillars decorated with exquisite 18th-century figures of the apostles. From the top of its 300-foot tower there's a fine view of the city and, in clear weather, the Alps. A notice at the entrance to the tower tells you whether the Alps can be seen and it's worth the long climb to the top. *Admission to the tower: DM 2. Open Mon.–Fri. 9–5, Sat. 8:30–7, Sun. and holidays 10–7.*

From Peterskirche, cross the busy street called Tal (it means "valley," and was an early route into the old city) and step into
15 Burgstrasse, and soon you're in the quiet, airy **Alter Hof,** the inner courtyard of the original palace of the Wittelsbach rulers

of Bavaria. They held court here starting in 1253, and something of the medieval flavor of those times has survived in this quiet corner of the otherwise busy downtown area. Don't pass through without turning to admire the medieval oriel (bay window) that hides modestly on the south wall, just around the corner as you enter the courtyard.

Time Out After all this sightseeing, take an opportunity to rest your legs and quench your thirst while at the same time continuing your tour of central Munich. On the little square called Am Platzl is Munich's most famous beer hall, the **Hofbräuhaus.** *Hofbräu* means "royal brew," a term that aptly describes the golden beer that is served here in king-size liter mugs. Duke Wilhelm V founded the brewery in 1589, and although it still boasts royal patronage in its title, it's now state-owned. If the downstairs hall is too noisy for you, there's a quiet restaurant upstairs. And if there are too many tourists, return on a Saturday night to join the locals at the weekly hop in the upstairs ballroom.

16 From the Hofbräuhaus, head north into **Maximilianstrasse,** Munich's most elegant shopping street, named after King Maximilian II, whose statue you'll see far down on the right. The king wanted to break away from the Greek-influenced classical style of city architecture favored by his father, Ludwig I, so he ingenuously asked his cabinet whether he could be allowed to create something original. Maximilianstrasse was the result. This broad boulevard, its central stretch lined with majestic buildings (now museums and government offices), culminates on a rise beyond the Isar River in the stately outlines of the Maximilianeum, a 19th-century palace now housing the Bavarian *Landtag* (parliament). Across Maximilianstrasse as you enter from the Hofbräuhaus stands another handsome city pal-
17 ace: the **Hotel Vier Jahreszeiten,** a historic watering hole for princes, millionaires, and the expense-account jet-set.

Turn left down Maximilianstrasse, away from the Maximilianeum, and you enter the square called Max-Joseph-Platz, dominated by the pillared portico of the 19th-century
18 **Nationaltheater,** home of the Bavarian State Opera Company. The statue in the center of the square is of Bavaria's first king, Max I Joseph. Along the northern side of this untidily arranged square (marred by the entrance to an underground parking lot)
19 is the lofty and austere southern wall of the **Residenz,** the royal palace of Wittelsbach rulers for more than six centuries. It began as a small castle, to which the Wittelsbach dukes moved in the 14th century, when the Alter Hof became surrounded by the teeming tenements of an expanding Munich. In succeeding centuries, the royal residence developed parallel to the importance, requirements, and interests of its occupants. As the complex expanded, it came to include the **Königsbau** (on Max-Josef-Platz) and then (clockwise) the **Alte Residenz;** the **Festsaal** (Banquet Hall); the **Altes Residenztheater** (Cuvilliés Theater); **Allerheiligenhofkirche** (All Soul's Church, now ruined); the **Residenztheater;** and the **Nationaltheater.** Building began in 1385 with the Neuveste (New Fortress), which comprised the northeast section; it burned to the ground in 1750, but one of its finest rooms survived: the 16th-century **Antiquarium,** which was built for Duke Albrecht V's collection of antique statues (today it's used chiefly for state receptions). The throne room of King Ludwig I, the **Neuer Herkulessaal,** is

now a concert hall. The accumulated treasures of the Wittelsbachs can be seen in the **Schatzkammer,** or Treasury (one rich centerpiece is a small Renaissance statue of St. George, studded with 2,291 diamonds, 209 pearls, and 406 rubies), and a representative collection of paintings and tapestries is housed in the **Residenzmuseum.** Antique coins and Egyptian works of art are located in the two other museums of this vast palace. In the center of the complex, entered through an inner courtyard where chamber-music concerts are given in summer, is a small Rococo theater, built by François Cuvilliés from 1751 to 1755. The French-born Cuvilliés was a dwarf who was admitted to the Bavarian court as a decorative "bauble." Prince Max Emanuel recognized his latent artistic ability and had him trained as an architect. The prince's eye for talent gave Germany some of its richest Rococo treasures. *Admission to Treasury and Residenzmuseum: DM 2.50 adults, DM 1.50 children. Open Tues.–Sat. 10–4:30, Sun. 10–1. Admission to Staatliche Münzsammlung (coin collection): DM 2.50 adults, 50 pf children, free Sun. and holidays. Open Tues.–Sun. 10–5. Admission to Staatliche Sammlung Ägyptischer Kunst (Egyptian art): DM 3 adults, 50 pf children, free Sun. and holidays. Open Tues.–Sun. 9:30–4 and Tues. 7 PM–9 PM. Admission to Cuvilliés Theater: DM 1.50 adults, DM 1 children. Open Mon.–Sat. 2–5, Sun. 10–5.*

20 Directly north of the Residenz on Hofgartenstrasse lies the former royal garden, the **Hofgarten.** Two sides of the pretty, formal garden are bordered by arcades designed in the 19th century by the royal architect Leo von Klenze. On the east side of the garden, dominated for years by the bombed ruin of the Bavarian Army Museum, workers are busy on Munich's most controversial public-works project: the new State Chancellery. Opponents say the enormous bulk of the planned new building will disturb the harmony of the Hofgarten and its historic surroundings.

In front of the ruins of the Army Museum stands one of Europe's most unusual—some say most effective—war memorials. Instead of looking up at the monument you are led down to it: It is a sunken crypt, covered by a massive granite block. In the crypt lies a German soldier from World War I.

Time Out Munich's oldest café, the **Annast,** is located where the Hofgarten is bordered by busy Odeonsplatz. In summer, tables under the trees of the Hofgarten offer a delightful retreat from the hum of city traffic only 100 yards away.

You can be forgiven for any confusion about your whereabouts ("Can this really be Germany?") when you step from the Hofgarten onto Odeonsplatz. To your left is the 19th-century 21 **Feldherrnhalle,** a local hall of fame modeled on the 14th-century Loggia dei Lanzi in Florence. In the '30s and '40s it was the site of a key Nazi shrine, marking the place where Hitler's abortive rising, or *Putsch,* took place in 1923. All who passed it had to give the Nazi salute.

Looking north up Ludwigstrasse, the arrow-straight avenue 22 that ends at the Feldherenhalle, you'll see the **Siegestor,** or victory arch, which marks the beginning of Ludwigstrasse. The Siegestor also boasts Italian origins; it was modeled on the Arch of Constantine in Rome. It was built to honor the achievements of the Bavarian army during the Wars of Liberation (1813–1815).

Completing this impressively Italianate panorama is the great yellow bulk of the former royal church of St. Kajetan, the
23 **Theatinerkirche,** a sturdily imposing Baroque building. Its lofty towers frame a restrained facade, capped by a massive dome. The church owes its Italian appearance to its founder, the Princess Henriette Adelaide, who commissioned it as an act of thanksgiving for the birth of her son and heir, Max Emanuel, in 1663. A native of Turin, the princess distrusted Bavarian architects and builders and thus summoned a master builder from Bologna, Agostino Barelli, to construct her church. He took as his model the Roman mother church of the newly formed Theatine order of Catholicism. Barelli worked on the building for 11 years but was dismissed before the project was completed. It was not for another 100 years that the Theatinerkirche was finished. Step inside to admire its austere, stucco interior.

Now head north up Ludwigstrasse. The first stretch of the street was designed by court architect von Klenze. Much as Baron Haussmann was later to demolish many of the old streets and buildings in Paris, replacing them with stately boulevards, so von Klenze swept aside the small dwellings and alleys that stood here to build his great avenue. His high-windowed and formal buildings have never quite been accepted by Müncheners, and indeed there's still a sense that Ludwigstrasse is an intruder. Most visitors either love it or hate it. Von Klenze's buildings end just before Ludwigstrasse becomes Leopoldstrasse, and it is easy to see where he handed construction over to another leading architect, von Gartner. The severe Neoclassical buildings that line southern Ludwigstrasse—including the Bayerische Staatsbibliothek (Bavarian State Library) and the Universität (University)—fragment into the lighter styles of Leopoldstrasse. The more delicate structures are echoed by the busy street life you'll find here in summer. Once the hub of the legendary artists' district of Schwabing, Leopoldstrasse still throbs with life from spring to fall, exuding the atmosphere of a Mediterranean boulevard, with cafés, wine terraces, and artists' stalls. In comparison, Ludwigstrasse is inhabited by the ghosts of the past.

At the southern end of Leopoldstrasse, beyond the Siegestor, lies the great open quadrangle of the university, Geschwister-Scholl-Platz, named after the founders of the student Weisse Rose (White Rose) movement, a group of anti-Nazi campaigners who fell victim to the Gestapo in the '30s. At its northern end, Leopoldstrasse leads into Schwabing itself, once Munich's Bohemian quarter but now distinctly upscale. Explore the streets of old Schwabing around Wedekindplatz to get the feel of the place. (Those in search of the young-at-heart mood that once animated Schwabing should make for Haidhausen, on the other side of the Isar.)

24 Bordering the east side of Schwabing is the **Englischer Garten.** Three miles long and more than a mile wide, it's Germany's largest city park, stretching from the central avenue of Prinzregentenstrasse to the city's northern boundary. It was designed for the Bavarian Prince Karl Theodor by a refugee from the American War of Independence, Count Rumford. While Count Rumford was of English descent, it was the open, infor-

mal nature of the park—reminiscent of the rolling parklands with which the English aristocracy of the 18th century liked to surround their country homes—that determined its name. It has an appealing boating lake, four beer gardens, and a series of curious decorative and monumental constructions, including a Greek temple, the Monopteros, designed by von Klenze for King Ludwig I and built on an artificial hill in the southern section of the park. In the center of one of the park's most popular beer gardens is a Chinese pagoda, erected in 1789, destroyed during the war, and then reconstructed. The Chinese Tower beer garden is world famous, but the park has prettier places in which to down a beer: the Aumeister, for example, along the northern perimeter. The Aumeister's restaurant is in an early 19th-century hunting lodge.

The Englischer Garten is a paradise for joggers, cyclists, and, in winter, cross-country skiers. The Munich Cricket Club's ground is in the southern section—proof perhaps that even that most British of games is not invulnerable to the single-minded Germans—and spectators are welcome. The park also has specially designated areas for nude sunbathing—the Germans have a positively pagan attitude to the sun—so don't be surprised to see naked bodies bordering the flower beds and paths.

On the southern fringe of Schwabing are Munich's two leading art galleries, the Alte Pinakothek and the Neue Pinakothek, located next to each other on Barerstrasse. They are as complementary as their buildings are contrasting. The Alte Pinakothek (old picture gallery) was built by Leo von Klenze between 1826 and 1836 to exhibit the collection of old masters begun by Duke Wilhelm IV in the 16th century, while the Neue Pinakothek (new picture gallery), a low brick structure, was opened in 1981 to house the royal collection of modern art left homeless when its former building was destroyed in the war.

25 The **Alte Pinakothek** is among the great picture galleries of the world. For many, a visit here will serve as the highlight of a Munich stay. The bulk of the works are northern European, though Italians and Spaniards—notably Giotto—are reasonably well represented. Nevertheless, it is the works of such painters as Van Eyck, Cranach, Duter, Rembrandt, and Rubens that constitute the star attractions. Among its richly filled rooms, seek out Altdorfer's *Alexanderschlacht*, centerpiece of the duke's original collection. The writer and critic Friedrich von Schlegel (1772–1829), seeing the painting, declared: "If Munich has any other paintings of this quality, then artists should make pilgrimages there as well as to Rome or Paris." Munich has many such paintings . . . and many such pilgrims. *Barerstr. 27. Admission: DM 4 adults, 50 pf children, free Sun. and holidays. Open Tues.–Sun. 9–4:30, also Tues. and Thurs. 7 PM–9 PM.*

26 Across a sculpture-studded stretch of lawn is the **Neue Pinakothek.** It's a low brick building that combines high-tech and Italianate influences in equal measure. From outside, the museum does not seem to measure up to the standards set by so many of Munich's other great public buildings. On the other hand, the interior offers a magnificent environment for picture gazing, not the least as a result of the superb natural light flooding in from the skylights. The highlights of the collection

are probably the Impressionist and other French 19th-century works—Monet, Degas, and Manet are all well represented. But there's also a substantial collection of 19th-century German and Scandinavian paintings—misty landscapes predominate—which are only now coming to be recognized as admirable and worthy products of their time. *Barerstr. 29. Admission: DM 4 adults, 50 pf children, free Sun. and holidays. Open Tues.–Sun. 9–4:30, also Tues. 9 PM–9 PM.*

Back on Barerstrasse, walk south toward the city center (turn right from the old gallery or left from the new gallery). Before
27 you stretches the circular **Karolinenplatz,** with its central obelisk; it's a memorial, unveiled in 1812, to those Bavarians killed fighting Napoléon. Turn right onto Briennerstrasse. Opening
28 up ahead is the massive **Königsplatz,** lined on three sides with the monumental Grecian-style buildings by von Klenze that gave Munich the nickname "Athens on the Isar." In the '30s the great parklike square was laid with granite slabs, which resounded with the thud of jackboots as the Nazis commandeered the area for their rallies. Only recently were the slabs torn up; since then the square has returned to something like the green and peaceful appearance originally intended by Ludwig I. The two templelike buildings he had constructed there are muse-
29 ums: the **Glyptothek** features a permanent exhibition of Greek
30 and Roman sculptures, and the **Antikensammlungen** (Antiquities Collection): has a fine group of smaller sculptures, Etruscan art, Greek vases, gold, and glass. *Glyptothek: Königspl. 3. Admission: DM 3.50 adults, 50 pf children, free Sun. and holidays. Open Tues., Weds., and Fri.–Sun. 10–4:30, Thurs. 12–8:30. Antiquities Collection: Königspl. 1. Admission: DM 3.50 adults, 50 pf children, free Sun. and holidays. Open Tues. and Thurs.–Sun. 10–4:30, Wed. noon–8:30.*

Return to Karolinenplatz and head south along Barerstrasse. You'll come to Lenbachplatz, a busy square scarred by road intersections and tramlines, and overlooked by a series of handsome turn-of-the-century buildings. At the point where Lenbachplatz meets Maximiliansplatz you'll see one of Munich's most impressive fountains: the monumental late-
31 19th-century **Wittelsbacher Fountain.**

At the southwestern corner of Lenbachplatz is the arched entrance to the park that was once the city's botanical garden, the
32 **Alter Botanischer Garten.** A huge glass palace was built here in 1853 for Germany's first industrial exhibition. In 1931 the immense structure burned down: six years later the garden was redesigned as a public park. Two features from the '30s remain: a small, square exhibition hall, still used for art shows; and the 1933 Neptune Fountain, an enormous work in the heavy, monumental style of the prewar years. At the international electricity exhibition of 1882, the world's first high-tension electricity cable was run from the park to a Bavarian village 30 miles away.

Time Out Tucked away on the northern edge of the Alter Boranischer Garten is one of the city's most central beer gardens. It's part of the **Park Café,** which at night becomes a fashionable disco serving magnums of champagne for DM 1,450 apiece. Prices in the beer garden are more realistic.

---

33 Opposite the southern exit of the park loom the freshly cleaned and ornate contours of the 1897 law courts, the **Palace of Justice.** Just around the corner is the **Hauptbahnhof** (main railway station)—and the end of our tour.

Outside the Center

The site of Munich's annual beer festival—the renowned Oktoberfest—is only a 10-minute walk from the main train station; alternatively, ride the U-5 subway one stop. The festival site is Munich's enormous exhibition ground, the **Theresienwiese,** named after a young woman whose engagement party gave rise to the Oktoberfest. The party celebrated the betrothal in 1810 of Princess Therese von Sachsen-Hildburghausen to the Bavarian crown prince Ludwig, later Ludwig I. It was such a success, attended by nearly the entire population of Munich, that it became an annual affair. Beer was served then as now, but what began as a night out for the locals has become a 16-day-and-night, nonstop international bonanza, attracting more than 6 million people. They knock back around 5 million liters of beer in enormous wooden pavilions that heave and pulsate to the combined racket of brass bands, drinking songs, and thousands of dry throats demanding more. Like most of life's questionable pleasures, it has to be experienced once. Only the brave return for more.

The site is overlooked by a 19th-century hall of fame—one of the last works of Ludwig I—and a monumental bronze statue of the maiden **Bavaria,** more than 100 feet high. The statue is hollow, and 130 steps take you up into the braided head for a view of Munich through Bavaria's eyes.

The major attraction away from the downtown area is **Schloss Nymphenburg,** a glorious Baroque and Rococo palace that was a summer home to five generations of Bavarian royalty. It's located in the northwest suburb. To reach it, take a number 12 streetcar or a number 41 bus. Nymphenburg is the largest palace of its kind in Germany, stretching more than half a mile from one wing to the other. The palace grew in size and scope over a period of more than 200 years, beginning as a summer residence built on land given by Prince Ferdinand Maria to his beloved wife, Henriette Adelaide, on the birth of their son and heir, Max Emanuel, in 1663. As mentioned earlier, she had the Theatinerkirche built as a personal expression of thanks for the birth. The Italian architect Agostino Barelli, brought from Bologna for that project, was instructed to build the palace. It was completed in 1675 by his successor, Enrico Zuccalli. Within that original building, now the central axis of the palace complex, is a magnificent hall, the Steinerner Saal, extending over two floors and richly decorated with stucco and swirling frescoes. In the summer, chamber-music concerts are given here. The decoration of the Steinerner Saal spills over into the surrounding royal chambers, in one of which is the famous Schönheitengalerie (Gallery of Beauties). The walls are hung from floor to ceiling with portraits of women who caught the roving eye of Ludwig I, among them a butcher's daughter and an English duchess. The most famous portrait is of Lola Montez, a sultry beauty and high-class courtesan who, after a time as mistress of Franz Liszt and later Alexandre Dumas, captivated Ludwig I to such an extent that he gave up his throne for her.

The palace is set in a fine park, laid out in formal French style, with low hedges and gravel walks, extending into woodland. Tucked away among the ancient trees are three fascinating structures built as Nymphenburg expanded and changed occupants. Don't miss the **Amalienburg,** or hunting lodge. It's a Rococo gem, built by François Cuvilliés, architect of the Residenztheater. The silver-and-blue stucco of the little Amalienburg creates an atmosphere of courtly high life that makes it clear that the pleasures of the chase here did not always take place out-of-doors. In the lavishly appointed kennels you'll see that even the dogs lived in luxury. For royal tea parties, another building was constructed, the **Pagodenburg.** It has an elegant French exterior that disguises a suitably Oriental interior in which exotic teas from India and China were served. Swimming parties were held in the **Badenburg,** Europe's first post-Roman heated pool.

Nymphenburg contains so much of interest that a day hardly provides enough time for it all. Don't leave without visiting the former royal stables, the **Marstallmuseum,** or Museum of Royal Carriages. It houses a fleet of vehicles, including an elaborately decorated sleigh in which King Ludwig II once glided through the Bavarian twilight, postilion torches lighting the way. On the floor above are fine examples of Nymphenburg porcelain, produced here between 1747 and the 1920s. *Admission to the entire Schloss Nymphenberg complex: DM 5 adults, DM 3 children. Open Tues.–Sun. 9–12:30 and 1:30–5. Pagodenburg and Badenburg are closed Oct.–Mar. Marstallmuseum and Nymphenburg porcelain exhibition are open Apr.–Sept., Tues.–Sun. 9–noon and 1–5; Oct.–Mar., Tues.–Sun. 10–noon and 1–4.*

Beyond Nymphenburg, on the northwest edge of Munich, lies medieval **Schloss Blutenburg,** now the home of an international collection of children's books. Take a suburban line S-2 train to Obermenzing to reach Blutenburg. The castle chapel, built in 1488 by Duke Sigismund, has some fine 15th-century stained glass. Sigismund loved the peace and quiet of Blutenburg (now disturbed by the roar of traffic on the nearby autobahn) and spent most of his time here rather than at the royal residence in Munich.

In 1597, Duke Wilhelm V also decided to look for a peaceful retreat outside Munich and found what he wanted at **Schloss Schleissheim,** then far beyond the city walls, today only a short ride on the suburban line S-1 (to Oberschleissheim station). A later ruler, Prince Max Emanuel, extended the palace and added a second, smaller one, the Lustheim. Separated from the main palace by a formal garden and decorative canal, the Lustheim houses Germany's largest collection of Meissen porcelain. *Admission: DM 4 adults, DM 3 children. Open Apr.–Sept., Tues.–Sun. 10–5; Oct.–Mar., Tues.–Sun. 10–4.*

Of all the controversial buildings that mark Munich's skyline, none outdoes the circus-tent-like roofs of the **Olympiapark.** Built for the 1972 Olympics, the park, with its undulating, transparent tile roofs and modern housing blocks, represented a revolutionary marriage of technology and visual daring when first unveiled. Today, though still striking, it seems almost dated, a state of affairs not helped by the dingy gray of the faded tiles, or indeed by the fact that many of them are given to falling off. Take the elevator up the 960-foot Olympia Tower for a view of the city and the Alps; there's also a revolving restaurant near the top. *Admission to stadium: DM 1 adults, 50 pf children. Open daily 8:30–6. Admission to Olympia Tower: DM 4 adults, DM 2.50 children. Open daily 8 AM–midnight. Restaurant open daily 11–5:30 and 6:30 PM–10:30 PM; tel. 089/308–1039 for reservations.*

Munich for Free

All **city-run museums** are free Sundays (though you still have to pay to see temporary exhibits). One of the best free evenings you'll ever have in Munich is a stroll along **Maximilianstrasse,** site of many of the best private art galleries. On the first Thursday of every month, when many of the galleries open their new exhibits, you can wander in and out of them all, attending the first-night parties and picking up as much free liquor as you can hold. It's a busy, colorful scene, when *tout le* Munich can be seen.

Free **music** and **concerts** are a regular feature of the city. There are free brass-band concerts at the **Chinese Tower** beer garden in the Englischer Garten every afternoon in summer and all day Sundays. On Sunday mornings the **Waldwirtschaft** beer garden, by the Isar River in the Grosshesselohe district (Georg-Kalb-Str. 3), has free jazz concerts (mostly of traditional jazz). Similarly, many of the beer halls in **Schwabing** have jazz bands Sunday afternoons. At least one Munich church will have a full sung **high mass** on Sunday mornings, often with an orchestra as well as a choir. The standards are remarkably high; moreover, church music of this quality performed in the Frauenkirche or the Theatinerkirche is a memorable experience. Notices outside churches give schedules.

The **Englischer Garten** is free any time but in winter offers an additional pleasure: free skating on its lakes and streams. Likewise, there's never a charge to visit the **Viktualienmarkt,** the noisy food market, but visit during the *Christkindlmarkt,* the lavish pre-Christmas market, to see it at its picturesque best. Finally, schedule one day of your visit to catch the **glockenspiel** on the Neues Rathaus. It goes through its elaborate paces at 11 every morning. It's one of the best free shows in town.

What to See and Do with Children

Take your children to the **zoo** (Tierpark Hellabrun). There are special areas where children can touch the animals and feed them and go for pony rides. It's a hands-on sort of place, just a 20-minute ride from downtown, too (*see* Parks and Gardens, below).

The **Deutsches Museum** rates as the city's number-one museum for children. Budding scientists and young dreamers alike will be delighted by its extensive collections and its many activities that provide buttons to push and cranks to turn. It's on the Museuminsel (Museum Island) in the Isar River, a 10-minute walk from downtown (*see* Museums and Galleries, below). The tower of the Gothic **Altes Rathaus** (old town hall) provides a satisfyingly atmospheric setting for a little toy museum. It includes several exhibits from the United States. *Marienpl. Admission: DM 3 adults, DM 1 children, DM 5 family tickets. Open daily 10–5.*

Munich has several theaters for children, where, with pantomime such a strong part of the repertoire, the language problem disappears. The best of them is the **Münchner Theater für Kinder** (Dachauerstr. 46, tel. 089/595–454 or 089/593–858). Two puppet theaters offer regular performances for children; the **Münchner Marionettentheater** (Blumenstr. 29a, tel. 089/265–712) and **Otto Bille's Marionettenbuhne** (Breiterangerstr. 15, tel. 089/150–2168 or 089/310–1278). Munich is the winter quarters of the **Circus Krone,** which has its own permanent building (Marsstr. 43, tel. 089/558–166). The circus performs there from Christmas until the end of March.

In summer, seek out the 100-year-old **carousel** at the edge of the Englischer Garten beer garden, a beer-mug's throw from the famous Chinese Pagoda.

For young roller skaters, Munich has a roller disco, the **Roll Palast,** in the western suburb of Pasing (Stockackerstr. 5); take the suburban rail line S-5 or S-6 to Westkreuz. Roller skates can be rented. Just east of Munich is **No-Name City** (Gruberstr. 60a), a mock-up western town, with saloons, corral, live country music, and daily duels (with blank ammunition) in the cowboy-populated streets. Take suburban line S-6 to Poing; from there it's only 200 yards. *Admission: DM 10.50 adults, DM 7 children. Open Tues.–Sun. 9:30–6.*

Munich is West Germany's leading **movie-making** center, and in the summer the studios at Geiselgasteig, on the southern outskirts of the city, open their doors to visitors. A "Filmexpress" transports you on a 1½-hour tour of the sets of *The Boat, Enemy Mine, The Endless Story,* and other productions. Take the number 25 streetcar to Bavariafilmplatz. *Admission: DM 10 adults, DM 6 children. Open Mar.–Oct., daily 9–4.*

Off the Beaten Track

For the cheapest sightseeing tour on wheels of the main sights of the city, board a **No. 19 streetcar** outside the main train station (on Bahnhofpl.) and make the 15-minute journey to Wienerplatz. Before heading back again, explore the streets around the square, part of the picturesque old residential area of Haidhausen. On a fine day, join the **chess players** at their open-air board at Schwabing's forumlike Münchner Freiheit square. On a rainy day, pack your swimming things and splash around in the art nouveau setting of the **Müllersches Volksbad,** on the corner of the Isar bridge known as Ludwigsbrücke. If it's Saturday, walk over to Blumenstrasse and visit the city's most unusual museum, the **Munich Fire Brigade's** permanent exhibit of antique fire-fighting equipment.

Also in this area is a museum-piece cemetery, the **Südfriedhof** where you'll find many famous names but few tourists. Four hundred years ago it was a graveyard beyond the city walls for plague victims and paupers. In the 19th century it was refashioned into an upscale last resting place by the city architect von Gärtner. The royal architect Leo von Klenze designed some of the headstones, and both he and von Gärtner are among the famous names you'll find there. The last burial took place here more than 40 years ago. The Südfriedhof is on the Thalkirchnerstrasse, a short walk from the Sendlinger-Tor-Platz U-bahn station.

Sightseeing Checklists

The points of interest listed here are all discussed in greater detail in Exploring Munich, above.

Historical Buildings and Sites

Alter Hof (Old Palace). The first of the Wittelsbach royal residences in Munich, today serving as local government offices.

Altes Rathaus (old town hall). Munich's first city hall, built in 1474, and restored after wartime bomb damage.

Bavaria. This monumental statue, Munich's Statue of Liberty, overlooks the Theresienwiese, site of the Oktoberfest.

Feldherrenhalle. Modeled on Florence's Loggia dei Lanzi, this arcade dominates the southern end of Odeonsplatz.

Friedensengel (Angel of Peace). This striking gilded angel crowns a marble column in a small park overlooking the Isar River. It marks one end of Prinzregentenstrasse, the broad, arrow-straight boulevard laid out by Prince Regent Luitpold at the end of the 19th century.

Königsplatz. An enormous city square, laid out by Ludwig I and flanked on three sides by Grecian temple–style exhibition halls and a massive Neoclassical arch (*see also* Museums and Galleries, below).

Marienplatz. This substantial square rates as the historic heart of Munich, invariably animated by visitors and locals alike.

Maximilianeum (Maximilianstr.). The Bavarian State Government meets in this lavish mid-19th-century arcaded palace. Built for Maximilian II as part of an ambitious city-planning scheme. Today only the terrace can be visited.

Münze (Pfisterstr. 4). Originally the royal stables, the Münze (mint) was created by court architect Wilhelm Egkl between 1563 and 1567. A stern Neoclassical facade was added in 1809; the courtyard retains its Renaissance look.

Nationaltheater. The sturdy Neoclassical bulk of the premier theater in Munich, home of the Bavarian State Opera Company, dominates the north side of Max-Joseph-Platz.

Neues Rathaus. The city's New Town Hall, with its famed glockenspiel, the largest musical clock in Germany.

Residenz. Massive palace complex of the Wittelsbach rulers of Bavaria, remodeled numerous times over the centuries, much of it open to the public (*see also* Museums and Galleries, below).

Schloss Blutenburg. A well-preserved walled and moated castle, formerly the hunting retreat of Duke Albrecht III. The castle's 15th-century chapel and Baroque hall can be visited.

Schloss Nymphenburg. Summer residence of the Wittelsbachs; Germany's largest Baroque palace (*see also* Museums and Galleries *and* Parks and Gardens, below).

Viktualienmarkt. Munich's open-air food market is among the most colorful and diverting sights in the city.

Museums and Galleries

Alte Pinakothek. One of the world's leading collections of old masters (*see* Exploring Munich, above).

Bayerisches Nationalmuseum. The Bavarian National Museum contains an extensive collection of Bavarian and other German art and artifacts. The highlight for some will be the medieval and Renaissance wood carvings, with many works by the great Renaissance sculptor Tilman Riemenschneider. Fine tapestries, arms and armor, a unique collection of Christmas crèches —(the Krippenschau), Bavarian arts and crafts, and folk artifacts compete for your attention. *Prinzregentenstr. 3. Admis-*

sion: DM 3 adults, 50 pf children, free Sun. and holidays. Open Tues.–Sun. 9:30–5.

BMW Museum. Munich is where BMWs are made, and the museum, adjoining the factory next to Olympia park, contains a dazzling collection of BMWs old and new. *Lerchenauerstr. 36. Admission: DM 4.50. Open daily 9–5.*

Deutches Jagd-und Fischerei Museum (German Museum of Hunting and Fishing). The world's largest collection of fishhooks and 500 stuffed animals make up just part of the attraction of one of Munich's most popular museums (*see* Exploring Munich, above).

Deutsches Museum (German Museum of Science and Technology). Founded in 1903 and housed in its present monumental building since 1925, this is one of the most stimulating and innovative science museums in Europe. Twelve miles of corridors, six floors of exhibits, and 30 departments make up the immense collections. Set aside a full day if you plan to do justice to the entire museum (*see* What to See and Do with Children, above). *Museumsinsel 1. Admission: DM 5 adults, DM 2 children. Open daily 9–5.*

Münchner Stadtmuseum (City Museum). Munich's history is illustrated by means of puppets, musical instruments, photographs, and documents. *Jakobspl. 1. Admission: DM 4 adults, children free; free Sun. and holidays. Open Tues.–Sat. 9–4:30, Sun. and holidays. 10–6.*

Neue Pinakothek. Late-18th- and 19th-century paintings, with strong French collections, make this one of the most compelling art galleries in Europe (*see* Exploring Munich, above).

Prähistorische Staatssammlung (State Prehistoric Collection). This is Bavaria's principal record of its prehistoric, Roman, and Celtic past. The perfectly preserved body of a young girl who was ritually sacrificed, recovered from a Bavarian peat moor, is among its more spine-chilling exhibits. Head down to the basement to see the fine Roman mosaic floor. *Lerchenfeldstr. 2. Admission: DM 2.50 adults, 50 pf children. Open Tues., Wed., and Fri.–Sun. 9–4, Thurs. 9–8* PM.

Paläontologisches Museum. The 10-million-year-old skeleton of a mammoth is the centerpiece of this paleontological and geological collection. *Richard-Wagner-Str. 10. Admission: free. Open Mon.–Thurs. 8–4, Fri. 8–3.*

Residenzmuseum. This is the former royal palace of the Wittelsbachs, with priceless collections of state treasures (*see* Historical Buildings and Sites in Sightseeing Checklists *and* Exploring Munich, above).

Schack-Galerie. Those with a taste for florid and romantic 19th-century German paintings will appreciate the collections of the Schack-Galerie, originally the private collection of one Count Schack. Others may find the gallery dull, filled with plodding and repetitive works by painters who now repose in well-deserved obscurity. *Prinzregentenstr. 9. Admission: DM 2.50 adults, 50 pf children, free Sun. and holidays. Open Wed.–Mon. 9–4:30.*

Staatliche Antikensammlungen und Glyptothek (State Collection of Antiquities and Sculpture). Ancient Greek and Roman collections are housed in two appropriately Neoclassical buildings on the vast Konigsplatz (*see* Exploring Munich, above).

Staatliche Graphische Sammlung (State Collection of Graphic Arts). A comprehensive collection of drawings and prints from the late Gothic period to the present day. *Meiserstr. 10. Admission free. Open Mon.–Fri. 9–1 and 2–4:30.*

Staatliches Museum für Völkerkunde (State Museum of Ethnology). Arts and crafts from around the world are displayed in this extensive museum. There are also regular ethnological exhibits. *Maximilianstr. 42. Admission: DM 3.50 adults, 50 pf children; free Sun. and holidays. Open Tues.–Sun. 9:30–4:30.*
Staatliche Sammlung Ägyptischer Kunst (State Collection of Egyptian Art). This is just part of the remarkable collection housed in the Residenz, the former royal palace (*see* Historical Buildings and Sites *and* Exploring Munich, above).
Staatsgalerie Moderner Kunst (State Gallery of Modern Art). The gallery is in the west wing of the Hitler-era Haus der Kunst, a monumental pillared building at the southern end of the Englischer Garten (the east wing has regular temporary exhibits). It features one of the finest collections of 20th-century paintings and sculptures in the world. *Prinzregentenstr. 1. Admission: DM 3.50 adults, 50 pf children; free Sun. and holidays. Open Tues.–Sun. 9–4:30, also Thurs. 7 PM–9 PM.*
Städtische Galerie im Lenbachhaus. This internationally renowned picture collection is housed in a delightful late-19th-century Florentine-style villa, former home and studio of the artist Franz von Lenbach. It contains a rich collection of works from the Gothic period to the present day, including an exciting assemblage of art from the early 20th-century *Blauer Reiter*, or Blue Rider, group: Kandinsky, Klee, Jawlensky, Macke, Marc, and Münter. *Luisenstr. 33. Admission: DM 4 adults, DM 2 children; free Sun. and holidays. Open Tues.–Sun. 10–6.*
Stuck Villa. Like the Lenbach Gallery, this museum is the former home of one of Munich's leading turn-of-the-century artists, Franz von Stuck. His work covers the walls of the haunting rooms of the Neoclassical villa, which is also used for regular art exhibits. *Prinzregentenstr. 60. Admission: varies from DM 5 to DM 7 according to exhibits. Open Tues., Wed., and Fri.–Sun. 10–5, Thurs. 10–7.*

Parks and Gardens

Alter Botanischer Garten. The city's former botanical garden is now a quiet downtown park (*see* Exploring Munich, above).
Englischer Garten. This is the largest city park in Germany, laid out at the end of the 18th century. Lakes, gravel paths, beer gardens, a Chinese pagoda, and a series of small, eye-catching temples number among its attractions (*see* Exploring Munich, above).
Botanischer Garten (Botanical Garden). A collection of 14,000 plants, including orchids, cacti, cyads, alpine flowers, and rhododendrons, makes up one of the most extensive botanical gardens in Europe. The park is located at the eastern edge of the Nymphenburg Palace park. *Menzingerstr. 63. Open daily 9–5; hothouses open daily 9–noon and 1–4.*
Hirschgarten. A former deer park, the Hirschgarten still has wild buck and roe deer in enclosures. There are children's playgrounds and an attractive beer garden. It's located in the suburb of Nymphenburg; take any of the westbound S-bahn train lines to Laim.
Hofgarten. This is the former royal palace garden, located just to the north of the Residenz (*see* Exploring Munich, above).
Isar Valley. Munich's Isar River is no built-up waterway but makes its way north past green, unspoiled banks, ideal territory for cyclists, joggers, and walkers. Nude sunbathing is tolerated on the banks and islands, although the river isn't recommended for swimming.

Luitpold Park (Karl-Theodor-Str.). This is Schwabing's city park. Its quiet and leafy paths and orderly flower beds make it ideal for long summer afternoons.

Olympiapark. Site of the 1972 Olympic Games and still very much the sporting center of the city (*see* Sports and Outdoor Activities, below, *and* Exploring Munich, above).

Schloss Nymphenburg. The 500 acres of Schloss Nymphenburg's park are popular with walkers and joggers. In winter, marked trails beckon cross-country skiers (*see* Historical Buildings and Sites; Museums and Galleries; *and* Exploring Munich, above).

Tierpark Hellabrun. This is the city zoo, among the finest in the world and one in which the animals are arranged according to geographical origin. Cages are kept to a minimum, with preference being given to enclosures wherever possible. The zoo's 170 acres include restaurants and children's areas. The number 52 bus from Marienplatz runs to the zoo. *Admission: DM 5 adults, DM 3 children. Open daily 8–6.*

West Park. Laid out for the 1983 International Horticultural Exhibition, this has become one of the most popular of the city's parks. It was designed to resemble the landscape of Upper Bavaria, with gently undulating hills (popular among joggers and cross-country skiers) and lakes and valleys, the whole planted with regional and international flora. There are restaurants, cafés, beer gardens, children's play areas, an open-air theater, and a concert arena. Take U-bahn lines 3 or 6 to West Park or Renlandstrasse.

Churches

Asamkirche. The most important and lavishly decorated late-Baroque church in the city, built by the brothers Asam. Don't miss it (*see* Exploring Munich, above).

Bürgersaal. Two churches in one, located in the heart of the city. The magnificently opulent Rococo upper church contrasts with the simple, cryptlike chapel below (*see* Exploring Munich, above).

Dreifaltigkeitskirche (Pacellistr.). This is the church of the Holy Trinity, built after a local woman prophesied doom for the city unless a new church was erected. It's a striking Baroque building, with heroic frescoes by Cosmas Damian Asam.

Franziskanerklosterkirche St. Anna im Lehel (St-Anna-Str.). Though less opulently decorated than the Asamkirche, this small Franciscan monastery church, consecrated in 1737, impresses with its sense of movement and its heroic scale. It was largely rebuilt after wartime bomb damage. The ceiling fresco by Cosmas Damian Asam was removed before the war, and, after restoration, now glows in all its original vivid joyfulness. The ornate altar was also designed by the Asam brothers.

Frauenkirche (Church of Our Lady). Munich's soaring, brick Gothic cathedral. Its two lofty towers, capped by onion-shape domes, are enduring symbols of the city (*see* Exploring Munich, above).

Ludwigskirche (Ludwigstr. 22). Planted halfway along the severe, Neoclassical Ludwigstrasse is this curious neo-Byzantine/early Renaissance-style church. It was built at the behest of Ludwig I to provide his newly completed suburb with a parish church. Though most will find the building a curiosity at best, it can be worth a stop to see the fresco of the *Last Judgement* in the choir. At 60 by 37 feet, it is one of the world's largest.

Michaelskirche. One of the most important and largest Renaissance churches in Germany, its construction began in 1583 (*see* Exploring Munich, above).

Peterskirche. Munich's oldest and smallest parish church was consecrated in 1368 on the site of four previous churches. Its tower, Alter Peter, is a local landmark (*see* Exploring Munich, above).

St. Kajetan's (Theatinerkirche). The dominating, ocher-yellow facade of the Theatinerkirche, framed by twin towers and a commanding dome, is one of the striking pieces of architecture in the downtown area (*see* Exploring Munich, above).

Salvatorkirche (Salvatorstr.). The bare brick exterior of this church points to the fact that it was almost certainly built by the same architect as the Frauenkirche. Today, it's the principal Greek Orthodox church in Munich.

Shopping

Gift Ideas Munich is a city of beer, and beer mugs and coasters make obvious choices for souvenirs and gifts. There are several specialty shops downtown. The best is **Ludwig Mory,** in the city hall on Marienplatz. Munich is also the home of the famous **Nymphenburg porcelain** factory. There's a factory outlet on Odeonsplatz, just north of Marienplatz; otherwise, you can buy direct from the factory, on the grounds of Schloss Nymphenburg (Nördliches Schlossrondell 8). Other German porcelain manufacturers also have outlets in the city. For Dresden and Meissen ware, go to **Kunstring Meissen** (Briennerstr. 4 and Karlspl. 5). For Bavarian arts and crafts, the **Bayerischer Kunstgewerberein** (Pacellistr. 7) is unbeatable. For wood carvings, pewter, painted glass, and molded candles, try **A. Kaiser** and **Sebastian Weseley** (Rindermarkt 1), or **Otto Kellnberger's Holzhandlung** and the neighboring **Geschenk Alm** (Heiliggeiststr. 7–8). All four are near the Viktualienmarkt. For the best chocolates, try **Confiserie Rottenhöfer** (Residenzstr. 26) or the **Café Schöne Münchnerin,** opposite the Haus der Kunst.

Antiques Bavarian antiques can be found in the many small shops around the Viktualienmarkt; Westenriederstrasse is lined with antique shops. Also try the area north of the university; Türkenstrasse, Theresienstrasse, and Barerstrasse are all filled with stores selling antiques. The weekend flea market on Dachauerstrasse can also be a good place to explore, though you won't find any bargains here. Munich's biggest antique outlet is the **Palais Bernheimer** (Ottostr. 4–8); the range of goods is immense and encompasses everything from simple and inexpensive pieces of pewter to old-master paintings. If you're looking for a piece of Bavarian farmhouse furniture, check out **Friedrich's Bauern Möbel Markt** (Emil-Riedel-Str. 5). Fine examples of antique German clocks can be found at **Kunsthandlung Schaller** (Prannerstr. 5). This is the area to explore if you're interested in upscale antiques. The **Carl Jagemann shop** (Residenzstr. 3), in the same neighborhood, has been in business for more than a century.

Folk Costumes Those with a fancy to deck themselves out in lederhosen or a dirndl or to sport a green loden coat and little pointed hat with feathers should head for **Loden-Frey** (Maffestr. 7–9) or **Wallach** (Residenzstr. 3). The aptly named **Lederhosen Wagner** (Tal 77) is another good bet.

Shopping Districts Munich has an immense central shopping area, a mile and a half of pedestrian streets stretching from the train station to Marienplatz and north to Odeonsplatz. There's talk, too, of extending it still farther. The two main streets here are **Neuhauserstrasse** and **Kaufingerstrasse.** This is where most of the major department stores are located (*see* Department Stores, below). For upscale shopping, **Maximilianstrasse, Residenzstrasse,** and **Theatinerstrasse** are unbeatable and contain a glittering array of classy and tempting stores, the equal of any in Europe. Schwabing, located north of the university, boasts two of the city's most intriguing and offbeat shopping streets: **Schellingstrasse** and **Hohenzollernstrasse,** the latter with a delightful open-air market at one end.

Department Stores **Hertie,** occupying an entire city block between the train station and Karlsplatz, is the largest and, some claim, the best department store in the city. **Ludwig Beck** (Marienpl. 11) is great any time but comes into its own as Christmas approaches. A series of booths, each delicately and lovingly decorated, contain craftsmen turning out traditional German toys. **Oberpollinger** (Kaufingerstr.) and **Kaufhof** (Marienpl.) are two longtime favorites.

Food Markets Munich's **Viktualienmarkt** is *the* place. Located just south of Marienplatz, it's home to an array of colorful stands selling everything from cheese to sausages, flowers to wine. A visit here is more than just an excuse to buy picnic makings: It's central to an understanding of the rough-and-ready, easy-come–easy-go nature of Müncheners.

Sports and Fitness

The **Olympiapark,** built for the 1972 Olympics, is the largest sports and recreation center in Europe. For general information about clubs, organizations, events, etc., contact the *Haus des Sports* (Briennerstr. 50, tel. 089/520–151) or the *Stadtischen Sportamt* (Neuhauserstr. 26, tel. 089/233–6224).

Beaches and Water Sports There is sailing and windsurfing on Ammersee and Starnbergersee. Windsurfers should pay attention to restricted areas at bathing beaches. Information on sailing is available from **Bayrischer Segler-Verband** (Augustinerstr. 46, tel. 089/5244). Information on windsurfing is available from **Verband der Deutschen Windsurfing Schulen** (Weilheim, tel. 0881/5267).

Golf **Munich Golf Club** has two courses that admit visitors, but not on weekends. Visitors must be members of a club at home. Its 18-hole course is at Strasslach in the suburb of Grünwald, south of the city (tel. 08170/450). Its nine-hole course is more centrally located, at Thalkirchen, on the Isar River (tel. 089/723–1304). The greens fee is DM 57 for either course.

Hotel Fitness Centers **Bayerischer Hof** (Promenadepl. 2–6, tel. 089/21200) has a rooftop pool, a sun terrace, and a sauna, and golf and tennis nearby.

Hilton International München (Am Tucherpark 7, tel. 089/340–051), facing the Englischer Garten, has marked running trails, an indoor pool, a sauna, and massage and spa facilities.

München Sheraton (Arabellstr. 6, tel. 089/924–011) has a large indoor pool that opens onto a garden. In the room with the pool are weights and some exercise equipment.

Vier Jahreszeiten Kempinski (Maximilianstr. 17, tel. 089/230–390) is proud of its rooftop swimming pool; it also has a gym

A. Kaiser, **10**
Barerstrasse, **31**
Bayerischer Kunstgewerberein, **4**
Café Schöne Münchnerin, **27**
Carl Jagemann, **19**
Confiserie Rottenhöfer, **23**
Friedrich's Bauern Möbel Markt, **28**
Geschenk Alm, **15**
Hertie, **1**
Hohenzollernstrasse, **33**
Kaufhof, **9**
Kaufingerstrasse, **7**
Kunsthandlung Schaller, **5**
Kunstring Meissen, **2**
Lederhosen Wagner, **16**
Loden-Frey, **20**
Ludwig Beck, **17**
Ludwig Mory, **18**
Maximilianstrasse, **26**
Neuhauserstrasse, **6**
Nymphenburg Porcelain, **25**
Oberpollinger, **8**
Otto Kellnberger's Holzhandlung, **14**
Palais Bernheimer, **3**
Residenzstrasse, **22**
Schellingstrasse, **32**
Sebastian Weseley, **11**
Theatinerstrasse, **21**
Theresienstrasse, **29**
Türkenstrasse, **30**
Viktualienmarkt, **12**
Wallach, **24**
Westenriederstrasse, **13**

Munich Shopping

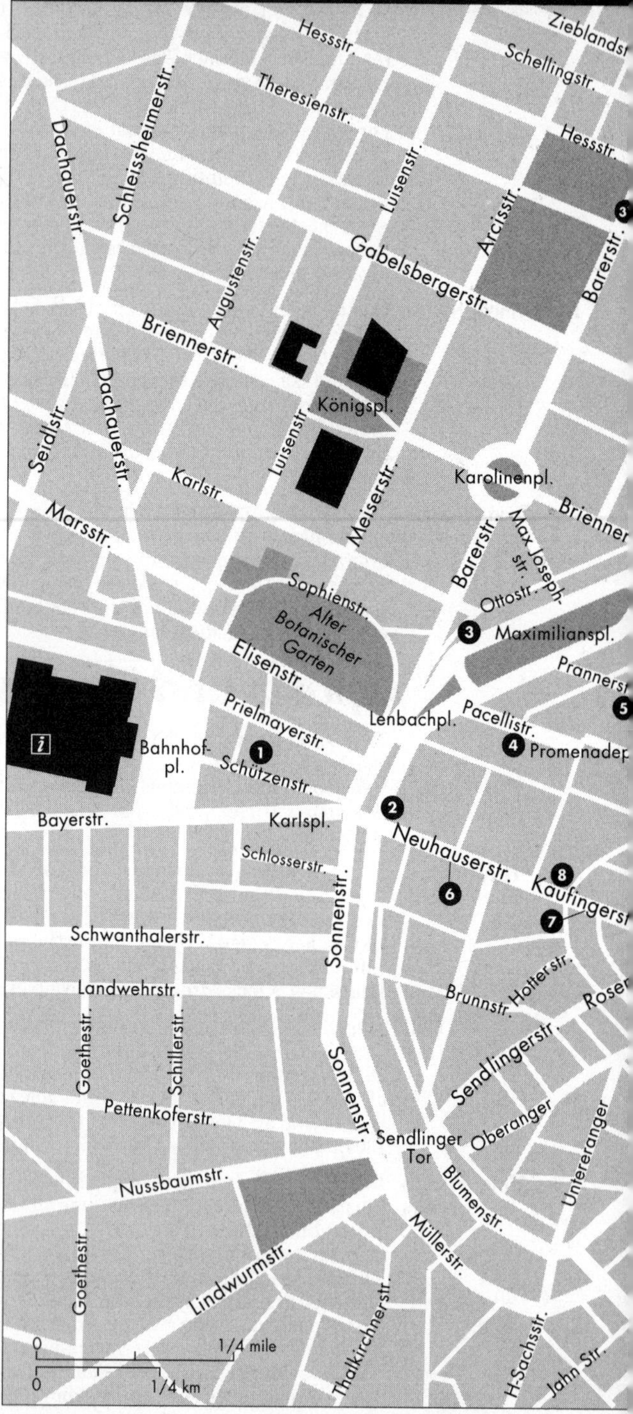

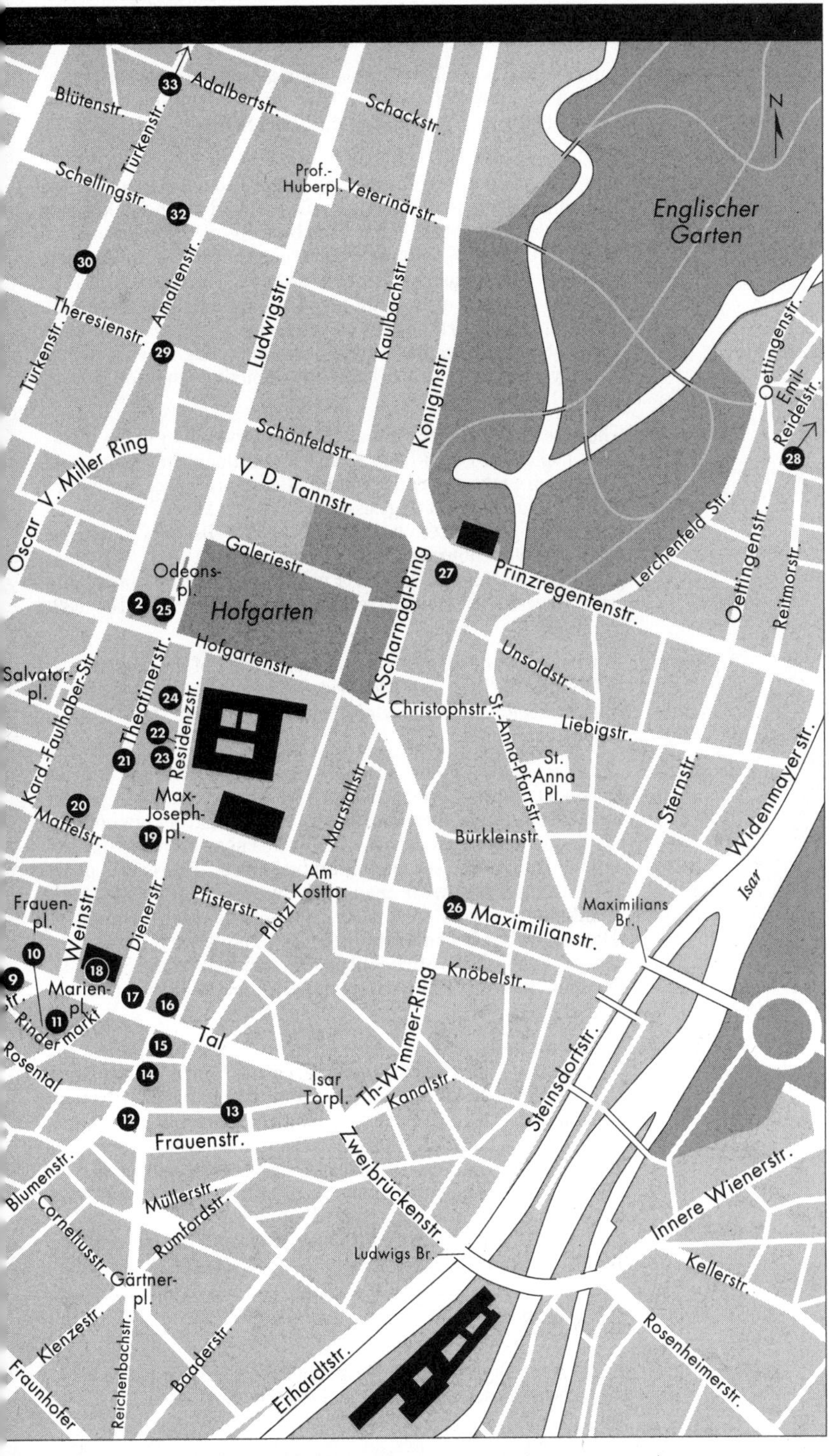
Adalbertstr.
Blütenstr.
Türkenstr.
Schackstr.
Schellingstr.
Prof.-Huberpl.
Veterinärstr.
Englischer Garten
Amalienstr.
Theresienstr.
Türkenstr.
Ludwigstr.
Kaulbachstr.
Königinstr.
Oettingenstr.
Emil-Reidelstr.
Schönfeldstr.
Oscar V. Miller Ring
V. D. Tannstr.
Lerchenfeld Str.
Oettingenstr.
Reitmorstr.
Galeriestr.
Odeons-pl.
Hofgarten
Prinzregentenstr.
K-Scharnagl-Ring
Hofgartenstr.
Unsoldstr.
Salvator-pl.
Kard.-Faulhaber-Str.
Theatinerstr.
Residenzstr.
Christophstr.
Liebigstr.
St.-Anna-Pfarrstr.
St. Anna Pl.
Sternstr.
Widenmayerstr.
Max-Joseph-pl.
Maffeistr.
Marstallstr.
Bürkleinstr.
Isar
Am Kosttor
Frauen-pl.
Weinstr.
Dienerstr.
Pfisterstr.
Platzl
Maximilianstr.
Maximilians Br.
Marien-pl.
Rindermarkt
Knöbelstr.
Th.-Wimmer-Ring
Tal
Rosental
Isar Torpl.
Kanalstr.
Steinsdorfstr.
Frauenstr.
Zweibrückenstr.
Blumenstr.
Müllerstr.
Corneliusstr.
Rumfordstr.
Innere Wienerstr.
Ludwigs Br.
Kellerstr.
Gärtner-pl.
Klenzestr.
Reichenbachstr.
Baaderstr.
Erhardtstr.
Rosenheimerstr.
Fraunhofer
N
2
9
10
11
12
13
14
15
16
17
18
19
20
21
22
23
24
25
26
27
28
29
30
32
33

with weights and exercise equipment, sauna, massage room, and solarium, and jogging maps in each room.

Hiking and Climbing Information is available from **Deutscher Alpeinverein** (Praterinsel, tel. 089/293–086) and from the sporting-goods stores **Sport Scheck** (tel. 089/21660) and **Sport Schuster** (tel. 089/237–070).

Jogging The best place to jog is the **Englischer Garten** (U-bahn stop: Münchner-Freiheit), which is 7 miles around and has lakes and dirt and asphalt paths. The broken blue line on the main asphalt path marks the 1972 Olympic marathon route. You can also jog through **Olympiapark** (U-bahn stop: Olympiazentrum.) A pleasant morning or evening jog is along the **Isar River,** a half mile from the Sheraton, or you can go for a jog in the 500-acre park of **Schloss Nymphenburg.** For a run through the Bavarian countryside, take the S-bahn to **Trentzing** and follow the marked trails.

Ice Skating There is an indoor ice rink at the **Eissportstadion** in Olympiapark (Spiridon-Louis-Ring 3) and an outdoor rink next to it, and indoor rinks at **Prinzregenten Stadium** (Prinzregentenstr. 80) and **Eisbahn-West** (Agnes-Bernauer Str. 241). There is outdoor skating in winter on the lake in the **Englischer Garten** and on the **Nymphenburger Canal.** Watch out for the *Gefahr* (danger) signs warning of thin ice. Further information is available from **Bayerischer Eissportverband** (Briennerstr. 52, tel. 089/521–336).

Rowing Rowboats can be hired on the southern bank of the **Olympiasee** in Olympiapark, at the **Kleinhesseloher See** in the Englischer Garten, and on the **Hinterbruler See** near the zoo in Thalkirchen.

Swimming You can try swimming outdoors in the Isar River at Maria-Einsiedel, but be warned that the river flows from the Alps and the water is frigid even in summer. Warmer natural swimming can be found off the beaches of the lakes near Munich—for example, the **Ammersee** and **Starnbergersee.** There are pools at: **Cosima Bad,** with man-made waves (corner of Englschalkingerstr. and Cosimastr., in Bogenhausen); **Dantebad** (Dantestr. 6); **Florian's Muhle** (Florianmuhlerstr., in the suburb of Freimann); **Michaelibad** (Heinrich-Wielnad-Str. 24); **Olympia-Schwimmhalle** (Olympiapark); and **Volksbad** (Rosenheimerstr. 1).

Tennis There are indoor and outdoor courts at: **Munchnerstrasse 15,** in Munchen-Unterfohring; at the corner of **Drygalski-Allee** and **Kistlerhofstrasse,** in Munchen-Furstenried; and at **Rothof Sportanlage** (Denningerstr.), behind the Arabella and Sheraton hotels. In addition, there are about 200 outdoor courts all over Munich. Many can be booked via **Sport Scheck** (tel. 089/21660), which has installations around town. Prices vary from DM 18 to DM 25 an hour, depending on the time of day. Full details on tennis in Munich are available from the **Bayerischer Tennis Verband** (Briennerstr. 50, tel. 089/524–420).

Dining

If it's generally true that Germans take their food seriously, then it's unquestionably true that Müncheners take it most seriously of all.

However, dining in Munich for the visitor turns out to be something of a split-level affair, offering haute cuisine on the one hand, unpretentious regional fare on the other.

With Munich rating as the Federal Republic's gourmet capital, it's no wonder that it is endowed with an inordinate number of Michelin-star restaurants for a non-French city—including two three-star establishments, real French-style operations, with chef-owners who honed their skills under such Gallic masters as Paul Bocuse.

For connoisseurs, to wine and dine at Aubergine or Tantris could well turn into the equivalent of a religious experience; culinary creations are accorded the status of works of art on a par with a Bach fugue or Dürer painting, with tabs worthy of a king's ransom.

Epicureans are convinced that one can dine as well in Munich as in any other city on the Continent, including Paris, Brussels, and Rome. And perhaps it's true. Certainly it is in a number of the top-rated restaurants listed below.

However, for many the true glory of Munich's kitchen artistry is to be experienced in those rustically decorated traditional eating places that serve down-home Bavarian specialties in ample portions.

The city's renowned beer and wine restaurants offer great atmosphere, low prices, and as much wholesome German food as you'll ever want. They're open at just about any hour of the day or night for easy eating in what many regard as the snack capital of the world.

Snacking in Munich

Munich is home to a type of pre-McDonald's fast food that derives from a centuries-old tradition. A tempting array of delectables is available at most hours of the day and night under various Bavarian names.

The generic term for Munich snacks is *Schmankerl*. And Schmankerl are served at *Brotzeit*, literally "bread time." According to a saying, "*Brotzeit ist die schonste Zeit*" (Bread time is the best time).

Very much in this tradition is a Teutonic version of the British elevenses, a mid-morning snack that goes by the name *Jause* in the German-speaking world and reaches its apogee as a minor feast in Bavaria, specifically Munich.

What one eats in the morning in Munich is *Weisswurst*, a tender minced veal sausage, made fresh daily, steamed, and served with sweet mustard, a crisp roll or pretzel, and frothy *Pils* (light beer).

Since 1857, when this tasty white sausage was invented by a local butcher, Weisswurst has ranked as Munich's number-one Schmankerl. The claim is that the genuine article is available only in and around Munich, served between midnight and noon and at no other time—a hard and fast rule. A complex protocol is involved in the ordering and eating of Weisswurst, but it need not be of concern here. The point is to enjoy this delicacy to which restorative qualities are attributed, hence its popularity with late-night revelers and those who imbibed inordinately the night before.

Another favorite Bavarian specialty is *Leberkas*, literally liver cheese, although neither liver nor cheese is involved in its construction. It is a spicy meat loaf, baked to a crusty turn each morning and served in succulent slabs throughout the day.

After that comes the repertoire of sausages indigenous to Bavaria, including types from Regensburg and Nürnberg.

More substantial repasts include *Tellerfleisch*, boiled beef with freshly grated horseradish, boiled potatoes on the side, served on wooden plates. (A similar dish is called *Tafelspitz*.)

Among roasts, sauerbraten (beef) and *Schweinsbraten* (pork) are accompanied by dumplings and red cabbage.

Haxn refers to ham hocks roasted over a beech fire for hours, until they're crisp on the outside, juicy on the inside. They are served with sauerkraut and potato puree.

You'll also find soups, salads, fish and fowl, cutlets, game in season, casseroles, hearty stews, desserts, and what may well be the greatest variety and highest quality of baked goods in Europe, including pretzels. No one need ever go hungry or thirsty in Munich.

Old Munich restaurants, called *Gastätten*, feature what's referred to as *Gutbürgerliche Küche*, loosely translated as good regional fare, and include brewery restaurants, beer halls, beer gardens, rustic cellar establishments, and *Weinstuben* (wine houses). More than a hundred such places brighten the scene.

Highly recommended restaurants in each price category are indicated by a star ★.

Category	**Cost***
Very Expensive	over DM 95
Expensive	DM 65–DM 95
Moderate	DM 45–DM 65
Inexpensive	DM 25–DM 45

**per person for a three-course meal, excluding drinks*

Our restaurant recommendations were compiled with the assistance of Gertrud Fein, the chief restaurant critic of West Germany's leading daily newspaper, the Süddeutsche Zeitung.

Very Expensive

Aubergine. German gourmets swear by the upscale nouvelle cuisine of Eckhart Witzigmann, chef and owner of the most sophisticated, if not exactly the most elegant, restaurant in town. The decor is streamlined modern—white and glittery. The service is appropriately polished. If you want a gastronomic experience on the grand scale, try the turbot in champagne or the breast of pigeon with artichoke and truffle salad. *Maximilianspl. 5, tel. 089/598–171. Reservations required. Jacket and tie required. MC. Closed Sun., Mon., Christmas and New Year's Day, and first 3 weeks of Aug.*

Boettner's. This is the oldest of Munich's classy restaurants, in business since 1905 and still going strong. There's a time-honored and quiet quality to its gracious bar and the dark, wood-paneled dining room. They provide a welcome contrast to the bustle of the city center outside. Seafood dominates the menu; try the lobster and sole served on a bed of tomato-flavored pasta. *Theatinerstr. 2, tel. 089/221–210. Reservations required. Jacket and tie required. AE, DC, MC, V. Closed Sat. evening, Sun., and holidays.*

Sabitzer's. Further evidence of upscale Munich's love affair with nouvelle cuisine, though with Bavarian influences, is provided by the classy offerings at Sabitzer's. Within its elegant gold-and-white 19th-century interior, you dine on such specialties as wild salmon with stuffed goose livers, and lamb with venison. *Reitmorstr. 21, tel. 089/298–584. Reservations required. Jacket and tie required. AE, DC, MC. Closed Sat., Sun., July, and Aug.*

★ **Tantris.** Chef Heinz Winkler presides almost regally over what most consider Munich's top restaurant. Here, too, nouvelle cuisine, served with panache, reigns supreme. Try the pigeon breast for a remarkable gastronomic experience. The downside is the setting, which bears an uncanny resemblance to an airport departure lounge, albeit one for VIPs. The restaurant is located in glitzy Schwabing. *Johann-Fichter-Str. 7, tel. 089/362–061. Reservations required. Jacket and tie required. AE, DC, MC. Closed Sat. lunch, Sun., Mon., first week in Jan., and 3 weeks in Aug.*

Expensive

★ **Austernkeller.** The nautical decor of this centrally located, vaulted cellar restaurant provides an appropriate setting for its delicate seafood specialties. Oysters—*Austern* in German—dominate the menu, but a wide range of other shellfish is featured, too. *Stollbergstr. 11, tel. 089/298–787. Reservations advised. Jacket and tie required. AE, DC, MC, V. Closed Mon. and Christmas.*

Bouillabaisse. There's little point in eating here if your tastes run to Bavarian and other German specialties. As its name makes clear, this restaurant's pungent and rich bouillabaisse—the garlicky fish stew from Provence, in the south of France—is the star attraction. The decor is striking, with imposing chandeliers lightening the otherwise somber and heavy-beamed dining room. *Falkenturmstr. 10, tel. 089/297–909. Reservations advised. Jacket and tie required. AE, DC, MC, V. Closed Sun., Mon. lunch, and Aug.*

Le Gourmet. Imaginative combinations of French and Bavarian specialties have won this little place substantial praise from local critics. Try chef Otto Koch's oxtails in champagne sauce or his zucchini and truffle salad. *Ligslazstr. 46, tel. 089/503–597. Reservations advised. Jacket and tie required. AE, DC, MC. Closed Sun. and first week in Jan.*

Käferschanke. Fresh fish, imported daily from the south of France, is the attraction here. Try the grilled prawns in a sweet-sour sauce. The rustic decor, complemented by some fine antiques, is a delight. The restaurant is located in the upscale Bogenhausen suburb, a 10-minute taxi ride from downtown. *Schumannstr. 1, tel. 089/41681. Reservations advised. Jacket and tie required. AE, DC, MC. Closed Sat. and holidays.*

★ **Preysing Keller.** Devotees of all that's best in modern German food—food that's light and sophisticated but with recognizably Teutonic touches—will love the Preysing Keller, the best hotel-restaurant in the city. The restaurant is in a 16th-century

Asternkeller, **21**
Aubergine, **5**
Bistro Terrine, **26**
Boettner's, **9**
Bouillabaisse, **18**
Donisl, **8**
Dürnbräu, **17**
Franziskaner, **12**
Goldene Stadt, **2**
Hamburger Fischstube, **22**
Haxnbauer, **20**
Hofbräuhaus, **19**
Hundskugel, **4**
Käferschanke, **25**
Kasak, **28**
Kay's Bistro, **15**
Le Gourmet, **1**
Max Emanuel Bräuerei, **27**
Nürnberger Bratwurstglöckl, **7**
Palais-Keller, **6**
Pfälzer Weinprobierstube, **10**
Preysing Keller, **23**
Ratskeller, **13**
Sabitzer's, **24**
Spatenhaus, **11**
Straubinger Hof, **14**
Tantris, **29**
Weinhaus Neuner, **3**
Weisses Bräuhaus, **16**

Munich Dining

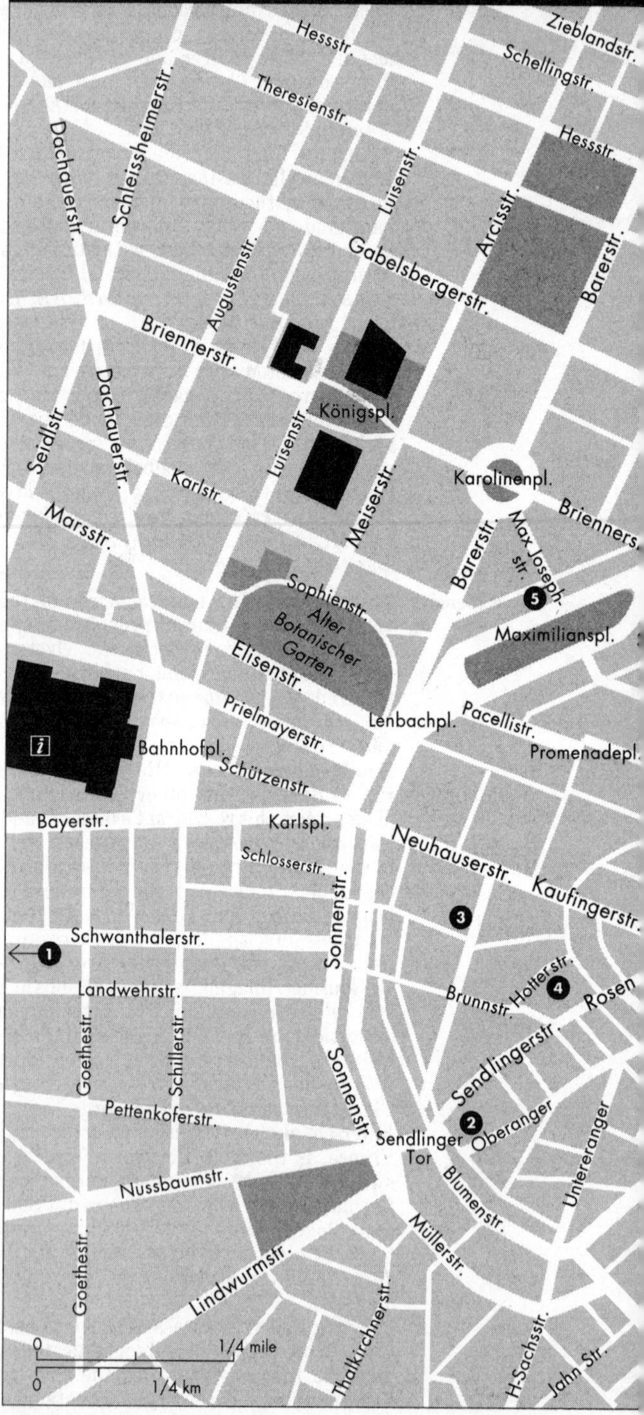

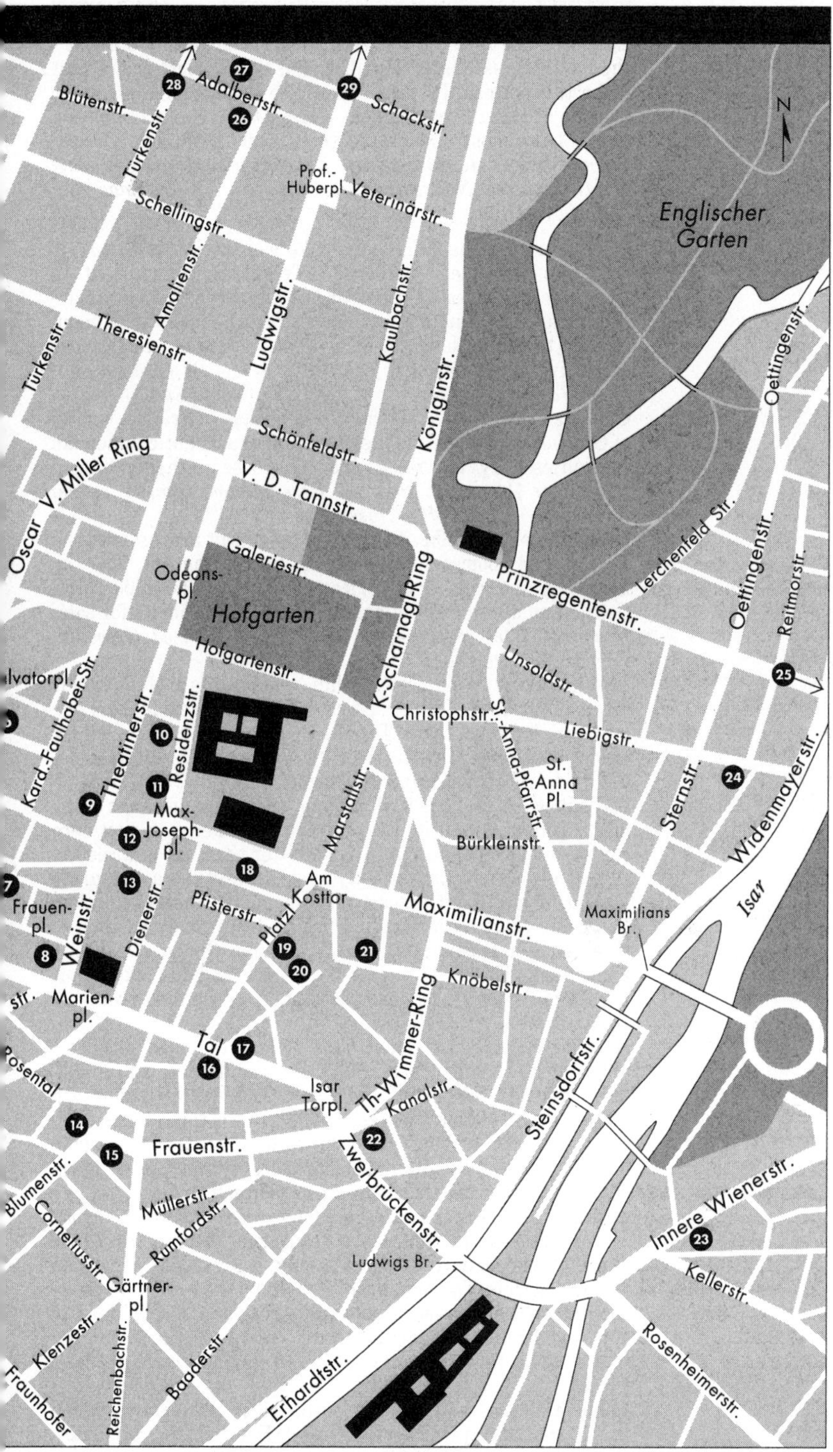
Blütenstr.
Türkenstr.
Adalbertstr.
Schackstr.
Prof.-Huberpl.
Veterinärstr.
Schellingstr.
Englischer Garten
Amalienstr.
Ludwigstr.
Kaulbachstr.
Theresienstr.
Türkenstr.
Königinstr.
Oettingenstr.
Schönfeldstr.
Oscar V. Miller Ring
V. D. Tannstr.
Lerchenfeld Str.
Galeriestr.
Odeons-pl.
Hofgarten
K-Scharnagl-Ring
Prinzregentenstr.
Oettingenstr.
Reitmorstr.
Hofgartenstr.
Unsoldstr.
Salvatorpl.
Kard.-Faulhaber-Str.
Theatinerstr.
Residenzstr.
Christophstr.
St.-Anna-Pfarrstr.
Liebigstr.
St. Anna Pl.
Marstallstr.
Sternstr.
Widenmayerstr.
Max-Joseph-pl.
Bürkleinstr.
Am Kosttor
Maximilianstr.
Maximilians Br.
Isar
Frauen-pl.
Weinstr.
Dienerstr.
Pfisterstr.
Platzl
Knöbelstr.
Marien-pl.
Tal
Th-Wimmer-Ring
Steinsdorfstr.
Rosental
Isar Torpl.
Kanalstr.
Frauenstr.
Zweibrückenstr.
Blumenstr.
Müllerstr.
Rumfordstr.
Corneliusstr.
Innere Wienerstr.
Ludwigs Br.
Kellerstr.
Gärtner-pl.
Klenzestr.
Reichenbachstr.
Baaderstr.
Erhardtstr.
Rosenheimerstr.
Fraunhofer
N
7
8
9
10
11
12
13
14
15
16
17
18
19
20
21
22
23
24
25
26
27
28
29

cellar, though it has been so over-restored that there's practically no sense of its age or original character. Never mind; it's the food, the extensive wine list, and the perfect service that make this special. Try the fixed-price seven-course menu—a bargain at DM 100 per person—for best value and a fine sampling of the most underrated restaurant in Munich. *Innere-Wiener-Str. 6, tel. 089/481–015. Reservations required. Jacket and tie required. No credit cards. Closed Sun., Christmas, and New Year's Day.*

Moderate

Bistro Terrine. The name may make you think that this is no more than a humble, neighborhood French-style restaurant. In fact, excellent classic French dishes are served within its appealing art-nouveau interior. Order from the fixed-price menu to keep the check low; à la carte dishes are appreciably more expensive. *Amalienstr. 40, tel. 089/281–780. Reservations advised. Jacket and tie required. AE, MC. Closed Sun.*

Goldene Stadt. Named for the "Golden City" of Prague, capital of Czechoslovakia, this is the place to find authentic Bohemian specialties. Try the roast duck or goose with dumplings. *Oberanger 44, tel. 089/264–382. Reservations advised. Dress: informal. AE, DC, MC. Closed Sun.*

Hamburger Fischstube. A breath of tangy salt air pervades the simple tiled rooms of this no-frills fish restaurant. Try the north German seafood; the prices are terrific. The ships in bottles add an appropriately nautical touch, and they're for sale. *Isartorpl. 8, tel. 089/225–420. Reservations advised. Dress: informal. AE, DC, MC, V.*

Kasak. Among the numerous ethnic restaurants in Munich, this is a real standout. Chef Anastatious Pistolas presides over the best Greek food in town. Try the three-course lunch menu for exceptional value. *Friedrichstr. 1a, tel. 089/391–771. Reservations advised. Dress: informal. AE, DC, MC, V.*

Kay's Bistro. The elegant vine-hung facade disguises one of the most bizarrely decorated restaurants in the city. A visit here can seem more like a trip to the theater than one to a restaurant. The decor changes weekly, embracing styles as disparate as Caribbean and Chinese. The menu is similarly varied. You could start with salmon à la Zizi Jeanmarie, move on to steak Ernest Hemingway, and finish with Queen Elizabeth's apple tart. This is the place for a chic and fun night out. *Utzschneiderstr. 1, tel. 089/260–584. Reservations required. Dress: casual. No credit cards.*

★ **Nürnberger Bratwurstglöckl.** This is about the most authentic old-time Bavarian sausage restaurant in Munich, and it's always crowded. Wobbly chairs, pitch-black wood paneling, tin plates, monosyllabic waitresses, and, downstairs, some seriously Teutonic-looking characters establish an unbeatable mood. If you want undiluted atmosphere, try for a table downstairs; if you want to be able to hear yourself think, go for one upstairs. The menu is limited, with *Nürnberger Stadtwurst mit Kraut*—finger-size Nürnberg sausages—taking pride of place. The beer, never in short supply, is served straight from wooden barrels. The restaurant is right by the Frauenkirche—the entrance is set back from the street and can be hard to spot—and makes an ideal lunchtime stop. *Frauenpl. 9, tel. 089/220–385. Reservations advised. Dress: informal. No credit cards.*

Palais-Keller. A wonderfully atmospheric cellar restaurant deep in the palatial Bayerischer Hof Hotel. Excellent Bavarian fare at Gastätten prices in a luxury hotel. Bakers working behind plate-glass windows turn out an array of breads, rolls, pretzels, and such, ready for the first customers at noon. A rare find. *Promenadenpl. 2, tel. 089/21200. Dress: informal. AE, DC, MC, V.*

Ratskeller. Munich's Ratskeller is one of the few city-hall cellar restaurants to offer vegetarian dishes alongside the normal array of hearty and filling traditional dishes. If turnip in cheese sauce is on the menu, you won't need to be a vegetarian to appreciate it. The decor is much as you would expect, with vaulted stone ceilings and flickering candles. *Marienpl. 8, tel. 089/220–313. Reservations advised. Dress: informal. AE, MC, V.*

Spatenhaus. A view of the opera house and the royal palace complements the Bavarian mood of Spatenhaus, with wood paneling and beams much in evidence. The menu is international, however, featuring more or less everything from artichokes to *zuppa Romana.* Strike a compromise and try the Bavarian Plate, an enormous mixture of local meats and sausages. *Residenzstr. 12, tel. 089/227–841. Reservations advised. Dress: informal. DC, MC, V.*

Inexpensive

Donisl. This place ranks high among the beer restaurants of Munich. It's located just off Marienplatz, and in summer its tables spill out onto the sidewalk. But the real action is inside. The large central hall, with painted and carved booths and garlands of dried flowers, is animated night and day by locals and visitors alike. The atmosphere, like the food, is rough-and-ready. The beer flows freely. *Weinstr. 1, tel. 089/220–184. No reservations. Dress: informal. AE, DC, MC, V.*

Dürnbräu. A fountain plays outside this picturesque old Bavarian inn. Inside, it's crowded and noisy. Expect to share a table; your fellow diners will range from millionaires to students. The food is resolutely traditional. Try the cream of spinach soup and the boiled beef. *Dürnbräugasse 2, tel. 089/222–195. Reservations advised. Dress: informal. AE, DC, MC, V.*

Franziskaner. Vaulted archways, cavernous rooms interspersed with intimate dining areas, bold blue frescoes, long wood tables, and a sort of spic-and-span medieval atmosphere —the look without the dirt—set the mood. This is the place for an early morning Weisswurst and a beer; Bavarians swear it will banish all trace of that morning-after feeling. The Franziskaner is located right by the State Opera. *Peruastr. 5, tel. 089/645–548. No reservations. Dress: informal. No credit cards.*

★ **Haxnbauer.** This is about the most sophisticated of the beer restaurants. There's the usual series of interlinking rooms—some large, some small—and the usual sturdy/pretty Bavarian decoration. But here, there is much greater emphasis on the food than in other similar places. Try the Leberkäs, meat loaf made with pork and beef, or *Schweinshaxe,* pork shanks. *Munzstr. 2, tel. 089/221–922. Reservations advised. Dress: informal. MC, V.*

Hofbräuhaus. The heavy stone vaults of the Hofbräuhaus contain the most famous of the city's beer restaurants. Crowds of singing, shouting, swaying beer drinkers—make no mistake; this is a place where beer takes precedence over food—fill the atmospheric and smoky rooms. Picking their way past the tables are hefty waitresses in traditional garb bearing frothing steins. Some people love it. Others deplore the rampant commercialization and the fact that the place is now so obviously aimed at the tourist trade. It's just north of Marienplatz. *Platz, tel. 089/221–676. No reservations. Dress: informal. No credit cards.*

Hundskugel. This is Munich's oldest tavern, dating back to 1640; history positively drips from its crooked walls. The food is surprisingly good. If *Spanferkel*—roast suckling pig—is on the menu, make a point of ordering it. This is simple Bavarian fare at its best. *Hotterstr. 18, tel. 089/264–272. Reservations advised. Dress: informal. No credit cards.*

Max Emanuel Bräuerei. Folk music and theater are featured in this time-honored Munich institution, located next to the university. The clientele is predominantly young, and the atmosphere is always lively. In summer you can eat in the delightful little beer garden. The food is wholesomely Bavarian, with some Greek and French touches. *Adalbertstr. 33, tel. 089/271–5158. Reservations advised. Dress: informal. DC, MC.*

Pfälzer Weinprobierstube. A warren of stone-vaulted rooms of various sizes, wood tables, flickering candles, dirndl-clad waitresses, and a vast range of wines add up to an experience as close to everyone's image of timeless Germany as you're likely to get. The food is reliable rather than spectacular. Local specialties predominate. *Residenzstr. 1, tel. 089/225–628. No reservations. Dress: informal. No credit cards.*

Straubinger Hof. Call early if you want a table at this famous old establishment. The Weisswurst is served fresh from 9 AM onward, and business is brisk, with stall holders from the Viktualienmarkt across the road jostling for the first out of the pan. In summer, the little beer garden outside is the place to be. *Blumenstr. 5, tel. 089/260–8444. No reservations. Dress: informal. No credit cards. Closed Sat. evenings and Sun.*

Weinhaus Neuner. Munich's oldest wine tavern serves good food as well as superior wines. Substantial renovations in 1988 made it hard to say if the time-honored atmosphere would survive unscathed, but first signs were that the Italian-influenced food would continue at its high levels. Try the homemade pasta with basil, cream, and salmon sauce. *Herzogspitalstr. 8, tel. 089/260–3954. Reservations advised. Dress: informal. AE, DC, MC. Closed Sun.*

★ **Weisses Bräuhaus.** This celebrated Munich inn has been serving its home-brewed beer for centuries, taking advantage of the fact that one of the main trading routes into the city ran right by its door. Modernization has in no way destroyed the atmosphere created by the dark wood paneling, stained glass, and little table lanterns. The waitresses wear traditional black outfits. If you want to do as the locals do, ask for suckling pig and strong beer. *Tal 10, tel. 089/299–875. Reservations advised. Dress: informal. No credit cards.*

Lodging

Make reservations well in advance, and be prepared for higher-than-average rates. Though Munich has a vast number of hotels in all price ranges, many of the most popular are full year-round; this is a major trade and convention city as well as a prime tourist destination. If you plan to visit during the *Mode Wochen* (fashion weeks) in March and September or during the Oktoberfest at the end of September, make reservations at least two months in advance.

Conversely, July and August could be considered practically off-season in this city that's geared to such a large extent to the business and conventions-and-meetings traveler. Such chain hotels as Sheraton and Hilton offer special discount packages at the top of the summer season, along with advantageous weekend arrangements year-round. Definitely worth checking out either through your travel agent or through the hotels' U.S. reservations systems.

The tourist office at Rindermarkt 5 has a reservations department, but note that it will not accept telephone reservations. There's also a reservations office at the airport. Best bet for finding a room if you haven't reserved in advance is the tourist office at Bayerstrasse, by the train station. You'll be charged a small fee, but the operation is supremely well organized.

The closer to the city center you stay, the higher the price. Consider staying in a suburban hotel and taking the U-bahn or S-bahn into town. Rates are much more reasonable, and a 15-minute train ride is no obstacle to serious sightseeing. Check out the city tourist office "Key to Munich" packages. These include reduced-rate hotel reservations, sightseeing tours, theater visits, and low-cost travel on the U- and S-bahn. Write to the tourist office at Rindermarkt 5.

Highly recommended lodgings in each price category are indicated by a star ★.

Category	**Cost***
Very Expensive	over DM 250
Expensive	DM 180–DM 250
Moderate	DM 120–DM 180
Inexpensive	under DM 120

**For two people in a double room, including tax and service.*

Very Expensive

Arabella. If you love traditional Bavarian style, this is not the place for you. The Arabella occupies the 22nd and 23rd floors of a high-rise apartment building in Bogenhausen, a suburb east of the city about 4 miles from the airport. The main feature is a "tropical island" leisure center around a palm-fringed pool and the obligatory Caribbean bar. Room styles range from Teutonic rustic to crisp, modern town house. *Arabellastr. 5, tel. 089/92320. 56 rooms and suites with bath. Facilities: restaurant, bar, sauna, solarium, pool, garage. AE, DC, MC, V.*

Bayerischer Hof. This is one of Munich's most traditional luxury hotels. It's set on a ritzy shopping street, with a series of exclusive shops right outside the imposing marble entrance. Public rooms are decorated with antiques, fine paintings, marble, and painted wood. Old-fashioned comfort and class abound in the older rooms; some of the newer rooms are more functional. *Promenadenpl. 2–6, tel. 089/21200. 440 rooms with bath. Facilities: 3 restaurants, nightclub, rooftop pool, garage, sauna, masseur, hairdresser. AE, DC, MC, V.*

City Hilton. Details were still vague at press time, but this brand-new Hilton, opened in April 1989, promises at least to prove something of a mecca for music lovers. The hotel is a two-minutes' walk from the Gasteig culture center and is connected to it by a covered walkway. *Rosenheimerstr. 15, tel. 089/38450.*

Adria, **23**
An der Oper, **11**
Arabella, **25**
Ariane, **6**
Bayerischer Hof, **10**
Bräufpanne, **20**
City Hilton, **19**
Daniel, **8**
Domus, **16**
Eden Hotel Wolff, **3**
Excelsior, **7**
Gästehaus am Englischer Garten, **15**
Grand Hotel Continental, **9**
Gröbner, **14**
Hilton International, **22**
Hotel Pension am Markt, **12**
Intercity, **4**
Kriemhild, **2**
Monopteros, **21**
Palace, **26**
Pension Beck, **18**
Prinzregent, **24**
Romantik Hotel Insel-Müble, **1**
Splendid, **13**
Trustee Park Hotel, **5**
Vier Jahreszeiten, **17**

Munich Lodging

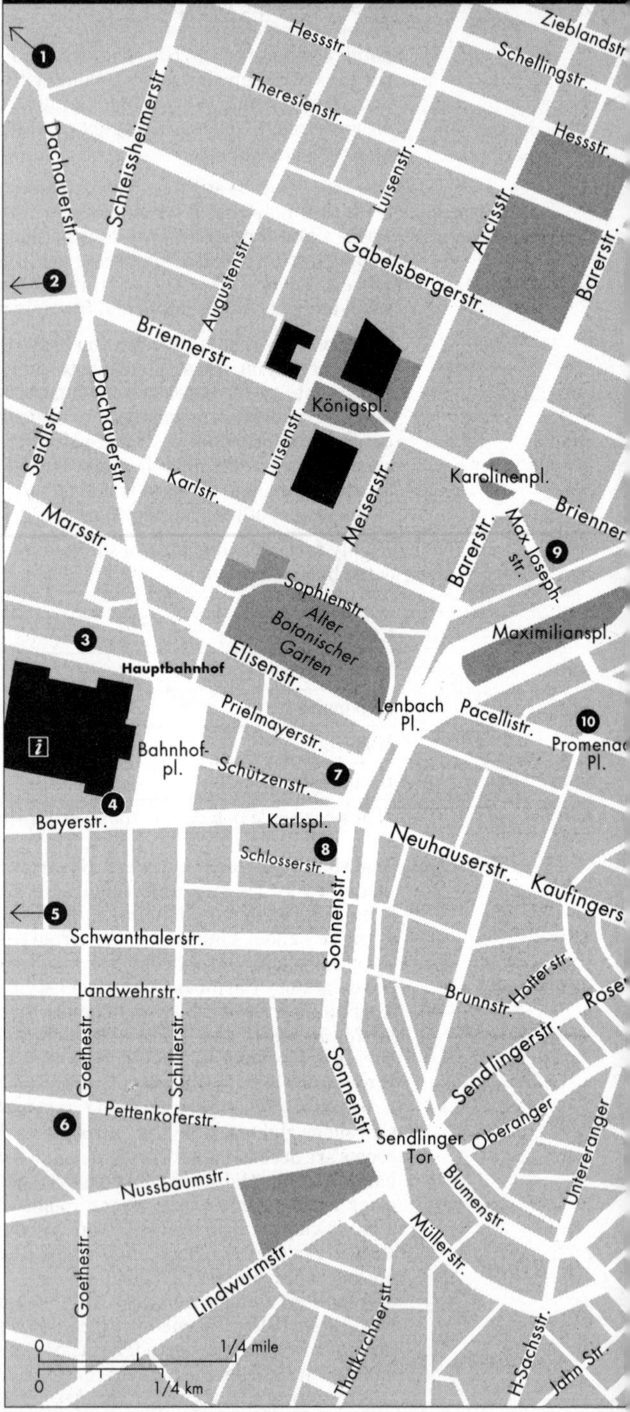

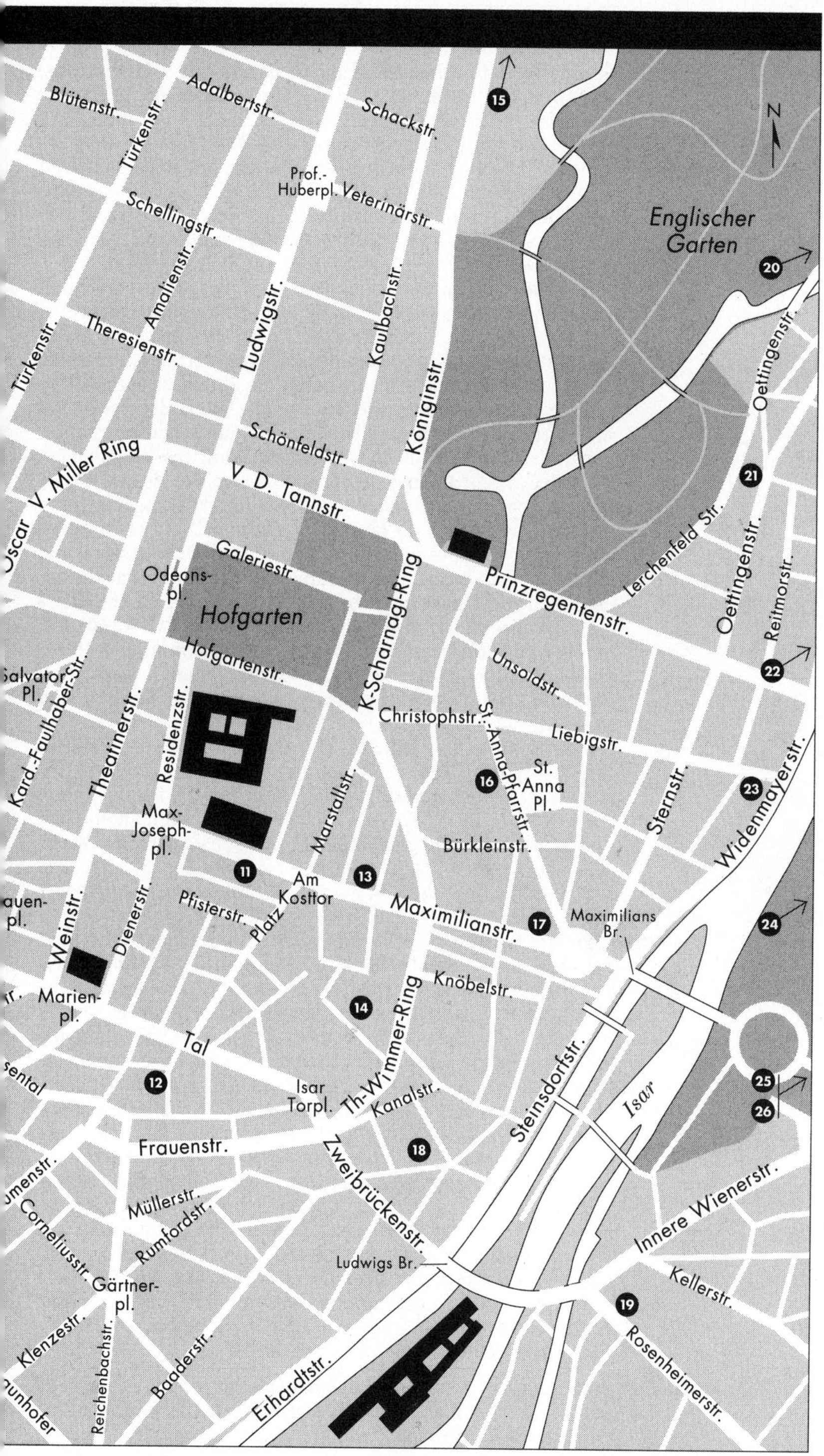
Blütenstr.
Adalbertstr.
Schackstr.
Türkenstr.
Prof.-Huberpl.
Veterinärstr.
Schellingstr.
Englischer Garten
Amalienstr.
Ludwigstr.
Kaulbachstr.
Theresienstr.
Türkenstr.
Oettingenstr.
Königinstr.
Schönfeldstr.
Oscar V. Miller Ring
V. D. Tannstr.
Lerchenfeld Str.
Galeriestr.
K-Scharnagl-Ring
Odeons-pl.
Prinzregentenstr.
Oettingenstr.
Reitmorstr.
Hofgarten
Hofgartenstr.
Unsoldstr.
Salvator-Pl.
Kard.-Faulhaber-Str.
Theatinerstr.
Residenzstr.
Christophstr.
St.-Anna-Pfarrstr.
Liebigstr.
St. Anna Pl.
Sternstr.
Widenmayerstr.
Max-Joseph-pl.
Marstallstr.
Bürkleinstr.
Am Kosttor
Maximilianstr.
Maximilians Br.
Pfisterstr.
Platz
Weinstr.
Dienerstr.
Knöbelstr.
Marien-pl.
Th.-Wimmer-Ring
Tal
Steinsdorfstr.
Isar
Isar Torpl.
Kanalstr.
Frauenstr.
Zweibrückenstr.
Innere Wienerstr.
Müllerstr.
Corneliusstr.
Rumfordstr.
Ludwigs Br.
Kellerstr.
Gärtner-pl.
Klenzestr.
Reichenbachstr.
Baaderstr.
Erhardtstr.
Rosenheimerstr.
N
11
12
13
14
15
16
17
18
19
20
21
22
23
24
25
26

487 rooms with bath. Facilities: swimming pool, restaurants and bars. AE, DC, MC, V.

Grand Hotel Continental. This relatively small (160 rooms) luxury hotel maintains the highest standards. Recently renovated, with what is considered the handsomest interior of any Munich hotel, it offers a convenient downtown location, antiques in the lobby and rooms, and the ultimate in personalized service. The hotel is a longtime favorite with high-level executives and government bigwigs. *Max-Joseph-Str. 5, tel. 089/557–911. 160 rooms with bath. Facilities: restaurant, bar, conference rooms, garage, hairdresser. AE, DC, MC, V.*

Hilton International. Recent renovations and revamping of management concepts have turned the Hilton into a marvel of sorts—big on the outside, intimate on the inside, with as cheerful, courteous, and accommodating a staff as you're likely to encounter in any European hotel, the glitziness of the lobby and reception area notwithstanding. The hotel is located on the rim of the city, with excellent public transportation connections. Ask for a room high up overlooking the neighboring English Garden, and in summer you'll be able to sleep with the windows open, undisturbed by sounds of traffic, hearing only the gentle whoosh of the fast-flowing stream that runs through the property. There's a beer garden alongside the stream, and the all-you-can-eat lunch and dinner gourmet buffet at the adjoining Isar Terrace may be the best bargain on the city's gastronomic scene. *Am Tucherpark 7, tel. 089/38450. 960 rooms with bath. Facilities: 3 restaurants, swimming pool, fitness center, sauna, massage, nearby tennis courts, golf packages, complimentary shuttle-bus service into city and back. AE, DC, MC, V.*

Romantik Hotel Insel-Müble. This former mill on the banks of the little Wurm River, in Munich's leafy Untermenzing suburb, is one of the most appealing of what, to many, is the best hotel chain in the country. Service is impeccable throughout; indeed, guests are positively pampered. The airy restaurant and riverside beer garden are a delight. *Von-Kahr-Str. 87, tel. 089/81010. 37 rooms with bath. Facilities: restaurant, beer garden. AE, DC, MC, V.*

★ **Vier Jahreszeiten.** The Vier Jahreszeiten—it means the Four Seasons—has been playing host to the world's wealthy and titled for more than a century. It has an unbeatable location, on Maximilianstrasse, Munich's premier shopping street, only a few minutes' walk from the heart of the city. Elegance and luxury set the tone throughout; many rooms have handsome antique pieces. A five-year, DM 30 million renovation of the entire hotel was completed in early 1989. All the rooms have been refurbished, new baths and soundproofing installed throughout, public areas rebuilt and redecorated, and a new restaurant, Bistro Eck, added on the main floor, joining the Theater restaurant in the cellar and the famed Walterspiel, long regarded as one of Munich's finest eating establishments. *Maximilianstr. 17, tel. 089/230–390; reservations in the U.S. from Kempinski Reservation Service, tel. 516/794–2670. 341 rooms with bath; 25 apartments; Presidential Suite. Facilities: restaurant, nightclub, rooftop pool, garage, sauna, car rental, Lufthansa check-in desk. AE, DC, MC, V.*

Expensive

An der Oper. A gem of a small hotel on a narrow, quiet, and elegant side street around the corner from the swank Maximilianstrasse. Big names from the opera stay here: conductors, dancers, singers. The French restaurant Bouillabaisse (*see* Dining, above) is a celebrity haunt, as is the atmospheric Opera Cellar. The rooms tend to be small and fairly spartan and offer little by way of view, but they are clean, comfortable, and nicely furnished, with soundproof double windows. *Falkenturmstr. 10, tel. 089/228–711. 55 rooms with bath. Run on bed-and-breakfast basis, with two restaurants loosely tied to the operation. AE, DC, MC.*

Eden Hotel Wolff. Chandeliers and dark wood paneling in the public rooms underline the old-fashioned elegance of this downtown favorite. It's located directly across the street from the train station and close to the fairgrounds of Theresienwiese. The rooms are comfortable; most are spacious. You can dine on excellent Bavarian specialties in the intimate Zirbelstube restaurant. *Arnulfstr. 4, tel. 089/551–150. 210 rooms with bath. Facilities: restaurant. No credit cards.*

Excelsior. It's no surprise that this modern hotel is a favorite among businesspeople. A sense of functional comfort pervades it, while the pedestrian-mall location, close to the train station, makes it convenient to downtown. Renovations in 1986 have helped maintain the hotel's reputation for efficiency and good service. *Schützenstr. 11, tel. 089/551–370. 116 rooms with bath or shower. Facilities: restaurant, bar. AE, DC, MC, V.*

Palace. This hotel opened in 1986, but the decor and mood lean toward old-fashioned elegance, with the accent firmly on Louis XVI styles and plush luxury. Most rooms overlook the little courtyard. The hotel is located in Alt-Bogenhausen, 4 miles from the airport. Downtown Munich is a 10-minute tram ride away (the tram stop is right by the door). *Trogerstr. 21, tel. 089/470–5091. 73 rooms and suites with bath. Facilities: bar, roof garden, Jacuzzi, sauna, gym. AE, DC, MC, V.*

Prinzregent. An air of slightly functional Bavarian rusticity pervades this small hotel. Carved wood, gilt angels, Rococo-style sconces and mirrors, and rough white plaster walls predominate. There's no restaurant, but the breakfast room, decked out with wood taken from an old farmhouse, makes for a soothing start to the day. The small bar off the lobby is a discreet rendezvous. The hotel is a 10-minute tram ride from downtown. *Ismaningerstr. 42–44, tel. 089/470–2081. 70 rooms with shower. Facilities: sauna, pool, bar. AE, DC, MC, V.*

★ **Splendid.** Chandelier-hung public rooms, complete with antiques and Oriental rugs, give this small hotel something of the atmosphere of a spaciously grand 19th-century inn. The service is attentive and polished. Have breakfast in the small courtyard in summer. There's no restaurant, but the bar serves snacks as well as drinks. The chic shops of the Maximilianstrasse are a five-minute stroll in one direction; an equally brief walk in the other brings you to the Isar River. *Maximilianstr. 54, tel. 089/296–6606. 37 rooms and 1 suite with bath. Facilities: bar. AE, MC, V.*

Trustee Park Hotel. Located close by the exhibit grounds, this newly opened hotel is first and foremost for businesspeople (and is correspondingly functional in decor); its high season coincides with trade fairs and conventions. Check out the weekend rates: Special family deals are often available. The rooms are spacious, and many have balconies or terraces. *Parkstr. 31, tel. 089/519–5421. 40 rooms with bath. Facilities: restaurant, bar. AE, DC, MC, V.*

Moderate

Adria. A modern and comfortable hotel, the Adria is located on the edge of Munich's museum quarter, in the attractive Lehel district, a short walk from the Isar River and the English Garden. There's no restaurant, but there is a large and bright breakfast room. *Liebigstr. 8, tel. 089/293–081. 51 rooms with bath. AE, DC, MC, V. Closed Dec. 24–Jan. 6.*

Braüfpanne. The plain concrete exterior of this hotel belies the considerable, if somewhat functional, comforts within. Though the rooms are sparsely furnished, they are intelligently designed, with writing desks and sofas. The restaurant offers excellent local specialties at affordable prices. Don't stay here if you want to be close to the center of things; it's a 25-minute tram ride from downtown in the northeast suburbs. *Oberföhringerstr. 107, tel. 089/951–095. 25 rooms with bath. Facilities: restaurant, bar, skittle alley. AE, DC, MC, V.*

Daniel. This is the place to stay if you value a downtown location; it's right on bustling Sonnenstrasse and the Stachus underground mall. The rooms are sleekly modern and comfortable. There's no restaurant. *Sonnenstr. 5, tel. 089/554–945. 80 rooms with bath. AE, DC, MC, V.*

Domus. Head here for home comforts and friendly, personal service. All the rooms have balconies. There's no restaurant, but drinks and snacks are available in the Tyrolean Room bar, which is decked out in appropriately rough-hewn and snug Alpine style. The hotel is located in the Lehel district, close to many museums and the English Garden. *St. Anna-Str. 31, tel. 089/221–704. 45 rooms with bath. Facilities: bar, garage. AE, DC, MC, V. Closed Christmas.*

★ **Gästehaus am Englischer Garten.** Not so long ago, only a handful of lucky initiates knew about this converted 200-year-old water mill. Today, despite the still slightly basic rooms, its fame is such that you need to reserve well in advance to be sure of getting a room. The hotel, complete with ivy-clad walls and shutter-framed windows, stands on the edge of the English Garden, no more than a five-minute walk from the bars and shops of Schwabing. There's no restaurant, but who needs one with Schwabing's numerous eating possibilities so close? Be sure to ask for a room in the main building; the modern annex down the road is cheaper but lacks charm. In summer, breakfast is served on the terrace. *Liebergesellstr. 8, tel. 089/392–034. 34 rooms, some with bath. No credit cards.*

★ **Hotel Pension am Markt.** Placido Domingo makes a point of checking into this little hotel whenever he's in town. It's located in one of Munich's prettiest and quietest squares and is run more like a private home than a hotel. A grand piano stands in the lobby; accompaniment is provided by a canary in a cage by the window. *Heiliggeiststr. 6, tel. 089/226–844. 30 rooms, most with bath. No credit cards.*

Intercity. Despite a location near the train station, double-glazing of all the windows ensures peace in this longtime downtown favorite. Try for one of the Bavarian-style rooms; the others are basic and little more than adequate. There's an excellent restaurant offering good-value Bavarian specialties. *Bahnhofpl. 2, tel. 089/558–571. 208 rooms and 4 apartments with bath. Facilities: restaurant, bar, skittle alley. DC, MC, V.*

Inexpensive

★ **Ariane.** Make reservations well in advance at this small pension, which is a five-minute walk due south of the train station. The standards of comfort are high, and many appreciate the excellent central location. *Pettenkoferstr. 44, tel. 089/535–529. 12 rooms, most with bath. No credit cards.*

Gröbner. You'll stay here because you appreciate not only the terrific central location—the Hofbräuhaus is just around the corner—but also the appeal of a friendly, family-run hotel. American guests are especially welcome. The rooms are basically furnished but clean. Try for one on the second floor; they are especially large and airy. *Herrnstr. 44, tel. 089/293–939. 30 rooms, some with bath. No credit cards.*

Kriemhild. If you're traveling with children, you'll appreciate the low rates of this welcoming, family-run pension in the western suburb of Nymphenburg. It's located just a few minutes' walk from the palace itself and from the Hirschgarten park, site of one of the city's best beer gardens. It's a 30-minute tram ride from downtown. There's no restaurant, but there is a small bar. An extensive breakfast buffet is included in the room rate. *Guntherstr. 16, tel. 089/170–077. 40 rooms, 20 with bath. Facilities: bar. MC.*

★ **Monopteros.** There are few better deals in Munich than this little hotel. It's located just south of the English Garden, with a tram stop for the 10-minute ride to downtown right by the door. The rooms may be basic, but the excellent service and warm welcome, added to the great location, more than compensate. There's no restaurant. *Oettingenstr. 35, tel. 089/292–348. 11 rooms, 3 with shower. No credit cards.*

Pension Beck. Frau Beck and her daughter run this rambling, friendly little pension with an authoritative but personal touch. It sprawls over several floors of a handsome Art Nouveau building in Lehel, within easy walking distance of downtown. Frau Beck aims to provide two essentials: "A comfortable bed and a good cup of coffee." If you share her priorities, this is a place you'll love. *Thierschstr. 36, tel. 089/225–768. 50 rooms, most with bath. No credit cards.*

The Arts and Nightlife

The Arts

Details of concerts and theater performances are listed in *Voschau* and *Monatsprogramm*, booklets available at most hotel reception desks, newsstands, and tourist offices. Some hotels will make ticket reservations; otherwise, use one of the ticket agencies in the city center, such as **Radio-RIM** (Theatinerstr., tel. 089/441–70253), **Residenz Bucherstube** (concert tickets only; Theatinerstr., tel. 089/220–868), or **Hieber Max** (Liebefrauenstr. 1, tel. 089/226–571).

Theater Munich has scores of theaters and variety-show haunts, although most productions will be largely impenetrable if your German is shaky. (An English-speaking company, the **Company,** presents about four productions a year; tel. 089/343–827). Listed here are all the better-known theaters, as well as some of the smaller and more progressive spots. A visit to one or more will underline just why the Bavarian capital has such an enviable reputation as an artistic hotspot. Note that most theaters are closed during July and August.

Bayerisches Staatsschauspiel/Neues Residenztheater (Bavarian State Theater/New Residence Theater) (Max-Joseph-Pl., tel. 089/218–5413). The box office is open Mon.–Fri. 10–1 and 3:30–5:30, Sat. 10–12:30, and one hour before the performance.

Cuvilliés-Theater/Altes Residenztheater (Old Residence Theater) (Max-Joseph-Pl.; entrance on Residenzstr.). The box office, at the Nationaltheater (Max-Joseph-Pl., tel. 089/221-316), is open Mon.–Fri. 10–1 and 3:30–5:30, Sat. 10–12:30, and one hour before the performance.
Deutsches Theater (Schwanthalerstr. 13, tel. 089/593–427). The box office is open Mon.–Fri. noon–6, Sat. 10–1:30.
Kleine Komodie (Bayerischer Hof Hotel, Promenadepl., tel. 089/292–810; Max-II-Denkmal, Maximilianstr., tel. 089/221-859). The box office at Bayerischer Hof is open Mon.–Sat. 11–8, Sun. and holidays 3–8. The box office at Max-II-Denkmal is open Tues.–Sat. 11–8, Mon. 11–7, Sun. and holidays 3–8.
Marionettentheater (Blumenstr. 29A, tel. 089/265–712). The box office is open Tues.–Sun. 10–noon.
Münchner Kammerspiele-Schauspielhaus (Maximilianstr. 26, tel. 089/237–21328). The box office is open Mon.–Fri. 10–6, Sat., Sun., and holidays 10–1.
Platzl am Platzl (Munzstr. 8–9, tel. 089/237–03355). Daily show (except Sat.) with typical Bavarian humor, yodeling, and *Schuhplattler* (the slapping of Bavarian leather shorts in time to the oompah music).
Prinzregententheater (Prinzregentenpl. 12). The box office is open Mon.–Fri. 10–1 and 3:30–5:30, Sat. 10–12:30, and one hour before the performance.
Theater der Jugend (Franz-Joseph-Str. 47, tel. 089/237–21365). The box office is open Tues.–Sat. 1:30–5:30.
Theater Kleine Freiheit (Maximilianstr. 31, tel. 089/221–123). The box office is open Mon.–Sat. from 11, Sun. from 2.

Concerts Munich and music go together. Paradoxically, however, it's only since 1984 that the city has had a world-class concert hall: the Gasteig center, a lavish brick complex standing high above the Isar River, east of downtown. It's the permanent home of the Munich Philharmonic Orchestra, which regularly performs in its Philharmonic Hall. There are two smaller halls at the Gasteig: the Carl-Orff Saal and the Black Box (less sinister than it sounds). In addition to the Philharmonic, the city has three other orchestras: the Bavarian State Orchestra, based at the National Theater; the Bavarian Radio Orchestra, which gives Sunday concerts at the Gasteig; and the Kurt Graunke Symphony Orchestra, which generally puts on operettas at the Gartnerplatz theater. The leading choral ensembles are the Munich Bach Choir, the Munich Motettenchor, and Musica Viva, the latter specializing in contemporary music. *see* The Arts, above, for details of programs and where to buy tickets.
Bayerischer Rundfunk (Rundfunkpl. 1, tel. 089/558–080). The box office is open Monday–Friday 9–noon and 1–5.
Galerie im Lenbachhaus (Luisenstr. 33, tel. 089/521–041). Though this is primarily an art gallery, chamber-music concerts are sometimes held here.
Gasteig Kulturzentrum (Rosenheimerstr. 13, tel. 089/418-1614). The box office is open Mon.–Fri. 10:30–2 and 3–6, Saturday 10:30–2.
Herkulessaal in der Residenz (Hofgarten, tel. 089/224–641). The box office opens one hour before performances.
Hochscule für Musik (Arcisstr. 12, tel. 089/559–101). Concerts featuring music students are given free of charge.
Kongressaal des Deutscher Museums (Museumsinsel 1, tel. 089/298–430 or 089/221–790). The box office opens one hour before performances.

Olympiahalle (tel. 089/306–13577). The box office is open Monday–Thursday 8–5, Friday 8–2. For pop concerts.

Nightlife

Munich's nighttime attractions vary with the seasons. The year starts with the abandon of *Fasching*, the Bavarian carnival time, when every night is party night. No sooner has Lent brought the sackcloth curtain down on Fasching than the local weather office is being asked to predict when the spring sunshine will be warm enough to allow the city's 50 beer gardens to open. From then until late fall the beer garden dictates the style and pace of Munich's nightlife. When it rains, the indoor beer halls and taverns absorb the thirsty like blotting paper.

The beer gardens and beer halls close at 1 AM, but there's no need to go home to bed then: Most bars and nightclubs are open until 3 AM, and some have all-night licenses. A word of caution about those bars, however: Munich's are no different from others in Europe. Just one round of drinks can break the holiday bank. Stick to beer or wine if you can, and pay as you go. And if you feel you're being duped, call the cops—the customer is usually, if not always, right. For a city with such a free-and-easy reputation, Munich lacks the raunchy, no-holds-barred forthrightness of Hamburg's Reeperbahn.

There are no live sex shows, nor wholesale sex-for-sale arrangements as in certain other German cities. Nevertheless, girls "in the trade" operate out of certain clubs, such as Leierkasten and Salambo, at 38 and 61 Ingolstadterstrasse, respectively. Call-girl services are advertised in the tabloids *AZ* and *tz*. There's a lively gay scene at a number of clubs and saunas that anyone with the inclination can easily discover. You might say the city has something for (just about) all tastes.

For striptease shows, explore the region south of the main railway station (Schillerstrasse, for example) or the neighborhood of the famous Hofbräuhaus (am Platzl). Many of the city's bars are ephemeral places that glitter mothlike for a season or two before vanishing.

Clubs **Intermezzo** (Maximilianpl. 16). It's said to have the prettiest strippers and most exotic dancers in town. Tall claim, but worth checking out.

Lola Montez (Am Platzl 1). Named after the gal who cost Ludwig I his crown, this cabaret and striptease night spot is also heading for a chapter in local history. Expensive, but no rip-off.

Maxim (Farbergraben 33). This club is tucked away behind the pedestrian shopping precinct, but leave the shopping basket at home—the girls cannot be bought (a rule that applies throughout the central city zone, by the way).

Discos Schwabing is discoland. There are three in a 50-yard stretch of Occamstrasse: **Albatros, Cockney,** and **Circo Valentino. Peaches,** on the neighboring Feilitzstrasse, and **Meddos,** on Marktstrasse, are also young and fun. Across town, **East Side** (Rosenheimerstr. 30) has an older clientele (well, not too old) and lots of plush and class. **PI** (on the east side of the Haus der Kunst) and the **Park-Café** (Sophienstr. 7) are the most fashionable discos in town, but you'll have to talk yourself past the doorman to join the chic crowds inside. The **Lenbach Palast** (Lenbachpl. 3) is less choosy and, frankly, more fun, with live bands nightly. The **Open Gate** (Maximilianpl. 5) has regular cabaret shows that frequently feature scantily clad young women and go-go girls. The noisiest disco in town: **Crash** (Lindwurmstr. 88). The youngsters love it, despite the risk of ruptured eardrums.

Bars and Singles Every Munich bar is singles territory. Try **Schumann's** (Maximilianstr. 36) anytime after the curtain comes down at the nearby opera house (and watch the barmen shake those cocktails), but wait till after midnight before venturing into the **Alter Simpl** (Turkenstr. 57) for a sparkling crowd despite the gloomy surroundings. **Harry's New York Bar** (Falkenturmstr. 9) offers escape from the German bar scene, and it serves genuine Irish Guinness. And for total escapists, there's always the **Hemingway Bar** (Rumfordstr. 17), with jungle decor and planter's punch at DM 12.50 a glass.

Jazz Munich likes to think it's Germany's jazz capital, and to reinforce the claim some beer gardens have taken to replacing their brass bands with funky combos. Purists don't like it, but jazz enthusiasts are happy. The combination certainly works at **Waldwirtshaft Grosshesselohe** (Georg Kalb-Str. 3), in the southern suburb of Grosshesselohe. Sundays are set aside for jazz, and if it's a fine day the excursion is much recommended. Some city pubs also set aside Sunday midday for jazz: Try **Doktor Flotte** (Occarstr. 8). The best of the jazz clubs are **Allotria** (Turkenstr. 33); **Domicile** (Leopoldstr. 19); **Nachtcafé** (Maximilianpl. 5); **Schwabinger Podium** (Wagnerstr. 1); **Unterfahrt** (Kirchenstr. 96); and **Jenny's Place** (Georgenstr. 50), which is run by a vivacious English actress and singer who has a great voice and a warm welcome for visitors from the United States and Britain.

Excursions

The excursions covered here are by no means the only ones you can make from Munich. Practically all the attractions in the Alps, for example, or those at the southern end of the Romantic Road—the resort town of Garmisch-Partenkirchen and Ludwig II's palaces and castles preeminently—make ideal destinations for one- or two-day trips out of town. For full details of these and many other destinations around Munich, *see* Chapters 4 and 8.

Tour 1: Ammersee and Andechs

The Ammersee is the country cousin of the better known, more cosmopolitan Starnbergersee, and many Bavarians (and tourists, too) like it all the more as a result. Fashionable Munich of past centuries thought it too far for an excursion, not to mention too rustic for its sophisticated tastes. So the shores remained relatively free of the villas and parks that ringed the Starnbergersee, and even though the upscale holiday homes of Munich's moneyed classes today claim some stretches of the eastern shore, the Ammersee still offers more open areas for bathing and boating than the bigger lake to the west. Bicyclists can circle the 12-mile-long lake (it's nearly 4 miles across at its widest point) on a path that rarely loses sight of the water. Hikers can spin out the tour for two or three days, staying overnight in any of the comfortable inns that crop up along the way.

Dinghy sailors and windsurfers can zip across in minutes with the help of the Alpine winds that swoop down from the mountains.

Getting There

By Car Take Autobahn 96—follow the signs to Lindau—and just before it ends, 20 kilometers (12 miles) west of Munich, take the exit for Herrsching, the lake's principal town. Herrsching is 40 kilometers (25 miles) from Munich.

By Train Herrsching, on the east bank of the lake, is the end of the S-5 suburban line, a half-hour ride from Munich's central Marienplatz. From Herrsching station, the number 952 bus runs north along the lake, and the number 956 runs south.

Exploring In Herrsching, head for the lake and the delightful promenade, part of which winds through the resort's park (its stately, 100-year-old elms now stand under a death sentence, victims of the Dutch elm disease that has carved a deadly path through Europe in the past 20 years). The fanciful 100-year-old villa that sits so comfortably in the park, overlooking the lake and the Alps beyond, seems almost as though it might have been built by Ludwig II, such is its romantic and fanciful mixture of medieval turrets and Renaissance-style facades. It was built for the artist Ludwig Scheuermann and is now a municipal cultural center and the scene of chamber-music concerts on some summer weekends.

Three miles south of Herrsching—you can reach it on the number 956 bus—is one of southern Bavaria's most famous places of pilgrimage, the Benedictine monastery of **Andechs.** The crowds of pilgrims are drawn not only by the beauty of the hilltop monastery and its 15th-century pilgrimage church, decked out with glorious Rococo decoration in the mid-18th century and a repository of religious relics said to have been brought from the Holy Land 1,000 years ago, but also by the beer brewed there. The monastery makes its own cheese as well, and it's an excellent accompaniment to the pale gold ale. You can enjoy both at large wood tables in the monastery tavern or on the terrace outside.

Follow the lake to its southeast corner and you'll find the little town of **Diessen,** with its magnificent Baroque abbey-church. Stop in to admire its opulent stucco decoration and sumptuous gilt and marble altar. Leonard Bernstein conducted the Mozart Requiem here in 1988. Visit the church in late afternoon, when the light falls sharply on its crisp gray, white, and gold facade, etching the pencil-like tower and spire against the darkening sky over the lake. Don't go without at least peeping into neighboring St. Stephen's courtyard, its cloisters smothered in wild roses. There's a delightful tearoom, too, which serves the excellent local beer.

Dining In Herrsching, the **Gasthof zur Post** (Andechstr. 1) is everything a Bavarian tavern should be. The weekday lunch menu is an unbeatable value, and the locally brewed dark beer is unbeatable, period. Along the lakeside promenade you'll find several idyllic terrace-restaurants; the **Alba-Seehotel** is the best. For the best *tirami su* outside Italy, stroll to the end of the promenade and call in at the **Restaurante da Mario.** In Diessen, make for the central Carl-Orff-Platz and pause to admire the rustic exterior of the **Gasthaus Unterbräu Gotsfried,** then venture inside for another indelible culinary impression (or, in summer, find a table outside in the leafy beer garden). The nearby **Hotel-Gasthof-Seefelder Hof** also has a delightful beer garden.

Tour 2: Dachau

Dachau residents complain, with some justification, that most visitors to their little city make straight for the site of the concentration camp and leave again without as much as a token visit to the attractions that distinguished their city long before the Nazis blighted it and its reputation. Dachau really doesn't deserve such treatment. It preserves the memory of the camp and the horrors perpetrated there with deep contrition while trying, with commendable discretion, to signal that it has far more to offer visitors. It's an older place than nearby Munich, for example, with local records going back to the time of Charlemagne in the 9th century. And it's a handsome town, too, built on a hilltop with fine views of Munich and the Alps.

Getting There

By Car Dachau is 20 kilometers (12 miles) northwest of Munich. Take the B-12 country road, or the Stuttgart autobahn to the Dachau exit.

By Train Dachau is on the S-2 suburban railway line, a 20-minute ride from Munich's Marienplatz.

Exploring Make for the town center and climb the hill to the **castle.** What you'll see is the one remaining wing of a palace built by the Munich architect Josef Effner for the Wittelsbach ruler Max Emanuel in 1715, a replacement for the original castle built in the 15th century. In the Napoleonic Wars at the beginning of the 19th century the palace served as a field hospital, treating French and Russian casualties from the Battle of Austerlitz (1805). The wars made a casualty, too, of the palace, and three of the four wings were demolished by order of King Max I Joseph. What's left now was the ballroom, and, on weekends in summer, it's still used for concerts. There's a 16th-century carved ceiling, with painted panels representing characters from ancient mythology.

Downtown, you'll find the parish church of **St. Jacob,** a towering 16th-century building that dominates the adjacent square, the former haymarket. Take a look at the colorful 18th-century sundial on the street-side wall.

Dachau served as a lively artists' colony in the 19th century, and the tradition lives on: There are art shops wherever you look. The **Dachauer Gemäldegalerie** in Konrad-Adenauer-Strasse is a good place to try.

To get to the site of the **concentration camp,** take a No. 722 bus from the train station. Photographs, contemporary documents, the few remaining cell blocks, and the grim crematorium create a somber and moving picture of the camp, where more than 200,000 people lost their lives. *Open Tues.–Sun. 9–5. A documentary film (in English) is shown at 11:30 and 3:30.*

Dining The **Bräustüberl,** 50 yards from the castle, has a shady beer garden for summer lunches. In the town center, the **Helferwirt** has a secluded garden and a cozy restaurant serving Bavarian fare. Next to the ivy-covered town hall, on Freisingerstrasse, is the solid, historic **Zieglerbraü,** once a 17th-century brewer's home, now a wood-paneled restaurant.

Tour 3: Landshut

If fortune had placed Landshut 40 miles south of Munich, in the protective folds of the Alpine foothills, instead of the same distance north, in the dull, flat wastes of Lower Bavaria, this delightful, historic town would have been overrun by visitors long ago. Landshut's geographical misfortune is the discerning visitor's good luck, for the town is never overcrowded, with the possible exception of the three summer weeks every four years 24 June–16 July 1989 was the last occasion) when the Landshuter Hochzeit is celebrated. The festival commemorates the marriage in 1475 of Prince George of Bayern-Landshut, son of the expressively named Ludwig the Rich, to Princess Hedwig, daughter of the king of Poland. The whole town gets swept away in a colorful reconstruction of the event that increased its already regal importance and that helped give it the majestic air you'll still find within its ancient walls.

Getting There

By Car Landshut is a 45-minute drive northwest from Munich on either Autobahn 92—follow the signs to Deggendorf—or the B-11 highway.

By Train Landshut is on the Plattling–Regensburg–Passau line, a 40-minute ride by express train from Munich.

Exploring A 10-minute bus ride will take you from the train station to the heart of the old town. There are parking lots right outside it, too. Landshut has not just one magnificent, cobbled market street but two: The one in **Altstadt** (Old Town) is considered by many to be the most beautiful city street in Germany; the one in **Neustadt** (New Town) projects its own special appeal. The two streets run parallel to each other, tracing a course between the Isar River and the heights overlooking the town. A steep path from Altstadt takes you up to **Burg Trausnitz,** sitting commandingly on the heights. This castle was begun in 1204 and accommodated the Wittelsbach dukes of Bayern-Landshut until 1503. *Admission, including guided tour: DM 1.50 adults, children free. Open daily 9–noon and 1–5.*

In the 16th century, the Wittelsbachs moved into a new palace (the *Stadtresidenz)* on **Altstadt,** the first Italian Renaissance building of its kind north of the Alps. The Renaissance facade of the palace forms an almost modest part of the architectural splendor and integrity of Altstadt, where even the ubiquitous McDonald's has to serve its hamburgers behind a baroque facade. *Admission to palace: DM 1.50 adults, children free. Open daily 9–noon and 1–5.*

Soaring over the street scene is the 436-foot tower and bristling spire of **St. Martin's** church, the tallest brick church tower in the world. The church contains some magnificent Gothic treasures and a 16th-century carved Madonna. Moreover, it is surely the only church anywhere in the world to contain an image of Hitler, albeit in devilish pose. The Führer and other Nazi leaders are portrayed as executioners in a 1946 stained-glass window showing the martyrdom of St. Kastulus. In the nave of the church is a clear and helpful description of its history and its treasures, an aid to English-speaking visitors that could profitably be copied by other churches and historical sites in Germany.

Dining There are several attractive Bavarian-style restaurants in Altstadt and Neustadt, most of them with charming beer gardens. The best are **Bräuereigasthof Ainmiller** (Altstadt 195), **Gasthaus Schwabl** (Neustadt 500), **Zum Hofreiter** (Neustadt 505), and the **Hotel Goldene Sonne** (Neustadt 520). The **Klausenberg Panorama-Restaurant** (Klausenberg 17) has a terrace with a fine view of the town and the surrounding country. For an inexpensive but satisfactory lunch, the **Buddha** (Apothekergasse) serves a good, fixed-price Chinese meal for around DM 10 per person. If you're looking for an authentic Bavarian dining experience, make your way to the old episcopal town of Freising, halfway between Landshut and Munich. It's the site of the world's oldest brewery, the **Bayerische Staatsbrauerei Weihenstephan.** Freising is the final stop on the S-1 suburban railway line from Munich, and one stop from Landshut by express train.

Lodging Landshut has four principal hotels, besides a handful of reasonably priced and comfortable inns. The hotels are: **Hotel Kaiserhof** (Papiererstr. 2, tel. 0871/6870; Expensive), a modern building on the banks of the Isar; **Romantik Hotel Fürstenhof** (Stethaimerstr. 3, tel. 0871/82025; Expensive), a tastefully modernized Art Nouveau villa; **Hotel Goldene Sonne** (Neustadt 520, tel. 0871/23087; Moderate), a historic inn in Old Town; and **Hotel Luitpold** (Luitpoldstr. 43, tel. 0871/61538; Inexpensive), a modern hotel between the train station and town.

Tour 4: Starnbergersee

The Starnbergersee was one of Europe's first pleasure grounds. Royal coaches trundled out from Munich to its wooded banks in the Baroque years of the 17th century; in 1663 Elector Ferdinand Maria threw a huge shipboard party in which 500 guests wined and dined as 100 oarsmen propelled them around the lake. Today, pleasure steamers perform the same task for visitors of less than noble rank. The lake is still lined with the Baroque palaces of Bavaria's aristocracy, but their owners now have to share the lakeside with public parks, beaches, and boat yards. The Starnbergersee is one of Bavaria's largest lakes, 12 miles long and 3 miles across at its widest point, so there's plenty of room for swimmers, sailors, and windsurfers. On its western shore is one of Germany's finest golf courses, but it's about as difficult for the casual visitor to play a game there as it was for a Munich commoner to win an invitation to one of Prince Ferdinand's boating parties. Those on the trail of Ludwig II should note that it was on the Starnbergersee that the doomed monarch met his watery death under circumstances that remain a mystery.

Getting There
By Car The northern end of the lake, where the resort of Starnberg sits in stately beauty, is a 30-minute drive from Munich on Autobahn 95. Follow the signs to Garmisch and take the Starnberg exit. Country roads then skirt the west and east banks of the lake.

By Train The S-6 suburban line runs from Munich's central Marienplatz to Starnberg and three other towns on the lake's west bank: Possenhofen, Feldafing, and Tutzing. The journey from Marienplatz to Starnberg takes 35 minutes. The eastern bank of the lake can be reached by bus from the town of Wolfratshausen, the end of the S-7 suburban line.

Exploring From Starnberg train station, take a stroll along the lakeside promenade for an overall impression of the shimmering beauty of this fascinating stretch of water, with the hazy hint of mountains at its southern rim. Rent bicycles at the station and pedal around the top of the lake to Percha, where a well-marked path will lead you south 2 miles to Berg. Leave the bicycles outside the castle park and stroll the half mile through thick woods to the **King Ludwig II Memorial Chapel,** built high above the point in the lake where the king's body was found on June 13, 1886. He had been confined in nearby Berg Castle after the Bavarian government took action against his withdrawal from reality and into expensive castle-building fantasy. A mile across the lake is the castle of **Possenhofen,** home of Ludwig's favorite cousin, Sissi. Local lore says they used to send affectionate messages across the lake to each other. Sissi married the Austrian Emperor Franz Joseph I but returned frequently to the Starnbergersee, to spend more than 20 consecutive summers in the lakeside villa that's now the Hotel Kaiserin Elisabeth. Just offshore is the tiny **Roseninsel**—(Rose Island), where King Maximilian II built a summer villa. You can swim to its tree-fringed shores or sail across in a dinghy or on a Windsurfer (Possenhofen's boat yard is one of the lake's many rental points).

Dining The most elegant dining in Starnberg is at the **Maximilian** (Osswaldstr. 16), where Bavarian fare with chic nouvelle touches is offered. For an airy tavern, try the **Gasthof in der Au** (Josef-Jager-Huber-Str. 15). If you fancy a view of the lake, make for the **Seerestaurant Undosa,** where the atmosphere is always boisterous. Farther down the lake, on the outskirts of Possenhofen, is the **Forsthaus am See** (Am See 1, Pocking-Possenhofen), where you dine beneath a carved panel ceiling imported from Austria's South Tyrol. The restaurant has a lakeside beer garden and its own pier for guests who arrive by boat. From Tutzing, at the end of the S-6 suburban line, a short walk up into the hills leads to the **Forsthaus Ilka-Höhe,** a rustic lodge with a fine view of the lake and excellent Bavarian food. On the other side of the lake, near the Berg Castle grounds and the King Ludwig II Memorial Chapel, try the **Dorint Seehotel Leoni** (Assenbucherstr. 44, Berg-Leoni) or the **Strandhotel Schloss Berg** (8137 Berg).

Tour 5: Wasserburg am Inn

Wasserburg floats like a faded ship of state in a benevolent, lazy loop of the Inn River, which comes within a few yards of cutting the ancient town off from the wooded slopes of the encroaching countryside. The river caresses the southern limits of the ancient town center, embraces its eastern boundary with rocky banks 200 feet high, returns westward as if looking for a way out of this geographical puzzle, and then heads north in search of its final destination, the Danube. Wasserburg sleeps on in its watery cradle, a perfectly preserved, beautifully set medieval town, once a vitally important trading post, later thankfully ignored by the industrialization that gripped Germany in the 19th century. Only one bridge connects the ancient town center with the newer suburbs across the river, a bridge, moreover, that regularly collapses under winter assaults by ice floes.

Getting There
By Car Take the B-304 highway from Munich, which leads directly to Wasserburg. It's a 45-minute drive.

By Train Take either the suburban line S-4 to Ebersberg and change to a local train to Wasserburg, or the Salzburg express, changing at Grafing Bahnhof to the local line. Both trips take 90 minutes.

Exploring You're never more than 100 yards or so from the river in Wasserburg's old town center. There are two large parking lots on the north and east banks, and it's only a few minutes' walk to the central Marienplatz. There you'll find Wasserburg's late-Gothic brick **town hall.** *Admission: DM 1 adults, 50 pf children. Guided tours Tues.–Fri. at 10, 11, 2, 3, and 4; Sat.–Sun. at 10 and 11.*

Marienplatz is also the site of the town's oldest church, the 14th-century **Frauenkirche,** which incorporates an ancient watchtower. Head up the hill to the imposing 15th-century parish church of **St. Jakob** to view its intricate Baroque pulpit, carved in 1640. Head south toward the river again; in two minutes you're at the walls of the **castle** that originally gave Wasserburg (Water Castle) its name. Take the river path back toward the town center, cross the bridge, and look back at the collection of Gothic and Renaissance buildings along the shore. It has a southern, almost Italian look, typical of many Inn River towns. At the end of the bridge, next to the 14th-century town gate, is one of Germany's most unusual museums, the **Erstes Imaginares Museum,** a collection of more than 400 world-famous paintings. There isn't an original among them: Every single one is a precise copy. *Admission: DM 2.50 adults, DM 1 children. Open May–Sept., Tues.–Sun. 11–5; Oct.–Apr., Tues.–Sun. 1–5.*

Wasserburg is a convenient base for enticing walks along the banks of the Inn River and into the surrounding countryside. A half-hour walk south leads to the village of **Attel.** Another half hour into the Attel River Valley and one reaches the enchanting castle-restaurant of **Schloss Hart** (tel. 08039/1774).

Dining You'll find the most compelling atmosphere for dining in Wasserburg at the **Herrenhaus** (Herrengasse 17, tel. 08071/2800; Moderate); it has a centuries-old wine cellar. For simple and traditional Bavarian fare, make for the **Gasthaus Zum Löwen** (Marienpl. 10, tel. 08071/7400; Inexpensive), a wood-paneled restaurant whose tables spill out onto the sidewalk in summer.

Lodging For solid comfort along with antiques in some of the rooms, good, hearty food, and a beer garden, try the **Hotel Fletzinger** (Fletzingergasse 1, tel. 08071/8010; Moderate). The **Hotel Paulanerstuben** (Marienpl. 9, tel. 08071/3903; Moderate) is centrally located, but ask for one of the quieter rooms that overlook the river.

4 The Bavarian Alps

Introduction

Oberbayern, or Upper Bavaria, is Germany's favorite year-round vacationland, for visitors and Germans alike.

This part of Bavaria, fanning south from Munich to the Austrian border, is arguably the most attractive area in the country. Scenically, it comes closest to what most of us think of when we see or hear the name Germany. In fact, upon initial exposure, the area may appear as something of a cliché. Stock images from tourist office posters—the fairy-tale castles you've seen in countless ads, those picturebook villages of too-good-to-be-true wood homes with brightly frescoed facades and window boxes filled with flowers in summer, sloping roofs heavy with snow in winter—are brought to life here. To complete the picture, onion-dome church spires rise out of the mist against the backdrop of the mighty Alps. Even the people sometimes appear to be actors completing a carefully staged scene. On Sundays and holidays they are often decked out in colorful regional costumes, listening to a brass band or zither player spin out tunes suited to the soundtrack of an old-fashioned travelogue. Indeed, the region can seem very much like a show turned on for the tourist trade, with *Gemütlichkeit* laid on with a trowel.

But it all turns out to be authentic: Southern Bavaria really is like that. Even Germans from the north consider the world south of Munich exotic; they, too, are attracted by the diversity of this popular playground, which has so much more to offer than simply local color.

The entire area, from close to Bodensee (Lake Constance) in the west, to Berchtesgaden in the east, is laced with possibilities for delightful excursions. Here, too, you will find a wide range of resorts at which to spend a weekend or week, to use either as bases for further explorations or as places to relax and take advantage of sporting opportunities.

Coming south from Munich, you will soon find yourself on a gently rolling plain leading to a lovely land of lakes fed by Alpine rivers and streams, surrounded by ancient forests. In time, the plain merges into foothills, which suddenly give way to a jagged line of Alpine peaks. In places such as Tegernsee, snow-capped mountains seem to rise straight up from the gem-like lakes.

If you continue south you will encounter cheerful villages with richly frescoed houses, some of the finest Baroque churches in Germany, and any number of minor spas where you can stay on to "take the waters" and tune up the system.

Accommodations run the gamut from luxury hotels in such sophisticated Alpine resort areas as Garmisch-Partenkirchen and Berchtesgaden, to cozy—and much less expensive—inns in simple villages. In addition, all through the region private homes offer Germany's own version of bed-and-breakfasts, indicated by signs of *Zimmer Frei* (rooms available). At these you'll find all the comforts anyone could ask for, pleasant surroundings, and hearty breakfasts—at some of the lowest prices in Europe.

You can eat and drink in high style at prestigious resort properties, such as those in Garmisch-Partenkirchen, or enjoy hearty regional fare and generous drafts of renowned Bavarian beer at rustic inns.

Sports possibilities are legion: downhill and cross-country skiing and ice-skating in winter; tennis, swimming, sailing, golf, and, above all, hiking in summer. Marked hiking trails lead through the glorious countryside, along rivers and lakes, through woods, and high into the Alps.

For those who enjoy driving, the *Deutsche Alpenstrasse* (German Alpine Road), makes for a spectacular journey by car. The entire route between Lindau, on Lake Constance, and Berchtesgaden adds up to about 485 kilometers (300 miles). The dramatic stretch between Garmisch-Partenkirchen and Berchtesgaden runs about 300 kilometers (185 miles) and affords wonderful views.

This tour of the Alps takes you east from Garmisch-Partenkirchen to Berchtesgaden. Oberammergau, the magnificent 18th-century abbey of Ettal, and Ludwig II's Versailles-style château at Herrenchiemsee are all covered, along with numerous villages, lakes, and other Alpine attractions. (Note that Neuschwanstein, the most famous of Ludwig's castles, is covered in our Romantic Road chapter. It's located just outside Füssen and makes an ideal day trip from Garmisch-Partenkirchen.)

Essential Information

Important Addresses and Numbers

Tourist Information The Bavarian regional tourist office in Munich, **FVV München Oberbayern** (Sonnenstr. 10, 8000 Munich 2, tel. 089/597–347), provides general information about Upper Bavaria and the Bavarian Alps. There are local tourist information offices in the following towns:

Bad Reichenhall: Kur-und-Verkehrsverein, im Hauptbahnhof–Nebenbau, 8230 Bad Reichenhall, tel. 08651/3003.
Bad Tölz: Kurverwaltung, Ludwigstrasse 11,8170 Bad Tölz, tel. 08041/70071.
Bayerischzell: Kuramt, Kirchplatz 2, 8163 Bayerischzell, tel. 08023/648.
Berchtesgaden: Kurdirektion, Königseerstrasse 2, 8240 Berchtesgaden, tel. 08652/5011.
Garmisch-Partenkirchen: Verkehrsamt der Kurverwaltung, Bahnhofstrasse 34, 8100 Garmisch-Partenkirchen, tel. 08821/18022.
Mittenwald: Kurverwaltung, Dammkarstrasse 3, 8102 Mittenwald, tel. 08823/1051.
Oberammergau: Verkehrsamt, Eugen-Papst-Strasse 9a, 8103 Oberammergau, tel. 08822/4921.
Prien am Chiemsee: Kurverwaltung, Am Bahnhof, 8210 Prien, tel. 08051/3031.
Reit im Winkl: Verkehrsamt, Rathausplatz 1, 8216 Reit im Winkl, tel. 08640/8207.
Rottach-Egern: Kuramt, Nördliche Hauptstrasse 9, 8183 Rottach-Egern, tel. 08022/671–341.

Car Rental **Avis:** Hindenburgstrasse 35, tel. 08821/55066, **Garmisch-Partenkirchen;** Balanstrasse 74, tel. 089/497–301, **Munich.**

Europcar: Schwanthalerstrasse 10A, tel. 089/594–72325, **Munich.**
Herz: Zugspitzstrasse 81, tel. 08821/18787, **Garmisch-Partenkirchen;** Nymphenburger-Strasse 81, tel. 089/129–5001, **Munich.**

Arriving and Departing by Plane

Munich, 95 kilometers (60 miles) northwest of Garmisch-Partenkirchen, is the main airport for the Bavarian Alps. There is easy access from Munich to the Autobahns that lead to the Alps (*see* By Car, below). If you're staying in Berchtesgaden at the eastern end of the Alps, the airports at Salzburg and Innsbruck in Austria are closer but have fewer international flights.

Arriving and Departing by Car, Train, and Bus

By Car Three Autobahns reach deep into the Bavarian Alps: E-7 from Ulm to Kempten at the west end of the Alps; E-6 from Munich to Garmisch; and E-11/E-17 from Munich to Salzburg and Innsbruck. All provide speedy access to the Alpine foothills, where they connect with a comprehensive network of well-paved country roads that penetrate high into the mountains. (Germany's highest road runs through Berchtesgaden at more than 5,000 feet.)

By Train Garmisch-Partenkirchen and Mittenwald are on the Inter-city network, which has regular direct service to all regions of the country. (Klais, just outside Garmisch, is Germany's highest Inter-city train station.) Bad Reichenhall and Berchtesgaden are linked directly to north German cities by the FD (Fern-Express) express service.

By Bus The Alpine region is not well served by long-distance bus services: Stick to trains if you plan to travel extensively. The southern section of the Europabus route, along the Romantische Strasse (Romantic Road), connects Frankfurt, Wiesbaden, Würzburg, Munich, and Augsburg with the resorts of Schongau and Füssen (*see* The Romantic Road). Seat reservations, which are obligatory, can be made through **Deutsche Touring GmbH** *(Am Römerhof 17. 6000 Frankfurt/Main 90, tel. 069/790–3240.)* Many travel agents—ABR in Bavaria, for instance—can also make reservations.

Getting Around

By Car The Deutsche Alpenstrasse, not a continuous highway but a series of roads, runs from Lindau in the west to the Austrian border beyond Berchtesgaden in the east, skirting the northern edge of the Alps for most of the way before heading deep into the mountains on the final stretch between Inzell and Berchtesgaden. Another route, the so-called Blaue Route (Blue Route), follows the valleys of the Inn and Salzach rivers along the German-Austrian border above Salzburg. This off-the-beaten-track territory includes three quiet lakes: the Tachingersee, the Wagingersee, and the Abstdorfersee. They are the warmest bodies of water in Upper Bavaria, ideal for family vacations. At Wasserburg, on the Inn River, you can join the final section of the Deutsche Ferienstrasse (German Holiday Road), another combination of roads that runs on to Traunstein, east of Chiemsee, and then into the Alps. The

Chiemsee and two other popular lakes, the Starnbergersee and the Ammersee, are within easy reach of Munich by Autobahn.

By Train Most Alpine resorts are connected with Munich by regular express and slower service. Munich's S–bahn (suburban service) extends as far as two lakes, the Starnbergersee and the Ammersee, where the Alpine foothills really begin.

By Bus Villages not served by train are connected by post bus. This is a fun and inexpensive way to get around, but service is slow and irregular. Larger resorts operate buses to outlying areas.

By Boat Passenger boats operate on all the major Bavarian lakes. They're mostly excursion boats and many run only in summer. However, there's an important year-round service on Chiemsee that links the mainland with the islands of Herreninsel and Fraueninsel. Four boats on the Starnbergersee and four on the Ammersee (including a fine old paddle steamer) make round trips of the lake several times a day between Starnberg and Stegen/Inning. Eight boats operate year-round on the Tegernsee, connecting Tegernsee town, Rottach-Egern, and Bad Wiessee. A fleet of 21 silent, electrically driven boats glides through the waters of the Königsee near Berchtesgaden to the most remote of Bavaria's lakes, the Obersee.

Guided Tours

Bus tours to King Ludwig II castles at Neuschwanstein and Linderhof and to the Ettal monastery near Oberammergau are offered by the **ABR** travel agencies in Garmisch-Partenkirchen (tel. 08821/55125) and Oberammergau (tel. 08822/4921). Tours to Neuschwanstein, Linderhof, Ettal, and into the neighboring Austrian Tyrol are also offered by a number of other Garmisch travel agencies: **Biersack** (tel. 08821/4920), **Frankl** (tel. 08821/51700), **Karrasch** (tel. 08821/2111), **Kümmerle** (tel. 08821/4955), **Roser** (tel. 08821/2926), **Teixeira** (tel. 08821/58580), and **Weiss-Blau** (tel. 08821/3766). The Garmisch mountain railway company, the **Bayerische Zugspitzbahn** (tel. 08821/52020) offers special excursions to the top of the Zugspitze, Germany's highest mountain, by cog rail and/or cable car (*see* Exploring, below). **German Federal Railways** (tel. 089/598–484 or 0821/96600) offers special excursion fares from Munich and Augsburg to the top of the Zugspitze; In Berchtesgaden, the **Schwaiger** bus company (tel. 08652/2525) offers bus tours of the area and over the Austrian border as far as Salzburg.

Exploring the Alps

Numbers in the margin correspond with points of interest on the Bavarian Alps map.

Highlights for First-time Visitors

Zugspitze
Kloster Ettal
Schloss Linderhof
Oberammergau
Tegernsee
Tatzelwurm gorge and waterfall
Kehlsteinhaus

Boat excursion on the Königsee in Berchtesgaden National Park

Tour 1: Garmisch-Partenkirchen

1 **Garmisch-Partenkirchen,** or Garmisch, as it's more commonly known, is the undisputed Alpine capital of Bavaria. This bustling, year-round resort and spa area is an ideal center from which to explore the Bavarian Alps. Once two separate communities, Garmisch and Partenkirchen were fused in 1936 to accommodate the winter Olympics. Today, with a population of 27,000, the area is large enough to offer every facility expected from a major Alpine resort, but is still small enough not to overwhelm.

For all that it seems an essentially modern town—few of its buildings pre-date World War I—Garmisch-Partenkirchen has a long history. Partenkirchen, the older half, was founded by the Romans. The road the Romans built between Partenkirchen and neighboring Mittenwald can still be followed. It was a major route well into the 17th century, the principal road between Rome and Germany. Much of the astounding wealth of the Fugger family in Augsburg (*see* The Romantic Road) resulted from trade between the south of Germany and Venice, which were connected by the Roman route.

Partenkirchen was economically devastated in the first half of the 17th century by the Thirty Years' War. The town was spared physical destruction, but went into a decline and became little more than a backwater. By the early 18th century, it was rejuvenated by the discovery of iron ore. Today, of course, tourism keeps Garmisch-Partenkirchen thriving.

Winter sports rank high on the agenda here. There are more than 62 miles of downhill ski runs, 40 ski lifts and cable cars, and 93 miles of cross-country ski tracks (called *Loipen*). One of the principal stops on the international winter sports circuit, the area hosts a week of international races every January. You can usually count on good skiing from November to early May.

2 The number-one attraction in Garmisch is the **Zugspitze,** the highest mountain (9,731 feet) in Germany. For those who want to make a night of it, there's a comfortable hotel at the top, the Schneefernhaus. There are two ways up the mountain: a leisurely 75-minute ride on a cog railway, or a 10-minute hoist by cable car. The railway journey starts from the train station in the center of town; the cable car begins its giddy ascent from the Eibsee, just outside town on the road to Austria. The round-trip fare for both is DM 42 adults, DM 26 children; there are sizable discounts for families. All fares include a day's ski pass. You can ride up on one route and down on the other.

If DM 42 stretches the vacation budget too much, take a cable car to one of the lesser peaks. The round-trip fare to the top of the **Alpspitze,** some 2,000 feet lower than the Zugspitze, is DM 25; to the top of the **Wank** and back costs DM 18 (you ride in four-seat cable cars). Both mountains can be tackled on foot, providing you're properly shod and physically fit. For details on other mountain hikes and on staying in mountain huts, contact Deutscher Alpenverein (German Alpine Association, Praterinsel 5, 8000 Munich, tel. 089/293–086).

Bavarian Alps

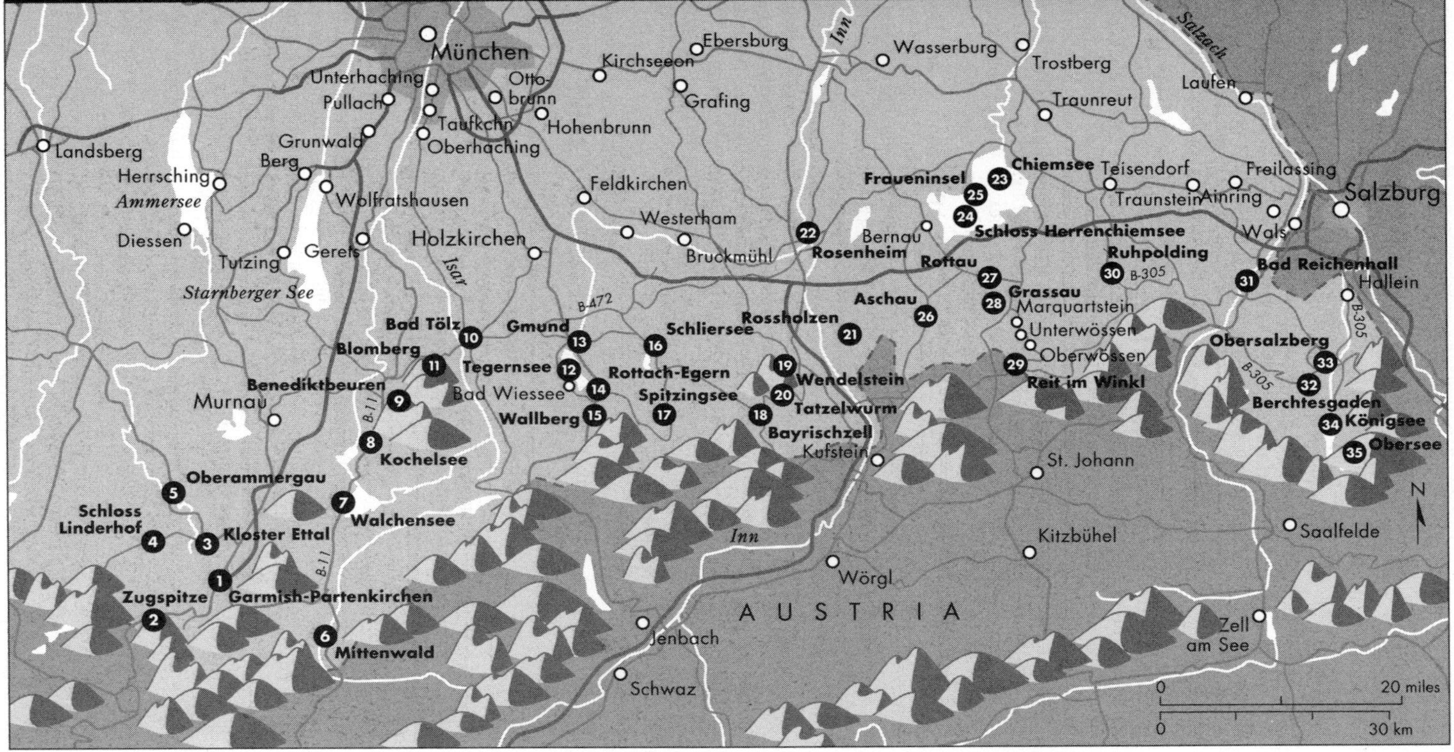

There are innumerable less-arduous but hardly less-spectacular walks (186 miles of marked trails) through the pine woods and upland meadows that cover the lower slopes of the mountains. If you have the time and stout walking shoes, try one of the two that lead to striking gorges. The **Höllentalklamm** route starts at the Zugspitze mountain railway terminal in town and ends at the top of the mountain (you'll want to turn back before reaching the summit unless you have mountaineering experience). The **Partnachklamm** route is even more challenging; if you attempt all of it, you'll have to stay overnight in one of the mountain huts along the way. It starts at the Olympic ice stadium in town and takes you through a series of **tunnels** and **galleries,** past a pretty little mountain lake, and far up the Zugspitze. An easier way to tackle this route is to ride part of the way up in the Eckbauer cable car that sets out from the Olympic ice stadium. There's a handy inn at the top where you can gather the strength for the hour-long walk back down to the cable car station. Horse-drawn carriages also cover the first section of the route in summer; in winter you can skim along it in a sleigh (tel. 08821/55917 for information).

Garmisch-Partenkirchen isn't all skiing, skating, and hiking, however. In addition to the two Olympic stadiums in the Partenkirchen side of the city, there are some other attractions worth seeing. In Garmisch, the 18th-century parish church of St. Martin, off the Marienplatz, contains some significant stucco work by the Wessobrunn artists Schmuzer, Schmidt, and Bader. Across the Loisach River on Pfarehausweg stands another, older St. Martin's, whose Gothic wall paintings include a larger-than-life-size figure of St. Christopher. Nearby, in Frühlingstrasse, are some beautiful examples of Upper Bavarian houses; at the end of Zöppritzstrasse lies the villa of composer Richard Strauss, who lived there until his death in 1949.

Not a culture-vulture? Then it might interest you to know that après-ski festivities begin as early as 4 PM, and the town boasts an active nightlife.

Excursions from Garmisch

Garmisch-Partenkirchen is an excellent center from which to tour the magnificent surrounding Alpine region. For many, a visit to the little village of Oberammergau, combined with a side trip to the monastery of Ettal and Ludwig II's jewel-like Linderhof château, is a highlight of their stay in Germany. This trip can be extended by visits to Ludwig II's most famous royal castle, Neuschwanstein, and the exquisite Rococo Wieskirche (*see* Chapter 8). Oberammergau is 20 kilometers (12 miles) north of Garmisch. To reach it, you must first pass the massive
3 walls of **Kloster Ettal,** the great monastery founded in 1330 by Holy Roman Emperor Ludwig der Bayer (Ludwig the Bavarian), for a group of knights and a community of Benedictine monks. The abbey was replaced with new buildings in the 18th century, and now serves as a school. However, the original 10-sided church was brilliantly redecorated in 1744–1753, becoming one of the foremost examples of Bavarian Rococo. It is open to visitors. The church's chief treasure is its enormous dome fresco (83 feet wide), painted by J. J. Zeiler in 1746. The mass of swirling clouds and the pink-and-blue vision of heaven is typ-

ical of the Rococo fondness for elaborate and luminous illusionistic ceiling painting.

A liqueur with legendary health-giving properties, made from a centuries-old recipe, is still distilled at the monastery by the monks. It's made with more than 70 mountain herbs. You can't get the recipe but you can buy bottles of the libation (DM 19 each) from the small stall outside the monastery.

Time Out Across the road, the **Hotel Ludwig der Bayer** (Kaiser-Ludwig Pl. 10, tel. 08822/4637) named after the monastery's founder, serves excellent coffee and monastery-brewed beer. For more solid refreshment, the menu runs the full gamut of Bavarian fare.

Some 10 kilometers (6 miles) west from Ettal, along a narrow
4 mountain valley road, is **Schloss Linderhof,** the only one of Ludwig II's royal residences to have been completed during the monarch's short life, and the only one in which he spent much time. It was built on the grounds of his father's hunting lodge between 1874 and 1878.

For a proper appreciation of Linderhof and the other royal castles associated with Ludwig's name, it helps to understand the troubled king for whom they were created.

"Mad" King Ludwig II is the haunting presence indelibly associated with Alpine Bavaria. He was one of the line of dukes, electors, and kings of the Wittelsbach dynasty who ruled Bavaria from 1180 to 1918. The Wittelsbachs are credited with having fashioned the grandiose look of Munich that exists today. This art-loving family started the city's great art collections, promoted music and the fine arts, and set up a building program that ran for centuries.

Ludwig II concentrated on building monumental edifices for himself rather than the people, and devoted a good part of his time and energies (along with an inordinate percentage of the royal purse) to this endeavor.

Grandest of his extravagant projects is Neuschwanstein, the monumental structure to the king's monumental ego that came close to breaking the Wittelsbach bank. It was built over a 17-year period starting in 1869, and today is one of Germany's top tourist attractions. (*See* Chapter 8).

Towering Neuschwanstein offered highly visible proof that the eccentric king had taken leave of his senses and was bleeding the treasury dry. In 1886, the government officially relieved Ludwig of his royal duties for reasons of insanity and had him confined in the small Schloss Berg on the shore of his beloved Starnbergersee, where he had spent summers in his youth.

On day two of the king's stay at the Schloss, he drowned under mysterious circumstances. A cross in the lake in front of the castle marks the place where it happened.

Although King Ludwig II is generally presented as a figure of ridicule in texts on travel in Bavaria, it should be noted that to Bavarians he remains the much-loved "Dream King." His romanticized likeness appears on banners at *Oktoberfest* parades and hangs in country inns and peasant homes.

Linderhof was the smallest of this ill-starred king's castles, and yet, ironically, his favorite country retreat. Set in grandiose sylvan seclusion, between a reflecting pool and the green slopes of a gentle mountain, this charming French-style Rococo confection is said to have been inspired by the Petit Trianon of Versailles. From an architectural standpoint, it could well be considered a disaster, a mish-mash of conflicting styles, lavish on the outside, vulgarly over-decorated on the inside: Ludwig's bedroom is filled with brilliantly colored and gilded ornaments; the Hall of Mirrors is a shimmering dreamworld; and the dining room boasts a fine piece of 19th-century engineering—a table that rises and descends from and to the kitchens below. The formal gardens contain further touches of Ludwig's love of fantasy: There's a Moorish Pavilion—bought wholesale from the 1867 Paris exhibition—and a grotto, said to have been modeled on Capri's blue grotto but with a rock that slides back at the touch of a button. The gilded Neptune fountain in the lake in front of the palace shoots a jet of water 105 feet into the air, higher than the roof of the building.

According to stories, while staying at Linderhof the eccentric king would dress up as Lohengrin to be rowed in a swan boat on the grotto pond; in winter, he took off on midnight sleigh rides behind six plumed horses and a platoon of outriders holding flaring torches. *Admission: DM 6 adults, DM 3 children. Open Apr.–Sept., 9–12:15 and 12:45–5:30, Oct.–Mar., 10–12:15 and 12:45–4.*

5 The renowned wood-carver's village of **Oberammergau** is magnificently situated above an Alpine valley, 11 kilometers (7 miles) east of Linderhof. Its main streets are lined with beautifully frescoed houses, occupied for the most part by families whose men are engaged in the highly skilled wood-carving craft, which has flourished here for three-and-a-half centuries. Wood-carving was Oberammergau's route to economic recovery after the depredations of the Thirty Years' War, and the art still flourishes here.

However, Oberammergau is best known not for its wood-carving, but for its Passion Play, which is performed once every decade in years ending with zero in faithful accordance to a solemn vow. The play started as an offering of thanks, commemorating the fact that the Black Plague stopped in 1634 as though by miracle, just short of the village.

The Passion Play was first performed that year, and since 1680 has been presented every 10 years, with an additional 350th anniversary performance in 1984.

The 16-act, five-and-a-half-hour play depicts the final days of Christ, from the Last Supper through the Crucifixion and Resurrection. It is presented on a partly-open-air stage against a mountain backdrop every day from late May to late September each Passion Play Year (the next is 1990).

A visit to Oberammergau during a play year may be considered something of a mixed blessing in view of the crowds attracted to this small village and the difficulty of obtaining tickets (most are available only through package tours).

Locals count on seeing half-a-million visitors or more in summers when the Passion Play is presented. The entire village is swept up by the play, with some 1,500 residents directly involved in its preparation and presentation. Men grow beards in hopes of capturing key roles; young ladies put off marriage to try to win the coveted role of Mary, awarded only to an unmarried applicant.

If you visit Oberammergau in a non-play year you can still visit the theater, the Oberammergau Passionspielhaus, and explore backstage. Tours of the huge building, with its vast stage open to the mountain air and 5,200-seat auditorium, are given by guides who will demonstrate the remarkable acoustics by reciting Shakespearean soliloquies. *Passionweise. Admission with guided tour: DM 4 adults, DM 2.50 children.. Open daily 10–noon and 1:30–4:30. Festival Information: Verkehrsbüro, Oberammergau, tel. 08822/4921.*

The preoccupation of villagers with the Passion Play doesn't totally push aside the wood-carvers. You can still find many at work even during play years. Oberammergau's shop windows are crammed with their creations. From June through September, a workshop is open free to the public at the Pilatushaus (Verlegergasse); potters and traditional painters can also be seen at work. If you speak some German you can even sign up for a week-long course in wood-carving, at a cost of between DM 425 and DM 605, bed and breakfast included.

Historic examples of the skill of Oberammergau craftsmen are on view at the Heimatmuseum, which also includes one of Germany's finest collections of Christmas creches, dating from the mid-18th century. *Dorfstr. 8. Admission: DM 2.50 adults, 50 pf children. Open May 10–Oct. 15, Tues.–Sat. afternoons only.*

Many of the exteriors of Oberammergau's homes, such as the 1784 Pilatushaus on Ludwig-Thoma-Strasse, are decorated with stunning frescoes. In late summer, geraniums pour from every window box, and the village explodes with color.

Oberammergau's 18th-century Catholic **church** is regarded as the finest work of Josef Schmuzer and has striking frescoes by Mathaus Gunther.

Along the Alps

A range of attractions line the Alps between Garmisch and Berchtesgaden to the east. Many of them lie on the Deutsche Alpenstrasse, the German Alpine Road, the most scenic of the west–east Alpine routes. All can be visited on day trips from Garmisch-Partenkirchen and/or Berchtesgaden. This tour
6 goes first to **Mittenwald,** 20 kilometers (12 miles) southeast of Garmisch and snugly set beneath the towering peaks of the Karwendel range, which separates Bavaria from Austria.

Many regard Mittenwald as the most beautiful town in the Bavarian Alps. It is situated on the spine of an important north–south trade route dating back to Roman times. In the Middle Ages, Mittenwald became the staging point for goods shipped up from Verona by way of the Brenner Pass and Innsbruck. From there, goods were transferred to rafts, which carried them down the Isar to Munich. As might be expected, Mittenwald grew rich on this traffic; its early prosperity is reflected to this day in the splendidly decorated houses with ornately carved gables and brilliantly painted facades that line its main street.

In the mid-17th century, however, the international trade route was moved to a different pass, and the fortunes of Mittenwald went into swift decline.

Prosperity returned to Mittenwald in 1684, when a farmer's son, Matthias Klotz, returned from a 20-year stay in Cremona as a master violin maker. In Cremona, Klotz had studied with Nicolo Amati, who gave the violin its present form. Klotz brought his master's pioneering ideas back to Mittenwald. He taught the art to his brothers and friends; before long, half the men in the village were making violins. With the ideal woods for violins coming from neighboring forests, the trade flourished. Mittenwald soon became known as "The Village of a Thousand Violins," and stringed instruments—violins, violas, and cellos—made in Mittenwald were shipped around the world. Klotz's craft is still carried on in Mittenwald, and the town has a fascinating museum, the **Geigenbau-und Heimatmuseum,** devoted to it. *Obermarkt 4, tel. 08823/8561. Admission: DM 2 adults, children free. Open Mon.–Fri. 10–11:45 and 2–4:45, weekends and public holidays 10–11:45.*

Ask the curator of the museum to direct you to the nearest of the several violin makers who are still active in Mittenwald. One of these craftsmen lives close to the museum and is happy to demonstrate the skills handed down to him by the successors of Klotz. The museum itself is next to Mittenwald's 18th-century church of **Sts. Peter and Paul.** Check the back of the altar and you'll find Klotz's name, carved there by the violin maker himself. In front of the church is a monument to Klotz. The church itself, with its elaborate and joyful stucco work, which coils and curls its way around the interior, is one of the most important Rococo structures in Bavaria. Note its Gothic tower, incorporated into the church in the 18th century. The bold frescoes on its exterior are characteristic of *Luftlmalerei*, an art form that reached its height in Mittenwald. You can see other fine examples of it on the facades of three famous houses: the Goethehaus, the Pilgerhaus, and the Pichlerhaus.

Time Out Just down the street from the museum and the church is the **Hotel Post.** Ask for their *Apfelkuchen* (apple cake) with morning or afternoon coffee. If you need something more substantial, the lunch menu will give you the strength for an afternoon hike in the surrounding mountains.

The road north from Mittenwald, B-11, runs between the 7 8 **Walchensee** and the **Kochelsee,** two of the most popular Bavarian Alpine lakes. They are longtime favorites for summer getaways, and offer good swimming, water sports, and mountain walks (the 5,900-foot-high Benediktinwand, east of Kochel, is a challenge for mountaineers; the 5,300-foot-high Herzogstand, above the Walchensee, is more suitable for the less adventurous). On the shores of the Kochelsee is one of the most extensive swimming lidos in Bavaria, with a collection of indoor and outdoor pools, water slides, and enough other games to keep a family amused the whole day long. *Trimini, Kochel. Admission: all-day ticket DM 8.50 adults, DM 6 children; 3-hour ticket DM 6 adults, DM 4 children; all-day family ticket DM 23. Open daily 9–8:30.*

The attractive little lakeside town of Kochel boasts a local hero, the Schmied von Kochel or Blacksmith of Kochel. His fame stems from his role—and eventual death—in the 1705 peasants' uprising at Sendling, just outside Munich. You can see his statue in the town center.

Some 10 kilometers (6 miles) north of Kochel on B-11 lies the Benediktenwand, a mountain that takes its name from the ancient Benedictine monastery at its foot. Founded in the mid-8th
9 century, the monastery of **Benediktbeuren** is thought to be the oldest Benedictine institution north of the Alps. It was a flourishing cultural center in the Middle Ages; paradoxically, it also gave birth to one of the most profane musical works of those times, the "Carmina Burana." The 1936 orchestration of the work by Bavarian composer Carl Orff is regularly performed in the monastery courtyard, the place where the original work was first heard in the 12th century. The father of the Asam brothers, whose church-building and artistic decoration made them famous far beyond the borders of 18th-century Bavaria, painted the frescoes of the monastery church. Cosmas Damian Asam, the eldest son, was born in Benediktbeuren.

Sixteen kilometers (10 miles) east of Benediktbeuren on B-472
10 lies the old market town of **Bad Tölz.** Visit, if you can, on a Wednesday morning—market day—when the main street is lined with stalls that stretch to the Isar River, the dividing line between the Old and New Towns. The New Town sprang up with the discovery in the mid-19th century of iodine-laden springs, which promoted Tölz into the ranks of German spas and allowed the locals to call their town Bad Tölz. You can take the waters, enjoy a full course of health treatment at any of the many specially equipped hotels, or just splash around in Bad Tölz's large lido, the **Alpamare,** where one of its indoor pools is disguised as a South Sea beach, complete with surf. *Ludwigstr. 13. Admission: 3-hour ticket DM 19 (weekends DM 22) adults, DM 14 children. Open daily 8AM–9PM.*

Bad Tölz clings to its ancient customs and traditions more tightly than any other Bavarian community. Folk costumes, for example, are not only preserved but are regularly worn. The town is also famous for its painted furniture, particularly farmhouse cupboards and chests. You can admire samples of painted furniture, as well as folk costumes and other historic crafts in the **Heimatmuseum,** housed in the Altes Rathaus (Old Town Hall). *Marktpl. Admission: free. Open Tues.–Sat. 10–noon and 2–4, Thurs. 10–noon and 2–6, Sun. 10–1.*

If you're in Bad Tölz on November 6, you'll witness one of the most colorful traditions of the Bavarian Alpine area: the Leonhardi-Ritt equestrian procession, which marks the feast day of St. Leonhard, the patron saint of horses. The procession ends north of the town at an 18th-century chapel on the Kalvarienberg, above the Isar River.

Drive 2 miles west of Bad Tölz along B-472 and you'll reach the
11 base of the town's local mountain, the **Blomberg.** It's an easy walk to the top, but you can also take a chair lift, which makes the journey in 12 minutes. If you're in a hurry to get down, rent a wheeled toboggan and try your luck on the dry run that snakes and curves its way down the mountain. It's great fun for kids, but can be expensive unless you ration the number of runs. *Admission: DM 5.50 a ride adults, DM 4.50 children. Open Apr.–Oct.*

About 17 kilometers (10 miles) east of Bad Tölz on B-472 is one
12 of the loveliest of the Alpine lakes, the **Tegernsee**, which is dotted with sails in summer and ice skaters in winter. Its wooded shores are lined with flowers in late spring; in fall, its trees provide a colorful contrast to the dark, snow-capped mountains. Elbowing each other for room on the banks of this heavenly stretch of water are expensive health clinics, hotels, and a former Benedictine monastery, which now houses a brewery and restaurant. The monastery, set in parklike grounds on the southeast shore of the lake, was founded in the 8th century. In the Middle Ages it was one of the most productive cultural centers in southern Germany; the musician and poet Minnesänger Walther von der Vogelweide (1170–1230) was one of its welcomed guests in the 12th century. Not so welcome were Hungarian invaders, who had laid the monastery to waste in the 10th century. Fire caused further damage in following centuries, and secularization sealed the monastery's fate at the beginning of the 19th century, when a Bavarian king, Maximilian I, bought the surviving buildings to use as a summer retreat. Now the site houses a brewery, a restaurant, and a beer tavern.

Time Out Follow King Max's footsteps into the vaulted rooms in which busy waitresses bustle around where Benedictine monks once meditated. The monastery beer is good and strong; the food is typically Bavarian.

The late-Gothic monastery **church** was refurbished in Italian Baroque style in the 18th century. Opinions remain divided as to the success of the remodeling, which was the work of a little-known Italian architect named Antonio Riva. Whatever you think of his designs, you'll admire the frescoes by Hans Georg Asam, whose work you saw at the monastery of Benediktbeuren. If you like what you've seen, you may also want to visit
13 the parish church of **Gmund**, at the northern end of the lake,
14 and the church of St. Laurentius at **Rottach-Egern**, on the southern shore. In both places you'll find further evidence of Asam's talents.

Rottach-Egern is a fashionable and upscale resort. Its classy shops, chic restaurants, and clutch of boutiques are as well-stocked and interesting as most of those in Munich. Also, its leading hotels are world-class. If you want to visit in style, Bachmair's, on the water's edge, is the place to stay; the flashy nightclub and casino at Bad Wiessee, on the western shore of the lake, can help you spend your money (*see* The Arts and Nightlife, below).

The mountain slopes above Bad Wiessee offer fine views, but
15 for the best vista of all climb the 5,700-foot **Wallberg**, at the southern end of the lake. It's a hard, four-hour hike, though anyone in good shape should be able to make it since it involves no rock climbing. If you don't wish to climb, ride the cable car, which makes the ascent in 15 minutes. At the summit there's a hotel, the Berggastof Sonnenbichel (tel. 08022/81365), with a restaurant and sun terrace. Several mountain trails set out from the summit; in winter the skiing is excellent.

From the Tegernsee you can follow an upland footpath 9 kilometers (6 miles) east to the next lake—the quieter, less-
16 fashionable **Schliersee.** Or you can drive the 27 kilometers (18

miles) there. The difference between the two lakes is made clear in the names local people have long given them: the Tegernsee is called the Herrensee (or Master's Lake), while the Schliersee is known as the Bauernsee (or Peasant's Lake). There are fine walking and ski trails on the mountain slopes that ring the Schliersee.

Like the Tegernsee, the Schliersee was the site of a monastery, built in the 8th century by a group of noblemen. It subsequently became a choral academy, which was eventually moved to Munich. Today, only the restored 17th-century **abbey church** recalls this piece of the Schliersee's history. The church has some fine frescoes and stucco work by Johann Baptist Zimmermann.

A spectacular 10-kilometer (6-mile) drive south from Schliersee takes you around hairpin bends to the tiny
17 **Spitzingsee,** cradled 3,500 feet up between the Taubenstein, Rosskopf, and Stumpfling peaks. The walking in this area is breathtaking in every sense. There's the skiing, too.

18 **Bayrischzell,** 10 kilometers (6 miles) east, is the next stop. To reach it, you pass one of the highest mountains of the area, the
19 6,200-foot **Wendelstein.** At its summit is a tiny stone-and-slate-roof chapel that's much in demand as an off-beat place to marry. The cross above the entrance was carried up the mountain by Max Kleiber, who designed the 19th-century church. Today, there are two easier ways up: a cable car (which sets out from the Schliersee–Bayrischzell road) and an historic old cog railway (catch it at Brannenburg, on the north side of the mountain).

While the slopes of the Wendelstein attract expert skiers, those above Bayrischzell beckon the rest. The town is in an attractive family resort area, where many a Bavarian first learns to ski. The wide-open slopes of the Sudelfeld mountain are ideal for those who enjoy undemanding skiing; in the summer and fall they offer innumerable upland walking trails.

A mile or two east of Bayrischzell on the Sudelfeld Road is the
20 **Tatzelwurm** gorge and waterfall, named after a winged dragon that supposedly inhabits these parts. This can be an eerie place to drive through at dusk. From the gorge, the road drops sharply to the valley of the Inn River and leads to another busy ski resort, Oberaudorf.

The Inn River Valley, one of Europe's most ancient trade routes, carries the most important road link between Germany and Italy. The wide, green Inn flows rapidly here, and in the
21 parish church of St. Bartholomew at **Rossholzen,** 16 kilometers (10 miles) north of Oberaudorf, you can see memorials to the local people who have lost their lives in its chilly waters. The church has a fine late-Gothic altar.

22 Rossholzen is 10 kilometers (6 miles) south of **Rosenheim,** a medieval market town that has kept much of its character despite the onslaught of industrial development. The arcaded streets of low-eaved houses are characteristic of Inn Valley towns.

Rosenheim is a good center from which to explore the Chiemgau region, an area of mountainous lakes dominated by the wide Chiemsee, Bavaria's largest stretch of water. Between

Rosenheim and the Chiemsee are a number of smaller lakes, set amid rich, rolling farmland and largely forgotten by the crowds
23 who make for the nearby Alps. The **Chiemsee,** which has long been popular, retains something of the quiet charm and strange melancholy that attracted Ludwig II in the last century. It was
24 here that he built the most sumptuous of his palaces, **Schloss Herrenchiemsee.** It was based on Louis XIV's great palace at Versailles. But this was the result of more than simple admiration of Versailles on Ludwig's part: with his name being the German for Louis, he was keen to establish that he, too, possessed the absolute authority of his namesake, the Sun King. As with most of Ludwig's projects, the building was never completed, and Ludwig was never able to stay in its state rooms. Nonetheless, what remains is impressive—and ostentatious. There are regular ferries out to the island from Stock, on the shore. If you want to make the journey in style, take the 100-year-old steam train—which glories in the name of Feuriger Elias, or Fiery Elias—from the neighboring town of Prien to Stock. A horse-drawn carriage takes you to the palace itself. The single most spectacular attraction in the palace is the Hall of Mirrors, a dazzling gallery (modeled on that at Versailles) where candle-lit concerts are held in the summer. Also of interest are the ornate bedroom Ludwig planned, and the stately formal gardens. The south wing houses a museum containing Ludwig's christening robe and death mask, as well as other artifacts of his life. *Palace and museum admission: DM 5 adults, DM 2.50 children. Open Apr.–Sept., daily 9–5; Oct.–Mar., daily 10–4.*

25 The smaller **Fraueninsel** (Ladies' Island) is a charming retreat. A Benedictine convent founded here 1,200 years ago now serves as a school. One of its earliest abbesses, Irmengard, daughter of King Ludwig der Deutscher, died here in the 9th century. Her grave was discovered in 1961. In the same year, early frescoes in the convent chapel were brought to light.

Just south of the Chiemsee, in a small, flat valley of the Chi-
26 emgauer Alps, is the enchanting village of **Aschau,** which lies in the protective shadow of a mighty castle, the 12th-century **Schloss Hohenaschau.** It is one of the few medieval castles in southern Germany to have been restored in the 17th century in Baroque style. The renovation gave its stately rooms a new elegance. Chamber-music concerts are presented regularly in the Rittersaal (Knights Hall) during the summer. *Tel. 08052/392. Admission: DM 1.50 adults, children free. Open May–Sept., Tues. and Fri. 9–5.*

At Aschau, you'll join the most scenic section of the Alpine Road, route B-305. It snakes through a series of towns and villages before ending at the Austrian border, just beyond Berchtesgaden. Rosenheim, Bad Reichenhall, and Berchtesgaden—all with good road connections to the rest of Germany—are ideal centers from which to explore this part of the Alps.

From Aschau, the Alpine Road heads into the mountains, passing through a string of villages—Bernau, Rottau, Grassau, Marquartstein, Unter- and Oberwössen—pretty enough to
27 make you want to linger. In summer, the farmhouses of **Rottau** virtually disappear behind facades of flowers, which have won
28 the village several awards. The houses of **Grassau** shrink beside

the bulk of the 15th-century church of the Ascension, worth visiting for its rich 17th-century stucco work. The 11th-century castle above Marquartstein is in private hands and can't be visited, so press on to the villages of Unter- and Oberwössen.

Time Out The **Hotel zur Post** at Unterwössen beckons the traveler at any time of day with strong coffee, delicious homemade pastries, locally brewed beer, and a menu that features some of the best of Bavarian fare.

Eight kilometers (5 miles) farther on, not much more than a snowball's throw from the Tyrolean border, lies the mountain
29 resort of **Reit im Winkl,** famous for the clarity of its light in summer and the depth of its snowfalls in winter. The Winklmoosalm mountain that towers above Reit im Winkl can be reached by bus or chair lift and is a popular ski area in winter and a great place for bracing upland walks in summer and fall.

The next stretch of the Alpine Road takes you past three shimmering mountain lakes—the Weitsee, the Mittersee, and the
30 Lödensee—before dropping down to busy **Ruhpolding,** once a quiet Alpine village and now a leading resort. This is where the Bavarian tourist boom began back in the '30s. Back then, tourists were welcomed at the train station by a brass band. The welcome isn't quite so extravagant these days, but it's still warm. In the 16th century, the Bavarian rulers journeyed out to Ruhpolding to hunt, and the Renaissance-style hunting lodge of Prince Wilhelm V still stands (it's now used for the offices of the local forestry service). The hillside 18th-century **Pfarrkirche St. Georg** (parish church of St. George) is one of the finest churches in the Bavarian Alps. In one of its side altars stands a rare 13th-century carved Madonna, the Ruhpoldinger Madonna. Note also the atmospheric crypt chapel in the quiet churchyard.

East of Ruhpolding lies a small portion of Bavaria that fits like a pocket into the fabric of Austrian territory that surrounds it on three sides. This southeastern corner of Germany is dominated by two resorts of international fame: Bad Reichenhall and Berchtesgaden. Although Berchtesgaden is more famous,
31 **Bad Reichenhall** is older and claims a more interesting history, thanks to the saline springs that made the town rich. The springs, which form Europe's largest saline source, were first tapped in pre-Christian times; the salt they provided in the Middle Ages supported the economies of cities as far away as Munich and Passau. King Ludwig I built an elaborate salt works and spa house here—the **Alte Saline** and **Quellenhaus**—in the early 19th century in vaulted, pseudo-medieval style. Their pump installations are astonishing examples of 19th-century engineering. *Admission: DM 3 adults, DM 1.50 children. Open daily 10–11:30 and 2–4.*

Bad Reichenhall even possesses a 19th-century "saline" chapel, part of the spa's facilities and built in exotic Byzantine style at the behest of Ludwig I. Salt is so much a part of the town that you can practically taste it in the air. Not surprisingly, most of the more expensive hotels offer special spa treatments based on the health-giving properties of the saline springs. The waters can also be taken in the attractive spa gardens throughout the year (Open Mon.–Sat. 8–12:15 and 3–5, Sun. and holidays 10–12:15). Bad Reichenhall's own symphony orchestra performs five days a week during the summer season and four days a week in winter. Like most resorts in the area, this one also has a casino. (*See* The Arts and Nightlife, below.)

It's ironic that Bad Reichenhall, which flourishes on the riches of its underground springs, has a 12th-century basilica dedicated to **St. Zeno,** patron saint of those imperiled by floods and the dangers of the deep. Much of this ancient church was remodeled in the 16th and 17th centuries, but some of the original cloisters remain.

32 **Berchtesgaden,** 18 kilometers (11 miles) south of Bad Reichenhall, is an ancient market town set in the noblest section of the Bavarian Alps. While as a high-altitude ski station it may not have quite the charm or cachet of Garmisch-Partenkirchen, in summer it serves as one of the region's most popular (and crowded) resorts, with top-rated attractions in a heavenly setting.

For American and British visitors, Berchtesgaden may have an image problem: Its name is indelibly linked to that of the notorious figure who terrorized much of the western world in the '30s and '40s—Adolf Hitler. Berchtesgaden was "Der Führer's" favorite mountain retreat. High on the slopes of Obersalzberg he built a luxurious headquarters hideaway, where many top-level Nazi staff meetings were held during World War II.

But Berchtesgaden had been a resort long before Hitler's time. Members of the ruling Wittelsbach dynasty started coming here in 1810. Their ornate palace stands today and is one of the town's major attractions, along with the former Nazi complex and a working salt mine.

Salt—or "white gold," as it was known in medieval times—was the basis of Berchtesgaden's wealth. In the 12th century the Emperor Barbarossa gave mining rights to a Benedictine abbey that had been founded here a century earlier. The abbey was secularized early in the 19th century, when it was taken over by the Wittelsbach rulers. The last royal resident, Crown Prince Rupprecht, who died here in 1955, furnished it with rare family treasures, which now form the basis of a permanent collection.

Königliches Schloss Berchtesgaden now serves as a museum. A number of fine Renaissance rooms provide the principal exhibition spaces for the Prince's collection of sacred art, which is particularly rich in wood sculptures by such great Renaissance artists as Tilman Riemanschneider and Veit Stoss. You can also visit the abbey's original, cavernous 13th-century dormitory and cool cloisters, which still convey something of the quiet and orderly life led by medieval monks. *Admission: DM 4.50 adults, DM 2 children. Open Easter–Sept., Sun.–Fri. 10–1 and 2–5; Oct.–Easter, Mon.–Fri. 10–1 and 2–5.*

The skill of wood carving in Berchtesgaden dates back to long before the time when Oberammergau established itself as the premier wood-carving center of the Alps. Examples of Berchtesgaden wood carvings and other local crafts are on display at one of the most interesting museums of its kind in the Alps, the *Heimatmuseum. Schroffenbergerallee 6. Admission: DM 3 adults, DM 1 children. Open Mon.–Fri.; with guided tours at 10 and 3.*

For many travelers, the pièce de résistance of a Berchtesgaden stay might well be a visit to its salt mine, the *Salzbergwerk*. In the days when the mine was owned by Berchtesgaden's princely rulers, only selected guests were allowed to see how the source of the city's wealth was won from the earth. Today, DM 11.50 will buy anyone a tour of the installation. Dressed in traditional miner's clothing, visitors sit astride a miniature train that transports them nearly half a mile into the mountain to an enormous chamber where the salt is mined. A couple of rides down wooden chutes used by the miners to get from one level to another, and a boat ride on an underground saline lake the size of a football field are included in the 1½-hour tour. *1 mi from Berchtesgaden on the B-305 Salzburg Rd. Admission: DM 11.50 adults, DM 6.50 children. Open May–mid-Oct., daily 8:30–5; mid-Oct.–Apr., Mon.–Sat. 10:30–3:30.*

For an experience of a different kind, a bus takes visitors up in
33 summer to **Obersalzberg,** site of Hitler's luxurious mountain retreat on the northern slope of the Hoher Goll. The hairpin bends of Germany's highest road lead to the base of the 6,000-foot peak on which sat the so-called Adlerhorst or Eagle's Nest, the Kehlsteinhaus. Hitler had the road built in 1937–39. It climbs more than 2,000 feet in less than 4 miles, and comes to an end at a lot that clings to the mountain about 500 feet below the Kehlsteinhaus. A tunnel in the mountain brings you to an elevator that whisks you up to the Kehlsteinhaus—and what appears to be the top of the world. There are refreshment rooms and a restaurant where you can steel yourself for the giddy descent to Berchtesgaden. The round-trip takes about an hour and costs DM 21.20 (half fare for children). A cable car also runs from Berchtesgaden to Obersalzberg (round-trip is DM 11 adults, DM 5.50 children).

The view from the Kehlsteinhaus is stunning: The jagged Watzmann slumbers above Berchtesgaden and, when the light and the mood are right, it's quite possible to believe the atavistic myth that surrounds the mountain. According to an ancient saga, the Watzmann range of nine distinct peaks is actually a royal family turned to stone by an angry god; their blood forms the two mountain lakes, the Obersee and the Königsee.

Both lakes lie within the Berchtesgaden National Park, 210 square kilometers of wild mountain country where flora and fauna have been left to develop as nature intended. The Berchtesgaden park is modeled on the United States' Yellowstone National Park; no roads penetrate the area, and even the mountain paths are difficult to follow. The National Park administration organizes guided tours of the area from June till September (contact the Nationalparkverwaltung, Doktorberg 6, 8240 Berchtesgaden, tel. 08652/61068).

One less-strenuous way into the National Park is by boat. A fleet of 21 excursion boats, electrically driven so that no noise
34 disturbs the peace of the lake, operate on the **Königsee.** Only the skipper of the boat is allowed to shatter the silence with a trumpet fanfare to demonstrate the lake's remarkable echo. The notes from the trumpet bounce back and forth from the almost vertical cliffs that plunge into the dark, green water. A cross on a rocky promontory marks the spot where a boatload of pilgrims hit the cliffs 100 years ago and sank. The voyagers, most of whom drowned, were on their way to the tiny, twin-

towered Baroque chapel of St. Bartholomä, built in the 17th century on a peninsula where an early Gothic church once stood. The princely rulers of Berchtesgaden built a hunting lodge at the side of the chapel; its rooms now serve as a tavern and a restaurant.

A narrow channel connects the Königsee and the Obersee. The
35 **Obersee** rivals the larger lake for sheer beauty. Its backdrop of jagged mountains and precipitous cliffs is broken by a waterfall, the Rothbachfall, that plunges more than 1,000 feet to the valley floor. *Boat service on the Königsee runs year-round, (except when the lake freezes over). Service operates to Obersee only in summer. Round-trips can be interrupted at St. Bartholomä and the Obersee. Full round-trip fare DM 15 adults, DM 7.50 children.*

What to See and Do with Children

If it's winter, rent skis or a sled from any resort sports shop and make for the slopes. Bayerischzell, Lengries, Neuhaus am Schliersee, and Oberammergau have excellent facilities for young beginners. Wishing you could take a **sleigh ride** through the snow? Call Harold Zischk at Bad Wiessee (tel. 08022/81096). His 2-hour tour high above the Tegernsee costs DM 23 for adults and DM 15 for children; on evening trips he serves mulled wine.

If it's summer, head for any of the lakes or, if the water's not warm enough for **swimming,** try one of the numerous lidos. The finest lidos are at Garmisch, Oberammergau, Kochel, Bad Tölz, and Penzberg. Also in summer, the ski slopes on the **Blomberg** mountain outside Bad Tölz create one of Europe's longest dry toboggan runs. You hurtle at great speed for nearly a mile down the mountain on a wheeled toboggan.

In winter, children can accompany foresters to **feed deer** at several points in the Alps. For Garmisch, tel. 08821/2038 or 08821/2135; Oberammergau, tel. 08822/515 or 08824/422; Schliersee, tel. 08026/356 or 08026/392; Ruhpolding, tel. 08663/1227.

For the very young, there's a charming **fairy-tale park** (Märchenwald) at Wolfratshausen, about 20 kilometers (12 miles) north of Bad Tölz on the B-11. Mechanical tableaux tell 24 favorite fairy tales in German and English. *Admission: DM 5 adults, DM 4 children. Open daily 9–5.*

Off the Beaten Track

On weekends year-round, Bavarian Alps resorts can be uncomfortably crowded. But there are still valleys and peaks where you can find solitude. Avoid anyplace with a cable car or funicular railway. Travel by water whenever possible. Board a boat at **Königsee,** for instance, and glide silently between the cliffs that plunge into the lake; then leave your fellow passengers behind at one of the two stopping points and strike out into **Berchtesgaden National Park.** No roads penetrate it, and the few hiking trails are refreshingly uncrowded. The Königsee itself is crowded at the resort end, but there are other lakes in the region where you can get away from it all. Try the **Wagingersee,** Germany's warmest lake. For campers, this is the place to pitch a tent.

Looking to trace your German roots? The **Deutsches Wappenmuseum** (Jennerbahnstr. 30, Königsee) has 4,000 German coats of arms and heraldic emblems, and can assist in ancestor-tracing. There are no fixed opening hours, so call (tel. 08652/61910) before visiting.

In the village of Hasslberg near Ruhpolding you can visit a 300-year-old **bell foundry,** now a fascinating museum of the ancient craft of the foundryman and blacksmith. *Admission: DM 2 adults, DM 4 children. Open Mon.–Sat. 10–noon and 2–4.*

Shopping

Berchtesgaden and Oberammergau have centuries-old **wood-carving** traditions. In both towns and in surrounding villages you'll find shops crammed with the work of local craftsmen. In Berchtesgaden, there's a central selling point at **Schloss Adelsheim** (Schroffenbergallee). Berchtesgaden is famous for its "Spanschachtel," delicate, finely constructed wood boxes made to contain everything from pins and needles to top hats. You'll find modern versions in every souvenir shop and, if you're lucky, you might even come across a 100-year-old example in one of the town's antique shops. In Oberammergau, you can buy wood carvings directly from craftsmen who demonstrate their skills from April to June and September to November in a "living workshop" at the **Pilatushaus** (Verlegergasse).

The **flowers** and **herbs** that grow in the Bavarian Alps have healing properties, and some long-established "apothecaries" put together herbal mixtures that are redolent of the elixir of life. **Josef Mack KG** (Innsbruckerstr. 37, Bad Reichenhall) has been in this business since 1856; **Dricoolo KG** (Ludwigstr. 27, Bad Reichenhall) is another established herb vendor. In Ruhpolding, there's an herb garden at **Gastehaus Jürgant** (Branderstr. 23a) where visitors can pick the basic ingredients of the preparations on sale, which include a potent herbal liqueur.

It's not the kind of gift every visitor wants to take home, but just in case you'd like a violin, cello, or even a double bass from a town that has been making these instruments for centuries—Mittenwald—the place to try is **Walther Georg** (Isarauenstr. 17). For traditional Bavarian costumes—dirndls, embroidered shirts and blouses, and lederhosen—try the **Trachtenstub'n** (Obermarkt 35, Mittenwald) or any of the **Dollinger** shops throughout southern Bavaria. In Ruhpolding the **Handweberei Fegg** (Seehauserstr. 33) turns out Bavarian-style tablecloths and furniture coverings directly from the loom.

Sports and Fitness

Bicycling Most local rail stations rent bikes for about DM 10 a day (half that if you have a valid train ticket). Many local sports shops also have bikes for rent: **Sport Eich** (Fendtgasse 5, Oberammergau) and **Sport Bittner** (Andreas-Fendt-Ring 1, Bischofswiesen, near Berchtesgaden) are two. The Bavarian regional tourist office in Munich (*see* Important Addresses, above) issues a regularly updated booklet on recommended cycling routes. A particularly striking route runs 32 kilometers (19 miles) between the resorts of Reit im Winkl, Ruhpolding, and Inzell. Bikes can be rented from the rail station at Ruhpolding.

Bowling Many resort hotels have their own bowling alleys (usually for English-style skittles; rarely tenpin). The **Hotel Bayerischer Hof** in Bad Reichenhall (tel. 08651/5084) organizes skittle weeks from March to June. The DM 535 cost includes half-pension, unlimited skittling, and two competitions with prizes.

Golf There are American-run golf courses at **Gmund,** on the Tegernsee, and at **Obersalzberg** (tel. 08652/2100) in Berchtesgaden. The latter has nine holes, set 3,300 feet up, and a distracting view of the Watzmann range. It is open for play from May through October. A spectacular 18-hole course is located at **Bad Wiessee,** high above the Tegernsee (tel. 08022/8769).

Hang gliding See the Alps from above. If hang gliding's your thing, Oberammergau's your place (tel. 08822/520 or 08822/4470).

Hiking The Bavarian Alps are veined with networks of marked paths. You can set off from just about any resort and find a number of scenic routes to follow. Check with local tourist office personnel for advice on the difficulty of various routes, and find out whether they have walking-tour maps. Oberammergau is an ideal starting point for hiking tours into the surrounding mountains. There are a variety of paths to choose from. Each year, on August 24, visitors can take part in an organized Mountain Hiking Day *(Gibirgswandertag)* called "In King Ludwig's Footsteps" in memory of Bavaria's "Dream King." At dusk, huge bonfires are set ablaze on surrounding mountains.

Mountain Climbing The Zugspitze climbing school in Garmisch-Partenkirchen (tel. 08824/344) organizes courses in rock climbing, ski touring, and deep-snow skiing, and provides guides for walking, skiing, or climbing tours of one day or longer. In the Berchtesgaden area, tel. 08652/2420 or 08652/5371.

Skiing The Bavarian Alps are Germany's winter playground. All you have to do is choose your resort and everything is laid out: ski rentals, ski school, lifts, and transportation. Vacations can be enjoyed for as little as DM 300. Contact local tourist offices for details. If you're a Nordic skier, match your speed against Bavaria's best in Oberammergau's annual "King Ludwig Race," held the first weekend in February. Oberammergau also hosts events over distances of 6 kilometers (4 miles) and 15 kilometers (9 miles) every Wednesday during the winter season.

Swimming The lakes are warm enough in summer for swimming, but Bavaria has fine lidos for year-round fun in the water. The best are in Garmisch-Partenkirchen, Oberammergau, Kochel, Penzberg, and Bad Tölz (*see* Exploring, above).

Water Sports **Sailing** schools can be found everywhere on Bavaria's lakes. **Captain Glas** (tel. 08157/8100) at Possenhofen on the western shore of the Starnbergersee has one of the largest fleets and can fix you up with anything from a small sailboat to a cabin cruiser. Surfboards can be hired for DM 15 an hour from the boat yard at **Seeshaupt** at the southern end of the lake, and for a similar fee at innumerable points on this and other lakes.

Dining and Lodging

Dining

Specialties here are much the same as in the rest of Bavaria, but local dishes to try are *Forelle* (trout), and *Lachsforelle* and *Bachsaibing* (freshwater salmon-trout). If you visit Chiemsee, try *Rekne* (a type of whitefish found only here).

Highly recommended restaurants are indicated by a star ★.

Category	Cost*
Very Expensive	over DM 90
Expensive	DM 55–DM 90
Moderate	DM 35–DM 55
Inexpensive	under DM 35

**per person for a three-course meal, including tax and tip but not wine*

Lodging

With few exceptions, all hotels and Gasthäuser in the Bavarian Alps and lower Alpine regions are traditionally styled, low-roofed chalets with wood balconies and multi-colored masses of flowers in summer. Standards are high, even in simpler lodgings. The choice is wide, from super-luxurious, world-class hotels to basic Gasthofs. Garmisch-Partenkirchen and Berchtesgaden are bountifully supplied with accommodations in all price ranges. Check out the special seven-day packages. Away from the main tourist centers you may sometimes be able to find accommodations for as little as DM 15. As a general rule, the farther from the Alps you stay, the lower the rates will be.

Highly recommended hotels are indicated by a star ★.

Category	Cost*
Very Expensive	over DM 180
Expensive	DM 120–DM 180
Moderate	DM 80–DM 120
Inexpensive	under DM 80

**For two people in a double room, including tax and service charge.*

Bad Reichenhall
Lodging

Alpenhotel Fuchs. Beautifully located outside the town amid Alpine meadows, with the mountain range at its back, the Fuchs assures guests they can sit out on its southern terrace and soak up the sun even in mid-winter. Inside, they can soak up the Bavarian style of the public rooms. *Nonn 50, tel. 08651/61048 or 08651/61049. 37 rooms, 35 with bath. Facilities: solarium, tennis courts, restaurant. AE, DC, MC, V. Closed Nov. 1–Dec. 22. Moderate.*

Hotel Bayerischer Hof. Centrally located (a short walk from the train station), this is a quiet, modern hotel with style and the expected Alpine atmosphere. *Bahnhofpl. 14, tel. 08651/5084. 64 rooms with bath or shower. Facilities: indoor pool, sauna, solarium, health farm with resident doctor, nightclub, restaurant. AE, DC, MC, V. Closed Jan. 5–Feb. 20. Moderate.*

Hotel Tiroler Hof. The '50s look of the Tiroler Hof does less than justice to the comforts within, where Alpine style combines with modern facilities. There's a charming, flower-covered courtyard for morning coffee or evening drinks. *Tirolerstr. 12, tel. 08651/2055. 45 rooms with bath or shower. Facilities: indoor pool, solarium, restaurant. AE, DC, MC, V. Moderate.*

Hotel Garni Carola. This is a modern, friendly hotel with basic comforts. There's no restaurant, but the town's pedestrian shopping area, with its restaurants and taverns, is nearby. *Friedrich Ebert Allee 6, tel. 08651/2629. 20 rooms, 15 with shower. No credit cards. Closed Nov. 1–Feb. 20. Inexpensive.*

Bad Tölz
Lodging
★ **Hotel Jodquellenhof.** *Jodquellen* are the iodine springs that have made Bad Tölz wealthy. You can take advantage of these revitalizing waters at this luxurious spa hotel. The imposing 19th-century building contains rooms of comfort and style. *Ludwigstr. 15, tel. 08041/5091. 78 rooms and 3 suites with bath. Facilities: outdoor and indoor pools, sauna, solarium, restaurant. AE, DC, MC, V. Expensive.*

Bad Wiessee
Dining
★ **Freihaus Brenner.** Proprietor and chef Josef Brenner has brought a taste of nouvelle cuisine to the shores of the Tegernsee, where his attractive restaurant sits, commanding fine views. Try any of his suggested dishes—they range from wild rabbit in elderberry sauce to fresh lake fish. *Freihausstr. 4, tel. 08022/82004. Reservations advised. Jacket and tie optional. MC. Moderate.*

Lodging
Hotel Rex. Standing high above the Tegernsee and backed by mountains, the Hotel Rex is ideal for those who value solitude and solid comfort. Fine Bavarian antiques give the hotel a special flair. *Münchnerstr. 25, tel. 08022/82091. 56 rooms and 2 suites with bath or shower. Facilities: restaurant (for guests only). No credit cards. Closed Nov. 1–Apr. 15. Expensive.*

Bergen
Lodging
★ **Hotel Säulner Hof.** A cheery wood-burning fire in the open fireplace, a cozy bar, and the enveloping comfort of thick rugs and brightly painted Bavarian antiques welcome the winter visitor to the Säulner Hof. In summer it also has attractions, not least of which is its ample terrace, with views of the mountains. *Säulnerweg 1, tel. 08662/8655. 15 rooms with bath or shower. Facilities: restaurant, bar. V. Closed Nov. Inexpensive.*

Berchtesgaden
Dining
Alpenhotel Denninglehen. Non-smokers will appreciate the special dining room set aside just for them in this mountain hotel's restaurant. The restaurant is 3,000 feet up in the resort area of Oberau, just outside Berchtesgaden, and its terrace offers magnificent views. *8240 Berchtesgaden-Oberau, tel. 08652/5085. Reservations advised. Dress: informal. No credit cards. Closed Dec. 1–20. Moderate.*

★ **Hotel-Restaurant Geiger.** Dine at this paneled, Bavarian-style restaurant under the baleful eyes of hunting trophies in the cozy Bauernstube, or enjoy the more elegant, antique-furnished Beidermeier Salon. The Geiger is a 15-minute bus ride from the center of town—and well worth the trip. *Stanggass,* *tel. 08652/5055. Reservations advised. Jacket and tie optional. AE, DC, V. Closed mid-Nov.–mid-Dec. Moderate.*

Hotel Post. This is a centrally located and solidly reliable hostelry with a well-presented international menu. If fish from the nearby Königsee is offered, order it. In summer you can eat in the beer garden. The Casablanca bar is ideal for a pre-meal aperitif. *Maximilianstr. 2, tel. 08652/5067. Reservations advised. Jacket and tie optional. AE, DC, MC, V. Moderate.*

Gasthof Bier Adam. Quality Bavarian fare served with style and care is what will draw you to the Bier Adam. *Marktpl. 22, tel. 08652/2390. No reservations. Dress: informal. AE, DC, MC, V. Closed Wed. in winter. Inexpensive.*

Lodging

Hotel Geiger. Early Victorian antiques and Bavarian peasant pieces mix well in the luxurious interior of this mountain hotel on the outskirts of town. *Stanggass, tel. 08652/5055. 40 rooms, 8 apartments, and 3 suites with bath. Facilities: indoor and outdoor pools, sauna, solarium, fitness room, restaurant. AE, DC, V. Closed Nov. Expensive.*

Stoll's Hotel Alpina. Set above the Königsee in the delightful little village of Schönau, the Alpina offers rural solitude and easy access to Berchtesgaden. Families are catered to: There are special family-size apartments and a playroom. *8240 Schonau am Konigsee, tel. 08652/5091. 41 rooms and 4 apartments, most with bath. Facilities: indoor and outdoor pools, sauna, solarium, sunbathing lawn, health farm, restaurant. AE, DC, MC, V. Closed Nov. 4–Dec. 17. Expensive.*

★ **Vier Jahreszeiten Hotel.** This centrally located, comfortably solid old hotel has been owned by the same family for more than 100 years. Antique furniture and an understated Bavarian accent make it a favorite. *Maximilianstr. 20, tel. 08652/5026. 62 rooms and 3 apartments with bath or shower. Facilities: indoor pool, sauna, solarium, fitness room, restaurant. AE, DC, MC, V. Expensive.*

Hotel-Café Grassl. Centrally located, the Grassl commands fine views. All the rooms are large and traditionally furnished, but ask for one away from the main street, which can be noisy. There's no restaurant, but the in-house café serves excellent pastries from its own bakery. *Maximilianstr. 15, tel. 08652/4071. 32 rooms, some with bath or shower. AE, DC, MC, V. Moderate.*

Hotel Watzmann. The USAAF Director of Operations in Berchtesgaden awarded the Hotel Watzmann a special certificate of appreciation for its hospitality to American servicemen. They, in turn, appreciate its cozy Bavarian style and good restaurant. *Franziskanerpl., tel. 08652/2055. 37 rooms, half with shower. Facilities: heated garden-terrace, restaurant. AE, MC, V. Closed Nov. 1–Dec. 22. Inexpensive.*

Weiherbach. Skiers are well cared for by the Weiherbach, which is near to cross-country trails and a five-minute walk from a ski lift. For summer visitors, there's a sunbathing lawn. *Weiherbachweg 6, tel. 08652/2333. 22 rooms, most with shower. No credit cards. Closed Nov. 3–Dec. 20. Inexpensive.*

Hotel zum Türken. The 10-minute bus or taxi ride from Berchtesgaden is worth it for the view from this quiet, comfortable little hotel on the Obersaltzberg mountain. *8240 Obersalzberg-Berchtesgaden, tel. 08652/2428. 17 rooms, half with bath or shower. AE, DC, MC, V. Closed Nov. 1–Dec. 20. Inexpensive.*

Chiemsee

Lodging

Pension Jägerhof. This comfortable, well-appointed pension is only 100 yards from the Chiemsee, in the village of Gstadt.

Breitbrunnerstr. 5. tel. 08054/242. 30 rooms, 11 with bath or shower. Facilities: sauna, solarium, fitness room. AE, DC, MC, V. Closed Nov. 1–Mar. Inexpensive.

Unterwirt zu Chieming. You can catch the boat to the islands of the Chiemsee right outside this small pension in the village of Chieming. It's located practically on the water's edge. *Hauptstr. 32, tel. 08664/551. 20 rooms, 8 with bath. No credit cards. Closed Oct. 21–Nov. 25. Inexpensive.*

Ettal
Dining

Bayerische Stube. Fresh mountain trout—Forelle—is the specialty of the Hotel Benediktenhof's traditional Bavarian restaurant. Try the venison when it's in season. *Zieglerstr. 1, tel. 08822/4637. Reservations advised. Dress: informal. No credit cards. Closed Nov. 1–Dec. 22. Moderate.*

★ **Hotel Ludwig der Bayer.** If the hotel's Bräustuberl is full, try it's neighboring Klosterstube. There should be a pillared, paneled corner where you can enjoy a plate of pork knuckle, Bavarian dumplings, and a mug of home-brewed beer. Wash it down with the locally distilled liqueur. *Kaiser Ludwig Pl. 10, tel. 08822/6601. Reservations advised. Dress: informal. No credit cards. Closed Nov. 9–Dec. 22. Moderate.*

Poststüberl, Hotel Zur Post. The most expensive midday meal in Andreas Fischer's Poststüberl is DM 20. This hearty fare and a mug of locally brewed beer will set you up for the rest of the day in the mountains around Ettal. *Kaiser Ludwig Pl. 18, tel. 08822/596. No reservations. Dress: informal. AE, DC, MC, V. Closed Nov. 10–Dec. 20. Inexpensive.*

Lodging

Benediktenhof. The open beams and colorfully painted walls are part of this former farmstead's 250-year history. Bedrooms are furnished in Bavarian Baroque or peasant style, with brightly decorated cupboards and bedsteads. *Zieglerstr. 1, tel. 08822/4637. 16 rooms and 1 apartment with bath or shower. Facilities: restaurant. No credit cards. Closed Nov. 1–Dec. 22. Moderate.*

★ **Hotel Ludwig der Bayer.** This large, comfortable hotel is run by the Benedictine order from the monastery across the road. There's nothing monastic about the furnishings, however, except for the carved religious figures that share the space with some fine antiques. *Kaiser Ludwig Pl. 10, tel. 08822/6601. 65 rooms with bath or shower. Facilities: indoor pool, sauna, solarium, card room, bowling alleys, restaurant. No credit cards. Closed Nov. 9–Dec. 20. Moderate.*

Hotel-Gasthof Zur Post. The Post is a comfortable, well-run Bavarian-style Gasthof located in the center of Ettal. *Kaiser Ludwig Pl. 18, tel. 08822/596. 18 rooms and 4 apartments, most with bath or shower. AE, DC, MC, V. Closed Nov. 10–Dec. 20. Moderate.*

Garmisch-Partenkirchen
Dining

★ **Posthotel Partenkirchen.** Hand-carved wood paneling encloses you in the rustic elegance of the Posthotel's restaurant. Traditional Bavarian dishes share the menu with Swiss and French regional specialties. *Ludwigstr. 49, tel. 08821/2075. Reservations advised. Jacket and tie optional. AE, MC, V. Expensive.*

Rotisserie Mühlenstube. Fresh salt-water fish in Upper Bavaria? It's possible at the Rotisserie Mühlenstube thanks to the restaurant's special salt-water tanks. The menu shows many other touches of individuality. *Mühlstr. 22, tel. 08821/7040. Reservations advised. Jacket and tie optional. AE, DC, MC, V. Expensive.*

Werdenfelser Hof. The picturesque exterior of this old Bavarian inn hides a restaurant of charm and style. Specialities from the neighboring Austrian province of Tyrol share the menu with such traditional Bavarian dishes as *Schweinshaxe. Ludwigstr. 58, tel. 08821/3621. Reservations advised. Dress: informal. DC, MC. Closed Thurs. Moderate.*

Stahl's Badstubn. Dive into a good, inexpensive meal here. The place is part of Garmisch's Alpspitz swimming lido and has made a big splash among the locals. Order from a menu that's nearly as long as the Olympic-size pool. *Klammstr. 47, tel. 08821/58700. Reservations advised. Dress: informal. No credit cards. Inexpensive.*

Lodging

★ **Clausings Posthotel.** This is one of the Romantik group—and romantic it certainly is, from the enveloping luxury of its rooms to its pastel pink Baroque facade, which faces Garmisch's central Marienplatz. The range of rare antiques in the public rooms is remarkable. *Marienpl. 12, tel. 08821/58071. 31 rooms, most with bath or shower. Facilities: Dance orchestra, beer garden, restaurant. AE, DC, MC. Expensive.*

Hotel Partenkirchner Hof. Located in the Partenkirchen section of town, this comfortable, well-appointed hotel combines elegance with a rustic, Bavarian touch. Its Reindl Grill is considered one of Bavaria's top restaurants. *Bahnhofstr. 15, tel. 08821/58025. 80 rooms with bath; 14 apartments in the Wetterstein annex. Facilities: indoor pool, sauna, beauty farm, restaurant. AE, DC, MC, V. Closed Nov. 15–Dec. 15. Expensive.*

★ **Kurhotel Bernrieder Hof.** Originally a farmhouse, the Bernrieder Hof has been transformed into one of Garmisch's most elegant hotels, complete with marble bathrooms. Spa treatments are available. *Von-Müller-Str. 12, tel. 08821/71074. 41 rooms with bath. Facilities: sauna, fitness room, medical facilities, restaurant. AE, DC, MC, V. Expensive.*

★ **Obermühle Hotel.** An ancient water wheel welcomes you at the front of the Obermühle, indicating the history of this charming old hotel, which dates back to 1634. It's quiet, set in its own park only five minutes from the town center. *Mühlstr. 22, tel. 08821/7040. 88 rooms, 6 apartments, and 4 suites, most with bath. Facilities: indoor pool, sauna, solarium, wine tavern. AE, DC, MC, V. Expensive.*

Hotel Aschenbrenner. The mountains rear up around this country-house hotel. Belle Epoque furnishings give it a comfortable elegance. There's no restaurant, but a generous breakfast buffet is served and evening snacks can be ordered. *Loisachstr. 65A, tel. 08821/58028. 24 rooms and 1 suite, most with bath. AE, DC, MC, V. Moderate.*

Hotel Garmischer Hof. Situated in the town center, within easy reach of the train and cable car stations, the swimming pool, and the spa park, the Garmischer Hof is a comfortable, traditional hotel, with an appealing garden and fine views. There's no restaurant. *Bahnhofstr. 53, tel. 08821/51091. 43 rooms with bath or shower. AE, DC, MC. Moderate.*

Gästehaus Kornmüller. American visitors are particularly fond of the Kornmüller, a traditional Bavarian guest house on the outskirts of town. *Höllentalstr. 36, tel. 08821/3557. 32 rooms, 8 apartments, and 4 suites, most with bath. AE, MC, V. Inexpensive.*

Grainau
Lodging
★

Hotel Post. Overshadowed by Germany's highest mountain, the mighty Zugspitze, the Post is set in some of the finest Bavarian countryside; two small, pretty lakes are only a short walk away. Bedrooms are large and airy; public rooms are comfortably furnished in the style of a country house. *Ober Grainau, tel. 08821/8853. 33 rooms and 7 apartments with bath or shower. Facilities: restaurant (for hotel guests only). AE, DC, MC. Closed Oct. 20–Dec. 20 and Jan. 10–Feb. 1. Moderate.*

Grassau
Dining

Sperrer. You'll have to tear yourself away from the magnificent mountain views here in order to study the menu. Solid Bavarian fare dominates it. Try the roast pork at any time; in summer, have it served in the Sperrer's pretty garden. *Ortenburgerstr. 5, tel. 08641/5011. Reservations advised. Dress: informal. No credit cards. Closed Mon. and Nov. Moderate.*

Hirschegg
Lodging
★

Hotel Walserhof. Hirschegg is located right on the German-Austrian border at the end of the lovely Kleinwalsertal Valley. The Walserhof looks one way toward Austria; the other way toward Germany. It's a four-star establishment, extremely comfortable, and has homey touches that make it special. *D-8985 Hirschegg/Kleinwalsertal, tel. 08329/5684. 28 rooms, 4 apartments, and 4 suites with bath. Facilities: indoor pool, sauna, solarium, fitness center, tennis court, restaurant. No credit cards. Closed Nov. 2–Dec. 15. Expensive.*

Kochel
Lodging

Alpenhotel Schmied von Kochel. The Schmied von Kochel (Blacksmith of Kochel) was a local folk hero, and the use of his name is one of several traditional touches that distinguish this 100-year-old Alpine-style hotel. A zither player can be heard most evenings in the intimate restaurant. *Schlehdorferstr. 6, tel. 08851/216. 34 rooms with bath or shower. Facilities: solarium, restaurant. MC, V. Moderate.*

Lenggries
Dining

Arabella Brauneck Hotel. Chef Rainer Maier offers Tuscan menus alongside Bavarian fare in the stylish dining room of this resort hotel. *Münchnerstr. 25, tel. 08042/2021. Reservations advised. Dress: informal. AE, DC, MC, V. Moderate.*

Mittenwald
Dining
★

Alpenrose. Drop in during the fall for the best venison you'll taste in these parts: The whole of October is devoted to venison dishes. Hearty Bavarian fare is offered year-round. *Obermarkt 1. tel. 08823/5055. Reservations advised. Dress: informal. Moderate.*

Post Hotel. Pause at the cozy bar for an aperitif and to make the difficult choice between the Post's wine tavern and its rustic Poststüberl. In summer, the charming terrace is the best spot. The menu offers mostly traditional Bavarian fare. *Obermarkt 9, tel. 08823/1094. Reservations advised. Dress: informal. No credit cards. Moderate.*

Lodging

Post Hotel. The 17th-century Post is the oldest and most attractive hotel in town. *Obermarkt 9, tel. 08823/1094. 90 rooms, 10 apartments, and 4 suites, most with bath. Facilities: indoor pool, sauna, solarium, restaurant. No credit cards. Expensive.*

Hotel Rieger. A rustic Bavarian hotel of great charm, the Rieger boasts modern health/cure facilities and deep-pile comfort. *Dekan-Karl-Pl. 28, tel. 08823/5071. 46 rooms with bath or shower. Facilities: indoor pool, sauna, solarium, restaurant. AE, DC, MC, V. Closed Nov.–3rd week of Dec. Moderate.*

Murnau
Lodging

Regina Hotel. From your balcony at the Regina you'll have a sweeping view of the Alps. The hotel is located on the edge of a park, within easy driving distance of the mountains and several lakes. *Seidlpark 2, tel. 08841/2011. 60 rooms and 2 suites with bath or shower. Facilities: indoor swimming pool, sauna, solarium, fitness room, bowling alley, restaurant. AE, DC, MC. Expensive.*

Oberammergau
Dining

Hotel Alois Lang. "Für Jeden Etwas" ("Something for all tastes") is the Alois Lang's motto. In fact, however, the real reason for eating here is the venison, specialty of chef Reinhard Michels. *St. Lukasstr. 15, tel. 08822/4141. Reservations advised. Dress: informal. AE, DC, MC, V. Moderate.*

Ammergauer Stubn. A homey beer tavern, the Stubn, located in the Wittelsbach hotel, offers a comprehensive menu that combines Bavarian specialties with international dishes. *Dorfstr. 21, tel. 08822/4545. Reservations advised. Dress: informal. AE, DC, MC. Closed Tues. and Nov. 7–Dec. 20. Moderate.*

Hotel Wolf. The restaurant of the Wolf hotel serves regional dishes in a traditional Bavarian ambience. Try the venison when it's in season, or the fat mountain trout at any time of year. *Dorfstr. 1, tel. 08822/6971. Reservations advised. Dress: informal. AE, DC, MC. Moderate.*

Lodging

Hotel Alois Lang. You should have no problem finding the Alois Lang, at least in summer: Its name is emblazened in the brilliant flower beds surrounding the large, Alpine-style building. Most of the rooms have balconies with fine views of the Ammergauer Alps. *St. Lukasstr. 15, tel. 08822/4141. 44 rooms with bath or shower. Facilities: sauna, solarium, restaurant. AE, DC, MC, V. Expensive.*

Hotel Turm Wirt. Rich wood paneling reaches from floor to ceiling in this popular and historic old hotel, located in the shadow of Oberammergau's mountain, the Kofel. The hotel's own band presents regular Bavarian folk evenings. *Ettalerstr. 2, tel. 08822/4291. 22 rooms with bath. Facilities: restaurant. AE, DC, MC, V. Closed Jan. 10–30. Moderate.*

★ **Hotel Wolf.** Americans in particular value this attractive old hotel—about 30% of guests are from the United States. Blue shutters punctuate its white walls; the steeply gabled upper stories bloom with flowers. *Dorfstr. 1, tel. 08822/6971. 31 rooms with bath. Facilities: outdoor pool, sauna, solarium, restaurant. AE, DC, MC, V. Moderate.*

Hotel-Gasthof Zur Rose. The Rose offers good value and great views. In addition to rooms in the main building, it has 10 apartments in two annexes. *Dedlerstr. 9, tel. 08822/4706. 29 rooms, most with bath. Facilities: restaurant. AE, DC, MC, V. Closed Nov. 1–Dec. 15. Inexpensive.*

Reit im Winkl
Dining

Kupferkanne. Outside, a garden surrounds the building; inside, you could be in an Alpine farmstead. The food is good country fare enhanced by some interesting Austrian specialties. Try the *Salzburger Brez'n* (spicy hard rolls) soup. *Weitseestr. 18, tel. 08640/1450. Reservations advised. Dress: informal. DC, MC. Closed Sat. and Nov. Inexpensive.*

Rosenheim
Dining

★ **Rossetti.** An Italian restaurant in Bavaria? There are plenty, of course, in Munich, but the Rossetti in out-of-the-way Rosenheim bears comparison with the best. Elegant without pretensions, it's attractively set in a turn-of-the-century villa. If you fancy pasta other than Swabian noodles, this is the place.

Münchenerstr. 66, tel. 08031/33388. Reservations advised. Jacket and tie optional. DC, MC, V. Closed Mon. Moderate.

Ruhpolding
Dining

Zur Post. Look for the Zur Post sign in any Bavarian town or village and you can be confident of abundant food. Ruhpolding's Zur Post is no exception. In business for more than 650 years, it has been in the hands of the same family for 150 years. *Hauptstr. 35, tel. 08663/1035. No reservations. Dress: informal. MC. Closed Wed. Inexpensive.*

Schliersee
Dining

Ratskeller. This is the place to meet the locals, who place more value on good, wholesome food than on chic furnishings. The menu is as solidly Bavarian as the decor: cabbage rolls, boiled beef, pork knuckle, and dumplings as large as your fists. *Rathausstr. 1a, tel. 08026/4786. No reservations. Dress: informal (or traditional Bavarian). No credit cards. Closed Mon., Feb., and last 3 weeks in Nov. Inexpensive.*

Seeon-Seebruck
Dining

Lambachhof. This fine old Bavarian homestead stands right on the banks of the Chiemsee, so fresh lake fish figures prominently on the menu. The Lambachhof also rears its own lambs, using only natural fodder; its roast lamb is exceptional. *Lambach 8–10, tel. 08667/427. Reservations advised. Dress: informal. No credit cards. Closed Tues. in May–Oct., and Dec. through Jan. Moderate.*

Tegernsee
Dining

Fischerstüberl am See. Fresh fish from the lake is the staple dish at this waterside hotel-restaurant, owned and run by the Götz family for almost a century. *Seestr. 51. tel. 08022/4672. Reservations advised. Dress: informal. No credit cards. Closed mid-Nov.–Dec. 24 and mid-Jan.–Feb. 20. Moderate.*

Seehotel Zur Post. This is another lakeside hotel-restaurant, with a fine winter garden and terrace. Fresh lake fish is recommended, but chef Hartmut Münchof would also like you to try some of his special creations, such as avocado salad. *Seestr. 3, tel. 08022/3951. Reservations advised. Dress: informal. AE, DC, MC, V. Closed last 3 weeks of Jan. Moderate.*

★ **Herzogliches Bräustuberl.** Once a monastery, then a royal retreat, the Bräustuberl is now a brewery-restaurant and popular excursion destination. If you're anywhere near the Tegernsee, seek it out. The food is simple but wholesome, and the beer is brewed on the premises. In summer, quaff it down beneath the huge chestnuts and admire the lake and mountains over the rim of your glass. *Schlosspl. 1, tel. 08022/4141. No reservations. Dress: informal. No credit cards. Inexpensive.*

Waging am See
Dining
★

Kurhausstüberl. This southeastern corner of Bavaria, around its warmest lake, the Wagingersee, was a quiet backwater before the Kurhausstüberl's fame spread. Now it's a place of pilgrimage for Munich's bons vivants. Yet the country-style restaurant's reticence is unchanged. Award-winning chef Alfons Schubeck bases his nouvelle cuisine on solid Bavarian foundations, rediscovering the possibilities of a tiny lake fish that anglers usually throw back, and making soups from cress and side dishes from wild asparagus. *Am See, tel. 08681/666. Reservations required. Jacket and tie optional. AE, DC, MC, V. Closed Mon. and Tues., and Jan. 6–mid-Feb. Expensive.*

The Arts and Nightlife

The Arts

Concerts Every summer, **Schloss Hohenaschau,** regarded as one of the finest castles of southern Germany, hosts a series of chamber concerts in its courtyard, its chapel, and its impressive banqueting hall. Contact the Kurverwaltung (8213 Aschau im Chiemgau, tel. 0805/392) for program details and reservations. King Ludwig's fantastic **Schloss Neuschwanstein** is the scene every September of a short season of chamber-music concerts, presented in the richly decorated minstrels' hall. (It was here that Ludwig hoped to stage concerts of music by his life-long hero, Richard Wagner, an ambition that, like so many of the doomed monarch's aims, remained unfulfilled). Contact the Schlossverwaltung Neuschwanstein (8959 Hohenschwangau, tel. 08362/81035) for details and tickets. Bavarian folk music and dancing are performed on Saturday evenings during the summer in the **Bayernhalle** (Brauhausstr. 19, Garmisch-Partenkirchen). Concerts of classical and popular music are presented Saturday through Thursday, mid-May through September, in the resort park bandstand in Garmisch, and on Fridays in the Partenkirchen resort park.

Theater Both **Berchtesgaden** and **Garmisch-Partenkirchen** have entertaining *Bauerntheaters* (folklore theaters). A working knowledge of German helps if you plan a visit. Berchtesgaden's theater company (Franziskanerpl., tel. 08652/2858) has daily performances in summer, and performs Thursday through Sunday in winter (except from November to Christmas). The Garmisch-Partenkirchen company (Rassensaal, Ludwigstr. 45) performs less frequently. Program details are available from the tourist office (tel. 08821/1800) or any hotel.

Nightlife

There are **casinos** in Garmisch-Partenkirchen (tel. 08821/-53099), Bad Reichenhall (tel. 08651/4091), and Bad Wiessee (tel. 08022/82P28). They are state-run and the same regulations apply in all. You'll need your passport to get in, and you must be respectably dressed (jacket and tie).

5 The Bodensee

Introduction

The Bodensee (Lake Constance) is the largest lake in the German-speaking world, 163 miles square, 210 miles around, and bordered by West Germany, Switzerland, and Austria. It's called a lake, but actually it's a vast swelling of the Rhine, gouged out by a massive glacier in the Ice Age and flooded by the river as the ice receded. The Rhine flows into its southeastern corner, where Switzerland and Austria meet, and leaves at its western end.

Visitors should be grateful: These immense natural forces have created one of the most ravishing corners of Germany, a natural summer playground, ringed with little towns and busy resorts. Gentle, vineyard-clad hills slope down to the lakeshore. To the south, the Alps provide a jagged and dramatic backdrop. It's one of the warmest areas of the country, too, the result not just of its geographic location—it's almost the southernmost region of Germany—but of the warming influence of the lake, which gathers heat in the summer and releases it in the winter like a massive radiator. There are corners of the Bodensee that enjoy a near-tropical climate, where lemons, bougainvillea, and hibiscus flourish and where vines grow in abundance. The lake itself practically never freezes (it has done so only once this century and twice in the last).

R&R may provide the major reason for visiting the Bodensee, but it's by no means the only one. The natural attractions of the lake, not least its abundance of fresh fish and its fertile soil, were as potent several thousand years ago as they are today. This is one of the oldest continually inhabited areas of Germany, and you'll want to pay your respects to at least part of this heritage. Highlights include the medieval island town of Lindau; Friedrichshafen, birthplace of the zeppelin; the Rococo abbey church of Birnau; and the town of Konstanz on the Swiss-German border. It would be a shame, too, once you're in Bodensee, not to take advantage of the area's closeness to Austria and Switzerland (and to little Liechtenstein). A day trip to one or more is easy to make, and formalities are few.

Essential Information

Important Addresses and Numbers

Tourist Information Information on the whole of the Bodensee region is available from the **Internationaler Bodensee-Verkehrsverein-Fremdenverkehrsamt** (8990 Lindau, tel. 08382/5022). For information on Upper Swabia, contact the **Fremdenverkehrsverband Bodensee-Oberschwaben** (Schützenstr. 8, Konstanz, tel. 07531/22232). There are local tourist information offices in the following towns:

Friedrischshafen: Tourist-Information, Friedrichstrasse 18, 7990 Friedrichshafen, tel. 07541/21729.
Konstanz: Tourist-Information Konstanz, Bahnhofplatz 13, 7750 Konstanz, tel. 07531/284–376.
Lindau: am Hauptbahnhof, 8990 Lindau, tel. 08382/5022.
Meersburg: Kur- und Verkehrsverwaltung, Schlossplatz 4, 7758 Meersburg, tel. 07532/82383.

Radolfzell: Städtisches Verkehrsamt, Rathaus, Marktplatz 2, 7760 Radolfzell, tel. 07732/3800.
Ravensburg: Städtisches Verkehrsamt, Marienplatz 54, 7980 Ravensburg, tel. 0751/82324.
Tuttlingen: Städtisches Verkehrsamt, Rathaus, 7200 Tuttlingen, tel. 07461/99203.
Überlingen: Verkehrsamt Überlingen, 7770 Überlingen, tel. 07551/63454.

Car Rental **Avis:** Siemenstrasse 3, **Friedrichshafen,** tel. 07541/56091; Zaehringer Platz 33–35, **Konstanz,** tel. 07531/57857.
Europcar: Eckenerstrasse 50, **Friedrichshafen,** tel. 07541/21841. Macaivestrasse 10, **Konstanz,** tel. 07531/62052.
Hertz: Loewentalerstrasse 49, **Friedrichshafen,** tel. 07541/31233.

Arriving and Departing By Plane

The nearest international airport to the Bodensee is Zurich, in Switzerland, 60 kilometers (40 miles) from Konstanz and with regular flights from the United States. Munich airport is 210 kilometers (130 miles) from Konstanz, Frankfurt airport is 375 kilometers (230 miles) from Konstanz. The little airport at Friedrichshafen, on the north shore of the lake, has flights from all three airports.

Arriving and Departing by Car and Train

By Car From Munich, take B-12 via Landsberg and Kempten; from Frankfurt, take Autobahn 81 to Memmingen, then B-18. If you want to take a more scenic but slower route from Frankfurt, take B-311 at Ulm and follow the Oberschwäbische Barockstrasse (the Upper Swabian Baroque Road) to Friedrichshafen. An alternative, no less scenic route to Lindau, at the east end of the lake, is on the Deutsche Alpenstrasse (the German Alpine Road). It runs east–west from Salzburg to Lindau, passing Garmisch-Partenkirchen and Füssen along the way.

By Train There are express Intercity trains to Lindau from Frankfurt (via Stuttgart and Ulm) and from Munich. There are also frequent and fast train services from Zurich and Basel in Switzerland.

Getting Around

By Car Lakeside roads in the Bodensee area are good, if crowded in summer; all offer scenic diversions to compensate for the occasional slow going in heavier traffic. You may want to drive around the entire lake, crossing into Switzerland and Austria; formalities at border crossing points are few. However, in addition to your passport, you'll need insurance and registration papers for your car. If you're taking a rental car, check with the rental company that it imposes no restrictions on crossing these frontiers. Car ferries link Romanshorn in Switzerland on the south side of the lake with Friedrichshafen, and Konstanz with Meersburg. Taking either saves substantial mileage driving around the lake.

By Train Local trains encircle the Bodensee, stopping at most towns and villages.

By Bus Railway and post buses serve most smaller communities that have no train links. Service is less than frequent, however; use local buses only if time is no object.

By Boat The German-Swiss-Austrian **Weissee Flotte** (White Fleet) line has been ferrying passengers around the lake for more than 120 years. Boats link most of the larger towns and resorts; numerous excursions are also available (*see* Guided Tours, below). If you plan to use the ferries extensively, buy a **Bodensee Pass.** It gives 15 days' unlimited travel on all ferries, as well as on many trains, buses, and some local mountain railways. Cost is DM 70 (DM 35 children from 6 to 16). Contact **Bodensee-Schiffsbetriebe der Deutschen Bundesbahn** (Hafenstr. 6, 7750 Konstanz, tel. 07531/281–389). There are also offices in Friedrichshafen (tel. 07541/201–389) and Lindau (tel. 08382/6099).

Guided Tours

City Tours Most of the larger tourist centers have regular tours with English-speaking guides. In **Friedrichshafen,** there are tours May through September on Tuesdays at 9:30, leaving from the tourist office (Friedrichstr. 18). There are tours of **Konstanz** May through September, daily, from the tourist office (Bahnhofpl. 13). **Lindau** offers tours, also starting from the tourist office (Am Hauptbahnhof), April through October, on Tuesdays and Fridays at 9:30 and 11. Meersburg tourist office (Schlosspl. 4) offers guided tours that include a visit to the wine museum; tours are held April through October, Wednesdays, at 10. The **Radolfzell** tourist office (Marienpl. 54) arranges tours, May through September, on Saturdays at 10 for groups of 10 or more.

Boat Tours There are numerous excursions around the lake organized by the Weissee Flotte lasting from one hour to a full day. Many cross to Austria and Switzerland, some head west along the Rhine to the Schaffhausen Falls, the largest waterfall in Europe. (*See* Getting Around by Boat, above, for addresses.) Information on excursions on the lake is also available from all local tourist offices and travel agencies.

Excursions Bus trips to destinations in and around the Bodensee can be booked from tour operators in all the larger towns. Typical tours include visits to cheese-makers in the Allgäu, the rolling Alpine foothills east of the Bodensee; tours around the Black Forest; tours to Baroque churches and castles around the lake; and tours to the ancient town of St. Gallen over the border in Switzerland. Operators include: **Seehas-Reisen** (Hussenstr. 46, Konstanz, tel. 07531/26016), **Autoreisen Bregenz** (Seepromenade 15, Überlingen, tel. 07551/4047), **Reisebüro Kast** (Münsterstr. 31–33, Überlingen, tel. 07551/63628).

Special-Interest Tours Flights around the Bodensee are offered by **Konair** (Flugpl., Konstanz, tel. 07531/61110). A 20-minute flight over Konstanz itself costs DM 40 per person. A 30-minute flight around the lake costs DM 80, a 45-minute flight costs DM 100. For DM 140, you can have the plane for an hour, easily time enough to fly south over parts of the Alps. A minimum of two passengers is required for all flights; reservations are essential.

Wine-tasting tours are also available. In Überlingen, tastings are held in the atmospheric Spitalweingut zum Heiligen Geist on Thursdays at 7 PM; contact the tourist office. In Konstanz, wine-tasting is offered Tuesdays at 5 PM in the half-timbered Spitalkellerei (Brückengasse 12, tel. 07531/28842). In Meersburg, tastings are held Tuesdays and Fridays at 6 PM; contact the tourist office or Georg Hack (tel. 07532/9097).

Exploring Bodensee

Numbers in the margin correspond with points of interest on the Bodensee map.

Highlights for First-time Visitors

Altes Schloss, Meersburg
Meersburg, from the lake
The gardens at Mainau
The Nikolausmünster, Überlingen
The Romanesque churches of Reichenau
The Rococo Wallsfahrtskirche at Birnau
The Zeppelin Museum at Friedrichshafen
At least one ride on the lake

Tour 1: Lindau and Environs

The showpiece of the Bodensee, and starting point of the tour,
1 is **Lindau,** located at the southeastern corner of the lake just a mile or two from the Austrian border. Lindau is an island town, tethered to the shore by a 210-yard causeway. Stand at the water's edge in its newer, mainland section, the so-called Gartenstadt (Garden Town—the name comes from its abundance of flowers and shrubs), on a hazy summer's day and the walls and roofs of old Lindau seem to float on the shimmering water, an illusion intensified by the miragelike backdrop of the Alps.

Lindau was originally three islands, on one of which the Romans built a military base. Under the Romans, the islands developed first as a fishing settlement, then as a trading center, a stage on the route connecting the rich lands of Swabia to the north with Italy. (It was a role that continued for hundreds of years: One of the most important stagecoach services between Germany and Italy in the 18th and 19th centuries was based here, the Lindauer Bote—Goethe traveled on it on his first visit to Italy in 1786). Commercial importance brought political power, and in 1275 little Lindau was made a Free Imperial City within the Holy Roman Empire. As the Empire crumbled toward the end of the 18th century, battered by Napoléon's Revolutionary armies, so Lindau fell victim to competing political groups. It was ruled (briefly) by the Austrian Hapsburg Empire before passing into Bavarian rule in 1806.

The proud symbol of Bavaria, a **seated lion,** is one of the most striking landmarks you'll see in Lindau. The lion in question, 20 feet high and carved from Bavarian marble, stares out across the lake from a massive plinth at the end of one of the harbor walls. At the end of the facing wall there's a lighthouse, the **Neuer Leuchtturm.** You can climb up to its viewing platform for a look out over the waters. On a clear day, you'll see the Three Sisters, three peaks in Liechtenstein. *Admission: DM 1, 40 pf children. Open daily 9:30–6.*

The Bodensee

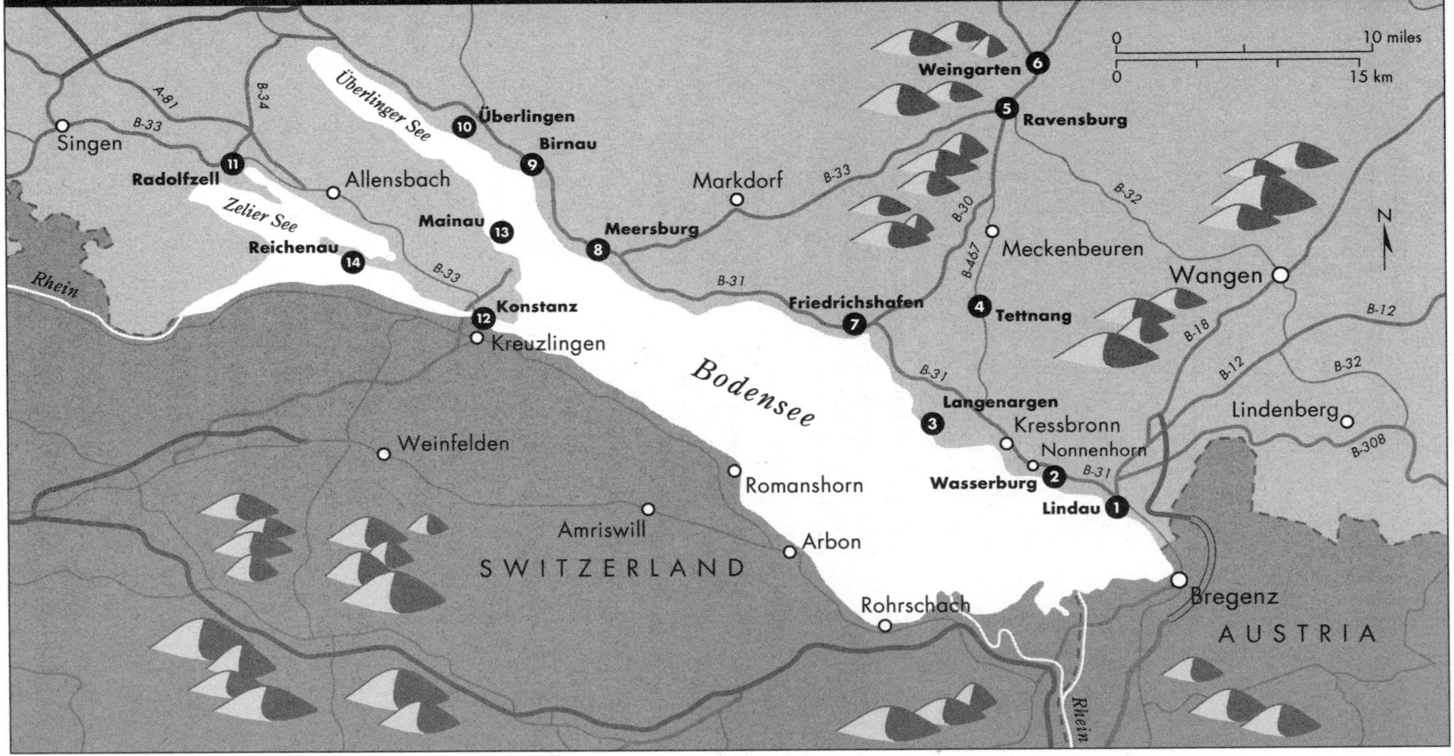

The **Alter Leuchtturm,** or old lighthouse, stands at the edge of the inner harbor on the weathered remains of the original 13th-century city walls.

From the harbor, plunge into the maze of ancient streets that make up the Altstadt (the Old Town). They all lead eventually to the **Altes Rathaus** (Old Town Hall), the finest of Lindau's handsome historical buildings. It was constructed between 1422 and 1436 in the midst of what was then a vineyard (now a busy thoroughfare) and given a Renaissance facelift 150 years later, though the original stepped gables were retained. The Emperor Maximilian I held an imperial council here in 1496; a fresco on the south facade depicts a scene from this highpoint of local history. The building was not always used for such noble purposes: Part of it served as the town prison. An ancient inscription, enjoining the townsfolk "to turn aside from evil and learn to do good," identifies it.

Face away from the town hall and walk down to the **Barfüsserkirche,** the Church of the Barefoot Pilgrims. Built from 1241 to 1270, it has for many years been Lindau's principal theater. The Gothic choir is a memorable location for concerts, especially of church music. The tourist office on Bahnhofplatz can provide details of performances.

Continue along Ludwigstrasse to Fischergasse, where you'll find a watchtower, once part of the original city walls. Pause in the little park behind it, the **Stadtgarten.** If it's early evening, you'll see the first gamblers of the night making for the neighboring casino.

Lindau's market square, Marktplatz, is just around the corner. A series of sturdily attractive old buildings line it, among them the 18th-century **Haus zum Cavazzen,** richly decorated with stucco and frescoes. Today, it's the municipal art gallery and local history museum. *Am Marktpl. Admission: DM 2 adults, DM 1 children. Open Apr.–Nov., Mon.–Sat. 9–noon and 2–5, Sun. 10–noon.*

Two contrasting churches also stand on Marktplatz: the simple, sparely decorated Gothic Stephanskirche and the more elaborate, Baroque Marienkirche. Both have charm—the Stephanskirche for its simplicity, the Marienkirche for its Baroque exuberance.

From Marktplatz, walk along pedestrians-only **Maximilianstrasse,** the main street of the old town, distinguished by half-timbered and gabled old houses.

Time Out The **Weinstube Frey** is a 16th-century wine tavern. Try fresh lake fish and a crisp white Bodensee wine for an excellent lunch. Smoked ham from the Black Forest is also a specialty. *Maximilianstr. 15.*

Turn right off Maximilianstrasse down cobbled Schafsgasse to reach the **Peterskirche** on Schrannenplatz. It's a solid Romanesque building, constructed in the 10th century and reputedly the oldest church in the Bodensee region. Step inside to see the frescoes by Hans Holbein the Elder (1465–1524). A number depict scenes from the life of St. Peter, the patron saint of fishermen and thus an important figure to the inhabitants of Lindau.

From Lindau, head west along the lake. The first attraction
2 you reach is **Wasserburg,** 6 kilometers (4 miles) away. It's a sort of Lindau in miniature, another jewel of a town that's actually *in* the lake, at the end of a narrow causeway. Wasserburg means "water castle," and that's exactly what this enchanting town once was, a fortress built on the site of a Roman watchtower. The original owners, the counts of Montfort zu Tettnang, sold it to the wealthy Fugger family of Augsburg to pay off mounting debts. When, in the 18th century, the Fuggers fell on hard times, too, the castle passed into the hands of the Hapsburgs. In 1805 it was taken over by the Bavarian government.

The Fuggers, when they bought Wasserburg, were among the richest families in Europe. During the final days of their ownership, they were so impoverished that they couldn't even afford to pay for the upkeep of the drawbridge that connected the castle with the shore. Instead, they built a causeway, linking the little castle permanently with the shore. Cars aren't allowed into Wasserburg these days, and one of the pleasures of a visit here is to wander undisturbed through its tangle of ancient streets. The castle itself is now a hotel, the Schloss Hotel Wasserburg (Hauptstr. 5), offering surprisingly reasonably priced accommodations.

The most unusual castle in the region stands at the water's
3 edge in **Langenargen,** 8 kilometers (5 miles) west. **Montfort Castle**—it was named after its original owners, the counts of Montfort-Werdenberg—was a conventional enough medieval fortification until it was rebuilt in the 19th century in pseudo-Moorish style by its new owner, King Wilhelm I of Württemberg. If you can, see it from the lake from a steamer: The castle is especially memorable in the early morning or late afternoon, when the softened, watery light gives additional mystery to its Oriental outline. These days, very unromantically, the castle is a municipal tourist center, with a café, a restaurant, and a disco.

Langenargen is worth visiting to see its central market square, Marktplatz, site of a Baroque parish church and the town museum. The museum contains a series of paintings by German painter Hans Purrmann (1880–1966), an admirer of the French painter Henri Matisse and cofounder of the Academie Matisse in Paris in 1908. The academy faltered soon after it was founded, and, between 1915 and 1935 (at which point Purrmann's work was outlawed by the Nazis), he lived in Langenargen. The museum may appeal only to those with an advanced taste for lesser-known 20th-century painting. *Marktpl. 20. Admission: DM 2.50 adults, DM 1 children. Open Apr.–Oct., Tues.–Sun. 10–noon and 3–5.*

Tettnang, Ravensburg, and Weingarten

Leave the lake now, and head north 12 kilometers (8 miles) on
4 B-467 to the little town of **Tettnang,** former ancestral home of the counts of Montfort zu Tettnang. By 1780 the dynasty had fallen on such hard times that it sold the entire town to the Hapsburgs. Twenty-five years later it passed to the Bavarian ruling dynasty, the Wittelsbachs. You'll principally want to visit to see what remains of the family's extravagant Baroque palace, the Neues Schloss. It was built in the early 18th centu-

ry, burned down in 1753, and then partially rebuilt before the family's finances ran dry. Enough remains, however, to give some idea of the Montfort's former wealth and positively Baroque lifestyle. *Admission: DM 2 (includes guided tour). Open Apr.–Oct., daily 10–5.*

Time Out The Last of the Montfort line, Count Anton IV, spent his declining years in a modest house in the town, now the **Gasthof Krone.** The inn has its own brewery, and you can try its excellent beer in the parlor where Count Anton dreamed of former glories. If you visit in the late spring, order up one of the asparagus dishes: Tettnang is one of Germany's leading asparagus-growing centers. *Bärenpl.*

5 Thirteen kilometers (8 miles) north of Tettnang on B-467, then B-30, is **Ravensburg,** an attractive city that once competed with Augsburg and Nürnberg for economic supremacy in southern Germany. It proved an uneven contest. The Thirty Years' War of the mid-17th century finally put an end to Ravensburg's remaining hopes of economic leadership; after the war, the city was reduced to little more than a medieval backwater. The city's loss proved fortuitous only in that many of its original medieval features have remained much as they were when built. Fourteen of the town gates and towers have survived, for example, while the Altstadt (the Old Town) is among the best preserved in Germany. Leave your car at the Untertor gate and explore the city on foot—cars have been banned from the Old Town. Head down Bachstrasse and you come to one of Ravensburg's most interesting churches, the former **Karmelitenklosterkirche,** once part of a 14th-century monastery, now a Protestant church. Ecclesiastical and commercial life were never entirely separate in medieval towns such as Ravensburg. The stairs on the west side of the chancel in the church, for example, lead to the former meeting room of the Ravensburger Gesellschaft (the Ravensburg Society), an organization of linen merchants established in 1400 to direct trade in the product that was largely responsible for the town's rapid economic growth.

The adjacent Marienplatz square has many old buildings that recall Ravensburg's wealthy years: the late-Gothic **Rathaus** (Town Hall), with a picturesque Renaissance bay window; the 14th-century **Kornhaus,** once the corn exchange for the whole of Upper Swabia; the 15th-century **Waaghaus,** the town's weighing station and central warehouse, incorporating a tower where the watchman had his lookout; and the colorfully frescoed **Lederhaus,** once the headquarters of the leather workers.

Time Out Among the historic facades of Marienplatz, you'll see the welcoming door of the **Posthotel Lamm.** Step inside for a taste of true Bodensee cooking in a traditional interior. Ask for a wine from any of the Bodensee vineyards or for a Ravensburg-brewed beer. *Marienpl.*

One of the city's defensive towers is visible from Marienplatz, the **Grüner Turm** (Green Tower), so called because of its green tiles; many are the 14th-century originals. Walk past the Grüner Turm and the neighboring Frauenturm to the **Liebfrauenkirche** (Church of Our Lady). It, too, is a 14th-century structure, elegantly simple on the outside but almost entirely rebuilt inside. Some of the original stained glass remains, however, as does the heavily gilded altar. Seek out the *Ravensburger Schutzmantelmadonna,* a copy of the 15th-century original that's now in Berlin's Dahlem Museum.

A short walk southeast of the Liebfrauenkirche is the massive **Obertor,** the oldest gate in the city walls. This was once one of Ravensburg's most secure defensive positions. From it, you can see another of the city's towers, the **Mehlsack,** or Flour Sack tower, 170 feet high and standing on the highest point of the city. If you can stand the 240-step climb, head up to the summit for the view south to the Bodensee and the Alps. *Admission free. Open mid-Mar.–mid-Oct., 1st and 3rd Sun. of the month only, 10–noon.*

Five kilometers (3 miles) north of Ravensburg on B-30 is the
6 pilgrimage town of **Weingarten,** site of the largest Baroque church in Germany, 220 feet high and over 300 feet long. It's the church of one of the oldest and most venerable convents in the country, founded in 1056 by the wife of Guelph II. (The Guelph dynasty ruled large areas of Upper Swabia; later, one line of the family, the Guelph-Wittins, found almost greater fame as the direct ancestors of Britain's current royal family, whose family name was Guelph-Wittin until as late as 1917, when it was changed to the more patriotic Windsor). Generations of Guelphs lie buried in the Weingarten basilica. Of greater significance, indeed the reason why the majestic basilica was built, is the little vial it possesses, said to contain drops of Christ's blood. First mentioned by Charlemagne, the vial passed to the convent in 1094, at a stroke making Weingarten one of Germany's foremost places of pilgrimage. On the Friday after Ascension (May 25 in 1990), the anniversary of the day the relic was entrusted to the convent, a huge procession of pilgrims, headed by 2,000 horsemen (many local farmers breed horses just for this procession) wends its way to the basilica. The interior of the basilica provides a suitably imposing stage for the climax of the procession. It was decorated by some of the leading German and Austrian artists of the early 18th century, with stucco by Franz Schmuzer, ceiling frescoes by Cosmas Damian Asam, and altar—itself among the most breathtakingly ornate in Europe; the towers on either side are nearly 80 feet high—by Donato Frisoni. The organ, installed between 1737 and 1750, is among the largest in the country.

Weingarten achieved additional recognition in the '50s, when archaeologists discovered hundreds of Alemann graves from the 6th, 7th, and 8th centuries just outside the town. If you want to learn about these early Germans, visit the **Alemannenmuseum** in the Kornhaus, a one-time granary. *Karlstr. 28. Admission free. Open Wed. and weekends 3–5.*

Tour 2: Friedrichshafen and Meersburg

7 The road back to the lake, B-30, takes you to **Friedrichshafen,** named after its founder King Friedrich I of Württemberg. It's a young city, founded by Friedrich in 1811, and almost wiped off the map by wartime air raids on its munitions factories. Curious though it may seem in an area otherwise given over to resort towns and agriculture, Friedrichshafen played a central role in Germany's aeronautic tradition, a tradition that saw the development of the zeppelin airship before World War I and the

Dornier flying boat in the '20s and '30s. In both cases, it was the broad, smooth waters of the lake that made Friedrichshafen attractive to the pioneer airmen: The zeppelins were built in enormous, floating hangars on the lake; the Dorniers were tested on its calm surface. The story of the zeppelins is fascinating. If you're interested, make for the **Städtisches Bodenseemuseum,** where the whole unlikely tale is told in detail, complete with models—one 26 feet long—plans, photographs, and documents. To most, the zeppelin is famous for the appalling fire that destroyed the hydrogen-filled *Hindenburg* in a matter of seconds at Lakehurst, New Jersey, in 1937. It was an accident that put a sudden stop to the airship as a practical means of air transport (ironically at the very moment when noninflammable gases were being developed). But, in fact, the story of the zeppelin began back in the last years of the 19th century, when Count (Graf) Ferdinand von Zeppelin, born in 1837 across the lake at Konstanz, built the first of his airships. Though he recognized its potential as a passenger-carrying aircraft—a potential that came to be realized only in the '20s and '30s—he was much more taken with its military applications. Few at the time shared his obsessive belief that the airship would transform modern warfare by being able to drop large numbers of bombs behind enemy lines, and the count was forced to risk a substantial part of his substantial fortune in the enterprise. By 1910, however, one man at least had come to share the count's vision—the Kaiser. Thus, in the years before World War I, the German military took over development of the airships—or zeppelins as they were by then known. In any event, their military uses proved distinctly limited. Though they were used for numerous bombing raids on London, for example, their crews were almost more at risk than those they were bombing. Slow-moving, cramped, and unreliable, the zeppelins were easy to shoot down, while the acute fire hazard was an ever-present risk. A statue of their strange aristocratic inventor—he looks suspiciously like the Kaiser—stares imperiously down at visitors to the museum. There's another monument to the count outside the museum, a plain, stone obelisk with the inscription "First we must wish, then we must believe, then it will happen." *Adenauerpl. 1. Admission: DM 2, free Wed. Open June–Aug. daily 10–5, Sept.–May Tues.–Sun. 10–noon and 2–5.*

From the museum, it's a short walk along the lakeside promenade to Friedrichshafen's **Schloss Hofen,** a small palace that served as the summer residence of the kings of Württemberg until 1918. The palace was formerly a priory—its foundations date back to the 11th century—and the adjoining priory church is a splendid example of local Baroque architecture. The swirling white stucco of the interior was executed by the Wessobrun Schmuzer family, whose master craftsman, Franz, was responsible for much of the finest work in the basilica of Weingarten. Franz Schmuzer also created the priory church's magnificent marble altar.

8 Your next stop, 18 kilometers (11 miles) west along the lake, is the historic old town of **Meersburg.** The most romantic way to approach Meersburg is from the lake. Seen from the water on a summer afternoon, with the sun slanting low across the water, the steeply terraced town can seem floodlit, like some elaborate stage setting. (There's little denying that Meersburg is well aware of its too-good-to-be-true charm—some may find

the gusto with which it has embraced tourism crass; indeed, the town can at times get unpleasantly crowded.) Assuming your visit is by boat, you'll step ashore in the Unterstadt, the lower town, which clings to the lake shore about 150 feet below the Oberstadt, or upper town. The climb between the two halves is not arduous, but there's a bus if you can't face the hike.

Meersburg is said to have been founded in 628 by Dagobert, king of the Franks, the man who, it's claimed, laid the first stone of the **Altes Schloss** (Old Castle), which watches majestically over the town and the lake far below. It's Germany's oldest inhabited castle, and one of the most impressive. The massive central tower, named after Dagobert, has walls 10 feet thick. In 1526, the Catholic bishop of Konstanz set himself up in the castle after Konstanz had embraced Protestantism and thrown him out. The castle remained the home of the bishops until the middle of the 18th century, when they had, as they saw it, a more suitable residence built, the Baroque Neues Schloss. Plans to tear down the Altes Schloss in the early 19th century were shelved when the castle was taken over by one Baron Joseph von Lassberg, a man much taken by its medieval romance. He turned it into a home for like-minded poets and artists, among them his sister-in-law, Annette von Droste-Hülshoff (1797–1848), generally considered Germany's finest female poet. Her small-scale, carefully crafted poems are drenched in impressions gained from the lake and the mountains laid out before the castle. The Altes Schloss is still private property, but much of it can be visited, including the richly furnished rooms where Annette von Droste-Hülshoff lived, as well as the imposing knights' hall, the minstrels' gallery, and the sinister dungeons. The **castle museum** contains a unique collection of medieval jousting equipment. *Schlosspl. Admission: DM 5 adults, DM 3 children. Open Mar.–Oct. daily 9–6, Nov.–Feb. daily 10:30–5.*

The spacious and elegant **Neues Schloss** is located directly across from the castle. It was built partly by Balthasar Neumann, the leading German architect of the 18th century, and partly by an Italian, Franz Anton Bagnato. Neumann's work is most obvious in the stately sweep of the grand double staircase, with its intricate grillwork and heroic statues. The other standout of the interior is the glittering Speigelsaal, the hall of mirrors, now the site of an international music festival held in the summer (*see* The Arts and Nightlife, below). In an unlikely combination of 18th-century grace and 20th-century technology, the top floor of the palace houses the **Dornier Museum.** It traces the history of the German aircraft and aerospace industries. *Schlosspl. Admission: DM 2.50 adults, DM 1.25 children. Open Easter–Oct., daily 10–12:30 and 1:30–5:30. Guided tours in English available.*

Sun-bathed, south-facing Meersburg has been a center of the Bodensee wine trade for centuries. You can pay your respects to the noble trade in the **Weinbau Museum,** one of the most comprehensive wine museums in Germany. A massive barrel, capable of holding 50,000 liters, and an immense wine press dating from 1607 are highlights of the collection. The museum has another claim to fame, too: It's located in the house where Dr. Frank Anton Mesmer (1734–1815), pioneer of hypnotism—"mesmerism"—lived in the early 19th century. *Vorburggasse*

11. Admission: DM 1 adults, children free. Open Apr.–Sept. Tues., Fri., and Sun. 2–5.

From the museum, it's only a short walk to Meersburg's picturesque market square, **Marktplatz,** surrounded by pretty, half-timbered houses, among them the medieval Rathaus, the town hall.

Time Out The **Weinkeller in Truben** continues the wine theme—its front door is one end of a huge wine barrel. Inside, wine racks stretch from the floor to the whitewashed, vaulted ceiling. Order a bottle of local wine and try one of the cheese-based dishes. *Steigstr.*

East of the Obertor, the town gate at the northern end of the town, is an idyllic retreat almost hidden among the vineyards, the **Fürstenhausen,** built in 1640 by a local vintner and later used as a holiday home by poet Annette von Droste-Hülshoff. It's now a museum containing many of her personal items and giving a vivid sense of Meersburg in her time. *Stettnerstr. 9. Admission: DM 3 adults, DM 1.20 children. Open Easter–mid-Oct. Mon.–Sat. 10–noon and 2–6, Sun. and holidays 2–6.*

Tour 3: Birnau, Überlingen, and Radolfzell

If you have any interest in the Rococo, you won't want to miss

9 **Birnau,** 10 kilometers (6 miles) along the lake. It's the site of the **Wallsfahrtskirche** pilgrimage church, the Rococo masterpiece of architect Peter Thumb. Built between 1746 and 1750, the church has a simple exterior, with plain gray and white plaster and a tapering clocktower spire over the main entrance; the interior, by contrast, is overwhelmingly rich, a Rococo gem, full of movement, light, and color. It's hard to single out highlights from such a profusion of ornament, but seek out the *Honigschlecker* (the Honey Sucker), a gold and white cherub beside the altar dedicated to St. Bernard of Clairvaux, "whose words are sweet as honey" (it's the last altar on the right as you face the high altar). The cherub is sucking honey from his finger, which he's just pulled out of a beehive. If this sort of dainty punning strikes you as misplaced in a place of worship, you'll probably find the small squares of glass set into the pink screen that rises high above the main altar; the gilt dripping from the walls; the swaying, swooning statues; and the swooping figures on the ceiling equally tasteless. If, like many, you are entranced by the plump cherub, odds are the rest of the building will be very much to your taste.

10 Birnau stands 2 miles or so along the lake from **Überlingen,** the German Nice, as the tourist office likes to call it. It's located midway along the northern shore of the Überlingersee, a narrow branch of the Bodensee that projects northwest out of the main body of the lake. Überlingen is an ancient city, a Free Imperial City since the 13th century, with no less than seven of its original city gates and towers left, as well as substantial portions of the old city walls. (What was once the moat is now a delightfully grassy place to walk, with the walls of the old town towering over you on one side and the Stadtpark—city park—stretching away on the other.) The heart of the city is the Münsterplatz, site of the Altes Rathaus (Old Town Hall) and the **Nikolausmünster** itself, the church of St. Nicholas. It's a

huge church for such a small town, built between 1512 and 1563 on the site of at least two previous churches. The interior is all Gothic solemnity and massiveness, with a lofty stone-vaulted ceiling and high pointed arches lining the nave. The single most remarkable feature is not Gothic at all, however, but opulently Renaissance—the massive high altar, fully four stories high, carved from white painted wood that looks almost like ivory. Statues, curlicues, and columns jostle for space on it.

Left of the church is the intricate, late-Gothic **Town Hall.** Go inside to see the **Ratsaal,** the council chamber, a high point of Gothic decoration. Its most striking feature amid the riot of carving is the series of figures representing the states of the Holy Roman Empire. There's a naivety to the figures—their beautifully carved heads are all just a little too large, their legs a little too spindly—that makes them easy to love. *Münsterpl. Admission free. Open daily 8–noon and 2:30–5. Closed Sat. afternoons in winter.*

From Überlingen, you can either drive the 10 kilometers (6 miles) back to Meersburg and take the ferry over to Konstanz, or you can continue around the end of the Überlingersee, drive across the neck of the Bodanrück peninsula—which juts into the western end of the Bodensee to Radolfzell—and continue from there to Konstanz. If you take the latter route, it's 23 kilometers (14 miles) from Überlingen to Radolfzell, and another 16 kilometers (10 miles) to Konstanz.

11 It's worth the extra mileage to see **Radolfzell,** an old lakeside town that wears its history with some style (aside from the ugly high rises surrounding it). It was an Austrian outpost for much of its existence, Austrian property from 1267 to 1415 and again from 1455 to the early 19th century. There are those same half-timbered buildings and sinewy old streets that you'll find in other historic Bodensee towns, that same elegant lakeside promenade and those same chic shops. But the tourist hype is less obtrusive—there's not the sense that Radolfzell has decided that it might as well give up being a real town and turn itself over entirely to the tourist trade. There are no outstanding sights here, it's true, but it's an appealing place for a night or two. And if you must have some culture, go and see the 14th-century **Liebfrauenmünster,** a sturdy Gothic church right on the lakeshore.

Tour 4: Konstanz

12 And so to **Konstanz,** the largest and most famous city on the Bodensee, the only Germany city on the southern shore, a German enclave almost in Switzerland (parts of the town actually *are* in Switzerland; the border runs across the southern half of Konstanz—crossing it is easy, with formalities reduced to a minimum). Because it's practically in Switzerland, Konstanz (or Kreuzlingen, as the Swiss call their part) suffered no wartime bombing—the Allies were unwilling to risk inadvertent bombing of neutral Switzerland—with the result that Konstanz is among the best-preserved major medieval towns in Germany. Its proximity to Switzerland also made this one of the most tense borders in the war. There's a famous story of a German Jew who, having crossed the border, was stopped by a Swiss policeman in Kreuzlingen. Having no papers, the German could do little more than pretend that he was Swiss,

out for a stroll and a beer. The policeman looked him up and down, and said *Ja, Schweizisches Bier ist gut.* Then he walked slowly away.

It's claimed that Konstanz was founded in the third century by the Emperor Constantine Chlorus, father of Constantine the Great. The story is probably untrue, though it's certain that there was a Roman garrison here. By the sixth century, Konstanz had become a bishopric; in 1192, it was made a Free Imperial City. But what really put Konstanz on the map was the Council of Konstanz, held between 1414 and 1418 and probably one of the most remarkable gatherings of the medieval world. Upwards of 100,000 people are said to have descended on the city during the great council. It was an assembly that was to have profound consequences, consequences that are still felt today. The council was not principally a political gathering so much as a religious one, though the point at which the politics stopped and the religion began was not always easy to identify: To enjoy either religious supremacy or political power in medieval Europe was, to a large extent, to enjoy both.

What was the council? It was convened to settle the Great Schism, the rift in the church brought about in the 14th century when the papacy moved from Rome to Avignon in the south of France. With the move, a rival pope declared himself in Rome. Whatever else it may not have done, the council did at least resolve the problem of the pope: In 1417, it elected Martin V as the true, and only, pope. What it failed to do, however, was to solve the underlying problems about the nature of the Church that, in part at least, had caused the schism in the first place. At stake was the primacy of the German Holy Roman Emperor in electing the pope (and thus in extending his, the emperor's, power) and the primacy of the pope in determining church affairs (and thus in extending the power of the Holy Roman Emperor still further).

Leading the rebel camp was John Hus (1372–1415), a theologian from Prague in Bohemia (modern Czechoslovakia), opposed both to the political power of the Holy Roman Emperor and to the religious primacy of the Pope. He was, in effect, a church reformer 100 years before his time, a man calling for a fundamental reinterpretation of Christian dogma and for the cleansing of the Church's corrupt practices.

What happened at Konstanz? Hus attended the council, having been promised safe-conduct by the Emperor Sigismund on condition that he would not say mass or preach. The emperor, however, needed a deal with the Church, one that would restore his role in electing the pope. The Church agreed, on condition that Hus be done away with. (Sigismund, too, had much to gain from Hus's death; with Hus out of the way, he hoped to restore his control of Bohemia.) So, safe-conduct notwithstanding, Hus was accused of having broken his side of the agreement—the emperor was seen to blush as the charges were read—and condemned to be burned at the stake, as indeed he duly was, in July 1415.

Neither the emperor nor the papacy gained much in the long run. Hus's death sparked violent uprisings in Bohemia that took until 1436 to suppress. Likewise, his reforming doctrines were the direct inspiration of Martin Luther a century later, a man whose actions caused a far greater schism than anything the Council of Konstanz had had to deal with—the Reformation itself, and the permanent division of the church between Catholics and Protestants. (Konstanz itself became a Protestant city in the Reformation, a revenge of sorts for the brutal treatment of Hus.)

Hus remains a key figure to Konstanz: There's a Hussenstrasse (Hus Street); the spot where he was killed is marked by a stone slab—the Hussenstein—and, appropriately, the square it's in is now the Lutherplatz; and the magnificent Konzilgebäude (Council Hall)—so called because it's claimed that the council of cardinals met here to choose the new pope, Martin V, in 1415 (they didn't; they met in the cathedral)—has a statue of Hus outside it. The Dominican monastery where Hus was held before his execution is still here, too, doing duty as a luxurious hotel, the Insel (*see* Dining and Lodging, below).

But for most visitors, Konstanz, for all its vivid history, is a town to be enjoyed for its more worldly pleasures—its elegant Alstadt (Old Town), trips on the lake, walks along the promenade, the classy shops, the restaurants, the views. The heart of the city is the **Gondelhafen,** the harbor, with the simple bulk of the Konzilgebäude looming behind it. Put up in 1388 as a warehouse, the building is now a concert hall. Alongside the Hus statue there's one of a more recent figure from the city's history, Graf Zeppelin, born in Konstanz in 1837.

Walk around the council building and take the street called Marktstatte. It leads to the **Rosgarten Museum,** the museum of local history. If you want to learn more about the Council of Konstanz, step inside. *Rosgartenstr. 3–5. Admission: DM 2.50. Open Tues.–Sat. 9–noon and 2–5, Sun. 10–noon.*

Continue up Marktstatte to the **Altes Rathaus** (Old Town Hall), built in the Renaissance and painted with boldly vivid frescoes—swags of flowers and fruits, shields, architectural details, sturdy knights wielding immense swords. Walk into the courtyard to admire its Renaissance restraint.

To see the spot where Hus was killed, continue past the Town Hall along Paradiesstrasse to Lutherplatz. Alternatively, turn right down Wessenbergstrasse, the main street of the Old Town. It leads to **St. Stephanskirche,** an austere, late-Gothic church with a very unGothic Rococo chancel. It stands in a little square surrounded by fine half-timbered houses. Look at the **Haus zur Katz** (on the right as you walk into the square). It was the headquarters of one of the city's trade guilds in the Middle Ages; now it houses the city archives.

Now walk through to the **Münster** (the cathedral), built on the site of the original Roman fortress. Building on the cathedral continued from the 10th century through the 19th, resulting in today's oddly contrasting building. The twin-towered facade, for example, is sturdily Romanesque, blunt and heavy looking; the elegant and airy chapels along the aisles are full-blown 15th-century Gothic; the complex nave vaulting is Renaissance; the choir is severely Neoclassical. Make a point of seeing the Holy Sepulchre tomb in the Mauritius Chapel at the far end of the church behind the altar. It's a richly worked 13th-century Gothic structure, 12 feet high, still with some of its original, vivid coloring and gilding, and studded with statues of the Apostles and figures from the childhood of Jesus.

Finally, you should walk up to the Rhine, through the **Niederburg,** the oldest part of Konstanz, a tangle of old, twisting streets. Once at the river, take a look at the two city towers here, the **Rheintor**—it's the one nearer the lake—and the aptly named **Pulverturm** (Powder Tower), the former city arsenal.

There are two easy island excursions you can make from Kon-
13 stanz. The first is to **Mainau,** "the island of flowers," 7 kilometers (4½ miles) north of Konstanz and easily reached by car (though cars aren't allowed on the island) and by boat. Mainau is one of the most unusual sites in Europe, a tiny island given over to the cultivation of rare plants. Not many people visit Germany expecting to find banana plantations, let alone such exotic flora as bougainvillea and hibiscus. But on Mainau these (and hundreds of more commonplace species) flourish, nurtured by the freakishly warm and moist climate. Visit in the spring and you'll find over a million tulips, hyacinths, and narcissi in bloom; rhododendrons and roses flower in May and June; dahlias dominate the late-summer display. The island was originally the property of the Teutonic Knights, who settled here in the 13th century. In the 19th century, Mainau passed to Grand Duke Friedrich I of Baden, a man with a passion for botany. He laid out most of the gardens and introduced many of the island's more exotic specimens. His daughter, Victoria, later queen of Sweden, gave the island to her son, Prince Wilhelm, and the island has remained Swedish ever since. Today, it's owned by Prince Wilhelm's son, Count Lennart Bernadette (who lives in the castle on the island, which can't be visited). There is a children's zoo to help keep younger visitors amused. Its wandering groups of tiny pot-bellied pigs are a hit with all visitors. *Admission: DM 8 adults, DM 6 senior citizens, DM 3 children 6–16, children under 6 free. Open Apr.–Oct., daily dawn–dusk.*

There's something of the same profusion of plant life to be seen
14 on the other excursion from Konstanz, **Reichenau,** though in this case it's vegetables that dominate rather than flowers. In fact, Reichenau is the single most important vegetable-growing area in Germany, with fully 15% of its area covered by greenhouses and practically the whole of the rest of the island growing something or other. Though it seems unlikely, amid the cabbages and the cauliflowers and the lettuces and the carrots and the potatoes, there are three of the most important and—for some, anyway—beautiful Romanesque churches in Europe on the island. Little Reichenau, 3 miles long and 1 mile wide, connected to the Bodanrück peninsula by just a narrow causeway, was one of the great monastic centers of the Dark Ages and the early Middle Ages. Secure from marauding tribesmen on its fertile island, the monastic community blossomed from the 8th century to the 12th, in the process developing into a major center of learning and the arts.

There are three villages on the island—Oberzell, Mittelzell, and Unterzell. Each is the site of one of the churches, with Mittelzell the site of the monastery itself. The first church you reach is the **Stiftskirche St. Georg** (the collegiate church of St. George), in Oberzell, built around 900. Cabbages grow in serried ranks up to its rough plaster walls. Small round-headed windows, a simple tower, and russet-color tiles provide the only exterior decoration. Inside, look for the wall paintings along the nave; they date from around 1000 and show the miracles of Christ. Their simple colors and unsteady outlines have an innocent, almost childlike charm. The striped backgrounds are typical of Romanesque frescoes.

The next church, begun in 816, is the largest and most important of the trio. It's the **Münster of St. Maria and St. Markus,** the monastery church itself. The monastery was founded in 725 by St. Pirmin; under the abbots Waldo (786–806) and Hatto I (806–23), it became one of the most important cultural centers of the Carolingian empire. It reached its zenith around 1000 under the rule of Abbot Hermanus Contractus, "the miracle of the century," when 700 monks lived here. It was then probably the most important center of book illumination in Germany. Though it's larger than St. Georg, the church here has much the same simplicity. It's by no means crude (though it can't be called technically sophisticated), just marvelously simple, a building that's utterly at one with the fertile soil in which it stands. Visit the **Schaztkammer** to see some of the more important treasures still here. They include a 5th-century ivory goblet with two carefully incised scenes of Christ's miracles and some priceless stained glass that is almost 1,000 years old. *Admission: DM 1 adults, 50 pf children. Open May–Sept. daily 11–noon and 3–4.*

The third church, the **Stiftskirche St. Peter and St. Paul,** at Unterzell, is a less perfect expression of the Romanesque, in part because it contains a number of later additions, most of them 15th century, and some Baroque stucco and frescoes. But it's worth a look anyway, if only to see the Romanesque frescoes in the apse, uncovered in 1990 during restoration work.

What to See and Do with Children

If your children are tired of swimming, racing paddleboats across the lake, and smashing balls around the miniature golf courses, take them to the zoo at **Affenburg** to feed the apes. It's about 8 kilometers (5 miles) north of Überlingen, in a forest. There are 200 Barbary apes here (the same sort of apes that live on the Rock of Gibraltar), and they're surprisingly friendly and trusting. Your admission price includes food you can give the apes. *Admission: DM 5 adults, DM 2.50 children. Open mid-Mar.–Oct. daily 9–noon and 1–6.*

There's another **zoo** halfway between Konstanz and Radolfzell. It features wild animals from all over Europe: bears, wolves, bison, and boars. It also has a petting zoo, with miniature goats, donkeys, and deer. There's an enormous playground, too. *Allensbach. Admission: DM 4 adults, DM 2 children 4–16, children under 4 free. Open Mar.–Sept. daily 9–6, Oct.–Feb. daily 10–5.*

For a day trip to Switzerland with the kids, try **Conny-Land,** just south of Konstanz on the road to Zurich. It's Europe's biggest dolphin aquarium, and also features go-carts, a minitrain, pony rides, a monorail, remote-controlled boats, and a petting zoo. The admission price allows unlimited use of all rides and facilities. Have lunch in the restaurant: huge glass panels allow a look into the dolphin pool. *Admission: 8 Swiss francs adults, Sfrs. 6 children. Open daily 9–6, dolphin and sea lion shows at 1:30 and 4:30.*

For a more sedate outing, take the kids on a cruise up the Rhine to Stein-am-Rhein in Switzerland to see the **Puppenmuseum.** It's the largest doll museum in Switzerland, with over 400 rare and antique dolls. *Schwarzhorngasse 136. Admission: Sfrs. 2. Open mid-Mar.–Oct. Tues.–Sun. 10–5.*

Off the Beaten Track

Head for the **Hat Museum** at Lindenberg, 16 kilometers (10 miles) northeast of Lindau in the Allgäu. It charts two centuries of hat-making. (Open Wed. 3–5:30 and Sun. 10–noon.) Or contemplate the achievements of the crusade for world peace as documented in Europe's first **Peace Museum.** It's in Bad Schachen, just outside Lindau. *Lindenhofweg 25. Open mid-Apr.–mid-Oct. Tues.–Sat. 10–noon and 2:30–5, Sun. 10–noon.*

If you're in Friedrichshafen you can make a nostalgic return to school with a visit to the **School Museum;** it's in the Schnetzenhausen suburb. There are convincing reconstructions of schoolrooms from 1830, 1880, and 1930—and not a pocket calculator in sight. *Open mid-June–mid-Sept. Tues.–Sat. 10–noon and 2:30–5, Sun. 10–noon, mid-Sept.–mid-June Sun 2–5.*

Just north of Konstanz on the Bodanrück Peninsula is the 1,000-acre **Wollmatinger Ried,** an area of moorland that's now a bird sanctuary. There are three-hour guided tours of the moor on Wednesdays and Saturdays, April through mid-October, at 4 PM, and two-hour tours June through mid-September on Tuesdays, Thursdays, and Fridays at 9 AM. Most of the birds you'll see are waterbirds, naturally; there are also remains of prehistoric stilt houses. Bring sturdy, comfortable shoes and mosquito repellent (if you can). Binoculars can be rented. Contact **DBV Naturschutzzentrum Wollmatinger Ried** (Fritz-Arnold-Str. 2e, Konstanz, tel. 07531/53550).

Shopping

The Bodensee is artists' territory, and shopping here means combing the many small galleries and artists' shops in lakeside towns and resorts for watercolors, engravings, and prints. Two reliable addresses are **Hans Müsken's** shop in Konstanz (Zollernstr. 3) and **Michael Zeller's** two shops in Lindau (Maximilianstr. and Cramergasse). Zeller organizes the celebrated, twice-yearly **Internationale Bodensee-Kunstauktion;** it's held in the spring and fall.

There's some fine local antiques and jewelry to hunt out, too. Two prominent craftsmen are **Christoph Rose** in Singen/Hohentwiel, just outside Radolfzell (Engestr. 1), and **Michael Zobel** in Konstanz (Augustinerstr. 4).

Pottery is a craft that's practiced in many places around the lake. You can find fine examples at **Angelika Ochsenreiter's** shop in Lindau (Ludwigstr. 29). On the island of Reichenau, there's loom producing highly individual weaving, at the **Werkgalerie Hochwart.**

Sports and Fitness

Bicycling Bikes can be rented from the train stations at Friedrichshafen, Konstanz, Lindau, and Überlingen for DM 10 a day (half that if you have a valid rail ticket). Some sports shops and tourist offices also rent bikes. In Konstanz, you can pick up bikes at three addresses: **Velotours** (Mainaustr. 34), **Radhaus** (Brückengasse 2), and **Rad-Lädele** (Komturweg 2a).

Boating There are more than 30 boatyards and sailing schools where you can rent boats; most will ask to see some kind of document (a proficiency certificate, for example, from a sailing school) to show you know how to handle a vessel under sail. Motorboats and rowboats can be rented in every resort without any such formalities. Windsurfers will also have no trouble finding boards to rent from any of the 35 rental points around the lake. Canoes can be rented from the **Huber** sports shop in Konstanz (Gottlieberstr. 32), as well as from some other places on the lake. Water-skiers are catered to on the lake, although the fun isn't inexpensive. The Bodensee is fine cruising water, too, and yachts can be chartered from the **Bodensee-Segelschule Wallhausen** (Zum Witmoos 10, 7750 Konstanz 19, tel. 07533/780).

Bowling Every resort has at least one hotel with a bowling alley. Konstanz has two bowling centers, each with eight alleys—the **Kegelzentrum Oberlohn** (Maybachstr. 18), and the **Kegel-und Freizeit-Center** (Markgrafenstr), which also has firing ranges, billiard tables, and dart boards.

Fishing Anglers agree the Bodensee is one of the biggest challenges Germany has to offer, with some fine sport in its mountain-fed waters. You'll need a license to fish; they are available, usually for a nominal fee, through the tourist office of the resort where you intend to fish. The Vordere Hörl tourist office offers vacations for anglers; contact the **Verkehrsverein Vordere Hörl** (Rathaus, 7761 Moos, tel. 07732/2544).

Golf Lindau has an 18-hole course on the grounds of a castle, **Schloss Schönbühl.** Guests are welcome. Contact the **Golf-Club Lindau-Bad Schachen** (Kemptenerstr. 125, 8990 Lindau, tel. 08382/6988). Konstanz also has a golf club, which welcomes foreign visitors provided they are members of clubs in their own countries. Contact the **Golf-Club Konstanz** (Langenrain, Hofgut Kargegg, 7753 Allensbach 3, tel. 07533/5124).

Horseback Riding There are riding stables in most Bodensee resorts, and some fine lakeside bridle paths, including a 12-mile trail from Konstanz to Radolfzell. You can rent horses from the **Reit-Club Konstanz** (Mainaustr. 78a, 7750 Konstanz, tel. 07531/61604).

Swimming The resorts of the Bodensee tell Germans they don't have to travel as far as the Mediterranean—the lake has comparable beaches and cleaner water. The beach's boast is debatable, but the water certainly sparkles. Open-air pools and lidos abound—at last count, there were 150 around the lake. Lindau's **Eichwald** lido has a lake beach a half-mile long and one acre of sunbathing lawns. The **Jakob** lido in Konstanz has a lakeside leisure area and heated pools.

Tennis Every resort has its tennis club, and you should have no difficulty getting onto a court. Konstanz has the biggest tennis center on the lake, the **Tennis Center Helle Müller** (Eichhornstr. 83, 7750 Konstanz, tel. 07531/54495).

Dining and Lodging

Dining

Fish specialties predominate around the Bodensee. There are 35 different types of fish in the lake, with *Renken* (lake trout) and *Felchen* the most highly prized. Felchen belongs to the salmon family and is best eaten *blau* (poached) in rosemary sauce or baked in almonds (*Müllerin*). Wash it down with a top-quality Meersburg white wine. If you venture north to Upper Swabia, you'll find *Pfannkuchen* and *Spätzle* are the most common specialties. Both are flour-and-egg dishes. Pfannkuchen, or pancakes, are generally filled with meat, cheese, jam, or sultanas, or chopped into fine strips and scattered in a clear consommé soup known as *Flädlesupp*. Spätzle, golden-roasted egg noodles, are the usual accompaniment for the Swabian Sunday roast-beef lunch of *Rinderbraten*. One of the best-known Swabian dishes is *Maultaschen*, a kind of ravioli, usually served floating in a broth strewn with chives.

Highly recommended restaurants are indicated by a star ★.

Category	Cost*
Very Expensive	over DM 90
Expensive	DM 55–DM 90
Moderate	DM 35–DM 55
Inexpensive	under DM 35

**per person for a three-course meal, including tax and tip but not wine*

Lodging

There's a wide range of hotels in all the towns and resorts around the lake, from venerable, wedding-cake-style Edwardian palaces to more modest and modern *Gasthöfe* (inns). If you're visiting in July and August, make reservations well in advance and expect higher-than-average prices. For lower rates and a more rural atmosphere, consider staying away from the lake in Upper Swabia or the Allgäu.

Highly recommended hotels are indicated by a star ★.

Category	Cost*
Very Expensive	over DM 180
Expensive	DM 120–DM 180
Moderate	DM 80–DM 120
Inexpensive	under DM 80

**All prices are for a standard double room for two, including tax and service charges.*

Friedrichshafen
Dining and Lodging

Buchhorner Hof. The 19th-century Buchhorner Hof is a resolutely traditional hotel in the center of Friedrichshafen. Hunting trophies on the walls, leather armchairs, and Turkish rugs decorate the public areas; bedrooms are large and comfortable. The restaurant is plush and subdued, with delicately carved chairs and mahogany-paneled walls. It offers a choice of menus that feature such dishes as pork medallions, perch fillet, and lamb chops. *Friedrichshafenstr. 33, tel. 07541/2050. 65 rooms with bath. Facilities: restaurant, bar, sauna, solarium. AE, DC, MC, V. Closed Dec. 20–Jan. 10. Expensive.*

City-Krone. This is a modern hotel with large rooms on a quiet, centrally located street about 200 yards from the lake. The public areas are sleekly furnished, with rug-covered marble floors and muted brass lights. The spiral staircase is almost overgrown with plants. Tile floors and peach tablecloths create a beguilingly old-fashioned mood in the restaurant; nonetheless, the emphasis remains firmly on the food, not the surroundings. Fish is the specialty—perch, pike, (something of an acquired taste), and Felchen—though some meat dishes are also served (try the Swabian pork fillet). *Schanzstr. 7, tel. 07541/22086. 80 rooms with bath. Facilities: restaurant, bar, sauna, pool. AE, DC, MC, V. Closed Dec. 12–Jan. 20; restaurant closed weekends. Expensive.*

Konstanz
Dining

Engstler's. Informal and friendly, Engstler's is a noisy, popular restaurant across the street from the Council Building. The food is distinctly red-blooded, with game dishes heavily featured. Venison goulash and roast boar are favorites; whitefish fillet numbers among the fish dishes. Special children's menus are also available. In summer, eat in the beer garden. *Fischmarkt 1, tel. 07531/23126. Reservations not required. Dress: informal. AE, DC, MC, V. Closed Jan. and Feb. Inexpensive.*

Dining and Lodging

★ **Seehotel Siber.** The most elegant dining in the region is offered at the Seehotel Siber. Though it's a little hotel, too, plushly furnished and smoothly run, it's the adjoining restaurant that's the major attraction. The food is part traditional, part nouvelle, with roast saddle of lamb and Barbary duck among the specialties. Other dishes are offered seasonally. The restaurant is divided in three: One room is done up like a library, with massive bookcases and peach tablecloths; the center room is airy and spacious, with a white ceiling and bold modern paintings; the third has mint-color walls, a deep green carpet, and enormous wood chairs. The mood throughout is formal and a little hushed. The Seehotel is located by the casino. *Seestr. 25, tel. 07531/63044. 11 rooms with bath. Facilities: restaurant (reservations essential, jacket and tie required). AE, DC. Hotel closed 3 weeks in Feb.; restaurant closed for dinner Mon. and Tues. Nov.–Jan. Very Expensive.*

★ **Steigenberger Insel-Hotel.** If the Seehotel offers the best dining in town, then this must be the best hotel, or at least the most luxurious. It's a former 13th-century monastery—the original cloisters are still here—where Hus was held before his execution and, much later, Graf Zeppelin was born. Bedrooms are spacious and stylish, more like those in a private home than in a hotel; service is appropriately polished. The restaurant is rather imposing, with some fine arches and great views over the lake. The Dominikaner Stube downstairs is rustic and there's the clubby, relaxed Zeppelin Bar. Gardens bright with flowers surround the hotel, keeping the bustle of Konstanz at bay. *Auf* *der Insel 1, tel. 07531/25011. Facilities: restaurant, 2 bars, beach, and garden. AE, DC, MC, V. Very Expensive.*

Lodging **Buchner Hof.** Elegant and well run, the small Buchner Hof is a 10-minute walk north of the old town just across the Rheinbrücke. It's a comfortable, quiet hotel, with spacious bedrooms featuring oak-veneer furniture (all of it new). There's no restaurant. *Bucherstr. 6, tel. 07531/51035. 13 rooms with bath. Facilities: wine bar, sauna, solarium. AE. Closed Christmas–Jan 10. Moderate.*

Lindau
Dining

★ **Restaurant Hoyerberg Schoessle.** A location offering a commanding view across the lake to Bregenz and the Alps combines with elegant nouvelle cuisine to make this about the best dining experience in Lindau. The specialties are fish and game, changing seasonally. There are fixed-price menus of six and eight courses; one offers lobster, noodles with white truffles and goose liver, and roast breast of squab. The decor features brick-trimmed arched windows, fresh flowers, and elegant, high-back chairs. Dine on the terrace for the terrific view. *Hoyerbergstr. 64, tel. 08382/25295. Reservations essential. Jacket and tie required. AE, DC, MC. Closed Feb. and Mon. Expensive.*

★ **Historische Bräugaststätte zum Schlechterbräu.** This is where the locals come for *Frühschoppen*, a Sunday brunch—and a vigorous tradition in this part of the country—of two fat sausages with sauerkraut and a tall glass of beer. The interior is authentically Teutonic, with oak booths and colorful stained-glass lamps. The food is every bit as robust, with Bavarian specialties predominating. Try the juicy *Schweinshaxen* (grilled pork knuckle). In summer, you can eat in the beer garden. The restaurant is located in the Old Town, on the island, near the Peterskirche. *In der Grub 28, tel. 08382/5842. Reservations not required. Dress: informal. No credit cards. Closed late Feb. and mid-Nov. Inexpensive.*

Gasthaus zum Sünfzen. Located in the heart of the Old Town, the Gasthaus zum Sünfzen is an appealing old inn with little leaded windows and a simple, wood-paneled interior. The food features such regional specialties as venison and lake fish, and sausages from the restaurant's own butcher shop. Try either the spinach Spätzle or the Felchen fillet. The menu changes daily and seasonally. *Maximilianstr. 1, tel. 08382/5865. Reservations advised. Dress: informal. AE, DC, MC, V. Closed Feb. Inexpensive.*

Lodging **Helvetia.** The sturdy old Helvetia is located on the harbor, looking out to the lighthouse and the lion. It's a popular resort hotel with a busy café/restaurant offering more of those same views and rooms with substantial four-poster pine beds and bold red-flowered prints. Some rooms also have pine bunk beds for children. *An der Seepromenade, tel. 08382/4002. 60 rooms with bath. Facilities: restaurant, bar, pool, sauna, solarium. AE, DC, MC, V. Closed mid-Nov.–Mar. Expensive.*

Lindauer Hof. The Lindauer is equally central but rather more restrained, with an elegant lounge filled with sturdy 19th-century furniture and spacious rooms. The building went up in the mid-18th century, and has shuttered windows and high gables. Front rooms afford the best views, naturally. *An der Seepromenade, tel. 08382/4064. 23 rooms with bath. Facilities: restaurant, bar, indoor pool, sauna, solarium. AE, MC, V. Closed mid-Nov.–mid-Mar. Moderate.*

Meersburg
Dining

Winzertrinkstube. The Winzertrinkstube is located down the steep hill from the Altes Schloss. The dining room is centered round an 18th-century wine press, now doing duty as a vast, geranium-filled flower pot. The food is heartily Swabian: Try *Käsespätzle* (cheese Spätzle) or Maultaschen. The terrace is a perfect spot for people-watching. *Steigstr. 33, tel. 07532/6484. Reservations advised. Dress: informal. No credit cards. Closed Dec.–Feb. Inexpensive.*

Lodging

Rothmund. The Rothmund has a hillside location east of the Old Town with a commanding view of the Alps. Don't be put off by the boxy exterior; inside, the hotel is tasteful and not a little plush, with antiques and Turkish rugs. The imposing breakfast room (complete with 17th-century armoire and tile fireplace) is decorated with paintings by owner Herr Rothmund. This is a place that's ideal for families (it's only a two-minute walk from a lakeside playground and minigolf) and those seeking a quiet atmosphere away from the bustle of the Old Town. *Uferpromenade 11, tel. 07532/6054. 21 rooms with bath. Facilities: restaurant, bar, garden, pool. AE. Closed Nov.–Mar. Moderate.*

Zum Bären. Built in the 16th century, the zum Bären will be the choice of those who value atmosphere over modern convenience. Creaking staircases and wood ceilings ensure maximum old-world charm, though colorful wallpapers and bright bedspreads lighten the mood. Service is excellent, the result perhaps of the fact that the hotel has been owned and run by the same family since the mid-17th century. *Marktpl. 11, tel. 07532/6044. 16 rooms with bath. Facilities: restaurant/wine bar. No credit cards. Closed mid-Nov.–mid-Mar. Moderate.*

Überlingen
Dining and Lodging

★ **Parkhotel St. Leonard.** Located about a mile from the lake on a vineyard-covered hillside, the modern St. Leonard offers elegance and style. All rooms have balconies, but try for one with a view of the lake. The restaurant is sleekly contemporary, with modern paintings and lavish place settings. In summer, you dine on a canopied terrace. Try the fresh trout with almond-butter sauce. Four- and six-course fixed-price menus are also offered. *Obere St. Leonardstr. 83, tel. 07551/8080. 158 rooms with bath. Facilities: restaurant, bar, indoor pool, sauna, solarium, indoor and outdoor tennis, billiards. AE. Expensive.*

★ **Romantik Hotel Hecht.** The little Hecht offers discreetly chic old-world comforts and superb food. It's a former Weinstube, built at the end of the 18th century and easy to spot with a magnificent sign (a gold fish clutching a bunch of grapes in its jaws). The restaurant is rustically decorated, with old plates and serving dishes ranged around the walls and a splendid grandfather clock. Fish is the main offering—try it either blau or Müllerin. If your tastes run to more exotic fare, Thai menus are also available—call a day or so ahead. *Münsterstr. 8, tel. 07551/63333. 9 rooms with bath. Facilities: restaurant (reservations advised). AE, DC, MC, V. Closed mid-Feb–mid-Mar. (restaurant also closed Mon.). Expensive.*

The Arts and Nightlife

The Arts

Music The region has its own orchestra, the **Bodensee Symphony Orchestra,** founded in 1932 and based in **Konstanz,** and with a season running from October through April. Program details and bookings are available from **Bodensee Symphonie Orchester** (Spanierstr. 3, 7750 Konstanz, tel. 07531/52855 or 07531/63031). Konstanz has an annual summer music festival, from mid-June to mid-July, with an international program of orchestral and chamber concerts and recitals. For program details and bookings contact the Konstanz tourist office (tel. 07531/284–377). Performances are held in the Council Building. **Überlingen** also has an international music festival, with concerts every Tuesday from May to September in the lakeside Kursaal. For program details and bookings, contact the **Städtische Verwaltung** (Landungspl. 7, 7770 Überlingen, tel. 07551/4041). **Meersburg** has an annual international chamber music festival in the magnificent Hall of Mirrors (Spiegelsaal) of the Neues Schloss. The concerts are held every Saturday from June to September. For program details and bookings, contact the **Städtische Kur-und Verkehrsverwaltung** (Schlosspl. 4, 7758 Meersburg, tel. 07532/82382). Several other castles and churches of the region are the scene of regular chamber music concerts and recitals, particularly in summer. For program details, contact the regional tourist office: the **Internationaler Bodenseeverkehrsverein und Fremdenverkehrsverband Bodensee-Oberschwaben** (Schützenstr. 8, 7750 Konstanz, tel. 07531/22232).

Theater **Konstanz** claims Germany's oldest active theater. Its **Stadttheater** (Konzilstr.) was originally a Jesuit college, where plays were staged as early as 1609. The theater has an annual repertory program of up to a dozen productions, and, apart from its main auditorium with seating for 400, it has a small workshop theater. For program details and bookings, contact the **Stadttheater Konstanz** (Konzilstr. 11, 7750 Konstanz, tel. 07531/200–750). **Lindau** and **Ravensburg** both have city theaters where touring productions are regularly staged.

Nightlife

Most of the towns and resorts of the Bodensee have regular evenings of entertainment for visitors, ranging from traditional folk music and dancing to more modern fare such as jazz and pop concerts. Local tourist offices have programs. Many resort hotels also organize regular *Heimatabende* (folk-music evenings) or *Gästeabende* (guests' evenings); in some, Saturday night really is dance night.

In summer, you can dance on the water—on one of the evening cruises organized by the Bodensee **Weisse Flotte** operators. The boats pick dancers and revelers up every Saturday night from May to September in Konstanz, Lindau, Meersburg, Rorschach, and Überlingen. For further details and bookings, contact the **Bodensee-Schiffsbetriebe der Deutschen Bundesbahn** (Hafenstr. 6, 7750 Konstanz, tel. 07531/281–389).

The **disco** scene is concentrated in Konstanz. **Flair** (Reichenauerstr. 212) is one of the biggest and best. Meersburg claims to have the most romantic disco—**Barcarole,** candlelit and overlooking the lake (Fährhaus Meersburg, Fährepl.).

Konstanz and Lindau have **casinos** (open daily till 2 AM), but the Las Vegas of the lake is at **Bregenz,** just over the Austrian border, on the southeastern shore. Perhaps the secret of its success lies in the generous practice of handing visitors their entrance money back in chips. You'll need a passport not only for the Bregenz casino but for the German ones, too.

6 The Bavarian Forest

Introduction

There are few areas in Europe where you can still wander undisturbed for days at a time, meeting no more than a handful of like-minded souls, and yet remain within short distance of an historic city or time-honored inn.

The *Bayerische Wald* (Bavarian Forest), in the southeast of Germany, is one such place. It's an ideal area to visit if you cherish the values of a more unhurried age and want to get close to the heart of an older Germany. This is central Europe's largest unbroken stretch of forest (although, like the Black Forest, it contains expansive sectors of rolling farmland). Czechoslovakia and, for a short stretch, Austria border it along its eastern rim; its southern limit is defined by the Danube. Unlike other border areas of Germany, however, this one has felt little influence from its neighbors. The region's flavor is also vastly different from the stock concept of the Bavaria of Munich and the deep south, a world supposedly populated by jolly peasants—men in Lederhosen and funny green hats with feathers and buxom women decked out in flowing dirndls—who spend their time singing along with oompah bands and knocking back great mugs of beer. The people of the Bavarian Forest are reserved, less effusive; even their accent is more refined than that of their southern countrymen.

This is a region for those in search of peace and quiet: hikers, nature lovers, skiers looking for uncrowded slopes, golfers distressed by the steep greens fees of more fashionable courses, and families on tight budgets with kids in tow.

The Bavarian Forest can be a welcome alternative to the tourist hype and crowds in places like Munich and Rothenburg. If the low-key and understated are your style, then you are sure to find this area very much to your taste.

Essential Information

Important Addresses and Numbers

Tourist Information

There are local tourist information offices in the following towns:

Bayerisch-Eisenstein: Verkehrsamt Bayerisch-Eisenstein, Schulbergstrasse, 8371 Bayerisch-Eisenstein, tel. 09925/327.
Bodenmais: Verkehrsverein Bodenmais, Bergknappenstrasse 10, 8373 Bodenmais, tel. 09924/214.
Cham: Verkehrsverein Cham, Rosenstrasse 1, 8491 Cham, tel. 09971/4933.
Deggendorf: Verkehrsverein Deggendorf, Oberer Stadtplatz 4, 8360 Deggendorf, tel. 0991/380169.
Freyung: Verkehrsamt Freyung, Rathausweg 1, 8393 Freyung, tel. 08551/4455.
Furth im Wald: Verkehrsverein Furth im Wald, Schlossplatz 1, 8492 Furth im Wald, tel. 09973/3813.
Grafenau: Verkehrsamt Grafenau, Am Rathaus, 8352 Grafenau, tel. 08552/2085.
Passau: Fremdenverkehrsverein Passau, Am Rathausplatz, 8390 Passau, tel. 0851/33421.

Regen: Verkehrsamt Haus des Gastes, 8370 Regen, tel. 09921/2929.
St. Englmar: Verkehrsamt St. Englmar, Rathausstrasse 6, 8449 St. Englmar, tel. 09965/221.
Straubing: Städtisches Verkehrsamt Straubing, Rathaus, Theresienplatz, 8440 Straubing, tel. 09421/16307.
Tittling: Verkehrsamt Tittling, Marktplatz 10, 8391 Tittling, tel. 08504/2666.
Viechtach: Städtisches Kur- und Verkehrsamt, Rathaus, 8374 Viechtach, tel. 09942/1622.
Waldkirchen: Fremdenverkehrsamt Waldkirchen, Hauzenbergerstrasse 1, 8392 Waldkirchen, tel. 08581/665.
Zwiesel: Verkehrsamt Zwiesel, Im Rathaus, 8372 Zwiesel, tel. 09922/1308.

Car Rental **Europcar:** Neuburgerstrasse 93, **Passau,** tel. 0851/6033.

Arriving and Departing by Plane

The nearest airports are at Munich and Nürnberg. Each is about 160 kilometers (100 miles) from the western edge of the Bavarian Forest.

Arriving and Departing by Car

The principal road links with the Bavarian Forest are the A-3 Autobahn from Nürnberg and the A-92 Autobahn from Munich (sections of the latter are still being completed). Nürnberg is 104 kilometers (65 miles) from Regensburg and 229 kilometers (140 miles) from Passau. Munich is 120 kilometers (75 miles) from Regensburg and 179 kilometers (110 miles) from Passau. Traffic on both roads is relatively light, even at peak periods.

Getting Around

By Car The small country highways and side roads within this region are less travelled, making the whole area something of a paradise for those who have experienced only the high-speed mayhem of most other German roads. B-85 runs the length of the Bavarian Forest from Cham in the northwest to Passau in the southeast and the Ostmarkstrasse has been designated a special scenic tourist route in Germany.

By Train Two main rail lines cross the region: One runs west to east via Nürnberg, Regensburg, Passau, and Vienna; the other runs south to north via Munich, Landshut, and Straubing. This latter route slices right through the heart of the Bavarian Forest on its way to Czechoslovakia (if you fancy overnighting in Prague, this is the train route to take). Plattling, just south of Deggendorf, is a main rail junction. Passau is the principal rail gateway on the border between southeast Germany and Austria.

By Bus Villages not on the railway line are well served by post bus. Passau has a municipal bus service that reaches into the hinterland.

By Boat The Danube, an important means of transport through East Bavaria, links the whole area with the rest of Germany and eastern Europe. Soviet ships, in fact, are a common sight in Passau. The Danube shipping company of **Ludwig Wurm** (Donaustr. 71, 8444 Irlbach, tel. 09424/1341) operates a passenger service in the summer between Regensburg and Passau. The company's comfortable motor ship *Agnes Bernauer* travels the Regensburg–Passau stretch on Sundays and the Deggendorf–Passau stretch on Tuesdays, Wednesdays, and Thursdays from July through September. (Wednesdays and Thursdays only in June). The Passau shipping company of **Wurm & Köck** (Höllgasse 26, 8390 Passau, tel. 0851/2066) operates a service between Passau and Linz in Austria. Ships of the **Erste Donau-Dampfschiffahrts-Gesellschaft,** or DDSG for short (DDSG Schiffstation, Postfach 1424, 8390 Passau, tel. 0851/33035), sail between Passau and Vienna. Wurm & Köck also operates short cruises on the Danube, the Inn, and the Ilz rivers (*see* Guided Tours, below).

Guided Tours

Several tourist offices in the Bavarian Forest organize bus tours of the region and excursions into Czechoslovakia. The Freyung tourist office (tel. 08551/4455) has weekly half-day trips to the Bavarian National Park and to the Dreisessel mountain for DM 8. The Freyung office also organizes regular trips to Prague in Czechoslovakia, as do the tourist offices of Grafenau (tel. 08552/2085) and Tittling (tel. 08504/2666). In Tittling, the **Hötl** bus company (tel. 08504/2092) has daily excursions in summer into the Bavarian Forest. Day trips throughout the area are also offered by **Manfred Eichberger** (tel. 08501/324), a bus operator in Kellberg, just outside Passau. The company will pick up passengers at Passau hotels.

Guided tours of Passau are organized from April through October by the city tourist office (tel. 0851/33421). There are two tours (at 10:30 and 2:30) from Monday to Friday, and one (at 2:30) on Saturdays and Sundays. Tours start at King Max Joseph monument in the Domplatz (the cathedral square), and last one hour. Cost is DM 3 adults, DM 1.50 children. A special tour for photographers is conducted on the last Saturday afternoon of every month from May through October. The two-hour tour starts at the Domplatz monument at 2 PM; cost is DM 6.

Cruises on Passau's three rivers begin and end at the Danube jetties on Fritz-Schäffer Promenade. March through October, regular 45-minute trips on the Danube, Inn, and Ilz are run by **Wurm & Köck** (Höllgasse 26, 8390 Passau, tel. 0851/2065). Cost is DM 6 adults, DM 3 children. Wurm & Köck also has regular cruises on the Austrian section of the Danube that reach as far as Linz. A two-day cruise to Linz, including overnight accommodations in a four-star hotel, costs DM 89. On Saturdays, April through October, evening cruises with music are offered. Duty-free cigarettes and alcohol can be bought during cruises to the Austrian sections of the Danube and Inn; a liter of Austrian rum costs just DM 20 at the ship's bar.

On the Inn River, an Austrian shipping operator, **M. Schaurecker** (A.-Stifterstr. 581, A-4780 Schärding, tel. 0043/771-23231), runs a daily service Tuesday through Sunday, mid-March through mid-November, between Passau and the enchanting Austrian river town of Schärding. The round-trip fare is DM 12.

Exploring the Bavarian Forest

Numbers in the margin correspond with points of interest on Bavarian Forest map.

Highlights for First-time Visitors

Heilige Grabkirche, Deggendorf
Metten Abbey library
Bavarian Forest National Park
Passau Cathedral organ
Neue Residenz, Passau
View from the Mariahilfberg, Passau

From Cham to Dreiburgenland

The gateway to the Bavarian Forest and the northernmost point of the Ostmarkstrasse—the tourist route that stretches
1 deep into the heart of the region—is the little town of **Cham.** Located on the Regen River, Cham is distinguished by intact sections of original 14th-century town walls, including a massive tower, the Straubinger Turm.

Heading southeast from Cham on B-85, look for the ruins of a
2 medieval castle perched on the 2,500-foot-high **Haidstein** peak. Around the year 1200, it was home to the German poet Wolfram von Eschenbach. On the slopes is a 1,000-year-old linden tree known as Wolframslinde (Wolfram's linden tree). With a circumference of more than 50 feet, its hollow trunk could easily shelter 50 people.

As you head south on B-85 you'll pass sunny villages with trim streets and gardens and see two sinuous lakes created by the dammed Regen River. From here the Weisser (white) Regen soon becomes the Schwarzer (black) Regen.

Between the village of Prackenbach and the little town of
3 Viechtach you'll see a dramatic section of the **Pfahl,** one of Europe's most extraordinary geological phenomena. The ridge of glistening white quartz juts dramatically out of the ground in an arrow-straight spur that extends more than 100 kilometers (60 miles) through the Bavarian Forest. Here the quartz rises in folds to heights of 100 feet or more.

4 Stop in **Viechtach** to see its spectacularly decorated Rococo church and to visit the **Kristall Museum,** which houses a glittering display of semi-precious stones and crystals from all over the world. *Bahnhofstr., tel. 09942/8107. Admission: DM 3 adults, DM 1 children. Open daily 10–5.*

Ten kilometers (6 miles) beyond Viechtach is Patersdorf. Here you can turn right (south) onto B-11 toward the historic Danube town of Deggendorf, 21 kilometers (13 miles) away, and the monastery of Metten, or turn left to visit the little spa of Bodenmais.

5 **Deggendorf** nestles between the Danube and the forested hills that rise in tiers to the Czech border. The town was once a settlement on the banks of the Danube, but repeated flooding forced its inhabitants to move to higher ground in the 13th cen-

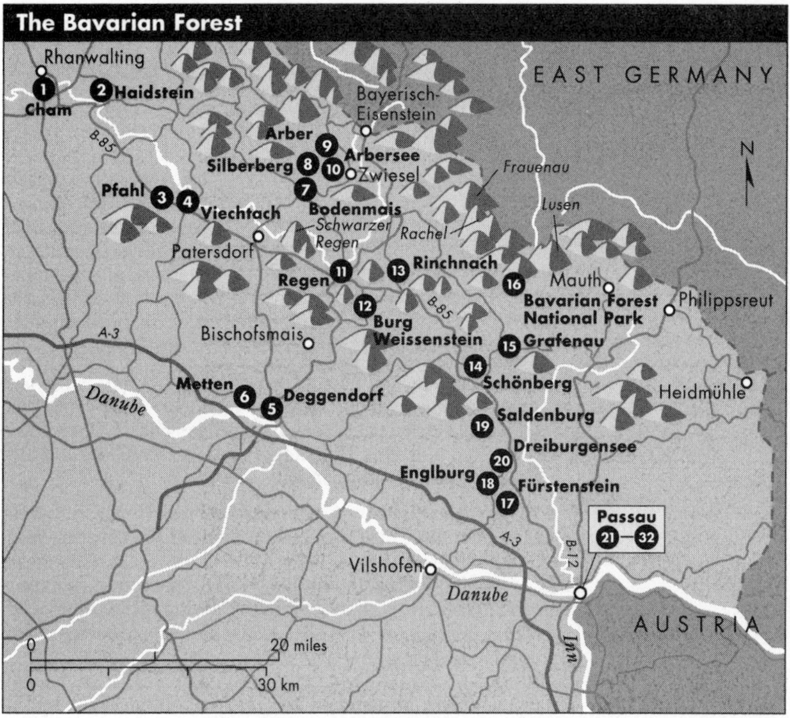

The Bavarian Forest

tury. A 30-yard stretch of the original town wall remains from those early years; there are other points of interest from later centuries, including a 16th-century **Rathaus** (Town Hall) located in the center of the wide main street, the Marktstrasse. *Tel. 0991/4004. Admission: DM1 adults, children. Tower open weekdays 10–noon and 2–4, Sat. 10–noon.*

At one end of the Marktstrasse stands the **Heilige Grabkirche,** which was originally built as a Gothic basilica in the 14th century. Its lofty tower—regarded as the finest Baroque church tower in southern Germany—was added 400 years later by the Munich master-builder Johann Michael Fischer. *Admission free. Open daily 9–sunset.*

Behind the church is the **Stadtmuseum** (City Museum) with exhibits tracing the history of the Danube people. *Admission free. Open Tues.–Sun. 10–4, Thurs. 10–8.*

Lovers of the Baroque may want to make a 7-kilometer (4-mile) side trip northwest of Deggendorf to the ancient Benedictine
6 abbey of **Metten**, founded in the 9th century by Charlemagne. Within its white walls and quiet cloisters is one of Germany's outstanding 18th-century libraries, with a collection of 160,000 books whose gilded leather spines are complemented by the heroic splendor of their surroundings: Herculean figures support the frescoed, vaulted ceiling, and allegorical paintings and fine stucco work identify different categories of books. In the monastery church is Cosmas Damian Asam's altar painting of *Lucifer Destroyed by St. Michael*, created about 1720. Its vivid

coloring and swirling composition are typical of the love of drama and movement in Baroque art. *Admission free (donations welcome). Guided tours daily at 10 and 3, except Easter.*

7 **Bodenmais,** 14 kilometers (9 miles) northeast of Patersdorf, is a health resort tucked into a valley below the Bavarian Forest's highest mountain, the 4,800-foot-high Arber. A nearby silver mine helped Bodenmais gain prosperity before tourism reached this isolated part of the country. The 700-year-old mine was closed in 1962 but you can still view its workings near
8 the summit of the 3,000-foot-high **Silberberg** (Silver Mountain). You can take the chair lift from the Arber Road, about 2 miles north of Bodenmais, or enjoy the easy, 15-minute walk from the road to the entrance of the mine. *Admission, including guided tour: DM 5 adults, DM 3 children. Open daily 10–4.*

Bodenmais also boasts a long tradition of glass making. Glass foundries have been busy in the Bavarian Forest for centuries; indeed, some Germans still call it the Glass Forest. Two glassworks can be visited in Bodenmais: the **Austen Glashütte** and the **Waldglashütte** (both open Mon.–Fri. 9–6, Sat. 9–2).

9 The **Arber**—the highest mountain of both the Bavarian Forest and the Bohemian Forest on the other side of the border—is located 13 kilometers (8 miles) north of Bodenmais. A bus service runs from Bodenmais to the base of the mountain, where a chair lift makes the 10-minute trip to the summit. A short walk
10 from the bottom of the lift leads to the **Arbersee lake,** surrounded by thick forest.

Time Out You can quench your thirst or fortify yourself for a hike up the Arber at the friendly **Gasthof** on the shores of the lake.

From Bodenmais, you'll join the Ostmarkstrasse again at
11 **Regen,** (20 kilometers/12 miles south) a busy market town with fine 16th-century houses around its large central square. On the last weekend in July the town celebrates an event that made culinary history: The creation in the 17th century of *Pichelsteiner Eintop* (pork and vegetable stew), a filling dish that has become a staple throughout Germany. The celebrations include sports events on the Regen River, so pack a swimsuit if you fancy joining in.

Regen has another claim to fame: a Christmas crèche created by Frau Maria-Elisabeth Pscheidl, who has been making the items for over 30 years. Today her collection is claimed to be the biggest—and (according to the local tourist office) best—of its kind in the world—even the Vatican has given it a seal of approval. Many of her creations are displayed in the **Pscheidl Bayerwald-Krippe Museum,** run by the town council in Frau Pscheidl's home. The collection grows from week to week. "I'll be adding to it as long as God allows me to," says Frau Pscheidl. *Ludwigsbrücke 3. Admission: DM 2 adults, DM 1.50 children. Open whenever Frau Pscheidl is at home.*

Just south of Regen, on the heights of Weissenstein, are the
12 ruins of **Burg Weissenstein.** The far, square tower rising from the surrounding rubble is all that remains of the original 11th-century castle, which was largely destroyed in the War of the Austrian Succession in the 18th century.

Eight kilometers (5 miles) east of Regen, still on the Ost-
13 markstrasse, lies the village of **Rinchnach.** Once the administrative center of church lands that extended deep into the Bavarian Forest, it is now a sleepy resort. Its importance began with the arrival in the 11th century of a monk who had left his monastery in search of greater solitude. Over the centuries, this once-lonely retreat grew (with royal Bavarian patronage) into an important monastery. The **monastery church** you see today was built in the 15th century. In 1727, Johann Michael Fischer was summoned from Munich to extend and renovate it in Baroque style. Visit its expansive and lordly interior to see his masterful wrought-iron work and some typically heroic frescoes.

Drive 17 kilometers (10 miles) south and turn left off the
14 Ostmarkstrasse to the village of **Schönberg,** set snugly within the encroaching forest. Linger in its Marktplatz (market square), where arcaded shops and houses present an almost Italian air. As you head farther south down the Inn Valley, this Italian influence—the so-called Inn-Valley style—becomes more pronounced.

Time Out Drop in at any time of day at the **Gasthof zur Post,** where you can eat well and inexpensively from a menu that reads like a guide to the cuisine of the Bavarian Forest. The local beer is about the best in the region.

Three miles east of Schönberg, deep in the Bavarian Forest, is
15 **15 Grafenau,** a typical little resort distinguished (for some people, anyway) as the favorite retreat of former West German Chancellor Willy Brandt.

Some 10 kilometers (6 miles) north of Grafenau is the main en-
16 trance to the **Bavarian Forest National Park**, a 32,000-acre stretch of the thickest forest in central Europe. Bears, wolves, and lynx roamed wild in these parts until well into the 19th century. Substantial efforts have been made to reintroduce these and other animals to the park, though today the animals are restricted to large enclosures. Well-marked paths lead to points where the animals can best be seen. Bracing walks also take you through the thickly wooded terrain to the two highest peaks of the park, the 4,767-foot **Rachel** and the 4,504-foot **Lusen.** Specially marked educational trails trace the geological and botanical history of the area, and picnic spots and playgrounds abound. In winter, park wardens will lead you through the snow to where wild deer from the mountains feed. A visitor center—**The National Park-Haus**—is located at the main entrance to the park. Slide shows and English-language brochures provide introductions to the area.

South of Grafenau lies the **Dreiburgenland,** (the Land of the
Three Castles). Its name comes from three famous castles:
17 18 19 **Fürstenstein, Englburg,** and **Saldenburg.** The little village of
Fürstenstein likes to call itself the "Pearl of the Dreiburgenland." You can get a fine view from the walls of its castle
of the Danube plain to the south, and the mountains of the Ba-
20 varian Forest to the north. On the shores of the **Dreiburgensee**
in Tittling, you'll find the **Freilichtmuseum** (Open-air Museum), which boasts 50 reconstructed Bavarian Forest houses. You can sit on the benches of a 17th-century schoolhouse, drink schnaps in an 18th-century tavern, or watch how grain was

ground in a 15th-century mill. *Museum-Dorf Bayerische Wald, Neben Hotel Dreiburgensee, Tittling tel. 08504/8482. Admission: DM 3. Open Easter–Oct., 9–5.*

Passau

Twenty kilometers (12 miles) south on the Ostmarkstrasse, at the eastern limit of lower Bavaria and the Bavarian Forest, lies
21 the ancient city of **Passau,** a remote yet important embarcation point for the traffic that has plied its way along the Danube River for centuries, traveling between Germany, central Europe, and the Black Sea. Two other rivers meet at Passau: the Inn and the much smaller Ilz. The town's strategic location at the confluence of these three rivers has inevitably given rise to comparison with other cities built on water, including Venice.

While Passau is no "Venice of the north," it does share with that Italian city a certain quality of light that painters throughout the centuries have been attracted to and tried to capture in their work. The typical Inn Valley buildings along its old streets, with their low, graceful arcades, give the city something of a Mediterranean air. It should come as no surprise that many of the architects who worked in Passau were Italian.

Settled first by the Celts, then by the Romans, Passau passed early on into the possession of prince-bishops, whose power once stretched beyond Vienna into present-day Hungary. The influence they wielded over nearly six centuries has left its traces in the town's Residenz (bishop's palace), Sommerschloss Freudenhain (the bishops' summer castle), and magnificent Dom (cathedral).

Passau is situated on a narrow point of land where the Inn and Danube meet, with wooded heights rising on the far sides of both rivers. Fine old homes line the waterfront, and streets of varying levels rise to a hill in the center of the old city. Picturesque archways join one house to another, adding to the harmoniously proportioned appearance of this delightful city. Little wonder that the 18th-century traveler Alexander von Humboldt included Passau in his list of the seven most beautifully situated cities in the world.

Today, Passau is considered one of Germany's most underrated cities, probably because of its location far from heavily traveled tourist tracks. At any rate, you will find it elegant and dignified; its grande-dame atmosphere has far more in common with the stately demeanor of Vienna or Prague than the brash approach of some cities in the Federal Republic.

Start your tour at a city square—the Kleiner Exerzierplatz—where progress has pushed aside a more gracious past. What was once a Benedictine monastery garden now houses a park-
22 ing lot and the enormous **Nibelungenhalle,** a vast Nazi-era hall that seats 8,000. Now headquarters of the city's tourist office, its name reflects the fact that the *Nibelungenlied (Song of the Niebelungs)* was written in Passau around 1200. It's an epic poem that encapsulates many central elements of German mythology. Among other things, it describes the love of Siegfried for Kriemhild and the overthrow of the Nibelungs—the Burgundians of France—by the German Hun tribes. Richard Wagner chose it as the theme for his immense 19th-century operatic cycle, *The Ring of the Niebelungs.* Later, Hitler appropriated

Passau

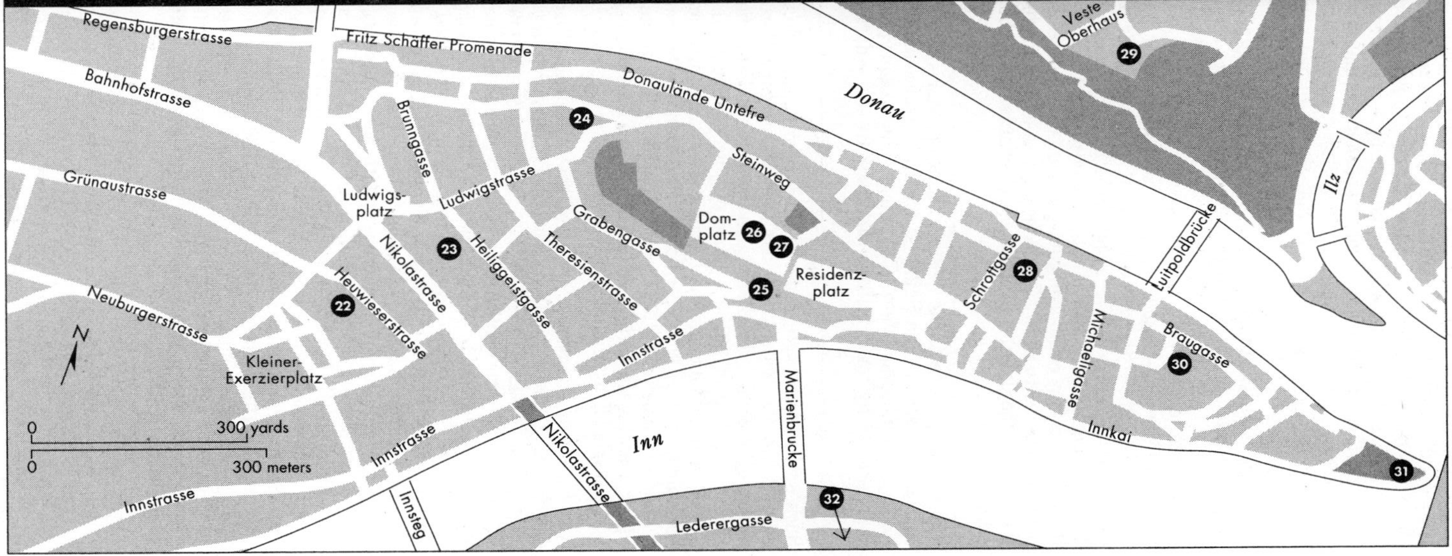

Alte Residenz, **26**
Dom, **25**
Dreiflusseck, **31**
Mariahilfberg, **32**
Neue Residenz, **27**
Nibelungenhalle, **22**
Niederburg Abbey, **30**
Rathaus, **28**
Rindermarkt, **24**
Spitalkirche Heiliger Geist, **23**
Veste Oberhaus, **29**

the legend, recasting it in Nazi dress in an attempt to legitimize the Nazi creed. His obsession with Wagner—almost surpassing that of Ludwig II's—was another example of his desire to see himself as an extension of an established Germanic tradition. Hence the name of the hall. It's an impressively monumental building, of the sort that Mussolini had a weakness for.

Turn right from the tourist office onto busy Ludwigsplatz. Beyond it stretches the city's main shopping street, Ludwigstrasse, part of an attractive pedestrian zone. The first street on the right leading off Ludwigstrasse is Heilig-Geist-Gasse,
23 the site of the 15th-century **Spitalkirche Heiliger Geist,** or Infirmary Church of the Holy Ghost. It has some fine 16th-century stained glass and an exquisite 15th-century marble relief depicting the Way of the Cross. Evidence of the influence of Passau's religious establishments—and of their central European, as opposed to purely Germanic interests—is provided by the fact that the church still possesses vineyards in neighboring Austria.

Time Out You can sample one of the Austrian wines produced from the church vineyards at the **Heilig Geist Stift-Schenke und Stifts-Keller,** a neighboring tavern. The union of church and vineyard is underlined by the crucifixes that hang from the darkened beams.

---

24 Back on Ludwigstrasse, walk to **Rindermarkt,** the old cattle market. On the way you'll pass the 17th-century Baroque **church of St. Paul** and walk through the medieval **Paulusbogen** (Paul's Arch), part of the original city walls. From Rindermarkt, turn right into narrow Luragogasse (named after one of the Italian builders who were busy in Passau in the 18th century) and continue on until you reach **Domplatz,** the expansive square fronting the cathedral. The statue you see in its center is of Bavarian King Maximilian Joseph I.

25 Now turn your attention to the **Dom,** the cathedral. A baptismal church stood here in the 6th century. Two hundred years later, when Passau became the seat of a bishop, the first basilica was built. It was dedicated to St. Stephan and became the original mother church of St. Stephan's Cathedral in Vienna. Little was left of the medieval basilica after a fire reduced it to smoking ruins in the 17th century. What you see today is an impressively heroic Baroque building, complete with dome and flanking towers. As you wander around its marble- and stucco-encrusted interior, you may feel like you're in an Italian cathedral. There's little here to remind you of Germany and much that proclaims the exuberance of Rome. Beneath the octagonal dome is the largest church organ in the world. Built between 1924 and 1928, and enlarged from 1979 to 1980, it claims no less than 17,388 pipes and 231 stops. Lunchtime concerts (DM 2 adults, DM 1 children) are given daily throughout the summer on the monstrous instrument and on Thursdays (DM 6 adults, DM 3 children) at 7:30 PM.

Bordering Domplatz are a number of sturdy 17th- and 18th-
26 century buildings, including the **Altes Residenz,** the former bish-
27 op's palace. Today it's a court house. The **Neue** (New) **Residenz** is next door, though its main entrance faces Residenzplatz, one of the most gracious and quiet corners of the town. Step

through the stately Baroque entrance of the palace to see the dazzling staircase, a scintillating study in marble, fresco, and stucco.

Outside again, turn into Schrottgasse and head toward the Danube. You'll soon find yourself staring at the bright Gothic
28 facade of Passau's 13th-century **Rathaus** (town hall). Originally the home of a successful merchant, it was taken over after an uprising in 1298 and declared the seat of city government. Two assembly rooms of the Rathaus contain wall paintings depicting scenes from local history and lore, including the (fictional) arrival in the city of Siegfried's fair Kriemhild. The Rathaus can only be visited on guided tours arranged by the tourist office (*see* Guided Tours, above).

Outside the Rathaus, face the Danube, cross the bridge on your right—the Luitpoldbrücke—and climb up to the
29 **Veste Oberhaus,** the powerful fortress commissioned by Bishop Ulrich II in 1219. Today, the Veste Oberhaus is Passau's most important museum, containing exhibits that illustrate the 2,000-year history of the city. It also commands a magnificent view of Passau and the three rivers that converge on it. A bus runs from Rathausplatz to the Vest Oberhaus from May–Oct. 15 at regular intervals. *Museum admission: DM 3 adults, DM 1.50 children. Open Apr.–Sept., Tues.–Sun. 9–5; Oct.–Mar., Tues.–Sun. 10–4.*

30 Walk back across the Luitpoldbrücke and turn left to **Niederburg abbey.** Founded in the 8th century as a convent, it was destroyed by fire and rebuilt in the last century in a clumsy Romanesque style. Today it's a girls' school. In its church you can see the 11th-century tomb of a queen who was once abbess here —Gisela, sister of the Emperor Heinrich II and widow of Hungary's first and subsequently sainted king, Stephan, who became the patron of Passau cathedral.

Head now to Passau's other major river, the Inn, just a few steps away. Follow the river to the point where the Danube,
31 Ilz, and Inn meet—the **Dreiflusseck** (Corner of the Three Rivers). For the Inn and the Ilz, it's the end of their journeys from the mountains and forests of Bavaria; from here their waters are carried by the Danube to the Black Sea. Interestingly, at this point the Inn is twice the width of the Danube. Its milky green water, the typical color of a mountain river, gives way slowly to the darker hues of the Danube, and the brownish Ilz adds its small contribution to this colorful natural phenomenon.

Another place to take in the meeting of the three rivers is the
32 **Mariahilfberg,** site of a 17th-century monastery pilgrimage church. It is located on the other side of the Inn, in the so-called Innstadt, or Inn City. It was here that in 1974 archaeologists uncovered the site of the Roman citadel of Boiotro, a stout fortress with five defense towers and walls more than 12 feet thick. A Roman well was also found, its water still plentiful and fresh. A 15th-century merchant's home has been converted into a museum to house the items brought to light by the continuing excavations. *Römermuseum Kastell Boiotro, Am Severinstor. Admission: DM 2 adults, DM 1 children. Open Mar.–Nov., Tues.–Sun. 10–noon and 2–5. A guided tour is given the 1st and 3rd Wed. of the month at 5 PM.*

What to See and Do with Children

Passau has a fascinating **toy museum,** which includes many exhibits from the United States. There is a good collection of dolls, as well as many ancient model steam engines and locomotives. *Residenzplatz. Admission: DM 3 adults, DM 1 children. Open daily 10–6 (Sat. and Sun. only in Feb.).*

At Ortenburg, 6 kilometers (10 miles) west of Passau, there's an extensive **deer park,** where children can feed the animals. (Admission: DM 4 adults, DM 2 children. Open daily 8–6.) In winter, children can accompany wardens into the **Bavarian Forest National Park** to feed the wild deer. Contact the Nationalparverwaltung Bayerischer Wald (8352 Grafenau, tel. 08552/2077).

In the hamlet of Irgenöd, just outside Ortenburg, there's the biggest **aviary** in eastern Bavaria. *Admission: DM 4.50 adults, DM 2.50 children. Open Apr.–Oct., 10–6.*

The Danube town of Straubing has a sizable **zoo** with various attractions for children. *Admission: DM 4 adults, DM 2 children. Open daily 8:30–6.*

Off the Beaten Track

Anywhere in the Bavarian Forest is off the beaten track but, if you're looking for something more than isolated forest walks and glades, seek out two extraordinary private collections. The world's largest **snuffbox collection** is to be found on the third floor of Weissenstein castle near Regen. The 1,300 snuffboxes on display were collected over a period of 46 years by Regen's former mayor, Alois Reitbauer. His reward was an entry in the "Guinness Book of Records." *Open late May–mid-Sept., daily 10–noon and 1–5.*

At Rhanwaltung, near Cham, you'll find one of Germany's most unusual collections of **clocks** and time-measuring machines. It's in the back room of a country pub, the Uhren-Wirt. The pub's *Wirt* (landlord), Gerhard Babl, has spent 30 years building up his collection of more than 400 timepieces. When he's not serving beers, he's winding his clocks and is happy to show you around.

Venture deep into the Bavarian Forest north of Passau and you'll be reminded that this is border country or, to be more exact, Iron Curtain country. From the heights of the Forest you'll see the heavily fortified frontier snaking through the landscape. Communist Czechoslovakia is on the other side. There's an incongruous gap in the frontier where it runs around the summit of the **Dreisessel** mountain. Part of the summit of the 4,300-foot-high mountain, a 100-yard stretch of road, marked at both ends by a barrier, is actually Czech territory. But there is no visible sign of Czech border guards. You can venture past the barrier if you're feeling daring, but it's not recommended: Just because you can't see the guards doesn't mean they aren't there.

Dreisessel means "three armchairs," an apt description of the summit and its boulders, which are shaped like the furniture of a giant's castle. If you're driving to the Dreisessel, take B-12 to Philippsreut, just before the frontier, then follow the well-marked country road. The mountain is about 67 kilometers (40 miles) from Passau.

Shopping

In virtually every resort of the Bavarian Forest you'll find shops selling **glassware,** local **pottery,** and **wood carving** as well. In Passau, make for the **Ludwigstrasse** pedestrian zone. In Deggendorf, the small streets of the old quarter around the Rathaus are prime territory for shoppers.

The Bavarian Forest is famous for its **glassware.** You'll get the best buys from the workshops, where you can often watch the article you order being made. The largest direct sales outlet is the **Joska** foundry in Bodenmais. There are two showrooms, one at the foundry itself, next to the post office, and the other in Arberseestrasse. The **Eisch** family in Frauenau, on the edge of the Bavarian Forest National Park, has been making glass since 1680 and their winged elephant trademark is internationally recognized as a mark of quality. Their glass foundry in Frauenau is open to visitors Mon.–Fri. 9–3 and Sat. 9:30–noon. You can buy directly from the showroom.

Sports and Fitness

Bicycling You can bicycle along the Danube from its source at Donaueschingen in southwest Germany to Passau on the Austrian border, a route that skirts the foothills of the Bavarian Forest for much of its final stretch. Excursion boats that ply the Danube between Regensburg and Passau carry bikes, enabling you to cycle one stage of the journey and let the Danube float you back. Bikes can be rented at most rail stations (DM 10 a day; half that if you have a valid ticket) and at many Bavarian Forest resorts.

Fishing The Weisser and Schwarzer Regen rivers are a challenge for anglers; there's also good fishing in the Danube, Inn, and Ilz rivers. Local tourist offices can supply permits.

Golf Golfers can enjoy at least two advantages in the Bavarian Forest: greens fees that are lower (sometimes a fraction of what's charged in Upper Bavaria), and clubs that welcome visitors. There's a challenging course at **Schaufling,** high above Deggendorf, that offers fine views of the Bavarian Forest and the Danube plain. **Furth im Wald** and **Waldkirchen** both have only nine-hole courses, but these are fun nonetheless, and scenically attractive.

Hiking The Bavarian Forest is prime hiking country, crisscrossed with trails of great variety and varied challenge. The longest, the **Pandurensteig,** runs nearly 167 kilometers (100 miles) from Waldmünchen in the northwest to Passau in the southeast, crossing the heights of the Bavarian Forest National Park. The trail can be covered in stages with the aid of a special tourist program that transfers hikers' luggage from one overnight stop to the other. Get details from **Fremdenverkehrsverband Ostbayern** (Landshuterstr. 13, 8400 Regensburg, tel. 0941/57186). Three resorts—Kellberg, Hauzenberg, and Buchelberg—have joined in a hiking-holiday scheme called **Wandern mit Tapetenwechsel** (Hiking with Change of Scene). The package consists of 14 days' hiking, bed-and-breakfast accommodations, tour assistance, and luggage transportation, all for around DM 450. For details, contact the **Verkehrsamt Kellberg** (8391 Thyrnau, tel. 08501/320).

Skiing Alpine skiers make for the World Cup slopes of the **Grosser Arber** (the summit is reached by chair lifts from Bayerisch-Eisenstein and from just outside Bodenmais). Other ski areas in the Bavarian Forest are not as demanding, but many resorts are ideal for family skiing vacations. St. Englmar, Frauenau, Furth im Wald, Waldmünchen, and the villages around the Brotjackelriegel, near Deggendorf, are the best. Cross-country trails are found everywhere in the Bavarian Forest; a map of 22 of the finest can be obtained free of charge from the **Fremdenverkehrsverband Ostbayern** (*see* Hiking, above). The pretty resort of Thurmansbang has a trail that stops at all of the best bargain inns of the area. For DM 200, Thurmansbang offers a week's bed-and-breakfast accommodations, cross-country ski instructions, and equipment rentals. Contact the **Verkehrsamt Thurmansbang** (tel. 08504/1642).

Swimming There are multi-pool lidos throughout the Bavarian Forest. The best are at Deggendorf, Passau, Vilshofen, Viechtach, and Waldkirchen. In summer, the forest lakes beckon swimmers, but avoid the Danube—it's doubly dangerous: There's a fast current, and the water is badly polluted.

Water Sports Sailboats and surfboards can be rented at most lakes; the Rannasee, the Perlsee, and the Egingersee are three of the prettiest. The Regen and the Inn rivers are perfect for canoeists. Canoes can be rented from **J. Denk** (Schmiedgasse 18, Passau, tel. 0851/31450) or through the tourist office in Roding, on the banks of the Regen (tel. 09461/1066)

Dining and Lodging

Dining

Food in the Bavarian Forest tends toward the wholesome and the hearty; large portions are very much the norm. Specialties include *Regensburger* (short, thick spicy sausages, rather like the *Bratwurst* of Nürnberg). Another sausage served here is *Bauernseufzer* (farmer's sigh). Dumplings, made out of virtually anything and everything, appear on practically every menu. Try *Deggendorfer Knödel* if you fancy something really local. The Danube provides a number of excellent types of fish, particularly *Donauwaller* (Danube catfish), from Passau. This is served *blau* (boiled) or *gebacken* (breaded and fried). The town of Tirschenreuth in the north of the region is the home of the equally delicious *Karpfen* (carp). Radishes are a specialty here, especially *Weichser Rettiche;* wash them down with one of the excellent local beers.

Highly recommended restaurants are indicated by a star ★.

Category	Cost*
Very Expensive	over DM 90
Expensive	DM 55–DM 90

Moderate	DM 35–DM 55
Inexpensive	under DM 35

**per person for a three-course meal, including tax and tip but not wine*

Lodging

Prices here are among the lowest in Germany. You'll find everything from humble bed-and-breakfasts and farmhouses to first class hotels. Many hotels offer special 14-day packages for the price of a 10-day stay, and 10-day packages for the price of a seven-day stay. There are also numerous packages available for riding, fishing, biking, tennis, and hiking vacations, with accommodations at low rates. All local tourist offices can supply lists of accommodations; most can help with reservations.

Highly recommended hotels are indicated by a star ★.

Category	Cost*
Very Expensive	over DM 180
Expensive	DM 120–DM 180
Moderate	DM 80–120
Inexpensive	under DM 80

**All prices are for a standard double room for two, including tax and service charges.*

Bayerisch-Eisenstein
Dining

Restaurant Waldspitze. On Tuesday and Friday nights the floor is cleared for dancing; on weekends there's a zither player. The mood, like the food, is very Bavarian, with excellent Austrian strudel representing about the only foreign influence. *Haupstr. 4, tel. 09925/714. Reservations advised. Dress: informal. No credit cards. Moderate.*

Lodging

★ **Sporthotel Brennes.** Ask for a room with a view of the Grosser Arber, the highest mountain of the Bavarian and Bohemian forests. The ski run begins virtually at the front door. *Brennes 14, tel. 09925/256. 33 rooms with bath. Facilities: solarium, restaurant. AE, DC, MC, V. Closed Nov.–mid-Dec. and Mar.–Apr. Moderate.*

Waldspitze. This is a large, comfortable, and well-appointed hotel, with a variety of sports facilities and a sauna and steam bath for relaxing tired muscles. *Hauptstr. 4, tel. 09925/308. 50 rooms and 100 apartments with bath. Facilities: indoor pool, table tennis, billiards, sauna, solarium, steam bath, restaurant. No credit cards. Moderate.*

Pension am Regen. The Czech border is only 150 yards from this small, quiet, and comfortable bed-and-breakfast pension. Rooms are spacious. *Anton Pech Weg 21, tel. 09925/464. 16 rooms and 6 apartments with bath. Facilities: indoor pool, sauna, solarium, fitness room. MC. Closed mid-Mar.–mid-May and mid-Oct.–mid-Dec. Inexpensive.*

Bischofsmais
Lodging

Hotel Wastlsäge. Rolling, forested countryside surrounds this extensive resort hotel. The cross-country skiing is great, and the walking trails are endless. *Lina-Müller–Weg 3, tel. 09920/170. 86 rooms and 5 apartments with bath or shower. Facilities:*

indoor pool, sauna, solarium, masseur, tennis courts, bowling alleys, table tennis, billiards, hairdressing salon, restaurant. AE, DC, MC, V. Moderate.

Pension Berghof-Plenk. Flowers smother both the timbered upper story of the Pension Berghof-Plenk and the meadows stretching out before it. If you arrive by train, owner Adolf Plenk will meet you at the station. *Oberdorf 18, tel. 09920/442. 17 rooms with bath or shower. Facilities: table tennis, croquet. No credit cards. Inexpensive.*

Cham
Dining

Bürgerstuben. The Stuben is in Cham's central Stadthalle (city hall). Tasty local dishes and an appealingly simple atmosphere add up to an authentic Bavarian experience. *Fürtherstr. 11, tel. 09971/1707. Reservations advised on weekends. Dress: informal. DC. Inexpensive.*

Lodging

Hotel-Restaurant Ratskeller. Church bells will shake you awake on Sunday mornings at the Ratskeller, which sits right next to the church in the center of this charming resort area. The hotel was renovated in 1987 and offers a high degree of comfort. *Am Kirchpl., tel. 09971/1441. 11 rooms with bath or shower. Facilities: restaurant. AE, DC, MC. Moderate.*

★ **Gästeheim am Stadtpark.** The most expensive room in this friendly guesthouse costs all of DM 28. The place is unbeatable for value and basic comfort. *Tilsiterstr. 3, tel. 09971/2253. 11 rooms with showers. No credit cards. Inexpensive.*

Deggendorf
Dining

Ratskeller. If you eat here, beneath the vaulted ceilings of the Rathaus (town hall), you could easily find yourself sharing a table with a town councillor, perhaps even the mayor. The menu is strictly Bavarian; the beer flows freely. *Oberer Stadpl. 1, tel. 0991/6737. No reservations. Dress: informal. MC. Closed Fri. Moderate.*

Zum Burgwirt. The Burgwirt, a snug, wood-paneled restaurant serving regional fare, is an established part of the Deggendorf scene. *Deggendorferstr. 7, tel. 0991/32236. No reservations. Dress: informal. No credit cards. Closed Sun. evening and Mon. lunch. Inexpensive.*

★ **Zum Grafenwirt.** In winter, ask the host for a place near the fine old tiled stove that sits in the dining room. Try filling dishes like roast pork and Bavarian dumplings. In summer, watch for the appearance of Danube fish on the menu. *Bahnhofstr. 7, tel. 0991/8729. Reservations advised on weekends. Dress: informal. Closed Tues. and late May/early June. AE, DC, MC. Moderate.*

Lodging

★ **Schlosshotel Egg.** The "Egg" of this castle-hotel's name isn't a reference to what you can expect in its excellent restaurant; it comes from Thiemo de Ekke, the original owner of the castle back in the 12th century. Today, the hotel is an atmospheric and memorable place to lay your head, but try for a room in the castle itself rather than in the adjoining guest house—all are large, and some have four-poster beds. The hotel is located 13 miles outside Deggendorf. *8351 Schloss Egg, tel. 09905/289. 19 rooms with bath. Facilities: restaurant. AE, DC, MC, V. Expensive.*

Berggasthof Rusel. This mountainside inn, high above Deggendorf and a 15-minute drive from the town center, is an ideal retreat for walkers, golfers, and skiers. A golf course is near at hand; mountain trails start at the front door; and the inn has its own ski lift, which is floodlit six nights a week. *8351 Schaufling* *(on B-11 north), tel. 09920/316. 35 rooms, 20 with bath. Facilities: restaurant. AE, DC, MC, V. Closed Nov. Inexpensive.*

Grafenau
Dining
★ **Säumerhof.** The Bavarian Forest isn't known for haute cuisine but here, in one of its prettiest resorts, is a restaurant that bears comparison with Germany's best. It's part of a small country hotel (with 10 moderately priced and homey rooms, if you want to stay the night) run by the Endl family. The kitchen is Gebhard Endl's territory, where he produces original, nouvelle-inspired dishes using mainly local produce. Try pheasant on champagne cabbage, for instance, or duck in raspberry vinegar sauce. *Steinberg 32, tel. 08552/2401. Reservations advised. Jacket and tie optional. No credit cards. Closed Mon., Tues., and Wed. lunch. Expensive.*

Lodging
Parkhotel am Kurpark. The modern exterior of this hotel disguises a cozy, traditional interior, with exposed wood beams and dark paneling. A large open fire in the lounge continues the rustic theme. *Freyungerstr. 51, tel. 08552/2444. 50 rooms with bath. Facilities: indoor pool, sauna, solarium, restaurant. AE, DC, MC, V. Moderate.*

Steigenberger Hotel Sonnenhof. If you have children, this is the hotel for you: The staff includes a *Spieltante* (playtime auntie) who keeps youngsters amused. It's a gracious, older hotel, set on extensive grounds, that offers rather understated comfort and a wide range of sports facilities. *Sonnenstr. 12, tel. 08552/2033. 196 rooms with bath. Facilities: indoor pool, indoor and outdoor tennis courts, minigolf, sauna, solarium, restaurant. AE, DC, MC, V. Moderate.*

Haidmühle
Dining
Adalbert Stifter. Named after a popular 19th-century Bavarian Forest poet, this friendly country restaurant at the foot of the Dreisessel mountain is at its best turning out the sort of time-honored dishes Stifter knew. Try one of the Bohemian-style roasts, for instance, served with fresh dumplings. *Frauenberg 32, tel. 08556/355. Reservations advised. Dress: informal. Closed Nov. and first half of Dec. MC. Moderate.*

Mauth
Dining
Barnriegel. This family-run restaurant is on the edge of the Bavarian Forest National Park and caters to appetites sharpened by a day's walking. If sauerbraten is on the menu, order it. Local lake fish is also a specialty. *Hauptstr. 2, Finsterau, tel. 08557/701. Reservations advised. Dress: informal. No credit cards. Moderate.*

Passau
Dining
★ **Passauer Wolf.** This riverside hotel-restaurant has big-city flair and a cuisine hard to match in this part of Germany. No Bavarian Gemütlichkeit here; instead, the elegance of starched linen and fine porcelain. Prices can be high, but quality is tops. Try any of the Danube fish dishes. *Rindermarkt 6–8, tel. 0851/34046. Reservations required. Jacket and tie required. AE, DC, MC, V. Closed Sun. evening. Expensive.*

★ **Heilig-Geist-Stiftsschenke.** For atmospheric dining, this one-time monastery, dating from the 14th century, is a must. In summer you eat beneath the chestnut trees of the charming beer garden. In winter, seek out the warmth of the vaulted dining rooms. The wines are excellent and suit all seasons. *Heilig-Geist-Gasse 4, tel. 0851/2607. Reservations advised. Dress: informal. AE, DC, MC. Closed Wed. and Jan 6–30. Moderate.*

★ **Gasthof Andorfer.** One of the finest wheat beers in lower Bavaria is brewed and served here, and you can drink it on a lime tree–shaded terrace overlooking the grain fields. The brewery-tavern is in Passau-Ries, on the northern heights of the city, next to the Veste Oberhaus fortress. The menu is basic, but the beer and the surroundings are what count. There are a few rooms if you fancy spending the night. *Rennweg 2, tel. 0851/51372. No reservations. Dress: informal. No credit cards. Inexpensive.*

Gasthaus zur Ries. This small, traditional inn, located across the road from the better-known Andorfer, has an equally appealing beer garden and a larger menu. There a few rooms, too. *Rennweg 1. No reservations. Dress: informal. No credit cards. Inexpensive.*

Ratskeller. The arched rooms of Passau's time-honored Ratskeller are a short walk from the Danube. Fish figures prominently on the menu; there are also imaginative meat dishes. Wash whatever you order down with a glass of beer. *Rathauspl., tel. 0851/34686. No reservations. Dress: informal. No credit cards. Inexpensive.*

Lodging

Hotel König. Though built only in 1984, the König blends successfully with the graceful Italian-style buildings alongside its elegant waterfront setting on the Danube. Rooms are large and airy; most have a fine view of the river. *Untere Donaulände 1, tel. 0851/85028. 40 rooms with bath. Facilities: sauna, solarium. AE, DC, MC, V. Expensive.*

★ **Wilder Mann.** Sleep beneath chandeliers and richly stuccoed ceilings in beds of carved oak or with ornate 19th-century decoration. The pool is memorably located in the 11th-century vaulted cellars of this one-time merchant's house. Class and comfort abound. *Am Rathauspl., tel. 0851/35071. 60 rooms with bath. Facilities: indoor pool, restaurant, café. AE, DC, MC, V. Expensive.*

★ **Schloss Ort.** Those with a yen to stay in a 13th-century castle that's been modernized with taste will appreciate not only the atmospheric surroundings of the Schloss Ort, but its great location at the Dreiflusseck, meeting point of the Danube, Ilz, and Inn. *Am Dreiflusseck, tel. 0851/34072. 58 rooms, most with bath or shower. Facilities: riverside terrace and garden, restaurant. No credit cards. Moderate.*

Weisser Hase. More than four centuries of tradition lie within the stout walls of the Weiser Hase (White Rabbit). It's centrally located, within easy walking distance of all Passau's attractions. *Ludwigstr. 23, tel. 0851/34066. 117 rooms, 95 with bath. Facilities: wine bar and restaurant. AE, DC, MC, V. Moderate.*

Regen
Lodging

Burggasthof Weissenstein. The ruins of the medieval Weissenstein castle loom over you as you breakfast on the sunny terrace of the Burggasthof, which overlooks the old town. Ask for a room with a view of either. *Weissenstein 32, tel. 09921/2259. 15 rooms with bath. Facilities: restaurant. No credit cards. Closed Nov.*

Gasthof-Pension Wieshof. A former farmhouse, the Wieshof retains a rural air while offering modern comfort. Wood paneling, beams, and antiques add to the rustic atmosphere. *Poschetsriederstr. 2, tel. 09921/4312. 15 rooms with bath. Facilities: bowling alley. No credit cards. Inexpensive.*

Schönberg
Dining and Lodging

★ **Hotel Merian.** The wood balconies of this chalet-style hotel, located on the edge of the Bavarian Forest National Park, provide a colorful contrast to its comfortably traditional interior. Wood is everywhere, from the low beams of the snug tavern to the carved pillars of the restaurant. Try the fish if you eat here: it comes directly from the hotel's own pond. *Unterer Marktpl. 12, tel. 08554/575. 40 rooms with bath. Facilities: indoor pool, sauna, solarium, bowling alleys, restaurant. No credit cards. Moderate.*

Viechtach
Dining

Dischinger. If it's the hunting season, order venison—the restaurant's Bavarian decor (lots of wood and primary colors) somehow matches its mood and taste. The fish dishes are also recommended. *Ringstr. 13, tel. 09942/1601. Reservations advised. Dress: informal. No credit cards. Closed Fri. and Sat. evenings in winter, last week of Feb. and first 2 weeks of Mar. Moderate.*

Vilshofen
Lodging

Bayerischer Hof. Vilshofen's Bayerischer Hof may be stars short of Munich's famous hotel of the same name, but it offers comfortable accommodations in a pleasant, park-like setting. *8358 Vilshofen, tel. 08541/5065. 31 rooms, half with bath or shower. Facilities: beer garden, restaurant. MC. Closed Dec. 27–Jan 10. Inexpensive.*

Zwiesel
Dining

Gasthof Deutscher Rhein. On Tuesdays, Wednesdays, and Saturdays there's live music in the cozy, rustic restaurant of this traditional Gasthof. The menu mixes Bavarian and Bohemian dishes—try the Bohemian dumplings. *Am Stadtpl., tel. 09922/1651. Reservations advised. Dress: informal. DC. Moderate.*

Bräustüberl. Sample the beers of one of the oldest—and, some say, best—breweries in the Bavarian Forest, the Erste Dampfbierbrauerie. The brewery is next door; visitors are welcome. There's a basic menu of Bavarian fare. *Regenerstr. 9, tel. 09922/1409. No reservations. Dress: informal. No credit cards. Inexpensive.*

Lodging

Hotel zur Waldbahn. The great-grandfather of the current owner, assisted by 13 children, built the Hotel zur Waldbahn more than 100 years ago to accommodate travelers on the trains connecting Czechoslovakia with all points south. Today, the emphasis is still put on making the traveler feel at home within the hotel's historic, wood-paneled walls. *Bahnhofpl. 2, tel. 09922/3001. 28 rooms with bath or shower. Facilities: restaurant, sauna. No credit cards. Closed Nov. Moderate.*

Kurhotel Sonnenberg. Located high above Zwiesel, the Sonnenberg offers fine views of the forest and quick access to mountain walks and ski runs. It's a sporty hotel, with numerous fitness facilities. *Augustinerstr. 9, tel. 09922/2031. 19 rooms, 1 apartment, 1 suite; all double rooms with bath or shower. Facilities: indoor pool, sauna, solarium, fitness room, restaurant. No credit cards. Moderate.*

The Arts

Passau is the cultural center of Lower Bavaria and its Europäische Wochen (European Weeks) festival is now a major event on the European music calendar. The festival runs from June to early August. For program details and reservations, write the **Kartenzentrale der Europäischen Wochen Passau** (Nibelungenhalle, 8390 Passau).

Passau also has a thriving theater company, the **Stadttheater,** which has its home in the beautiful little Baroque opera house of Passau's prince-bishops. Program details and reservations from **Stadttheater Passau** (Gottfried-Schäffer-Str. 8390 Passau).

The city's cabaret company, the **Theater im Scharfrichter-Haus,** is nationally famous and hosts a German cabaret festival every fall. Fall is also the time for Passau's annual Kirmes (fair), followed in December by a **Christkindlmarkt** in the beautiful setting of the Residenzplatz.

Jazz fans make for nearby Vilshofen every June for the annual international jazz festival, staged in a special tent on the banks of the Danube. For program details and reservations, tel. 08541/2080.

7 The Black Forest

Introduction

The Black Forest, or Schwarzwald, as it's called in German, is one of those magic names that evokes for everyone a vague feeling of romance. However, if it should also conjure up for you the somewhat sinister image of a formidable wilderness that the sun never pierces, you are quite wrong.

The Black Forest isn't black in that sense. Although there are some somber woods, this is smiling, gentle terrain. Valleys green with pastureland stretch against a backdrop of fairly steep mountains. Your chief impression is likely to be that it's picturesque—a much-abused term, but fitting in this case to describe farmhouses with steeply pitched thatched roofs, and narrow, winding roads that pass through tunnels of trees to reach sparkling mountain lakes and hidden villages that double as resorts.

Located deep in the southwest corner of Germany, the Black Forest follows the east bank of the Rhine from the Swiss border as far north as Karlsruhe. It could be said to have been discovered as a vacationland in the 19th century, although the Romans had been enjoying the salubrious effects of its thermal springs as early as the 3rd century, when the Emperor Caracalla and his staff stayed at what is today Baden-Baden to recover from the rigors of battle.

Celebrated names have long been associated with the Black Forest. In 1770 the 15-year-old daughter of the Empress Maria Theresa, traveling between Vienna and Paris with an entourage of 250 officials and servants in some 50 horse-drawn carriages, made her way along the coach road through the Hollental (Hell Valley) to spend the night at Hinterzarten, where the future Queen Antoinette checked into a renowned coach inn that had been in business since 1446; now called the Park Hotel Adler, it's still number one in that prestigious resort town (*see* Lodging, below).

Starting early in the 19th century, just about everyone who mattered in Europe gravitated to Baden-Baden: kings, queens, emperors, princes and princesses, members of Napoléon's family, and the Russian nobility, along with actors, actresses, writers, and composers. Turgenev, Dostoevsky, and Tolstoy were among the Russian contingent. Victor Hugo was a frequent visitor. Brahms composed lilting melodies in this calm setting. Queen Victoria spent her vacations here. This is still a favorite vacation setting for millionaires, movie stars, and the new corporate royalty.

Mark Twain could be said to have put the Black Forest on the tourist map for Americans. In his 1880 book *A Tramp Abroad,* he waxed poetic on the haunting beauties of this forest fairyland.

Today you can come here for rest and relaxation and to "take the waters," as the Romans first did, at thermal resorts large or small. The Black Forest offers a wide range of sporting activities, catering particularly to the German enthusiasm for hiking with its virtually limitless trails wending their way in and out of the woods. In winter these same trails serve as tracks for cross-country skiing on some of the most ideally suited terrain in all of Europe for this popular sport.

You can also enjoy downhill skiing in the Black Forest, where, according to a local claim, it all started. The first person went flying down a mountainside on two wood boards right here, and the world's first ski lift was set up on the slopes of the Feldberg, the region's highest mountain.

The Black Forest's enviable sporting scene is blessed by dependable snow in winter, warming sun in summer. Freudenstadt, at the center of the Black Forest, claims the greatest number of annual hours of sunshine of any town in Germany. Most resorts offer tennis, swimming, and bicycle riding, and some boast golf courses of international standards.

If you are merely passing through the area, count on a rare driving experience on the kind of roads you see in the ads for European sports cars. You'll zip through a scenic landscape on tightly curved roads seemingly designed to test the skill of the driver but offering enormous satisfactions for those up to the challenge.

The Black Forest is Germany's southernmost wine region and home to some of the country's finest traditional food. Black Forest smoked ham and Black Forest cake are both world famous, and that's only the beginning.

The Black Forest also happens to be home of the cuckoo clock, despite Orson Welles's claim in *The Third Man* that all Switzerland managed to create in 500 years of peace and prosperity was this trivial timepiece. Cuckoo clocks are still made (and sold) here as they have been since more or less time immemorial, along with hand-carved wood artifacts and exquisite examples of glassblowing *(see* Shopping, below).

For all its fame, the Black Forest still offers great value. It's possible to stay at a modest, family-run country inn or farmhouse where you'll start the day with an enormous breakfast to keep you going for the better part of the day for not much more than the price of a meal in a German city restaurant.

Essential Information

Important Addresses and Numbers

Tourist Information Information for the whole of the Black Forest is available from **Fremdenverkehrsverband,** Bertoldstrasse 45, 7800 Freiburg, tel. 0761/31317. There are local tourist information offices in the following towns:

Baden-Baden. Kurverwaltung, Augustaplatz 8, 7570 Baden-Baden, tel. 07221/275–200.
Badenweiler. Kurverwaltung, Ernst-Eisenlohr-Strasse 4, 7847 Badenweiler, tel. 07632/72110.
Bad Herrenalb. Kurverwaltung, 7506 Bad Herrenalb, tel. 07083/7933.
Bad Liebenzell. Kurverwaltung, Kurhausdamm 4, 7263 Bad Liebenzell, tel. 07052/2015.
Feldberg. Kurverwaltung im Ortsteil Altgalshütten, Kirchgasse, 1, 7821 Feldberg, tel. 07655/1092.
Freiburg. Verkehrsamt, Rotteckring 14, 7800 Freiburg im Breisgau, tel. 0761/216–3289.
Freudenstadt. Kurverwaltung, Lauterbadstrasse 5, 7290 Freudenstadt, tel. 07441/6074.

Pforzheim. Stadtinformation, Rathaus, Marktplatz 1, 7530 Pforzheim, tel. 07321/392–190.
Schluchsee. Kurverwaltung, Fischbacherstrasse, 7826 Schluchsee, tel. 07656/301.
Titisee-Neustadt. Kurverwaltung, in Kurhaus, 7820 Titisee-Neustadt, tel. 07651/8101.
Triberg. Kurverwaltung im Kurhaus, Luisenstrasse 10, 7740 Triberg, tel. 07722/81230.
Wildbad. Verkehrsamt, König-Karl-Strasse 7, 7547 Wildbad, tel. 07081/10281.

Car Rental **Avis:** in **Baden-Baden,** Langestrasse 93, tel. 07221/31717; in **Freiburg,** St.-Georgenerstrasse 7, tel. 0761/42288.
Europcar: in **Baden-Baden,** Langestrasse 65, tel. 07221/25311; in **Freiburg,** Zaehringerstrasse 42, tel. 0761/57038.
Hertz: in **Baden-Baden,** Lichtenalerstrasse 39, tel. 07221/22471; in **Freiburg,** Eschholzstrasse 42, tel. 0761/272–020.

Arriving and Departing by Plane

The nearest international airports are at Stuttgart and the Swiss border city of Basel, the latter just 70 kilometers (40 miles) from the largest city in the Black Forest, Freiburg.

Arriving and Departing by Train and Car

By Train The main rail route through the Black Forest runs north–south, following the Rhine valley. There are fast and frequent trains to Freiburg and Baden-Baden from most major German cities.

By Car The Rhine Valley Autobahn, A-5, runs the length of the Black Forest, connecting with the rest of the Autobahn system at Karlsruhe, north of the Black Forest.

Freiburg, the region's major city, is 410 kilometers (260 miles) from Munich and 275 kilometers (170 miles) from Frankfort.

Getting Around

By Train Local lines connect most smaller towns. Two east–west routes—the Black Forest Railway and the Höllental Railway—are among the most spectacular in the country. Details are available from **Deutsche Bundesbahn** (German Railroads) in Freiburg, (tel. 0761/36440).

By Car Good two-lane highways crisscross the entire region, making driving here easy and fast. The region's tourist office *(see* Important Addresses and Numbers, below) has established a series of specially designated tourist driving routes: the High Road, the Low Road, the Spa Road, the Wine Road, and the Clock Road. Though intended primarily for drivers, most points along them can also be reached by train or bus.

Guided Tours

Bus tours of the Black Forest are available in **Freiburg** and **Baden-Baden.** The Freiburg tourist information office offers one-day tours of the Black Forest and parts of neighboring Switzerland. Tours start from DM 40 adults, DM 29 children. In Baden-Baden, contact **Deutsche Reisebüro** (Sofienstr. 16, tel. 07221/24666). Half-day tours to the French city of Strasbourg are also available.

Exploring the Black Forest

Numbers in the margin correspond with points of interest on the Black Forest map.

Highlights for First-time Visitors

Pforzheim Schmuckmuseum
Erzgrube lake
Die Woltacher Glashütte (Glassblowing factory), Wolfach
Freiburg Münster
Baden-Baden

Pforzheim to Freiburg

1 Our tour begins at **Pforzheim,** an ancient city founded by the Romans and standing on a hilly site at the meeting place of three rivers, the most important of which is the Würm. The city is located on the A-8 Autobahn, the main Munich–Karlsruhe route. Pforzheim was almost destroyed in World War II, but painstaking reconstruction has restored much of its former elegance. For an example of the thoroughness of this postwar restoration work, visit the church of **St. Michael** in the center of the city. The original not-altogether-happy mixture of 13th- and 15th-century styles has been faithfully reproduced; contrast the airy Gothic choir with the church's sturdy Romanesque entrance. However, by no means are all the postwar buildings here faithful echoes of traditional styles. Take a look at another Pforzheim church, **St. Matthew's,** a striking, tentlike construction built in 1953, long before the designers of the similarly styled Olympic stadium in Munich were at their drawing boards.

Pforzheim is known as the Gold City because of its association with the jewelry trade. Explore the jewelry shops on streets around Leopoldplatz and you'll see how important that business has been and is to Pforzheim. The Reuchlinhaus, the city cultural center, has a jewelry museum, the **Schmuckmuseum.** Its glittering collection of 17th- to 20th-century jewelry is one of the finest in the world. *Admission free. Open Tues.–Sat. 10–5, Wed. 10–8, Sun. 10–1 and 3–5.*

Pforzheim's other major claim to fame is as a center of the German clock-making industry. In the **Technisches Museum,** one of the country's leading museums devoted to the craft, you can see watch- and clock-makers at work; there's also a reconstructed 18th-century clock factory. *Admission free. Bleichstr. 81. Open Wed. 9–noon and 3–6, and every 2nd and 4th Sun. of the month 10–noon and 2–7.*

Leave Pforzheim on the road south, B-463, which follows the twists and turns of the pretty little Nagold river. Gardeners should look for the signs to the **Alpine Garden** (on the left as you leave the city limits). The garden, located on the banks of the Würm river, stocks more than 100,000 varieties of plants, including the rarest Alpine flowers. *Open Apr.–Sept., daily 9–7.*

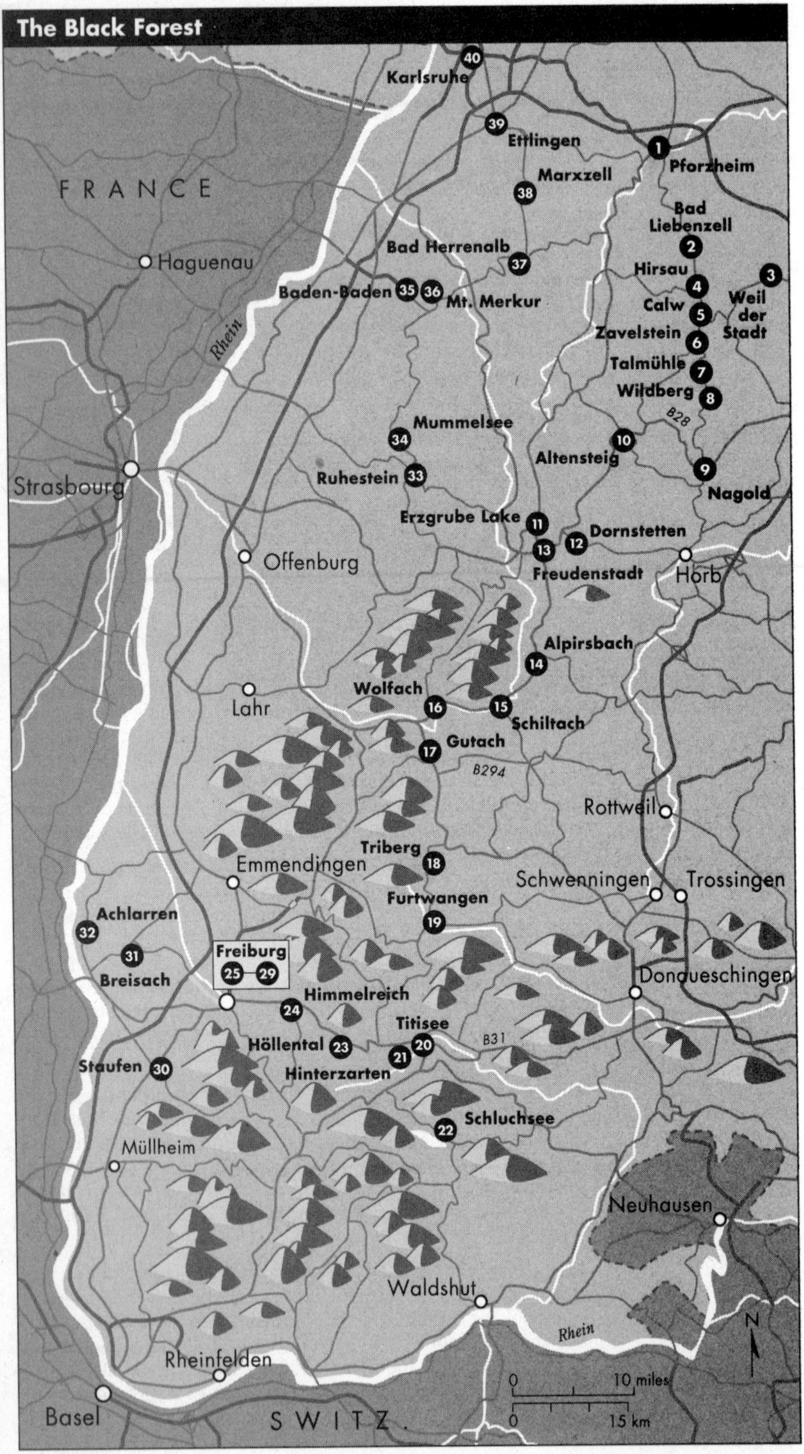
The Black Forest
FRANCE
Karlsruhe
Ettlingen
Pforzheim
Marxzell
Bad Liebenzell
Bad Herrenalb
Hirsau
Haguenau
Baden-Baden
Mt. Merkur
Calw
Weil der Stadt
Zavelstein
Rhein
Talmühle
Wildberg
B28
Mummelsee
Altensteig
Strasbourg
Ruhestein
Nagold
Erzgrube Lake
Dornstetten
Offenburg
Horb
Freudenstadt
Alpirsbach
Wolfach
Lahr
Schiltach
Gutach
B294
Rottweil
Triberg
Emmendingen
Schwenningen
Trossingen
Furtwangen
Achlarren
Freiburg
Breisach
Donaueschingen
Himmelreich
Titisee
B31
Höllental
Staufen
Hinterzarten
Schluchsee
Müllheim
Neuhausen
Waldshut
Rhein
N
Rheinfelden
0
10 miles
Basel
SWITZ.
0
15 km
1
2
3
4
5
6
7
8
9
10
11
12
13
14
15
16
17
18
19
20
21
22
23
24
25
29
30
31
32
33
34
35
36
37
38
39
40

2 Back on B-463, you'll soon reach picturesque **Bad Liebenzell,** one of the Black Forest's oldest spas. Bathhouses were built here as early as 1403. Nearly six centuries later the same hot springs feed the more modern installations that have taken the place of these medieval originals. Apart from medicinal baths (highly recommended for the treatment of circulatory problems), there is a lido with outdoor and indoor hot-water pools. *Paracelsus Baths. Admission: DM 9.80 for 2 hours. Open Apr.–Oct., daily 7:30 AM–9 PM; Nov.–Mar., daily 8:30 AM–9 PM.*

The other principal pastime in and around Bad Liebenzell is walking along the Nagold River Valley. Winding through the thick woods around the little town, a path leads to the partially restored 13th-century castle of **Liebenzell,** today an international youth center and youth hostel.

Time Out For morning coffee or afternoon tea, the **Café Schweigert** is ideally situated in the town center, overlooking the river. For lunch or dinner, try the nearby **Kronen Hotel,** with its riverside terrace.

If you have time, drive into the hills behind Bad Liebenzell to
3 the former imperial city of **Weil der Stadt,** a small, sleepy town with only its well-preserved city walls and fortifications to remind the visitor of its onetime importance. The astronomer Johannes Kepler, born here in 1571, was the first man to track and explain accurately the orbits of the planets; the **Kepler Museum** in the town center is devoted to his discoveries. *Keplergasse 2. Admission free. Open Apr.–Sept., daily 9–5; Oct.–Mar, 1st and 3rd Sun. of the month 9–5.*

4 **Hirsan,** 5 kilometers (3 miles) south on B-463, is the site of the ruins of a 9th-century monastery, now the setting for open-air theater performances in the summer.

5 **Calw,** 3 kilometers (2 miles) farther south, is one of the prettiest towns of the Black Forest. The novelist Hermann Hesse (1877–1962) claimed it was "the most beautiful of all I know." Pause on the town's 15th-century bridge over the Nagold River; if you're lucky you'll see a local tanner spreading hides on the river wall to dry, as his ancestors have done for centuries. The town's market square, with its two sparkling fountains, is an ideal spot for relaxing, picnicking, or people-watching, surrounded by 18th-century half-timbered houses, whose sharp gables stab the sky on all sides.

6 On the road south again, watch for a sign to **Zavelstein,** 3 miles out of Calw. The short detour up a side valley to this tiny town is well worth taking, particularly in spring, when surrounding meadows are carpeted with wild crocuses.

Back on the main road south, you come next to the village of
7 **Talmühle.** Here a side road leads to one of the oldest and, until it closed in 1924, most productive silver mines of the Black Forest, the **Neublach** mine. Since then a new use has been found for the mine's extensive workings. Doctors discovered that the dust-free interior of the mine helped in the treatment of asthma patients. Today, rather incongruously, a therapy center is located in the mine. The ancient shafts can also be visited. *Admission: DM 4 adults, DM 3 children. Open Apr.–Nov., Mon–Fri. 10–4, Sun. 9:30–5.*

8 Arrive in **Wildberg,** 8 kilometers (5 miles) farther south, on the third Sunday of July in an even-numbered year and you'll witness one of Germany's most picturesque contests, the **Schäferlauf,** in which Black Forest shepherds demonstrate their skills and speed in managing their flocks. Those unable to time their arrival quite so precisely will find that the appealing little fortified town nonetheless has much to command attention, including a 15th-century wooden town hall and the remains of a medieval castle.

Time Out In the town of **Nagold,** 10 kilometers (7 miles) farther south, drop in at the half-timbered **Alte Post** inn on the main street. Kings and queens have taken refreshment here on journeys through the Black Forest. Order a glass of the local beer and a plate of Black Forest smoked ham, or a pot of strong coffee and a slice of the famous Black Forest cake.

9 Leaving **Nagold,** head west toward Freudenstadt on local highway B-28, a road that skirts another jewel of the Black Forest,
10 the ancient town of **Altensteig,** on a sunny terracelike slope above the Nagold River. Climb up the hill and you will discover the peace and beauty of the medieval town square below the fine Gothic castle.

11 In summer, pause at **Erzgrube lake,** 9 kilometers (6 miles) farther along B-28, for a swim or a picnic. Boats and sailboards can be rented. The Black Forest is at its thickest here, with 200-year-old trees towering to heights of 150 feet or more.

B-28 skirts the oldest town of the northern Black Forest,
12 **Dornstetten.** If you fancy another dip into the past, stop to see the 17th-century town hall, flanked by equally venerable old buildings, their low, red-roofed eaves framing magnificent half-timbered facades. The fountain dates from the 16th century.

13 The road snakes through lush farmland to **Freudenstadt,** another war-torn city rebuilt with painstaking care. It's a young city by German standards, founded in 1599 to house workers from the nearby silver mines and refugees from religious persecution in what is now the Austrian province of Carinthia. You'll find the streets still laid out in the checkerboard formation decreed by the original planners, the vast central square still waiting for the palace that was intended to stand there. It was to have been built for the city's founder, Prince Frederick I of Württemberg; he, unfortunately, died before work could begin. Don't miss Freudenstadt's Protestant parish church, just off the square. Its lofty nave is L-shaped, a rare architectural liberty in the early 17th century, when this imposing church was built. Freudenstadt claims to enjoy more annual hours of sunshine than any other German resort, so sit in the sun-bathed Renaissance arcades of the fine main square and bask in the warmth of the rays.

Time Out Sixteen kilometers (10 miles) farther on, take a break for a glass of beer at any of the small taverns in the village of **Alpirsbach.** The unusually soft water here gives the locally brewed beer a purity that is acclaimed far beyond the village's boundaries. Visitors are gladly shown around the brewery. In summer, concerts are held regularly in Alpirsbach's fine 11th-century parish church.

14 15 South of **Alpirsbach,** stop at **Schiltach,** 10 kilometers (6 miles) along, to admire the frescoes on the 16th-century town hall. They tell the town's history more vividly than any local chronicle could. Look for the figure of the Devil, who was blamed for burning down the town on more than one occasion.

Leaving Schiltach, follow the B-294 highway 14 kilometers (9
16 miles) to **Wolfach.** It's the site of **Die Woltacher Glashütte,** the only remaining Black Forest factory where glass is blown using the centuries-old techniques that were once common throughout the region. *Admission: DM 2.50 adults, DM 1.50 children. Open Apr.–Nov., daily 9–3:30.*

Just outside Wolfach is one of the most diverting museums in the Black Forest, the **Vogtsbauernhof Freilichtmuseum** (Open-air Museum). Farmhouses and other rural buildings from all parts of the region have been transported here from their original locations and reassembled, complete with traditional furniture, to create a living museum of Black Forest building types through the centuries. *Admission: DM 4 adults, DM 2 children. Open Apr.–Nov., daily 8:30–6.*

The road south from Wolfach follows the **Gutachtal,** a valley famous for the traditional costume worn by its women on feast days and holidays. If you're curious why some women wear black pom-poms on their hats and others wear red, the answer's simple: Married women wear black pom-poms; unmarried wear
17 red. The village of **Gutach** is one of the best spots in the Black Forest to see traditional thatched roofs. Escalating costs caused by a decline in thatching skills, in addition to the ever-present risk of fire, mean that there are already substantially fewer thatched roofs in Guttach than there were 20 years ago. But you'll still find more here than in just about any other town in the region.

At the head of the valley, 13 kilometers (9 miles) south, lies the
18 town of **Triberg,** site of Germany's highest waterfall, where the Gutach River plunges nearly 500 feet over seven huge granite steps. The pleasant 30-minute walk from the center of Triberg to the top of the spectacular falls is well signposted.

For some, however, the most compelling reason for visiting Triberg is to see the **Heimatmuseum** (Wallfahrtstr. 4), the local history museum. This is cuckoo-clock country, and the museum has an impressive collection of clocks. The oldest dates from 1640; its simple wooden mechanism is said to have been carved with a bread knife. Die-hard clock enthusiasts will want to con-
19 tinue on to the **Uhrenmuseum** in **Furtwangen,** 16 kilometers (10 miles) south. It's another clock museum, the largest in Germany, and charts the development of Black Forest clocks, the cuckoo clock taking pride of place. Its massive centerpiece is a 25-hundredweight astronomical clock built by a local master. *Admission: DM 3 adults, DM 1 children. Open Apr.–Oct., daily 10–5.*

From Furtwangen, you're only 21 kilometers (13 miles) from
20 the Black Forest's lakeland, with the **Titisee,** a rare jewel among lakes, as star attraction. Set in a mighty forest, the 1½-mile-long lake is invariably crowded in summer with boats and windsurfers. Boats and boards can be rented at several points along the shore.

From Titisee it's 5 kilometers (3 miles) to the lovely 800-year-
21 old town of **Hinterzarten,** the most important resort in the southern Black Forest. Some buildings date back to the 12th century, such as **St. Oswald's** church, built in 1146. Hinterzarten's oldest inn, **Weisses Rossle,** has been in business since 1347. The **Park Hotel Adler,** established in 1446, has been under the same family management for 14 generations, although the original building was burned down during the Thirty Years' War and the inn where Marie Antoinette and her retinue put up in 1770 has been considerably altered since her visit.

Hinterzarten is situated at the highest point along the Freiburg–Donaueschingen road, and from it a network of far-ranging hiking trails fans out into the surrounding forest. In winter Hinterzarten is one of Germany's most popular centers for *Langlauf* (cross-country skiing).

From Hinterzarten, it's 25 kilometers (16 miles) to the
22 mountain-enclosed **Schluchsee.** Take highway B-317 along the lower slopes of the 4,500-foot Feldberg, the Black Forest's highest mountain, then pick up B-500. Schluchsee is the name of both the lake and its lakeside resort, where there's a heated pool for those who find the icy Alpine waters of the lake too daunting.

From Schluchsee head toward the largest city in the southern Black Forest, Freiburg. To get there by the shortest route
23 you'll have to brave the satanically named **Höllental** (Hell Valley). The first stop at the end of the valley is a little village
24 called, appropriately enough, **Himmelreich,** or Kingdom of Heaven. The village is said to have been given its name by railroad engineers in the 19th century, who were grateful that they had finally laid a line through Hell Valley. At the entrance to Höllental is a deep gorge, the **Ravennaschlucht.** It's worth scrambling through to reach the tiny 12th-century chapel of **St. Oswald,** the oldest parish church in the Black Forest.

Back on B-31, watch for the appearance of a bronze statue of a deer high on a roadside cliff, 3 miles on. It commemorates the local legend of a deer that amazed hunters by leaping the deep gorge at this point. Another 16 kilometers (10 miles) brings you to Freiburg.

25 **Freiburg,** or Freiburg in Breisgau, to give the town its full name, was founded in the 12th century. Despite extensive wartime bomb damage, skillful restoration has helped re-create the original and compelling medieval atmosphere of one of the most appealing historic towns in Germany. Freiburg has had its share of misadventures through the years, especially in the 17th and 18th centuries. In 1632 and 1638 Protestant Swedish troops in the Thirty Years' War captured the city; in 1644 it was taken by Catholic Bavarian troops; and in 1677, 1713, and 1744 French troops captured it. For Americans, Freiburg has a particular significance: The 16th-century geographer Martin Waldseemüller, who first put the name America on a map in 1507, was born here.

Towering over the rebuilt medieval streets of the city is its most
26 famous landmark, the **Münster,** Freiburg's cathedral. The pioneering 19th-century Swiss art historian Jacob Burckhardt described its delicately perforated 370-foot spire as the finest in Europe. If you've seen the Salisbury cathedral spire in En-

Kaufhaus, **27**
Münster, **26**
Rathaus, **29**
Rathaus Platz, **28**

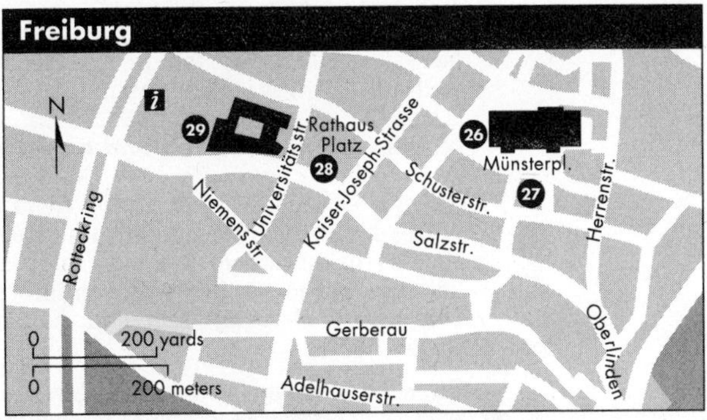

gland, you'll want to decide for yourself whether Burckhardt was right. The cathedral took three centuries to build, from around 1200 to 1515. You can easily trace the progress of generations of builders through the changing architectural styles, from the fat columns and solid, rounded arches of the Romanesque period to the lofty Gothic windows and airy interior of the choir, the last parts of the building to be completed. Of particular interest are the luminous 13th-century stained-glass windows; a 16th-century triptych (three-panel painting) by Hans Baldung Grien; and paintings by Holbein the Younger and Lucas Cranach the Elder. If you can summon the energy, climb the tower; the reward is a magnificent view of the city and the Black Forest beyond. Go on a Friday and you'll see the colorfully striped awnings of the market stalls spread out below, a fitting accompaniment to the 16th-century market house, the
27 **Kaufhaus.** The four statues you see on the fine facade beneath its steeply pitched roof are of Hapsburg monarchs.

Time Out Stroll to Oberlinden square and visit Germany's most ancient inn, **Zum Roten Bären,** the Red Bear. Order a *Viertel*—a quarter-liter glass—of the local wine and perhaps a plate of locally smoked ham. The inn is also a small hotel.

28 The city's other main square is **Rathaus Platz,** where Frei-
29 burg's famous **Rathaus** (Town Hall) stands, constructed from two 16th-century patrician houses joined together. Among its attractive Renaissance features is an oriel, or bay window, clinging to a corner and bearing a bas-relief of the romantic medieval legend of the Maiden and the Unicorn.

Having braved Hell Valley to get to Freiburg, a visit to the
30 nearby town of **Staufen,** where Dr. Faustus is reputed to have made his pact with the Devil, should hold no horrors. It's 20 kilometers (12 miles) south of Freiburg via B-31. The legend of Faustus is remembered today chiefly because of Goethe's drama of the same name, written in the early 19th century. The play depicts the doctor as a man driven by fear of death to make a pact with the Devil; in return for immortality, Faustus sells his soul. In fact, the original Faustus was an alchemist, an early scientist, in the 16th century. He made a pact not with the Devil but with a local baron who was convinced Faustus could make his fortune by discovering the secret of how to make gold from base metals. In his attempts Dr. Faustus died in an explosion that produced such noise and sulphurous stink that the townspeople were convinced the Devil had carried him off. You can

visit the ancient inn, the **Löwen,** on the market square, Marktplatz, that Faustus used to frequent. Frescoes on its walls tell his story in vivid detail.

North to Baden-Baden and Karlsruhe

Staufen is on the Wine Road, the **Weinstrasse,** another of the routes drawn up by the tourist authorities of the Black Forest. It's also the southernmost point of this Black Forest tour. From here the tour makes its way north through the southernmost vineyards of Germany, source of the prized Baden wine, to Baden-Baden.

Twenty kilometers (12 miles) northwest of Freiburg on B-31 is
31 the town of **Breisach.** It stands by the Rhine river; everything you see to the west on the opposite bank is in France. Towering high above the town and the surrounding vineyards is the **Stephansmünster,** the cathedral of St. Stephen, built between 1200 and 1500 (and almost entirely rebuilt after World War II). As at Freiburg, the transition from sturdy Romanesque styles to airy and vertical Gothic styles is easy to see. North of the town rises the **Kaiserstuhl,** or Emperor's Chair, a volcanic outcrop clothed in vineyards that produce high-quality wines.
32 Sample some in one of the taverns of the village of **Achlarren,** 2 or 3 miles north of Breisach; you can also visit the fine little **wine museum** in the village. *Admission to the museum: DM 2 adults, DM 1 children. Open Apr.–Oct., Mon–Fri. 2–5, Sat. and Sun. 10:30–4.*

You'll be driving past numerous vineyards and wine villages as you make your way north. Most of the vineyards offer tastings. There's no obligation to buy, and you certainly won't be pressured into it. But fulsome praise is considered polite. You leave the Weinstrasse at **Lahr,** 40 kilometers (25 miles) north of the Kaiserstuhl. Here you should turn right (east) onto B-415 and head along the narrow **Shuttertal** valley to **Zell,** 15 kilometers (10 miles) away. A winding mountain road takes you the 21 kilometers (13 miles) to the A-28 highway. Turn right to **Freudenstadt,** then left for B-500 and Baden-Baden.

You're back on the Black Forest High Road now, the Schwarzwald Hochstrasse, in the land of myth and fable. At the village
33 of **Ruhestein,** the side road left leads to the **Allerheiligen** monastery ruins. This 12th-century monastery was secularized in 1803, at which point plans were drawn up to turn it into a prison. Two days later, lightning started a fire that burned the monastery to the ground. To this day the locals claim it was divine intervention.

Three miles north of Ruhestein you reach another potent
34 source of local myth. This is the **Mummelsee,** a small, almost circular lake that has fascinated local people and visitors alike for centuries. Because of the lake's high mineral content, there are no fish in it. According to legend, however, sprites and other spirits of the deep find it to their liking. The Romantic lyric poet Mörike (1804–1875) immortalized it in his ballad *The Spirits of the Mummelsee.* The lake is a popular destination in the summer; visit if you can during the mist-laden days of spring and fall to capture its full mysterious appeal.

From the Mummelsee, it's downhill all the way to the famous
35 and fashionable spa of **Baden-Baden,** set in a wooded valley of

the northern Black Forest and sitting atop the extensive underground hot springs that gave the city its name. The Roman legions of the Emperor Caracalla discovered the springs when they settled in here on R&R. The leisure classes of the 19th century rediscovered the bubbling waters, establishing Baden-Baden as the unofficial summer residence of many of Europe's royal families, who left their imprint on the city in the palatial homes and stately villas that still grace its tree-lined avenues.

The small, neat city, so harmoniously set within the surrounding forest, has a flair and style all its own. As Germany's ultimate high-fashion resort, it lives unashamedly on leisure and pleasure. Here, the splendor of the Belle Epoch lives on to a remarkable extent. Some claim that one out of five residents is a millionaire. In the evening, Baden-Baden is a soft-music-and-champagne-in-a-silver-bucket kind of place, and in the daytime, it follows the horseback-riding-along-the-bridle-paths tradition. It features a crowded season of ballet performances, theater, concerts, and recitals, along with exciting horse racing and high-stakes action at its renowned casino.

Baden-Baden claims that the casino, Germany's first, is the most beautiful in the world, a boast that not even the French can challenge, for it was a Parisian, Jacques Benazet, who persuaded the sleepy little Black Forest spa to build gambling rooms to enliven its evenings. In 1853, Benazet commissioned the architects of the Paris opera house to come up with a design along the lines of the greatest French imperial palaces. The result was a series of richly decorated, chandelier-hung gaming rooms in which even an emperor could feel at home—and did. Kaiser Wilhelm I was a regular visitor, as was his wordly-wise chancellor, Bismarck. Visitors as disparate as the Russian novelist Dostoevsky, the Aga Khan, and Marlene Dietrich have all been patrons.

Few people visit Baden-Baden to go sightseeing (though those who feel the urge might want to see the **Neues Schloss,** or New Castle, a 19th-century fortress that was rebuilt in the Renaissance style for the grand dukes of Baden; today it's a museum of local history). If you come here to take the waters, still have a flutter in the casino *(see* The Arts and Nightlife, below) and perhaps swim in the positively palatial **Caracalla Baths,** a vast complex with no fewer than seven pools, opened in 1985 *(see* Sports and Outdoor Activities, below). Above all, you'll want to stroll around this supremely elegant resort and sample the gracious, old-world atmosphere of a place that, more than almost anywhere else in Europe, retains the feeling of a more unhurried, leisured age. Anyone who knew the south of France before the war will feel very much at home here. If the frantic pace of Las Vegas is more your idea of fun, you'll find Baden-Baden slow, but for many, the more relaxed tempo has an appeal of its own.

Time Out Step into the warm elegance of the **Café König.** Order a pot of coffee and a wedge of Black Forest cake and listen to the hum of money and leisure from the spa crowd, who have made this quiet corner their haunt.

Leaving Baden-Baden, take the road to **Gernsbach,** a couple of miles to the east. The road skirts Baden-Baden's own mountain
36 peak, the 2,000-foot-high **Merkur.** You can take the cable car to

the summit. *Cost round-trip: DM 5 adults, DM 3 children. Open daily 10–6.*

37 Drive the 15 kilometers (10 miles) to **Bad Herrenalb,** another popular Black Forest spa, set amid the wooded folds of the Alb River Valley. Railway enthusiasts will admire the train station here; it's actually Baden-Baden's original 19th-century station. It was saved from destruction during the modernization of the Baden-Baden station when it was transported here and put up in all its former glory.

Eight kilometers (5 miles) north on the road to Karlsruhe, the
38 final point of the tour, lies the village of **Marxzell.** A group of ancient locomotives and other old machines at the side of the road announces the presence of the **Karl Benz Museum,** a wonderland for the technically-minded. Every kind of early engine is represented in this museum dedicated to the German automobile pioneer Karl Benz (1844–1929), the man who the Germans claim built the first practical automobile in 1888, a claim hotly disputed by the French. The museum has no fixed opening times; just ring the bell.

39 From Marxzell, head for **Ettlingen,** a 1,200-year-old town that's now practically a suburb of its newer and much larger neighbor, **Karlsruhe.** Ettlingen, bordered by the Alb River, is a jewel of a town, its ancient center a maze of traffic-free cobbled streets. Visit in summer for the annual theater and music festival in the beautiful **Baroque Schloss** (palace) (*see* The Arts and Nightlife, below). The palace was built in the mid-18th century, and its striking domed chapel, today a concert hall, was designed by Cosmas Damian Asam, a leading figure of south German Baroque. Its ornate, swirling ceiling fresco is typical of the heroic, large-scale, illusionistic decoration of the period.

40 **Karlsruhe,** founded at the beginning of the 18th century, is a young upstart compared to ancient Ettlingen. But it makes up in industrial and administrative importance what it lacks in years, and sits astride a vital Autobahn and railroad crossroads. Its major attraction for the visitor is the former palace of the Margrave Karl Wilhelm, today the **Badische Landesmuseum,** the museum of local history. The town quite literally grew up around the palace, which was begun in 1715; 32 avenues radiate out from it, 23 leading into the extensive grounds, the remaining nine forming the grid of the old town. It's said that the margrave fell asleep under a great oak while searching for a fan lost by his wife and dreamed that his new city should be laid out in the shape of a fan. True or false, the fact is that the city is built on a fan pattern, and all the principal streets, with one exception, lead directly to the palace. The exception is the Kaiserstrasse, constructed in 1800, which runs parallel to the palace.

Despite wartime bomb damage, faithful restoration has ensured that much of the old town retains its original and elegant 18th-century appearance. Walk to the **Marktplatz,** the central square, to see the austere stone pyramid that marks the margrave's tomb and the severe Neoclassical **Stephanskirche,** the church of St. Stephen, modeled on the Pantheon in Rome and built around 1810. The interior, rebuilt after the war, is incongruously modern.

What to See and Do with Children

Take a slide down the dry toboggan run at **Poppeltal,** located on the Schwarzwald-Baderstrasse, 20 kilometers (12 miles) south of Wildbad. The narrow, twisting run descends more than half a mile through the forest. There are one- and two-seat toboggans for rent. Paradoxically, the run has to be shut down in the winter, when snow and ice make it dangerous.

Tour the disused silver mines at **Neublach,** at Talmühle *(see* Exploring the Black Forest, above). Ride the **Black Forest Railway** through "Hell Valley" from Freiburg to the mountain resort of Hinterzarten. Spend a few hours, or even the day, at the Black Forest's own Disneyland, **Europa Park,** at Ettenheim, 40 kilometers (25 miles) north of Freiburg on the Karlsruhe-Basel Autobahn. It's open April–October. Visit the **Open-air museum** of Black Forest farmhouses near Wolfach *(see* Exploring the Black Forest, above).

Off the Beaten Track

Take any minor road in the Black Forest and you're off the beaten track. Hikers can lose themselves for days in the thick woodland.

At **Schapbach,** in the enchanting Wolf River Valley, head up into the hills to **Glaswald Lake** and you should have this tree-fringed stretch of water all to yourself. Parts of the neighboring Poppel Valley are so wild that carnivorous flowers number among the rare plants that carpet the countryside. Visit the valley's **Hohloh Lake** nature reserve, near Enzklösterle, in July and August and you'll find the bug-eating *Sonnentau* in full bloom. Farther north, just off B-500 near **Hornisgrinde** mountain, a path to the remote and romantic **Wildsee** passes through an experimental area of forest where the trees are left untended. Scientists are interested to learn just how the Black Forest would develop if it were left untouched; it's the equivalent of a jungle in the center of Europe.

Germany's only **bee museum** is to be found near St. Trudpert (open Wed., Sat., and Sun. afternoons). The world's finest collection of trumpets can be seen (and heard) at the **Hochrheinmuseum** in Bad Säckingen (open Tues., Thurs., and Sun. afternoons).

You can even get off the beaten track in fashionable **Baden-Baden**—wait for dusk to fall and take a stroll along the tiny **Oos River** through the **Kurpark** gardens. Watch the gaslights flicker into life as the first gamblers of the night arrive at the pillared casino.

Buy a Black Forest smoked ham as an aromatic souvenir. It's a specialty that's prized all over Germany. You can buy one at any butcher shop in the region, but it's more rewarding to visit a *Schinkenräucherei* (smokehouse), where the ham is cured. **Hermann Wein's Schinkenräucherei** in Freudenstadt sells smoked hams, and the staff is glad to show people around. You'll need to call in advance (tel. 07443/8041).

The region's wines, especially the dry Baden whites and delicate reds, are highly prized in Germany. Buy them directly from any vintner on the Wine Road *(see* Exploring the Black Forest, above).

Shopping

Shopping in the Black Forest means cuckoo clocks. For the widest range in the whole area try **Hansen** (Münsterpl. 6) in Freiburg. The staff speaks English and will ship goods to the United States and Canada; they can also arrange tax refunds.

Wood carvings, glass, and pottery are all good buys in the Black Forest. **Gaisser** (Langestr.), located in Baden-Baden's attractive pedestrian shopping zone, stocks glass and porcelain from all over Germany, with many specialties form the Black Forest.

Sports and Fitness

Bicycling Bicycles can be rented at nearly all the train stations in the Black Forest. Cost is DM 10 a day, half that if you have a railway ticket. Some tourist offices also rent bicycles. Biking in the Black Forest is not for the unfit, although several regional tourist offices offer tours where the biker's luggage is transported separately from one overnight stop to the next. Six- to 10-day tours are available for as little as DM 174 per person including bed-and-breakfasts and bike rental. Contact the **Fremdenverkehrsverband Schwarzwald** in Freiburg for full details *(see* Important Addresses and Numbers, above). For the super-fit, Titisee-Neustadt organizes a tour through 12 of the Black Forest's mountain passes. Contact **Kurverwaltung** (7821 Titisee-Neustadt, tel. 07651/20668) for details.

Fishing The Black Forest, with its innumerable mountain rivers and streams, is a fisherman's paradise. Fishing without a license is forbidden, and fines are automatically levied on anyone caught doing so. Licenses cost DM 8 a day and are available from most local tourist offices, which can usually also provide maps and rent out equipment. Contact the **Fremdenverkehrsverband Schwarzwald** (Bertodstr. 45, Freiburg, tel. 0761/31317) for details.

Golf There are courses at Baden-Baden, Bad Herrenalb, Badenweiler, Donaueschingen, Freiburg, and Freudenstadt. The Baden-Baden course is considered one of Europe's finest. Contact the **Golf Club** (Fremersbergstr. 127, Baden-Baden, tel. 07221/23579).

Horseback Riding Farms throughout the Black Forest offer riding holidays; addresses are available from local tourist offices and the **Fremdenverkehrsverband Schwarzwald** in Freiburg. Many of the larger towns have riding clubs and stables where visitors can rent horses, including **Baden-Baden** (Balgerhauptstr. 77, tel. 07221/64666). The resort of **Wehr** offers 14 days' stay in a bed-and-breakfast and 10 hours of riding for DM 405; similar vacation packages are offered throughout the region.

Swimming Most of the larger resorts and towns in the Black Forest have pools, either indoor or outdoor. You can also swim in any of the region's lakes, if you can stand the cold. The most lavish swimming pool in the region is the **Caracalla** complex in Baden-Baden. Opened in 1985, it has five indoor pools and two outdoor pools, a sauna, a solarium, and Jacuzzis. *Römerpl. 11, tel.*

07221/275–940. Admission: DM 13 for 2 hours. Open daily 8 AM–10 PM.

The **Friedrichsbad** swimming pool in Baden-Baden offers mixed nude bathing. *Römerpl. 1, tel. 07221/2751. Admission: DM 25; children under 16 not admitted. Open Mon. and Wed.–Sat. 8 AM–10 PM, Tues. 8–4.*

Winter Sports Despite Swiss claims to the contrary, the Black Forest is the true home of downhill skiing. In 1891 a French diplomat was sighted sliding down the slopes of the **Feldberg**, the Black Forest's highest mountain, on what are thought to be the world's first downhill skis. The idea caught on among the locals, and a few months later Germany's first ski club was formed. In 1907, the world's first ski lift was opened at Schollach. There are now more than 200 ski lifts in the Black Forest. The slopes of the Feldberg are still the top ski area. Five days' skiing lessons in Hinterzarten cost from DM 120, with ski passes from DM 70 for a full week. Accommodations can be had for about DM 130 a week. (Call the **Verkehrsamt**, Hintergarten, tel. 07652/1501, for details.) Cross-country ski instruction is given in every resort, and tours of two days and more are offered by many tourist offices. Schonach's three-day trip includes a party in a mountain hut and two nights in bed-and-breakfasts for DM 258. (Call the **Kurverwaltung, Schonach im Schwarzwald**, tel. 07722/6033, for details.)

Walking The Black Forest is ideal country for walkers. The three principal trails are well marked and cross the region from north to south, the longest stretching from Pforzheim to the Swiss city of Basel, 280 kilometers (175 miles) away. Walks vary in length from a few hours to a full weekend. The **Clock-carriers' Road**, following the path of early Black Forest clock dealers, is a perennial favorite. Three nights' lodging in bed-and-breakfasts plus transport of your luggage is available for DM 166 and up. Contact the **Kurverwaltung**, in Freiburg (tel. 07722/81230), for details.

Dining and Lodging

Dining

Restaurants in the Black Forest range from the well-upholstered luxury of Baden-Baden's chic eating spots to simple country inns. Some specialties here betray the influence of neighboring France, but if you really want to go native, try *z'Nuni*, the local farmers' second breakfast, generally eaten around 9 AM. It consists of smoked bacon, called *Schwarzwaldgeräuchertes*—the most authentic is smoked over fir cones—a hunk of bread, and a glass of chilled white wine. No visitor to the Black Forest will want to pass up the chance to try *Schwarzwalderkirschtorte*, Black Forest cherry cake. *Kirschwasser*, locally called *Chriesewässerle* (from the French *cerise*, meaning cherry), is cherry brandy, the most famous of the region's excellent *Schnaps* (brandies).

Ratings Highly recommended restaurants in each price category are indicated by a star ★.

Category	Cost*
Very Expensive	over DM 90
Expensive	DM 55–DM 90
Moderate	DM 35–DM 55
Inexpensive	DM 20–DM 35

**per person for a three-course meal, excluding drinks, service, and tax*

Lodging

Accommodations in the Black Forest are varied and numerous, from simple rooms in farmhouses to five-star luxury. *Gasthofs* (inns), all offering as much local color as you'll ever want and low prices, abound. In summer, Schluuchsee and Titisee are crowded, so make reservations well in advance. Some spa hotels close for the winter.

Ratings Highly recommended lodgings in each price category are indicated by a star ★.

Category	Cost*
Very Expensive	over DM 180
Expensive	DM 120–DM 180
Moderate	DM 80–DM 120
Inexpensive	under DM 80

**All prices are for two people in a double room, excluding service charge.*

Baden-Baden
Dining

Merkurius. The owner-chef here is Czech-born; appropriately his menu features the best of Bohemian cooking. The comfortable, homey restaurant, complete with fireplace, is part of a small country-house hotel 5 miles south of Baden-Baden. Bohemian dumplings compete with German potato pancakes for top honors. *Klosterberg 2, tel. 07223/5474. Reservations required. Jacket and tie required. AE, DC, MC. Closed Sun., Mon., and Tues. evenings. Very Expensive.*

★ **Stahlbad.** This is one of the most elegant restaurants in Baden-Baden. French oil paintings from the 19th century hang on its walls, and the mahogany gleam of its antique tables and sideboards provides a foil for the fine china. Green velvet furnishings predominate. The restaurant is located in a gracious mansion surrounded by extensive grounds. The food is part French (mostly nouvelle) and part German. *Augustapl. 2, tel. 07221/24569. Reservations required. Jacket and tie required. AE, DC, MC, V. Closed Sun. evening and Mon. Expensive.*

Zum Alde Gott. The draw here is the classy combination of upscale rustic appeal with distinctive nouvelle German cooking; figs in beer pastry make for a memorable dessert. With only 12 tables, the mood is intimate and sophisticated. You can dine outside in the summer. The restaurant is located in the suburb of Neuweier. *Weinstr. 10, tel. 07223/5513. Reservations advised. Dress: casual. AE, DC, MC, V. Closed Fri. lunch and Thurs. Moderate.*

La Terrazza. You'll find this glass-enclosed oasis tucked away at the end of the elegant Augusta Arcade. As the name suggests, Italian food is served here, and very fine Italian food at that. There's a charming, fountain-cooled courtyard for summer dining. *Augusta-Arkaden, Lichtentalerstr., tel. 07221/32727. Reservations advised. Jacket and tie required. AE, DC, MC, V. Moderate.*

Bratwurstglöckle. Hunt out the large bronze bell—the *Glöckle*—that hangs outside this traditional beer and wine tavern. It signals good food and drink at reasonable prices. *Steinstr. 7, tel. 07221/2968. Dress: informal. No credit cards. Inexpensive.*

Löwenbräukeller. This Bavarian-style restaurant with a small, tree-shaded beer garden serves only one beer—Munich's famous Löwenbräu—along with a wide selection of Baden wines. The food is simple and filling, with regional specialties predominating. *Gernsbacherstr. 9. No reservations. Dress: informal. No credit cards. Inexpensive.*

Zur Traube. Located in the suburb of Neuweier, Zur Traube offers generous portions. Steaks are its specialty—try the veal steak in wild mushroom sauce. *Mauerbergstr. 107, tel. 07223/57216. Reservations advised. Dress: informal. AE, DC, MC, V. Closed Mon. and late Jan.–early Feb. Inexpensive.*

Lodging

★ **Brenner's Park Hotel.** This hotel claims, with some justification, to be one of the best in the world. It's a stately mansion off Baden-Baden's leafy Lichtentaler Allee, set on spacious private grounds. Luxury abounds, and all the rooms and suites (the latter costing up to DM 1,950 a day) are luxuriously furnished and appointed. *Schillerstr. 6, tel. 07221/3530. 109 rooms with bath. Facilities: sauna, health farm, indoor pool, parking, bar, 2 restaurants. No credit cards. Very Expensive.*

★ **Der Kleine Prinz.** This is a beautifully modernized, small 19th-century mansion. Each of its rooms is decorated in a different style, ranging from art nouveau to Manhattan modern. The tower room has a spiral staircase; two rooms have fireplaces; a number have Jacuzzis. The restaurant (closed Jan.) is small and sophisticated and offers award-winning German nouvelle food. *Lichtentalerstr. 36, tel. 07221/3464. 30 rooms with bath. Facilities: restaurant. AE, DC, MC, V. Very Expensive.*

Hotel Bischoff. The Friedrichsbad Roman baths are right across the street, and most other attractions in Baden-Baden are only a short walk away from this solidly comfortable, fin de siècle villa-hotel. The bedrooms are basically but adequately furnished; there's a cozy breakfast room, but no restaurant. *Römerpl. 2, tel. 07221/22378. 25 rooms with shower. AE, DC, MC, V. Closed Dec. and Jan. Moderate.*

★ **Laterne.** This is one of Baden-Baden's oldest hotels (it dates from the late 17th century), as well as one of its smallest. The public rooms, the restaurant, and some of the bedrooms have original beams and woodwork and antique Black Forest furnishings. It's centrally but quietly located in a pedestrian zone. *Gernsbacherstr. 10, tel. 07221/29999. 10 rooms with bath or shower. Facilities: restaurant. AE, DC, MC, V. Moderate.*

Zum Felsen. Located 2 miles from downtown Baden-Baden in the Lichtental suburb, this is a great choice for families. It's a simple and small guest house, offering reliable comfort and low rates. *Geroldsauerstr. 43, tel. 07221/71641. 7 rooms with bath or shower. Facilities: restaurant (closed Christmas–mid-Jan.). No credit cards. Inexpensive.*

Am Markt. This is a historic, 250-year-old hotel in the center of town; it's been run by the Bogner family for more than three decades. *Marktpl. 17–18, tel. 07221/22747. 27 rooms, 9 with bath or shower. Facilities: restaurant. AE, DC, MC, V. Inexpensive.*

Bad Herrenalb
Lodging

Schwarzwald-Kulm Hotel. Set high above the forest resort of Bad Herrenalb, this luxury hotel boasts full sports and fitness facilities. *Doblerstr. 26, tel. 07083/7420. 170 rooms with bath. Facilities: indoor pool, sauna, solarium, steam bath, squash court, tennis courts, bowling alleys, restaurants. AE, DC, MC, V. Expensive.*

Bad Liebenzell
Lodging

Thermen-Hotel. Idyllically located between the spa park and the forest, this striking 16th-century half-timbered mansion opened as a luxurious hotel in 1988. *Postfach 1260, tel. 07052/408–300. 22 rooms with bath. Facilities: indoor pool, hot springs, restaurant. AE, DC, MC, V. Expensive.*

Baiersbronn
Dining
★

Baveiss. This is one of the most elegant and sophisticated restaurants in Germany, one that has been winning plaudits for many years. It's in the Mitteltal hotel—itself a substantial luxury hotel—and offers magnificent French nouvelle cuisine prepared under the direction of leading chef Manfred Schwarz. The fixed-price *gastronomique* menu, at DM 110 per person, represents surprisingly good value, too. *Kurhotel Mitteltal, Gärtnerbuhlweg 14, tel. 07442/471. Reservations required. Jacket and tie required. AE, DC. Closed Mon., Tues., and late Nov.–Christmas. Very Expensive.*

Traube Tonbach. French cuisine is offered here, too. You dine at antique tables beneath a ceiling of gnarled beams and straw thatch. Try for a table by the large window overlooking the Tonbach valley. *Tonbachstsr. 237, tel. 07442/4970. Reservations required. Jacket and tie required. AE, DC, MC, V. Closed Thurs., Fri. lunch, and Jan. 10–Feb. 10. Expensive.*

Buhl
Dining
★

Burg Windeck. Dine where medieval knights once celebrated hunting successes, in a hilltop 13th-century castle with spectacular views of the Rhine valley. The food is sophisticated German with nouvelle touches; the atmosphere is sturdily authentic. *Kapelwindeckstr. 104, tel. 07223/23671. Reservations required. Dress: informal. AE, DC, MC. Closed Mon., Tues., and Jan–mid-Feb. Expensive.*

Lodging
★

Badischer Hof. The last of the knights of Windeck set up housekeeping in this historic building in the 16th century. Set beside a mountain stream, the hotel has a quiet courtyard where you can breakfast or enjoy the wine of the vineyards that stretch out to the Black Forest beyond. *Haupstr. 36, tel. 07223/23063. 25 rooms with bath. Facilities: restaurant. AE, DC, MC, V. Expensive.*

Cafe-Pension Jägersteig. Magnificent views of the wide Rhine valley as far as the French Vosges mountains are included in the reasonable room rate at this spectacularly located mountain pension, high above the town of Bühl and its surrounding vineyards. *7580 Bühl-Kappelwindeck, tel. 07223/24125. 10 rooms with bath or shower. No credit cards. Moderate.*

Ettlingen
Dining

Ratsstuben. Dine in a 16th-century cellar by the fast-flowing Als River; it was originally used to store salt. The food is heartily Teutonic. *Am Markt/Kirchgasse 1–3, tel. 07243/14754. Reservations advised. Dress: informal. DC, MC, V. Moderate.*

Lodging
★ **Hotel-Restaurant Erbprinz.** This is one of the most historic hotels in Ettlingen, one that even has its own trolley-car stop. For many, the real reason for staying here is the excellent restaurant, which offers magnificent nouvelle German specialties. In the summer, dine in the charming garden, hidden away behind the hotel's green and gilt fencing. *Rheinstr. 1, tel. 07243/12071. 50 rooms with bath or shower. Facilities: restaurant. AE, DC, MC, V. Expensive.*

Stadthotel Engel. A modern hotel, tucked away on the edge of Old Town, the Engel offers stylish comfort in cozy rooms. For the most atmosphere, try for one of the top-floor rooms. *Kronenstr. 13, tel. 17243/3300. 64 rooms with bath. Facilities: sauna, restaurant. AE, DC, MC, V. Moderate.*

Freiburg
Dining
★ **Falkenstube.** You'll find the most elegant dining in Freiburg here; it's the restaurant of the Colombi Hotel. The gracious atmosphere is set by softly lit oak paneling; the food is distinctive French nouvelle. Veal with foie gras and truffles makes for a memorable meal. For best value, try the 10-course "gourmet menu." *Rotteckring 16, tel. 0761/31415. Reservations required. Jacket and tie required. AE, DC, MC, V. Expensive.*

★ **Greiffenegg-Schlossle.** You'll come here for a potent Teutonic experience. The restaurant is in Freiburg castle and offers striking views from its terrace. The specialty is venison, though if you prefer something less intimidatingly rich, try the special "gourmet menu." *Schlossbergring 3, tel. 0761/32728. Reservations advised. Dress: informal. AE, DC, MC, V. Closed Mon. and Feb. Moderate.*

Kühler Krug. Venison also dominates the proceedings at this restaurant, which has even given its name to a distinctive saddle-of-venison dish. Those who prefer fish can choose from the imaginative range of freshwater varieties available. *Torpl. 1, tel. 0761/29103. Reservations advised. Dress: informal. AE. Closed Thurs. and 3 weeks in June. Moderate.*

Ratskeller. For typical Black Forest ambience, make for the Ratskeller, nestling in the shadow of the cathedral on Münsterplatz. The dark interior, with wood paneling and exposed beams, is complemented by the time-honored dishes, with roast meats and rich sauces predominating. *Münsterpl. 11, tel. 0761/37530. Reservations advised. Dress: informal. Closed Sun. evening and Mon. Moderate.*

★ **Zum Roten Baren.** The Red Bear claims to be the oldest inn in Germany, able to trace its history back to 1311. True or not, it's the archetypal German history-book inn, with a traditional menu to match. Prices are surprisingly low given the high quality, with fixed-price meals starting at DM 25 per person. There's a "surprise" menu, too, at DM 50 per person. Swabian (southwest German) *Spätzle*—a variety of noodle—comes with most dishes. *Oberlinden 12, tel. 0761/36913. Reservations advised. Dress: informal. AE, DC, MC, V. Moderate.*

Weinstube Karcher. Though a wine tavern first and foremost, this place nonetheless also offers tasty local fare at reasonable prices. Traditional jazz is featured at Sunday lunch. *Eisenbahnstr. 43, tel. 0761/22773. Dress: informal. No credit cards. Closed Christmas. Inexpensive.*

Lodging
Panorama Hotel am Jägerhäusle. The commanding view of Freiburg is the principal attraction of this sturdily comfortable old hotel. All the rooms face south and enjoy the same fine view. *Wintererstr. 89, tel. 0761/51030. 85 rooms with bath. Facilities:*

indoor pool, sauna, solarium, tennis, table tennis, restaurant. AE, DC, MC, V. Very Expensive.

Novotel. Stay here if you value the convenience of a downtown location and the functional comfort of a better-than-average chain hotel. It's located a few minutes' walk from Old Town. *Am Karlspl. 1, tel. 0761/31295. 112 rooms with bath. Facilities: parking, restaurant. AE, DC, MC, V. Expensive.*

Rappen. Located in the heart of the pedestrian-only Old Town, this hotel features brightly painted farmhouse-style rooms. The appealing rustic theme extends to the excellent restaurant. Wine lovers will appreciate the wide choice—more than 200—of regional vintages. *Münsterpl. 13, tel. 0761/31353. 20 rooms with bath. Facilities: restaurant. AE, DC, MC, V. Moderate.*

Freudenstadt
Dining

★ **Ratskeller.** Ask for a table near the *Kachelofen* if it's cold outside; that's a large, traditional tiled heating stove, and a central feature of this atmospheric haunt on picturesque Marktplatz. Swabian dishes and venison are featured prominently on the menu, but try the homemade trout roulade with crab sauce if it's available. The fixed-price menu, starting from DM 15, offers the best value. *Marktpl. 8, tel. 07441/2693. Reservations advised. Dress: informal. AE, DC, MC, V. Closed Tues. and Feb. Moderate.*

Baren. Fish—local trout is a specialty—and traditional, simple Swabian dishes are the main attractions of this robustly Teutonic restaurant. If you want to eat as the locals do, try *Maultaschen*, a delicious ravioli dish that Swabians swear by. For best value, try one of the daily specials; they start at DM 25. *Langestr. 33, tel. 07441/6585. Reservations advised. AE, DC, MC, V. Closed Sun. evening, Mon., and last 2 weeks in Jan. Moderate.*

Lodging

★ **Schwarzwaldhotel Birkenhof.** If you need to recharge tired batteries, there are few better places in which to do so than this superbly equipped hotel. Old-fashioned comfort and a woodland setting complement a wide range of sports facilities. The two restaurants offer a choice between classic French cuisine and sturdy Black Forest fare. *Wildbaderstr. 95, tel. 07441/4074. 60 rooms with bath. Facilities: indoor pool, sauna, solarium, Jacuzzi, massage room, squash, golf, table tennis, bowling alley, 2 restaurants. AE, DC, MC, V. Expensive.*

Golfhotel-Waldlust. This is a hotel with tradition, a spacious villa with its own extensive grounds and fine views of the Black Forest. In its pillared lounge, tea dances are held most days; an orchestra plays in the evenings. Some rooms are furnished with antiques. *Lauterbachstr. 92, tel. 07441/4051. 110 rooms, most with bath. Facilities: restaurant. No credit cards. Expensive.*

Schwanen. Owned and run by the Bukenberger family since 1900, the centrally located Schwanen, only a two-minute walk from the train station, offers good value and above-average comfort. *Forststr. 6, tel. 07441/2267. 17 rooms with bath or shower. Facilities: restaurant. No credit cards. Inexpensive.*

Gutach im Elztal
Dining and Lodging

★ **Romantik Hotel Stollen.** The flower-strewn balconies and low roofs of this hotel disguise a distinctive and luxurious interior. Run by the same family for 140 years, it combines understated comfort—some rooms have four-poster beds—with attentive service: You are treated as if you were staying in a family home rather than a hotel. The restaurant—which comes complete with a roaring log fire—offers regional food with nouvelle touches. The hotel is located 10 kilometers (6 miles) north of Freiburg. *7809 Gutach im Elztal, tel. 07685/207. 10 rooms with bath. Facilities: restaurant. AE, MC, V. Expensive.*

Hinterzarten
Lodging
★

Park Hotel Adler. The Riesterer family has owned this historic property since 1446. It's one of Germany's finest hotels, standing on nearly two acres of grounds that are ringed by the Black Forest. Marie-Antoinette once ate here, and the highest standards are kept up in the French restaurant and a paneled 17th-century dining room. An orchestra accompanies dinner and later moves to the bar for dancing. All rooms are sumptuously appointed. *Adlerpl., tel. 07652/711. 75 rooms with bath. Facilities: indoor pool, sauna, solarium, indoor and outdoor tennis, table tennis, golf range, 2 restaurants, bar. AE, DC, MC, V. Very Expensive.*

Sassenhof. Traditional Black Forest styles reign supreme here. The rooms are furnished with rustic pieces, brightly painted and decoratively carved. There's no restaurant, but guests are welcome to use the kitchen. *Adlerweg 17, tel. 07652/1515. 15 rooms and 6 suites with bath. Facilities: indoor pool, solarium, sauna. No credit cards. Expensive.*

Kesslermuhle. The Muhle, or mill, was first mentioned in local records in the 12th century. In the 15th century it passed from the Kessler family to the Birkenbergers, whose descendants still run the hotel that the original mill became. Extensive modernization has produced a snug place to lay your head. The wood-paneled restaurant is atmospheric. *Erlenbruckerstr. 45, tel. 07652/1290. 31 rooms with bath. Facilities: indoor pool, sauna, gym, table tennis, billiards, restaurant, café, bar. No credit cards. Expensive.*

Nagold
Dining
★

Romantik Restaurant Alte Post. This is a centuries-old half-timbered inn that has the kind of ambience lesser establishments believe can be built in with false beams. The menu ranges from traditional Swabian dishes to classic (and expensive) French offerings. For best value try the local food; the veal in mushroom sauce and venison (in season) are reliable favorites. *Bahnhofsstr. 2, tel. 07452/4221. Reservations advised. Jacket and tie required. AE, DC, MC, V. Closed Sat. lunch and 2 weeks in Jan. Moderate.*

Lodging

Hotel Post Gästhaus. Run by the former proprietors of the neighboring Alte Post restaurant, this hotel is part of a historic and charming old coach inn. Parts of the ivy-clad building are modern, but the same standards of comfort are offered throughout. *Bahnhofstr. 3, tel. 07452/4048. 24 rooms with bath. AE, DC, MC, V. Expensive.*

Pforzheim
Dining
★

Rotisserie le Canard. Superb classic French cuisine and sophisticated Swabian fare are offered in the gracious surroundings of this restaurant of the Gute Hoffnung hotel. Try the homemade Spätzle with fresh herbs for a surprisingly delicate version of what's normally a hearty and filling dish. *Dillsteinerstr. 9–11, tel. 07231/22011. Reservations required. Jacket and tie required. AE, DC, MC, V. Closed Sun. Expensive.*

★ **Pic-Pic.** People in the know come here for imaginative dishes at low prices. There are about 40 of them on the vast menu; none costs more than DM 36. *Zerrennerstr. 6, tel. 07231/101-939. Reservations advised. Dress: informal. No credit cards. Closed lunch. Moderate.*

Lodging **Ruf.** When it opened at the beginning of the century, this hotel was described by a visiting English journalist as "A house that is aware of its importance for the numerous German and foreign visitors . . . to Pforzheim." Whether or not it is still "aware of its importance," it still aims to offer the same degree of reliable comfort—the hotel is nothing fancy, but it is dependably efficient and welcoming. The excellent restaurant is decorated with intricate wrought iron and stained glass. *Am Schlossberg, tel. 07231/16011. 51 rooms with bath. Facilities: restaurant. No credit cards. Expensive.*

Titisee
Dining and Lodging **Romantik Hotel Adler Post.** Located in the Neustadt district of Titisee, about 3 miles from the lake, this solid old building has been owned and run by the Ketterer family for 140 years. All the rooms are comfortably and traditionally furnished. The restaurant, the Rotisserie zum Postillon, offers excellent local specialties. *Hauptstr. 16, tel. 07651/5066. 32 rooms with bath. Facilities: indoor pool, sauna, solarium, restaurant. AE, DC, MC, V. Expensive.*

The Arts and Nightlife

The Arts

Music Freiburg's annual **Zeltmusick** festival is a musical jamboree held in June or July in tents—*Zelt* is German for tents—that sprout on the city outskirts. The accent is on jazz, but most types of music are featured, including classical. The city also has a Philharmonic orchestra; it gives concerts year-round in the city theater. Chamber-music concerts are presented in the summer in the courtyard of the ancient Kufhaus, opposite the Münster. For program details and tickets for all the above, contact **Freiburg Verkehrsamt,** Rotteckring 14, tel. 0761/216–3281. For jazz, make for the **Jazz Haus** (Schnewlinstr. 1); live music is featured nightly. Baden-Baden's orchestra performs regularly at the **Kurhaus** (Werderstr.) and also presents an annual two-week summer festival, the **Musikalische Sommer.** For program details and tickets, call 07221/275–2500.

Theater Freiburg has an annual summer theater festival. Performances are given in the city's theater complex and spill out onto the streets and squares as well. Street theater is also featured in the annual **Schlossberg** festival, held in August, a popular and informal carnival-like event centering on the castle. Baden-Baden's **Theater am Goetheplatz** presents a regular program of drama, opera, and ballet. Call 07221/275–260 for program details and tickets.

Movies English-language movies are regularly shown at Freiburg's **German-American Institute** (Kaiser-Joseph-Str. 266, tel. 0761/31645).

Nightlife

Black Forest nightlife means Baden-Baden's elegant **casino,** first and foremost. There's a DM 5 admission charge; bring your passport as ID. You'll have to sign a form guaranteeing you can meet any debts you run up. There's a strict dress code, too. If your tastes run to less intimidatingly formal nightlife, the city's leading disco, the **Club Taverne** (closed Mon. and

Tues.), is located in the same building. For a more muted evening, try the **Oleander Bar** in Baden-Baden's top hotel, Brenner's Park-Hotel (Lichtentaler Allee); a piano offers a soothing accompaniment to the tinkle of ice in your glass.

Nightlife in Freiburg revolves around the city's wine bars and wine cellars. **Oberkirch's Weinstuben** and **Die Zwiebel,** both located on Münsterplatz, are typically atmospheric; you can also look for night spots on any of the streets around the cathedral. The top discos are **El PI** (Schiffstr. 16) and **Lord Nelson** (Bertoldtstr. 26). **Sam's Dance Palace** (Humboldtstr. 2) is fun if you don't mind crowds. **The Playboy Bar** (Möltkestr. 3) is Las Vegas–tacky and expensive; a pool keeps excited customers cool.

8 The Romantic Road

Introduction

Of all the specially designated tourist routes that crisscross Germany, none rivals the aptly named Romantische Strasse, or Romantic Road. It's not so much the road itself that is the big attraction, for the scenery to be encountered along the way (with a few exceptions) is more domestic and rural than spectacular. What makes the Romantic Road so memorable are the medieval towns, villages, castles, and churches that stud its 420-kilometer (260-mile) length. Many of these are tucked away beyond low hills, their spires and towers poking up through the greenery.

Within the massive gates of formerly fortified settlements, half-timbered houses lean against each other along narrow cobbled lanes. Ancient squares are adorned with fountains and flowers, and formidable walls are punctuated by watchtowers built to keep out marauding enemies.

Today's invaders turn out to be tourists, and who can blame them for coming to visit a string of towns that had until comparatively recent times been bypassed by progress and remained an all but forgotten backwater of history?

The Romantic Road's sights add up to a pageant of marvels of history, art, and architecture, providing a concentrated essence of Germany at its most picturesque and romantic.

The road runs south from Würzburg in the north of Bavaria to Schwangau in the Alps along the Austrian border. You can, of course, follow it in the opposite direction, as a number of bus tours do.

Either way, among the major sights, you'll see one of Europe's most scintillating Rococo palaces, in Würzburg. Rothenburg-ob-der-Tauber may well be the best-preserved medieval town on the Continent. Then there's the handsome Renaissance city of Augsburg. Finally, for most visitors, the highlight will be Ludwig II's captivating fantasy castle of Neuschwanstein.

For much of its length the Romantic Road follows age-old trade routes. Once this was a main overland passage across the Continent. The sector through the Lech Valley between Füssen and Donauwörth started as the old Roman road known as Via Claudia, along which merchants moved to deliver spices from the Indies to the great cities of the north. In the Middle Ages, knights and minnesingers traveled this route as well.

The concept of the Romantic Road could be considered something of a marketing ploy. At a time when West Germany was trying to rebuild its tourist industry in the wake of the devastation of World War II, an enterprising public-relations type dreamed up the name to apply to this historic passage through several regions of southern Germany that could be advertised as a single package with a catchy title. And that was how, in 1950, the Romantic Road was born, soon to evolve into one of Europe's most heavily traveled tourist trails.

The name itself refers not so much to the kind of romance lovers engage in as to a variation of the word meaning wonderful, fabulous, imaginative. And, of course, the Romantic Road started as a road on which the Romans traveled. By any name, this passage can make for a memorable journey.

On its way the road crosses former battlefields where armies fought for control of the region and the towns that dot it. Paradoxically, it was the most cataclysmic of these conflicts, the Thirty Years' War of the mid-17th century, that by destroying their economic base assured the survival of the most historic of the Romantic Road towns, such as the gemlike Rothenburg-ob-der-Tauber, all but forgotten over the centuries until fairly recently, when it emerged as a star attraction of the Romantic Road tour. Today, armies of tourists may disrupt the town's tranquillity, but they cannot obliterate its exquisitely preserved medieval attributes. The age-old stones have not been tampered with. And, if you travel the Romantic Road off-season, you may yet find this lovely place slumbering as it did in the dim and distant past.

As you travel the Romantic Road, two names crop up again and again: Walther von der Vogelweide and Tilman Riemenschneider. To help you appreciate more about their lives and works, it might be helpful to know a little about these masters of the Middle Ages and Renaissance, respectively, whose names are forever associated with Würzburg and the Romantic Road. Walther von der Vogelweide, who died in Würzburg in 1230, was the most famous of the German *Minnesänger*, the poet-musicians who wrote and sang of courtly love in the age of chivalry, when knights and other nobles hired them for their artistic services to help win the favors of fair ladies.

Von der Vogelweide broke with this tradition by writing love songs to maidens of less-than-noble rank; he also accepted commissions of a political nature, producing what amounted to medieval political manifestos. His work was romantic, lyrical, witty, and filled with a sighing wistfulness and philosophical questioning. "Oh, you long years," he once wrote, "where did you disappear? Was my life a reality, or did I dream it?" And this was three centuries before Shakespeare concerned himself with similar thoughts.

Tilman Riemenschneider, Germany's master of late-Gothic sculpture, lived an extraordinary life. His skill with wood and stone was recognized at an early age. His success became so great that he soon presided over a major Würzburg workshop, with a team of assistants. Riemenschneider worked alone, however, on the lifesize figures that dominate his sculptures. His characteristic grace and harmony of line can be picked out in such features as the folds of a robe.

At the height of his career, Riemenschneider was appointed city councillor; later he became mayor of Würzburg. In 1523, however, he made the fateful error of siding with the revolutionaries in the Peasants' Revolt. He was arrested and held for eight weeks in the dungeons of the Marienburg fortress above Würzburg, where he was frequently tortured. Most of his wealth was confiscated, and he returned home a broken man, with little will to continue his work. Times and artistic tastes were changing. Late-Gothic styles gave way to the greater refinement of the Renaissance.

Riemenschneider died six years after his fall from favor, in 1531. For nearly three centuries he and his sculptures were ignored and all but forgotten. Only when, in 1822, ditchdiggers uncovered the site of his grave did Riemenschneider once again come to be included among Germany's greatest artists.

The discovery sparked a wave of interest. Riemenschneider was enthusiastically resurrected and championed by the Romantics of the 19th century. His works were sought out, catalogued, and guarded with zealous admiration. Today he is recognized as the towering giant of early-Renaissance German sculpture. The richest collection of his works is in Würzburg, although other masterpieces are on view in churches and museums in many parts of Germany; for example, the renowned Windsheim Altar of the Twelve Apostles is found in the Palatine Museum in Heidelberg.

Essential Information

Important Addresses and Numbers

Tourist Information Two regional tourist information offices cover the towns along the Romantic Road. These are: **Fremdenverkehrsverein Allgäu Bayerisch-Schwaben,** Fuggerstrasse 9, D-9800 Augsburg, tel. 0821/33335; and **Fremdenverkehrsverein Bodensee-Oberschwaben,** Schützenstrasse 8, 7750 Konstanz, tel. 07531/22232. For information on the Romantic Road itself, *see* Getting Around by Car, above. Local tourist offices include:

Augsburg: Verkehrsverein, Bahnhofstrasse 7, tel. 0821/502–070.
Dinkelsbühl: Tourist-Information, Marktplatz, tel. 09851/90240.
Donauwörth: Städtisches Verkehrsamt, Rathausgasse 1, tel. 0906/789–0145.
Feuchtwangen: 8805 Fremdenverkehrsamt, Marktplatz 1, tel. 09852/90444.
Füssen: Kurverwaltung, Augsburgerstrasse 2, tel. 08362/7077.
Harburg: Fremdenverkehrsverein, Schlossstrasse 1, tel. 09003/101.
Landsberg am Lech: Fremdenverkehrsamt, Hauptplatz 1, tel. 08191/128–246.
Nördlingen: Städtisches Verkehrsamt, Marktplatz 2, tel. 09081/84114.
Rothenburg-ob-der-Tauber: Tourist-Information, Marktplatz 2, tel. 09861/40492.
Schongau: Verkehrsverein, Bahnhofstrasse 44, tel. 08861/7216.
Schwangau: Kurverwaltung, Rathaus, Münchenerstrasse 2, tel. 08362/81051.
Würzburg: Fremdenverkehrsamt, Falkenhaus am Markt, tel. 0931/37335.

Car Rental **Avis:** Klinkerberg 31, tel. 0821/38241, **Augsburg;** Schuererstrasse 2, tel. 0931/50661, **Würzburg.**
Europacar: Leonardsberg 17, tel. 0821/313–015, **Augsburg;** Friedenstrasse 15, tel. 0931/88150, **Würzburg.**
Hertz: Ulmerstrasse 21, tel. 0821/407–707, **Augsburg;** Hoechberger Strasse 10, tel. 0931/415–221 or 414–145, **Würzburg.**

Arriving and Departing

By Plane The major international airports serving the Romantic Road are Frankfurt, at its northern end, and Munich, at its southern end. Regional airports include Nürnberg and Stuttgart.

By Car The northernmost city of the Romantic Road—and the natural starting point for a tour—is Würzburg on the Frankfurt–Nürnberg Autobahn. It's 115 kilometers (72 miles) from Frankfurt and 280 kilometers (175 miles) from Munich. Augsburg, the largest city on the Romantic Road, is 70 kilometers (44 miles) from Munich and 365 kilometers (228 miles) from Frankfurt. Full information on the Romantic Road is available from **Tourist Information Land an der Romantischen Strasse,** Kreisverkehrsamt, Crailsheimerstrasse 1, 8800 Ansbach, tel. 0981/68232.

By Train Both Würzburg and Augsburg are on the Intercity network and have fast, frequent service to and from Frankfurt, Munich, and Stuttgart. Less frequent trains link most of the other major towns of the Romantic Road.

By Bus From mid-March until the beginning of November, daily bus service runs the length of the Romantic Road. One bus leaves Würzburg at 9 AM and reaches Füssen at 7:35 PM; a second starts from Wiesbaden at 7 AM, stops in Frankfurt, and arrives in Munich at 6:55 PM after following the northern section of the route. In the other direction, buses leave Füssen at 8:15 AM (arriving in Würzburg at 7:20 PM) and Munich at 9 AM (arriving in Wiesbaden at 8:45 PM). All buses stop at the major sights along the road. Reservations are essential; contact **Deutsche Touring GmbH** (Am Römerhof 17, 6000 Frankfurt/Main 90, tel. 069/790–3240). Local buses cover much of the route but are infrequent and slow.

Getting Around

By Car The Romantic Road is most easily traveled by car, starting at Würzburg as outlined below and following the B-27 country highway south to meet roads B-290, B-19, B-292, and along the Wörnitz River on B-25.

Guided Tours

City Tours All the cities and towns on the Romantic Road offer guided tours, either on foot or by bus. Details are available from the local tourist information offices. Following is a sample of the more typical.

Augsburg has self-guided walking tours, with routes of varying lengths posted on color-coded signs throughout the downtown area. A twice-daily bus tour—"2,000 Years in Two Hours"—takes in all the main sights. Tours start from the Rathaus; the cost is DM 12 adults, DM 6 children.

Rothenburg-ob-der-Tauber's night watchman, dressed in traditional garb, conducts visitors on a nightly tour of the town, leading the way with a lantern. Tours begin at 9 PM and cost DM 2. The night watchman in **Dinkensbühl** also does a nightly round, and though he doesn't give official tours he is always happy to answer questions from inquisitive visitors. Daily guided tours of Dinkensbühl in horse-drawn carriages are a fun way to see the little town.

Bus Tours From mid-March to the beginning of November, the **Deutsche Touring** company *(see* Getting Around by Bus, above) operates a daily bus excursion from Frankfurt to Rothenburg, leaving Frankfurt at 8:15 AM and returning around 8 PM. The bus has an English-speaking guide, and the DM 89 fare (DM 69 children) includes lunch, a guided tour of Rothenburg, and admission charges to various museums.

Train Tours **Deutsche Bundesbahn** (German Railways) offers special weekend excursion rates covering travel from most German railroad stations to Würzburg and hotel accommodations for up to four nights. Details are available at any train station.

Boat Trips Three shipping companies offer excursions on the Main River from Würzburg. The **Fränkische Personenschiffahrt** (Kranenkai 1, tel. 0931/51722) and the **Würzburger Personenschiffahrt Kurth & Schiebe** (Am Alten Kranen, tel. 0931/58573) operate excursions to the vineyards in and around Würzburg; wine tasting is included in the price. Fränkische Personenschiffahrt (FPS for short) also offers cruises of up to two weeks on the Main, Neckar, and Danube rivers, and the Main–Danube canal. **Veitschöchheimer Personenschiffahrt Heinrich Herbert** (Am Alten Kranen, tel. 0931/55633) offers daily service to Veitschöchheim, site of the palace that was once the summer residence of the bishops of Augsburg.

Exploring the Romantic Road

Highlights for First-time Visitors

Würzburg Residenz
Rothenburg-ob-der-Tauber
Dinkelsbühl
Augsburg Cathedral
Wieskirche
Schloss Neuschwanstein

Würzburg

Numbers in the margin correspond with points of interest on the Romantic Road map.

Our tour of the Romantic Road begins at its northern extremi-
1 ty, in the basically Baroque city of **Würzburg,** the pearl of the Romantic Road, a heady example of what happens when great genius teams up with great wealth.

Situated at the confluence of two age-old trade routes, Würzburg has been a prosperous city since more or less time immemorial. And it still shows. Starting in the 10th century Würzburg was ruled by the powerful (and rich) prince-bishops who created the city with all the glittering attributes that you see today.

Set on the banks of the Main River as it passes through a calm valley backed by vineyard-covered hills, this glorious old city is overlooked by a fortified castle on dominating high ground on the far side of the river. This is Festung Marienberg, constructed between 1200 and 1600, and for 450 years residence of the prince-bishops.

From the start, you should be advised that present-day Würzburg is by no means 100% original. In fact, the city you will visit turns out to be largely restored. It happened this way: At the very end of World War II, in one of those unfortunate strategic

The Romantic Road

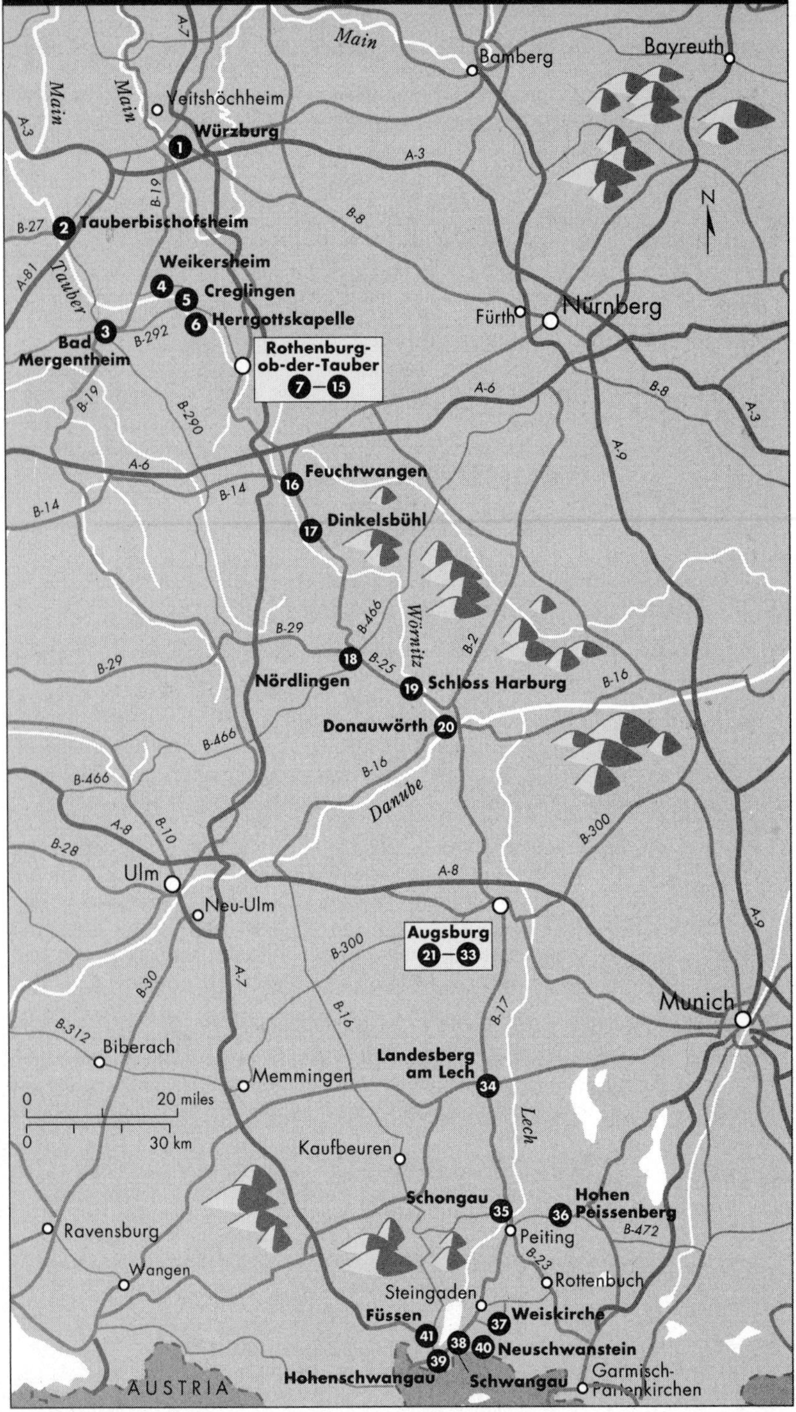

decisions, Würzburg was all but obliterated in a saturation bombing raid. The date was March 16, 1945. While the bombing lasted no more than 20 minutes, 87% of Würzburg was wiped off the map, with some 4,000 buildings destroyed and at least that many people killed.

Painstaking reconstruction has returned most of the city's famous sights to their former splendor, in many cases using original stones from the bombed-out structures.

In fact, those who knew prewar Würzburg insist that the heart of the city now is every bit as impressive as it was prior to 1945 and, except for a new pedestrian zone, remains a largely authentic restoration.

High on the list of compelling reasons for visiting Würzburg is the **Residenz,** the glorious Baroque palace where the line of prince-bishops lived after coming down from their hilltop fortress Festung Marienberg.

Pleasure-loving Prince-Bishop Johann Phillip Franz von Schonborn financed the venture. Construction started in 1719 under the brilliant direction of Balthasar Neumann, the German architectural genius of his age. Most of the interior decoration was entrusted to the Italian stuccoist Antonio Bossi and the Venetian painter Giovanni Batista Tiepolo. But the man whose spirit infuses the Residenz is von Schonborn, who unfortunately did not live to see the completion of what has come to be considered the most beautiful palace of Germany's Baroque era and one of Europe's most sumptuous buildings, frequently referred to as the "Palace of Palaces." This dazzling structure is located a 10-minute walk from the railway station, along Kaiserstrasse and then Theaterstrasse.

Anyone harboring doubts as to whether the prince-bishops of 18th-century Würzburg were bishops first and princes only incidentally will have them swept aside in a hurry. The Residenz is irrefutable evidence of the worldly power of these glamorous rulers and men of God.

From the moment you enter the building, the splendor of the Residenz is evident, as the largest Baroque staircase in the country, the **Treppenhaus,** stretches away from you into the heights. Halfway to the second floor, the stairway splits and peels away at 180 degrees to the left and right.

Dominating the upper reaches of this vast space is Tiepolo's giant fresco of **The Four Continents,** a gorgeous exercise in blue and pink with allegorical figures at the corners representing the continents (only four were known of at the time).

Next, make your way to the *Weissersaal* (the White Room) and then beyond to the grandest of the state rooms, the **Kaisersaal** (Throne Room). The Baroque/Rococo ideal of *Gesamtkunstwerk*—the fusion of the arts—is illustrated to perfection here. Architecture melts into stucco, stucco invades the frescoes, the frescoes extend the real space of the room into their fantasy world. Nothing is quite what it seems, and no expense was spared to make it so. Tiepolo's frescoes show the visit of the Emperor Frederick Barbarossa to Würzburg in the 12th century to claim his bride. The fact that the characters all wear 16th-century Venetian dress hardly seems to matter. Few interiors anywhere use such startling opulence to similar effect. The room is airy, magical, intoxicating. You'll find more of this same expansive spirit in the **Hofkirche,** the chapel, which offers further proof that the prince-bishops experienced little or no conflict between their love of ostentation and their service to God. Among the lavish marbles, rich gilding, and delicate stuccowork, note the Tiepolo altarpieces, ethereal visions of *The Fall of the Angels* and *The Assumption of the Virgin.* Finally, tour the palace garden, the **Hofgarten;** the entrance is next to the chapel. This 18th-century formal garden, with its stately gushing fountains and trim, ankle-high shrubs outlining geometrical flower beds and gravel walks, is the equal of any in the country. *Admission, including guided tour: DM 3.50 adults, DM 2.50 students over 14 and senior citizens. Open Apr.–Sept., Tues.–Sun. 9–5; Oct.–Mar., Tues.–Sun. 10–4.*

Time Out From the square fronting the Residenz, take the first street on the right, Theaterstrasse, and make for the **Bürgerspital;** it's about halfway down the street on the right. Originally this was a medieval hospice established by wealthy burghers for Würzburg's poor and old. Not only did they get a roof over their heads, they received a daily allowance of one liter of wine (two on Sundays). Today, there's no free wine, but buying a quarter liter of good Franconian white wine from the Bürgerspital's own vineyards won't make a dent in anyone's budget. Ask for a tour of the wine cellar: Its barrels are as big as a small German car. Just down the road, on Juliuspromenade, is another of these charitable institutions, the **Juliusspital** (Julius Hospice), established in 1576 by a Würzburg bishop.

To the left is Würzburg's attractive pedestrian shopping area, Schönbornstrasse, named after the bishop who commissioned Neumann to build the Residenz. On the left as you enter the street is another example of Neumann's work, the distinctive Baroque **Augustinerkirche** (Church of St. Augustine). The church was a 13th-century Dominican chapel; Neumann's additions date from the early 18th century. At the end of Schönbornstrasse is Würzburg's Romanesque cathedral, the **Dom,** begun in 1045. Step inside and you find yourself, somewhat disconcertingly, in a shimmering Rococo treasure house. This is, perhaps, only fitting: Prince-Bishop von Schönborn, who came up with the concept of the Residenz, is buried here, and it's hard to imagine him slumbering amid the dour weightiness of a Romanesque edifice.

Alongside the cathedral is the **Neumünster,** built above the grave of the early Irish martyr St. Kilian, who brought Christianity to Würzburg and, with two companions, was put to death here in 689. Their missionary zeal bore fruit, however, for 17 years after their deaths, a church was consecrated in their memory. By 742, Würzburg had become a diocese; over the following centuries 39 churches flourished throughout the city. Once an abbey church, the Neumünster's former cloistered churchyard contains the grave of Walther von der Vogelweide, the most famous minstrel in German history.

Across the pedestrian zone toward the river lies Würzburg's market square, the **Markt,** with shady trees and a framework of historic old facades. At one end, flanked by a Rococo mansion, are the soaring late-Gothic windows of the 14th-to-15th-century **Marienkapelle** (St. Mary's Chapel), where architect Balthasar Neumann lies buried. Pause beneath its finely carved portal and inspect the striking figures of Adam and Eve; you shouldn't have great difficulty recognizing the style of Tilman Riemenschneider. The original statues are in Würzburg's museum, the Mainfränkische Museum, on the Marienberg, across the river; the ones in the portal of the Marienkapelle are copies.

On your explorations along the edge of the pedestrian zone and market square note the exquisite "house Madonnas," small statues of the Virgin set into corner niches on the second level of many old homes. So many of these lovely representations of the city's patron saint can be seen that Würzburg is frequently referred to as "the town of Madonnas."

On the way to the **Marienburg Fortress,** you'll cross the Old Main Bridge, already standing before America was discovered. Among the city's glories are the twin rows of infinitely graceful statues of saints that line the bridge. Note particularly the "Weeping Madonna," known as *Patronna Franconiae.* There's also a great view of the fortress from the bridge—statues in the foreground, Marienburg and its surrounding vineyards as the focal point—to make for the perfect photograph to treasure as a souvenir of this historic city.

To reach the Marienburg, you can make a fairly stiff climb on foot or take the bus from the Old Main Bridge. It runs every half hour starting at 9:45 AM.

The Marienburg was the original home of the prince-bishops beginning in the 13th century. The oldest buildings—note especially the **Marienkirche,** the core of the complex—date from even earlier, around 700. In addition to the rough-hewn medieval fortifications, there are a number of fine Renaissance and Baroque apartments. The highlight of a visit to the Marienburg is the **Mainfränkische Museum** (the Main-Franconian Museum). The rich and varied history of Würzburg is brought alive by this remarkable collection of art treasures. The standout is the gallery devoted to Würzburg-born Renaissance sculptor Tilman Riemenschneider, including the originals of the great Adam and Eve statues, copies of which adorn the portal of the Marienkapelle. You'll also be exposed to fine paintings by Tiepolo and Cranach and exhibits of porcelain, firearms, and antique toys. Wine lovers won't want to miss the old winepresses, some of them enormous. Other exhibits chart the history of Franconian wine. *Admission to Marienburg Fortress: DM 1.50 adults, DM 1 students over 14 and senior citizens. Open Apr.–Sept., Tues.–Sun. 9–noon and 1–5; Oct.–Mar., Tues.–Sun. 10–noon and 1–5. Admission to Mainfränkische Museum: DM 2.80 adults, DM 2 students over 14. Open Apr.–Oct., daily 10–5; Nov.–Mar., daily 10–4.*

To see the original summer palace of the prince-bishops, you have to go a little north of Würzburg, to Veitshöchheim. Though it has little of the glamorous appeal of the Residenz, the sturdy Baroque building provides further evidence of the great wealth of the worldly rulers of Würzburg. *Admission, including guided tour: DM 2.50 adults, DM 1.50 students over 14 and senior citizens. Open Apr.–Sept., Tues.–Sun. 9–noon and 1–5.*

The Tauber Valley

The Romantic Road heads south from Würzburg, following the B-27 country highway, to the lovely valley of the Tauber at the
2 small town of **Tauberbischofsheim,** 36 kilometers (22 miles) southwest. There are no major sights here. What you'll want to do is linger in its shady pedestrian mall; stroll down to the sleepy Tauber River; and visit the parish church, site of a side altar richly carved by a follower of Tilman Riemenschneider.

Follow B-290 16 kilometers (10 miles) south to **Bad Mergen-**
3 **theim,** the premier resort of this region. Between 1525 and 1809, Bad Mergentheim was the home of the Teutonic Knights, one of the most successful of the medieval orders of chivalry. Their greatest glories came in the 15th century, when they had established themselves as one of the dominant powers of the Baltic, ruling large areas of present-day East Germany, Poland, and Lithuania. The following centuries saw a steady decline in the order's commercial success. In 1809 Napoléon expelled the Teutonic Knights from Bad Mergentheim. The French emperor had little time for what he considered the medieval superstition of orders such as this and had no compunction in disbanding them as he marched east through Germany in the opening stages of his ultimately disastrous Russian campaign. The expulsion of the order seemed to be the death knell of the little town. But in 1826 a shepherd discovered mineral springs on the north bank of the river. They proved to be the strongest sodium sulphate and bitter-salt waters in Europe, with health-giving properties that ensured the little town's future prosperity. Excavations subsequently showed that the springs had been known in the Iron and Bronze Ages before becoming choked with silt.

Eleven kilometers (7 miles) southeast of Bad Mergentheim stands the village chapel that guards one of the great Renaissance German paintings, the so-called *Stuppacher Madonna* by Matthias Grünewald (c. 1475–1528). The painting is believed to have been produced for a church in nearby Aschaffenburg; no one seems clear on how it found its way here. It was only in 1908 that experts finally recognized it as the work of Grünewald; repainting in the 17th century had turned it into a flat and unexceptional work. Grünewald was one of the leading painters of the early Renaissance in Germany. Though he was familiar with the developments in perspective and natural lighting of Italian Renaissance painting, his work remained resolutely anti-Renaissance in spirit: tortured, emotional, dark. You'll want to compare it with that of Dürer, his contemporary, if you visit Munich's Alte Pinakothek museum. Where Dürer used the lessons of Italian painting to reproduce its clarity and rationalism, Grünewald used them to heighten his essentially still Gothic imagery.

B-19 and B-292 lead the 12 kilometers (8 miles) to the little town
4 of **Weikersheim,** which provides another excuse to linger on the long road south. The town is dominated by the castle of the counts of Hohenlohe. The great hall of the castle is the scene each summer of an international youth music festival, and the Rittersaal (Knight's Hall) contains lifesize wall sculptures of animals, reflecting the counts' love of hunting. In the cellars you can drink a glass of cool wine drawn from the huge casks

that seem to prop up the building. Outside again, stroll through the enchanting gardens and enjoy the view of the Tauber and its leafy valley.

Follow the Tauber valley 20 kilometers (12 miles) farther to
5 **Creglingen.** Here you can detour up a side valley, the Herrgottstal (Valley of the Lord). The valley has been an important place of pilgrimage since the 14th century, when a farmer had a vision of a heavenly host plowing his field. A chapel, the
6 **Herrgottskapelle** (Chapel of Our Lord), was built by the counts of Hohenlohe. In the early 16th century Tilman Riemenschneider was commissioned to carve an altarpiece for it. This is the reason you come here. This enormous work, 33 feet high, depicts in minute detail the life and ascension of the Virgin Mary. Riemenschneider entrusted much of the background detail to the craftsmen of his Würzburg workshop, but he allowed no one but himself to attempt the lifesize figures of this masterpiece. Its intricate detail and attenuated figures are a high point of late-Gothic sculpture.

Now drive the remaining 20 kilometers (12 miles) to Rothenburg-ob-der-Tauber, for most people the quintessential town of the Romantic Road.

Rothenburg-ob-der-Tauber

Numbers in the margin correspond with points of interest on the Rothenburg-ob-der-Tauber map.

7 **Rothenburg-ob-der-Tauber** (literally, "the red castle on the Tauber") is the kind of gemlike medieval town that even Walt Disney might have thought too good to be true, with gingerbread architecture galore and a wealth of fountains and flowers against a backdrop of towers and turrets. The reason for its survival is simple. Rothenburg was a small but thriving 17th-century town that had grown up around the ruins of two 12th-century churches that had been destroyed by an earthquake. Then it was laid low economically by the havoc of the Thirty Years' War, the cataclysmic religious struggle that all but destroyed Germany in the 17th century. Its economic base devastated, the town slumbered, an all-but-forgotten backwater, until modern tourism rediscovered it. And here it is, milking its "best-preserved-medieval-town-in-Europe" image to the full, undoubtedly something of a tourist trap, but real enough for all that. There really is nowhere else quite like it. Whether Rothenburg is at its most appealing in the summer, when the balconies of its ancient houses are festooned with flowers, or in the winter, when snow lies on its steep gables and narrow streets, is a matter of taste. Few people are likely to find this extraordinary little survivor from another age anything but remarkable.

8 Begin your visit by walking around the **city walls,** more than a mile long. Stairs every 200 or 300 yards provide ready access. There are great views of the tangle of pointed and tiled roofs
9 and of the rolling country beyond. Then make for the **Rathaus** (Town Hall), the logical place to begin an exploration of Rothenburg itself. Half the building is Gothic, begun in 1240, the other half classical, begun in 1572. A fire in 1501 destroyed part of it the structure, hence the newer, Renaissance section, which faces the main square. Go inside to see the **Histori-**

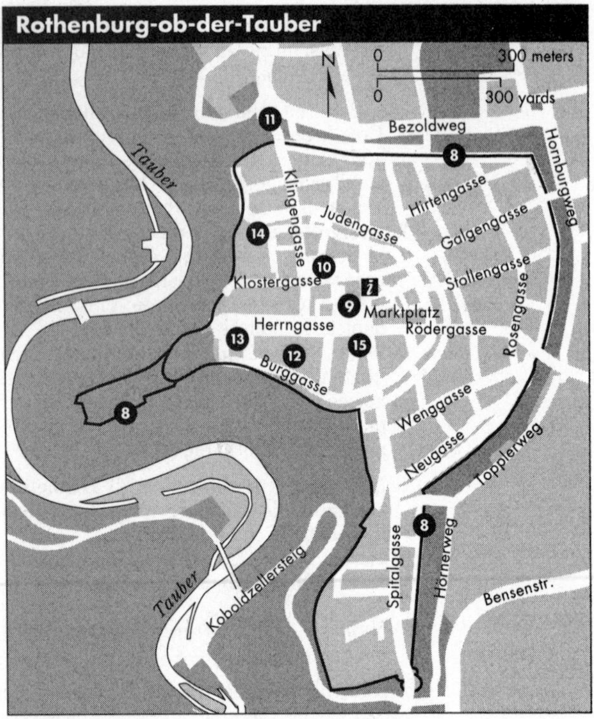

engewölbe, a museum housed in the vaults below the building that charts Rothenburg's role in the Thirty Years' War. Great prominence is given to the Meistertrunk (Master Drink). This event will follow you around Rothenburg. It came about when the Protestant town was captured by Catholic forces. During the victory celebrations, so the story goes, the conquering general was embarrassed to find himself unable to drink a great tankard of wine in one go, as his manhood demanded. He volunteered to spare the town further destruction if any of the city councillors could drain the mighty draught. The mayor, a man by the name of Nusch, took up the challenge and succeeded, and Rothenburg was preserved. The tankard itself is on display at the Reichsstadtmuseum (*see* below). As it contains fully 3¼ liters, the wonder is not so much that the conquering general was unable to knock it back but that he should ever have tried it in the first place. An annual pageant celebrating the prodigious feat, with townsfolk parading the streets dressed in 17th-century garb, helps keep the legend alive. The festival begins in the courtroom of the town hall, where the event is said to have occurred. *Rathauspl. Admission: DM 2 adults, DM 1 children. Open mid-Mar.–Oct., daily 9–6.*

10 Just north of the town hall is the **Stadtpfarrkirche St. Jakob** (parish church of St. James), the repository of further works by Tilman Riemenschneider, including the famous Heiliges Blut (Holy Blood) altar. Above the altar a crystal capsule is said to contain drops of Christ's blood. The church has other items of interest, including three fine stained-glass windows dating

from the 14th and 15th centuries in the choir, and the famous Herlin-Altar, with its 15th-century painted panels. *Open Easter–Oct., daily 9–5; Nov.–Easter, daily 10–noon and 2–4.*

11 Another of Rothenburg's churches, **St. Wolfgang's,** is built into the defenses of the town. From within the town it looks like a peaceful parish church; from outside it blends into the forbidding city wall. Through an underground passage you can reach the sentry walk above and follow the wall for almost its entire length.

12 Two museums you won't want to miss are the **Mittelalterliches**
13 **Kriminalmuseum** and the **Puppen und Spielzeugmuseum.** The former sets out to document the history of German legal processes in the Middle Ages and contains an impressive array of instruments of torture. The latter is an enchanting doll and toy museum housed in a 15th-century building near the Rathaus. There are 300 dolls, the oldest dating from 1780, the newest from 1940. *Mittelalterliches Kriminalmuseum: Burggasse 3. Admission: DM 3.50 adults, DM 2 children. Open Apr.–Oct., daily 9:30–6; Nov.–Mar., daily 2–4. Puppen und Spielzeugmuseum: Hofronnengasse 13. Admission: DM 3.50 adults, DM 1.50 children. Open Mar.–Dec., daily 9:30–6; Jan.–Feb., daily 11–5.*

14 The **Reichsstadtmuseum** (Imperial City Museum) turns out to be two attractions in one. It's the city museum and contains artifacts that illustrate Rothenburg and its history. Among them is the great tankard, or *Pokal*, of the Meistertrunk. The setting of the museum is the other attraction; it's a former convent, the oldest parts of which date from the 13th century. Tour the building to see the cloister, the kitchens, and the dormitory, then see the collections. *Hafronnengasse 13. Admission: DM 3.50 adults, DM 1.50 children. Open Mar.–Dec., daily 9:30–6; Jan.–Feb., daily 11–5.*

Cobbled Hofronnengasse runs into the Marktplatz (Market
15 Square), site of an ornate Renaissance fountain, the **Herterlichbrunnen.** To celebrate some momentous event—the end of a war, say, or the passing of an epidemic—the *Schäfertanz* (Shepherds' Dance) was performed around the fountain. The dance is still done, though for the benefit of tourists rather than to commemorate the end of a threat to Rothenburg. It takes place in front of the Rathaus several times a year, chiefly at Easter, in late May, and throughout June and July.

Feuchtwangen, Dinkelsbühl, and Nordlingen

Numbers in the margin correspond with points of interest on the Romantic Road map.

Our next main stop on the Romantic Road is the captivating little town of Dinkelsbühl, within a ring of tower-capped ramparts and a moat. However, if you're driving there from
16 Rothenburg, stop first at **Feuchtwangen,** the town just before it. Its central market square, with a splashing fountain and an ideal setting of half-timbered houses, rivals even the attractions of Rothenburg and Dinkelsbühl. Summer is the time to go, when open-air theater productions are staged in the low, graceful cloisters next to the **Stiftskirche,** the collegiate church, from mid-June to the beginning of August. Inside the church is a 15th-century altar carved by Albrecht Dürer's

teacher, Michael Wohlgemut. Don't miss the **Heimatmuseum** (Regional Museum), with its excellent collection of folk arts and crafts.

17 **Dinkelsbühl** is only 12 kilometers (8 miles) farther south. Within its mellow walls the rush of traffic seems an eternity away. There's less to see here than in Rothenburg, but the mood is much less tourist-oriented, less precious. It's thought that the town originated in the 6th century as the court of a Franconian king. Like Rothenburg, Dinkelsbühl was caught up in the Thirty Years' War, and, again like Rothenburg, it preserves a fanciful episode from those bloody times. Local lore says that when Dinkelsbühl was under siege by Swedish forces and in imminent danger of destruction, a young girl led the children of the town to the enemy commander and implored him in their name for mercy. The commander of the Swedish army, Colonel Klaus Dietrich von Sperreuth, is said to have been moved almost to tears, and he spared the town. Whether or not it's true, the story is a charming one, and it is retold every year in a pageant by the children of Dinkelsbühl during a 10-day festival in July.

Touring Dinkelsbühl is not so much a matter of taking in specific sights—museums, palaces, parks, and churches, say—as of simply wandering around the historic area, pausing to admire a facade, a shop window, or the juxtaposition of architectural styles, from Gothic through Baroque, that makes this little town memorable. Altrathausplatz, Seringerstrasse, Bahnhofstrasse, Marktplatz, and Turrngasse will all reward lovers of quaint, picture-postcard Teutonic townscapes. The one standout sight for many is **St. Georg's Kirche** (Marktpl.). Big enough, at 235 feet long, to be a cathedral, St. Georg's is among the best examples in Bavaria of the late-Gothic style. Note especially the complex fan vaulting that spreads sinuously over the ceiling. If you can face the climb, head up the 200-foot tower for amazing views over the jumble of Dinkelsbühl's rooftops.

The cry of *So G'sell so*—"All's well"—still rings out every night
18 across the ancient walls and turrets of **Nördlingen,** the next stop along the Romantic Road. The town employs sentries to sound out the traditional message from the 300-foot-high tower of the central parish church of St. Georg at half-hour intervals between 10 PM and midnight. The tradition goes back to an incident during the Thirty Years' War, when an enemy attempt to slip into the town was detected by an alert townswoman. From the church tower—known locally as the Daniel (open 8 AM–dusk)—you'll get an unsurpassed view of the town and surrounding countryside, including, on clear days, all of 99 villages. However, the climb is only for the fit: The tower has 365 steps, one for each day of the year. The ground plan of the town is two concentric circles, like the rings of a tree. The inner circle of streets, whose central point is St. Georg's, marks the earliest boundary of the medieval town. A few hundred yards beyond it is the outer boundary, a wall built to accommodate the expanding town. Fortified with 11 towers and punctuated by five massive gates, it's one of the best-preserved town walls in Germany. You can stroll along it for about 2 miles of its length.

For an even more spectacular view of Nördlingen, contact the local flying club, the **Rieser Flugsportverein** (tel. 09081/4099), and take to the sky in a light aircraft. The sight of Nördlingen nestling in the trim, green Swabian (southwestern Germany) landscape is well worth the cost. You'll notice another phenomenon from the air: the basinlike formation of the **Ries,** a 15-mile-wide crater caused by a huge meteorite nearly 15 million years ago. Until the beginning of this century, it was believed that the crater was the remains of an extinct volcano. In 1960 it was proven that the Ries was caused by a meteorite at least ½ mile in diameter that hit the ground at more than 100,000 miles per hour. The impact had the destructive energy of 250,000 atomic bombs of the size that obliterated Hiroshima. It also turned the surface rock and subsoil upside down, hurling debris as far as Czechoslovakia and wiping out all plant and animal life within a radius of 300 miles. The compressed rock, or *suevit,* formed by the explosive impact of the meteorite was used to construct many of the town's buildings, including St. Georg's tower.

The next stop on the Romantic Road is where the little Wörnitz River breaks through the Franconian Juran mountains, 20 kilometers (12 miles) south. Here you'll find one of southern
19 Germany's best-preserved medieval castles. **Schloss Harburg** was already old when it passed into the possession of the counts of Oettingen in 1295; before that time it had belonged to the Hohenstaufen emperors. The ancient and noble house of Oettingen still owns the castle, and treasures collected by the family through the centuries can be seen in it. The collection includes some works by Tilman Riemenschneider, along with illuminated manuscripts dating as far back as the 8th century and an exquisite 12th-century ivory crucifix. *Admission, including guided tour: DM 8 adults, DM 2 children. Open mid-Mar.–Oct., daily 9–11:30 and 1:30–5:30.*

Eleven kilometers (7 miles) south, the Wörnitz River meets the
20 Danube at the old walled town of **Donauwörth.** If you're driving, pull off into the clearly marked lot on B-25, just north of town. Below you sprawls a striking natural relief map of Donauwörth and its two rivers. The oldest part of town is on an island in the river, connected to the rest of town by a wood bridge and greeted on the northern bank by the single surviving town gate, the Riederstor. North of the gate is one of the finest avenues of the Romantic Road: Reichsstrasse (Empire Street), so named because it was once a vital link in the Road of the Holy Roman Empire between Nürnberg and Augsburg. The broad street—known by the locals as the Gute Stube ("front room") of their town—is lined by solid, centuries-old houses and shops that tell their own tales of Donauwörth's prosperous past. The Fuggers, a famous family of traders and bankers from Augsburg, acquired a palatial home here in the 16th century; its fine Renaissance-style facade under a steeply gabled roof stands proudly at the upper end of Reichsstrasse.

Augsburg

Numbers in the margin correspond with points of interest on the Augsburg map.

21 **Augsburg,** 50 kilometers (30 miles) south, is the next stop on the Romantic Road. Home of the Fuggers, who led the city into the Renaissance, Augsburg is Bavaria's third-largest city, after Munich and Nürnberg. Augsburg's history dates back to 15 years before the birth of Christ, when one Drusus, son of the Roman Emperor Augustus, set up a military camp here on the banks of the Lech River. The settlement that grew up around it

Deutsche Barockgalerie, **25**
Dom St. Maria, **31**
Fuggerei, **29**
Maximilian-Museum, **23**
Mercury Fountain, **24**
Mozarthaus, **32**
Oblatter Wall, **33**
Rathaus, **30**
Rotes Tor, **27**
St. Annakirche, **22**
Sts. Ulrich and Afra, **26**
Vogeltor, **28**

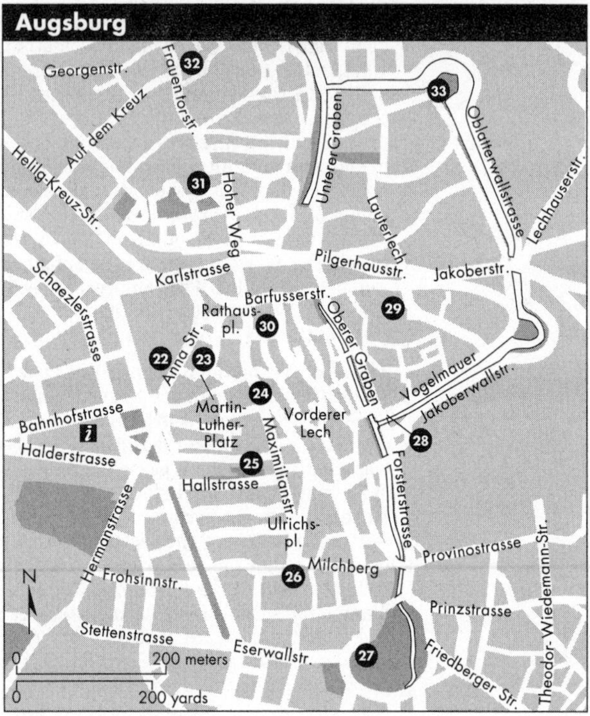

was known as Augusta, a name Italian visitors to the city still give to it. It was granted city rights in 1156, and 200 years later, first mention can be found in municipal records of the Fugger family, who were to Augsburg much as the Medicis were to Florence. On your tour of the city you will encounter traces of that extraordinary family at almost every turn.

Begin at the Verkehrsverein (city tourist office), on Bahnhofstrasse, the street running into the city center from the Hauptbahnhof (train station). The maps and information you can pick up include a pamphlet listing three tours that are signposted in three different colors. Follow the blue route first
22 to one of Augsburg's many historic churches, **St. Annakirche.** This former Carmelite monastery dates from the 14th century. Visitors can wander through its quiet cloisters and view the chapel used by the Fugger family until the Reformation. In 1318, Martin Luther stayed in the monastery during his meetings with Cardinal Cajetanus, the papal legate sent from Rome to persuade the reformist to renounce his heretical views. Luther refused, and the place where he publicly declared his rejection of papal pressure is marked with a plaque on Augsburg's main street, the Maximilianstrasse.

Outside St. Annakirche, follow the green route southward,
23 along Martin-Luther-Platz, past the **Maximilian-Museum,** a permanent exhibition of Augsburg arts and crafts. *Phillipine-Welser-Str. 24. Admission free. Open Tues.–Sun. 10–4.*

At the end of the square in front of you is Maximilianstrasse; here you'll notice one of the three monumental and elaborate

fountains that splash amid the buzz of traffic on this historic old
24 street. The **Mercury fountain** was designed by the Dutch master Adriaen de Vries in 1599, showing winged Mercury in his classic pose. Farther up Maximilianstrasse is another de Vries fountain: a bronze Hercules struggling to defeat the many-headed Hydra. The lantern-lined street was once the scene of a wine market; today the high-gabled, pastel facades of the 16th-century merchant houses assert themselves against encroaching postwar shops. On the right, as you walk up the slight incline of the street, stands the former home and business quarters of the Fuggers. The 16th-century building now houses a restaurant in its cellar and offices on the upper floors. In the ground-floor entrance are busts of two of Augsburg's most industrious Fuggers, Raymund and Anton, tributes from a grateful city to the wealth these merchants brought the community. Beyond a modern glass door is a quiet courtyard with colonnades, originally reserved for the Fugger womenfolk.

Another wealthy family, the von Liebenhofens, built a rival palace only a few paces up the street. The 18th-century palace now bears the name of a baron who married into the banking family, von Schaezler. The von Liebenhofens wanted to outdo the Fuggers—but not at any price. Thus, to save money in an age when property was taxed according to the size of the street frontage, they constructed a long, narrow building running far back from Maximilianstrasse. The palace is comprised of a series of interconnecting rooms that lead into an astonishing green-and-white Rococo ballroom: an extravagant, two-story hall heavily decorated with mirrors, chandeliers, and wall sconces. Marie Antoinette, on her way from Vienna to Paris to marry Louis XVI, was guest of honor at the inauguration ball in 1770.

Descendants of the von Liebenhofens bequeathed the palace to the city of Augsburg after the war; today its rooms contain the
25 **Deutsche Barockgalerie** (German Baroque Gallery), a major art collection that features works of the 17th and 18th centuries. The palace adjoins the former church of a Dominican monastery. A steel door behind the banquet hall of the palace leads into another world of high vaulted ceilings, where the Bavarian State Collection highlights an exhibition of early Swabian old master paintings. Among them is a Dürer portrait of one of the Fuggers. *Maximilianstr. 46. Admission free, but donations are encouraged. Open May–Sept., Tues.–Sun. 10–5; Oct.–Apr., Tues.–Sun. 10–4.*

At the top of Maximilianstrasse on Ulrichsplatz, at the highest
26 point of the city, is the former monastery church of **Sts. Ulrich and Afra,** two churches built on the site of a Roman cemetery where St. Afra was martyred in AD 304. The original, Catholic building was begun as a late-Gothic construction in 1467; a Baroque-style preaching hall was added in 1710 as the Protestant church of St. Ulrich. St. Afra is buried in the crypt, near the tomb of St. Ulrich, a 10th-century bishop credited with helping stop a Hungarian army at the doors of Augsburg in the battle of the Lech River. The remains of a third patron of the church, St. Simpert, are preserved in one of the church's most elaborate side chapels. From the steps of the magnificent altar, look back along the high nave to the finely carved Baroque wrought-iron and wood railing that borders the entrance. As you leave, pause to look into the separate but adjacent Protestant church of St.

Ulrich, the former monastery assembly hall taken over and reconstructed by the Lutherans after the Reformation.

Turning to the color-coded tour guides, follow the green route south for a few hundred yards and you'll reach the city's ancient fortifications and its most important medieval entrance gate, the
27 **Rotes Tor** (Red Gate), which once straddled the main trading road to Italy. From here you can follow the traces of the early city fortifications northward and back to the city center, pass-
28 ing the Gothic **Vogeltor** (Bird Gate) on Eserwell-Strasse and, on the street called Vorderer Lech, the rebuilt 16th-century home of Hans Holbein the Elder, one of Augsburg's most famous sons (homes of two others, Leopold Mozart and Bertolt Brecht, are also on our route). The Holbein house is now a city art gallery with a regularly changing program of exhibitions. *Vorderer Lech 20. Open May–Oct., Tues.–Sun. 10–5; Nov.–Apr., Tues.–Sun. 10–4.*

At the end of Vorderer Lech, make a sharp right, and follow the green route over a small stream into the tranquility of the
29 **Fuggerei.** This is the world's oldest social housing scheme, established by the Fugger family to accommodate the city's deserving poor. The 147 homes still serve the same purpose; the annual rent of "one Rheinish Guilder" (DM 1.72) hasn't changed either. Understandably, there's quite a demand to take up residence in this peaceful, leafy estate. There are four requirements: Residents must be Augsburg citizens, Catholic, and destitute through no fault of their own, and they must pray daily for their original benefactors, the Fugger family.

From the Fuggerei, follow the green route back into the city center, stopping at the **Brecht** family home, a modest artisan's house. Here the renowned playwright Bertolt Brecht, author of *The Threepenny Opera*, was born and lived until he moved on, first to Munich and then, under Hitler, to Scandinavia and later the United States. After the war he settled in East Berlin, to direct the Berliner Ensemble. Today the house serves as a memorial center dedicated to Brecht's life and work. *Auf dem Rain 7. Admission: DM 2 adults, DM 1 children. Open May–Oct., Tues.–Sun. 10–5; Nov.–Apr., Tues.–Sun. 10–4.*

Two left turns bring you to Rathausplatz, the center of Augsburg, dominated by the 258-foot-high **Perlachturm** (open Apr.–
30 Sept., daily 10–6) and the adjacent massive, square **Rathaus** (Town Hall). The great building, Germany's largest city hall when it was built in the early 17th century, is one of the finest Renaissance structures north of the Alps. (The Rathaus can be visited between 10 and 6 on days when no official functions are taking place.)

Time Out Behind the Rathaus, down the street called Hunoldsgraben, is one of Augsburg's oldest wine taverns, the **Augsburger Schmuckkastchen.** It used to belong to a 14th-century monastery; now it's the realm of Bacchus. Beer, light meals, and coffee are served, but wine is what you're expected to order. *Closed Mon.*

From the great square in front of the Rathaus (its 16th-century fountain commemorates the 1,600th anniversary of the founding of Augsburg), turn north again along the shopping streets
31 of Karolinenstrasse and Hoher Weg to the **Dom St. Maria** (Ca-

thedral of the Virgin Mary); its square Gothic towers will signal the way. An Episcopal church stood here in the 9th century, and a 10th-century Romanesque crypt, built in the time of Bishop Ulrich, remains from those early years. The heavy bronze doors on the south portal date from the 11th century; 11th-century windows on the south side of the nave depict the prophets Jonah, Daniel, Hosea, Moses, and David, to form the oldest cycle of stained glass in central Europe. Five altarpieces by Hans Holbein the Elder are among the cathedral's other treasures.

A short walk from the cathedral, still following the green route, will take you to the quiet courtyards and small raised garden of the former Episcopal residence, a series of fine 18th-century buildings in Baroque and Rococo styles that now serve as the offices of the Swabian regional government. Although less than 40 miles from the capital of Bavaria, we're now firmly in Swabia, once such a powerful dukedom under the Hohenstaufens that its territory covered virtually all of present-day Switzerland. Today Swabia has become an administrative district of Bavaria, and Augsburg has yielded the position it once held to the younger city of Munich.

32 Head north again, along Frauentorstrasse, to the **Mozarthaus,** birthplace of Leopold Mozart, father of Wolfgang Amadeus Mozart. A comfortable 17th-century home, it now serves as a Mozart memorial and museum, with some fascinating contemporary documents on the Mozart family. *Frauentorstr. 30. Admission free. Open Mon., Wed., Thurs. 10–noon and 2–5; Fri. 10–noon and 1–4; Sat. and Sun. 10–noon.*

Tired? Retrace your steps to the city center. If you've time and energy, you can continue your tour with a walk along the remains of the city's ancient northern and eastern defenses. For part of the way a pleasant walk follows the moat, which was
33 once part of the fortifications. At the **Oblatter Wall** you can rent a boat and row between the green, leafy banks, a welcome break and a fine way to say farewell to Augsburg.

Toward the Alps

Numbers in the margin correspond with points of interest on the Romantic Road map.

Leaving Augsburg southward on B-17—the southern stretch of the Romantic Road—you'll drive across the Lech battlefield, where the Hungarian invaders were stopped in 955. Rich Bavarian pastures extend as far as the Lech River, which follows the country road for much of its way. About 32 kilometers (20
34 miles) south is the historic old town of **Landsberg am Lech,** in whose prison Adolf Hitler wrote much of *Mein Kampf.* The town was founded by the Bavarian ruler Heinrich der Löwe (Henry the Lion) in the 12th century and grew wealthy from the salt trade. You'll see impressive evidence of Landsberg's early wealth among the solid old houses packed within its turreted walls; the early 18th-century Altes Rathaus (Old Town Hall) is one of the finest of the region.

The German artist Sir Hubert von Herkomer was born in a small village just outside Landsberg. Within the town walls is an unusual monument—not to Sir Hubert (he was knighted in England in 1907) but to his mother, Josefine. It's a romantic, medieval-style tower, bristling with turrets and galleries, built by Sir Hubert himself. He called it his Mutterturm, or "mother tower." The young Hubert was taken by his parents to the United States and later, when they couldn't happily settle in America, to England. He died in Devon in 1914. The 100th anniversary of the completion of the Mutterturm was in 1988, and an exhibition on the life and work of this remarkable man was held within its rough-stone walls.

Beyond Landsberg, the Bavarian Alps rise along the southern horizon, signaling the end of the Romantic Road. Some 30 ki-
35 lometers (18 miles) south is another old walled town, **Schongau,** founded at about the same time as Landsberg, with virtually intact wall fortifications, together with towers and gates. In medieval and Renaissance times, the town was an important trading post on the route from Italy to Augsburg. The steeply gabled, 16th-century Ballenhaus was a warehouse before it was elevated to the rank of Rathaus (Town Hall).

If you're driving, leave the Romantic Road just beyond Schongau, at the village of **Peiting,** and take B-472 to the nearby sum-
36 mit of the 3,000-foot-high **Hohen Peissenberg,** the first real peak of the Alpine chain. A pilgrimage chapel was consecrated on the mountain in the 16th century; a century later a larger church was added, with a fine ceiling fresco and delicate carvings by local Bavarian masters.

After returning to Peiting, take B-23 to **Rottenbuch,** where the Augustinian order built an impressive monastery on the Ammer River in the 11th century. The Gothic basilica was redecorated in Rococo style during the 18th century. The lavish interior of cream, gold, and rose stuccowork and statuary is stunning.

Rottenbuch is a worthy preparation for the next—and most glor-
37 ious—example of German Rococo architecture, the **Wieskirche** (Church of the Meadow). It stands in an alpine meadow just off the Romantic Road near Steingaden, its yellow and white walls and steep red roof set off by the dark backdrop of the Trauchgauer mountains. The architect Dominicus Zimmermann (former mayor of Landsberg and creator of much of that town's Rococo architecture) was commissioned in 1745 to build the church on this spot, where, six years earlier, a local woman claimed to have seen tears running down the face of a picture of Christ. Although the church was dedicated as the Pilgrimage Church of the Scourged Christ, it is now known as the Wieskirche. Visit it on a fine day, when alpine light streaming through its high windows displays the full glory of the glittering interior. It's Bavarian Rococo at its scintillating best. Together with the pilgrimage church of Vierzehnheiligen in north Bavaria, the Wieskirche represents the culmination of German Rococo ecclesiastical architecture. As at Vierzehnheiligen, the simple exterior gives little hint of the ravishing interior. A complex oval plan is animated by a series of brilliantly colored stuccos, statues, and gilt. A luminous ceiling fresco completes the decoration. Note the beautifully detailed choir and organ loft. Concerts are presented in the church in the summer. Contact the Städtische Musikschule Schongau (tel. 08861/8173) for details. Zimmermann, the architect of the church, is buried in the 12th-century former abbey church of Steingaden. Although his work was the antithesis of Roman-

esque architecture, he was laid to rest in a dour, late-Romanesque side chapel.

From Steingaden, the road runs beneath the Ammergau range
38 22 kilometers (13 miles) to **Schwangau,** a lakeside resort town and an ideal center from which to explore the surrounding mountains. Schwangau is where you encounter the heritage of Bavaria's famous 19th-century king, Ludwig II. Both his childhood home and the most spectacular of his exotic castles are at the town's doorstep. Ludwig spent much of his youth at Schloss Hohenschwangau; it is said that its neogothic atmosphere provided the primary influences that shaped the construction of the wildly romantic Schloss Neuschwanstein, the fairy-tale castle Ludwig built across the valley after he became king.

39 **Hohenschwangau** palace was built by the knights of Schwangau in the 12th century. Later it was remodeled by Ludwig's father, the Bavarian crown prince (and later king) Maximilian, between 1832 and 1836. It was here that the young Ludwig met the composer Richard Wagner. Their friendship shaped and deepened the future king's interest in theater, music, and German mythology—the mythology upon which Wagner drew for his "Ring" cycle of operas. Wagner saw the impressionable Ludwig principally as a potential source of financing for his extravagant operas rather than a kindred spirit. For all his lofty idealism, the composer was hardly a man to let scruples interfere with his self-aggrandizement.

Ludwig's love of the theater and fantasy ran so deep that when
40 he came to build **Neuschwanstein,** he employed a set designer instead of an architect. The castle soars from its mountainside like a stage creation—it should come as hardly a surprise that Walt Disney took it as the model for his castle in the movie *Sleeping Beauty* and later for the Disneyland castle itself.

The life of the proprietor of this spectacular castle reads like one of the great Gothic mysteries of the 19th century. Here was a king, a member of the Wittelsbach dynasty that had ruled Bavaria since 1180, who devoted his time and energies to creating architectural flights of fancy that came close to bankrupting the Bavarian government. Finally, in 1886, before Neuschwanstein was finished, members of the government became convinced that Ludwig had taken leave of his senses. A medical commission set out to prove that the king was insane and forced him to give up his throne. Ludwig was incarcerated in the much more modest lakeside castle of Berg on the Starnbergersee. Then, on the evening of June 13, 1886, the king and the doctor attending him disappeared. Late that night their bodies were pulled from the lake. The circumstances of their deaths remain a mystery to this day.

The interior of Ludwig's fantasy castle is a fitting setting for this grim tale. His bedroom is tomblike, dominated by a great Gothic-style bed. The throne room is without a throne; Ludwig died before one could be installed. Corridors are outfitted as a ghostly grotto, reminiscent of Wagner's *Tannhauser*. During the 17 years from the start of construction until his death, the king spent only 102 days in this country residence. Chamber concerts are held at the beginning of September in the gaily decorated minstrels' hall, one room at least that was completed as Ludwig conceived it. (Program details are available from the Verkehrsamt, Schwangau, tel. 08362/81051.) There are some spectacular walks around the castle. Make for the **Marienbrücke** (Mary's Bridge), spun like a medieval maiden's hair across a deep, narrow gorge. From this vantage point, there are giddy views of the castle and the great Upper Bavarian plain beyond. *Admission to Schloss Hohenschwangau, including a guided tour: DM 6 adults, DM 2.50 children and senior citizens. Open Apr.–Sept., daily 9–5:30; Oct.–Mar., daily 10–4. Admission to Schloss Neuschwanstein, including a guided tour: DM 6 adults and children over 14. Open Apr.–Sept., daily 9–5:30; Oct.–Mar., daily 10–4. The two castles are ½ mi from each other and about 1 mi from the center of Schwangau. Cars and buses are barred from the approach roads, but the 1-mi journey to Neuschwanstein can be made by horse-drawn carriages, which stop in the village of Hohenschwangau. A bus from the village takes a back route to the Aussichtspunkt Jugend; from there, it's only a 10-minute walk to the castle. The Schloss Hohenschwangau is a 15-minute walk from the village.*

If you plan to visit Hohenschwangau or Neuschwanstein, bear in mind that more than 1 million people pass through the two castles every year. Authorities estimate that on some summer weekends the number of people who tour Neuschwanstein is matched by the number who give up at the prospect of standing in line for up to two hours. If you visit in the summer, get there early. The best time to see either castle is a weekday in January, February, or early March.

The castles are only 5 kilometers (3 miles) from the official end
41 of the Romantic Road, the border town of **Füssen,** set at the foot of the mountains that separate Bavaria from the Austrian Tyrol. Füssen also has a notable castle, the Hohes Schloss, one of the best-preserved late-Gothic castles in Germany. It was built on the site of the Roman fortress that once guarded this Alpine section of the Via Claudia, the trading route from Rome to the Danube. The castle was the seat of Bavarian rulers before Emperor Heinrich VII mortgaged it and the rest of the town to the bishop of Augsburg for 400 pieces of silver. The mortgage was never redeemed, and Füssen remained the property of the Augsburg episcopate until secularization in the early 19th century. The castle was put to good use by the bishops of Augsburg as their summer Alpine residence. It has a spectacular 16th-century Rittersaal (Knights' Hall) with a fine carved ceiling, and a princes' chamber with a Gothic tiled heating oven. *Magnuspl. 10. Admission: DM 4 adults, DM 2 children. Open daily 2–4.*

The presence, at least in summer, of the bishops of Augsburg ensured that Füssen received an impressive number of Baroque and Rococo churches. A Benedictine abbey was built in the 9th century at the site of the grave of St. Magnus, who spent most of his life ministering in Füssen and the surrounding countryside. A Romanesque crypt beneath the Baroque abbey church has a partially preserved 10th-century fresco, the oldest in Bavaria.

The abbey was secularized and never reclaimed by the Catholic church, and today it serves as Füssen's Rathaus (Town Hall). In summer, chamber concerts are held in the high-ceilinged, Baroque splendor of the abbey's Fürstensaal (Princes' Hall). *Program details are available from the Kurverwaltung Füssen, tel. 08362/7077.*

Complete your tour of the Romantic Road with a stroll down a street that—like Augsburg's Maximilianstrasse—was once part of the Roman Via Claudia. Now it's Füssen's main shopping street—a cobblestone pedestrian walkway, lined by high-gabled medieval houses and backed by the bulwarks of the castle and the easternmost buttresses of the Allgäu Alps. The Lech River, which has accompanied you for much of the final section of the Romantic Road, rises in those mountains and embraces the town as it rushes northward. One of several lakes in the area, the Forggensee is formed from a broadening of the river. *A pleasure boat makes 2-hour cruises on the lake from the beginning of June through September. Fare is DM 10 adults, DM 5 children.*

What to See and Do with Children

In **Würzburg,** take a boat trip on the Main River (*see* Guided Tours, above). In **Rothenburg-ob-der-Tauber,** young imaginations soar while roaming through the dungeons beneath the Rathaus and the grisly exhibits in the **Mittelalterliches Kriminalmuseum** (Medieval Criminal Museum). A rack, thumbscrews, and various other torture devices will keep you busy answering questions. The town also has the enchanting **Puppen und Spielzeugmuseum** (Doll and Toy Museum), with enough dolls to keep youngsters amused for hours (*see* Exploring the Romantic Road, above). You might also seek out the adventure playground in the dry moat in front of the **Würzburger Tor,** where, on a fine day, you can sun yourself while the children play in the shadow of Rothenburg's ancient walls.

If you're in **Dinkelsbühl** in July, the annual **Kinderzeche** (Children's Tribute) festival makes for a fascinating experience for youngsters. It recreates the event during the Thirty Years' War in which the children of the town saved it from destruction (*see* Exploring the Romantic Road, above).

Augsburg has an excellent **puppet theater** and a **zoo** with more than 1,900 animals. *Admission: DM 5 adults, DM 3 children. Open Apr.–Sept., daily 8:30–6; Oct.–Mar., daily 8:30–5.*

At **Königsbrunn,** just outside Augsburg, is a lido with five heated pools, complete with water cannons, chutes, and geysers. *Admission for 2 hours: DM 14 adults, DM 8 children. Open daily 10:30–9:30.*

A mile outside **Schongau,** suitably set in a wood, is one of the popular **Märchenwälder** (fairy-tale forests) that dot the German landscape, complete with mechanical models of fairy-tale scenes, deer enclosures, and an old-time miniature railway. *Schongau Märchenwald, Diessenstr. 6. Admission: DM 4 adults, DM 2 children. Open Easter–Oct. daily 9–7.*

If you're in Schongau during the winter, take a sleigh ride into the mountains to feed the wild deer. Josef Kotz sets off daily from the Karbrücke bridge at 2:30 (tel. 08362/8581).

Off the Beaten Track

Getting off the beaten track in one of Germany's most popular tourist areas is not as hard as you might think. Even in Rothenburg-ob-der-Tauber there are corners where the world passes you by. Pull on the bell at the **Staudthof** in Herrngasse, hand over DM 1, and you'll gain admittance to the town's oldest patrician home, a 1,000-year-old haven of peace that's belonged to the von Staudt family for three centuries. The yew trees in the quiet courtyard have been there that long, too. The shutters are painted in the yellow and black of the Habsburgs as tribute to the fact that it was the Habsburgs who raised two members of the von Staudt family to the nobility. Linger at the low wall along Rothenburg's **Burggasse** as dusk falls on the valley below. Watch the sun set from the western defense walls of the lovely little hilltop town of **Schillingsfurst,** halfway between Feuchtwangen and Rothenburg.

Visit Bavarian forester Siegfried Niestroj's **butterfly farm** in Dinkelsbühl (open daily 9–7). It's next to the town's Rothenburger Tor.

Shopping

Hümmel **porcelain** figures are a perennial favorite among visitors to this area of Germany. Prices vary dramatically, so be sure to shop around. You'll find a wide selection at competitive prices at **Otto Wolf** (Marktpl.) in Nördlingen. Hümmel figures and other German porcelain and glassware can be found in Dinkelsbühl at **Weschcke and Ries** (Segringerstr.) and, in Rothenburg, at **Unger's** (Herrngasse) and the **Kunstwerke Friese** (Grüner Markt, near the Rathaus). The Kunstwerke Friese also stocks a selection of the beautifully crafted porcelain birds made by the Hümmel manufacturers, the Goebel Porzellanfabrik.

Locally made **pottery** is enjoying a renaissance in some of the Romantic Road towns. **Jürgen Pleinkies** (Segringerstr.) in Dinkelsbühl is energetically trying to restore his town's former reputation for fine earthenware; he also offers courses at the potter's wheel. Local artists don't lack for inspiration in these beautiful Romantic Road towns; a large selection of their work can be found at the **Reichstadt** gallery (Segringerstr.).

Children will love the wonderland of **Käthe Wohlfahrt's** shop (Herringasse) in Rothenburg. **Her Weihnachtsdorf** (Christmas village) is a wonderland of locally made toys and decorations; even in summer there are Christmas trees hung with brightly painted wood baubles. In Rothenburg, the centuries-old home of **Georg Nusch** (Burggasse)—the councillor who saved the town by accepting General Tilly's wine-drinking challenge— is a shop stacked high with local glassware and other handicrafts.

In Augsburg the place to shop is the broad **Maximilianstrasse,** once the city's wine market. The Romantic Road's true **wine** center is Würzburg. Visit any of the vineyards that rise from the Main River and choose a *Bochsbeutel*, the distinctive green, flagon-shape wine bottles of Franconia. It's claimed that the shape came about because wine-guzzling monks found it the easiest to hide under their robes. In Würzburg itself, you'll want to linger on traffic-free **Schönbornstrasse** and the adjacent marketplace. Wine and the familiar goblets in which it is served in this part of the world are sold in many of the shops here. You can buy directly from two ancient city institutions: the **Bürgerspital** (Theaterstr.) and the **Juliusspital** (Juliuspromenade). Both sell wine from their own vineyards, as well as the glasses from which to drink it.

Sports and Fitness

Bicycling Bikes can be rented at all train stations on the Romantic Road. Rental is DM 10 a day (DM 5 if you have a valid rail ticket). Some tourist offices—Dinkelsbühl is one—have a limited number of bikes for rent. You'll need ID, such as a passport, as a deposit against the safe return of the bike.

Canoeing The Lech River, which follows the southern stretch of the Romantic Road for much of its way, offers excellent canoeing. There's good sport, too, to be had on the Tauber and Wörnitz rivers. Contact the **DON canoe club** at Donauwörth (tel. 0906/5962).

Golf **Augsburg Golf Club** (tel. 08234/5621) welcomes visiting members of overseas golf clubs. For scenery and a mild challenge, try the nine-hole course at **Schloss Colberg** (tel. 0981/5617). It's 20 kilometers (12 miles) east of Rothenburg.

Hang Gliding Although there are eagles in those mountains, the winged forms you see in the skies above Füssen and Schongau are more likely to be hang gliders. This is a leading center of the sport. For information contact the **Allgäu Drachenflugschule** (tel. 08364/107).

Mountain Climbing and Walking The mountains above Füssen and Schwangau beckon climbers and walkers. Contact the **Bergschule Ostallgäu** in Schwangau (tel. 08362/81463) for guides, maps, and other information.

Sailing and Windsurfing The lakes around Füssen offer excellent sailing and windsurfing. **Lutz Selbach** has boathouses renting sailing dinghies and Windsurfers at two of them, Hopfensee and Weissensee (tel. 08363/5429). For boats and Windsurfers on the larger Forggensee, **Egon Ganahl** (tel. 08367/471) is the man to contact.

Skiing Füssen, Schwangau, and surrounding villages are popular ski resorts. All have sport shops offering lessons and equipment. Schwangau has its own ski school (tel. 08362/8455).

Dining and Lodging

Dining

The best Franconian and Swabian food combines hearty regional specialties with nouvelle elements. Various forms of pasta are common. Try *Pfannkuchen* (pancakes) and *Spätzle* (noodles), the latter often served with roast beef, or *Rinderbraten,* the traditional Sunday lunchtime dish. One of the best regional dishes is *Maultaschen,* a Swabian version of ravioli, usually served floating in broth strewn with chives. Würzburg is one of the leading wine-producing areas of Germany, and beer lovers will want to try Kulmbacher, one of the best Franconian beers.

All the historic cities and towns along the Romantic Road have a wide selection of good-value restaurants. This being such an important tourist area and the heartland of picture-postcard Germany, a great many are firmly in the heavy-beamed, open-fireplace mold. If you want classy, international-style restaurants you may be disappointed.

Ratings Highly recommended restaurants in each price category are indicated by a star ★.

Category	Cost*
Very Expensive	over DM 90
Expensive	DM 55–DM 90
Moderate	DM 35–DM 55
Inexpensive	DM 20–DM 35

**per person for a three-course meal, including tax and excluding drinks*

Lodging

The Romantic Road is Hansel and Gretel land. The best hotels are accordingly more rustic and basic than slickly modern. You'll find high standards of comfort and cleanliness throughout the region. Make reservations as far in advance as possible if you plan to visit in the summer. Hotels in Würzburg, Rothenburg, and Füssen in particular are often full year-round. Tourist information offices can sometimes help with accommodations, even in high season, especially if you arrive early in the day.

Ratings Highly recommended hotels in each price category are indicated by a star ★.

Category	Cost*
Very Expensive	over DM 180
Expensive	DM 120–DM 180
Moderate	DM 80–DM 120
Inexpensive	under DM 80

**All prices are for two people in a double room, excluding service charges.*

Augsburg *Dining*

★ **Cheval Blanc.** Located on the southeast outskirts of Augsburg, 4 miles from downtown, this first-class restaurant has big-city flair thanks to the skill and imagination of its Austrian chef, Franz Fuchs. Try the shrimp ravioli on a bed of fresh spinach, or tenderloin of rabbit with lightly sautéed vegetables. *Landsbergerstr. 62, Haunstetten, tel. 0821/80050. Reservations required. Jacket and tie required. AE, DC, MC. Closed Sun., Mon. lunch, and first 3 weeks of Aug. Expensive.*

Agnes-Bernauer-Stuben. Named after the legendary maiden drowned in the Danube by her beloved's father, this centrally located restaurant combines traditional decor (wood paneling, chintz curtains, wrought-iron well) with traditional fare. Try one of the fixed-price lunch menus, a good value at under DM 25. *Ludwigstr. 19, tel. 0821/516–579. Reservations advised. Dress: informal. AE, DC, MC, V. Closed Sun. and Mon. Moderate.*

Fuggerkeller. The vaulted cellars of the former Fugger home on Augsburg's historic Maximilianstrasse are now a bright and comfortable restaurant, owned and run by the luxurious Drei

Mohren Hotel above it. The midday specials are a particularly good value; try the Swabian-style stuffed cabbage rolls in a spiced meat sauce. Prices for dinner are higher. *Maximilianstr. 40, tel. 0821/510–031. Reservations advised. Dress: informal. AE, DC, MC, V. Closed Sun. and first 3 weeks of Aug. Moderate.*

★ **Welser Kuche.** You can practically hear the great oak tables groan under the eight-course menus of Swabian specialties offered here. You'll need to give a day's notice if you want the eight-course menu, however. Be sure to try Spätzle, the Swabian version of pasta. *Maximilianstr. 83, tel. 0821/33930. Reservations advised. Dress: informal. Open evenings only. Moderate.*

Lodging

★ **Steigenberger Drei Mohren Hotel.** Kings, princes, even Napoléon slept here; so did the British commander who defeated him at Waterloo, the duke of Wellington. The historic hotel, however, takes its name from three very early guests of less renown: three Abyssinian bishops who sought shelter in this worldly German city. *Maximilianstr. 40, tel. 0821/510–031. 110 rooms with bath. Facilities: parking, restaurant, bar. AE, DC, MC, V. Very Expensive.*

Alpenhof Ringhotel. Located on the outskirts of Augsburg, right on the Romantic Road, this hotel has easy access to the city center. Modern and well appointed, it has a nostalgic, almost Romantic restaurant, where you dine amid carved pillars and wrought iron. *Donauwörtherstr. 233, tel. 0821/413–051. 136 rooms with bath or shower. Facilities: indoor pool, sauna, solarium, fitness room, billiards, table tennis, casino, playground, restaurant. AE, DC, MC, V. Expensive.*

Dom Hotel. Just across the street from Augsburg's cathedral, this is a snug, comfortable establishment with a personal touch. Ask for one of the attic rooms, where you'll sleep under beam ceilings and wake to a rooftop view of the city. *Frauentorstr. 8, tel. 0821/153–031. 43 rooms with bath or shower. MC, V. Moderate.*

Holiday Inn. At 35 stories, this is Germany's tallest high-rise hotel. It's no place to stay if you value personal service or intimate atmosphere, but those in search of comfort and assured levels of service will feel at home. *Wittelsbacherpark, tel. 0821/577–087. 185 rooms with bath. Facilities: indoor swimming pool, sauna, solarium, sun terrace, restaurant. AE, DC, MC, V. Moderate.*

Hotel Post. Centrally located on a tree-lined avenue, this hotel offers modern, comfortable accommodations in friendly, well-run surroundings. The breakfast room, decked out in crisp blue-and-white checks, makes for a good start to the day. *Fuggerstr. 5/7 (Am Konigspl.), tel. 0821/36044. 45 rooms, most with bath or shower. AE, DC, MC, V. Closed Christmas and New Year's Day. Inexpensive.*

Bad Mergentheim

Dining

★ **Zirbelstuben Hotel Victoria.** The warm glow of pine-paneled walls and (at least in winter) a fine tiled stove will envelop you in this excellent hotel-restaurant. The menu is a successful combination of classic French haute cuisine and no-nonsense Franconian specialties. Fish dishes predominate; try the salmon and asparagus. *Poststr. 2–4, tel. 07931/5930. Reservations advised. Jacket and tie required. AE, DC, MC, V. Moderate.*

Kettler's Altfränkische Weinstube. You'll want to come here to try the Nürberger Bratwürste—finger-size, spicy sausages—and to enjoy the atmosphere of a snug 180-year-old Franconian tavern. The wine list is enormous. *Krumme Gasse 12, tel. 07931/7308. Reservations advised. Dress: informal. No credit cards. Closed Dec. 23–Jan. 15. Inexpensive.*

Dinkelsbühl
Lodging

Hotel Goldene Kanne. Many American visitors favor this small, attractive hotel, with its modern facilities and convenient location close to the train station. The atmospheric wine tavern is a popular rendezvous. *Segringerstr. 8, tel. 09851/6011. Facilities: restaurant. AE, DC, MC, V. Moderate.*

Blauer Hecht. Built in 1750, this hotel has lately been renovated to a high standard of comfort. It's central but quiet. *Schweinmarkt 1, tel. 09851/811. 28 rooms, 1 apartment, 1 suite, all with bath or shower. AE, DC, MC, V. Closed Jan. Inexpensive–Moderate.*

Donauwörth
Dining

Traube. This restaurant recently celebrated its 300th anniversary, although it began life under a different name. Within its old walls you'll be offered home-style Swabian-Bavarian fare at low prices. *Kapellstr. 14, tel. 0906/6096. Reservations advised. Dress: informal. AE, DC, MC, V. Inexpensive.*

Lodging
★

Hotel-Restaurant Park-Café. A new group has been formed in Germany to bring together hotels having one feature in common: an idyllic location. This one qualifies because of its fine site high above Donauwörth. *Sternschanzenstr. 1, tel. 0906/6037. 25 rooms with bath or shower. Facilities: wine tavern, bowling alleys, public swimming pool next door. AE, DC, MC. Moderate.*

Feuchtwangen
Dining

Greifen-Stube. You'll dine here within walls decorated with frescos of Feuchtwangen's past; the pictures will tell you that the Emperor Maximilian and dancer Lola Montez were also guests. Dine as they must have done, on local Franconian dishes such as lambs' kidneys in a mustard sauce or tender breast of partridge. *Marktpl. 8, tel. 09852/2002. Reservations required. Jacket and tie required. AE, DC, MC, V. Closed Jan. 2–Feb. 12 and Christmas. Moderate.*

Lodging
★

Romantik Hotel Greifen Post. The solid, market-square exterior of this hotel gives little hint of the luxuries within. Ask for the room with the four-poster or, if that's taken, settle for one of the other so-called "romantic" rooms. If you've got two days to spare, try one of the "Romantic Weekend" packages for the best value. *Marktpl. 8, tel. 09852/2002. 41 rooms, 2 apartments, 1 suite, all but one with bath. Facilities: indoor pool, sauna, solarium, restaurant. AE, DC, MC, V. Expensive.*

Füssen
Dining

Alpen-Schlössle. A *Schlössle* is a small castle, and although this comfortable, rustic restaurant doesn't exactly qualify as such, it is located on a mountain site, just outside Füssen, that King Ludwig might well have chosen for one of his homes. If wild duck is on the menu, don't leave without tasting it. *Alatseestr. 28, tel. 08362/4017. Reservations advised. Dress: informal. No credit cards. Closed Tues. and Nov.–mid-Dec. Moderate.*

Gasthaus zum Schwanen. This modest, cozy establishment offers good regional cooking with no frills at low prices. The Swabian *Maultaschen*—a kind of local ravioli—are made on the premises and are excellent. *Brotmarkt 4, tel. 08362/6174. Dress: informal. No credit cards. Closed Sun. evening, Mon., and Nov. Inexpensive.*

Lodging

Hotel Hirsch. You'll know you're in the depths of Bavaria by the traditional peasant-style painting on your bed's headboard and on the rustic-looking closets. The friendly tavern is relaxed, too, serving beer rather than wine. *Schulhausstr. 2–4, tel. 08362/6055. 47 rooms, about half with bath. Facilities: restaurant. AE, DC, V. Closed Nov. 15–Dec. 20. Expensive.*

Hotel Sonne. *Sonne* means sun, and this is an appropriately bright, cheerful, and modern hotel in Bavarian style with traditional furnishings. *Reichenstr. 37, tel. 08362/6061. 32 rooms with bath or shower. Facilities: café (but no restaurant), disco/nightclub. AE, DC, MC, V. Moderate.*

Landsberg
Dining

Alt Landtsperg. The Bavarian national colors of blue and white decorate not only the timber-clad walls but the tables, too, in this 100% Bavarian tavern-restaurant. Owner and chef Heinz Sättler is something of a Bavarian nationalist but still finds room on his menu for "fine new German-French cuisine" alongside "solid Bavarian." *Alte Bergstr. 435, tel. 08191/5838. Reservations required. Dress: informal. AE, MC. Closed Wed. and Sun. lunch, last 2 weeks in Feb., and Aug. Moderate.*

Nördlingen
Dining

Mayer's Keller. Don't be put off by the plain interior of this unassuming restaurant, a short walk from Nördlingen's Altstadt: The menu is welcoming enough. Try any of the fish dishes, all prepared with flair. *Marienhöhe 8, tel. 09081/4493. Reservations advised. Dress: informal. No credit cards. Closed Mon. Moderate.*

Lodging

Hotel Schützenhof. This small, comfortable hotel in traditional style, on the outskirts of town, is known for its excellent restaurant, which specializes in fresh fish from the surrounding lakes and rivers. *Kaiserwiese 2, tel. 090781/3940. 15 rooms with bath. Facilities: bowling alley. AE, DC, MC, V. Closed first 2 weeks of Aug. Moderate.*

★ **Hotel Sonne.** The great German poet Goethe stayed here, only one in a long line of distinguished guests, headed by Emperor Friedrich III in 1487. The vaulted cellar wine-tavern is a reminder of those days. Today the historic old hotel is in the loving hands of an Englishwoman and her Anglophile husband. *Marktpl., tel. 09081/5067. 40 rooms, all with bath or shower. Facilities: wine tavern. AE, MC. Closed Dec. 26–mid-Jan. Moderate.*

Rothenburg-ob-der-Tauber
Dining

★ **Baumeisterhaus.** In summer, you can dine in one of Rothenburg's loveliest courtyards, a half-timbered oasis of peace that's part of a magnificent Renaissance house. If the weather's cooler, move inside to the paneled dining room. The menu, changed daily, features Bavarian and Franconian specialties. *Marktpl., tel. 09861/13404. Reservations advised. Dress: informal. AE, DC, MC, V. Moderate.*

★ **Die Blaue Terrasse.** The view of the Tauber Valley from the window tables of the Blue Terrace restaurant rivals the magnificent offerings—part regional, part nouvelle—of master-chef Günther Koch. Snails and asparagus (in season) are perennial favorites. *Untere Schmiedgasse 16/25, tel. 09861/2051. Reservations advised. Jacket and tie required. AE, DC, MC, V. Closed mid-Dec.–Jan. Moderate.*

Reichs-Küchenmeister. Master chefs in the service of the Holy Roman Emperor were the inspiration for the name of this restaurant. Test the skills of the present chef by ordering any of the game dishes. *Kirchpl. 8, tel. 09861/2046. Reservations advised. Dress: informal. AE, DC, MC, V. Closed Mon. and Tues. in winter months. Moderate.*

Lodging **Burg Hotel.** Five minutes away from the town center, yet located in the peace of the Tauber Valley, this hotel offers easy access to Rothenburg as well as a sense of tranquil isolation. Ask for one of the rooms overlooking the river. There's no restaurant. *Taubertal, Klostergasse 1, tel. 09861/5037. 15 rooms, 8 suites, all with bath. AE, DC, MC, V. Expensive.*

★ **Hotel Eisenhut.** It's appropriate that the prettiest small town in Germany should have the prettiest small hotel in the country. It stands in the center of town and is located in what were originally four separate town houses, the oldest dating from the 12th century, the newest from the 16th. Inside, there are many antiques, along with other typical Bavarian decorations, the whole fusing to create a distinctively Teutonic yet classy quality. The hotel has a fine restaurant. *Heringasse 3, tel. 09861/2041. 82 rooms, 3 suites, all with bath or shower. Facilities: restaurant. AE, DC, MC, V. Closed Jan.–Feb. Expensive.*

Hotel Goldener Hirsch. This lantern-hung, green-shuttered 15th-century patrician house is an inextricable part of Rothenburg's history: It was here that the Meistertrunk play was first performed. Baroque antiques are everywhere, from the lobby to the uppermost, bay-windowed bedroom. *Untere Schmiedgasse 16/25, tel. 09861/2051. 80 rooms, most with bath or shower. AE, DC, MC, V. Closed mid-Dec.–Jan. Expensive.*

★ **Romantik Hotel Markustrum.** This hotel is one of the Romantic group, and romantic it certainly is: a 13th-century (but fully modernized) sharp-eaved house that is practically embraced by the ancient Markus tower and gate. If you stay at the height of the season, you'll hear the nightwatchman making his rounds. *Rödergasse 1, tel. 09861/2370. 26 rooms, most with bath. Facilities: restaurant; riding stables nearby. AE, DC, MC. Closed Jan. 10–Mar. 18. Expensive.*

★ **Adam das Kleine Hotel.** Ask for the room with the carved four-poster. If that's already taken, then settle for one of the two rooms with leaded windows and views of the castle gardens. You may have trouble finding the hotel: In summer it's smothered in flowers that hide its half-timbered facade. Officially, the hotel provides a bed and breakfast only, but here's a tip: Owner Hans-Karl Adam is a fantastic chef (the author of many books), and if you feign great hunger he'll soften and prepare a dream of a meal for you. *Burggasse 29, tel. 09861/2364. 13 rooms, 12 with bath or shower. No credit cards. Closed Nov. 1–Easter. Moderate.*

Hotel Reichs-Küchenmeister. If there's no room in the wood-paneled main building, don't worry about settling for the annex: It's a garden house set amid green lawns. *Kirchpl. 8, tel. 09861/2046. 32 rooms, 2 suites, most with bath. Facilities: sauna, whirlpool, solarium. AE, DC, MC, V. Moderate.*

Schongau
Dining **Hotel Holl.** Hotelier Alexander Holl takes full advantage of the local lakes and rivers to stock the menu with fresh and imaginative fish dishes. The restaurant is on the outskirts of town, but it's worth the stroll. There is a small hotel attached. *Altenstadterstr. 39, tel. 08861/7292. Dress: informal. AE, DC, MC, V. Closed Sat.–Sun. and last 2 weeks in Aug. Moderate.*

Schwangau
Dining **König Ludwig.** The restaurant (and hotel) carries the name of the king so closely associated with the Schongau area, and the kitchen can be relied upon to produce some dishes bordering on the regal, particularly when game is in season. *Kreuzweg 11,*

tel. 08362/81081. Reservations advised. Dress: informal. AE. Moderate.

Coloman. Not only the regional nature of many of the dishes but the country-house style of this paneled, wood-beamed restaurant tell you you're in the Allgäu area of Bavaria. In summer, the outdoor beer garden is a shady delight. *Kroeb 2, tel. 08362/8288. Dress: informal. No credit cards. Closed Nov. 3–Dec. 11. Inexpensive.*

Weikersheim
Dining

Laurentius. St. Laurentius is the patron saint of cooks, and his patronage is much in evidence in this delightful, vaulted hotel-restaurant. If you're in the area at lunchtime, stop in for a three-course menu that includes imaginative meat dishes and homemade pastry for under DM 30. *Marktpl. 5, tel. 07934/7007. Reservations advised. Dress: informal. AE, DC, MC, V. Closed Feb. 1–Mar. 5. Moderate.*

Würzburg
Dining

Juliusspital Weinstuben. The wine you drink here is from the tavern's own vineyard; the food—predominantly hearty Franconian specialties—takes second billing to the excellent local wines. *Juliuspromenade 19, tel. 0931/54080. Reservations advised. Dress: informal. No credit cards. Closed Wed. and Feb. Moderate.*

★ **Ratskeller.** The vaulted cellars of Würzburg's Rathaus shelter are one of the city's most popular restaurants. Beer is served, but Franconian wine is what the regulars drink. The food is staunch Franconian fare. *Beim Grafeneckart, Langgasse 1, tel. 0931/13021. No reservations. Dress: informal. AE, DC, MC, V. Closed first 2 weeks of Feb. Moderate.*

Schiffbäuerin. River fish feature prominently on the menu of this restaurant, whose name means "shipbuilder's wife." Try its Franconian fish specialty, *Meersfishli*, or "little sea fish." *Katzengasse 7, tel. 0931/42487. Reservations advised on weekends. Dress: informal. No credit cards. Closed Sun. evening, Mon., and mid-July–mid-August. Moderate.*

Backofele. More than 400 years of tradition are sustained by this historic old tavern. You can dine well and inexpensively on such dishes as oxtail in Burgundy sauce, and homemade rissoles in wild mushroom sauce. *Ursulinergasse 2, tel. 0931/59059. Reservations advised. Dress: informal. No credit cards. Inexpensive.*

Stadt Mainz. Recipes from the original proprietor's own cookbook, dated 1850, form the basis of the imaginative menu of the Stadt Mainz hotel's restaurant. Eel from the Main River, prepared in a dill sauce, and Würzburg roast beef with fried onions are two reliable staples. *Semmelstr. 39, tel. 0931/53155. Reservations advised on weekends. Dress: informal. No credit cards. Closed Dec. 20–Jan. 20. Inexpensive.*

Lodging

★ **Hotel Rebstock.** More than five centuries of hospitality are contained behind this hotel's Rococo facade. The spacious lobby, with its open fireplace and beckoning bar, sets the tone. If you fancy opulent living, ask for one of the two luxury suites. All rooms are individually decorated. *Neubaustr. 7, tel. 0931/30930. 81 rooms, 2 suites, all with bath or shower. Facilities: restaurant, bar. AE, DC, MC, V. Closed first 2 weeks of Jan. Expensive.*

Hotel Schloss Steinburg. Set above the Main River Valley, the hotel looks over hillside vineyards, and guests are encouraged to make the acquaintance of the wines that come from them. There are tastings and classes, and diplomas for those who complete the latter. *Auf dem Steinberg, tel. 0931/93061. 44 rooms, 2 apartments. Facilities: swimming pool, sauna, solarium, bowling alley. DC, MC, V. Expensive.*

Hotel Walfisch. You'll breakfast on the banks of the Main in a dining room that commands views of the river valley and the vineyard-covered Marienberg above Würzburg. For lunch and dinner, try the hotel's cozy Walfischstube restaurant. *Am Pleidenturm 5, tel. 0931/50055. 41 rooms, most with shower. Facilities: restaurant. AE, DC, MC, V. Expensive.*

Gasthof Russ. This solid old inn is centrally placed for reaching all Würzburg's attractions. Since 1909 it's been owned and run by the same family, who take great pride in the warmth of their hospitality. *Wolfhartsgasse 1, tel. 0931/50016. 30 rooms, about half with bath or shower; those without are considerably cheaper. Facilities: restaurant. No credit cards. Moderate.*

Franziskaner. This comfortable and friendly family-run hotel was fully renovated in 1983. It's centrally located, a two-minute walk from the city's pedestrian shopping area. *Franziskanerpl. 2, tel. 0931/15001. 47 rooms, most with bath or shower. AE, DC, MC, V. Inexpensive.*

Stadt Mainz. This traditional Franconian inn dates back to the 15th century. Its bedrooms are simply but comfortably furnished. *Semmelstr. 39, tel. 0931/53155. 21 rooms. No credit cards. Closed Dec. 20–Jan. 20. Inexpensive.*

The Arts

Most of the towns on the Romantic Road have annual arts festivals. Local tourist information offices can supply details of programs and make ticket reservations. The leading festivals are Würzburg's Mozart Festival, held in the Residenz in June; Augsburg's Mozart Festival, in June and July; Rothenburg's Meistertrunk drama festival, in June; and Dinkelsbühl's Kinderzeche festival, in July. Those in Rothenburg and Dinkelsbühl celebrate historical events when the towns were saved from conquest and destruction, and combine plays, concerts, and carnival-like attractions. Every other year—1990 is the next—Nördlingen and nearby villages host the Rieser Cultural Season.

Music Augsburg has chamber and symphony orchestras, plus a ballet and opera companies. Performances are given September through July in the Kongresshalle (Göggingerstr. 10, tel. 0821/3604). Würzburg's music school has an orchestra that gives regular performances; call 0931/37436 for details and tickets. Chamber-music concerts are given year-round at Oettingen Castle (tel. 09082/20000) and at Neuschwanstein Castle (tel. 08362/81035).

Theater Augsburg and Würzburg both have city-theater companies offering a regular repertoire of German classics, modern drama, and comedy. Good knowledge of German is required if you plan a visit. Augsburg also has an annual open-air drama season, with the old city walls as a backdrop, in June and July; it moves to the romantic setting of the inner courtyard of the Fugger Palace in July and August. Dinkelsbühl has an open-air theater season from late June to mid-August.

9 Franconia: The Romantic Heart

Introduction

In a way, Franconia—or Franken, as it's called in German—could be considered the forgotten province of Germany. You may have trouble finding it on the average German map.

Technically, Franconia is part of Bavaria, comprising a good part of so-called Lower Bavaria (i.e., the northern part of the state), running across the country from just east of Frankfurt to the boundary with Czechoslovakia, its northern border forming the frontier with East Germany, its southern extremity reaching to the Danube, all still far north of Munich and what most of us think of as Bavaria.

Franconia could be called a state of mind; it could also be regarded as a country of its own within the confines of the Federal Republic. Many feel that it is the romantic heart of Germany, and the fountainhead of some of its greatest art.

Once upon a time this was, of course, the land of the Franks, who had important kingdoms of their own; much later it was to emerge as the domain of the powerful prince-bishops, who created fortified city-states studded with the magnificent palaces that are now the tourist highlights of the region, along with brooding hilltop castles, splendid country homes, and exquisite pilgrimage churches.

In the early 19th century, when Napoléon dismembered the Holy Roman Empire, Franconia was taken over by Bavaria, but it retains its own special character. There's a sophistication that may seem lacking elsewhere in this hearty, fun-loving former empire.

The cultural legacy of Franconia's various periods forms a continuing theme of any visit to the region. For here the minnesingers created Germany's lyric poetry in the early Middle Ages, followed by the poets-craftsmen known as the Meistersingers, who carried on the tradition.

Great sculpture abounds, as by the Renaissance master Tilman Riemenschneider, native son of Würzburg. Other names in the arts include architect Balthasar Neumann; Germany's greatest painter, Albrecht Dürer; and sculptor Veit Stoss. Here, too, Richard Wagner built his spectacular opera house, a fitting symbol of this epicenter of German mythology.

Finally there's the look and lay of the land itself: pastoral countryside laced with rivers large and small, including the Main and the Danube, along with others most of us have never heard of. The rolling hills are capped with medieval castles and monasteries. The fact that part of the area is named Franconian Switzerland should tell us something. It is in part a land of minor mountains and forests but to a large extent remains low-key and nondazzling, which may well be the reason why, with a few dramatic exceptions, Franconia should be so little known to tourists from beyond its boundaries.

Franconia rates high with in-the-know epicures in search of authentic German regional cuisine. And it produces extraordinary wines, such as a dry, flinty white bottled in stubby, flat bottles known as *Bocksbeutel* and considered one of the glories of the region.

Franconia includes within its orbit the northern section of the Romantic Road, beginning at Würzburg; and, considerably farther to the east, Bayreuth, which during the Wagner Festival in July is overrun by music lovers. Otherwise Franconia is certainly among Germany's less-visited areas and still makes for one of the Continent's happiest journeys of discovery.

Our coverage of Franconia begins at Aschaffenburg, 40 kilometers (25 miles) southeast of Frankfurt, in the northwestern part of the region. It ends at Regensburg, on the Danube River, in the southeastern part of the region, 310 kilometers (195 miles) from Aschaffenburg as the crow flies. En route, it covers the historic cities of Coburg, Bayreuth, Bamberg, and Nürnberg, as well as such memorable sights as the magnificent Baroque abbey of Weltenburg and the Rococo pilgrimage church of Vierzenheiligen. The unspoiled hills and valleys of the Spessart, the sinuous Main River Valley, and the Frankenwald (Franconian Forest) provide bucolic relief from the competing urban attractions of Franconia. (For information on Würzburg, perhaps the most celebrated of all the historic cities of Franconia, *see* Chapter 8.)

Essential Information

Important Addresses and Numbers

Tourist Information

The principal regional tourist office for Franconia is **Fremdenverkehrsverband Franken,** Am Plärrer 14, 8500 Nürnberg 80, tel. 0911/264–202. There are local tourist-information offices in the following towns:

Amorbach. Rathaus, 8762 Amorbach, tel. 09373/778.
Ansbach. Martin-Luther-Platz 1, 8800 Ansbach, tel. 0981/51243.
Aschaffenburg. Dalbergstrasse 6, 8750 Aschaffenburg, tel. 06021/30426.
Bamberg. Hauptwachstrasse 16, 8600 Bamberg, tel. 0951/21040.
Bayreuth. Luitpoldplatz 7–9, 8580 Bayreuth, tel. 0921/88588.
Ingolstadt. Hallstrasse 5, 8070 Ingolstadt, tel. 0841/305–415.
Coburg. Herrngasse 4, 8630 Coburg, tel. 09561/74180.
Kloster Banz and **Vierzenheiligen.** Bambergerstrasse 25, 8623 Staffelstein, tel. 09573/4192.
Kronach. Marktplatz, 8640 Kronach, tel. 09261/97236.
Kulmbach. Stadthalle, Suttestrasse 2, 8650 Kulmbach, tel. 09221/802–218.
Lichtenfels. Am Marktplatz 1, 8620 Lichtenfels, tel. 09571/7950.
Mespelbrunn. Hauptstrasse 173, 8751 Miltenberg, tel. 09371/400–119.
Nürnberg. Frauentorgraben 3, 8500 Nürnberg 70, tel. 0911/23360.
Regensburg. Altes Rathaus, 8400 Regensburg, tel. 0941/507–2141.
Wertheim. Stadtverwaltung, 6980 Wertheim, tel. 09342/301–230.
Weissenburg. Friedrich-Ebert-Strasse 1, 8832 Weissenburg, tel. 09141/2031.

Travel Agencies **American Express,** Alderstrasse 2, Nürnberg, tel. 0911/232–397.

Car Rental **Avis:** Markgrafenalle 6, tel. 0921/26151, **Bayreuth;** Mainzer Landstrasse 170, tel. 069/230–101, **Frankfurt;** Allersbergerstrasse 139, tel. 0911/49696, **Nürnberg;** Friedenstrasse 8, tel. 0941/97001, **Regensburg;** Schuererstrasse 2, tel. 0931/50661, **Würzburg.**
Europcar: Mainzer Landstrasse 160, tel. 069/234–002, **Frankfurt;** Nürnberg airport, tel. 0911/528–484, **Nürnberg;** Ziegelsdorferstrasse 118, tel. 0941/35085, **Regensburg;** Friendenstrasse 15, tel. 0931/881–150, **Würzburg.**
Herz: Mainzer Landstrasse 139, tel. 069/233–151, **Frankfurt;** Nürnberg airport, tel. 0911/527–710, **Nürnberg;** Ladehofstrasse 4, tel. 0941/22151, **Regensburg.**

Arriving and Departing by Plane

The major international airports for Franconia, with regular flights from the United States, are at Frankfurt and Munich. The most important regional airports are at Nürnberg and Bayreuth. There are frequent flights between Frankfurt and Nürnberg.

Arriving and Departing by Car and Train

By Car Franconia is served by five main autobahns: A-7 from Hamburg; A-3 from Köln and Frankfurt; A-81 from Stuttgart; A-6 from Heilbronn; and A-9 from Munich. Nürnberg is 167 kilometers (104 miles) from Munich and 222 kilometers (139 miles) from Frankfurt. Regensburg is 120 kilometers (75 miles) from Munich and 332 kilometers (207 miles) from Frankfurt.

By Train Fast Intercity trains run hourly between Frankfurt and Munich, with stops at Würzburg and Nürnberg. The trip takes about four hours. There are also hourly trains from Munich to Regensburg and from Regensburg to Nürnberg.

Getting Around

By Car The most famous scenic route in Franconia is the Romantic Road *(see* Chapter 8), but almost as interesting are the eastern section of the Burgenstrasse; the Castle Road, that runs west to east from Heidelburg to Nürnberg; and the Bocksbehtel Strasse, the Franconian Wine Road, that follows the course of the Main River from Zeil am Main along the wine-growing slopes of the valley to Aschaffenburg.

By Train If you start in Frankfurt and plan to visit the wine towns along the Main River, there are good local trains to Aschaffenburg, Miltenberg, and other small river towns. There are no direct train links to either Bayreuth or Bamberg. To explore south Franconia, use the local trains from Nürnberg to Trehchtlingen, Ansbach, and Ingolstadt.

By Bus The bus service between major centers in Franconia is poor; it's better to drive or ride the train. Other than the buses along the Romantic Road, the only major service is from Rothenburg-ober-Tauber to Nürnberg. However, local buses run from most train stations to smaller towns and villages, though the service isn't frequent. Buses for the Fichtelgebirge in north Franconia leave from Bayreuth's post office near the train station.

By Bicycle Renting bicycles is popular in Franconia, and the tourist authorities have made great efforts to attract cyclists. The terrain of the Altmühltal valley is particularly suitable for biking, and the tourist office in Eichstätt (Residenzpl. 1) issues leaflets on suggested cycling tours and lists of outlets where you can rent bikes. Bicycles can also be rented from most major train stations (the cost is DM 10 per day, half that if you have a rail ticket). Other tourist offices can supply details of special cycling routes in their regions.

By Boat A total of 15 different lines operate cruises through the region from April to October. Contact the **Fremdenverkehrsverband Franken** (Am Plärrer 14, Nürnberg, tel. 0911/264–202) and ask for details of their "Weisse Flotte" cruises. Or contact a travel agent in advance.

Guided Tours

The two most popular excursions are boat trips on the Danube from Regensburg to Ludwig I's imposing Greek temple of Walhalla, and one to the monastery at Weltenburg. There are regular sailings to both, March through October. The round-trip fare to Walhalla is DM 10 adults, DM 5 children; tel. 09424/1341 for information. The round-trip fare to Weltenburg is DM 7 adults, DM 4.50 children; tel. 09441/5858 for information.

There are also regular trips in the summer along the Main River from Aschaffenburg to Würzburg and from Würzburg to Bamberg. These are scenic routes worth considering for those with the time to do so. For information, contact **Fränkische Personen-Schiffahrt,** Kranenkas 1, Würzburg, tel. 0931/55356 and 0931/51722.

For boat tours around Bamberg, contact **Fritz Kropf,** Kapuzinerstrasse 5, tel. 0951/26679. Tours leave at 2:30 and 4 daily; the cost is DM 5.50 adults, DM 4 children.

Exploring Franconia

Numbers in the margin correspond with points of interest on the Franconia map.

Highlights for First-time Visitors

The *Bamberg Rider* statue, Bamberg
Hauptmarkt, Nürnberg
Dürer's House, Nürnberg
The Margräfliche's Opera House, Bayreuth
Regensburg Cathedral
The Stone Bridge, Regensburg
Vierzenheiligen Pilgrimage Church
Walhalla
Weltenburg Abbey Church

Aschaffenburg to Würzburg

If you're touring Franconia from Frankfurt, the first town
1 you'll reach is **Aschaffenburg,** on the Main River, gateway to both Franconia and the streams and woods of the Spessart hills. It's a small town, which, despite the ring of factories encircling it—Aschaffenburg is a major textile-producing cen-

Franconia

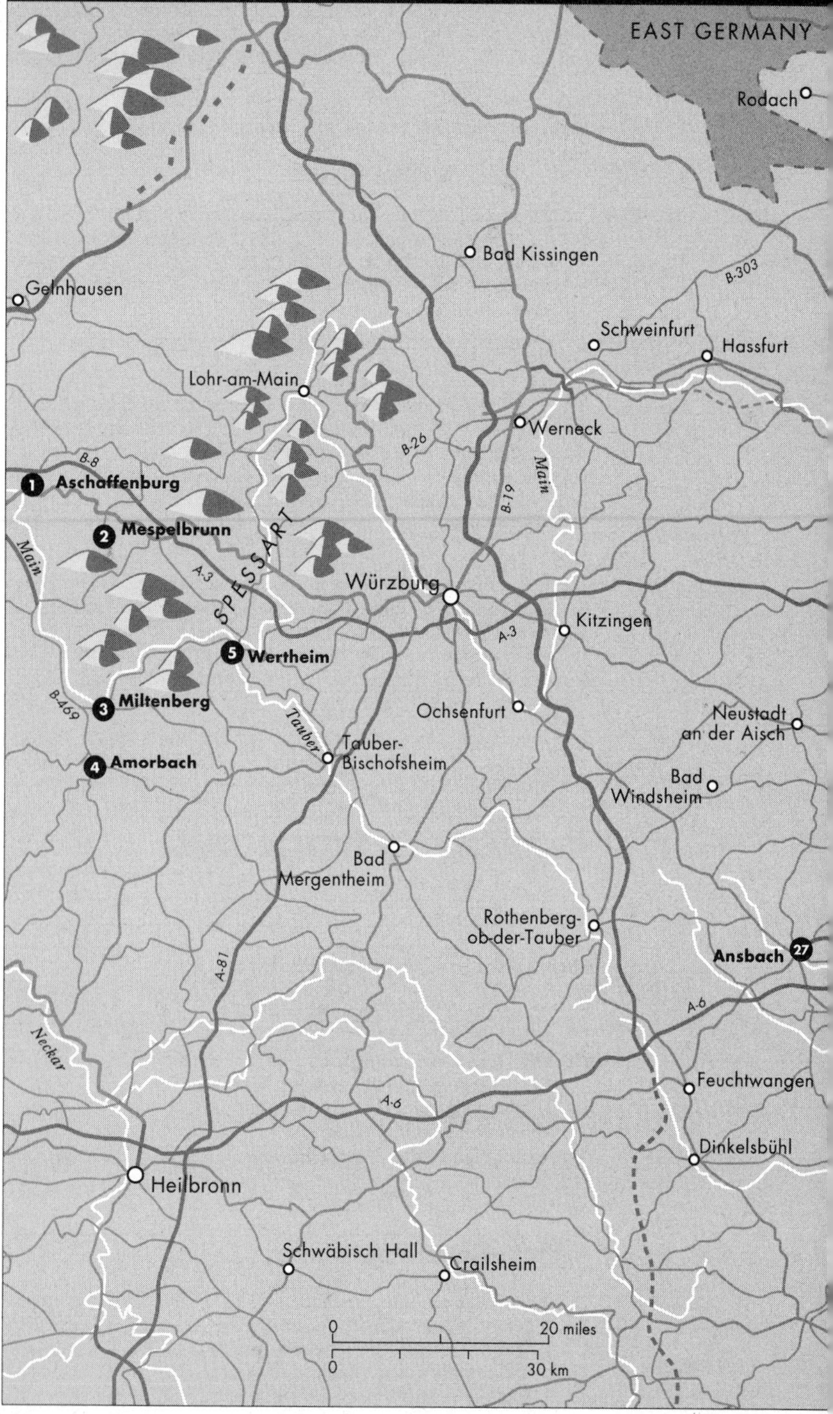
EAST GERMANY
Rodach
Bad Kissingen
B-303
Gelnhausen
Schweinfurt
Hassfurt
Lohr-am-Main
Werneck
B-26
B-8
Main
1 Aschaffenburg
B-19
2 Mespelbrunn
Main
SPESSART
A-3
Würzburg
Kitzingen
A-3
5 Wertheim
B-469
3 Miltenberg
Tauber
Ochsenfurt
Neustadt an der Aisch
Tauber-Bischofsheim
4 Amorbach
Bad Windsheim
Bad Mergentheim
Rothenberg-ob-der-Tauber
Ansbach 27
A-81
A-6
Neckar
Feuchtwangen
A-6
Dinkelsbühl
Heilbronn
Schwäbisch Hall
Crailsheim
0
20 miles
0
30 km

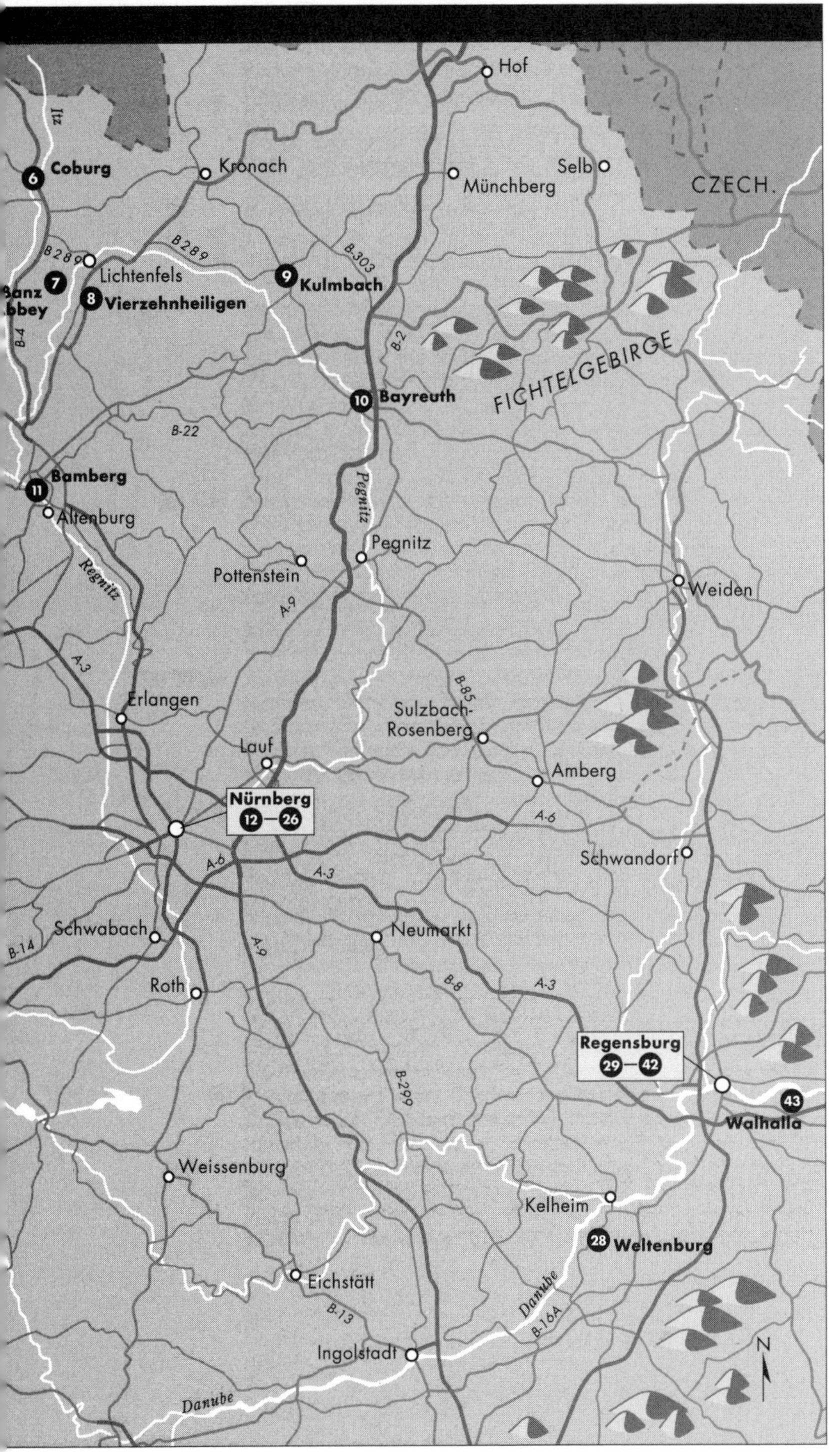
Hof
Coburg
6
Itz
Kronach
Münchberg
Selb
CZECH.
B289
B289
B-303
Lichtenfels
Kulmbach
9
7
Banz Abbey
8
Vierzehnheiligen
B-4
B-2
FICHTELGEBIRGE
10
Bayreuth
B-22
11
Bamberg
Altenburg
Pegnitz
Regnitz
Pegnitz
Pottenstein
Weiden
A-9
A-3
B-85
Erlangen
Sulzbach-Rosenberg
Lauf
Amberg
Nürnberg
12—26
A-6
A-6
A-3
Schwandorf
Schwabach
Neumarkt
B-14
A-9
B-8
A-3
Roth
Regensburg
29—42
43
Walhalla
B-299
Weissenburg
Kelheim
28
Weltenburg
Eichstätt
B-13
Danube
B-16A
Ingolstadt
N
Danube

ter—has retained its quiet, market-town atmosphere. The historic center has been carefully preserved, with much of it now an elegant pedestrian mall.

Begin your visit at **Schloss Johannisburg.** This imposing Renaissance castle, built between 1605 and 1615, was the residence of the prince-electors of Mainz, hereditary rulers of Aschaffenburg. The exterior of the doughty sandstone castle looks back to the Middle Ages, appearing more fortress than palace. Four massive corner towers guard the inner courtyard. The interior contains two small museums. The **Schloss Museum** (Castle Museum) charts the history of the town and contains a representative collection of German glass. The **Staatsgalerie** (City Art Gallery) has a small section devoted to Lucas Cranach (1472–1553), a leading painter of the German Renaissance, including typical enigmatic nudes and haunting landscapes. The palace grounds contain a striking copy of the temple of Castor and Pollux in Pompeii, constructed for Ludwig I of Bavaria in 1840. If you've admired the lavish Neoclassical buildings Ludwig put up in Munich, this powerful structure will appeal. *Admission to castle and museums: DM 3 adults. Open Apr.–Sept., Tues.–Sun. 9–noon and 1–5; Oct.–Mar., Tues.–Sun. 10–noon and 1–4.*

Time Out For an ideal introduction to Franconian wines and regional specialties, stop at the **Schlossweinstuben** (tel. 06021/12440), a wine cellar/restaurant in the castle. There's a fine view from the terrace over the Main Valley.

To reach the center of Aschaffenburg, start on Karlsstrasse and continue along Fürstengasse, which leads to Landlingstrasse and the **Stiftskirche** (collegiate church) of Sts. Peter and Alexander, on a small hill. Little remains of the original Romanesque building here save the cloisters; most of what you see dates from the 16th and 17th centuries. Pause before you go in to admire the tapering green spire and the imposing, slightly out-of-kilter facade. Inside, the **Lamentation of Christ,** a gaunt and haunting painting by Mathias Grünewald (c. 1475–1528), is the most notable of a number of paintings on view. It was part of a much larger and now lost altarpiece. As with the work of Grünewald's contemporary, Cranach, see how, in spite of the lessons of Italian Renaissance painting, naturalism and perspective still produce an essentially Gothic image, attenuated and otherworldly.

Castle lovers may enjoy a 17-kilometer (10-mile) excursion southeast from Aschaffenburg on B-8 to the small, romantic
2 castle of **Mespelbrunn.** This lies in the still sparsely populated forest area of the Spessart, the former hunting grounds of the archbishops of Mainz.

The castle of Mespelbrunn, surrounded by a moat and dominated by a massive round tower, is in an appealingly isolated spot. The **Rittersaal** (Knight's Room) on the first floor displays Teutonic suits of armor, assorted weapons, and massive, dark furniture. A more delicate note is struck by the 18th-century **Chinesiche Salon** (Chinese Room) upstairs. From the castle, hiking paths lead into the forested surroundings, for Spessart is a walker's paradise. *Admission: DM 3 adults, DM 1.50 children. Open Apr.–Sept., Mon.–Sat. 9–noon and 1–5, Sun. 9–5.*

From Aschaffenburg you can take the A-3 Autobahn 63 kilometers (40 miles) direct to Würzburg and then head east to Coburg, Bayreuth, and Bamberg *(see* below), or head south on route 4669, along the banks of the Main, to Miltenberg. From Miltenberg you can drive east past a succession of riverside towns to Würzburg. If you have time or inclination only for the Rococo glories of Würzburg, take the first route. If a more leisurely drive through the Main Valley is more your style, take the second. Our coverage describes the second route.

3 The little town of **Miltenberg** stands amid the hills and forests of the Odenwald. If you've seen Rothenburg-ob-der-Tauber and loved it but hated the crowds, Miltenberg will provide the antidote. For most, the Marktplatz, the steeply sloping town square, is the standout. A 16th-century fountain, bordered by geraniums, splashes in its center; all around, tall half-timbered houses, some six stories high, their crooked windows bright with yet more flowers, stand guard. To see more of these appealing buildings, stroll down Hauptstrasse, site of the Rathaus (Town Hall) and the 15th-century Haus zum Riesen (House of the Giant). The town takes its name from its castle, the entrance to which is on the Marktplatz. You can peek into the courtyard (open in the summer only) to see the standing stone in it. Though its origins and meaning are obscure, most scholars agree that it's probably Roman and connected with a fertility rite (there's no denying its phallic qualities).

Time Out The **Haus zum Riesen** (Hauptstr.) is one of the oldest inns in Germany. Stop in for a glass of beer or wine and to admire its gnarled and ancient timbers.

4 From Miltenberg, you can take a side trip to **Amorbach,** 8 kilometers (5 miles) south on B-469. The town itself is not the attraction; rather, it's the massive onetime Benedictine abbey church of **St. Maria** that will claim your attention. The building is interesting chiefly as an example of the continuity of German architectural traditions, the superimposition of one style on another. You'll see examples of work here from the 8th century through the 18th. The facade of the church, for all that it seems a run-of-the-mill example of Baroque work, with twin domed towers flanking a lively and well-proportioned central section, is in fact a rare example of the Baroque grafted directly onto a Romanesque building. Look closely and you'll notice the characteristic round arches of the Romanesque marching up the muscular towers. It's the onion-shape domes at their summits and the colored stucco applied in the 18th century that make them seem Baroque. There are no such stylistic confusions in the interior, however: All is Baroque power and ornamentation. *Admission: DM 3 adults, DM 2 children. Tours of the church and former monastery buildings are given Apr.–Sept., Mon.–Sat. 9–noon and 1–6, Sun. 11–6; Mar. and Oct., Mon.–Sat. 9–noon and 1:30–5:20, Sun. 11–6; Nov.–Feb., Mon.–Fri. 11 and 2:15, Sat. 11 and 2–4, Sun. 2–4.*

From Amorbach, backtrack to Miltenberg and follow B-469 for 70 kilometers (43 miles) to Würzburg. For most of the drive, you'll be sticking close to the Main River. A succession of riverside towns remind you that this is among the most appealingly
5 unspoiled regions of Germany. The largest town is **Wertheim,** 30 kilometers (18 miles) from Miltenberg, located where the Main and Tauber rivers meet. It was founded in 1306 and pro-

claims its medieval origins through a jumble of half-timbered houses with jutting gables. Those in the central Marktplatz are the most attractive. The principal sight is the ruined **Kurmainzisches Schloss** (castle), built for the counts of Wertheim in the 11th century. The ruins are convincingly romantic; the view from them over the Main Valley is memorable. Now drive the remaining 40 kilometers (24 miles) to Würzburg.

Coburg, Bayreuth, and Bamberg

6 **Coburg,** reached from Würzburg on B-19 and B-303, is a historic town, standing on the Itz River, just a few miles from the East German border. Whether glittering under the summer sky or frosted white with the snows of winter, Coburg is a jewel, and surprisingly little known. It was founded in the 11th century and remained in the possession of the dukes of Saxe-Coburg-Gotha until 1918; the present duke still lives there. In fact, it's as the home of the Saxe-Coburgs, as they are generally known, that the town is most famous. They were a remarkable family. Superficially just one among dozens of German ruling families, they established themselves as something of a royal stud farm, providing a seemingly inexhaustible supply of blue-blooded marriage partners to ruling houses the length and breadth of Europe. The most famous of these royal mates was Prince Albert, husband of Queen Victoria. Their numerous children, married off among more of Europe's kings, queens, and emperors, helped spread even farther afield the tried-and-tested Saxe-Coburg stock. There's a statue of the high-minded prince in the Marktplatz, the main square. (Queen Victoria has a further, special claim to fame in the annals of Coburg: On a visit to her new husband's hometown, she had the first flush toilet in Germany installed.)

The Marktplatz, ringed with gracious Renaissance and Baroque buildings, is the place to start your tour. The **Rathaus** (Town Hall), begun in 1500, is the most imposing structure. A forest of ornate gables and spires projects from its well-proportioned facade. Look at the statue of the **Bratwurstmännla** on the building; the staff he carries is claimed to be the official length against which the town's famous bratwurst sausages are measured.

Time Out If you think this is the sort of story that appears only in guidebooks, console yourself by trying a bratwurst from one of the stands that sell them in the square.

Just off the square, on Schlossplatz, you'll find **Schloss Ehrenburg,** the ducal palace. Built in the mid-16th century, it has been greatly altered over the years, principally following a fire in the early 19th century. The then duke took this opportunity to rebuild the palace in a heavy Gothic style. It was in this dark and imposing heap that Prince Albert spent much of his childhood. The throne room; the Hall of Giants, named for its larger-than-life frescoes; and the Baroque-style chapel can all be visited. *Schlosspl. Admission: DM 3.50 adults, children (with parents) free. Tours Apr.–Sept., daily at 10, 11, 1:30, 2:30, 3:30, and 4:30; and Oct.–Mar., daily at 10, 11, 1:30, 2:30, and 3:30.*

The major attraction in Coburg, however, is the **Veste Coburg** (the fortress), one of the largest and most impressive in the country. To reach it, you pass through the **Hofgarten** (Palace Gardens), today the site of the **Naturwissentschaftliches Museum** (Natural History Museum). It's the country's leading museum of its kind, with more than 8,000 exhibits of flora and fauna, and geological, ethnological, and mineralogical specimens. *Admission: DM 2. Open Apr.–Oct., daily 9–6; Nov.–Mar., daily 9–5.*

The brooding bulk of the castle lies beyond the garden on a small hill above the town. The first buildings were constructed around 1055, but with progressive rebuilding and remodeling through the centuries, today's predominantly late-Gothic/early Renaissance edifice bears little resemblance to the original rude fortress. It contains a number of museums (all open the same hours as the castle). See the **Fürstenbau,** or Palace of the Princes, where Martin Luther was sheltered for six months in 1530. Among the main treasures are paintings by Cranach. Dürer, Rembrandt, and Cranach (again) are all represented at the **Kunstsammlungen,** the art museum in the fortress, as are many examples of German silver, porcelain, arms and armor, and furniture. Finally, there's the **Herzoginbau,** the duchess's building, a sort of 18th-century transportation museum, with carriages and ornate sledges for speeding in style through the winter snows. *Admission to Veste Coburg: DM 2.50 adults, children (with parents) free. Open Apr.–Oct., Tues.–Sun. 9–noon and 2–4; Nov.–Mar., Tues.–Sun. 9–noon and 2–3:30.*

Time Out For a taste of old Coburg, make for **Klosterschänke** (Nägleinsgasse 4, tel. 09561/92665), a historic vaulted cellar in the center of town. Coburg grilled sausages are a specialty, and there is a wide range of chilled wines.

From Coburg, take B-4 south for a mile or so, then turn left (southwest) onto B-289 and follow the signs to Lichtenfels, 9 kilometers (5 miles) away. Lovers of Baroque and Rococo church architecture should make a right here to see Banz Abbey and Vierzenheiligen, probably the two most remarkable churches in Franconia. They stand on opposite sides of the Main River Valley, 3 or 4 miles southwest of Lichtenfels. The larger,
7 though in some ways the less impressive, is **Banz Abbey,** standing high above the Main on what some call the "holy mountain of Bavaria." There had been a monastery here since 1069, but the present buildings—now home to a lucky group of senior citizens—dates from the end of the 17th century. The highlight of the complex is the **Klosterkirche** (Abbey Church), the work of architect and stuccoist Johann Dientzenhofer. Two massive onion-dome towers soar over the restrained yellow sandstone facade. Note the animated statues of saints set in niches, a typical Baroque device. Inside, the church shimmers and glows with lustrous Rococo decoration. *Open Apr.–Sept., daily 8:30–11:30 and 1–5:30; Oct.–Mar., Mon.–Sat. 8:30–11:30 and 1–4:30.*

From the terrace there's a striking view over the Main to
8 **Vierzehnheiligen.** What you're seeing is probably the single most ornate Rococo church in Europe, although you might not know it just from looking at the exterior. There are those same onion-dome towers, the same lively curving facade, but little to suggest the almost explosive array of paintings, stucco, gilt, statuary, and rich rosy marble inside. The church was built by Balthasar Neumann (architect of the Residenz at Würzburg;

see Chapter 8) between 1743 and 1772 to commemorate a vision of Christ and 14 saints—Vierzehnheiligen means "14 saints"—that appeared to a shepherd back in 1445. Your first impression will be of the richness of the decoration and the brilliance of the coloring, the whole more like some fantastic pleasure palace than a place of worship. Notice the way the whole building seems to be in motion—almost all the walls are curved—and how the walls and ceiling are alive with delicate stucco. Much as the builders of Gothic cathedrals aimed to overwhelm through scale, so Neumann wanted to startle worshipers through beauty, light, color, and movement. Anyone who has seen the gaunt Romanesque cathedrals of Protestant north Germany will have little difficulty understanding why the Reformation was never able to gain more than a toehold in Catholic south Germany. There are few more uplifting buildings in Europe.

If it was beer that brought you to Germany, you'll want to drive the 32 kilometers (20 miles) east from Lichtenfels along B-289
9 to **Kulmbach.** In the country that produces—and drinks—more beer per capita than any other on Earth, the burghers of Kulmbach have the rare distinction of drinking more per head than those of any other German town. More beer is brewed here than anyplace else in the country. The locals claim it's the sparklingly clear spring water from the nearby Fichtelgebirge hills, combined with centuries of experience, that makes their beer so special. Put their claims to the test by trying any one of the numerous beers produced here. Pride of place must go to the frightening-sounding Kulminator brew, the strongest beer in the world. Other unique quaffs include Kloster, a thick black beer, quite unlike any other brewed in Germany, and Eisbock, which gives even Kulminator a run in the potency stakes. Kulmbach celebrates its beer every year in a nine-day festival that starts the last Saturday in July. With less-than-exquisite wit, they've christened the mammoth tent where the serious swilling takes place the Festspulhaus, or, literally, "festival swallowing house," a none-too-subtle dig at nearby Bayreuth and its Festspielhaus, where Wagner's operas are performed.

It would be unfair to pretend that Kulmbach is nothing but beer, beer, and more beer. The old town, for example, contains a warren of narrow streets that merit exploration. Likewise, no visitor here will want to miss the **Plassenburg,** symbol of the town and the most important Renaissance castle in the country. It's located a 20-minute hike from the old town on a rise overlooking Kulmbach. The first building here, begun in the mid-12th century, was torched by marauding Bavarians, who were anxious to put a stop to the ambitions of Duke Albrecht Alcibiades, a man who seems to have had few scruples when it came to self-advancement and who spent several years murdering, plundering, and pillaging his way through Franconia. His successors built today's castle starting in about 1560. Externally, there's little to suggest the graceful Renaissance interior, but as you enter the main courtyard the scene changes abruptly. The tiered space of the courtyard is covered with precisely carved figures, medallions, and other intricate ornaments, the whole comprising one of the most remarkable and delicate architectural ensembles in Europe. Inside, you may want to see the **Deutsches Zinnfingurenmuseum** (Tin Figures Museum), with more than 300,000 mini-statuettes, the largest collection of its kind in the world. *Admission: DM 2 adults, DM 1 chil-*

dren. Open Apr.–Sept., daily 10–4:40; Oct.–Mar., daily 10–3:30.

Twenty-two kilometers (14 miles) south of Kulmbach on route
10 303, then route 2, is **Bayreuth,** pronounced "Bay-roit." Bayreuth means Wagner. This small Franconian town was where 19th-century composer and man of myth Richard Wagner finally settled after a lifetime of rootless shifting through Europe, and here he built his great theater, the Festspielhaus, as a suitable setting for his grandiose and heroic operas. The annual Wagner festival, first held in 1876, regularly brings the town to a halt as hordes of Wagner lovers descend on Bayreuth, pushing prices sky-high, filling hotels to bursting, and earning themselves much-sought-after social kudos in the process (to some, it's one of *the* places to be seen). The festival is usually held in July, so unless you plan to visit the town specifically for it, this is the time to stay away *(see* The Arts and Nightlife, below). Likewise, those whose tastes do not include opera and the theater will find little here to divert them. Bayreuth has no picture-postcard setting, and there is little here that is not connected in some way with music, specifically Wagner's.

As it's Wagner who brings most visitors to Bayreuth, it's only fitting to start a tour of the town with a visit to the house he built here, the only house he ever owned, in fact: **Wahnfried,** or Vision of Peace. It's a simple, austere Neoclassical building, constructed in 1874, just south of the town center. Today it's a museum celebrating the life of this maddening and compelling man, though, after wartime bomb damage, only the facade remains of the original construction. Here Wagner and his wife, Cosima, daughter of composer Franz Liszt, lived; and here, too, they are buried. Hitler, whose admiration for Wagner knew few limits, stayed here during visits to the Wagner festival, the guest of the by then near-senile Cosima. The other great figure with whom Wagner is associated, King Ludwig II of Bavaria, the young and impressionable "dream king" who provided much of the financial backing for Wagner's vaultingly ambitious works, is remembered, too; there's a bust of him in front of the front door. Though the house is something of a shrine to Wagner, even those who have little interest in him will find it intriguing and educational. Standout exhibits include the original scores for a number of his operas, including *Parsifal, Tristan, Lohengrin, The Flying Dutchman,* and *Götterdämmerung.* You can also see designs, many of them original, for productions of his operas, as well as his piano and huge library. At 10, noon, and 2, excerpts from his operas are played in the living room. *Richard-Wagner-Str. 48. Admission: DM 2.50 adults (DM 3.50 in July and Aug.), DM 1 children. Open daily 9–5.*

From the museum, you are close to the **Neues Schloss** (New Palace). If Wagner is the man most closely associated with Bayreuth, then it's well to remember that had it not been for the woman who built this glamorous 18th-century palace, he would never have come here in the first place. She was the Magravina Wilhelmina, sister of Frederick the Great of Prussia and wife of the margrave (marquis) of Brandenburg. While the margrave was an altogether unremarkable man, his wife was a woman of enormous energy and decided tastes. She devoured books; wrote plays and operas (which she directed and, of course, acted in); and built, transforming much of the town and bringing it near bankruptcy. Her distinctive touch is much in evidence at the New Palace, built when a mysterious fire conveniently destroyed parts of the original palace. Anyone with a taste for the wilder flights of Rococo decoration will love it. The **Staatsgalerie** (State Art Gallery), containing a representative collection of mainly 19th-century Bavarian paintings, is also housed in the palace. *Ludwigstr. 21. Admission: DM 2 adults, DM 1.50 children. Open Apr.–Sept., daily 10–noon and 1:30–4:30; Oct.–Mar., daily 1:30–3.*

Wilhelmina's other great architectural legacy is the **Markgräfliche's Opernhaus** (Margravina's Opera House), just a step or two from the New Palace. Built between 1745 and 1748, it is a Rococo jewel, sumptuously decorated in red, gold, and blue. Apollo and the nine Muses cavort across the frescoed ceiling. It was this delicate 500-seat theater that originally drew Wagner to Bayreuth, since he felt that it might prove a suitable setting for his own operas. In fact, while it may be a perfect place to hear Mozart, it's hard to imagine a less suitable setting for Wagner's epic works. Catch a performance here if you can *(see* The Arts and Nightlife, below); otherwise, take a tour of the ravishing interior. *Admission: DM 2 adults, DM 1.50 children. Open Apr.–Sept., daily 9–11:30 and 1:30–4:30; Oct.–Mar., daily 10–11:30 and 1:30–3.*

Now you'll want to head up to the **Festspielhaus;** it's located a mile or so north of the downtown area at the head of Niebelungstrasse. This plain, almost intimidating building is the high temple of the cult of Wagner. The building was conceived, planned, and financed by the great man specifically as a setting for his monumental operas. Today, it is very much the focus of the annual Wagner festival, still masterminded by descendants of the composer. The spartan look is partly explained by Wagner's near-permanent financial crises, partly by his desire to achieve perfect acoustics. For this reason, the wood seats have no upholstering, and the walls are bare of all ornament. The stage is enormous, capable of holding the huge casts required for Wagner's largest operas. *Auf dem Grünen Hügel. Admission: DM 2 adults, DM 1.50 children. Open Jan.–mid-June, Sept., and Nov.–Dec., Tues.–Sun. 10–11:30 and 1:30–3. Closed mid-June–Aug. and in Oct.*

The **Altes Schloss Ermitage** (Old Castle and Hermitage), 5 kilometers (3 miles) north of Bayreuth, makes an appealing change from the sonorous and austere Wagnerian mood of much of the town. It's an early 18th century palace, built as a summer palace and remodeled in 1740 by the Margravina Wilhelmina. While her taste is not much in evidence in the drab exterior, the interior, alive with light and color, displays her guiding hand in every elegant line. The standout is the extraordinary **Japanese room,** filled with Oriental treasures and chinoiserie furniture. The park and gardens, partly formal, partly natural, are enjoyable for idle strolling in summer. *Admission: DM 2 adults, DM 1.50 children. Open Apr.–Sept., daily 9–11:30 and 1–4:30; Oct.–Mar., daily 10–11:30 and 1–2:30.*

Time Out For simple regional specialties and a wide choice of beers, try the restaurant of the **Weihenstephan** hotel (Bahnhofstr. 5, tel. 0921/82288), located close by the train station. You can sit on the terrace in summer.

11 **Bamberg,** the next major city on the tour, is 60 kilometers (37 miles) west of Bayreuth on B-22. Bamberg is one of the great historic cities of Germany, filled with buildings and monuments that recall its glorious days as the seat of one of the most powerful ruling families in the country. Though founded as early as the 2nd century AD, Bamberg rose to prominence only in the 11th century, under the irresistible impetus provided by its most famous son, Holy Roman Emperor Heinrich II. His imperial cathedral still dominates the historic area.

The city lies on the Regnitz River, about 80 kilometers (50 miles) north of Nürnberg. The historic center is a small island in the river; to the west is the so-called Bishops' Town, to the east the so-called Burghers' Town. Connecting them is a bridge on which stands the Altes Rathaus (Old Town Hall), strategically positioned between ecclesiastical and secular strongholds. Though there are many attractions, the preeminent pleasure of a visit is to stroll through the narrow, sinewy streets of old Bamberg, past half-timbered and gabled houses and formal 18th-century mansions. Peek into cobbled, flower-filled courtyards or take time out in a waterside café, watching the little steamers as they chug past the colorful row of fishermen's houses that comprise Klein Venedig (Little Venice).

Start your tour at the **Dom,** the imperial cathedral, on Domplatz, heart of Bishops' Town. It's one of the most important of Germany's cathedrals, a building that tells not only Bamberg's story but that of much of Germany as well. The first building here was begun by Heinrich II in 1003, and it was in this partially completed cathedral that he was crowned Holy Roman Emperor in 1012. In 1237 it was mostly destroyed by fire, and the present late-Romanesque/early Gothic building was begun. From the outside, the dominant features are the massive towers at each corner. Heading into the dark interior, you'll find one of the most striking collections of monuments and art treasures of any European church. The most famous is the *Bamberg Rider,* an equestrian statue, carved—no one knows by whom—around 1230 and thought to be an allegory of knightly virtue. The larger-than-life-size figure is an extraordinarily realistic work for the period, more like a Renaissance statue than a Gothic piece. Compare it to the mass of carved figures huddled in the tympana, the semi-circular spaces above the doorways of the church; while these are stylized and obviously Gothic, the *Bamberg Rider* is poised and calm. In the center of the nave you'll find another great sculptural work, the massive tomb of Heinrich and his wife, Kunigunde. It's the work of Tilman Riemenschneider, Germany's greatest Renaissance sculptor. Pope Clement II is also buried in the cathedral, in an imposing tomb under the high altar; he is the only pope to be buried north of the Alps.

After you've toured the cathedral, go next door to see the **Diözesan Museum** (Cathedral Museum). In addition to a rich collection of silver and other ecclesiastical objects, the museum contains a splinter of wood and the *heilige Nagel,* or holy nail, both reputedly from the cross of Jesus. A more macabre exhibit is Heinrich's and Kunigunde's skulls, mounted in elaborate metal supports. The building itself was designed by Balthasar Neumann, the architect of Vierzenheiligen church, and constructed between 1730 and 1733. *Dompl. 5. Admission: DM*

2.50 adults, DM 1.50 children. Open Apr.–Sept., daily 9–noon and 1:30–5; Oct.–Mar., daily 9–noon and 1:30–4.

Keep your ticket for the cathedral museum to visit the adjoining **Neue Residenz** (Dompl. 8; open same hours). This immense Baroque palace was the home of the prince-electors. Their wealth and prestige are easily imagined as you tour the glittering interior. Most memorable is the **Kaisersaal** (Throne Room), complete with impressive ceiling frescoes and elaborate stuccowork. You'll also be able to visit the rose garden in back of the building, which offers a fine view of the Benedictine abbey church of St. Michael.

The palace also houses the **Staatsbibliothek** (State Library). Among the thousands of books and illuminated manuscripts are the original prayer books belonging to Heinrich and his wife, a 5th-century manuscript by the Roman historian Livy, and handwritten manuscripts by the 16th-century painters Dürer and Cranach.

End your tour of Domplatz with a visit to the **Alte Hofaltung,** the former imperial and episcopal palace. It's a sturdy and weather-worn half-timbered Gothic building, with a graceful Renaissance courtyard. Today it contains the **Historisches Museum,** with a collection of documents and maps charting Bamberg's history that will appeal most to avid history buffs and/or those who read German well. *Dompl. 7. Admission: DM 1 adults, 50 pf children. Open Dec.–Apr., Tues.–Fri. 9–1, Sat. and Sun. 9–4:30; May–Oct., Tues.–Sun. 9–5. Closed Nov.*

From Domplatz, walk down the hill to the **Altes Rathaus,** 200 or so yards away, one of the most bizarrely situated municipal buildings in Europe. It is perched on a little island in the Regnitz River, a stone bridge connecting it to the onetime rival halves of Bamberg. Half the building is Gothic, half is Renaissance; between them is an ornate Baroque gateway topped by an elegantly tapering spire. While here you'll get just about the best view of the fishermen's houses of Klein Venedig (Little Venice).

From the bridge you can walk over to the **Hoffmann-Haus** on Schillerplatz. Hoffmann, a Romantic writer and poet, lived in this little house between 1809 and 1813. Unusually, he is best remembered not for one of his own works but for an opera written *about* him by composer Jacques Offenbach, *The Tales of Hoffmann*. The house has been preserved much as it was when Hoffmann lived here—complete with the hole in the floor of his study through which he talked to his wife below. *Schillerpl. 26. Admission: DM 1 adults, 50 pf children. Open May–Oct., Tues.–Fri. 9:30–5:30, Sat. and Sun. 9:30–10:30.*

Time Out The **Historischer Brauereiausschank Schlenkerla,** (Dominikanerstr. 6, tel. 0951/56060), a 15th-century monastery converted into the ultimate beer hall, offers plenty of authentic, mug-banging atmosphere and low prices. The rough-hewn wood tables, plaster walls, and rowdy mood add up to a fun atmosphere in which to down a liter of the unique, almost black *Rauchbier* (smoked beer), which tastes as though it has been barbecued. Rauchbier is brewed only in Bamberg, and is made according to a lengthy and complex process virtually unchanged since early in the 16th century. The malt is smoked over a fire of beech wood from the sunny side of the nearby

Steigerwald, and this smoking gives the heavy brew its distinctive, pungent flavor. With it order a *Bierbrauvesper*, composed of smoked meat, sour-milk cheese, and black bread and butter, all served on a wood platter. *Prost!*

Tour Three: Nürnberg to Regensburg

Numbers in the margin correspond with points of interest on the Nürnberg map.

12 **Nürnberg** is the principal city of Franconia, and second in size and significance in Bavaria only to Munich. Its origins date back at least to 1040. It's among the most historic and visitable of Germany's cities; the core of the old town, through which the Pegnitz River flows, is still surrounded by its original medieval walls. Nürnberg has always taken a leading role in German affairs. It was here, for example, that the first "diet," or meeting of rulers, of every Holy Roman Emperor was held. And it was here, too, that Hitler staged the greatest and most grandiose Nazi rallies and the Allies held the war trials. Wartime bombing destroyed much of medieval and Renaissance Nürnberg, though faithful reconstruction has largely re-created the city's prewar atmosphere.

The city grew because of its location at the meeting point of a number of medieval trade routes. With prosperity came a great flowering of the arts and sciences. Albrecht Dürer, the first indisputable genius of the Renaissance in Germany, was born here in 1471, and he returned in 1509 to spend the rest of his life here. (His house is one of the most popular tourist shrines in the city.) Other leading Nürnberg artists of the Renaissance include woodcarver Michael Wolgemut and sculptors Adam Kraft and Peter Vischer. Earlier the minnesingers, medieval poets and musicians, chief among them Tannhäuser, had made the city a focal point in the development of German music. In the 15th and 16th centuries their traditions were continued by the Meistersingers. Both groups were celebrated much later by Wagner. Among a great host of inventions, the most significant were the pocket watch, gun casting, the clarinet, and the geographical globe (the first of which was made before Columbus discovered the Americas).

Nürnberg is rich in special events and celebrations. By far the most famous is the Christkindlmarkt, an enormous pre-Christmas market that runs from November 27 to Christmas Eve. The highlight is the December 10 candle procession, in which thousands of children march through the city streets. There are few sights in Europe to compare with the flickering of their tiny lights in the cold night air, the whole scene played out against the backdrop of centuries-old buildings.

The historic heart of Nürnberg is compact; all principal sights are within easy walking distance. To get a sense of the city begin your tour by walking around all or part of the **city walls.** Finished in 1452, they come complete with moats, sturdy gateways, and watchtowers. Year-round floodlighting adds to their
13 brooding romance. Stop at the **Königstor** (Royal Gate), by the Hauptbahnhof (main train station), to see the **Handwerkerhof,** a "medieval mall" with craftsmen busy pretending it's still the Middle Ages. They turn out puppets, baskets, pewter mugs and plates, glassware, and *Lebkuchen* (gingerbread cookies).

Albrecht-Dürer-Haus, **23**
Alt-Stadt-Museum, **21**
Altes Rathaus, **19**
Die Kaiserburg, **22**
Frauenkirche, **17**
Gansemännchen-brunnen, **20**
Germanisches Nationalmuseum, **25**
Helig-Geist-Spital, **15**
Königstor, **13**
St. Lorenz Kirche, **14**
St. Sebaldus Kirche, **18**
Schöner Brunnen, **16**
Spielzeug Museum, **24**
Verkehrsmuseum, **26**

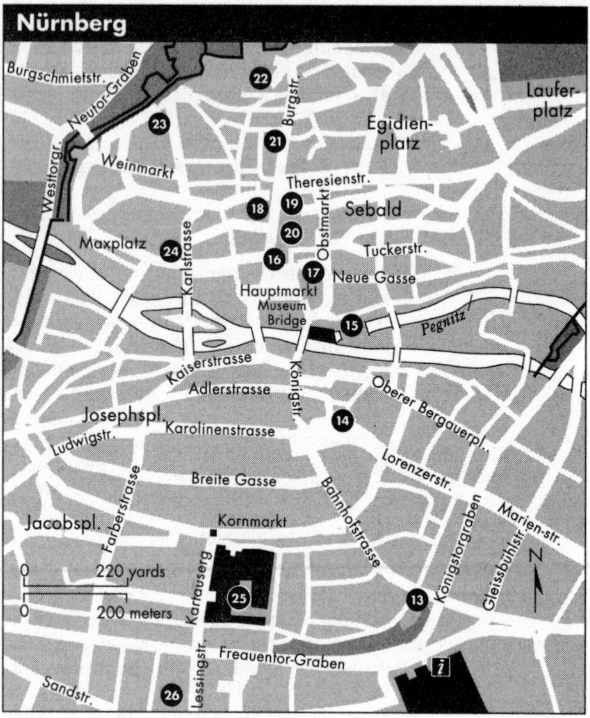

Time Out The **Bratwurstglöcklein** (Am Königstor), located in the Handwerkerhof, offers some of the best bratwurst in Nürnberg. Sauerkraut and potato salad are the traditional accompaniments. Wash it all down with a glass of beer.

14 From the Königstor, head up Königstrasse to **St. Lorenz Kirche.** Opinions are divided as to the most beautiful church in the city; but many think St. Lorenz Kirche deserves the honor. If you visit it and St. Sebaldus Kirche *(see* below) you can make up your own mind. St. Lorenz was begun around 1220, completed about 1475. It's a sizable church; two towers flank the main entrance, which is covered with a forest of carving. In the lofty interior, note the works by sculptors Adam Kraft and Veit Stoss: Kraft's great stone tabernacle to the left of the altar, and Stoss's *Annunciation* at the east end of the nave are considered their finest works. There are many other carvings throughout the building, a fitting testimonial to the artistic richness of late-medieval Nürnberg.

From the church, walk up to the Hauptmarkt, crossing the little museum bridge over the Pegnitz River. To your right, set on
15 graceful arcades over the river, is the **Helig-Geist-Spital** (Holy Ghost Hospital), begun in 1381. It's worth looking into the courtyard to admire its elegant wood balconies and spacious arcades. Continue the few paces to the **Hauptmarkt** (Main Market). Like Munich's Viktualienmarkt, Nürnberg's market is more than just a place to do the shopping. Its colorful stands, piled high with produce and shaded by striped awnings, are a

central part of the city. The red-armed market women, whose acid wit and earthy homespun philosophy you'll have to take on trust unless your command of German extends to an in-depth familiarity with the Nürnberg dialect, are a formidable-looking bunch, dispensing flowers, fruit, and abuse in about equal measure. It's here that the Christkindlmarkt is held.

16 There are two principal sights in the market. One is the **Schöner Brunnen** ("Beautiful Fountain"). It's an elegant, 60-foot-high Gothic fountain carved around the year 1400, looking for all the world as though it should be on the summit of some lofty Gothic cathedral. Thirty figures arranged in tiers stand sentinel on it. They include prophets, saints, local noblemen, sundry electors of the Holy Roman Empire, and one or two strays, such as Julius Caesar and Alexander the Great. A gold ring is set into the railing surrounding the fountain, reputedly placed there by an apprentice carver. Stroking it is said to bring good luck. Cynics will enjoy the sight of Germans and tourists alike examining the railing for the ring and surreptitiously rubbing it.

17 The other major attraction is the **Frauenkirche** (Church of Our Lady), which was built, with the approval of Holy Roman Emperor Charles IV, in 1350 on the site of a synagogue burned down in a pogrom in 1349. (The area covered by the Hauptmarkt was once the Jewish quarter of the city.) These days, most visitors are drawn not so much by the church itself as by the **Männleinlaufen,** a clock dating from 1500 that's set in its facade. It's one of those colorful mechanical marvels at which the Germans have long excelled—a perfect match between love of punctuality and ingenuity. Every day at noon the electors of the Holy Roman Empire glide out of the clock to bow to the Emperor Charles IV before sliding back under cover. It's worth scheduling your morning to catch the display.

From the Hauptmarkt, continue the short distance north to
18 the 13th-century **St. Sebaldus Kirche,** on Sebaldkircheplatz. Though the church lacks the number of art treasures boasted by rival St. Lorenz, its lofty nave and choir are among the purest examples of Gothic ecclesiastical architecture in Germany: elegant, tall, and airy. Veit Stoss carved the crucifix at the east end of the nave, while the elaborate brass shrine, containing the remains of St. Sebaldus himself, was cast by Peter Vischer around 1520.

19 Abutting the rear of the church is the **Altes Rathaus** (Old Town Hall), built in 1332, destroyed in World War II, and subsequently painstakingly restored. Visit its dungeons, hacked from the underground rock. *Rathauspl. Admission: DM 2. Open May–Sept., Mon.–Sat. 10–4, Sun. 10–1.*

20 Facing the town hall is the bronze **Gansemännchenbrunnen** (Gooseman's Fountain). It's an elegant work of great technical sophistication, cast in 1550.

Walk north from the Altes Rathaus along Burgstrasse. On your
21 left you'll pass the Fembohaus, now the **Alt-Stadt-Museum** (Old City Museum). It's one of the finest Renaissance mansions in Nürnberg, a dignified, patrician dwelling completed in 1598. The story of the city is told in its museum. *Burgstr. Admission: DM 2. Open year-round, Tues.–Fri. and Sun. 10–5, Sat. 10–1.*

22 At the end of Burgstrasse you reach Nürnberg's number-one sight, **Die Kaiserburg** (the Imperial Castle). This immense cluster of buildings, standing just inside the city walls, was the residence of the Holy Roman Emperors. Impressive rather than beautiful, the complex comprises three separate groups of buildings. The oldest, dating from around 1050, is the **Burggrafenburg,** the Burgrave's Castle, with a craggy, ruined seven-sided tower and bailiff's house. It stands in the center of the complex. To the east is the **Kaiserstallung** (Imperial Stables). These were built in the 15th century as a granary, then converted into a youth hostel after the war. The real interest, however, centers on the Imperial Castle itself, the westernmost part of the fortress. The standout feature here is the Renaissance **Doppelkappelle** (Double Chapel). The lower part of the chapel was used by the castle minions and is accordingly austere, befitting their lowly status. The adjoining upper part, correspondingly richer, larger, and more ornate, was where the emperor and his family worshiped. Visit also the **Rittersaal** (Knight's Hall) and the **Kaisersaal** (Throne Room). Their heavy oak beams, painted ceilings, and sparse interiors have changed little since they were built in the 15th century.

23 Descending from the western part of the castle, walk across the cobbled square to the **Albrecht-Dürer-Haus,** located opposite the Tiergärtner gate. This was the home of the great German painter from 1509 to his death in 1528. It is also about the best-preserved late-medieval house in the city, typical of the prosperous merchants' homes that once filled Nürnberg. Admire the half-timbering of the upper stories and the tapering gable before stepping inside. Dürer was the German Leonardo, the Renaissance man incarnate, bursting with curiosity. His greatest achievement was in woodcuts, a notoriously difficult medium that he raised to new heights of technical sophistication, combining great skill with a haunting, immensely detailed drawing style and complex allegorical subject matter. A number of original prints adorn the walls. The house also offers a convincing sense of what life was like in early 16th-century Germany. *Albrecht-Dürer-Str. 39. Admission: DM 3 adults, DM 2 children and senior citizens. Open Mar.–Oct. and Christkindlmarkt, Tues. and Thurs.–Sun. 10–5, Wed. 5–9; Nov.–Feb., Tues., Thurs., and Fri. 10–5, Wed. 9–1.*

24 The **Spielzeug Museum** (Toy Museum) is located on Sigmundstrasse. To reach it, walk down the street that runs past Dürer's house. There are few places where a toy museum seems more appropriate. Nürnberg likes to call itself the toy capital of the world, and this museum does its best to prove why. One or two exhibits date from the Renaissance; most, however, are from the 19th century. Simple dolls vie with mechanical toys of extraordinary complexity. There's even a little Ferris wheel. *Sigmundstr. 220. Admission: DM 3. Open Tues. and Thurs.–Sun. 10–5, Wed. 10–9.*

25 A final sight in the historic area for those with interest in German cultural achievements is the **Germanisches Nationalmuseum** (Germanic National Museum), located close by the Hauptbahnhof. You could spend an entire day visiting this vast and fascinating museum. It is the largest of its kind in Germany, and about the best arranged. The setting gets everything off to a flying start; the museum is located in what was once a Carthusian monastery, complete with cloisters and monastic

outbuildings. Few aspects of German culture, from the Stone Age to the 19th century, are not covered here, and quantity and quality are evenly matched. For some, the highlight may be the superb collection of Renaissance German painting (with Dürer, Cranach, and Altdorfer well represented). Others may prefer the exquisite medieval ecclesiastical exhibits—manuscripts, altarpieces, statuary, stained glass, jewel-encrusted reliquaries—or the collections of arms and armor, or the scientific instruments, or the toys. Few will be disappointed. *Kornmarkt. Admission: DM 3 adults, DM 1 children. Open Tues., Wed., and Fri.-Sun. 9–5, Thurs. 8* AM*–9:30* PM.

26 Children love the **Verkehrsmuseum** (Transportation Museum), located just south of the National Museum outside the city walls. December 7, 1835, saw the first-ever train trip in Germany, from Nürnberg to nearby Fürth. A model of the epochal train is here at the museum, along with a series of original 19th- and early 20th-century trains and stagecoaches. Stamp lovers will also want to check out some of the 40,000-odd stamps in the extensive exhibits on the German postage system. *Lessingstr. 6. Admission: DM 4 adults, DM 2 children. Open Apr.-Sept., Mon.-Sat. 10–5, Sun. 10–4; Oct.-Mar., daily 10–4.*

Numbers in the margin correspond with points of interest on the Franconia map.

Leave Nürnberg on route 14 and drive the 37 kilometers (23
27 miles) to **Ansbach.** It's a small, quiet town whose medieval origins are still evident in half-timbered and gabled buildings. The principal attraction here is the 18th-century **Residenz,** palace of the margraves of Ansbach-Bayreuth, begun in 1731 by the Margrave Carl Wilhelm Friedrich, brother of Wilhelmina of Bayreuth *(see* Coburg, Bayreuth, and Bamberg, above). The highlights are the **Spiegelkabinett** (Hall of Mirrors), a ravishing, shimmering room—originally lit by hundreds of candles—and **Gekachelter Saal,** the porcelain gallery. It was the next margrave, Carl-Alexander, who was responsible for the porcelain here. Upon Carl Wilhelm's death, the new margrave inherited both his father's palace and his enormous debts. He tried to settle them by starting a porcelain factory, the results of which you see here. The Hofgarten (Palace Gardens) can also be visited. *Admission: DM 2.50 adults, DM 1.50 children. Palace open for guided tours only, Apr.-Sept., Tues.-Sun. at 9, 10, 11, 2, 3, and 4; Oct.-Mar., Tues.-Sun. at 10, 11, 2, and 3.*

The trip from Ansbach to Regensburg (the focal point of this tour) takes you via the towns of Weissenburg, Eichstätt, and Ingolstadt, which offer little by way of outstanding sights, although all convey the mellow flavor of old Franconia.

As you near Regensburg, however, there's one highlight everyone should visit—the great abbey church of St. George and St.
28 Martin by the banks of the Danube at **Weltenburg.** The most dramatic approach to the abbey is by boat from Kelheim, 10 kilometers (6 miles) downstream *(see* Guided Tours, above). On the stunning ride, the boat winds between towering limestone cliffs that rise straight up from the tree-lined riverside. The abbey church, constructed between 1716 and 1718, is commonly regarded as the masterpiece of the brothers Cosmas Damian and Egid Quirin Asam, the two leading Baroque architects and decorators of Bavaria (Cosmas Damian was the architect, Egid Quirin was the painter, sculptor, and stuccoworker). If you've

seen their little church of St. John Nepomuk in Munich you know what pyrotechnics to expect here, albeit on a substantially larger scale. To some, this kind of frothy confection, with painted figures whirling on the ceiling, lavish and brilliantly polished marble, highly wrought statuary, and stucco dancing rhythmic arabesques across the curving walls, seems more like high kitsch than high art. To others, the exuberance, drama, and sheer technical sophistication of this concentrated style may appear like Mozart's music in stone. Whichever view you take, it's hard not to be impressed by the bronze equestrian statue of St. George, reaching down imperiously with his flamelike, twisted gilt sword to dispatch the winged dragon at his feet, over the high altar.

Numbers in the margin correspond with points of interest on the Regensburg map.

29 **Regensburg** is one of the best-preserved cities in Germany. Everything here is original, since the city suffered no major damage in World War II. It is also one of Germany's most historic cities. The mystery, then, would appear to be: Why is Regensburg not better known? It happens to be among the most consistently underrated destinations in the Federal Republic. Few visitors to Bavaria (or even Franconia) venture this far off the well-trod tourist trails that take in Munich, the Alps, and the Romantic Road. For this reason, Regensburg may well come as the big surprise of a tour of Franconia. Even Germans are astonished that such a remarkable city should exist in comparative obscurity.

The key to Regensburg is the Danube. The city marks the northernmost navigable point of the great river, and it was this simple geographical fact that allowed Regensburg to control trade along the Danube between Germany and central Europe. The great river was a highway for more than commerce, however: It was a conduit of ideas as well. It was from Regensburg, for example, in the 7th and 8th centuries that Christianity was spread across much of central Europe. By the Middle Ages, Regensburg had become a political, economic, and intellectual center of European significance. Today the city may long since have given way to Munich in political clout and sheer size, but for many centuries it was the most important city in southeast Germany, eclipsed by Munich only when Napoléon ordered the dismemberment of the Holy Roman Empire in the early years of the 19th century. That he presided over its decline from Regensburg, a Free Imperial City since the 13th century and meeting place of the Imperial Diet (parliament) since the 17th, was an irony he appreciated.

Regensburg's story begins with the Celts in around 500 BC. They called their little settlement Radasbona. In AD 179, as an original marble inscription in the Museum der Stadt Regensburg proclaims, it became a Roman military post called Castra Regina. Little remains of the Roman occupation save a fortified gate, the Porta Praetoria, in the old town. When Bavarian tribes migrated to the area in the 6th century, they occupied what remained of the Roman town and, apparently on the basis of its Latin name, called it Regensburg. Irish missionaries led by St. Boniface in 739 made the town a bishopric before heading down the Danube to convert the heathen in lands even more far-flung. Charlemagne, first of the Holy Roman Emperors, arrived at the end of the 8th century,

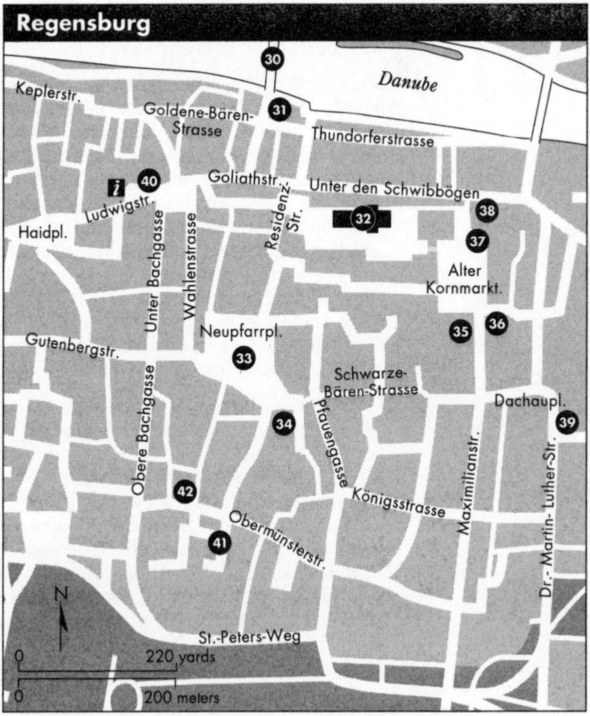

incorporating Regensburg into his burgeoning lands. And so, in one form or another, prospering all the while and growing into a glorious medieval and, later, Renaissance city, Regensburg remained until Napoléon turned up.

Any serious tour of Regensburg—not for nothing is it known as "the city of churches"—involves visiting an unusually large number of places of worship. If your spirits wilt at the thought of inspecting them all, you should see at least the Dom (cathedral) and then go on to the remaining attractions.

30 Begin your tour at the **Steinerne Brücke** (Stone Bridge). It leads south over the Danube to the almost-too-good-to-be-true
31 **Brückturm** (Bridge Tower): all tiny windows, weathered tiles, and pink plaster. (The brooding building with a massive roof to the left of the tower is an old salt warehouse.) The bridge is a central part of Regensburg history. Built in 1141, it was rightfully considered a miraculous piece of engineering at the time—and, as the only crossing point over the Danube for miles, effectively cemented Regensburg's control of trade in the region.

32 From the bridge, look up at the commanding towers of the **Dom St. Peter.** The cathedral, modeled on the airy, vertical lines of French Gothic architecture, is something of a rarity this far south in Germany. It wouldn't look out of place in Köln or Bonn. Begun in the 13th century, it stands on the site of a much earlier Carolingian church. Construction dragged on for almost 600 years, and it was finally finished when Ludwig I of Bavaria, then the ruler of Regensburg, had the towers built. (These

were replaced in the mid-'50s after their original soft limestone was found to be badly eroded.)

Walk under the Bridge Tower to Domplatz, the cathedral square. Before heading into the building, admire its intricate and frothy facade, embellished with delicate and skillful carving. A remarkable feature of the cathedral is its size, able to accommodate 7,000 people, three times the population of Regensburg when construction began. Standouts of the austere interior are the glowing 14th-century stained glass in the choir and the exquisitely detailed statues of the Archangel Gabriel and the Virgin in the crossing (the meeting point of nave and choir). The **Domschatzmuseum** (Cathedral Museum) contains more valuable treasures. The entrance is in the nave. *Admission: DM 2.50. Open Apr.–Oct., Tues.–Sat. 10–5, Sun. 11:30–5; Dec.–Mar., Fri. and Sat. 10–4, Sun. 11:30–4; closed Nov.*

Complete your tour of the cathedral with a visit to the **cloisters,** reached via the garden. These contain a small octagonal chapel, the **Allerheiligenkappelle** (All Saints' Chapel), a typically solid Romanesque building, all sturdy grace and massive walls. You can barely make out the faded remains of stylized 11th-century frescoes on its ancient walls. The equally ancient shell of St. Stephan's church, the **Alter Dom** (Old Cathedral), can also be visited. *Admission: DM 2.50. The cloisters, chapel, and Alter Dom can be seen only on guided tours: mid-May–Oct., daily at 10, 11, and 2; Oct.–Mar., daily at 11 and noon; Apr.–mid-May, daily at 11 and 2.*

To the south of the cathedral are the Neupfarrkirche and the church of St. Kassian. To the east lie the Niedermünster
33 church, the Karmelitenkirche, and the Alte Kappelle. The **Neupfarrkirche** (Neupfarrpl.), built between 1519 and 1540, is the only Protestant church in Regensburg, indeed one of a very few in Franconia. It's an imposing building, still substantially less ornate than any other in the city. Some may find its restraint welcome after the exuberance of so many of the other places of
34 worship. **St. Kassian** is a much older building, the oldest church in the city, in fact, founded in the 8th century. Don't be fooled by its dour exterior; inside, the church has been endowed with delicate Rococo decoration.

From St. Kassian, turn right onto the pedestrians-only Schawarze-Bären-Strasse, one of the best shopping streets in the
35 city. Turn left at the end. This brings you to the **Alte Kappelle,** the Old Chapel. This, too, is a Carolingian structure, put up in the 9th century. As at St. Kassian, the doughty exterior gives little hint of the joyous Rococo treasures within, an extravagant concoction of sinuous gilt stucco, rich marble, and giddy frescoes, the whole illuminated by light pouring in from the upper windows.

36 The adjoining **Karmelitenkirche** is Baroque from crypt to cupola. Finally, head north through the Alter Kornmarkt square to
37 the former parish church, the **Niedermünster,** another ancient structure (construction started in 1150) with a Baroque interior. Here in 1982 workmen discovered a Roman altar, dating from between AD 180 and 190, dedicated to the Emperor Commodus; a little stone plinth indicates that the altar was used for incense offerings. The site is open to the public.

38 A substantial Roman relic is located just round the corner from the church (turn right as you leave it). This is the **Porta Praetoria,** one of the original city gates, a rough-hewn and blocky structure. Look through the grille on its eastern side to see a section of the original Roman street, located about 10 feet below today's street.

Time Out For a taste of old Regensburg, make for the **Historische Wurstküche** (literally, "sausage kitchen"); it's located just by the Stone Bridge. It's the oldest and most authentic sausage restaurant in Regensburg. This is the place to try *Schweinebratwurste über Buchenholzohle gebraten,* finger-size pork sausages grilled over beech-wood charcoal; they are easier to eat than to pronounce. Sit on the terrace for the view over the Danube while enjoying these tidbits. Prices are low. *Thundorferstr. 3. Closed Sat.*

39 From the Porta Praetoria, you can either backtrack through Kornmarkt to the **Museum der Stadt Regensburg** or continue along Goldene-Bären-Strasse to the Fischmarkt and Altes Rathaus (Old Town Hall). For many, the museum is one of the highlights of a visit to the city, both for its unusual and beautiful setting—a former Gothic monastery—and for its wide-ranging collections, from Roman artifacts to Renaissance tapestries, all helping to tell the story of Regensburg. The most significant exhibits are the paintings by Albrecht Altdorfer (1480–1538), a native of Regensburg and, along with Cranach, Grünewald, and Dürer, one of the leading painters of the German Renaissance. His work has the same sense of slight distortion—of heightened reality—you find in that of his contemporaries, in which the lessons of Italian painting are used to produce an emotional rather than a rational effect. What's really significant about Altdorfer is his interest in landscape not merely as the background of a painting but as its subject. Figures in many of his works are simply incidentals. What's even more intriguing is that Altdorfer's obviously emotional response to landscape would not have seemed out of place in the 19th century. Far from seeing the world around him as essentially hostile, or at least alien, like the Romantics of the 19th century he saw it as something intrinsically beautiful, to be admired for its own sake, whether wild or domestic. *Dachaupl. 2–4. Admission: DM 2.50 adults, DM 1 children. Open Tues.–Sat. 10–4, Sun. and holidays 10–1.*

40 The **Altes Rathaus,** a picture-book complex of medieval buildings with half-timbering, windows large and small, and flowers in tubs, is among the best-preserved of its kind in the country, as well as one of the most historically important. It was here, in the imposing Gothic **Reichsaal** (Imperial Hall), that the "everlasting Imperial Diet" met from 1663 to 1805. This could be considered a forerunner of the German parliament, where representatives from every part of the Holy Roman Empire—plus the emperor and the prince-electors—assembled to discuss and determine the affairs of the far-reaching German lands. The hall is sumptuously appointed with tapestries, flags, and heraldic designs. Note especially the wood ceiling, built in 1408. If you have kids in tow, they'll want to see the adjoining torture chamber, the **Fragstatt,** and execution room, the **Armesünderstübchen.** Medieval notions of justice can be gauged by the fact that any prisoner who withstood three days of "ques-

tioning" here without confessing was released. *Rathauspl. Admission: DM 3 adults, DM 1.50 children. Open for guided tours only, Apr.–Oct., Mon.–Sat. at 9:30, 10, 10:30, 11, noon, 1:30, 2:15, 2:30, and 4, Sun. at 10, 11, and noon.*

41 There's one more major sight in the downtown area, the **Schloss** Thurn-und-Taxis. To reach it from the Rathaus, head down Bachgasse for 500 yards. Members of the Thurn-und-Taxis family still live in this enormous structure, originally the Benedictine monastery of St. Emmeram. The Thurn-und-Taxis were not only the leading family of Regensburg from around 1600 onward but one of the most influential in Germany; their fortune came from running the German postal system, a monopoly they enjoyed until 1867. The former abbey cloisters are probably the architectural treasure of the palace itself, with their elegant and attenuated late-Gothic carving. As for the rest of the building, much of which was extensively rebuilt at the end of the 19th century, opinions remain divided. Some consider it the most vulgar and ponderously overdecorated specimen of its kind in Germany. Others admire its Victorian bombast and confidence. You can also visit the **Marstallmuseum** (Transport Museum) in the palace if you have a weakness for 18th- and 19th-century carriages and sleighs. *Admission to palace and cloisters: DM 2.50. Open for guided tours only, Mon.–Fri. at 2:15 and 3:30, Sun. and holidays at 10:15 and 11:30. Admission to Marstallmuseum: DM 3.50. Open for guided tours only, Mon.–Fri. at 2, 2:40, and 3:15, Sun. at 10, 10:40, and 11:15.*

42 Next to the palace there's one more church to be visited, **St. Emmeramus.** It's the work of the Asam brothers and is decorated in their customary and full-blown late-Baroque manner.

Numbers in the margin correspond with points of interest on the Franconia map.

One excursion from Regensburg you won't want to miss if you have an interest in the wilder expressions of 19th-century German nationalism is by Danube riverboat (*see* Guided Tours,
43 above) to the incongruous Greek-style temple of **Walhalla,** 11 kilometers (7 miles) east of the city. To get to the temple from the river, you'll have to climb 358 marble steps; this is not a tour to take if you're not in good shape. Walhalla—a name resonant with Nordic mythology—was where the god Odin received the souls of dead heroes. And this monumental temple on a commanding site high above the Danube was erected to honor German heroes through the ages, in the prevailing Neoclassical style of the 19th century. Walhalla, built in 1840 for Ludwig I, turns out to be a copy of the Parthenon in Athens. Even if you consider the building more a monument to kitsch than a tribute to the great men of Germany, you will at least be able to muse on the fact that it is a supremely well-built structure, its great, smooth-fitting stones and expanses of costly marble evidence of both the financial resources and the craftsmanship that were Ludwig's to command.

What to See and Do with Children

The number-one attraction for children is the **Spielzeug Museum** (Toy Museum) in Nürnberg (*see* above). Nürnberg also has a **zoo;** children love its dolphinarium. *Am Tiergarten 30, tel.*

0911/571–346. Admission: DM 6 adults, DM 3 children. Open daily 9–sunset.

If you're in Franconia during the weeks prior to Christmas, by all means consider taking your children to Nürnberg's **Christkindlmarkt,** the most lavish and spectacular Christmas market in Germany. The highlight is the December 10 candle procession.

In Regensburg, visit the **Figurentheater,** or Puppet Theater (Dr.-Johann-Maier-Str. 3). There are performances May through September, Saturday and Sunday at 3. And the torture chamber at the **Altes Rathaus** can be a great place for kids to unlock their imaginations.

Children may not be too struck by the Abbey Church at Weltenburg or Ludwig I's grandiose Walhalla, but they'll appreciate the **boat rides** to them on the Danube *(see* Guided Tours, above). For trips on the Main River between Aschaffenburg and Würzburg, call 0931/91553.

Coburg has little appeal for most children (unless you think they'll appreciate stern lessons on Prince Albert's grim childhood), but the **Naturwisstschaftlichen** (Natural History Museum) can provide a diverting hour or two *(see* above).

Finally, all children can appreciate the sense of medieval and Renaissance life in the narrow, atmospheric streets of Nürnberg and Regensburg. Let the past come alive for them.

Off the Beaten Track

The area between Aschaffenburg and Würzburg is wine country. Though many of the local wineries offer tours, few beat the one at Miltenburg's **St. Killian Kellerei** offered by wine master Bernard Lorenz. Call two days in advance to be sure of getting his services (tel. 09371/2120). In addition to giving you the full story of how the wines are made, he'll take you to the wine cellars set in the cliffs along the river, time permitting.

Though the whole of Franconia offers many delightful small medieval towns, few tourists visit **Kronach,** east of Coburg. It was here that Renaissance master painter Lucas Cranach was born at the end of the 15th century; you can visit his house at Marktplatz 1. A cluster of half-timbered buildings and a fine Renaissance town hall complete the appeal of this flower-strewn square. Outside the town, see the **Rosenberg fortress.** *Admission: DM 3 adults, DM 1.50 children. Open Apr.–Dec., daily 10–5.*

If you fancy a hike to a Disney-style castle, visit **Altenburg,** 2 miles outside Bamberg (or take the number 10 bus). It's a "medieval" castle built on the site of a much older castle in the 19th century, during the full flood of Romantic enthusiasm for the days of chivalry and courtly love. *Admission free. Open Apr.–Oct., daily 9–5.*

For a change of pace after Franconia's castles, palaces, and churches, take a look at the **Teufelhöhle** (Devil's Cave) at Pottenstein, midway between Bayreuth and Nürnberg. The skeleton of a bear found in the cave guards the entrance. (Tours Apr.–Oct., daily 8–6). There's another cave 3 miles outside

Kelheim, near Regensburg. This is the **Schulerloch** (Schoolboy's Cave). It was inhabited by Neanderthal man and a series of Ice Age creatures. (Tours Easter–Oct.)

If all this sightseeing has worn you out, spend time at the thermal baths at **Rodach,** just a mile from the East German border in the north of Franconia. *Admission: DM 8. Open Mon. and Fri.–Sun. 9–7, Tues.–Thurs. 9–9. Children under 10 must have a doctor's certificate.*

Shopping

Specialties in **Coburg** include some delicious foods (not all of which you'll be permitted to bring home with you; check to see that you're not infringing customs regulations). For bratwurst, smoked ham, *Schmätzchen* (gingerbread), and *Elizenkuchen* (almond cake), try **Grossman's** (Ketchinggasse 20–24). For other traditional German goods, take a look at **Franz Denk's** shop (Kirchhof 4); his stoneware is expensive but exceptional. Around the corner is **Blumen Körble** (Steingasse 5). It has a wide range of wreaths and bouquets made from dried flowers. Off the market square, you'll find **Kaufmann's** (Judengasse). Run by a husband-and-wife team, it has fine hand-blown glass and homemade jewelry.

Lichtenfels, southeast of Coburg, is the place for baskets; there's even a state-run basket-weaving school here. The outlet where you can find German perfection in baskets of all shapes and sizes is **Es Körbla** (Stadtknechtgasse), just off the market square.

If you've enjoyed a visit to **Kulmbach's** Plassenburg museum, the world's largest collection of tin figures, visit **Wanderer und Ranning** (Obere Stadt 34) and buy some to take home. The shop boasts more than 1,000 tin figures in all shapes and sizes. Traditional *Trachtenschmuck* silver jewelry is sold in three shops in town: **Brückner** and **Juvelier Hubschmann** (both on Langgasse) and **Giorgio Canola** (Kressinsteinerstr. 11), which also has a selection of semiprecious stones.

Bayreuth's main shopping streets are Maximilianstrasse and Richard-Wagner-Strasse, both with department stores and sophisticated boutiques. The Hofgarten Passage, an arcade off Richard-Wagner-Strasse, has several fine shops, including **Piccola Tazza,** which sells puppets, and **Laurenstein,** with chocolates from Germany, Belgium, and Switzerland. **C. V. Brocke** (Operastr. 18) has painted-glass pictures and pewter figurines. **Döring's** (corner of Kammererstr. and Kirchgasse) sells stoneware and figurines.

Bamberg's main shopping area runs along Hauptwachstrasse. Across from the tourist information center is **Pappenberg's,** a shop selling communion, wedding, and baptism candles, all of which can be engraved. It also features beeswax candles, pewter, and wood carvings. An excellent place to shop for pottery is **Der Topferladen** (Untere Brücke 1), near the Altes Rathaus. The shop sells decorative plates, mugs, and bowls from more than 70 potters. If you want a small gift, around the corner is **Renate's Allereli** (Untere Brücke 7). It has stuffed animals, porcelain, nutcrackers, and linen tablecloths. **Zensinger's** (Katzenberg 4) has unusual decorative glass and a large assortment of polished stone necklaces and crystals. **Pierron Goldsmith**

(Hauptwachstr. 6) has polished-stone necklaces, garnets, and the ornate silver jewelry worn with traditional costumes. There's a small **flea market** on Saturdays on the Untere Brücke.

Across from the main train station in **Nürnberg** is the famous **Handwerkerhof** (Handicraft Court). It has many shops where engravers, glassblowers, silversmiths, goldsmiths, and other craftsmen make their wares. You can watch them work and buy examples of their art. (The market is closed Christmas–March 20). The historic area has numerous quality shops, especially on Königstrasse and Karolinenstrasse. Children will love the **Spielwaren Virnich** toy store (corner of Königstr. and Luitpoldstr.) For a wide range of souvenirs, try **Elsässer** (Königstr.). If you don't find what you're looking for there, try **Ostermayr** (Königstr. 33–37), or turn down Karolinenstrasse, where there are three more large stores selling souvenirs. Department stores and bakeries sell Nürnberg's famous *Lebkuchen* (gingerbread cookies). During the month before Christmas, you can shop at the **Christkindlmarkt** for tree decorations, toys, polished stones, socks, mittens, spices, and much more.

Regensburg is famous for its crafts. **Gewürz-Eckerl** (Unter d. Schwibbögen) sells attractive handmade puppets, glass ornaments, and fine jewelry. **Wiedamann Zinn und Keramik** (Brückstr. 4), offers a wide selection of pewter and pottery. If you fancy yourself in a dirndl or sporting a pair of lederhosen, try **Emess Moden** (Wahlenstr. 12).

Sports and Fitness

Bicycling Bikes can be rented at train stations for DM 10 per day; half that if you have a valid rail ticket. Local tourist offices can suggest other places to rent bikes. *See* Getting Around, above, for further information on biking in Franconia.

Fishing Various areas along the Main River have good fishing. The Miltenburg tourist office offers a seven-day fisherman's vacation, with reduced prices for board and lodging; call 09371/67272 for details. The fishing around Coburg is good, with up to 13 different kinds of fish to catch. Contact the **Angelfachgeschäft** (Schemannstr. 11, tel. 09561/60494), which can also give information on fishing in Lake Wüstenahorn, where a permit for a day's fishing is available for DM 11. Note that you'll need a license to fish anywhere in Germany. Contact any tourist office for one; the cost is DM 10 for one year.

Golf Coburg has a nine-hole course (tel. 09561/1277) across from Schloss Tambach on B-303. There's an 18-hole course at Bayreuth-Thurnau (tel. 09228/319).

Hang Gliding and Gliding Hang-gliding enthusiasts can take part in a 14-day training course at Stadtsteinach in the Frankenwald. Contact the tourist office (Badstr. 5, 8652 Stadtsteinach, tel. 09225/774). The air currents of the Rhön and Spessart regions are ideal for gliding, and you can take part in round-trip flights by contacting the tourist offices at Aschaffenburg and Miltenburg *(see* Important Addresses and Numbers, above). Alternatively, write the Spessart regional tourist office (Promenadenweg 11, 8776 Heigenbrücken).

Hiking The vast stretches of forest and numerous nature parks in much of north Franconia make this an ideal destination for hiking vacations, a fact that the Germans have not been slow to exploit. There are more than 25,000 miles of hiking trails, the greatest concentration in the Altmühltal Nature Park—Germany's largest—and in the Frankenwald. There are also marked trails in the Fichtelgebirge mountains, in Swiss Franconia, and in and around Coburg, including the romantic valleys of the Upper Main and Rodach, bordering the foothills of the vast Thüringer Forest of East Germany.

Dining and Lodging

Dining

Franconia offers a wide range of dining experiences, though with a preponderance of *Gasthaüser*, inns offering simple but good local specialties. Most offer inexpensive lunch menus. Traditional dishes you'll want to try include sauerbraten (marinated slices of beef), *Schweinshaxe* (pig's knuckle), and the ever-present *Knödel* (dumplings). A wide selection of local beers is always available—try Kulmbacher and, especially in Bamberg, smoky Rauchbier. In the Main Valley towns, you should try the delightfully dry wines produced there; they are served in the familiar bulbous green bottles known as *Bocksbeutel*.

Highly recommended restaurants in each price category are indicated by a star ★.

Category	Cost*
Very Expensive	over DM 90
Expensive	DM 55–90
Moderate	DM 35–55
Inexpensive	under DM 35

**per person for a three-course meal, including sales tax and excluding drinks and service*

Lodging

Make reservations well in advance for hotels in all the larger towns and cities if you plan to visit anytime between June and September. If you're visiting Bayreuth during the annual Wagner festival in July, consider making reservations up to a year in advance. And remember, too, that prices can be double the normal rates during the festival. Standards of comfort and cleanliness are high throughout the region, whether you stay in a simple pension or a modern, international chain hotel.

Highly recommended hotels in each price category are indicated by a star ★.

Category	Cost*
Very Expensive	over DM 180
Expensive	DM 120–DM 180

Moderate	DM 80–DM 120
Inexpensive	under DM 80

**All prices are for two people in a double room.*

Aschaffenburg
Dining and Lodging
★ **Romantik Hotel Post.** This is the number-one choice in town for both dining and lodging. Despite extensive wartime damage, the restored Post exudes class and that inimitable German coziness. All rooms are individually furnished. Eating here can be an experience not just for the excellent local specialties but because there's an original 19th-century mail coach in the rustic-looking restaurant. *Goldbachstr. 19–21, tel. 06021/21333. 71 rooms with bath. Facilities: sauna, indoor pool, restaurant, parking. AE, DC, MC, V. Expensive.*

Aschaffenburger Hof. This modern hotel offers high standards of comfort and service. Try for one of the rooms facing the courtyard. The restaurant provides better-than-average local specialties. *Weissenburgerstr. 20–22, tel. 06021/21441. 65 rooms with bath. Facilities: restaurant, parking. AE, DC, MC, V. Moderate.*

Zum Wilden Mann. The ancient exterior of this place promises rather more than the functional interior delivers; there's little feeling that you're in a 16th-century building. Nonetheless, standards are good, and service is polished. The restaurant serves excellent trout from the Main. *Doherstr. 51, tel. 06021/21555. 50 rooms with bath. Facilities: sauna, restaurant, parking. AE, DC, MC, V. Closed Dec. 23–Jan. 7. Moderate.*

Bamberg
Dining
★ **Bottingerhaus.** Dine on classy nouvelle specialties in the upscale Baroque surroundings of the most sophisticated restaurant in Bamberg, or pay a visit to the simpler wine cellar in the bowels of the building. In summer, try for a table on the terrace overlooking the garden. *Judengasse 14, tel. 0951/54074. Reservations advised. Jacket and tie required (informal dress in wine cellar). AE, DC, MC, V. Expensive (Moderate in wine cellar).*

Michels Küche. Local specialties and delicate nouvelle cuisine are offered in this appealingly old-fashioned former brewery. Try the venison in season. *Markusstr. 13, tel. 0951/26199. Reservations advised. Dress: informal. AE, DC. Closed Sun. and Mon. Moderate–Expensive.*

Gasthof Weierich. Located alongside the walls of the towering cathedral, the Weierich boasts three charmingly decorated restaurants, each offering game (in season), fish, and other Franconian specialties. *Lugbank 5, tel. 0951/54004. Reservations advised. Dress: informal. No credit cards. Moderate.*

Würzburger Weinstuben. This should be your choice for unmistakably German, half-timbered old-world atmosphere and good-value local specialties. A wide range of wines are available, and there's a garden for romantic summer dining. *Zilnkenwörth 6, tel. 0951/22667. Reservations advised. Dress: informal. AE, DC, MC, V. Closed late Aug.–mid-Sept., Tues. for dinner, and Wed. Moderate.*

Lodging
Barock Hotel am Dom. Standing close by the cathedral in the heart of the old town, this hotel offers a stylish combination of old-world elegance and discreet modern luxury. No restaurant. *Luitpoldstr. 37, tel. 0951/24112. 41 rooms with bath. AE, DC, MC, V. Expensive.*

★ **Romantik Hotel Weinhaus Messerschmitt.** Built in 1422 and owned and run by the same family since 1832, this will be the choice of anyone who values small, one-of-a-kind hotels. The 18th-century exterior is opulent; the dark paneled interior is tasteful and soothing. The restaurant is exceptional. For a culinary adventure, try the eels in sage. *Langestr. 41, tel. 0951/27066. 12 rooms with bath. Facilities: restaurant. AE, DC, MC, V. Closed Jan. 11–24. Expensive.*

Altenburgblick. You'll stay in this modern hotel chiefly for the view of the castle (all rooms have balconies). While the decor is insignificant, the levels of service are high. There's a beer garden for summer evenings, complete with stately chestnut trees. The cellar beer restaurant is smokily atmospheric. *Panzerleite 59, tel. 0951/54023. 45 rooms, most with bath. No credit cards. Moderate.*

Café und Gasthaus Graupner. This hotel offers simple accommodations at low prices in the heart of the old town. There's no restaurant; the café provides hearty breakfasts. A modern, 10-room annex without noticeable charm houses overflow guests. *Langestr. 51, tel. 0951/26056. 28 rooms, most with bath. AE, MC. Inexpensive.*

Bayreuth
Dining
★

Schloss Hotel Thiergarten. Located 4 miles from Bayreuth in the Thiergarten suburb, this small, onetime hunting lodge, now beautifully converted into a hotel (*see* Lodging, below) and two stunning restaurants, provides one of the most elegant dining experiences in Franconia. The intimate Kamlin (the name means fireplace, a reference to the lavishly ornate one here) and the Venezianischer Salon, dominated by a glittering 300-year-old Venetian chandelier, both offer sophisticated and memorable regional and nouvelle specialties. *Tel. 09209/1314. Reservations required. Jacket and tie required. AE, DC, MC, V. Closed Feb. 13–Mar. 12, Sun. for dinner, and Mon. Very Expensive.*

Bayerischer Hof. You can eat in the elegantly classical surroundings of the hotel's French restaurant or in the informal and rustic Hans Sachs Stube, a traditional-style inn (actually no more than a few years old—and with very unmedieval air-conditioning—but convincing enough nonetheless). *Bahnhofstr. 14, tel. 0921/22081. Reservations advised. Jacket and tie required (informal dress in Hans Sachs Stube). AE, DC, MC, V. Closed Sun. Expensive.*

Weihenstephan. Long wood tables, fulsome regional specialties, and beer straight from the barrel (from the oldest brewery in Germany) make this a perennial favorite with tourists and locals. In summer, the flower-strewn and crowded terrace is the place to be. *Bahnhofstr. 5, tel. 0921/82288. Reservations advised. Dress: informal. No credit cards. Moderate.*

Wolffenzacher. The rowdy, wood-paneled atmosphere and the good-value local specialties—this is a great place to try Schweinshaxe—make this traditional haunt a good low-cost bet. The city-center location is a plus. *Badstr. 1, tel. 0921/64522. Reservations advised. Dress: informal. MC. Inexpensive.*

Lodging
★

Schloss Thiergarten. If you plan to stay in this near-regal little hotel, be sure to make reservations well in advance. Some may find the furnishings a trifle faded, but there's no denying the class of this baronial spot. Staying here is like staying with your favorite elderly millionaire aunt. (*See* Dining, above, for details of the two restaurants.) *Tel. 09209/1314. 8 rooms with bath. Facilities: sauna, terrace, 2 restaurants. AE, DC, MC, V. Closed Feb. 13–Mar. 12. Very Expensive.*

★ **Goldener Anker.** No question about it: If you've booked far enough in advance, this is *the* place to stay in Bayreuth if you're here for the Wagner festival. The hotel is located right by the Festspielhaus and has been entertaining composers, singers, conductors, and players for more than 100 years, as the signed photographs in the lobby and the signatures in the guest book make clear. Rooms are small but individually decorated; many have antique pieces. The restaurant is justly popular. *Opernstr. 6, tel. 0921/65500. 28 rooms with bath. Facilities: parking, restaurant. No credit cards. Closed Dec. 20–Jan. 10. Expensive.*

Am Hofgarten. This delightful small establishment is more like a private home than a hotel. All rooms are individually decorated and have many personal touches. There's an appealingly rustic bar and a small garden out back (but no restaurant). Composer Franz Liszt lived in the house opposite. *Lisztstr. 6, tel. 0921/69006. 18 rooms, 9 with bath. Facilities: bar. AE, DC, MC. Closed mid-Dec.–mid-Jan. Moderate.*

Gasthof Vogel. This is probably the best low-cost bet in town. It's centrally located (near the Stadthalle) and offers basic, well-run comfort. There's a noisy beer restaurant and a tree-shaded courtyard. *Friedrichstr. 13, tel. 0921/68268. 8 rooms, with bath. Facilities: beer restaurant. No credit cards. Inexpensive.*

Coburg
Dining

★ **Coburger-Tor Restaurant Schaller.** Located just south of the city center, this hotel-restaurant provides surprisingly upscale dining in a softly lit and distinctly well-upholstered ambience. The food is sophisticated nouvelle, especially good value if you order one of the fixed-price menus. The desserts are luscious. *Ketschendorfer-Str. 22, tel. 09561/25074. Reservations required. Jacket and tie required. No credit cards. Closed Fri. dinner and Sat. lunch. Expensive.*

Ratskeller. An entirely different experience is offered in the stone vaults this establishment, the sort of emphatically Teutonic place where local specialties always taste better. Try the sauerbraten, along with a large glass of frothy beer. *Markt 1, tel. 09561/92400. Reservations advised. Dress: informal. No credit cards. Moderate.*

★ **Goldenes Kreuz.** In business since 1477, this restaurant boasts all the rustic decor you'll ever want and large portions of Franconian food. Goose with dumplings provides an authentically hearty experience. Not for lovers of nouvelle cuisine. *Herrngasse 1, tel. 09561/90473. Reservations advised. Dress: informal. No credit cards. Inexpensive.*

Lodging

★ **Blankenburg.** Solid, reliable, and comfortable, this hotel, located north of the town center, provides probably the best accommodations in Coburg. The rustic restaurant offers local specialties. *Rosenauerstr. 30, tel. 09561/75055. 38 rooms with bath. Facilities: restaurant, parking. AE, DC, MC, V. Expensive.*

Goldene Traube. High levels of comfort are provided by this sturdy favorite, plus an excellent central location. Some of the cheaper rooms are plain, however. *Am Viktoriabrunnen 2, tel. 09561/9833. Facilities: sauna, restaurant, parking. AE, DC, MC, V. Moderate.*

Miltenberg
Dining and Lodging

★ **Zum Riesen.** You won't find many more atmospheric places to stay than this little half-timbered, family-run inn, in business since the 16th century—it's straight from the pages of the

Brothers Grimm. The considerable promise of the fairy-tale exterior is matched by the interior, though modern necessities have been thoughtfully and unobtrusively provided. The service has just that touch of informality that makes the difference between a good and a memorable hotel. The adjoining restaurant continues the old-world theme. *Hauptstr. 97, tel. 09371/3644. 14 rooms with bath. Facilities: restaurant, parking. DC. Closed Jan.–mid-Mar. Moderate.*

Nürnberg
Dining

★ **Goldenes Posthorn.** Though rebuilt after the war, the authentic heart of old Nürnberg still beats in this ancient restaurant by the cathedral. In their day, both Dürer and Hans Sachs ate here. The food is nouvelle Franconian; try the pigeon terrine or quail stuffed with walnuts and goose livers. The wine list is extensive. *An der Sebalduskirche, tel. 0911/225–153. Reservations required. Jacket and tie required. AE, DC, MC. Closed Sun. Very Expensive.*

★ **Essigbrätlein.** Some rank this as the top restaurant in the city, indeed one of the best in Germany. As the oldest restaurant in Nürnberg, built in 1550, it is unquestionably one of the most atmospheric, having been used originally as a meeting place for wine merchants. Today, its elegant period interior is *the* place to eat *Essigbrätlein* (roast loin of beef). Other dishes blend Franconian and nouvelle recipes. *Weinmarkt 3, tel. 0911/225–131. Reservations required. Jacket and tie required. AE, DC. Closed Mon. and three weeks in May. Expensive.*

Nassauer Keller. The exposed-beam-and-plaster decor complements the resolutely traditional cooking. Try the duck and the apple strudel. The restaurant has a memorable location in the cellar of a 12th-century tower by the church of St. Lorenz. *Karolinenstr. 2–4, tel. 0911/225–967. Reservations advised. Jacket and tie required. AE, DC, MC. Moderate.*

Bratwurst Haüsele. There are few better places to try Nürnberg's famous grilled sausages—roasted over an open fire and served on heavy pewter plates with horseradish and sauerkraut—than this dark, wood-paneled old inn. The mood is noisy and cheerful. *Rathauspl. 1, tel. 0911/227–625. Dress: informal. No credit cards. Inexpensive.*

★ **Helig-Geist-Spital.** Heavy wood furnishings and a choice of more than 100 wines makes this authentic and picturesque wine tavern a popular spot for visitors. It may be touristy, but it's the real thing for all that. *Spitalgasse 12, tel. 0911/221–761. Dress: informal. No credit cards. Inexpensive.*

Lodging

Carlton. This stylish old hotel, sturdy in a grande-dame way, is quietly efficient and offers thick-carpeted, old-fashioned luxury. The restaurant is plushly expensive and a pleasure in the summer, when you can sit out on the shaded terrace. It's located on a quiet side street close by the train station. *Eilugstr. 13, tel. 0911/200–333. 187 rooms with bath. Facilities: restaurant, bar, sauna. AE, DC, MC, V. Very Expensive.*

Maritim. If you value modern convenience over old-world charm, consider staying in this luxuriously modern hotel, opened in 1986. You won't find so much as a hint of the medieval glories of old Nürnberg here, but the service is impeccable, the spacious rooms are tastefully (if blandly) furnished, and the public areas are elegantly well-heeled. It's located just south of the historic area. *Frauentorgraben 11, tel. 0911/26630. 316 rooms with bath. Facilities: 2 restaurants, bar, sauna, indoor pool, solarium, parking. AE, DC, MC, V. Very Expensive.*

Deutscher Kaiser. The old-world mood of this distinctive, turn-of-the-century hotel will appeal to those who value charm over modern luxury. The rooms are simple in a fresh-faced way, with views of the jumbled roofs of the old town. *Königstr. 55, tel. 0911/203–341. 81 rooms with bath. Facilities: restaurant. AE, DC, MC, V. Moderate.*

Drei Raben. This is one of the best budget bets in Nürnberg. It's basic but more than adequate for a night or two, with the added benefit of a good location in the old town. The hotel is family-owned and -run. There's no restaurant. *Königstr. 63, tel. 0911/204–583. 31 rooms with bath. AE, DC, MC, V. Inexpensive.*

Regensburg

Dining

Ratskeller. Regensburg is short on upscale restaurants, so you may as well enjoy the typical offerings of this establishment. The decor is the usual hefty, Teutonic vault, complete with larger-than-life heraldic designs on the walls; the food is the usual hefty Teutonic fare. You can eat in the courtyard in the summer. *Rathauspl. 1, tel. 0941/51777. Reservations advised. Dress: informal. AE, DC, MC. Closed Sun. for dinner and Mon. Moderate.*

Reissbierbrauer. The atmosphere in this former church is pure Bavarian, down to the checked blue-and-white tablecloths. The menu features pork, sausages, and dumplings. *Am Schwanenpl., tel. 0941/55581. Reservations advised. Dress: informal. No credit cards. Moderate.*

★ **Historische Wurstküche.** This is one place no visitor will want to miss. It serves traditional sausages mostly, in a rowdy, fun-filled atmosphere by the Stone Bridge. *Lammgasse 1, tel. 0941/59098. No reservations. Dress: informal. No credit cards. Inexpensive.*

Lodging

★ **Parkhotel Maximilian.** This is the most elegant and sophisticated hotel in Nürnberg, a handsome 18th-century building in the old town with memorably exotic public areas. Bedrooms are less opulent, but all are intelligently and comfortably decorated. If you're feeling homesick, there's an American-style steakhouse. *Maximilianstr. 28, tel. 0941/51042. 53 rooms with bath. Facilities: 2 restaurants, café, parking. AE, DC, MC, V. Very Expensive.*

Bischofshof am Dom. Some rate this complex, formerly part of the bishops' palace, one of the most appealing and classy hotels in the city; others find it drab and gloomy, weighed down rather than buoyed up by its setting. There's no arguing over the merits of its location, however, close to the Porta Praetoria. Another plus is the dramatically decorated restaurant, its ceiling supported by a massive column. *Krauterermarkt 3, tel. 0941/59086. 67 rooms with bath. Facilities: restaurant, terrace. AE, DC, MC, V. Expensive.*

Kaiserhof am Dom. Stay here for the great view of the cathedral. The building itself oozes period charm, with exposed beams, stone walls, and rough plaster; however, some rooms are dull. Try to get one with a view, and you'll be happy. *Kramgasse 10, tel. 0941/54027. 31 rooms with bath. Facilities: restaurant. AE, MC. Moderate.*

The Arts

Opera Opera lovers cheerfully admit that there are few more intense operatic experiences than that offered by the annual **Wagner festival** in Bayreuth. The festival is held in July. If you want tickets, write to **Theaterkasse** (Luitpoldpl. 9, 8580 Bayreuth) no later than September the year before. Then hope for the best—the computer decides (though the more applications you make, the better your chances). If you get tickets, make hotel reservations at once: Rooms can be nearly impossible to find during the festival. Ticket prices are steep; DM 250 is not unusual. If you don't get tickets, you can console yourself with visits to the exquisite 18th-century **Margravine's Opera House;** performances are given most nights in July and August. Check with the tourist office for details. A wide repertoire of opera is also offered at the **Landestheater** in Coburg, October through mid-July. Call 09561/95021 for tickets.

Concerts Ansbach hosts a **Bach Week** in odd-numbered years in early August. Contact **Geschäftsstelle im Rathaus** (Postfach 1741, 8800 Ansbach, tel. 0981/3587) for tickets. Bamberg is a city of music. The **Bamberg Symphony Orchestra** gives regular concerts; those in the cathedral, normally given with the Bamberg Choir, can be memorable. Call 0951/25256 for tickets. Organ concerts are given in the cathedral at noon every Saturday, May through October. You can catch opera and operetta at the **Hoffmann Theater** (Schillerpl. 7, tel. 0951/87499), September through July. In June and July, open-air performances are also given at the **Alte Hofhalting.** Call 0951/25256 for tickets. Regensburg offers a range of musical experiences, though none so moving as a performance by the famous **Domspatzen** (Cathedral Sparrows). The best sung mass is Sunday at 9 AM. It can be a remarkable experience, and it's worth scheduling your visit to the city to hear the choir.

Theater The best theaters in Franconia are in Nürnberg and Regensburg. In Nürnberg, call 0911/22988 for tickets for all theaters. The leading theater in Regensburg is the **Stadttheater** (Bismarckpl. 7, tel. 0941/59156).

10 Germany's Other Rhineland

Introduction

The Rhine, castles, and vineyards—the combination immediately suggests the picture-postcard scenery of Germany's best-known stretch of the Rhine, between Bingen and Koblenz. But there's another part of the Rhineland where vineyards climb slopes crowned by ancient castles. This is the Rhineland Palatinate. It lacks the spectacular grandeur of the river above Bingen, the elegance of the resorts of Boppard and Koblenz, and the cachet of the wines of the Rheingau. But for that reason the crowds are smaller, the prices lower, and the pace slower. And there are attractions here you won't find in the more popular stretch of the river farther north, including the warmest climate in Germany. The south-facing folds of the Palatinate hills shelter communities where lemons, figs, and sweet chestnuts grow alongside vines. It's a region where few autobahns penetrate and where most other roads lead to truly off-the-beaten-track territory. One of these roads is Germany's first specially designated Weinstrasse (Wine Road), a winding, often narrow route with temptations—vineyards and farmsteads that beckon the traveler to sample the current vintage. If you're covering the route by car, take along a nondrinker as codriver, or split the driving between you. And take your time.

Where the Wine Road ends, three of Germany's oldest cities beckon: Speyer, Worms, and Mainz. They are among the Rhineland's great imperial centers, where emperors and princes met and where the three greatest Romanesque cathedrals in Europe stand. After covering the Wine Road, this chapter explores these cities. From the most northerly, Mainz, you are poised to explore the remainder of the Rhineland. (For full details, *see* Chapter 13.)

Essential Information

Important Addresses and Numbers

Tourist Information Information on the Wine Road can be obtained from the **Weinstrasse Zentrale fur Tourismus,** Postfach 2124, 6740 Landau; **Fremdenverkehrsverband,** Bezirksstelle Pfalz, Hindenburgstrasse 12, 6730 Neustadt an der Weinstrasse; and **Mittelhaardt-Deutsche Weinstrasse,** Weinstrasse 32, 6705 Deidesheim an der Weinstrasse. There are local tourist information offices in the following towns:

Bad Dürkheim. Verkehrsamt, Mannheimerstrasse 24, 6702 Bad Dürkheim, tel. 06322/793–275.
Deidesheim. Verkehrsamt im Rathaus, Marktplatz, 6705 Deidesheim, tel. 06326/1921.
Landau. Verkehrsamt, Marktstrasse 50, 6740 Landau, tel. 06341/13295.
Neustadt an der Weinstrasse. Verkehrsamt, Exterstrasse 4, 6730 Neustadt an der Weinstrasse, tel. 06321/855–329.
Mainz. Verkehrsverein Mainz, Bahnhofstrasse 15, 6500 Mainz, tel. 06131/23741.
Speyer. Verkehrsamt der Stadt Speyer, Maximilianstrasse 11, 6720 Speyer, tel. 06232/14395.
Worms. Verkehrsverein der Stadt Worms, Neumarkt 14, 6520 Worms, tel. 06241/25045.

Car Rental **Avis:** Mainzer Landstrasse 170, tel. 069/23010, **Frankfurt;** Wormser Landstrasse 22, tel. 06232/32068, **Speyer;** Alzeyer Strasse 44, tel. 06241/591–081, **Worms.**
Europcar: Mainzer Landstrasse 160, tel. 069/234–002, **Frankfurt.**
Hertz: Hanuer Landstrasse 106–108, tel. 069/449–090, **Frankfurt;** Bernsheimerstrasse 1, tel. 06241/43750, **Worms.**

Arriving and Departing by Plane

Frankfurt is the nearest major international airport for the whole of the Rhineland, with regular flights from the United States. Autobahn access to Mainz, the northernmost point of the itinerary, is fast and easy. Stuttgart Airport serves the southern half of the region. Take Autobahn 8 to Karlsruhe and then drive the 36 kilometers (22 miles) to the southern point of the wine route.

Getting Around

By Car Most roads in the region are narrow and winding, a far cry from the highways of much of the rest of Germany. Autobahn 6 runs northeast/southwest across much of the southern part of the region, from Saarbrücken on the French border to the Rhine, reaching it just above Mannheim. Halfway along, a spur—Autobahn 63—branches north to Mainz. Driving conditions are good everywhere, with all roads well surfaced.

By Train Mainz is the only major city in the region with regular Intercity services; there are hourly connections to and from major German cities. To reach the southern part of the region, travel through Karlsruhe and Landau. Railroad buses service those towns not on the rail network.

By Bus Buses crisscross the region, with most services running to and from Mainz. Post buses connect smaller towns and villages. For information, timetables, and reservations, contact **Deutsche Touring GmBH.,** Am Römerhof 17, 6000 Frankfurt/Main 90, tel. 069/79030.

Guided Tours

A number of the smaller towns and villages offer sightseeing tours in the summer, some including visits to neighboring vineyards. At Annweiler, for example, tours of the town are given Wednesdays, beginning at the Rathaus at 10 AM, where you are given a glass of wine. The tourist office also organizes tours to Trifels castle. Details of this and all other tours in the region are available from local tourist information offices. There are city tours of Speyer, Mainz, and Worms. Mainz also offers a walking tour of the old town Saturdays starting at 10 AM. For details of all Rhine River tours, contact **Köln-Düsseldorfer Deutsche Rheinschiffahrt,** Frankenwerft 15, 5000 Köln 1, tel. 0221/208–8288.

Exploring Germany's "Other" Rhineland

Highlights for First-time Visitors

The Romanesque Cathedrals of Speyer, Worms, and Mainz
Dörrenbach Village
Burg Trifels
Village of St. Martin
Gutenberg Museum, Mainz
Synagogue, Worms

Along the Wine Road

Numbers in the margin correspond with points of interest on the "Other" Rineland map.

Although the northern end of the Wine Road is a favored starting point for many visitors because of its proximity to Mainz and Frankfurt, the logical place to begin your tour is at its southern point, at the town where the Wine Road itself began,
1 **Schweigen-Rechtenbach** on the French border. It was in this little wine village, in July 1935, that a group of vintners hit on the idea of establishing a tourist route through the vineyards of the region. To get the road off to a suitable start they put up a massive stone arch, the **Deutsches Weintor** (German Wine Gate). There's an open gallery halfway up the arch that offers a fine view of the vineyards that crowd the countryside between the Vosges mountains, over the French border, and the Rhine, away to the east. Some of Schweigen's best wine comes from the vineyards on the French side of the border; you can walk across the frontier—it's only 200 yards from the arch—with no formalities and compare vintages. For a further investigation of the region's wines, follow the **Weinlehrpfad,** the "wine inspection path." It begins in Schweigen and ambles for about a mile through the vineyards of the nearby Sonnenberg. It was the first of scores of such walking routes that you'll find in wine-producing areas throughout Germany. The path is well marked and easy to follow.

Drive north on B-38 to Bad Bergzabern, 10 kilometers (6 miles) away. A mile before you reach the town, turn left to see the vil-
2 lage of **Dörrenbach.** It's an enchanting place, tucked snugly in a protective fold of the Palatinate hills. The Renaissance **Rathaus** (Town Hall) has a flower-hung facade, crisscrossed with so much timber there's hardly room for the tiny-paned windows.

Time Out The little spa town of Bad Bergzabern rivals any in Germany for harmonious Renaissance streets of half-timbered old houses. One of the most appealing—it has a distinctive painted bay window—houses the **Zum Engel** tavern. Its ancient interior makes an excellent layover for a cup of coffee, a beer, a glass of wine, and/or a bite to eat.

3 Drive north, following the signs to **Klingenmünster,** 8 kilometers (5 miles) away. The village has the ruins of a 7th-century Benedictine monastery, with a (still intact) Baroque chapel. If castles are your thing, you can walk from the monastery to the

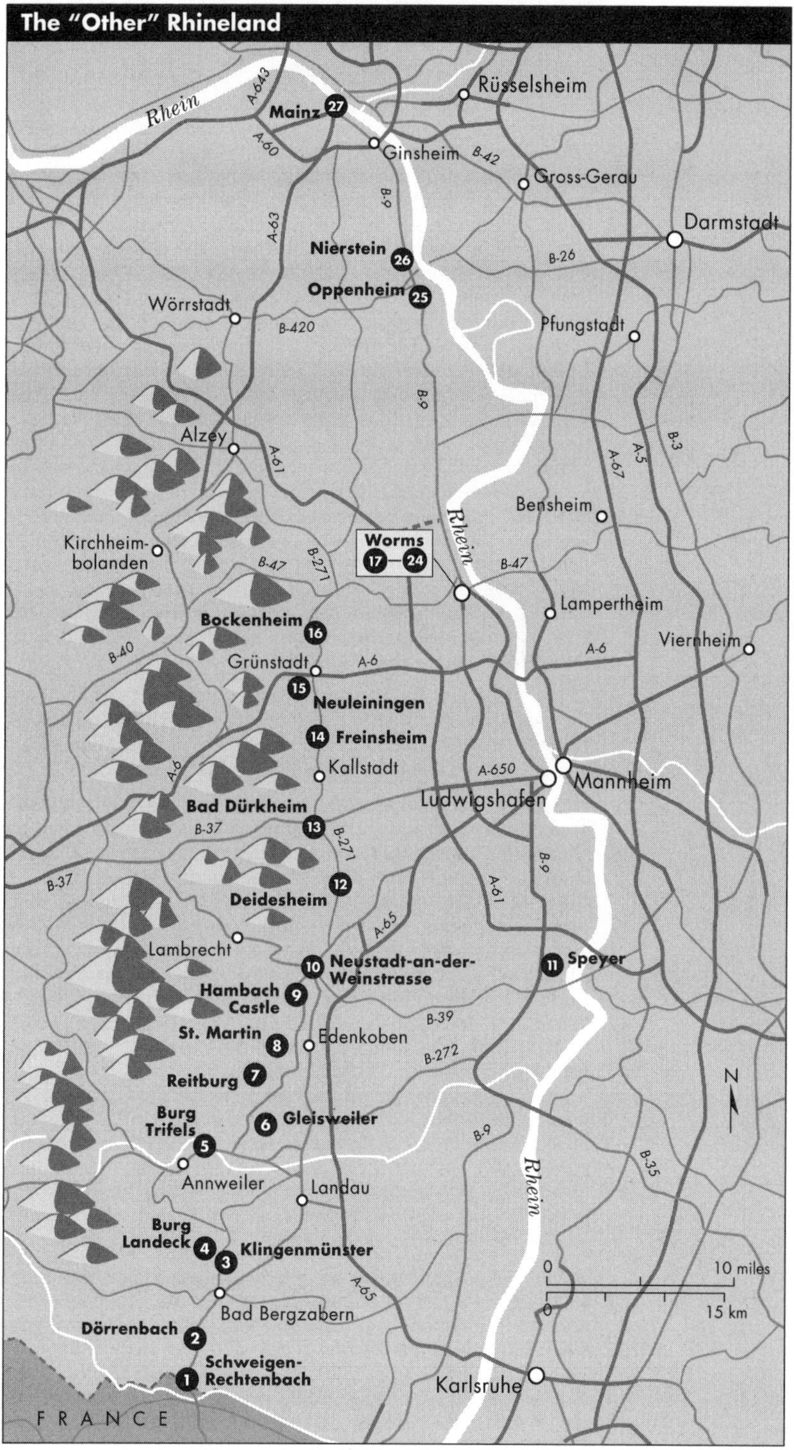
The "Other" Rhineland
Rhein
A-643
A-60
A-63
Mainz 27
Rüsselsheim
Ginsheim
B-42
Gross-Gerau
Darmstadt
B-9
Nierstein 26
Oppenheim 25
B-26
Wörrstadt
B-420
Pfungstadt
Alzey
A-61
A-67
A-5
B-3
Bensheim
Kirchheim-
bolanden
B-47
B-271
Worms
17—24
Rhein
Lampertheim
Bockenheim 16
B-40
Grünstadt
A-6
Viernheim
15 Neuleiningen
14 Freinsheim
Kallstadt
A-650
Mannheim
Ludwigshafen
Bad Dürkheim
13
B-37
12
Deidesheim
A-65
Lambrecht
10 Neustadt-an-der-
Weinstrasse
11 Speyer
Hambach
Castle 9
B-39
St. Martin 8
Edenkoben
B-272
Reitburg 7
Burg
Trifels 5
6 Gleisweiler
Annweiler
Landau
B-35
Burg
Landeck 4
3 Klingenmünster
0
10 miles
15 km
Bad Bergzabern
Dörrenbach 2
Schweigen-
Rechtenbach 1
Karlsruhe
FRANCE
N

4 ruins of **Burg Landeck.** The walk, through silent woods of chestnut trees, takes about half an hour. Your reward will be a magnificent view from the castle over the Rhine Valley and south as far as the Black Forest.

There's a more spectacular, and more famous, castle another 8 kilometers north, outside the village of Annweiler. This is
5 **Burg Trifels,** one of the most romantic buildings in the country, its drama only slightly spoiled by the fact that what you see today is a rather free reconstruction of the original Romanesque castle, rebuilt in 1937 (a period when a lot of Germans were keen on re-establishing what they saw as the glories of their "race"). The original castle was constructed in the mid-12th century by the Emperor Barbarossa, whose favorite castle it was said to have become. In 1193, English King Richard the Lion-heart, captured by Barbarossa on one of Richard's endless forays across Europe, was held for ransom here (the English treasury grudgingly paid the immense sum). Of more lasting significance was the fact that from 1126 to 1273 Burg Trifels housed the imperial crown jewels. That's what's said to have led to the legend that Burg Trifels was the site of the Holy Grail, the bowl used by Christ at the Last Supper. In the Middle Ages, the Holy Grail was the object of numerous knightly quests, the purpose of which was not so much to find the Grail as to prove one's steadfastness and Christian virtue by embarking on an impossible task. *Admission: DM 3 adults, DM 1.50 children. Open Apr.–Sept., Tues.–Sun. 9–1 and 2–6; Oct.–Mar., Tues.–Sun. 9–1 and 2–5.*

If you visit Burg Trifels, you'll pass the ruins of two neighboring castles as you head up the hill. These are the castles of **Scharfenberg** and **Anebos.** Their craggy, overgrown silhouettes add greatly to the romance of a visit to Burg Trifels.

Head back to the Wine Road and follow the signs to **Edenkoben.** Twelve kilometers (8 miles) brings you to the little town of
6 **Gleisweiler,** reputedly the warmest spot in Germany. A flourishing subtropical park supports the claim. Further proof of the mild climate hereabouts is supplied by the fig trees that grow in abundance on many south-facing walls. This is also about the only area in Germany where lemons are grown. The sun-drenched charms of the region attracted Bavaria's King Ludwig I in the middle of the 19th century. He called it "a garden of God" and compared its light to that of Italy. In the 1850s he built himself a summerhouse in the hills above the town; Edenkoben responded by putting up a statue of its royal guest in the main square. You can pay your respects to the Bavarian monarch by visiting his handsome Neoclassical villa. Today, it houses paintings by the German Impressionist Max Slevogot (1868–1932). The paintings have a certain dreamy charm, but many visitors will find the grandiose setting more diverting. *Villa Ludwigshohe. Admission: DM 3. Open Apr.–Sept., Tues.–Sun. 9–1 and 2–6; Oct.–Mar., Tues.–Sun. 9–1 and 2–5.*

On the opposite (north) side of the valley, facing the Villa
7 Ludwigshohe, are the ruins of **Rietburg castle.** The only chair lift in the Rhineland Palatinate will whisk you up to them if you feel like checking out the terrific view.

Time Out The other reason for visiting Rietburg castle is to have lunch on the terrace of the **café** here. Drink in the view as you eat.

Back on the Wine Road, a mile or two brings you to the village
8 of **St. Martin.** It's said to be the most beautiful in the area, a reputation it nurtures by encouraging the surrounding vineyards to encroach on its narrow streets. You'll find vines clinging everywhere, linking the ancient houses with curling green garlands. Visit the little 15th-century church to see the imposing Renaissance tomb of the Dalberg family. Their castle, now romantically ruined, stands guard over the village.

There's another castle hereabouts you can visit, especially if your blood is stirred by tales of German nationalism and the
9 overthrow of tyranny. It's **Hambach castle,** standing about a half mile outside the village of Hambach, itself about 5 miles north of St. Martin. It's not the castle, built in the 11th century and largely ruined in the 17th, that's the attraction. Rather, you'll visit to honor an event that happened here in May 1832. Fired by the revolutionary turmoil that was sweeping across Europe and groaning under the repressive yoke, as they saw it, of a distant and aristocratic government, 30,000 stalwart Germans assembled at the castle demanding democracy, the overthrow of the Bavarian ruling house of Wittelsbach, and a united Germany. The symbol of their heroic demands was a flag, striped red, black, and yellow, which they flew from the castle. The old order proved rather more robust than these proto-democrats had reckoned on; the crowd was rapidly dispersed with some loss of life. The new flag was banned. It was not until 1919 that the monarchy was ousted and a united Germany became fully democratic. Fittingly, the flag flown from Hambach nearly 90 years earlier was adopted as that of the new German nation. (It was a short-lived triumph: Hitler did away with both democracy and the flag when he came to power in 1932, and both were restored only in 1949, with the creation of the Federal Republic of Germany.) The castle remains a focus of the democratic aspirations of the Germans. Exhibits chart the progress of democracy in Germany. *Admission: DM 2 adults, DM 1 children. Open Mar.–Nov., daily 9–5.*

A mile or two north of Hambach, high rises announce the presence of the biggest town on the Wine Road and the
10 most important wine-producing center in the region, **Neustadt-an-der-Weinstrasse.** It's a bustling town, the narrow streets of its old center still following the medieval street plan. It's wine that makes Neustadt tick, and practically every shop seems linked with the wine trade. A remarkable 5,000 acres of vineyards lie within the official town limits. If you need to get your sightseeing fix, make for central Marktplatz to see the Gothic **Stiftskirche** (Collegiate Church). It's an austere Gothic building, constructed in the 14th century for the elector of the Rhineland Palatinate. Inside, a wall divides the church in two, a striking reminder of former religious strife. The church, indeed the whole region, became Protestant in the Reformation in the 16th century. At the beginning of the 18th century, the Catholic population of the town petitioned successfully to be allowed a share of the church. The choir (the area around the altar) was accordingly designated the Catholic half of the church, while the nave, the main body of the church, was reserved for the Protestants. To keep the squabbling communities apart, the wall was built inside the church. Is it an instance of religious tolerance or intolerance? And who got the better deal? As you wander round the church—be sure to look

at the intricate 15th-century choir stalls and the little figures, monkeys, and vine leaves carved into the capitals of the nave columns—you can ponder these matters.

Time Out Duck into the ancient confines of the **Herberge aus der Zunftzeit** (Mittelgasse), a 14th-century tavern offering excellent local wines and specialties. Try a slice of *Zwiebelkuchen* (onion tart) and a glass of Kirchberg wine.

11 If you have time, make the side trip to **Speyer,** 29 kilometers (18 miles) east of Neustadt on the west bank of the Rhine. Speyer was one of the great cities of the Holy Roman Empire, founded probably in Celtic times, taken over by the Romans, and expanded in the 11th century by the Ottonian Holy Roman Emperors. Between 1294 and 1570, no fewer than 50 full diets (meetings of the rulers of the Holy Roman Empire) were convened here. The focus of your visit will be the imperial cathedral, the **Kaiserdom,** one of the largest medieval churches in Europe, certainly the finest Romanesque cathedral in Europe, and a building that more than any other in Germany conveys the pomp and majesty of the early Holy Roman Emperors. It was built in only 30 years, between 1030 and 1060, by the emperors Konrad II, Heinrich III, and Heinrich IV. A four-year restoration program in the 1950s returned the building to almost exactly its condition when first completed. If you have any interest in the achievements of the early Middle Ages, this is not a building to miss. Speyer cathedral, thanks chiefly to the fact that later ages never saw fit to rebuild it, and partly to the intelligent restorations of the '50s, embodies all that is best in Romanesque architecture.

There's an understandable tendency to dismiss most Romanesque architecture as little more than a cruder version of Gothic, the style that followed it and that many consider the supreme architectural achievement of the Middle Ages. Where the Gothic is seen as delicate, soaring, and noble, the Romanesque by contrast seems lumpy, earthbound, and crude, more fortresslike than divine. It's true that even the most successful Romanesque buildings are ponderously massive, but they possess a severe confidence and potency that can be overwhelming. What's more, look carefully at the decorative details and you'll see vivid and often delicate craftsmanship.

See as much of the building from the outside as you can before you venture inside. You can walk most of the way around it, and there's a fine view from the east end from the park by the Rhine. If you've seen Köln cathedral, the finest Gothic cathedral in Germany, you'll be struck at once by how much more massive Speyer cathedral is in comparison. What few windows there are are small, as if crushed by the surrounding masonry. Notice, too, their round tops, a key characteristic of the style. The position of the space-rocket-like towers, four in all (two at either end), and the immense, smoothly sloping dome at the east end give the building a distinctive, animated profile; it has a barely supressed energy and dynamism. Notice, too, how much of a piece it is; having been built all in one go, the church remains faithful to a single vision. Inside, the cathedral is dimly mysterious, stretching to the high altar in the distance. In contrast to Gothic cathedrals, whose walls are supported externally by flying buttresses, allowing the interior the minimum of masonry and the maximum of light, at Speyer the columns supporting the roof are massive. Their bulk naturally disguises the side aisles, drawing your eye to the altar. Look up at the roof; it's a shallow stone vault, the earliest such vaulted roof in Europe. Look, too, at the richly carved capitals of the columns, filled with naturalistic details—foliage, dogs, birds, faces.

No fewer than eight Holy Roman Emperors are buried in the cathedral, including, fittingly enough, the three who built it. They lie in the crypt. This, too, should be visited to see its simple beauty, uninterrupted by anything save the barest minimum of decorative detail. The entrance is in the south aisle. *Kaiserdom. Admission to crypt: 50 pf adults, 30 pf children. For guided tours, tel. 06232/102–259. Cost is DM 1 adults, 50 pf children. Open Apr.–Sept., weekdays 9–5:30, Sat. 9–4, Sun. 1:30–3; Oct.–Mar., weekdays 9–11:30 and 2–4:30, Sat. 9–11:30 and 1:30–4, Sun. 1:30–4:30.*

Treasures from the cathedral and the imperial tombs are kept in the city's excellent museum, the **Historisches Museum der Pfalz,** on nearby Grosses Pfaffengasse. Beneath its ornate, turreted roof there's also one of the region's most comprehensive **wine museums.** The museum will reopen in 1990 following renovations. *Contact the tourist office for times and admissions; tel. 06232/14395.*

North to Worms

12 Back on the Wine Road, the wine town of **Deidesheim,** 6 kilometers (4 miles) from Neustadt, is the next stop north. It was here that the bishops of Speyer, among the most powerful clerics in Germany in the Middle Ages, had their administrative headquarters. Their former palace is now mostly a ruin, its moat a green and shady park. Make sure you see the town square, Marktplatz. It's bordered on three sides by flower-smothered, half-timbered houses, the whole forming one of the most picturesque ensembles in the Rhineland-Palatinate. Climb the impressive stairway to the Rathaus (Town Hall); the entrance is through a curious porch crowned by a helmetlike roof and spire. Ask to view the fine wood-paneled assembly hall where councillors and envoys of successive bishops of Speyer haggled over church finances.

Time Out Look for the golden sign of the **Deidesheimer Hof** (Marktpl.) on the right side of the three-cornered market square. In the cool interior of this ancient inn you'll eat and drink in quiet comfort. Look, too, for the names Gerümpel and Goldbächel on the wine list: They are the very best the area has to offer.

Don't leave Deidesheim without strolling down the street called Feigengasse. It's named after the fig trees (*Feigen*) that grow in front of practically every house.

Eight kilometers (5 miles) and two charming wine villages (Forst and Wachenheim) farther on, you reach another bustling
13 little Wine Road town: **Bad Dürkheim.** Bad Dürkheim has a boast that's hard to beat: a wine-cask so big it contains a restaurant with seating for 420 (the Bad Dürkheimer Riesenfass, am Wurstmarktgelände). On weekends it reverberates to the music of a brass band. In mid-September, it's the focal point of

what the locals claim is the world's biggest wine festival, a week of revelry and partying when the wine flows freely.

The **Pfälzerwald** nature park begins just beyond Bad Dürkheim's town limits. It's Germany's largest uninterrupted area of forest, and a favorite area for hiking. If you don't fancy a full-fledged walking tour, at least give yourself an hour or two to experience its lonely, rugged grandeur.

Head north from Bad Dürkheim a couple of miles to Kallstadt.
14 Turn right to see **Freinsheim,** 4 kilometers (2½ miles) away. The little town is one of the best preserved in the region, a winning combination of winding medieval streets and high-gabled, half-timbered buildings. A counterpoint to this toy-town charm is provided by the stately Baroque Rathaus (Town Hall), an elegantly classical building with an unusual covered staircase leading up to the imposing main entrance. Take a look, too, at the original medieval walls that still encircle the old town; conical-roofed towers punctuate them at rhythmic intervals.

More too-good-to-be-true charm is provided by the town of
15 **Neuleiningen,** 10 kilometers (6 miles) north of Kallstadt. Until quite recently, this was among the most backward and impoverished areas of the country. The people were called *Geesbocke,* or "billy goats," a mocking reference to the fact that these were the only animals they could afford to keep. The name lives on today in the village's most historic inn, Zum Geesbock. Stop in to sample a glass or two of local wine and to admire the Renais-
16 sance interior. The Wine Road ends at **Bockenheim,** 10 kilometers (6 miles) north of Neuleiningen.

Worms to Mainz

Numbers in the margin correspond with points of interest on the Worms map.

From Bockenheim, you can continue north along B-271 to Mainz and the Rheingau or make the detour to the ancient im-
17 perial city of **Worms** (pronounced "Va-rms"). Why visit Worms? First, to see the great, gaunt Romanesque cathedral; it presents a less perfect expression of the Romanesque spirit than Speyer cathedral but exudes much of the same craggy magnificence. Second, because Worms, though devastated in World War II, is among the most ancient cities in Germany, founded as far back perhaps as 5,000 years ago, settled by the Romans, and later one of the major centers of the Holy Roman Empire. More than 100 diets of the empire were held here, including the one in 1521 before which Martin Luther came to plead his "heretical" case. Third, because Worms is one of the most important wine centers in Germany; anyone who has fallen under the spell of the Rhineland Palatinate's golden wines will want to sample more here. There's some industry on the outskirts of the city, but the rebuilt old town is compact and easy to explore.

It was the Romans who made Worms important, but it was a Burgundian tribe, established in Worms from the 5th century, who gave the city its most compelling legend—the Nibelungen. The story, written probably in the 12th century and considerably elaborated down the years, is complex and sprawling, telling of love, betrayal, greed, war, and death. It ends when

Cathedral, **18**
Dreifaltigkeit Church, **19**
Judenfriedhof, **22**
Liebfrauenkirche, **24**
Lutherdenkmal, **20**
Städtisches, **23**
Synagogue, **21**

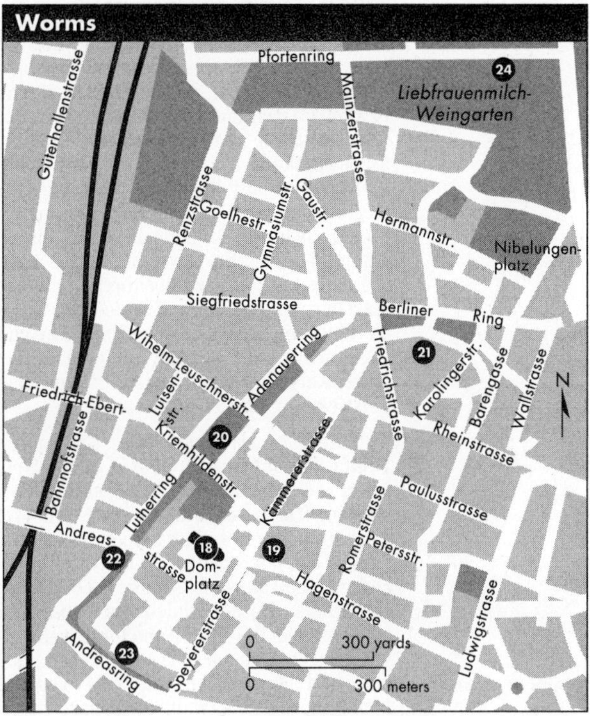

the Nibelungen—the Burgundians—are defeated by Attila the Hun, their court destroyed, their treasure lost, their heroes dead. (One of the most famous incidents tells how Hagen, treacherous and scheming, hurls the court riches into the Rhine; there's a bronze statue of him, caught in the act, by the Nibelungen bridge.)

The Nibelungen may be legend, but it's based on historical fact. For instance, it's known that a Burgundian tribe was defeated, in present-day Hungary, by Attila the Hun in 437. Not until Charlemagne resettled Worms almost 400 years later, making it one of the major cities of his empire, was the city to prosper again. Worms wasn't just an administrative and commercial center, it was a great ecclesiastical city, too. The first expression of this religious importance was the original cathedral, begun in 1020. In 1171 a new cathedral was started. This is the one you come to Worms to see.

18 If you've seen Speyer cathedral, you'll quickly realize that **Worms cathedral,** by contrast, contains many Gothic elements. In part this is simply a matter of chronology. Speyer cathedral was completed more than 100 years before that at Worms was even begun, long before the lighter, more vertical lines of Gothic were developed. But there's another reason. Once built, Speyer cathedral was left largely untouched in later periods; at Worms, the cathedral was remodeled frequently as new styles in architecture and new values developed. Nonetheless, as you walk around the building, you'll find that same muscular confidence, that same blocky massiveness as at Speyer. The ground plan of the church is similar, too, with two towers at each end, a

prominent apse at the east end, and short transepts (the "arms" of the church). The Gothic influence is most obvious inside, especially in the great rose window at the west end (over the main entrance). It could almost be in a French church and presents a striking contrast to the tiny, round-headed windows high up in the nave. Notice, too, how a number of the main arches in the nave are pointed, a key characteristic of the Gothic. It wasn't only in the Gothic period that the cathedral was altered, however. As you near the main altar you won't miss seeing the lavish Baroque screen of columns supporting an opulent gold crown that towers above the altar. This is the Baroque at its most potent. Is the church diminished in any way by this startling juxtaposition of styles? Do these rival styles clash or do they complement one another? The choir stalls, installed in 1760, are equally opposed in spirit to the body of the church. Intricately carved and gilded, they proclaim the courtly and sophisticated glamour of the Rococo.

Outside the cathedral, cross the square to see the simple
19 **Dreifaltigkeit Church** (Church of the Holy Trinity). Remodeling of the church in the 19th century produced today's austere building (the facade and tower are still joyfully Baroque). It's a Lutheran church and as good a place as any in the city to recall Luther's appearance in 1521 before the Holy Roman Emperor and massed ranks of Catholic theologians to defend his heretical beliefs. Luther ended his impassioned plea against the corruption of the church and for its reform (hence Reformation) with the ringing declaration, "Here I stand, I can do no different. God help me. Amen!" He was duly excommunicated. From the church, walk back past the cathedral to see the
20 **Lutherdenkmal,** a 19th-century group of statues of Luther and other figures from the Reformation. It's on the little area of grass next to the street called, appropriately enough, Lutherring.

Worms was also one of the most important Jewish cities in Germany, a role that came to a brutal end with the rise of the Nazis. From the Luther monument you can walk along
21 Lutherring to see the rebuilt **synagogue,** the oldest in the country. It was founded in the 11th century; in 1938 it was entirely destroyed. In 1961, the synagogue was rebuilt, using as much of the original masonry as had survived. The ancient Jewish
22 cemetery, the **Judenfriedhof,** can also be visited. *Admission free. Open daily 10–noon and 2–4.*

23 To bone up on the history of the city, visit the **Städtisches** Museum (Municipal Museum). It's housed in the cloisters of a former Romanesque church. *Weckerlingpl. Admission: DM 2 adults, DM 1 children. Open May.–Sept., Tues.–Sun. 9–noon and 2–5; Oct.–Apr., Tues.–Sun. 10–noon and 2–4.*

If you visit the city in late August or early September, you'll find it embroiled in its carnival, the improbably named Backfischfest, or Baked Fish Festival. The highlight is the **Fischerstechen,** a kind of water-borne jousting in which contestants spar with long poles while balancing on the wobbly decks of flat-bottom boats. The winner is crowned King of the River; the losers get a dunking. Baked fish is the culinary highlight of the festival, of course. The wine is never in short supply.

Don't leave Worms without visiting the vineyard that gave birth to Germany's most famous export wine, Liebfraumilch

(Our Lady's Milk). The vineyard encircles the Gothic pilgrim-
24 age church of the **Liebfrauen** convent, the **Liebfrauenkirche,** an easy 20-minute walk north from the old town. Buy a bottle or two from the shop at the vineyard.

Numbers in the margin correspond with points of interest on the "Other" Rhineland map.

Two of Germany's most famous wine towns—Oppenheim and Nierstein—lie between Worms and Mainz, the end of this
25 tour. **Oppenheim** is 26 kilometers (16 miles) north of Worms on B-9; Nierstein is a mile or two beyond. Oppenheim is said to have been the center of Charlemagne's wine estates. Take a look at the fine market square, fussily bordered on all sides by time-honored half-timbered buildings. Then climb the steep stepped streets to the Gothic church of St.
26 Catherine, the **Katharinenkirche. Nierstein** is a town that lives for wine; whole streets contain shops that sell nothing but the precious liquid. Many have ornate wood or wrought-iron signs, brilliantly painted and gilded, advertising their wares.

27 Sixteen kilometers (10 miles) north lies the city of **Mainz,** site of the third of the great Romanesque cathedrals of the Rhine, a sturdy, turreted structure that watches with the dignity of age over the hustle and bustle of the rebuilt market square and shopping streets that jostle it for room. Step inside and silence falls about you like a cloak. One thousand years of history accompany you through the aisles and chapels. The first cathedral here—dedicated to Sts. Martin and Stephan—was built at the end of the 10th century. In 1002, Heinrich I, the last Saxon emperor of the Holy Roman Empire, was crowned in the still-far-from-complete building. In 1009, on the very day of its consecration, the cathedral burned to the ground. Rebuilding began almost immediately. The cathedral you see today was largely finished at the end of the 11th century. Substantial sections were rebuilt at the end of World War II. Before that, in the 18th century, an imposing Baroque spire was constructed; similarly, in the Gothic period, rebuilding and remodeling did much to alter the Romanesque purity of the original. With all these additions and modifications, can the cathedral really be considered Romanesque? The answer has to be "yes," if only because its ground plan links it so firmly to the cathedrals at Speyer and Mainz. Notice the towers at each end and the spires that rise between them; one may be Baroque, but its positioning and something of its bold impact produce an effect that is nothing if not Romanesque. Inside, though pointed arches proliferate, the walls have the same grim, fortresslike massiveness of Speyer. True, there's more stained glass—more light generally—but the weight of masonry is full-fledged Romanesque. The **Dom und Diozesän Museum** (Cathedral Treasury and Museum) contains a series of rich ecclesiastical objects that will appeal to anyone with a taste for the intricate skills of medieval and Renaissance craftsmen. *Admission free. Open Mon.–Sat. 9–noon and 2–5.*

Opposite the east end of the cathedral on Liebfrauenplatz is one of the most popular attractions in the Rhineland, the **Gutenburg Museum.** It charts the life and times of Mainz's most famous—and unquestionably most influential—son, Johannes Gutenburg (1390–1468). It was in Mainz, in 1460, that Gutenburg built the first machine that could print from movable type. The significance of his invention was immense, leading to an explosion in the availability of information. This wasn't actually the building in which Gutenburg worked; that's long since disappeared, but a vivid sense of his original workshop is conveyed. There's a fine reconstruction of his printing machine, as well as exhibits charting the development of printing and bookbinding. But the highlight must be the copy of the Gutenburg Bible, one of only 47 extant, not only one of the most historically significant books in the world but surely one of the most beautiful, too. *Liebfrauenpl. 5. Admission free. Open Tues.–Sat. 10–6, Sun. 10–1.*

From the Gutenburg Museum, return to the 20th century by crossing Rheinstrasse to the **Rathaus** (Town Hall). This is no ancient structure but an unashamedly modern glass-and-concrete building put up in the 1970s. Opinions have been divided over its merits for as long as the building's been here.

For another example of modern Mainz, take a look at the church of **St. Stephen.** It's on Willigisplatz, a half mile south of the Rathaus. You walk through the rebuilt old town on your way there, a sensitive example of reconstruction following near-total destruction in the war. The church itself is one of the oldest single-nave Gothic buildings in this part of the Rhineland. But look at the stained glass in the choir; it was designed by French painter Marc Chagall in the '50s. Its vivid and bold coloring is a strangely beautiful complement to the austere Gothic design of the rest of the church.

Mainz claims to put on the wildest pre-Lent carnival in Germany. Be here in early February if you want to put that boast to the test. The city erupts in a Rhineland riot of revelry, the high point of which is the procession through the old town.

What to See and Do with Children

On the Wine Road you'll find one of Germany's biggest leisure parks, the **Hassloch Holidaypark,** so big most people call it Germany's Disneyland. It's at Hassloch, on B-39 between Neustadt and Speyer. A circus, a dolphinarium, an adventure playground, and an elaborate medieval mock-up, the "Robber Knights of Falkenstein Mountain," number among the attractions. *6733 Hassloch-Pfalz, tel. 06324/599–390. Admission: DM 18 adults, DM 16 children. Open mid-Mar.–Oct., daily 9–6.*

There's another, smaller park, the **Kurpfalz Park,** close by at Wachenheim, between Deidesheim and Bad Dürkheim. It has all the fun of the fair, plus a wildlife park. *Tel. 06325/2077. Admission: DM 11 adults, DM 8 children. Open Easter–Oct., daily 9–6.*

Nierstein has two museums, both in the Altes Rathaus on Marktplatz, that seem to fascinate youngsters. One is the **Palaeontological Museum,** considerably more interesting than it sounds, with a 265-million-year-old fly, one of only three ever found, among the exhibits. *Admission free. Open Sun. only 10–1.*

The other is the **Schiffarfemuseum,** the Shipping Museum, which charts in graphic form the history of shipping on the Rhine. *Admission free. Open Sun. only 10–noon.*

If **zoos** are your thing, there's a little one at Landau. *Hinderburgstr. 12. Admission: DM 3.50 adults, DM 1.50 children. Open daily 9–6.*

There's a charming wildlife park at Silz, the **Wildpark Südliche Weinstrasse.** *Admission: DM 4 adults, DM 2 children. Open 8:30–dusk.*

Off the Beaten Track

Climb through the woods above the town of **Frankenstein** on A-37, between Kaiserslautern and Mannheim, to the ruins of the medieval castle that watches over the ugly, brooding town. Whether it's the castle that helped inspire Mary Shelley, author of *Frankenstein,* no one knows, but it's easy to imagine how a Romantic soul might be stirred by the ruin.

Stroll through the groves of sweet **chestnut trees** in the hills above Bad Dürkheim. They're among the few remaining in Germany, the descendants of saplings planted by the Romans 2,000 years ago.

The click and whir of roulette balls may not suggest an off-the-beaten-track activity, but Bad Dürkheim's little **casino** is definitely a change for the high rollers of Baden-Baden and Mainz. If you fancy a quiet flutter, try your luck here.

If plants are your passion, seek out **Kakteenland Bisnaga** at Steinfeld, just north of the French border. Unusual? This is cactus country, with more than 1,000 different spiny and spiky species. *Wengelspfad 1. Admission free. Open weekdays 8–5.*

In nearby Nothweiler there's an ancient iron mine, the **St. Anna Ironworks,** that's now open to visitors. The mine is said to date from Celtic times, before the birth of Christ. *Open Apr.–mid-Nov., Mon.–Sat. 2–6, Sun. noon–6.*

Shopping

Shopping in the Rhineland Palatinate means **wine.** This is a region that's given over to wine, and you'll find entire streets in many towns and villages that are dominated by shops devoted to the product of the grape. Likewise, vineyards along the roadside invite you in to pass judgment on the year's vintage. These can be great places to totter from barrel to barrel in search of the perfect wine. Once found, the wine can be decanted into plastic containers for easy transport. **Karl Sauter** in Neustadt an der Weinstrasse (118 Hampstr.) is a walking encyclopedia of knowledge, and his shop is one of the best places to pick up a gift box of bottles of the area's best. The **Winzergenossenschaft Vier Jahreszeiten-Kloster Limburg** is a group of vintners that won a federal gold medal of honor in 1986 for its wine promotion; you're in very good hands with any of its members. The organization has its headquarters and cellars at Limburgerstrasse. 8, Bad Dürkheim. It's open Monday–Friday 8–noon, and 1–5, Saturday 8:30–12:30. One of its leading members, **Heinz Kroning,** opens his extensive cellars Tuesday for visitors.

Wineglasses, bottle openers (some of them elaborately carved from local wood), and **wine coolers** are among other gift ideas. Worms' tourist office (Neumarkt 14) sells the most original wine cooler, a terra-cotta replica of a Roman example unearthed by archaeologists.

Antique hunters report that it's worthwhile digging through two shops in Worms: **Antik in Worms** (Wilhelm Leuschner-Str. 3) and **Antik Schimmel** (Kammererstr. 48). The city also has a **flea market;** it's held Saturdays in March, June, September, and December in the city's main parking lot, near the Rhine. Mainz has a famous **flea market,** the Krempelmarkt, held along the banks of the Rhine every third Saturday of the month (except Apr. and Oct.).

Pirmasens, on the edge of the Palatinate forest, the Pfalzerwald, is Germany's shoe center; it can be worth a detour from the Wine Road to stock up on a pair or two. While in the area, why not make the trip 32 kilometers (20 miles) northwest to Homberg, on the Saarbrucken–Kaiserslautern road, for a homberg from the town that gave the famous hat its name?

Sports and Fitness

Bicycling The vineyard-lined country roads on either side of the Wine Road are a cyclist's dream. You can rent bikes at any of the main train stations for DM 10 a day (half that if you have a valid train ticket). In Bad Dürkheim, try **Fahrradverleih Thyssen,** (Schlossgartenstr. 3).

Climbing The sandstone cliffs of the Palatinate forest, the Pfalzerwald, are fun and relatively safe to tackle. The tourist office in **Annweiler am Trifels** (tel. 06346/2200) will tell you where the best climbing can be found.

Golf The Palatinate has its own golf club, the **Golf Club Pfalz e.V.,** with an 18-hole course at Geinsheim, near Neustadt an der Weinstrasse (tel. 06327/2973). Visitors are welcome. There's also a club at Bad Kreuznach (tel. 06708/2145).

Hiking You can cover the whole Wine Road on foot, along a clearly marked trail that winds its way between the vineyards covering the slopes of the Palatinate forest. Maps and information can be obtained from the **Fremdenverkehrsverband** (Bezirkstelle Pfalz, Hindenburgstr. 12, 6730 Neustadt an der Weinstrasse). The **Wasgau nature park** on the edge of the Palatinate forest is also fine walking country, and the tourist office at Dahn offers a vacation package that includes not only overnight stops but a walking stick and a bottle of locally made schnapps to help you cover the distance between them. Contact the **Fremdenverkehrsbüro Dahn** (Schulstr. 20, 6783 Dahn, tel. 0639/5811).

Horseback Riding There are ample opportunities, and fine riding country. Recommended stables include **Gerd Helbig's Reiterhof,** at Silz (tel. 06346/5927); the **Gut Hohenberg** (tel. 06346/2592); and the **Ferien und Reiterhof Münz** (tel. 06346/5272). All are near Annweiler am Trifels.

Swimming There are open-air and indoor pools in many parts of the Rhineland Palatinate. One of the biggest swimming complexes in Germany is in **Wörth** (on Autobahn 65, between Landau and Karlsruhe). The **Wörth Badepark** (Bad-Allee) has 10 pools, a wave machine, and two water slides, each more than 80 yards long. **Speyer's** lido (Geibstr. 4) also has a spectacular water slide. There are thermal baths at **Bad Bergzabern** and **Bad**

Dürkheim (here you can splash around in warm pools overlooking the sun-drenched vineyards that clothe the hills around the town).

Tennis Tennis players will find courts in most towns and villages. Those at **Bad Dürkheim** are so beautifully located that you might have difficulty concentrating on the game; make reservations at the **Papillon Cafe** (tel. 06322/793–275). Speyer has a tennis club that accepts visitors—the **Tennisclub Weiss-Rot** (Holzstr., tel. 06232/67979).

Dining and Lodging

Dining

Though Mainz can offer more elegant dining, in most of the towns and villages of the Rhineland Palatinate you'll eat local specialties in local inns. Sausages are more popular here than in almost any other area of the country, with the herb-flavored *Pfalzer* a favorite. *Hase im Topf*, a highly flavored rabbit pâté made with port, Madeira, brandy, and red wine, is another specialty to look for. The Rhineland Palatinate, though not geographically the largest wine-producing area in the country, nonetheless produces more wine than any other region in Germany, and all restaurants will have a range of wines to offer.

Highly recommended restaurants in each price category are indicated by a star ★.

Category	Cost*
Very Expensive	over DM 90
Expensive	DM 55–90
Moderate	DM 35–55
Inexpensive	under DM 35

**per person for a three-course meal, not including drinks*

Lodging

Accommodations are plentiful, with those along the Wine Road mostly simple and inexpensive inns. The region has many bed-and-breakfasts; keep an eye open for signs reading "Zimmer Frei," meaning "rooms available." If you plan to visit during any of the wine festivals in the late summer and fall, make reservations well in advance, and expect higher prices.

Highly recommended hotels in each price category are indicated by a star ★.

Category	Cost*
Very Expensive	over DM 180
Expensive	DM 120–DM 180
Moderate	DM 80–DM 120
Inexpensive	under DM 80

**Prices are for two people in a double room.*

Annweiler
Dining

Burg-Restaurant Trifels. Eat in the shadows of Burg Trifels, where Richard the Lion-heart once stayed in less happy circumstances. In summer, try for a table on the terrace; the view is terrific. Palatinate specialties—including delicious dumplings—are featured on the menu. *Auf den Schlossackern, tel. 06346/8479. Dress: informal. No credit cards. Moderate.*

s'Reiwerle. Tuesday is *Schlachtfest* day at this charming cellar restaurant, which means the menu is given over to huge meat dishes, including ample helpings of local sausage. Wednesdays and Fridays are *Flammkuchenhessen*—literally, "flaming cake"—days. The wine list features some of the best the region can offer. *Flitschberg 7, tel. 06346/8871. Dress: informal. No credit cards. Inexpensive.*

Lodging

Haus Anebos. This family-run pension overlooks the spa park; some rooms also have views of the Palatinate forest. The mood throughout is simple and old-fashioned, but rooms are ample and comfortable. *Anebosstr. 12, tel. 06346/7368. 16 rooms, 15 with bath. Facilities: restaurant, sauna, solarium. No credit cards. Moderate.*

Haus Bergterrasse. The Michel family runs this quiet country pension like a real home-away-from-home and are ready with holiday help, ranging from the best wines to try to the most picturesque forest paths to walk. They'll even loan you a bike. *Trifelsstr. 8, tel. 06346/7219. 25 rooms with bath. Facilities: restaurant, wine bar, garden. No credit cards. Inexpensive.*

Bad Dürkheim
Dining
★

Bad Dürkheimer Riesenfass. This must be Germany's most unusual restaurant, located in the biggest wine barrel in the world, with room for 420 people inside and a further 230 on the terrace. The food, like the wine, is robustly local. It's touristy but fun. *Am Wurstmarktgelände, tel. 06322/2143. Reservations advised. Dress: informal. AE, DC, MC. Moderate.*

Restaurant-Weinstube Käsbüro. Despite the name—it means "cheese office"—this historic old tavern specializes in fish and game dishes. It's located about a mile from the center of Bad Dürkheim, in Seebach, and is well worth hunting out. *Dorfpl., Seebach, tel. 06322/8694. Reservations advised. Dress: informal. AE, DC, MC, V. Moderate.*

Zum Winzer. In late summer and fall, you can pick the grapes that hang from the vines that enfold the terrace of this restaurant, whose name means "vintner." It's the headquarters of one of the leading local winegrowing associations, a guarantee of good value and high-quality wines. The food features local specialties. *Kaiserslauterer-Str. 12, tel. 06322/2171. Reservations advised. Dress: informal. AE, DC, MC. Closed Thurs. Moderate.*

Lodging

Dorint-Hotel. This establishment offers reliable standards of comfort and service, though it's otherwise an impersonal chain hotel. The location, right by Bad Dürkheim's thermal pools, is terrific. *Kurbrunnenstr. 30–32, tel. 06322/6010. 98 rooms and 2 suites, all with bath. Facilities: restaurant, bar, nightclub, café, terrace, sauna, solarium, indoor and outdoor pools. AE, DC, MC, V. Moderate.*

Kurparkhotel. Ask for a room overlooking the little spa park; on summer evenings you'll be serenaded by the orchestra that plays on its bandstand. Rooms are large and airy, and some have views of the vineyards above the town. *Schlosspl. 1–4, tel. 06322/7970. 109 rooms, most with bath. Facilities: restaurant,* *bar, terrace, garden, sauna, solarium, indoor thermal pool. AE, DC, MC, V. Moderate.*

Deidesheim
Dining
★
Zur Kanne. Seasoned Wine Road travelers know that this place is worth making time for. The historic walls of what claims to be the oldest inn in the Rhineland Palatinate contain a small restaurant whose fame has spread throughout the region. Try any of the local specialties; they're prepared with flair and imagination. *Brennessel* (nettle) soup is a reliable favorite. *Weinstr. 31, tel. 06326/396. Reservations advised. Dress: informal. AE, DC, MC. Closed Tues. Moderate.*

Lodging
★
Deidesheimer Hof. This is the showpiece hotel of the Deidesheim-based Hahnhof group, a country-wide chain of wine restaurants. It's a traditional old Deidesheimer house, immaculately clean and comfortable and run with slick but friendly efficiency. *Am Marktpl., tel. 06326/1811. 26 rooms, most with bath. Facilities: restaurant, wine tavern. AE, DC, MC, V. Moderate.*

Neustadt-an-der-Weinstrasse
Dining
Ratsherrenstuben. On Mondays in the quiet courtyard of the half-timbered building that houses the Ratsherrenstuben you'll find a corner where a fraternity of Neustadt vintners have met for centuries to discuss business. Afterward, they adjourn to the restaurant. Join them in sampling the local wines and full-bodied local specialties. *Marktpl. 10–12, tel. 06321/2070. Reservations advised. Dress: informal. DC, MC, V. Closed Wed. and Aug. Moderate.*

Panorama. The centrally located Panorama is on the top floor of the Kurfürst Hotel. True to its name, it offers a sweeping view of Neustadt and the surrounding countryside. In summer, you can eat on the terrace. In fall, try any of the game dishes. *Mussbacher Landstr. 2, tel. 06321/7441. Reservations advised. Dress: informal. AE, DC, MC, V. Moderate.*

Weinstube Eselsburg. A consummate artist is in charge here. The tavern's jovial landlord finds time between serving creative Palatinate dishes to sketch and paint. He sings, too—the evenings can lengthen into quite a party. The tavern is in the Musbach area of Neustadt, a 10-minute drive from the town center. *Kurpfalzstr. 62, Neustadt-Mussbach, tel. 06321/66984. Dress: informal. No credit cards. Inexpensive.*

Lodging
Haardter Schloss. Despite the name, this charming old hotel is not exactly a castle, more a 19th-century villa. Nonetheless, it has the time-honored air associated with castle living. Antiques abound; even the newer furniture was made in the castle workshops. The restaurant enjoys a wide reputation. It's located in the Haardt section of Neustadt. *Mandelring 35, tel. 06321/32625. 10 rooms with bath. Facilities: restaurant, terrace, gardens. AE, DC, MC. Moderate.*

Hotel Garni Tanner. Also located in the Haardt district, this hotel has its own small park of rare and exotic trees and shrubs. Stretching beyond it is the wild expanse of the Palatinate forest. Green carpets of vineyards stretch in other directions. Rooms are modern and functional, but comfort is assured. *Mandelring 216, Neustadt-Haardt, tel. 06321/6541. 40 rooms with bath. Facilities: indoor pool, sauna, solarium, terrace. AE, DC, MC. Moderate.*

Pfalzgraf. Centrally located in the pedestrian zone, no more than a one-minute walk from the train station, this hotel is in a tastefully modernized turn-of-the-century building. Ask for a mansard room; they're small but cozy. *Friedrichstr. 2, tel.*

06321/2185. 40 rooms with bath. Facilities: restaurant, café. AE, DC, MC, V. Inexpensive.

Mainz *Dining*

★ **Gourmet Restaurant Rheingrill.** This is the restaurant of the Hilton. Ask for a table overlooking the Rhine. The food is distinctly upscale and nouvelle. If lobster with black noodles is on the menu, be sure to try it. The game dishes are also good. *Rheinstr. 68, tel. 06131/245–129. Reservations advised. Jacket and tie required. AE, DC, MC, V. Expensive.*

Restaurant Walderdorff. Head here for a touch of French culinary flair. It's a bistro-style restaurant, serving classy nouvelle cuisine, much of it featuring fish. For dessert, try the *Apfelkuchen* (apple cake). *Karmeliterpl. 4, tel. 06131/222–515. Reservations advised. Jacket and tie required. AE, DC, MC, V. Expensive.*

★ **Rats-und Zunftstuben Heilig Geist.** The most atmospheric dining in Mainz is offered here. Parts of the building date from Roman times, but most of it is Gothic, with vaulted ceilings and stone floors. The menu features Bavarian specialties with nouvelle touches. *Rentengasse 2, tel. 06131/225–757. Reservations advised. Dress: informal. AE, DC, MC. Closed Sun. dinner. Moderate.*

Lodging

Hilton International. A terrific location right by the Rhine, allied with the reliable standards of comfort and service expected of the chain, make the Hilton the number-one choice in Mainz. Don't expect to find much in the way of old-German atmosphere. The restaurant is exceptional (*see* above). *Rheinstr. 68, tel. 06131/2450. 435 rooms and 14 suites, all with bath. Facilities: 3 restaurants, hair salon, shopping mall, gym, sauna, solarium, casino. AE, DC, MC, V. Very Expensive.*

Novotel Mainz-Sud. Stay here if you value the amenities of an above-average chain hotel. The location—the hotel is in the Bretzenheim suburb, a 15-minute ride from downtown—may discourage those who want to be in the thick of things. *Essenheimerstr., tel. 06131/361–054. 121 rooms with bath. Facilities: restaurant, bar, outdoor pool. AE, DC, MC, V. Expensive.*

Hammer. The Hammer is a basic, few-frills downtown hotel by the train station. Rooms are modern and comfortable—and soundproof. There's no restaurant. *Bahnhofpl. 6, tel. 06131/611–061. 40 rooms with bath. Facilities: sauna, solarium. AE, DC, MC, V. Moderate.*

Speyer *Dining*

Restaurant Backmulde. For best value, try the fixed-price, six-course menu. It offers an appealing mixture of regional and nouvelle-inspired dishes. Fish predominates. *Karmeliterstr. 11, tel. 06232/71577. Reservations advised. Jacket and tie required. AE, DC, MC, V. Closed Sun. and 3 weeks in summer (times vary depending on school vacations). Expensive.*

★ **Wirstschaft zum Alten Angel.** Regional dishes from the Palatinate and the French Alsace region dominate the menu in this historic cellar tavern in the heart of the city. Try the mushroom gratinée. *Mühlturmstr. 27, tel. 06232/76732. Reservations advised. Dress: informal. AE, DC, MC. Closed Sat. and Aug. Moderate.*

Lodging

Hotel Kurpfalz. This is a turn-of-the-century villa, fully renovated in 1987, and given a convincing old-world atmosphere. It's family-run and small. There's no restaurant. *Mühlturmstr. 27, tel. 06232/24168. 10 rooms and 1 suite, all with bath. AE, DC, MC. Moderate.*

Goldener Engel. The "Golden Angel" has been in business since 1701 and offers simple, time-honored atmosphere allied with appealing modern comfort (it was renovated in 1987). There's no restaurant. *Am Postpl., tel. 06232/76732. 39 rooms with bath. AE, DC, MC, V. Inexpensive.*

Worms
Dining
★ **Rotisserie Dubs.** Make the trek to Wolfgang Dubs's sleekly appointed restaurant to eat his excellent steak in snail sauce, a substantially more appetizing dish than it sounds. The restaurant is located in the suburb of Rheindürkheim, a 10-minute ride from downtown. *Kirchstr. 6, tel. 0624/2032. Reservations required. Jacket and tie required. No credit cards. Expensive.*

Bacchus. The name here is apt: This is the place to drink some of the best wine in the region. The food is ample, with local specialties predominating. *Obermarkt 10, tel. 06241/6913. Reservations advised. Jacket and tie required. AE, DC, MC, V. Moderate.*

Lodging **Dom Hotel.** This is the best hotel in Worms, modern and centrally located, though offering little more than functional comfort. The Bacchus restaurant (*see* above) compensates. *Obermarkt 10, tel. 06241/6913. 58 rooms with bath. Facilities: restaurant. AE, DC, MC, V. Moderate.*

Nibelungen. The Nibelungen is chic-modern, though in other respects nothing special. Rooms are ample, and the downtown location is a plus. There's no restaurant. *Martinsgasse 16, tel. 06241/6977. AE, DC, MC. Moderate.*

The Arts and Nightlife

The Arts

Music Regular organ and chamber-music concerts are given in the three great Romanesque cathedrals of the area—in **Mainz, Speyer,** and **Worms.** Mainz also has an annual **cathedral music festival** lasting through the summer. Organ recitals are given in the cathedral every Saturday at noon from mid-August to mid-September. Classical-music concerts are also given regularly at the **Kurfürstliches Schloss** (Diether-von-Isenburg-Str., tel. 06131/228–729). In 1990, Speyer is celebrating the 2,000th anniversary of its foundation with a full musical program in September and October: The focus will be a festival of religious music in the cathedral.

Theater The area's theatrical activity is concentrated in Mainz. The city's resident company, the **Theater der Landeshauptstadt Mainz,** performs regularly in the Grosses Haus, Gutenbergerplatz, and two other smaller venues; tel. 06131/123–365 or 06131/123–366 for program details and tickets. Worms has a city theater, the **Städtisches Spiel und Festhaus,** where concerts and drama productions are staged. For program details and tickets, contact the box office on Rathenaustrasse or phone 06241/22525. In Speyer, the city's theater is the **Stadthalle** (Obere Langgasse); contact the local tourist office, the Verkehrsamt (Maximilianstr. 11), for program details and tickets.

Nightlife

Mainz and Bad Dürkheim both have **casinos,** with adjacent bars for celebrating a lucky evening or drowning loser's sorrows.

Bad Dürkheim's nightlife is otherwise crammed into Friday and Saturday nights at the Dorint Hotel's **Cotton Club** dance bar. In **Mainz,** night owls make for the Altstadt, the old town. The central Marktplatz is the scene from May through September of a nightly program of open-air pop music, jazz, and street cabaret. Worms has a square-dance club, **The Crackers,** which welcomes guests. Phone 06241/23400 if you'd like to join in. The discotheques and bars of **Worms** are concentrated around Judengasse. If you tire of the wine taverns of the Wine Road try the exotic **Bahama Club** (Landauerstr. 65) in Neustadt an der Weinstrasse. Neustadt has surprisingly upbeat nightlife; **Madison** (am Kartoffelmarkt 2) is the in place.

Wine Festivals

The wine festivals of the towns and villages of the Wine Road are numerous enough to take up several vacations. From late May through October the whole area seems to be caught up in one long celebration. The most important festivals are: the **Dürkheimer Wurstmarkt** (Germany's biggest wine festival), in mid-September; the **Weinlesefest,** in Neustadt an der Weinstrasse (with the coronation of the local Wine Queen), in the first week of October; Schweigen-Rechtenbach's **Rebenblütenfest,** in the first week of July; Bad Bergzabern's **Böhammerfest,** in early July; Landau's **Herbstmarkt,** in mid-September; Edenkoben's **Südliches Weinstrasse Grosses Weinfest,** in late September; and the **Mainzer Weinmarkt** in Mainz's Volkspark, the last weekend of August and the first weekend of September.

11 The Neckar Valley

Introduction

It may lack the dramatic beauty and historic resonance of the Rhine, but the Neckar River has attractions enough to make a tour along its banks a memorable vacation. This chapter covers its most distinctive stretch, from Mannheim, where the Neckar empties into the Rhine, just 55 miles south of Frankfurt, to Heilbronn. For much of the route, you'll be driving along the Burgenstrasse, the Castle Road (this section of the Neckar has proportionately more castles than any comparable stretch of the Rhine). From Mannheim, whose industrial suburbs enclose a city of surprising charm, the route runs southeast to the ancient university town of Heidelberg, for many the apotheosis of romantic Germany. With the exception of a detour south to the town of Schwetzingen (glorying in the name "Germany's asparagus capital"), the route next snakes its scenic way east, then south, between the river and the wooded slopes of the Odenwald Forest, before hitting the rolling, vine-covered countryside around Heilbronn.

It's a busy road—this is not off-the-beaten-track territory—but there are plenty of opportunities along the way to escape into quiet side valleys and to visit little towns that sleep in leafy peace. You'll find just as much to charm you here as along the Romantic Road, but little of the tourist hype. Scarcely one of these towns is without its guardian castle, standing in stern splendor above medieval streets. This is a region that can delight—and sometimes surprise—even the most hardened traveler.

Essential Information

Important Addresses and Numbers

Tourist Information For information on the whole of the Burgenstrasse, contact **Arbeitsgemeinschaft Burgenstrasse,** Rathaus, Marktplatz, 7100 Heilbronn, tel. 07131/562–271. There are local tourist information offices in the following towns and cities:

Bad Wimpfen: Verkehrsamt, Marktplatz 1, 7107 Bad Wimpfen, tel. 07063/7051.
Heidelberg: Verkehrsverein Heidelberg, Friedrich-Ebert-Anlage 2, 6900 Heidelberg, tel. 06221/10821.
Heilbronn: Verkehrsverein Heilbronn, Rathaus, Marktplatz, 7100 Heilbronn, tel. 07131/562–270.
Mannheim: Tourist-Information, Bahnhofplatz 1, 6800 Mannheim 1, tel. 0621/101–011.
Mosbach: Städtisches Verkehrsamt, Rathaus, 6950 Mosbach, tel. 06261/82236.

Car Rental **Avis:** Karlsruherstrasse 43, tel. 06221/22215, **Heidelberg;** Salzstrasse 112, tel. 07131/72077, **Heilbronn;** Augartenstrasse 112–114, tel. 0621/442091, **Mannheim.**
Europcar: Neckarauerstrasse 79–81, tel. 0621/851–047, **Mannheim;** Wiesenbacherstrasse 33, tel. 06223/7052, **Neckargemünd.**
Hertz: Kurfürstenanlage 1, tel. 06221/23434, **Heidelberg;** Karl-Wüst-Strasse 30, tel. 07131/76061, **Heilbronn;** Friedrichsring 36, tel. 0621/22997, **Mannheim.**

Arriving and Departing by Plane

The nearest airports to the Neckar Valley are at Frankfurt and Stuttgart. There's fast and easy access by car and train to all major centers along the Neckar from both.

Getting Around

By Car Mannheim is a major junction of the Autobahn system, easily reached from all parts of the country. Heidelberg and Heilbronn are also served by Autobahn. A 10-minute drive on A-656 speeds you from Mannheim to Heidelberg; Heilbronn stands aside the east–west A-6 and the north–south A-81. The route followed in this chapter, the Burgenstrasse, also unromantically designated A-37, follows the north bank of the Neckar from Heidelberg to Mosbach, from where it runs down to Heilbronn as A-27. It's a busy road, and fast. If you need a change of pace, cross the river at Mosbach to Obrigheim, and continue south on the slower B-39.

By Train Mannheim is West Germany's most important rail junction. Along with nearby Heidelberg, there are hourly Intercity trains to it from all major German cities. There are express trains to Heilbronn from Heidelberg and Stuttgart. Local services link many of the smaller towns along the Neckar.

By Bus Europabus 189 runs the length of the Burgenstrasse May through September. There are stops at towns and villages all along the Neckar. For information, timetables, and reservations, contact **Deutsche Touring GmBH** (Am Römerhof 17, 6000 Frankfurt/Main 90, tel. 069/79030). Local buses run from Mannheim, Heidelberg, and Heilbronn to most places along the river; post buses connect the rest.

Guided Tours

City Tours There are guided tours of **Heidelberg** at 10 and 2 daily May through October (at 2 only November through April) from the train station and Bismarckplatz. Contact **Heidelberg Service** (tel. 06221/29641) or the tourist office (tel. 06221/10821) for details.

In Heilbronn, the tourist office offers a "Viertal nachs Sachs" tour, meaning "quarter after six," which is just when the tour begins (that's 6 PM!). July 5 through September 27 tours are given Tuesdays; April 26 through June 21, tours are given alternate Tuesdays. The cost is DM 5, and all tours start with a free glass of wine. On the first Thursday of May, June, July, August, and September, tours are offered in a 1927 Paris city bus. The cost of DM 17.50 (DM 12.50 for children) includes a welcome-aboard drink. Contact the tourist office for details (tel. 07131/562270). Ten times a year (contact the tourist office for 1990 timings), a "Heilbronn by Night" tour is offered. The DM 66 cost gives entry to no less than seven wine taverns and restaurants, with drinks in each and food in three; the tour ends at a strip club. There are daily bus tours of Mannheim, May through September, at 10. Tours leave from the Wasserturm and cost DM 12 (DM 9 for children).

Boat Tours The **Rhein-Neckar-Fahrgastschiffahrt** (RNF) company (tel. 06221/20181) offers boat rides from Heidelberg along the Neckar and down the Rhine to Speyer and Worms. Easter through

October, there are regular trips on the Neckar from Heilbronn. Contact **Personenschiffahrt Stumpf** (tel. 07131/85430) or the tourist office (tel. 07131/562–270) for details.

Exploring the Neckar Valley

Highlights for First-time Visitors

Apothekenmuseum, Heidelberg

Hotel zum Ritter, Heidelberg

Klostergasse, Bad Wimpfen

Twelve Apostles Altar-Piece, Kurpfälzisches Museum, Heidelberg

The Renaissance Clock, Heilbronn Rathaus

The Quadrastadt, Mannheim

The views from the Philosophenweg and the Königstuhl, Heidelberg

Mannheim

Numbers in the margin correspond with points of interest on the Neckar Valley map.

The tour begins where the Neckar and the Rhine meet—at
1 **Mannheim**, a major industrial center and the second largest river port in Europe. Inside its industrial sprawl lurks an elegant old town, carefully rebuilt after wartime bomb damage. Mannheim is unusual among the cities of the Rhine for having been founded only in 1606, but it's even more unusual for having been laid out on a grid pattern. It was the forward-looking Palatinate Elector Friedrich IV who built the city, imposing on it the rigid street plan that forms the heart of the old town, or Quadrastadt (literally, "squared town"). Streets running northeast–southwest—from one river to the other—are labeled A through U; those running northwest–southeast are numbered 1 through 7. So, if you're looking for the central Marktplatz, it's G-1 on your map; if you're looking for the best restaurant in town—Da Gianni—it's R-7. Rationalism rules. The only exception to this system is Kurpfalzstrasse, which cuts through the heart of the town, leading southwest from the Neckar to the Schloss (palace). There's a terrific view down it from the main staircase of the palace.

Though it was the Elector Friedrich IV who built Mannheim, his court was at Heidelberg. In 1720, the Elector Carl Philip went one stage further, moving the court to Mannheim rather than rebuilding what remained of his castle at Heidelberg after it had been sacked by Louis XIV's French troops in 1689 and again in 1693. (What, ironically, helped prompt his decision was the desire to build a palace modeled on the absolutist, classical lines of Louis XIV's great palace at Versailles; like many German 18th-century rulers, Carl Philip eagerly seized the example provided by Louis XIV to reinforce his own absolute right to rule.) The palace was 40 years in the building, com-

The Neckar Valley

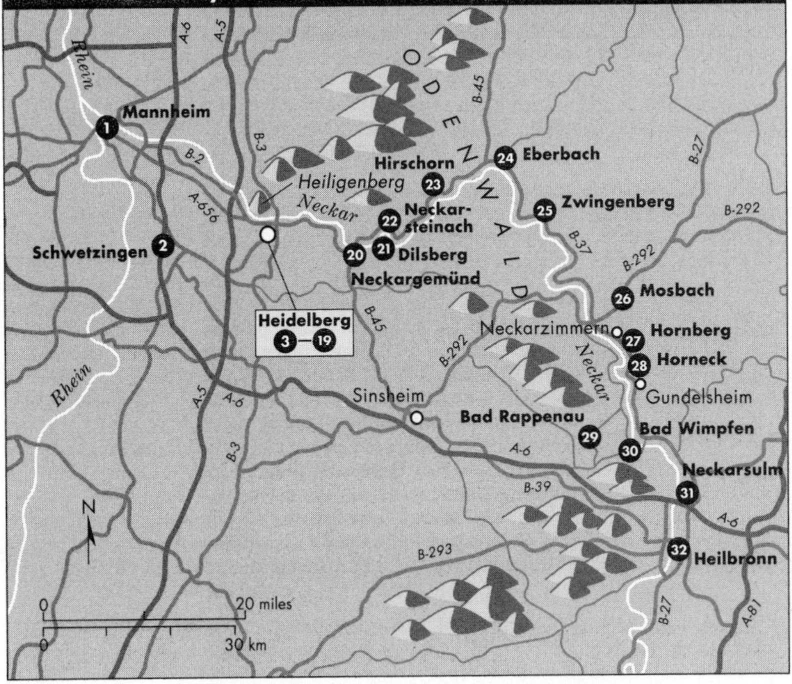

pleted only in 1768. Five separate architects were employed, their combined efforts producing one of the largest buildings in Europe, a vast, relentlessly symmetrical edifice containing more than 400 rooms and 2,000 windows, and with a frontage more than a quarter-mile long. The palace was reduced to a smoking ruin in World War II, and rebuilt in the '50s. Today, it belongs to Mannheim University. The great hall and some of the state rooms can be visited; they're impressive, but strangely lifeless now. *Furfürstlichtes Schloss. Admission: DM 1.50 adults, 80 pf children. Open Apr.–Oct. Tues.–Sun. 10–noon and 3–5; Nov.–Mar. Sat. and Sun. only 10–noon and 3–5.*

From the palace, you can either head off to the right to visit the Städtische Kunsthalle (City Art Museum) or make a left to see the Jesuitenkirche (Jesuit church) three blocks away at A-4. The **Jesuitenkirche** is the largest and most important Baroque church in Germany, its immense, rigorously classical facade flanked by graceful domed spires (known as *Spitzhelm*, after their resemblance to old-time German helmets) and topped by a massive dome. It was begun in 1733, commissioned by the Elector Carl Philip to commemorate his family's return to Catholicism. The church, too, was severely bombed in the war, and most of the internal decorations were lost (including what were probably the most lavish ceiling and dome paintings in the country). But, though plainer now, the airy grandeur of the interior suggests something of its former magnificence. Pause as you go in to look at the ornate wrought-iron gates at the entrance.

The **city art museum** is located at Friedrichsplatz, at the eastern fringe of the Quadrastadt, a 10-minute walk from the Jesuit church. The building itself is a prime example of Jugendstil (Art Nouveau) architecture, constructed in 1907. Provocative and large-scale modern sculptures stand outside. Inside, you'll find one of the largest and best collections of modern art in Germany. All the big names are here, from Manet to Warhol. *Moltkestr. 9. Admission free. Open Tues.–Sun. 10–5 (Thurs. 10–8).*

2 Heidelberg is the next major stop of this tour, but detour south to **Schwetzingen** on A-6—it's only five miles—to see the palace there, a formal 18th-century building constructed as a summer residence by the Palatinate electors. It's a noble, rose-colored building, imposing and harmonious, but the real interest centers on the park, a blend of formal French and informal English styles, with neatly bordered gravel walks trailing off into the dark woodland. The 18th-century planners of this delightful park had fun with the construction of an exotic mosque, complete with minarets and a shimmering pool. Somewhere along the line they got more than a little muddled, however, and gave the building a very German Baroque portal. Be sure to see the charming Rococo theater, the scene each June of an international music festival. Another rare pleasure awaits you if you're in Schwetzingen in June: The town is Germany's asparagus center, and fresh asparagus dishes dominate the menu of every local restaurant.

Heidelberg

Numbers in the margin correspond with points of interest on the Heidelberg map.

3 And so on to **Heidelberg,** 10 kilometers (six miles) northeast. If any one city in Germany can be said to encapsulate the spirit of the country, it must be Heidelberg. Scores of poets and composers—virtually the entire 19th-century German Romantic movement—have sung its praises. And others, too. Goethe and Mark Twain both fell in love here: the German writer with a beautiful young woman, the American with the city itself. Sigmund Romberg set his play *The Student Prince* in the city; Carl Maria von Weber wrote his lushly Romantic opera *Der Freischütz* ("The Marksman") here. Composer Robert Schumann was a student at the university. It was the university, the oldest in the country, that gave impetus to the artistic movement that claimed Heidelberg as its own, but the natural beauty of the city—embraced by mountains, forests, vineyards, and the Neckar River, and crowned by its ruined castle—provided the materials of their trade. The campaign they waged on behalf of the town has been astoundingly successful. Heidelberg's fame is out of all proportion to its size; over 2.5 million visitors crowd its streets every year. If you want to find the *feine Heidelberg* ("fine Heidelberg") of poet Viktor von Scheffel's day, avoid visiting in summer. Late fall, when the vines turn a faded gold, or early spring, with the first green shoots of the year appearing, can both be captivating. Best of all, visit in the depths of winter, when hoary river mists creep through the narrow streets of the old town and awaken the ghosts of a romantic past.

Alte Brücke, **19**
Castle, **13**
Heiliggeistkirche, **17**
Hotel zum Ritter, **18**
Königstuhl, **15**
Königstuhl funicular, **12**
Kurpfälzisches Museum, **6**
Molkenkur, **14**
New University, **9**
Old University, **7**
Rathaus, **16**
St. Peter, **11**
Studentenkarzer, **8**
Universitätsbibliothek, **10**
University, **4**
Wormser Hof, **5**

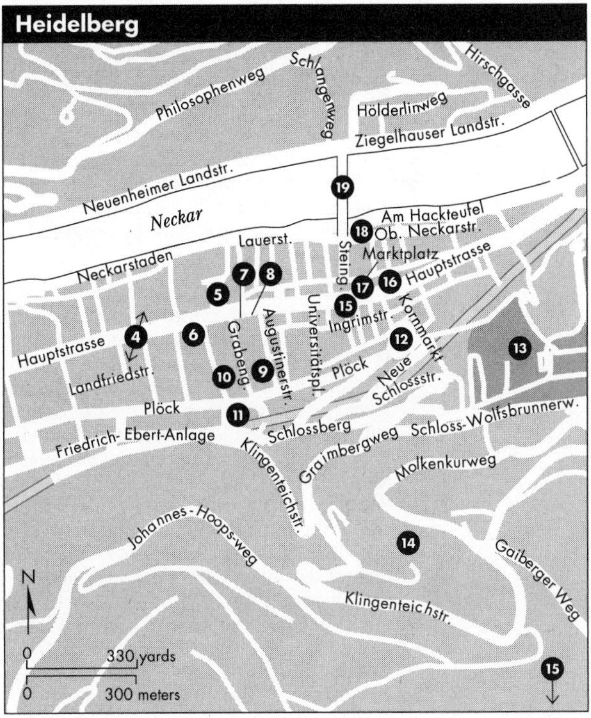

The city was the political center of the Rhineland Palatinate. At the end of the Thirty Years' War (1618–1648), the Elector Carl Ludwig married his daughter to the brother of Louis XIV in the hope of bringing peace to the Rhineland. But when the elector's son died without an heir, Louis XIV used the marriage alliance as an excuse to claim Heidelberg, and, in 1689, the town was sacked and laid to waste. Four years later, he sacked the town again. From its ashes arose the town you see today: a Baroque town built on Gothic foundations, with narrow, twisting streets and alleyways. The new Heidelberg is changing under the influence of U.S. Army barracks and industrial development stretching into the suburbs, but the old heart of the city remains intact, exuding the spirit of romantic Germany.

Extending west to east through the old town is **Hauptstrasse,** an elegant pedestrian mall that runs straight as an arrow for a half mile to the main square, **Marktplatz.** This tour takes you down Hauptstrasse, where you can explore the attractions along it and on its narrow side streets, before leading you to the number-one sight, the castle. You can then visit the rest of the town around Marktplatz.

4 As you walk down Hauptstrasse, the **university**—or part of it anyway; there are four separate university complexes in the town—enfolds you almost immediately. On Brunnengasse, a lane to your left, is the anatomy wing, a former monastery taken over by the university in 1801. What had been a chapel became a dissecting laboratory; the sacristy became a morgue.

Out on Hauptstrasse again, pause in front of the **Haus zum Riesen** (the Giant's House), so called because the local worthy who built it in 1707 (using stone from the destroyed castle) put up the larger-than-life statue of himself that you see over the front door. Wander on down Hauptstrasse. On your right you'll pass the Protestant **Providence Church** (built by the Elector Carl Ludwig in the mid-16th century) and the richly ornate
5 doorway of the **Wormser Hof,** former Heidelberg seat of the bishops of Worms. Look at its lead-paned Renaissance oriel window (bay window) on the second floor: It's one of the finest in the city.

Opposite, on the left, is Heidelberg's leading museum, the
6 **Kurpfälzisches Museum** (Electoral Palatinate Museum), housed in a Baroque palace. Its collections chart the history of Heidelberg. Among the exhibits are two contrasting standouts. One is a replica of the jaw of Heidelberg Man, a key link in the evolutionary chain and thought to date from half a million years ago; the original was unearthed near the city in 1907. You'll need rare powers of imagination to get much of a sense of this early ancestor from just his (or her) jaw, however. The other presents no such problems. It's the *Twelve Apostles Altarpiece,* one of the largest and finest works of early Renaissance sculptor Tilman Riemenschneider. Its exquisite detailing and technical sophistication are matched by the simple faith that radiates from the faces of the Apostles. On the top floor of the museum there's a rich range of 19th-century German paintings and drawings, many of Heidelberg. *Hauptstr. 97. Admission: DM 1 adults, children free. Open Tues.–Sun. 10–5 (Thurs. 10–9).*

Time Out Turn down the small street next to the museum and slip into the cool, dark interior of the **Schnitzelbank.** It's been a favorite student haunt for more than a century, and the walls are covered with photographs of the student fraternities who have met here down the years. Try a glass of wine from a Neckar vineyard or any of the locally brewed beers. *Bauamgasse.*

7 From the museum, you're two blocks from the **Old University,** founded in 1386 and rebuilt in the early 18th century for the Elector Johann Wilhelm. Behind it, in Augustinerstrasse, is
8 the former students' prison, the **Studentenkarzer,** where, from 1712 to 1914, unruly students were incarcerated (tradition dictated that students couldn't be thrown in the town jail). The students could be held for up to 14 days; they were left to subsist on bread and water for the first three but thereafter were allowed to attend lectures, receive guests, and have food brought in from the outside. A stay in the jail became as coveted as a scar inflicted in the university fencing clubs. There's bravado, even poetic flair, to be deciphered in the graffiti of two centuries that cover the walls and ceiling of the narrow cell. *Admission: DM 1 adults, 70 pf children. Open Mon.–Sat. 9–5.*

9 Across Universitätsplatz (University Square) is the **New University,** built from 1930–32 with funds raised in the United States by a former American student at the university, the U.S. Ambassador to Germany, J. G. Schurman. The ancient section you see incorporated in the new building is all that remains of the old city walls. It's the **Hexenturm,** the Witches' Tower, where witches were locked up in the Middle Ages.

Opposite the New University, at the end of the street called
10 Plöck, is the university library, the **Universitätsbibliothek.** Its 1.5 million volumes include the famous *Manesse Codex*, a collection of medieval songs and poetry once performed in the courts of Germany by the Minnesänger. *Plöck 107–109. Admission free. Open Mon.–Sat. 10–noon.*

Opposite the library is the city's oldest parish church, the
11 Gothic church of **St. Peter.** Linger in its graveyard; the graves of many leading citizens are here, some dating back 500 and more years. The Baroque building you see immediately east of the church, originally a Jesuit seminary, later a lunatic asylum, is a students' dormitory.

12 From here, continue along Plöck to the **Königstuhl funicular,** which hoists visitors to the Königstuhl heights, 1,860 feet
13 above Heidelberg, stopping at the ruined **castle** on the way. The two-minute ride to the castle costs DM 2 (DM 1.30 for children); the 17-minute ride to the top costs DM 4 (DM 2.40 for children). The funicular leaves every 20 minutes in the morning, and every 10 minutes in the afternoon. The funicular may be the quickest way to get to the castle, but you can also take the winding road up, following in the footsteps of generations of earlier visitors. (You can always walk down from the castle if you want to pretend to be Mark Twain but don't fancy the hike up.)

The castle was already in ruins when Germany's 19th-century Romantics fell under its spell, drawn by the mystery of its Gothic turrets and Renaissance walls etched against the verdant background of the thick woodland above Heidelberg. The oldest parts still standing date from the 15th century, though most of the great complex was built in the Renaissance and Baroque styles of the 16th and 17th centuries, when the castle was the seat and power base of the Palatinate Electors. What's most striking is the architectural variety of the building, vivid proof of changing tastes (and uses) down the years. There's even an "English wing," built in 1610 by the Elector Friedrich V for his teenage Scottish bride, Elizabeth Stuart; its plain square-windowed facade appears positively foreign in comparison to the more opulent styles of the rest of the castle. (The enamored Friedrich also had a charming garden laid out for his young bride; its imposing arched entryway, the Elisabethentor, was put up overnight to surprise her on her 19th birthday.) The architectural highlight, however, remains the Renaissance courtyard—harmonious, graceful, and ornate.

Leave at least two hours to tour the complex—and expect long lines in summer (up to 30 minutes is usual). On no account miss the **Heidelberger Fass** or the fascinating **Apothekenmuseum.** The Heidelberger Fass is an enormous wine barrel in the cellars, made from 130 oak trees and capable of holding 49,000 gallons. It was used to hold wines paid as tax by wine growers in the Palatinate. In the rule of the Elector Carl Philip, the barrel was guarded by the court jester, a Tyrolean dwarf called Perkeo. Legend has it that, small or not, he could consume frighteningly large quantities of wine—he was said to have been the most prodigious drinker in Germany—and that he died when he drank a glass of water by mistake. A statue of Perkeo stands opposite the massive barrel. The Apothekenmuseum is a delight, filled with containers (each with a carefully painted enamel label), beautifully made scales, little drawers, shelves, a marvelous reconstruction of an 18th-century apothecary's shop, dried beetles and toads, and a mummy with a full head of hair. *Castle admission: DM 4 adults, DM 2 children (this qualifies you for the tour and for entry to the Heidelberger Fass). Open daily 9–5. Guided tours from 9–noon and 1:30–4. Apothekenmuseum admission: DM 2 adults, DM 1 children. Open daily 10–5.*

The castle is floodlit in the summer, and in June and September firework displays are given from the terraces. In August, the castle is the setting for an open-air theater festival. Performances of *The Student Prince* figure prominently.

There are fine views of the old town from the castle terraces, but for an even better view, ride the funicular up to either of the
14 15 next two stops, **Molkenkur** and, at the summit, **Königstuhl.** If the weather's clear, you can see south as far as the Black Forest, and west to the Vosges mountains of France.

Time Out Both the Lokenkur and Königstuhl stops have comfortable restaurants with terraces commanding sweeping views. If you don't want lunch, stop in for just a cup of coffee and a pastry.

Back in town, walk toward the river from the funicular station to **Kornmarkt.** It's one of the oldest squares in Heidelberg, graced with a fine Baroque statue of the Virgin Mary. The impressive building on the corner of Mittelgasse was once Heidelberg's foremost hostelry, the Prinz Karl, where Mark Twain stayed in 1874. A few years earlier it had been used as a barracks by Bismarck's triumphant Prussian army, as they swept through the Rhineland forcibly uniting Germany. The young Prince Wilhelm von Preussen, later Kaiser Wilhelm I, was among the soldiers stationed there; prudently, he brought
16 along his own camp bed. The **Rathaus** (Town Hall), a stately Baroque building dating from 1701, faces you now. Be here at 7 PM to hear the melodious chimes that ring out from the building. The west side of the Rathaus fronts Heidelberg's market square, the Marktplatz. It was here, in the towering shadow of
17 the 14th-century **Heiliggeistkirche** (Church of the Holy Ghost) that criminals were tortured and decapitated and witches were burned. The church itself, dominating the west side of the square, fell victim to the plundering General Tilly, leader of the Catholic League, in the Thirty Years' War. Tilly loaded the church's greatest treasure, the *Biblioteka Palatina,* at the time the largest library in Germany, onto 500 carts and trundled it off to Rome, where he presented it to the Pope. Few of the volumes found their way back to Heidelberg. At the end of the 17th century, French troops plundered the church again, destroying the family tombs of the Palatinate electors; only the 15th-century tomb of Elector Ruprecht III and his wife Elisabeth von Hohenzollern remain today.

Opposite the church, on Hauptstrasse, you'll see the elaborate
18 Renaissance facade of the **Hotel zum Ritter,** all curlicues, columns, and gables. It takes its name from the statue of a Roman knight ("Ritter") atop one of the many gables. Its builder,

Carolus Belier, had the Latin inscription *Persta Invicta Venus* added in gold letters to the facade—"Beauty, Remain Unconquerable." It was an injunction that seems to have had the desired effect: This was the only Renaissance building in the city to have been spared the attentions of the invading French in 1689 and 1693. Between 1695 and 1705 it was used as Heidelberg's town hall; later, it became an inn. Today, it's the most atmospheric hotel in town (*see* Dining and Lodging, below).

Skirt the cathedral, cross the former fish market, the Fischmarkt, and turn down picturesque Steingasse. Within a
19 few steps you're at the river and the romantically turreted **Alte Brücke** (Old Bridge). It's the fifth bridge built here since medieval times, its predecessors having suffered various unhappy fates (one was destroyed by ice floes). The Elector Carl Theodor, who built it in 1786–88, must have been confident it would last: He had a statue of himself put on it, the plinth decorated with Neckar nymphs (river maidens). Just to be on the safe side, he also put up a statue of the saint appointed to guard over it, St. John Nepomuk. You can walk onto the bridge from the Old Town under a portcullis spanned by two Baroque towers, each capped with a *Spitzhelm* spire. In the left (west) tower are three dank dungeons that once held common criminals. Between the towers, above the gate, were more salubrious lock-ups, with views of the river and the castle; these were reserved for debtors. Above the portcullis you'll see a memorial plaque paying warm tribute to the Austrian forces who helped Heidelberg beat back a French attempt to capture the bridge in 1799. Walk onto the bridge and turn to soak up one of the finest views in Heidelberg, across the river to the old town and the castle above. There are equally good views from the road that runs along the far side of the river. For the best view of all, climb up Schlangenweg—it means Snake Path—to **Philosophenweg,** a path through the woods above the river. Be here as the sun sets, turning the castle to gold, for a vision to cherish for a lifetime.

Along the Burgenstrasse

Numbers in the margin correspond with points of interest on the Neckar Valley map.

From Heidelberg, you drive down the Neckar Valley on the Burgenstrasse, following the north bank of the river through a gentle landscape of orchards and vineyards. Wooded hills crowned with castles rise above the soft-flowing water.

20 The first town you reach is **Neckargemünd,** just 12 kilometers (8 miles) upstream from Heidelberg. Once it was a bustling river town; today, it's a sleepy sort of place, though it can make a good base from which to see Heidelberg if you want to avoid the summertime crowds there. Eight kilometers (5 miles) on,
21 perched impregnably on a hill, is **Dilsberg** castle, one of the few hereabouts to have withstood General Tilly's otherwise all-conquering forces in the Thirty Years' War. Until the students' jail in Heidelberg was built, its dungeons were used to accommodate the university's more unruly students. The view from its battlements over the valley and the green expanse of the Odenwald forest beyond is well worth the climb.

22 Opposite Dilsberg is **Neckarsteinach,** known as the Vierburgenstadt (Town of the Four Castles), for the fairly obvious reason that there are four castles here. They form one large complex—the **Schadeck**—most of which dates from the 12th century. Today, it's mostly ruined, but those sections still intact are the baronial residence of an aristocratic German family.

Time Out As along the Rhine, a number of the castles that stand on the Neckar have been converted into hotels. The castle above the 23 pretty little town of **Hirschorn,** 10 kilometers (16 miles) east of Neckarsteinach, is one such. If you don't plan to stay here (*see* Dining and Lodging, below), it can be worth stopping off for lunch. The view is superb. If you prefer a less formal lunchtime 24 layover, carry on to the next village—**Eberbach—** just a few miles up the valley, and make for the **Krabbenstein.** It's a 17th-century inn, one of the oldest along the river. The walls are decorated with frescoes that illustrate trades carried on in the village since the Middle Ages.

Eight kilometers (5 miles) beyond Eberbach, there's another 25 castle, standing above the village of **Zwingenberg,** its medieval towers thrusting through the dark woodland. Some say it's the most romantic along the Neckar (the one at Heidelberg excepted). It's owned by the margraves of Baden and is open limited times only but if you happen along when the castle is open, stop in to admire the frescoed 15th-century chapel and the collection of hunting trophies. *Admission: DM 3. Open May–Sept., Tues., Fri., and Sun. only 2–4.*

26 The little town of **Mosbach** is 16 kilometers (10 miles) up the valley. It's one of the most charming towns on the Neckar, and its ancient market square, Marktplatz, contains one of Germany's most exquisite half-timbered buildings. It's the early 17th-century **Palmsches Haus,** its upper stories smothered with intricate timbering. The **Rathaus,** built 50 years earlier, is a modest affair in comparison.

Three miles east of Mosbach you'll see the massive circular bulk 27 of **Hornberg** castle rising above the woods that drop to the riverbank. The road up to the castle leads through vineyards that have been providing excellent dry white wines for centuries. Today, the castle is part hotel and restaurant (*see* Dining and Lodging, below) and part museum. In the 16th century it was home to the larger-than-life knight Götz von Berlichingen (1480–1562). Von Berlichingen was a remarkable fellow. When he lost his right arm fighting in a petty dynastic squabble, the Landshut War of Succession, in 1504, he had a blacksmith fashion him an iron one. The original designs for this fearsome artificial limb are on view in the castle, as is a suit of armor that belonged to him. Scenes from his life are also represented. For most Germans, the rumbustious knight is best remembered for a remark he delivered to the Palatinate elector and that was faithfully reproduced by Goethe in his play about von Berlichingen (called, simply, *Götz von Berlichingen).* Responding to a reprimand from the elector, von Berlichingen told him, more or less, to "kiss my ass" (the original Germany is substantially more earthy). To this day, the polite version of this insult is known as a "Götz von Berlichingen"; practice it on the Autobahn when a BMW screeches on its brakes, headlights flashing, inches from your rear bumper. *Admission: DM 2.50 adults, DM 1 children. Open Mar.–Nov. daily 9–5.*

During the Peasants' War (1525), Götz von Berlichingen and his
28 troops destroyed the fine medieval castle of **Horneck,** 5 kilometers (3 miles) upriver. It was subsequently rebuilt and stands in all its medieval glory. Once it was owned by the Teutonic Order of Knights; today, it has a more mundane role as the retirement home of a German charity.

29 Two spas now await the tired traveler: **Bad Rappenau** and **Bad**
30 **Wimpfen.** Bad Rappenau's brine baths are said to ease not just aching limbs but asthma, rheumatism, and circulatory problems, too. It's an attractive little town, with a picturesque Rathaus (Town Hall) that was once a moated castle. However, Bad Wimpfen, 10 kilometers (6 miles) farther on, is of greater interest, a town rich in history and beauty. The Romans founded it, building a fortress here and a bridge across the Neckar in the first century AD. By the early Middle Ages, Bad Wimpfen had become an imperial center; the 12th-century Emperor Barbarossa built his largest palace here. Much of what remains of it can be visited, including the imperial living quarters with their stately pillared windows, from which the royal inhabitants enjoyed fine views of the river below. *Kaiserpl. Admission: DM 2. Open Apr.–Sept., Tues.–Sun. 9–noon and 2–5.*

After you've seen the fortress, you'll want to explore the small, winding streets of the historic center, a picture-postcard jumble of Gothic and Renaissance buildings. **Klostergasse,** a stage set of a street, is the standout. If you want to see the town in more detail, follow the marked walking tour; it begins at the Rathaus and is marked by signs bearing the town arms, an eagle with a key in its beak. Highlights of the tour are two churches: the early Gothic Ritterstiftskirche (Knights' Church) of **Sts. Peter and Paul;** and the **parish church** on the market square, Marktplatz. Sts. Peter and Paul stands on a charming square, shaded by gnarled chestnut trees. The rough-hewn Romanesque facade is the oldest part of the church, left standing when the town ran out of money after rebuilding the remainder of the church in Gothic style in the 13th century. The outline of the walls of this original building are clearly visible on the floor inside. The cloisters are delightful, an example of German Gothic at its most uncluttered and pure. In the parish church, be sure to see the 13th-century stained glass; it's among the oldest in the country.

31 Motorbike fans won't want to miss the town of **Neckarsulm,** 10 kilometers (6 miles) up the valley. It's a busy little industrial center, home of the German automobile manufacturer Audi and site of the **Deutsches Zweirad Museum,** the German Motorcycle Museum. It's located close by the NSU factory, where motorbikes were first manufactured in Germany. Among its 180 exhibits is the world's first mass-produced machine (the Hildebrand and Wolfmüller), a number of famous racing machines, and a rare Daimler machine, the first one made by that legendary name. The museum also has an exhibit of old bicycles, the oldest dating back to 1817, and early automobiles. All are arranged over four floors in a handsome 400-year-old building that belonged to the Teutonic Order of Knights until 1806. *Urbanstr. 11. Admission: DM 5 adults, DM 3 children, DM 10 for a family ticket. Open daily 9–noon.*

32 It's 6 kilometers (4 miles) now to the city of **Heilbronn** and the end of the Neckar tour. The city owes its name to a "holy well," or Heiligen Brunnen, a little fountain that bubbles up out of the ground by the church of St. Kilian; it owes its fame to the Romantic German classic *Kätchen von Heilbronn,* by early 19th-century writer Heinrich von Kleist. The virtuous, put-upon Kätchen was modeled by von Kleist on the daughter of Heilbronn's lord mayor, and the family home still stands on the west side of the central square, Marktplatz. It's ornate oriel window, decorated with figures of four of the prophets, makes it easy to spot.

Most of the leading sights in Heilbronn are grouped in and around Marktplatz, dominated by the sturdy **Rathaus,** built in Gothic style in 1417 and remodeled in the Renaissance. Set into its clean-lined Renaissance facade beneath the steeply eaved red roof is a magnificently ornate 16th-century **clock.** It's divided into four distinct parts. The lowest is an astronomical clock, showing the day of the week, the month, and the year. Above it is the main clock; note how its hour hand is larger than the minute hand, a convention common in the 16th century. Above this, there's a smaller dial that shows the phases of the sun and the moon. Then, at the topmost level, suspended from a delicate stone surround, there's a bell, struck alternately by the two angels that stand on either side of it. Be here at noon when the whole elaborate mechanism swings into action. As the hour strikes, an angel at the base of the clock sounds a trumpet; another turns an hour glass and counts the hours with a scepter. Simultaneously, the twin golden rams between them charge each other and lock horns while a cockerel spreads its wings and crows.

Time Out Heilbronn is one of the largest wine-producing cities in Germany, with more than 1,000 acres of vineyards within the city limits. Try any of the local wines in the historic tavern **Schwarzer Kater,** a short walk from the market square. *Lammgasse 2.*

Behind the market square is Heilbronn's most famous church, the **Kilianskirche** (church of St. Kilian), dedicated to the Irish monk who brought Christianity to the Rhineland in the Dark Ages and who lies buried in Würzburg. Its lofty Gothic tower was capped in the early 16th century with a fussy, lanternlike structure that ranks as the first major Renaissance work north of the Alps. At its summit there's a soldier carrying a banner decorated with the city arms. Walk around the church to the south side (the side opposite the main entrance) to see the well that gave the city its name.

What to See and Do with Children

The **Heidelberg** tourist office issues a special publication, *Heidelberg fur Kinder* ("Heidelberg for Children"), that lists activities and attractions. Pick it up free from any of the city's three tourist offices. The city has a **zoo** on the banks of the Neckar on Tiergartenstrasse. *Admission: DM 6 adults, DM 3 children, DM 4 senior citizens and students. Open Apr.–Sept. Mon.–Thurs. and Sat. 9–7, Fri. 9–9, Sun. 10–6; Oct.–Mar. Mon.–Sat. 9–5.*

On the Königstuhl heights above the city there's a children's fair, the **Märchen-paradies,** with fairy-tale tableaux, rides, a miniature railroad, and more. (Admission: DM 3 adults, DM 2 children. Open mid-Mar.–mid-Oct. daily 10–6.) Children love the ride up the mountain on the funicular, too (*see* Exploring, above).

The **Auto and Technik Museum** at Sinsheim, 20 kilometers (12 miles) south of Neckargemünd, is worth the detour if you're driving the Neckar Valley. There are more than 1,000 exhibits, encompassing the whole history of mechanized transportation. *Admission: DM 13 adults, DM 8 children. Open daily 9–6.*

Twenty kilometers (12 miles) south of Heilbronn, on B-27, you'll find one of south Germany's best fun parks, the **Freizeitpark Tripsdrill,** located at Cleeborn/Tripsdill. It's great for families, with a wine museum to amuse parents while children enjoy the rides. (Admission: DM 14 adults, DM 12 children. Open Easter–Nov. daily 9–6.) North of Heilbronn on the same road are some intriguing caves, the **Eberstädter Höhlen** (open daily 10–4).

Off the Beaten Track

In **Heidelberg,** escape the crowds by crossing the Theodor Heuss Bridge to the north bank of the Neckar and climbing the heights above the river along the path called **Philosophenweg.** Many painters were here before you, capturing the views the route gives of the city below. Strike off into the woodland above you in the direction of the summit of the **Heiligenberg.** On the way you'll pass a curious Nazi-era relic, the **Germanische Thingstätte,** an open amphitheater originally intended for woodland festivals.

Along the Neckar Valley road, all the small valleys—the locals call them "Klingen"—that cut north into the Odenwald are off-the-beaten-track territory. The most atmospheric of them all is the **Wolfsschlucht,** which starts below the castle at Zwingenberg. The dank, shadowy little gorge features in Carl Maria von Weber's opera *Der Freischütz.* If you see a vulture circling overhead, don't be alarmed. It's likely to be from Claus Fentzloff's unusual **aviary** at Guttenberg castle, farther along the Neckar Valley. He keeps vultures, eagles, and rare breeds of owl, showing them daily at 11 and 3, March through October. They give demonstration flights for the delight of the visitors, and sometimes disappear for days on end. "But they always come home," says Fentzloff.

For unusual museums in Neckarland, try the **Lucky-Charm Museum** in Bad Wimpfen (Kronengässchen 2. Open Fri. 4–8, Sat.–Sun. 11–8) and the **Bonsai** museum of miniature trees in Heidelberg (Mannheimerstr. 401. Open daily 10–4).

Shopping

Wine is the chief product of the Neckar region, and Heilbronn is the place to buy it. The city has an internationally renowned wine festival in the second week of September, the "Weindorf," where more than 200 wines from the Heilbronn region alone are offered. Outside festival time, you'll find numerous shops stocking wine in Heilbronn's central shopping zone, and you can also buy direct from vineyards. A good one to try is the **Amalienhof** (Lukas-Cranach-Weg 5).

There are numerous vineyards along the Neckar Valley road between Heidelberg and Heilbronn. Those around **Gundelsheim** are judged to be the best, but for sheer historical worth you can't beat a bottle from the **Hornberg** castle estate, which once stocked the table of the knight Götz von Berlichingen (*see* Exploring, above).

The Neckar Valley is also famous for its **glass** and **crystal.** You can buy directly from the factory at Neckarzimmern or from Heidelberg shops such as **Crystal** (Hauptstr. 135) and **König** (Universitätspl.). Both are in Heidelberg's excellent pedestrian shopping zone, which stretches for more than a half mile through the ancient heart of the city. Heilbronn also has an extensive central pedestrian shopping mall. In both cities, you can find interesting and often reasonably priced German **antiques.** In Heidelberg try **Spiess & Walther** (Friedrich-Ebert-Anlage 23a); in Heilbronn, take time to comb **Monika Finkbeiner's** well-stocked shop (Allee 38). Heidelberg has a **flea market** in the Dehner suburb every second Saturday. The U.S. Army base in the city organizes a rummage sale in March.

Heidelberg has two tempting **markets.** On Wednesday and Sunday mornings, make for the central market square, Marktplatz; on Tuesday and Friday mornings, make for Friedrich-Ebert-Platz.

Sports and Fitness

Bowling You can scatter the pins at Heidelberg's **Euro-Bowling Center** (Bergheimerstr. and Mittermaierstr., tel. 06221/23233).

Golf Visiting golfers tee off with no problem at two Heidelberg clubs, the **Golfclub Heidelberg** in the neighboring village of Lobbach-Lobenfeld (tel. 06226/40490), and the **Hohenhardter Hof Club** (Wiesloch 4, tel. 06222/72081). In Heilbronn you can play at the **Golfclub Heilbronn-Hohenlohe,** in the village of Friedrichsruhe (tel. 07132/3680).

Horseback Riding In Heidelberg, there are stables at the city **zoo** (tel. 06221/42728) and at Pleikartsforstenhof 5 (tel. 06221/32059). Heilbronn has a riding club where you can hire horses and also take lessons, the **Reiterverein Heilbronn** (Im Sternberg 5, tel. 07131/78469).

Roller-skating Wednesday night is disco-night at the roller-skating rink at Heilbronn's **Europaplatz.** It's great fun. The rink is open daily from 9 to 9.

Swimming You'll find open-air and indoor swimming pools in all towns and most villages along your way. Heidelberg has a pool fed by thermal water at Vangerowstrasse 4, and pools at the extensive **Tiergartenschwimmbad** next to the zoo. Heilbronn's favorite lido, the **Freibad Neckarhalde,** has a view of the river. It's not advisable to swim in the Neckar River.

Tennis Most towns and villages along the Neckar have local tennis clubs that accept visitors. In Heidelberg, you can play at the **Kirchheimerweg** courts (tel. 06221/12106). In Heilbronn, the tennis schools at Böckingerstrasse 170 (tel. 07131/46166) and Viehweide 91 (tel. 07131/42905) can arrange lessons and partners.

Dining and Lodging

Dining

Heidelberg and Mannheim offer the most elegant dining in the region, though in Heidelberg you'll be dining with tradition at your table: There are few restaurants in the city that don't have decor to match the stage-set atmosphere of the town. Elsewhere, you'll find atmospheric and frequently excellent food in the restaurants of the castle hotels along the Neckar. In smaller towns along the valley, simple inns, dark and timbered, are the norm. Outside Heidelberg and Mannheim, prices can be low. Specialties in the Neckar Valley are much the same as along the Wine Road, with sausages and local wines figuring prominently.

Highly recommended restaurants are indicated by a star ★.

Category	Cost*
Very Expensive	over DM 90
Expensive	DM 55–DM 90
Moderate	DM 35–DM 55
Inexpensive	under DM 35

**per person for a three-course meal including tax but not drinks*

Lodging

If you plan to visit Heidelberg in summer, make reservations well in advance and expect to pay top rates. To get away from the crowds, consider staying out of town—at Neckargemünd, say—and driving or taking the bus into the city. Staying in a castle hotel can be fun. This is an area that's second only to the Rhine for baronial-style castle hotels studding the hilltops. Most have terrific views as well as stone-passageways-and-four-poster-bed atmosphere.

Highly recommended hotels are indicated by a star ★ .

Category	Cost*
Very Expensive	over DM 180
Expensive	DM 120–DM 180
Moderate	DM 80–DM 120
Inexpensive	under DM 80

**Prices are for two people in a double room.*

Heidelberg
Dining

Der Kurfürstenstuben-Grill. The hand-carved wood ceiling and paneled walls of this elegantly rustic restaurant in the Europäischer Hof Hotel provide an unlikely setting for sophisticated nouvelle cuisine. Dine on the leafy terrace in summer.

Brunch is featured Sundays. *Friedrich-Ebert-Anlage 1, tel. 06221/27101. Reservations advised. Jacket and tie required. AE, DC, MC, V. Expensive.*

Giardino. An Italian restaurant in Heidelberg? A paradox maybe, but also quite an experience. Il Giardino is the elegant and smoothly run restaurant of the Prinzhotel, and offers classic Italian cuisine. For best value, try the gourmet menu (the first course is a salad of fish and black truffles) at DM 118 per person. *Neuenheimer Landstr. 5, tel. 06221/40320. Reservations advised. Jacket and tie required. AE, DC, MC, V. Closed Tues. and Nov. Expensive.*

★ **Gaudeamus Igitur.** Elegant rusticity, complete with high-class nouvelle cuisine, obligatory exposed beams, stone walls, and wood ceilings, sums up the restaurant of the Hirschgasse Hotel. Herbs from the hotel's own garden are used extensively. The name, by the way, means "Let us be happy." *Hirschgasse 3, tel. 06221/49921. Reservations advised. Jacket and tie required. AE, DC, MC, V. Closed Sun., public holidays, and Dec. 23–Jan. 7. Expensive.*

★ **Romantik-Restaurant zum Ritter St. Georg.** The venison you eat here—dine in either the Knight's Tavern or the Alderman's Hall—comes from the restaurant's own hunting grounds outside Heidelberg. This is the restaurant of the most emphatically Teutonic hotel in town, and offers a full-bodied taste of old-time Germany. *Hauptstr. 178, tel. 06221/20203. Reservations advised. Jacket and tie required. AE, DC, MC, V. Moderate.*

Perkeo. Ask for a table in the atmospheric Schlosstube, and, if suckling pig is on the menu, ask for that, too. You'll then be dining in the style for which this historic old restaurant has been known for close to three centuries. *Hauptstr. 75, tel. 06221/160613. Reservations advised. Dress: informal. AE, DC, MC, V. Inexpensive.*

★ **Zum Roten Ochsen.** This is about the most famous and time-honored of Heidelberg's old taverns. Bismarck and Mark Twain ate here; so, too, many years later, did John Foster Dulles. It's been run by the Spengel family for more than a century, and they jealously guard the rough-hewn, half-timbered atmosphere. Many of the oak tables have initials carved into them, legacy of thousands of former visitors. The mood is festive and noisy, with rowdy singing most nights. *Hauptstr. 217, tel. 06221/20977. Reservations essential. Dress: informal. No credit cards. Closed Sun., public holidays, and mid-Dec.–mid-Jan. Inexpensive.*

★ **Schnookelooch.** This picturesque and lively old tavern dates back to 1407 and is inextricably linked with Heidelberg's history and its university. Most evenings a piano player joins the fun. *Haspelgasse 8, tel. 06221/22733. Reservations essential. Dress: informal. No credit cards. Inexpensive.*

Lodging

★ **Europäischer Hof.** This is the classiest and most luxurious of Heidelberg's hotels, handy for about everything in town and with a wide range of facilities. Public rooms are sumptuously furnished, while bedrooms are spacious and tasteful. If you fancy a splurge, go for one of the suites; the best have Jacuzzis. *Friedrich-Ebert-Anlage 1, tel. 06221/27101. 150 rooms with bath. Facilities: 2 restaurants, bar, indoor pool, gym, sauna, solarium, shopping mall. AE, DC, MC, V. Very Expensive.*

★ **Hotel Hirschgasse.** Located across the river on the edge of town (which you may find inconvenient if you want to go back and forth more than once a day), the Hirschgasse is one of the oldest hotels in Heidelberg, dating back to 1472. Renovations in 1988 have produced an elegantly chic mood, though something of the older more simple atmosphere remains in some rooms. One has a four-poster bed. The restaurant is exceptional. *Hirschgasse 3, tel. 06221/49921. 23 rooms and 2 suites, all with bath. Facilities: restaurant. AE, DC, MC, V. Closed Dec. 23–Jan. 7. Expensive.*

Prinzhotel. Cool pastel shades establish a discreetly upscale mood in this turn-of-the-century villa. It's located across the river from the Old Town; fight for a room with a view of the river. *Neuenheimer Landstr. 5, tel. 06221/40320. 47 rooms and 3 suites, all with bath. Facilities: restaurant, indoor pool, sauna, steam bath, solarium. AE, DC, MC, V. Expensive.*

★ **Romantik Hotel zum Ritter St. Georg.** If this is your first visit to Germany, stay here. It's the only Renaissance building in Heidelberg and offers atmosphere by the barrel-load. The Red Baron would feel right at home in the dining room, complete with suit of armor, rough plaster walls, arched doorways, and exposed beams. Bedrooms are clean and comfortable, some traditional, some more modern. *Hauptstr. 178, tel. 06221/20201. 31 rooms with bath. Facilities: restaurant. AE, DC, MC, V. Expensive.*

Perkeo. The mood may be a bit motel-like, but some homey, old-fashioned touches that you may find more agreeable than the relentless Lederhosen-look of many Heidelberg hotels makes this a good low-cost bet. It's located on the busy pedestrian main street, so ask for a quiet room. *Hauptstr. 75, tel. 06221/22255. 25 rooms with bath. AE, DC, MC, V. Moderate.*

Heilbronn
Dining

★ **Wirtshaus am Götzenturm.** This is no ordinary *Wirtshaus* (meaning "inn"), but a charming and classy restaurant run with imagination and skill by owner-chef Gerhard Münch. Try any of his four-course, fixed-price fish dishes. *Allerheiligenstr. 1, tel. 07131/80534. Reservations essential. Jacket and tie required. No credit cards. Closed lunch and all day Sun. Expensive.*

Festhalle Harmonie. Eat on the terrace in summer to enjoy the view of the city park. Inside, the decor fuses traditional and modern styles. For best value, try one of the fixed-price menus. *Friedrich-Weber-Allee 28, tel. 07131/86890. Reservations essential. Jacket and tie required. No credit cards. Closed most of Aug. Moderate.*

★ **Ratskeller.** For sturdy and dependable regional specialties—try Swabian *Maultaschen,* a kind of local ravioli—and as much Teutonic atmosphere as you'll ever want, you won't go wrong in this, the basement restaurant of the town hall. *Marktpl. 7, tel. 07131/84628. Reservations advised. Dress: informal. No credit cards. Closed Sun. dinner. Inexpensive.*

Lodging

Hotel Götz. The Götz is a modern high rise, located close by the historic area, and about the best hotel in town, much favored by business types. What it lacks in atmosphere it makes up for with dependable levels of service and comfort. *Möltkestr. 52, tel. 07131/1550. 90 rooms with bath. Facilities: restaurant, bar. AE, DC, MC, V. Moderate.*

Hirschhorn
Dining and Lodging

Schlosshotel Hirschhorn. Not so much a castle hotel as a pleasant if undistinguished modern hotel in a castle, the Hirschhorn is perched on a hilltop overlooking the Neckar, 14 miles east of Heidelberg. Hallways have that rough-plaster medieval look, lest you forget you're in a castle; rooms are furnished in approved Student Prince style. The views are terrific, and the restaurant much better than average. *6932 Hirschhorn/Neckar, tel. 06272/1373. 25 rooms with bath. V. Closed Dec.–Jan. Expensive.*

Mannheim
Dining
★ **Da Gianni.** Sophisticated Italian dishes, with a distinctly nouvelle accent, are served in this classy haunt in the Quadrastadt. Try pigeon with artichoke or any of the fish specialties for a meal you won't forget. *R-7 34, tel. 0621/20326. Reservations essential. Jacket and tie required. AE, MC. Closed Mon. and 3 weeks in July. Expensive.*

★ **L'Epi d'Or.** French nouvelle cuisine and sophisticated local specialties are the hallmark of Norbert Dobler's city-center restaurant. The warm lobster salad is a classic; or try the saddle of lamb. *H-7 3, tel. 0621/14397. Reservations essential. Jacket and tie required. AE, DC, MC, V. Expensive.*

Alte Munz. For old German atmosphere, local specialties, and a wide range of beers, the Alte Munz is hard to beat. Try the suckling pig if it's available. *P-7 1, tel. 0621/28262. Reservations advised. Dress: informal. AE, MC, V. Moderate.*

Goldene Gans. Freshly made local dishes (Pfälzer liver-dumpling and home-cured sausage are two to try) and wines from the tavern's own vineyards combine with surprisingly low prices to make this a terrific low-cost bet. *Tattersallstr. 19, tel. 0621/105–277. Reservations not required. Dress: informal. No credit cards. Closed Sun. and Dec. 23–Jan. 6. Inexpensive.*

Lodging
★ **Maritim Parkhotel.** It may be part of a chain, but the turn-of-the-century Parkhotel is the number-one choice in town, offering opulent comforts very much in the grand manner. The pillared, chandelier-hung lobby sets the mood; rooms are spaciously elegant. *Friedrichspl. 2, tel. 0621/45071. 184 rooms and 3 suites, all with bath. Facilities: restaurant, bar, indoor pool, sauna, steam bath, solarium, beauty salon. AE, DC, MC, V. Very Expensive.*

Steigenberger Hotel Mannheimer Hof. The combination of the great location, overlooking Friedrichsplatz, and the reliable standards of the Steigenberger chain make this a good choice for solid comfort. *Augusta-Anlage 4–8, tel. 0621/45021. 166 rooms and 4 suites, all with bath. Facilities: bar, restaurant. AE, DC, MC, V. Expensive.*

Novotel Mannheim. Built in 1980 and fully renovated in 1988, the Novotel is a reliable standby. Rooms are standardized, but well designed and comfortable. *Auf dem Friedenspl., tel. 0621/417–001. Facilities: restaurant, bar, indoor pool. AE, DC, MC, V. Moderate.*

Neckargemünd
Lodging
Hotel zum Ritter. Built in the 16th century, the half-timbered zum Ritter is an appealingly historic hotel with exposed beams, simple plaster walls, and creaking passages. Ask for a room with a view. *Neckarstr. 40, tel. 06223/7035. 40 rooms with bath. AE, MC, V. Expensive.*

Neckarzimmern
Dining and Lodging
★ **Burghotel Neckarzimmern.** Midway between Heidelberg and Heilbronn stands the ancient castle where knight Götz von Berlichingen, immortalized by Goethe, spent his declining years. Some complain that it hasn't much panache for an 11th-century castle, but rooms are comfortable and some have great views over the vineyards to the river. The restaurant features venison (in season) and fresh fish. *6951 Neckarzimmern, tel. 06261/406–465. 29 rooms with bath. Facilities: restaurant. AE, DC, MC. Expensive.*

Obrigheim
Dining and Lodging

Hotel Schloss Neuburg. The Neuburg is another castle hotel, standing high above the Neckar and the Odenwald. Sensitive modernization has ensured that many original features have been retained while many essential comforts have been built in. Many bedrooms have oak beams. *Obrigheim 06952, tel. 06261/7001. 13 rooms with bath. Facilities: restaurant. AE, DC, MC. Moderate.*

The Arts and Nightlife

Information on all upcoming events in **Heidelberg** is listed in the monthly *Ketchup* magazine (which costs DM 3); the monthly *Konzerte im Heidelberger Stern* (available free—pick it up at the tourist office); and *Heidelberg Aktuell* (also free and available from the tourist office). The **Heilbronn** tourist office publishes a similar monthly listings magazine, *Heilbronn Today & Tomorrow;* it, too, is available free. Tickets for theaters in Heidelberg are available from **Theaterkasse** (Theaterstr. 4, tel. 06221/20519). In Heilbronn, you can buy tickets from the tourist office.

The Arts

Theater and Music

Heidelberg has a thriving theater scene. The **Theater der Stadt** (Friedrichstr. 5) is the best-known theater in town; others include the **Zimmer Theater** (Hauptstr. 118, tel. 06221/21069) and the **Theater in Augustinum** (Jasperstr. 2, tel. 06221/3881). For information on performances at the castle during the annual Schloss-Spiele festival, tel. 06221/58976. Heilbronn's **Stadttheater** (Berliner Pl. 1, tel. 07131/563–001) is the leading venue in the city. In summer, **classical concerts** are given in the gardens behind the Festhalle; contact the tourist office for details of performances and tickets.

Nightlife

Heidelberg's nightlife is concentrated around the Heiliggeistkirche (the Church of the Holy Ghost), in the Old Town. For a fun night out, try the **Hard Rock Café** (Hauptstr.); it's not exactly Student Prince country, but it's a good place for videos and burgers. For blues, jazz, and funk, try **Hookemann** (Fischmarkt 3); admission is free. Germany's oldest jazz cellar is **Cave 54** (Krämergasse 2). The **Goldener Reichsapfel** nearby is always crowded after 10 PM; the mood is smokey and loud. **Club 1900** (Hauptstr.) is a well-established disco. For most, however, nightlife in Heidelberg means a visit to one of the student taverns to drink wine and beer, lock arms, and sing. There are no better places to try than **Zum Roten Ochsen** and **Schnookelooch,** both in business for several centuries and both offering low-beamed Teutonic fun and games.

12 Frankfurt

Introduction

Frankfurt-am-Main, to give this thriving metropolis its full name, is West Germany's financial and commercial capital. Despite a long and distinguished past, it's also an unashamedly modern city, the sort of place where a Japanese businessman making his first visit to Europe would feel very much at home. It's not a city with a great deal of local charm. Neither does it have much that could be termed elegant, shops and restaurants aside. Where other German cities, pummeled by Allied bombing, went to painstaking lengths to restore as much as possible of their prewar heritage, Frankfurt in the chaotic postwar years threw itself into high-rise construction with a vengeance, sweeping away large areas of the war-torn old town and replacing them with aggresive glass and steel. The hope was that the city would be chosen as the new capital of West Germany (it very nearly was). In any event, Bonn was selected, leaving Frankfurt's city fathers not a little shamefaced as they contemplated their new skyscrapers.

None of which suggests that Frankfurt is a city that visitors are likely to warm to. The sort of subtle charm Munich possesses in such abundance, for example, just doesn't exist here. The fact that Frankfurt has the busiest airport in Germany, five train stations, the largest inland port in Europe, and the two tallest buildings and biggest hotel in the country may (and does) appeal to any number of multinational corporations, but it hardly recommends it as a tourist city.

So why come to Frankfurt? First, because it *is* a deeply historic city, one of the joint capitals of Charlemagne's empire, the city where no fewer than 30 Holy Roman Emperors were elected and crowned, the city where Gutenburg set up his print shop, the city where Goethe was born, the city where the first German parliament met. There may be only faint shadows of this original Frankfurt for you to see today, but they are here nonetheless and, this being Germany, beautifully cared for, too.

Frankfurt's commercial clout has its historic side as well. The city was a major trading center as early as the 12th century. Its first international Autumn Fair was held in 1240; in 1330 its Spring Fair was inaugurated. Both are still going strong today. The stock exchange, one of the half dozen most important in the world, was established back in 1595. The Rothschilds opened their first bank here, in 1798.

Second, while Frankfurt may be a city of balance sheets and share prices, it still possesses something of the glitzy panache and high living that are such conspicuous features of today's Germany cities. It's more than just a question of expense-account restaurants and sleek cars. Rather, there's the feeling that you are in the heart of a powerful, sophisticated, and cosmopolitan nation. There may not be much here to remind you of the Old World, but there's a great deal that explains Germany's astonishing success story.

Essential Information

Important Addresses and Numbers

Tourist Information For advance information, write to the **Verkehrsamt Frankfurt/Main** (Gutleutstr. 7–9, tel. 069/212–8849). The main tourist office is located at the **Hauptbahnhof** (main train station). It runs a hotel reservations service and can arrange sightseeing tours of the city as well as excursions (tel. 069/212–8849). It's open April–October, Monday–Saturday 8 AM–10 PM; November–March, Monday–Saturday 8 AM–9 PM, Sunday and holidays 9:30–8. A secondary tourist office is located at the **Hauptwache** train station downtown (tel. 069/ 212–8708). It's open weekdays 9–6, Saturday 9–2.

Consulates **U.S. Consulate General,** Seismayerstrasse 21, tel. 069/74007.

British Consulate General, Bockenheimer Landstrasse 51–53, tel. 069/72046.

Emergencies **Police:** tel. 110. **Fire:** tel. 112. **Medical Emergencies:** tel. 069/792–0200.

Pharmacies: tel. 069/11500. **Dental Emergencies:** tel. 069/660–727.

English-Language Bookstores **British Bookshop,** Börsenstrasse 17, tel. 069/280–492.
Internationale Buchhandel, Münchnerstrasse 56, tel. 069/252–914.
America Haus (library, newspapers, cultural events), Staufenstrasse 1, tel. 069/722–860.

Travel Agencies **American Express International,** Steinweg 5, tel. 069/210–548.
Thomas Cook, Kaiserstrasse 11, tel. 069/13470.
D.E.R. Deustches Reisebüro, Eschersheimer Landstrasse 25–27, tel. 069/156–6289.
Hapag-Lloyd Reisebüro, Rossmarkt 21, tel. 069/216–2286.

Lost and Found **Fundbüro Stadt,** Mainzer Landstrasse 323, tel. 069/750–02403; **Fundbüro Bahn,** at the train station, tel. 069/265–5831; **Fundbüro Flughafen,** at the airport, tel. 069/960–2413.

Car Rental **Avis,** Mainzer Landstrasse 170, tel. 069/230–101.
Europcar, Mainzer Landstrasse 160, tel. 069/234–00204.
Hertz, Hanauer Landstrasse 106–108, tel. 069/449–090.

Arriving and Departing by Plane

Frankfurt airport is the biggest on the Continent, smaller only among all European airports than London's Heathrow. There are direct flights to it from many U.S. cities and from all major European cities. It's located 6 miles southwest of the downtown area, by the Köln–Munich Autobahn.

Between the Airport and Downtown Getting into Frankfurt from the airport is easy. There are two S-Bahn lines (suburban trains) that run from the airport to downtown Frankfurt. One line, S-14, goes to Hauptwache square in the heart of Frankfurt. Trains run every 20 minutes; the trip takes about 15 minutes. The other line, S-15, goes to the Hauptbahnhof (main train station), just west of the downtown area. Trains run every 10 minutes; the trip takes 11 minutes. One-way fare for both services is DM 3.30 (DM 4.40 during rush hours). Intercity express trains to and from most major West German cities also stop at the airport. There are hourly services to Köln, Hamburg, and Munich, for example. City bus 61 also serves the airport, running between it and the Südbahnhof train station in Sachsenhausen, south of the downtown area. The trip takes about 30 minutes. A taxi from the airport into the city center normally takes around 20 minutes; allow double that in rush hours. The fare is around DM 35. If you're picking up a rental car at the airport, getting into Frankfurt is easy. Take the main road out of the airport and follow the signs for Stadtmitte (downtown).

By Train All long-distance trains arrive at and depart from the Hauptbahnhof. For information, call **Deutsche Bahnhof** (German Railways), tel. 069/23033, or ask at the information office in the station.

Arriving and Departing by Bus and Car

By Bus More than 200 European cities—including all major West German cities—have bus links with Frankfurt. Buses arrive and depart from the south side of the Hauptbahnhof. For information and tickets, contact **Deutsche Touring,** Am Römerhof 17, tel. 069/79030.

By Car Frankfurt is located at the meeting point of a number of major autobahns, of which the most important are A-3, running south from Köln and then on to Würzburg, Nürnberg, and Munich, and A-5, running south from Giessen and then on to Mannheim, Heidelberg, Karlsruhe, and the Swiss-German border at Basel. A complex series of beltways surrounds the city. If you're driving to Frankfurt on A-5 from either north or south, exit at Nordwestkreuz and follow A-66 to the Nordend district, just north of downtown. Driving south on A-3, exit onto A-66 and follow the signs to Frankfurt-Höchst and then the Nordend district. Driving north on A-3, exit at Offenbach onto A-661 and follow the signs for Frankfurt-Stadtmitte.

Getting Around

On Foot Downtown Frankfurt is compact and easily explored on foot. There are fewer pedestrians-only streets in the downtown area than in some other major German cities; the most important radiate from Hauptwache square. The Römer complex, south of Hauptwache, is also pedestrianized. From here, you can easily cross the river on the Eisener Steg (Iron Bridge) to Sach--senhausen, most of whose tangle of small streets are best explored on foot. For sights and attractions away from the downtown area, make use of the excellent public-transportation system.

By Public Transportation Frankfurt lays claim to a smooth-running, well-integrated public transportation system, consisting of the U-bahn (subway), S-bahn (suburban railway), and Strassenbahn (streetcars). Fares for the entire system are uniform, though based on a complex zone system that can be hard to figure out. A basic one-way ticket for a ride in the inner zone costs DM 1.70 (DM 2.20 during rush hours). For rides of just a stop or two, buy a **Kurzstrecken Karte;** cost is DM 1.20. The best buy of all is a 24-hour ticket, a **24-Studen.** It costs DM 7 and allows unlimited travel in the inner zone for DM 7 in any 24-hour period. For information and assistance, call 069/26940.

By Taxi Fares start at DM 3.60 and increase by DM 1.80 per kilometer. There is an extra charge of 50 pfennigs per piece of baggage. You can hail taxis in the street or call them at tel. 069/250–001, tel. 069/230–033, tel. 069/545–011. Note that there's an extra charge for the drive or coming to the pickup point.

By Bike In summer, you can rent bikes at the **Goetheturm** (Goethe Tower) at the edge of the Frankfurt Stadtwald (tel. 069/49111).

Guided Tours

Orientation Tours Two-and-a-half-hour bus tours taking in all the main sights with English-speaking guides are offered by the tourist office, March through October. Tours leave from the main train station daily at 10:15 and 2. November through February, tours leave at 2 only. Cost is around DM 30. Call 069/212–8849 for reservations.

Special-Interest Tours The city transit authority (tel. 069/136–82425) runs a brightly painted old-time streetcar—the **Ebbelwei Express** (Cider Express)—Saturdays and Sundays every 45 minutes between 1:30 and 5:30. Departures are from the Ostbahnhof (east train station) and the fare—it includes a free glass of cider (or apple juice) and a pretzel—is DM 3. All the major attractions in the city are covered as the streetcar trundles along. The ride lasts just over 30 minutes. The **Historische Eisenbahn Frankfurt** (Eschborner Landstr. 140, tel. 069/539–147) runs a vintage steam train along the banks of the Main River on occasional weekends January through mid-May and every weekend mid-May through September. The train runs from the Eisener Steg west to Frankfurt-Griesham and east to Frankfurt-Mainkur. Fare is DM 5 one-way, DM 9 round-trip.

Walking Tours The tourist office arranges walking tours on demand (tel. 069/212–8849). Tours are tailored to suit individual requirements, and costs vary accordingly.

Excursions **Dema-Reisen Sightseeing** (Mannheimerstr. 7–9, tel. 069/231–322) and **Deutsche Touring** (Am Römerhof 17, tel. 069/79030) offer a variety of tours into the areas immediately around Frankfurt as well as farther afield. Destinations include the Rhine Valley, with steamship cruises and wine tasting and day trips to the historic towns of Heidelberg and Rothenburg-ob-der-Tauber. Deutsche Touring's "Frankfurt Panorama Tour," for example, takes in both the city and the towns of Höchst, Bad Soden, and Kronberg in the lovely Taunus Valley. Full information is available from both organizations. A **Casino Bus** service operates daily to the casino at Bad Homburg in the Taunus. It leaves every hour between 2:15 and 11:15 PM (the last bus back to Frankfurt leaves Bad Homburg at 3 AM) from Baslerplatz. The fare of DM 7 includes entry to the casino.

Boat Trips There are a variety of round-trips and excursions on the Main River. The **Köln-Dusseldorfer** line (tel. 069/282–420) offers the most trips; they leave from the Frankfurt Mainkai am Eisernen Steg, just south of the Romer complex. The **Fahrgastschiff Wikinger** company (tel. 069/282–886) and the **Frankfurter Personenschiffahrt Anton Nauheimer Company** (tel. 069/281–884) also offer trips along the Main and excursions to the Rhine. Combined boat trips and wine-tasting trips are offered by **Deutsche Touring** (tel. 069/79030).

Exploring Frankfurt

Numbers in the margin correspond with points of interest on the Frankfurt map.

Highlights for First-time Visitors

Hauptwache
Romerberg
Goethehaus und Goethemuseum
Sachsenhausen
Stadelsches Kunstinstitut und Stadtische Galerie

The Old Town

1 Start your tour of Frankfurt in the reconstructed old town, at the square called **Hauptwache,** hub of the city transportation network. The Hauptwache is a handsome 18th-century building a single story high under a steeply sloping roof. It was built as the city's guardhouse and prison; today, it serves as a café. An underground shopping mall stretches below the square. Head into it to the tourist office to pick up a city map and other information on Frankfurt.

2 To the south of the square is the **Katerinenkirche** (church of St. Katherine), the most important Protestant church in the city. What you see today is a simplified version of the second church on the site, put up after the war. It was in the original church here that the first Protestant sermon was preached in Frankfurt, in 1522. Step inside to see the simple, postwar stained glass. *Open daily 10–5.*

3 Head south from the church along Berlinerstrasse to the circular bulk of the **Paulskirche** (Church of St. Paul's), a handsome, mostly 18th-century building that, church or not, is more interesting for its political than for its religious significance. It was here that the short-lived German parliament met in May 1848. The parliament was hardly a success—it was disbanded within a year, having achieved little more than offering the Prussian king the crown of Germany, but it remains a focus for the democratic aspirations of the German people. The building you see today, modeled loosely on the original, was rebuilt after the war in the expectation that it would become the home of the new German parliament. The German Book Dealers' annual Peace Prize is awarded in the hall, as is the Goethe Prize. *Open daily 10–3.*

Walk along the pedestrian street called Neue Krame and over Braubachstrasse. On your left you pass the Gothic turrets and crenellations of the **Steinernes Hays** (Stone House), built in 1464. Today it is the home of the Frankfurt Kunstverein (Arts Association). *Markt 44. Admission: DM 6. Open Tues.–Sat. 11–6.*

4 You are now entering the historic heart of Frankfurt, the ancient **Römerberg Square,** which has been the center of civic life for centuries. Immediately on your right and occupying most of
5 the square is the city hall, called the **Römer.** It's a modest-looking building compared with many of Germany's city halls, though it has a certain charm. Its gabled Gothic facade with ornate balcony is widely known as the city's official emblem.

Frankfurt

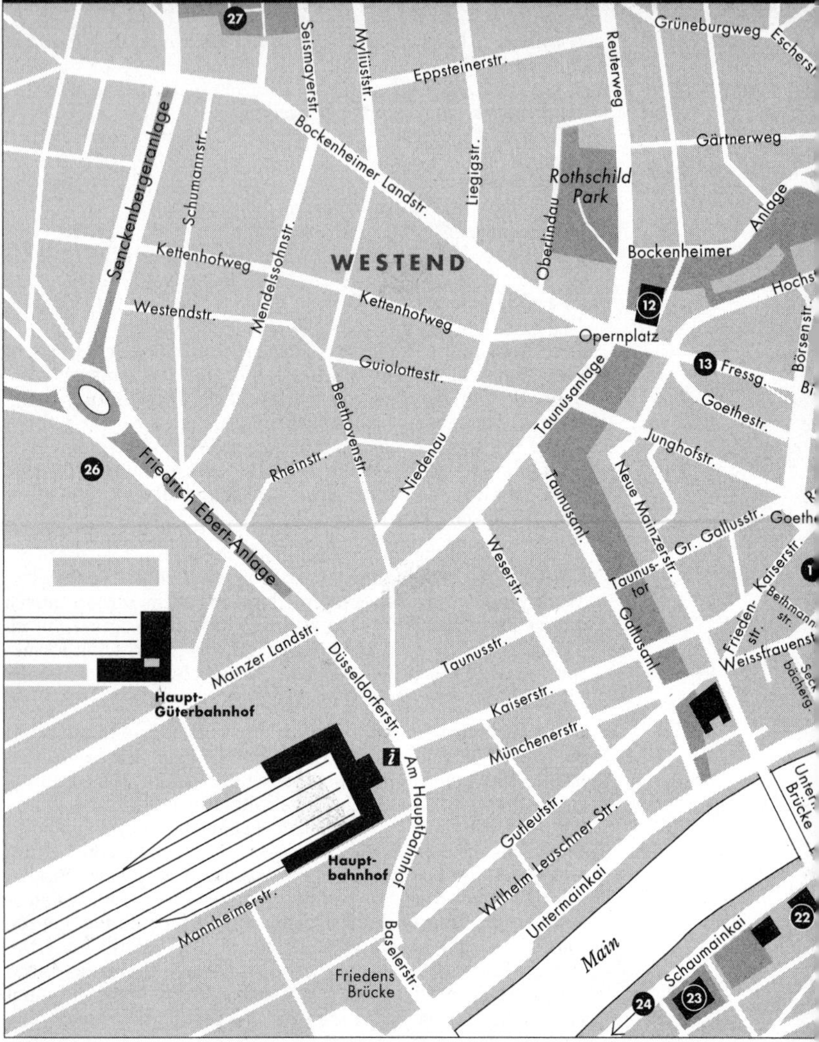

Alte Oper, **12**
Börse, **14**
Deutsches Architektur-museum, **21**
Deutsches Filmmuseum, **22**
Dom St. Bartholomäus, **18**
Eiserner Steg, **8**
Fressgasse, **13**
Goethehaus und Goethemuseum, **11**
Hauptwache, **1**
Historisches Museum, **7**
Karmeliterkirche, **10**
Katerinenkirche, **2**
Kuhhirtenturm, **19**
Leonardskirche, **9**
Liebfrauenkirche, **16**
Messe, **26**
Museum für Kunsthandwerk, **20**
Nikolaikirche, **6**
Palmengarten/ Botanischer Garten, **27**
Paulskirche, **3**
Römer, **5**
Römerberg Square, **4**
Schweizer Platz, **25**
Städelsches Kunstinstitut und Städtische Galerie, **23**
Städtische Galerie Liebieghaus, **24**
Staufenmauer, **17**
Zoologischer Garten, **15**

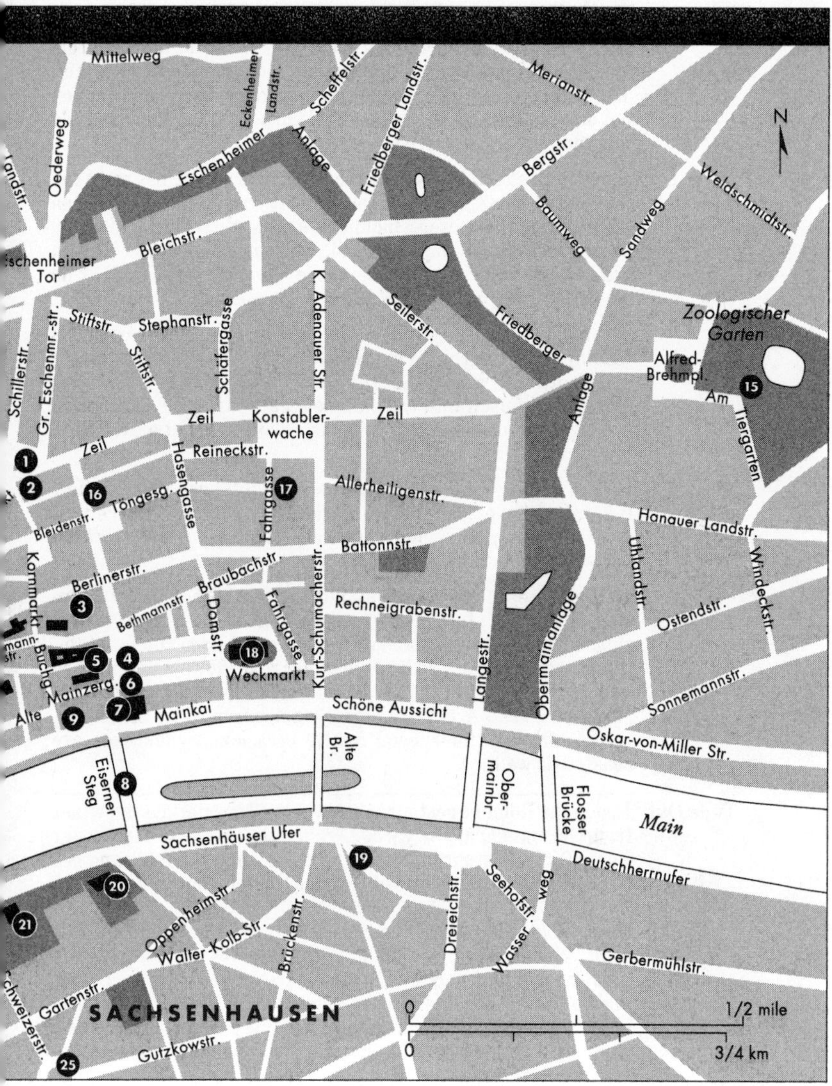
Mittelweg
Oederweg
Eckenheimer Landstr.
Scheffelstr.
Friedberger Landstr.
Merianstr.
Eschenheimer Anlage
Bergstr.
Baumweg
Sandweg
Weldschmidtstr.
Bleichstr.
Eschenheimer Tor
K. Adenauer Str.
Seilerstr.
Friedberger Anlage
Zoologischer Garten
Alfred-Brehmpl.
Am Tiergarten
15
Stiftstr.
Stephanstr.
Schäfergasse
Schillerstr.
Gr. Eschenmr.-str.
Zeil
Konstablerwache
Reineckstr.
Hasengasse
Fahrgasse
Allerheiligenstr.
Anlage
Hanauer Landstr.
Töngesg.
Bleidenstr.
Battonnstr.
Uhlandstr.
Windeckstr.
Berlinerstr.
Braubachstr.
Domstr.
Rechneigrabenstr.
Ostendstr.
Kornmarkt
Bethmannstr.
Kurt-Schumacherstr.
Langestr.
Obermainanlage
Weckmarkt
Sonnemannstr.
Buchg.
Mainzerg.
Alte
Mainkai
Schöne Aussicht
Oskar-von-Miller Str.
Eiserner Steg
Alte Br.
Obermainbr.
Flosser Brücke
Main
Sachsenhäuser Ufer
Deutschherrnufer
Dreieichstr.
Seehofstr.
Wasserweg
Oppenheimstr.
Walter-Kolb-Str.
Brückenstr.
Gerbermühlstr.
Gartenstr.
Schweizerstr.
SACHSENHAUSEN
Gutzkowstr.
0
1/2 mile
0
3/4 km
1
2
3
4
5
6
7
8
9
16
17
18
19
20
21
25

Three individual patrician buildings make up the Römer. From left to right they are the Alt-Limpurg, the Zum Römer (from which the whole structure takes its name), and the Lowenstein. The mercantile-minded Frankfurt burghers used the complex not only for politcal and ceremonial purposes, but also for trade fairs and other commercial ventures.

The most important events to take place in the Römer were the banquets held to celebrate the coronations of the Holy Roman Emperors. These were mounted in the glittering and aptly named **Kaisersaal** (Imperial Hall), starting in 1562, last used in 1792 to celebrate the election of the Emperor Francis II, who would later be forced to abdicate by Napoléon.

The most vivid description of the ceremony was by Germany's leading poet, Goethe, in his "Dichtung und Wahrheit" ("Poetry and Truth"). It is said that the young Goethe, as a 16-year-old, smuggled himself into the banquet celebrating the coronation of Emperor Joseph II by posing as a waiter, to get a first hand impression of the festivities.

Today, visitors can see the impressive full-length 19th-century portraits of the 52 emperors of the Holy Roman Empire that line the walls of the banqueting hall. *Admission: DM 1 adults, 50 pf children. Open Mon.–Sat. 9–6, Sun. 10–4.*

In the center of the square stands the fine 16th-century **Fountain of Justitia** (Justice). At the coronation of Emperor Matthias in 1612, wine instead of water flowed from the fountain. The crush of thirsty citizens was so great, however, that they had to be restrained to prevent damage from being done to the stonework. This event has recently been revived by the city fathers, but only for special festive occasions, when oxen are roasted as well.

Time Out Inside the Römer a restaurant serves local specialties and wines from the municipal vineyards. Around the corner at Limpurger Gasse 2, the restaurant's shop sells the same products and is a good place to buy a bottle of Hock or Hochheimer wine.

6 On the south side of the Römerberg is the **Nikolaikirche** (Church of St. Nicholas). It was built in the late 13th century as the court chapel for the Holy Roman Emperors, and it's worth trying to time your visit to coincide with the chimes of the glockenspiel carillon, which ring out three times a day. It's a wonderful sound. *Carillon chimes daily at 9 AM, noon and 5 PM. Nikolaikirche open Mon.–Sat. 10–5.*

7 Beside the Nikolaikirche is the **Historisches Museum** (History Museum), where you can see a perfect scale model of the old town, complete with every street, house, and church. There is also an astonishing display of silver, exhibits covering all aspects of the city's life from the 16th to the 20th century, and a children's museum. *Saalgasse 19. Admission free. Open Tues. and Thurs.–Sun. 10–5, Wed. 10–8.*

Behind the church, on the eastern side of the square, is a row of painstakingly restored half-timbered houses, dating from the 15th and 16th centuries. They are an excellent example of how the people of Frankfurt have begun, albeit belatedly, to take seriously the reconstruction of their historic buildings.

Leaving the square, walk the short distance to the Main River. At Mainkai, the busy street that runs parallel to the tree-lined river, you will see on your left the **Rententurm,** one of the city's medieval gates, with its pinnacled towers at the base of the main spire extending out over the walls. To your right and in
8 front is the **Eiserner Steg,** an iron bridge built as a pedestrian walkway to connect central Frankfurt with the old district of Sachsenhausen. From here river trips and boat excursions start, as well as the old steam train. (For details, *see* Tours and Excursions, above.)

9 Stroll along Mainkai, past the Eiserner Steg, to **Leonardskirche** (St. Leonard's Church), which is a magnificently preserved 15th- and 16th-century building, with a fine 13th-century porch. Its main treasure is the beautifully carved Bavarian altar, circa 1500.

Continue a short way along Mainkai, then turn right into the
10 narrow Karmeliter Gasse, which brings you to the **Karmeliterkirche** (Carmelite Church and Monastery). Within its quiet cloisters is the largest religious fresco north of the Alps, a 16th-century representation of the birth and death of Christ. Jörg Ratgeb, the creator of this 262-foot-long fresco, was one of the most important artists of his time, but it did not prevent his brutal death by quartering in 1526 for his part in the Peasants' Rebellion. The church and monastery buildings were secularized in 1803 and now house the city archives and the Early and Prehistory Museum. *Admission free. Cloisters open weekdays 8–4.*

11 From here, it's a short way to the **Goethehaus und Goethemuseum** (Goethe's House and Museum). Coming out of the Karmeliterkirche into Münzgasse, turn left and go to the junction of Bethmannstrasse and Berliner Strasse. Use the pedestrian walkway and cross over to the north side of Berliner Strasse, then turn left again onto Grosser Hirschgraben. Outside No. 23 there will probably be a small crowd of visitors entering and leaving. This is where Johann Wolfgang von Goethe was born in 1749. Although the original house was destroyed by Allied bombing, it has been carefully rebuilt and restored in every detail as the young Goethe would have known it. The furnishings are all period pieces, many belonging to the poet's family. The room where Goethe was born has been turned into a memorial, and the one where he wrote is set up as it used to be. In Goethe seniors' study, look for the little window that was installed so he could keep an eye on the street outside and, in particular, on young Johann, who was well known to wander afield. The adjoining museum contains a permanent collection of manuscripts, paintings, and memorabilia documenting the life and times of Germany's outstanding poet. *Grosser Hirschgraben 23, tel. 069/28284. Admission: DM 3 adults, DM 1.50 children. Open Apr.–Sept., Mon.–Sat. 9–4, Sun. 10–1; Oct.–Mar., Mon.–Sat. 9–4.*

On leaving the Goethehaus turn left, and at the end of Grosser Hirschgraben bear left again and retrace your steps up Rossmarkt. Cross over to the Gutenberg Memorial and continue along the pedestrian zone to Rathenau-Platz. From here take a window-shopping stroll past the elegant shops and boutiques of Goethestrasse, which ends at Opernplatz and Frank-
12 furt's reconstructed opera house, the **Alte Oper.** Wealthy Frankfurt businessmen gave generously for its original con-

struction in the 1870s, provided they were given priority for the best seats. Kaiser Wilhelm II traveled all the way from Berlin for the gala opening in 1880. Destroyed by incendiary bombs in 1944, the opera house remained in ruins for many years while controversy raged over its reconstruction. The new building, in the classical proportions and style of the original, was finally opened in 1981. It now has the most modern facilities for opera, ballet, concerts, and conferences.

The steps of the opera house, or the Rothschild Park opposite, are a good spot from which to take in the impressive sight of Frankfurt's modern architecture. In this part of the new town you are close to the financial center (the West End), and if you look down Taunusanlage and Mainzer Landstrasse, the view both to the right and left is dominated by gleaming skyscrapers that house the headquarters of West Germany's biggest and richest banks. More than 365 international banks also have offices here, confirming Frankfurt's position as the country's financial capital. If you have a camera, take a photo, especially in the early evening, when the setting sun is mirrored in the glass and metal facades.

Return to the beginning of the pedestrian zone. This is the site of Bockenheimer Tor, one of the gateways in the old walled city. Wander at leisure down Bockenheimer Strasse, known lo-
13 cally as **Fressgasse** "Food Street"). It's a gourmet shopper's paradise and one of Frankfurt's liveliest streets.

Time Out Stop at any one of the attractive cafés, restaurants, or delicatessens that line Fressgasse; the selection is enormous, and you're certain to find something to your taste. In the summer you can sit at tables on the sidewalk and dine alfresco. *Prost!*

Next, cross over onto Biebergasse, a continuation of the main
14 shopping center. Just around the corner is the Frankfurt **Börse** (Stock Exchange), Germany's leading stock exchange and financial powerhouse. The Borse was founded by Frankfurt merchants in 1558 to establish some order in their often chaotic dealings, but the present building dates from the 1870s. In the past, the trading was hectic on the dealers' floor. These days, computerized networks and international telephone systems have removed the frenetic action to rooms behind the scenes. There is a visitors' gallery. *Admission free. Open weekdays Mon.–Fri. 11:30–1:30.*

From here there is a choice of two routes. You can continue along Biebergasse, past the Hauptwache, and walk east along the **Zeil,** the city's largest pedestrian zone and main shopping street. It is lined with department stores selling every conceivable type of consumer goods and can get very crowded. The far end of the Zeil brings you to Alfred-Brehm Platz and the en-
15 trance to the **Zoologischer Garten** (Zoological Garden). This is one of Frankfurt's chief attractions, ranking among the best zoos in Europe. Its remarkable collection includes some 5,000 animals of 600 different species, a Bears' Castle, an Exotarium (aquarium plus reptiles), and an aviary, reputedly the largest in Europe. Many of the birds can be seen in a natural setting. The zoo is an ideal place for a family outing, as it also has a restaurant, and a café, along with afternoon concerts in summer. *Zoo admission: DM 7 adults, DM 3 children. Exotarium admission: DM 3.50 adults, DM 1.50 children. Combined ticket*

price: DM 8.50 adults, DM 4 children. Open mid-Mar.–Sept., daily 8–7; mid-Nov.–mid-Feb., daily 8–5; between seasons open daily 8–6.

Alternatively, if you don't want to go all the way down the Zeil, just after the Hauptwache turn right down Liebfrauenstrasse. Here, in more peaceful surroundings, you will come to the
16 **Liebfrauenkirche** (Church of Our Lady), a late-Gothic church dating from the end of the 14th century. Among its few surviving features of interest are the fine tympanum relief over the south door, the ornate Rococo furnishings, the 16th-century choir, and the frieze work around the pointed arches. Outside, there is also a delightful Rococo fountain.

Turn off onto Töngesgasse and walk to Fahrgasse. Follow the
17 signs to the **Staufenmauer,** which is one of the few surviving stretches of the old city wall. The Staufenmauer and the Saalhof-kapelle (Chapel) (near the Eiserner Steg bridge) are the two oldest parts of the medieval city in evidence today. *Admission free. Saalhofkapelle. Open Tues. and Thurs.–Sat. 10–5, Wed. 10–8, Sun. 10–5.*

Continue down Fahrgasse, cross Berliner Strasse at a convenient point, bear left along Braubachstrasse for a few yards,
18 and then turn right onto Domstrasse. You are now at the **Dom St. Bartholomäus** (Cathedral of St. Bartholomew) or Kaiserdom (Imperial Cathedral), as it is more popularly known. This grand Gothic structure dates from 1290 and was used primarily for imperial coronations, hence the name. It was built to replace an earlier church established by Charlemagne's son, Ludwig the Pious, on the present site of the Römerberg. The cathedral suffered little damage during World War II and still contains most of its original treasures, including a life-size crucifixion group and a fine 15th-century altar. Its most impressive exterior feature is its tall, red sandstone tower (almost 300 feet high), which was added between 1415 and 1514. Excavations in front of the main entrance in 1953 revealed the remains of a Roman settlement and the foundations of a Carolingian imperial palace. *Admission free. Open Mar.–through Oct., daily 9–noon and 3–6; Nov.–Feb., daily 9–noon and 3–5.*

Walk on now, down the lane called Zum Pfarrturm, and head toward the river. On the Mainkai, cross to **Sachsenhausen** over the Alte Brücke. Formerly a village separate from Frankfurt, Sachsenhausen is said to have been established by Charlemagne, who arrived here with a group of Saxon families in the 8th century and formed a settlement on the banks of the Main. It was an important bridgehead for the crusader Knights of the Teutonic Order and, in 1318, officially became part of Frankfurt. After crossing the bridge, look along the bank to your left
19 and you'll see the 15th-century **Kuhhirtenturm** (Shepherd's Tower), the only remaining part of Sachsenhausen's original fortifications. The composer Paul Hindemith lived in the tower from 1923 to 1927 while working at the Frankfurt Opera.

Sachsenhausen is now largely residential but is also renowned for its collection of museums, most of which are threaded along the river bank. The district has a distinctly medieval air, with narrow back alleys, quaint little inns, and quiet squares that have escaped the destructive tread of the modern developer. There is much of authentic historical interest here. For both Frankfurters and visitors alike, it is where you'll find the best the city has to offer in nightlife—from clubs and discos to traditional taverns and restaurants, tucked in among the half-timbered houes.

Time Out Sachsenhausen is the home of the famous *Ebbelwei* (apple-wine or cider) taverns. Look for a green pine wreath over the entrance to tell pasersby that a freshly pressed—and alcoholic—apple juice is on tap. You can eat well in these small inns, too, though the menu might need some explanation. For example, *Handkas mit Musik* does not promise music at your table. The *Musik* means that the cheese, or *Kas* (from Käse) will be served with raw onions, oil, vinegar, and bread and butter. Most traditional apple-wine taverns serve this specialty without a fork, and those who ask for one give themselves away as strangers. There are about 15 of these taverns; two of the best known are **Zum Gemalten Haus** (Schweizerstr. 67,) and **Lorsbacher Tal** (Grosse Rittergasse 49). One word of warning: don't underestimate the potency of apple wine. Three or four glasses will be quite enough if you want to enjoy the rest of the tour and leave Frankfurt with a clear head.

No fewer than seven top-ranking museums line the Sachsenhausen side of the Main, on Schaumainkai, known locally as the Museum Bank. These range from exhibitons of art, crafts, and architecture to the German Film Museum.

20 One of Frankfurt's newest museums is the **Museum für Kunsthandwerk** (Museum of Applied Arts), which was opened in 1985. This award-wining building, designed by the American architect Richard Meier, contains a vast collection of European and Asian handicrafts, including furniture, glassware, and porcelain. *Schaumainkai 17. Admission free. Open Tues. and Thurs.–Sun. 10–5, Wed. 10–8.*

21 A little further along is the **Deutsches Architekturmuseum** (Museum of German Architecture), currently Frankfurt's most popular museum. It is housed within a period villa, though the interior is entirely modern. There are five floors of drawings, models, and audiovisual displays that chart the progress of German architecture through the ages, as well as many special exhibits. *Schaumainkai 43. Admission free. Open Tues. and Thurs.–Sun. 10–5, Wed. 10–8.*

Next door is Germany's first museum devoted exclusively to the
22 cinema, **Deutsches Filmmuseum** (German Film Museum). The exhibits include an imaginative collection of film artifacts. The museum has its own movie theater. *Schaumainkai 41. Admission free. Open Tues. and Thurs.–Sun. 10–5, Wed. 10–8.*

23 Farther on you will come to the **Städelsches Kunstinstitut und Städtische Galerie** (Städel Art Institute and Municipal Gallery). This houses one of the most significant art collections in Germany, with fine examples of Flemish, Dutch German, and Italian old masters, plus a sprinkling of French Impressionists. *Schaumainkai 63. Admission: DM 2. Open Tues. and Thurs.–Sun. 10–5, Wed. 10–8.*

24 Finally, it's worth stopping at the **Städtische Galerie Liebieghaus** (Liebieg Municipal Museum of Sculpture). Here, in this charming 17th-century villa, is housed the city's internationally famous collection of classical, medieval, and Renaissance sculpture. Some pieces are exhibited in the lovely gar-

dens surrounding the house. *Schaumainkai 71. Admission free. Open Tues. and Thurs.–Sun. 10–5, Wed. 10–8.*

If you have time and energy, there is more to explore in Sachsenhausen. It's very much the up-and-coming district—
25 take a short detour down to **Schweizer Platz;** you'll find it full of new shops, boutiques, cafés, and bars thronging with people and activity.

Retrace your steps back to Schaumainkai and return to the north bank of the river by way of Friedens Brücke, which leads you, via Baseler Strasse, to the main train station, in Frankfurt's West End.

From here, three avenues lead to the center of town: Kaiserstrasse, Münchenerstrasse, and Taunusstrasse. They are lined with fast-food joints, shops, strip clubs, cinemas, and restaurants and at night, with neon lights flashing and rock music blaring, have a rather seedy atmosphere.

Continue past the main train station and wander north along
26 Friedrich-Ebert-Anlage to the **Messe,** a vast complex of exhibition halls where some of the world's greatest trade fairs are held annually. In addition to the two major fairs in spring and fall, among the more important smaller ones are the Automobile Show in March, the Fur Fair at Easter, and the International Book Fair in early fall.

Further north still, along Senckenbergeranlage, is the delight-
27 ful **Palmengarten und Botanischer Garten** (Tropical Garden and Botanical Garden). The large greenhouses enclose a variety of lush tropical and sub-tropical flora, including 800 species of cactus, while the surrounding park offers numerous leisure facilities. During most of the year there are flower shows and exhibitions; in summer, concerts are held in an outdoor bandshell. Situated between the Palmengarten and the adjoining Grüneburgpark, the botanical gardens contain a wide assortment of wild, ornamental, and rare plants from around the world. *Entrance at Siesmayerstr. 61. Admission: DM 4 adults, DM 1.50 children. Open daily 9–7.*

Frankfurt for Free

Finding something for nothing in Frankfurt, a town of high finance and commerce, is a bit of a challenge. With some imagination and planning, though, you can enjoy much of what Frankfurt has to offer without spending too much.

You can spend hours roaming through the **city-run museums** and not have to spend a cent—they don't charge admission except for special exhibitions. *Strandgut* magazine is your best bet for finding out about free or low-cost events in Frankfurt. This free magazine, available in many of Frankfurt's *Kneipen* (pubs) and at most movie theaters, will let you know what's happening around town. Movie and theater programs, as well as live music and other events are listed here. Look for "Eintritt Frei" (admission free) alongside the listings, and you'll know you've found one of Frankfurt's freebies.

Live jazz concerts are held every Sunday morning in the **Historic Museum on Römerberg.** These concerts are very popular and tend to get rather crowded, but the atmosphere is always lively and friendly and the music enjoyable—a fine way to spend a relaxing Sunday morning, especially if you have been out on the town Saturday night.

Check out the **Kleinmarkthalle** close to Liebfrauenberg for a taste of a real old Frankfurt institution. This covered market hall is a feast for the eyes as well as the stomach, with everything from fresh fruits and vegetables and butchers selling homemade Hessian sausages to brilliantly colored flowers. The hearty, red-faced men and women here are a striking contrast to your typical Frankfurt banker. The gallery upstairs is reserved for more exotic products from such foreign countries as Turkey and Lebanon. It's open 8–6.

All you'll need to invest is energy when you climb the **Goetheturm** (Goethe Tower) on the Sachsenhäuser Berg hill. Climbing the many steps up to the top of the 141 meter tower yields a sweeping view of all of Frankfurt and its environs, and on a clear day, as far as the Taunus.

What to See and Do with Children

Your children can see birds and animals up close at the Frankfurt **Zoologischer Garten.** Of special interest to boys and girls is the **Exotarium,** where special climate conditons are created for rare or exotic creatures, such as penguins, reptiles, and insects. In association with the zoo is the **Natural History Museum of Senckenberg,** where exhibitions on prehistoric animals have been designed partly with children in mind. The displays will take your children back to dinosaur times and get their imaginations going (*see* Parks and Gardens, and Museums and Galleries, below).

For outdoor activity and a chance to run and play, Frankfurt's parks offer ample room. The **Palmgarten** has wide open lawns landscaped with shrubs, flower borders, and trees. There is a little lake where you can rent rowboats, a play area for kids, and a wading pool. Concerts take place in the music pavilion, and there is much to see in the Palm House itself (*see* Parks and Gardens, below).

Excursions on the **vintage streetcar,** the **steam train** along the river, or a **boat** will be fun and exciting for the kids and provide a chance for you to sit and enjoy the scenery (*see* Guided Tours, above).

Off the Beaten Track

The old quarter of **Höchst** is Frankfurt's most western suburb. Located on the Main River, it was in the Middle Ages a town in its own right, governed by Mainz until it was engulfed by the spread of Frankfurt. Unlike Frankfurt, however, Höchst was not devastated by wartime bombing and still possesses many of its original historic buildings. It's worth taking the time to explore the picturesque Altstadt (Old Town), with its attractive market and half-timbered houses.

Höchst has long been a manufacturing center and in the 18th century was particulary noted for its porcelain. The famous **Höchster Porzellan Manufaktur** (Bolongarostr. 186, tel. 069/ 300–9020) is located in Dalberghaus. Call to arrange for a guided tour of the works. You can also see a fine exhibit of porcelain at the **Bolongaropalast** (Bolongaro Palace), a magnificent residence facing the river. It was built in the late 18th century by an Italian snuff manufacturer. Its facade—almost the size of a football field—is nothing to sneeze at. Also on Bolongaro Strasse is the **Höchster Schloss.** Built in 1360, this castle was originally the seat and customs house of the Archbishop of Mainz. Destroyed and rebuilt several times, it now houses the **local history museum** and the **Hoechst AG company museum.** *Admission free. Open daily 10–4.*

Of greater interest is the **Justiniuskirche,** Frankfurt's oldest church, located at the corner of Justiniusplatz and Bolongaro Strasse. Dating from the 7th century, the church is part early Romanesque, part 15th-century Gothic. The view from the top of the hill is well worth the walk.

The major attraction to the southwest of the city is the **Stadtwald** (City Forest), which is threaded with lovely paths and trails, as well as containing one of Germany's most impressive sports stadiums. Of particular interest is the Waldehrpfad—a trail leading past a series of rare trees, each identified by a small sign. The Stadtwald was the first place in Europe where trees were planted from seed (they were oaks, sown in 1398), and there are still many extremely old trees in evidence. In addition to bird sanctuaries and wild-animal enclosures, the forest also boasts a number of good restaurants and is a pleasant place to eat and linger. *Take bus 36 from Konstabler Wache to Hainer Weg.*

North of Frankfurt is the district of Seckbach. The 180-meter Lohrberg hill is a favorite among Frankfurters, as the climb yields a fabulous view of the town and the Taunus, Spessart, and Odenwald hills. Along the way you'll also see the last remaining vineyard within Frankfurt, the **Seckbach Vineyard.** *Take the subway to Seckbacher Landstr., and then bus No. 43 or 38.*

Still within Frankfurt but definitely off the beaten track is scenic **Holzhausen Park.** This small park is quiet and peaceful, complete with willow trees and a little moated palace, the **Holzhausen Schlösschen.** *Take the subway to Holzhausenstr.*

Also within Frankfurt, visit the **old Jewish quarter** near Börneplatz. The **Alte Jüdische Friedhof** (Old Jewish Cemetery) is located on the east side of the square. Partly vandalized in the 1940s, it is nearly all that remains of prewar Jewish life in Frankfurt. The cemetery can be visited by prior arrangement only. *Corner of Kurt-Schumacher-Str. and Battonstr, tel. 069/740–2125.*

During excavation, a Jewish **ritual bath,** or *Mikwe* was uncovered. Citizens' groups went to work to make sure that it was preserved, and it remains, incorporated into the office block, dwarfed by modern buildings. *Eckenheimer Landstr.*

Sightseeing Checklists

Historic Buildings and Sites

All of the historic buildings and sites listed below appear in the Exploring Frankfurt section of this chapter unless otherwise noted.

Alte Oper (Old Opera House). Built between 1873 and 1880 and destroyed during World War II, Frankfurt's old opera house has been beautifully reconstructed in the style of the original.

Bolongaropalast (Bolongaro Palace). A grand and aristocratic residence built by a family of Italian snuff manufacturers in the 1770s. (*See* Off the Beaten Track, above.)
Börneplatz. This is the historic center of Frankfurt's Jewish community. (*See* Off the Beaten Track, above.)
Börse (Stock Exchange). For those interested in international finance, this is the center of West Germany's stock and money market.
Deutschordenshaus (House of the Teutonic Order). A Baroque building, it once belonged to the Knights of the Teutonic Order. It was built in 1709 above a Gothic cellar. Next door is a church that dates back to 1309. *Brueckenstr. 3–7. The church can be visited by prior arrangement only (tel. 069/609–10830).*
Eiserner Steg (Iron Bridge). A pedestrian walkway, the bridge connects the center of Frankfurt to Sachsenhausen.
Eschenheimer Turm (Eschenheimer Tower). Built in the early 15th century, this tower remains the finest example of the city's original 42 towers. *Eschenheimer Tor.*
Fernmeldeturm (Telecommunications Tower). At 1,086 feet, this is the fourth-highest tower in the world. It is no longer open to the public. *Wilhelm-Epstein-Str.*
Fressgasse (Food Street). The street's proper name is Bockenheimer Strasse, but Frankfurters have given it this sobriquet because of the amazing choice of delicatessens, wine merchants, cafés, and restaurants to be found here.
Goetheturm (Goethe's Tower). Located at the edge of the Stadtwald on the Sachsenhauser Berg, this is Germany's highest wood tower. (*See* Off the Beaten Track, above.)
Hauptwache (Guardhouse). An attractive Baroque building, it was originally constructed as a municipal guardhouse in 1729.
Höchster Schloss (Höchst Castle). This 14th-century castle, destroyed and rebuilt several times, now houses the Höchst city museum and the Hoechst AG company museum. (*See* Off the Beaten Track, above.)
Kuhhirtenturm (Shepherd's Tower). This is the last of nine towers, built in the 15th century, that formed part of Sachsenhausen's fortifications.
Messe (Exhibition Halls). A huge complex of buildings holds some of the most important trade fairs in the world.
Rententurm (Renten Tower). Another of the city's fortifications, the Rententurm was built in 1456 along the Main River.
Römer (City Hall). With its gabled Gothic facade, the Römer is the traditional symbol of Frankfurt and has been the center of civic life here for 500 years.
Römerberg. This square, lovingly restored after wartime bomb damage, is the historical focal point of the city.
Sachsenhausen. The old quarter of Sachsenhausen, on the south bank of the Main River, is of great historical interest, sensitively preserved and very popular with residents and tourist alike.
Steinernes Haus (Stone House). This Gothic-style patrician house has also served as a trading post.
Zeil. This pedestrian shopping street ranks among Germany's busiest and best. (*See* Shopping, below.)

Churches and Cathedrals

Dom St. Bartholomäus (Cathedral of St. Bartholomew). Also known as the Kaiserdom (Imperial Cathedral), the Dom was built largely between the 13th and 15th centuries and survived the bombs of World War II with most of its original treasures intact.

Justiniuskirche (Church of St. Justinius). Situated in the old quarter of Höchst, this church dates back to the days of the Carolingians and is older than anything that remains in Frankfurt proper. (*See* Off the Beaten Track, above.)

Karmeliterkirche (Carmelite Church and Monastery). The cloisters of this former monastery contain one of the most significant religious frescos north of the Alps.

Katherinenkirche (Church of St. Catherine). This church was originally built in 1678, the first independent Protestant church in the Gothic style.

Leonardskirche (St. Leonard's Church). This beautifully preserved 14th- and 15th-century building with five naves boasts some fine old stained glass.

Liebfrauenkirche (Church of Our Lady). Dating form the 14th century, this late-Gothic church still possesses a few of its original treasures.

Nikolaikirche (Church of St. Nicholas). The glockenspiel rings out three times a day at this small red sandstone church, which dates from the late 13th century.

Paulskirche (Church of St. Paul). Site of the first all-German parliament in 1848, the church is now used mainly for formal ceremonial occasions.

Saalhofkapelle (Saalhof Chapel). Near the Eiserner Stegbridge and behind the Rententurm, this small 12th-century chapel is one of the oldest buildings in the city. *Saalgasse 31.*

Museums and Galleries

Bundespost Museum (Postal Museum). On display are the various means of transporting mail through the ages—from the mail coach to the airplane. There's also an exhibition of stamps and stamp-printing machines, as well as a reconstructed 19th-century post office. *Schaumainkai 53. Admission free. Open Tues.–Sun. 10–4. Reopens after renovation in September 1990.*

Deutsches Architekturmuseum (Museum of German Architecture). The Architecture Museum houses an impressive collection of drawings, models, and audiovisual displays tracing the development of German architecture.

Deutsches Filmmuseum (German Film Museum). Germany's first museum of cinematography houses an exciting collection of film artifacts.

Goethehaus und Goethemuseum (Goethe's House and Museum). The birthplace of Germany's most famous poet has been faithfully restored and is furnished with many original pieces that belonged to his family. The museum next door contains a comprehensive collection of Goethe memorabilia.

Heinrich Hoffmann Museum or **Struwwelpeter-Museum.** This museum contains a collection of letters, sketches, and manuscripts by Dr. Heinrich Hoffmann, physician and creator of the children's-book hero Struwwelpeter. *Schubertstr. 20. Open Tues.–Sun. 10–5. Admission: DM 1 adults and children over 13.*

Historisches Museum (History Museum). This fascinating museum encompasses all aspects of the city's history over the last four centuries.

Kaisersaal (Imperial Hall). Inside the Römer, this former banquet hall now holds a gallery of portraits of the 52 emperors of the Holy Roman Empire.

Museum für Kunsthandwerk (Museum of Applied Arts). More than 30,000 objects, representing European and Asian handicrafts, are exhibited in displays with changing themes.

Museum fuŕr Volkerkunde (Ethnological Museum). The exhibits depict the lifestyles and customs of primitive societies from different parts of the world. The collection includes masks, cult objects, and jewelry. *Schaumainkai 29. Open Tues. and Thurs.–Sun. 10–5, Wed. 10–8. Admission free.*

Naturkundermuseum Senckenberg (Natural History Museum). This is the largest natural-history museum in Germany, with Europe's most impressive collection of dinosaurs, whales, and other large mammals. Fossils, animals, plants, and geological exhibits are all displayed in an exciting, hands-on environment. The most important single exhibit is the diplodocus, imported from New York and the only complete specimen of its kind in Europe. *Senckenberganlage 25. Admission: DM 2. Open Tues. and Thurs.–Sat. 9–4, Wed. 9–8, Sun. 9–6.*

Schirn Kunsthalle (Schirn Art Gallery). One of Frankfurt's most modern museums houses a fine collection of 20th-century art. Located opposite the cathedral. *Am Römerberg 6a. Admission: DM 3–DM 6, depending on current exhibition. Open Tues. and Thurs.–Sun. 10–5, Wed. 10–8.*

Städelsches Kunstinstitut and Städtische Galerie (Städel Art Institute and Municipal Gallery). One of West Germany's most important art collections, with paintings by Dürer, Vermeer, Rembrandt, Rubens, Monet, Renoir, and other great masters.

Städtische Galerie Liebieghaus (Liebieg Municipal Museum of Sculpture). The sculpture collection from different civilizations and epochs here is considered one of the most important in Europe.

Parks and Gardens

Anlagenring. When the fortification wall surrounding Frankfurt was demolished in the 19th century, the open space on both sides of the structure was turned into a park. A 3-mile ring of green now encircles the city center, north of the Main. It's an ideal circuit for joggers and fitness enthusiasts.

Nizza. On the north bank of the Main, directly opposite the museums on Schaumainkai, is this pretty promenade bordered by a wide variety of Mediterranean trees and shrubs. There are footpaths and benches, too.

Palmengarten und Botanischer Garten (Tropical Garden and Botanical Gardens). A splendid cluster of tropical and semi-tropical green-houses contain a wide variety of flora, including cacti, orchids, and palms. The surrounding park has many recreational facilities. In the botanical gardens are a number of special collections, including a 2½-acre rock garden and rose and rhododendron gardens.

Stadtwald (City Forest). With its innumerable paths and trails, bird sanctuaries, and sports facilities, the Stadtwald is used by citizens and visitors alike for recreation and relaxation. (*See* Off the Beaten Track, above.)

Volkspark Niddertal. This park was the site of the 1989 *Bundesgartenschau* (Bu'ga'schau), the annual federal garden show, which takes place in a different German city each year. The fairgrounds become a public park area after the exhibition.

Zoologischer Garten (zoo). Founded in 1858, this is one of the most important and attractive zoos in Europe, with many of the animals and birds living in a natural environment.

Shopping

Gift Ideas Frankfurt, the financial capital of Germany, is not best known for gifts and souvenirs. It is, however, the home of the largest selection of **Meissen porcelain** outside of East Germany, found, improbably, in the Japanese department store **Mitsukoshi** (Kaiserstr.). More typical Frankfurt specialties include **Apfelwein,** or apple wine; it can be purchased in most supermarkets and in the taverns in Sachsenhausen, south of the river. Look, too, for **Bethmännchen und Brenten** (marzipan cookies) and **Frankfurter Kranz** (a sort of creamy cake) in local bakeries and sweetshops. **Jewelry** designed and made by local craftsmen is an unusual gift to take home. **La Galleria** (Berlinerstr.) and **Luise Schloze** (Kaiserstr.) both have good selections. A **Struwelpeter** puppet or doll, named after the character in the famous children's book by Heinrich Hoffmann, also makes a good gift to take home. If you want to stock up on wine, stop in at **Limpurger Gasse 2,** next to the Römer, where wine produced in the municipal vineyards is sold. This is the place to buy a genuine bottle of Hocheimer for no more than a few marks.

Shopping Districts The heart of Frankfurt's shopping district is the ritzy pedestrian street called **Zeil,** running east from Hauptwache square. It is one of the busiest shopping streets in the country—the so-called "shopping mile"—turning over more than 1 billion Deutsche Marks' worth of business every year. The mall under the **Hauptwache** is hardly less classy and busy.

The streets running off Zeil and the Hauptwache are home to a series of upscale fashion shops. Try **Goethestrasse** and **Steinweg** for designer clothing, shoes, and leather goods; **Rossmarkt** and **Kaiserstrasse** for jewelry and watches; **Schillerstrasse** for glass and porcelain; **Braubachstrasse, Fahrgasse,** and **Weckmarkt** for art and antiques; and **Dusseldorfer Strasse** for furs.

There's another elegant shopping mall, extending over three stories, in the **BfG building** on the corner of Theaterplatz and Neue-Mainzer-Strasse.

Extending west from the Hauptwache is **Grosse Bockheimer Strasse** (or Fressgass to the locals). Cafés, restaurants, and above all, food shops are the draw here. This is the place for fish—fresh or smoked—French cheeses, smoked hams from Italy, and a wide range of local specialties, including frankfurters.

Sachsenhausen over the river boasts a multitude of ever-more-chic stores. Check out probably the most classy butcher shop in Germany, the **Metzgerei Meyer** on Schweizer Strasse. With its stark green-and-black Italian tiles and subtle spotlighting, it's more like a jewelry store than a place to buy sausages.

Flea Markets A flea market is held Saturdays between 8 and 2 at the **Schlachthof** (Deutschherrenaufer, corner of Wasserweg). Get there early if you're looking for bargains. There's a wide range of goods on display, most of it pretty junky, though you can sometimes find better-quality goods, too. In any event, it's a colorful and vivid place to explore.

Sports and Fitness

For information on all sports in Frankfurt, call the city sports office, tel. 069/212–3565.

Bicycling Opportunities for biking in the city are limited, but get away from the downtown area and Frankfurt's parks and forests offer terrific places to bike. In summer, you can rent bikes at the **Goetheturm** on the northern edge of the Stadtwald (tel. 069/49111).

Hotel Fitness Centers ***Steigenberger Airporthotel*** (Unterschweinsteige 16, tel. 069/69851), about 1 mile from the Frankfurt Airport, has an indoor pool, sauna, and solarium and jogging paths in the nearby woods.

Intercontinental (Wilhelm-Leuschner-Str. 43, tel. 069/230-561) overlooks the Main River, along whose banks you can jog. The hotel has an indoor pool, health club, gym, and sauna.

Hotel Gravenbruch Kempinski (Neu-Isenburg 2, tel. 06102/5050) is about 15 minutes by car outside of Frankfurt. It's located in a 37-acre park, with tennis courts, two Olympic-size pools, and jogging paths through the woods.

Frankfurter Hof (Kaiserpl. 17, tel. 069/20251) is a venerable hotel without fitness facilities; however, it can arrange for guests to use the **Judokan Sport und Fitness Center,** a 10-minute walk away. An hourly fee is charged.

Jogging A good place to jog morning or evening is along the Main River. You can stick to one side or do a loop, crossing a bridge, going down the other bank, and crossing another bridge back over. **Grüneberg Park,** in the city center, is part of the old Rothschild estate. It's 1 mile around, with a Trimm Disch exercise facility in the northeast corner. For a vigorous forest run, take the Strassenbahn (streetcar) to **Hohemark** (a 30-minute ride). For jogging, swimming, and tennis, take the Strassenbahn to the **Stadtwald,** a 4,000-acre forest park south of the city.

Skating The **Eissporthalle** (Bornheimer Hang 4, Ratsweg, tel. 069/241-9141) has two rinks, one outdoor, the other indoor. It's open in winter 9 AM–10:30 PM.

Swimming Frankfurt has several well-equipped swimming-pool complexes. The **Rebstockbad** (August-Euler-Str. 7, tel. 069/708-078) has an indoor pool, a pool with a wave machine and palm-fringed beach, and an outdoor pool with giant water chutes. There's also a solarium, a Japanese sauna, a gym, billiard tables, and a restaurant, where you can fortify yourself after your workout. A similar center is the **Stationbad** (Morfelder Landstr. 362, tel. 069/678–040), which has an outdoor pool, solarium, and exercise lawns. The **Brentanobad** (Rödelheimer Parkweg, tel. 069/783–695) has an outdoor pool surrounded by lawns and old trees; it's often crowded in summer.

Tennis Courts are available at the **Nidda Park** sports center. Next to the **Stationbad** (*see* Swimming) you'll find 20 courts (cost: DM 14 per hour). Call 069/67840 for reservations.

Dining

Dining in Frankfurt—the expense-account city par excellence—can be expensive. You'll need to make reservations well in advance, too, if you plan to eat in any of the fancier restaurants: With business in the city a year-round affair, there are few moments when most restaurants are not booked solid. The good news is that the range and quality of the city's dining experiences is terrific. You can find everything from the most sophisticated French haute cuisine to earthy and pungent local dishes in street-corner *Gasthofs*.

Highly recommended restaurants in each price category are indicated by a star ★.

Category	Cost*
Very Expensive	Over DM 95
Expensive	DM 65–DM 95
Moderate	DM 45–DM 65
Inexpensive	DM 25–DM 45

**per person for a three-course meal, excluding drinks*

Very Expensive

★ **Erno's Bistro.** Erno's (prop. Erno W. Schmitt) is something of a Frankfurt institution. It's small and chic—and *very* popular with visiting power brokers—and offers classy nouvelle specialties (or "cuisine *formidable*," as Erno prefers to call it). Fish dishes predominate—all the fish is flown in daily, most of it from Paris—with specialties varying according to what's available in the markets that day. This is also one of those rare restaurants where you can sit back with confidence and let the staff—all the waiters speak English—choose your meal for you. You won't regret it. *Liebigstr. 15, tel. 069/721–997. Reservations required. Jacket and tie required. AE, DC, MC, V. Closed Sat. and Sun. and mid-June–mid-July.*

★ **Gourmet.** For style and quality in the grand manner, there are few restaurants in Germany that rival this place, the best of the three restaurants in the Hotel Gravensbruch Kempinski, located 7 miles out of town in the Neu Isenburg suburb. Small and intimate, the restaurant offers subtle French nouvelle food. The decor is subdued, the service is polished. *Hotel Gravensbruch Kempinski, Neu Isenburg 2, tel. 06102/5050. Reservations required. Jacket and tie required. AE, DC, MC, V. Closed lunch and Wed.*

Humperdinck. Those in search of affluent and oh-so-tasteful Frankfurt need look no farther than the soothingly chic Humperdinck (named after the 19th-century composer Engelbert Humperdinck, whose house this was, not the '60s crooner). The food fuses nouvelle and classic French elements; choose one of the fixed-price menus for the best value. The restaurant is located just south of Grüneburg Park. *Grüneburgweg 95, tel. 069/722–122. Reservations required. Jacket and tie required. AE, DC, MC, V. Closed Sat. lunch and Sun.*

★ **Restaurant Français.** The green-and-gold surroundings of this restaurant of the incomparably luxurious Steigenberger Hotel Frankfurter, with crystal chandeliers and tapestries on the

Atschel, **12**
Bistro 77, **10**
Börsenkeller, **6**
Casa Nova, **4**
Erno's Bistro, **2**
Gourmet, **13**
Gütsschanke Neuhof, **9**
Humperdinck, **1**
Jacques Offenbach, **3**
Leiter, **5**
Restaurant Français, **7**
Weinhaus Brückenkeller, **11**
Zum Gemalten Haus, **8**
Zum Rad, **15**
Zur Eulenberg, **14**

Frankfurt Dining

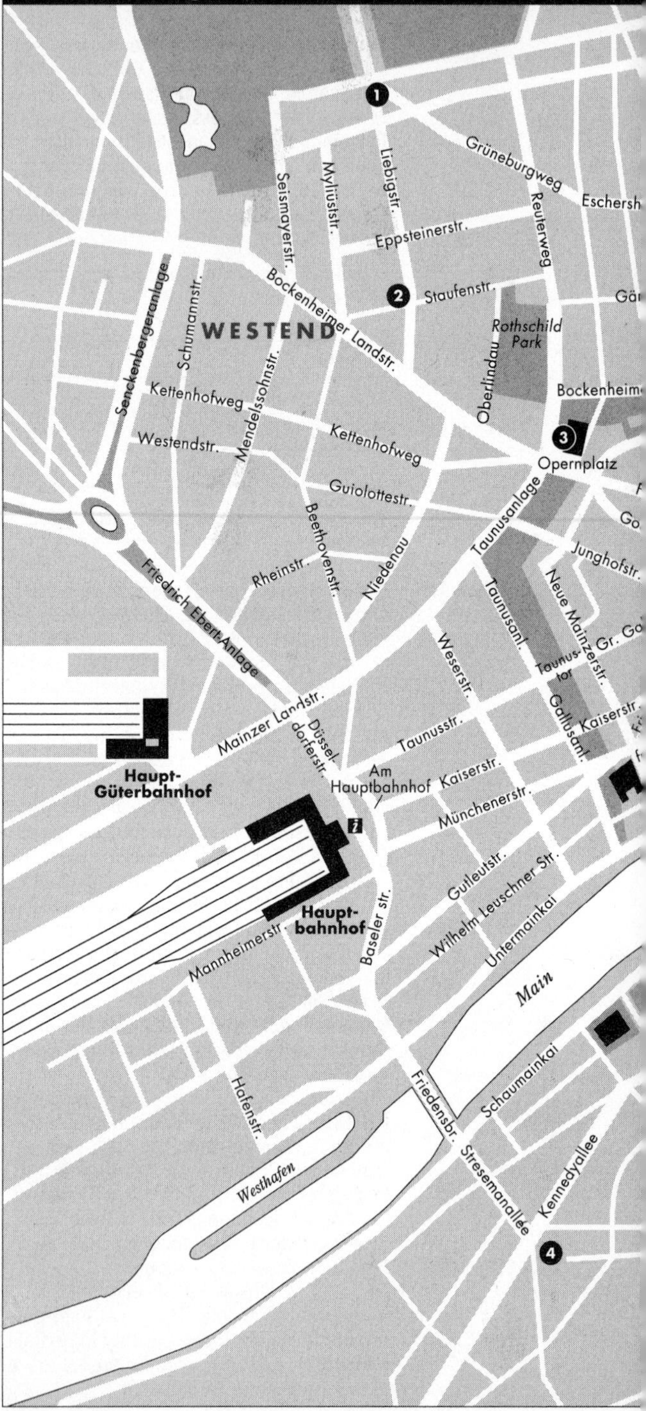

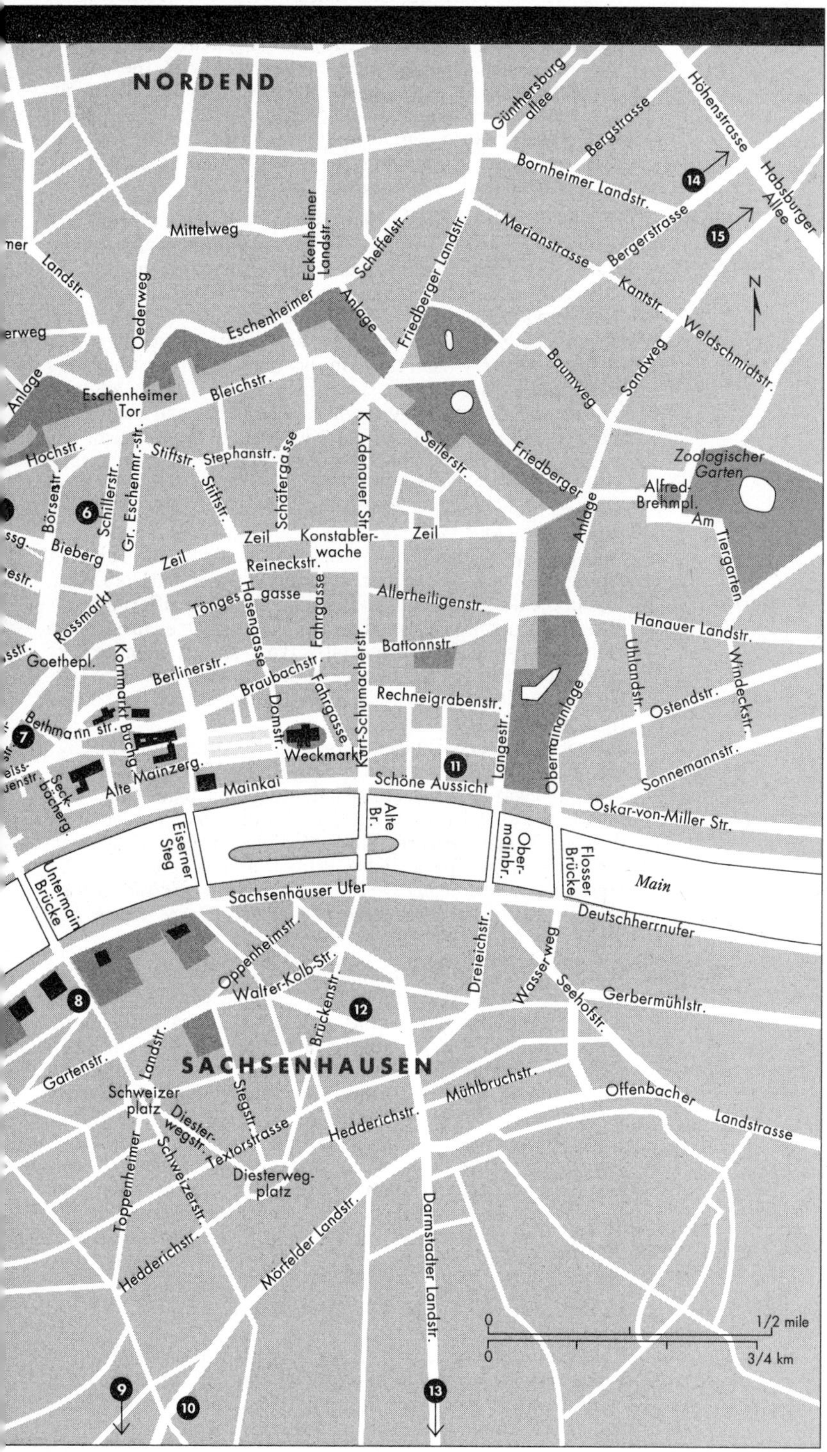
NORDEND
SACHSENHAUSEN
Main
Günthersburg allee
Bergstrasse
Höhenstrasse
Habsburger Allee
Bornheimer Landstr.
Merianstrasse
Bergerstrasse
Kantstr.
Weldschmidtstr.
Sandweg
Baumweg
Friedberger Landstr.
Scheffelstr.
Eckenheimer Landstr.
Mittelweg
Landstr.
Oederweg
Eschenheimer Anlage
Anlage
Eschenheimer Tor
Bleichstr.
Hochstr.
Stiftstr.
Stephanstr.
Schäfergasse
K. Adenauer Str.
Seilerstr.
Friedberger Anlage
Zoologischer Garten
Alfred-Brehmpl.
Am Tiergarten
Börsenstr.
Schillerstr.
Gr. Eschenmr.-str.
Bieberg
Zeil
Konstablerwache
Reineckstr.
Töngesgasse
Hasengasse
Fahrgasse
Allerheiligenstr.
Hanauer Landstr.
Rossmarkt
Goethepl.
Kornmarkt
Berlinerstr.
Braubachstr.
Battonnstr.
Uhlandstr.
Windeckstr.
Domstr.
Kurt-Schumacherstr.
Rechneigrabenstr.
Langestr.
Obermainanlage
Ostendstr.
Bethmann str.
Büchg.
Weckmarkt
Sonnemannstr.
Alte Mainzerg.
Seckbächerg.
Mainkai
Schöne Aussicht
Oskar-von-Miller Str.
Eiserner Steg
Alte Br.
Obermainbr.
Flosser Brücke
Untermain Brücke
Sachsenhäuser Ufer
Deutschherrnufer
Oppenheimstr.
Walter-Kolb-Str.
Brückenstr.
Dreieichstr.
Wasserweg
Seehofstr.
Gerbermühlstr.
Gartenstr.
Landstr.
Schweizer platz
Diesterwegstr.
Stegstr.
Textorstrasse
Hedderichstr.
Mühlbruchstr.
Offenbacher Landstrasse
Diesterwegplatz
Toppenheimer
Schweizerstr.
Hedderichstr.
Mörfelder Landstr.
Darmstadter Landstr.
0
1/2 mile
0
3/4 km
6
7
8
9
10
11
12
13
14
15

walls, provide an appropriately sumptuous setting for some of the finest food in Frankfurt. The food is French (of course), traditional rather than nouvelle, and served with the sort of panache you might expect in one of the best restaurants in Paris. For a memorable gastronomic treat, try the stuffed quail in truffle butter sauce. *Am Kaiserpl. 17, tel. 069/20251. Reservations required. Jacket and tie required. AE, DC, MC, V. Closed Sun., July, and holidays.*

Expensive

★ **Weinhaus Brückenkeller.** Sophisticated dining in Frankfurt isn't just a matter of refined French food in expense-account restaurants. This establishment offers magnificent German specialties in the sort of time-honored, arched cellar that would have brought a lump to Bismarck's throat. What's more, though the food may be unmistakably Teutonic, it's light and delicate, a far cry from the giant portions of stomach-bursting dishes most traditional German restaurants offer. In addition to the terrific antique-strewn surroundings and the classy food, there's a phenomenal range of wines to choose from: The cellars—don't be shy about asking to see them—hold around 85,000 bottles. *Schutzenstr. 6, tel. 069/284–238. Reservations advised. Jacket and tie required. AE, DC, MC, V. Closed lunch, Sun., and 3 weeks in July.*

Gütsschanke Neuhof. Sheep graze within sight of the elegant dining room of this country restaurant, 8 miles south of Frankfurt in the Götzhain suburb. The menu is varied, offering a mix of German and international dishes. Try the home-cured meats from the restaurant's own estates (you can buy them to take home, too). Dine on the terrace in the summer. *6072 Dreieich-Götzenhain, tel. 06102/3214. Reservations advised. Jacket and tie required. AE, DC, MC, V.*

Jacques Offenbach. Dine in this gourmet restaurant in the bowels of the lavishly restored Opera House. The mood is low-key but classy, with subdued lighting and pale walls. The food is mostly French, featuring traditional and nouvelle dishes in equal measure. This is *the* place to eat after a performance at the Opera House; it takes orders up to midnight. *Opernpl. 1, tel. 069/284–820. Reservations advised. Jacket and tie required. Reservations advised. Closed lunch and July.*

Moderate

Bistro 77. Specialties from Alsace are served at this subtly chic and light French restaurant in Sachsenhausen. The featured dishes change daily according to what's available in the morning markets, but standards remain consistently high. Chef-owner Dominique Mosbach is always happy to advise diners on what to order. *Ziegelhüttenweg 1–3, tel. 069/614–040. Reservations advised. Dress: informal. AE, DC, MC, V. Closed Sat. lunch, Sun., and mid-June–mid-July.*

★ **Börsenkeller.** The dark, rather masculine atmosphere of this restaurant reflects its favored status among businessmen from the nearby stock exchange. Soft lighting, heavy arches, and high-backed booths establish the mood. The food is traditional and substantial, though always prepared with some style. Steaks are a specialty. *Schillerstr. 11, tel. 069/281–115. Reservations advised. Jacket and tie required. AE, DC, MC, V. Closed Sun.*

Casa Nova. The inviting exterior of this little Sachsenhausen restaurant is matched by the cozy interior. It's an Italian restaurant, offering mostly fish specialties, all prepared with flair and imagination. If the pasta seems as if it might prove too plentiful, half portions are available. *Stresemannallee 38, tel. 069/632–473. Weekend reservations required. Dress informal. MC. Closed Sat. and 2 weeks in Aug.*

Leiter. Located right by the pedestrians-only Fressgass in the heart of the old town, this is among the most relentlessly trendy places for style leaders to be seen. The atmosphere and the menu are contemporary, with a sprinkling of Paris bistro ambience, the food is light, and the wines are good. In summer, sit outside to watch the passing parade. *Kaiserhofstr. 11, tel. 069/292–121. Reservations advised. Dress: informal. AE, DC, MC, V. Closed Sun.*

Inexpensive

Atschel. Long wood tables, a boisterously noisy atmosphere, and daily specials chalked on a blackboard signal this establishment's homey, tavernlike style. The food, like the mood, is hearty. The restaurant is located in Sachsenhausen in a former apple-wine tavern. *Wallstr. 7, tel. 069/619–201. Dress: informal. No credit cards. Closed lunch and Mon.*

★ **Zum Gemalten Haus.** This is the real thing, a traditional apple-wine tavern in the heart of Sachsenhausen. Its name means "At the Painted House," a reference to the frescoes that cover the walls inside and out. In summer, the courtyard is the place to be; in winter, you sit in the noisy tavern proper at long tables with benches. It's often crowded, so if there isn't room when you arrive, order a glass of apple wine and hang around until someone leaves: It's worth the wait. Portions are ample and prices are low. *Schweizerstr. 67, tel. 069/614–559. No reservations. Dress: casual. No credit cards. Closed Mon. and Tues.*

Zur Eulenburg. Take the subway or a streetcar out to Seckbacher Landstrasse, in the district of Bornheim, a mile northeast of the old town, to eat in this popular apple-wine tavern. You'd better be hungry, though: The portions would satisfy a caveman. Meat dishes cram the menu; try the Frankfurt-style *Rippchen* (ribs). *Eulengasse 46, tel. 069/451–203. Dress: informal. No credit cards. Closed lunch, Mon., and Tues.*

Zum Rad. This is another traditional apple-wine tavern, a 19th-century inn in the pretty suburb of Seckbach, a couple of miles northeast of the old town. Its tree-shaded courtyard is a delight in the summer and on warm fall days. *Leonhardtsgasse 2, tel. 069/479–128. Dress: informal. No credit cards. Closed lunch.*

Lodging

With a host of businesspeople descending on Frankfurt year-round, most hotels in the city are expensive (though many also offer significant reductions on weekends, an option worth checking out) and are frequently booked up well in advance. The majority of the larger hotels are located around the main train station, close to the business district and the trade-fair building and a 15- to 20-minute walk from the old town. Lower prices and—for some, anyway—more atmosphere are offered by smaller hotels and pensions in the suburbs; the efficient public transportation network makes them easy to reach. With some significant exceptions, the farther from the downtown area your hotel is, the fewer facilities it is likely to have.

The tourist offices at the airport, the main train station, and the Hauptwache train station can all help with accommodations if you show up without reservations. There are also hotel reservation machines at the airport and at the main train station. There's a DM 10 charge for all reservations made using these machines, of which DM 6 is deducted from your hotel bill.

Highly recommended hotels in each price category are indicated by a star ★.

Category	Cost*
Very Expensive	over DM 250
Expensive	DM 180–DM250
Moderate	DM 120–DM 180
Inexpensive	under DM 120

**All prices are for two people in a double room, including tax and service.*

Very Expensive

★ **Hotel Gravenbruch Kempinski.** Located a 15-minute drive south of the downtown area in its own leafy grounds, this hotel offers elegance and sophistication. It's built around a 16th-century manor house and combines substantial modern luxury with Old World charm. All the rooms are spacious and classy; those in the newer annexes have views of the lake. Of the three restaurants, the Gourmet (*see* Dining, above) is the most formal. *6078 Neu Isenburg 2, tel. 06102/5050. 298 rooms with bath. Facilities: 3 restaurants, bar, indoor and outdoor pools, tennis, sauna, masseur, hairdresser, Lufthansa check-in desk, limo service to and from airport and city. AE, DC, MC, V.*

★ **Hessischer Hof.** This is the choice of many businesspeople, not just because of its location opposite the trade-fair building but for the air of class and style that pervades its handsome and imposing interior (the exterior is nondescript). The public rooms are subdued and traditional; bedrooms are elegantly chic, and many of them are furnished with antiques. The restaurant features excellent nouvelle cuisine; it also has a fine display of Sèvres porcelain ranged around the walls. *Friedrich-Ebert-Anlage 40, tel. 069/75400. 167 rooms with bath. Facilities: restaurant, 2 bars. AE, DC, MC, V.*

Mövenpick Parkhotel Frankfurt. This is another businessman's favorite, conveniently located just south of the train station. The hotel comes in two parts, a sturdy 19th-century building and, right next to it, a sleekly modern building. Rooms in the older building have more atmosphere and are larger, but all are elegantly comfortable and decorated in soothingly subdued tones. The more expensive restaurant—*La Truffe*—is one of the classiest in the city. *Wiesenhüttenpl. 36, tel. 069/26970. 310 rooms with bath. Facilities: 2 restaurants, bar, beer cellar, wine restaurant. AE, DC, MC, V.*

★ **Steigenberger Frankfurter Hof.** The combination of an old-town location, an imposing 19th-century Renaissance-style building, and full-bodied luxury makes this the leading choice for many visitors. It's the flagship of the Steigenberger chain, though offering the sort of personal service that wouldn't seem out of place in a family-run hotel. The atmosphere throughout is of old-fashioned, formal elegance, with burnished woods, fresh flowers, and thick-carpeted hush. The Restaurant Français (*see* Dining) is among the gourmet high spots of Germany; the bar is a classy late-night rendezvous. *Am Kaiserpl. 17, tel. 069/*

20251. 359 rooms with bath. Facilities: 4 restaurants, bar, shopping mall. AE, DC, MC, V.

Expensive

Altea Hotel. This high-rise hotel, opened in 1987, is located close to the trade fair building. The bedrooms are simply and elegantly furnished and feature mahogany veneers. Some rooms come complete with kitchenette. Stay here for convenience, not atmosphere. *Voltastr. 29, tel. 069/79260; in the U.S. tel. 800/223–9802. 414 rooms with bath. Facilities: restaurant, bar/bistro, terrace, gym, Jacuzzi, sauna. AE, DC, MC, V.*

Frankfurt Savoy Hotel. Precisely the sort of well-run, slightly anonymous modern hotel you'd expect to find in Frankfurt, this establishment is eminently comfortable but has little discernible personality. It's very much a businessperson's hotel, located close to the train station and with a wide range of restaurants, bars, and other facilities to soothe away the stresses of power brokering. *Wiesenhüttenstr. 42, tel. 069/230–511. 151 rooms with bath. Facilities: 2 restaurants, bar, disco, pool, sauna, solarium, hairdresser. AE, DC, MC, V.*

★ **An der Messe.** This little place—the name means "at the fairgrounds"—is a pleasing change from the giant hotels of the city. It's stylish, with a distinctive pink marble lobby and chicly appointed bedrooms. The staff is courteously efficient. The only drawback is the absence of a restaurant. *Westenstr. 104, tel. 069/747–979. 46 rooms with bath. Facilities: terrace. AE, DC, MC, V.*

★ **Hotel National.** Class and style set the tone at this hotel, located just south of the train station. It's set in a former school and has some fine antiques in the public rooms and some of the larger bedrooms. The restaurant offers excellent local and international dishes. *Baselerstr. 50, tel. 069/234–841. 71 rooms with bath. Facilities: restaurant. AE, DC, MC, V.*

★ **Turm Hotel.** Stay here for the excellent location—just north of the old town—not for local charm or atmosphere. It's a newer hotel, efficiently run but with slightly functional rooms. The basement restaurant features good-value international specialties. *Erschersheimer Landstr. 20, tel. 069/154–050. 75 rooms with bath. Facilities: restaurant. AE, DC, MC, V.*

Moderate

Arcade. This modern hotel is just a five-minute walk from the train station. Rooms are furnished basically, though all have TV, and two are specially equipped for disabled guests. *Speicherstr. 3–5, tel. 069/273–030. 193 rooms with bath. Facilities: restaurant, bar. MC, V.*

Liebig. A comfortable, family-run hotel, this establishment has spacious, high-ceilinged rooms and a friendly feel. Ask for a room at the back—it's much quieter. Try the Weinstube restaurant for excellent Hessen wine. *Liebigstr. 45, tel. 069/727–551. 20 rooms with bath. Facilities: restaurant. MC, DC, V.*

Maingau. This excellent-value hotel is within easy reach of the downtown area, close to the lively Altstadt quarter, with its cheery apple-wine taverns. Rooms are basic, but clean and comfortable, some with TV. Families with children are welcome. *Schifferstr. 38–40, tel. 069/617–001. 100 rooms with bath. Facilities: restaurant. AE, MC.*

Neue Kräme. The reason for staying in this distinctly basic little hotel is, quite simply, the terrific location in the heart of the old town. It's on a pedestrian street, meaning that traffic noise is minimal. There's no restaurant, but drinks and snacks are available. *Neue Kräme 23, tel. 069/284–046. 21 rooms with bath. AE, DC, MC, V.*

Frankfurt Lodging

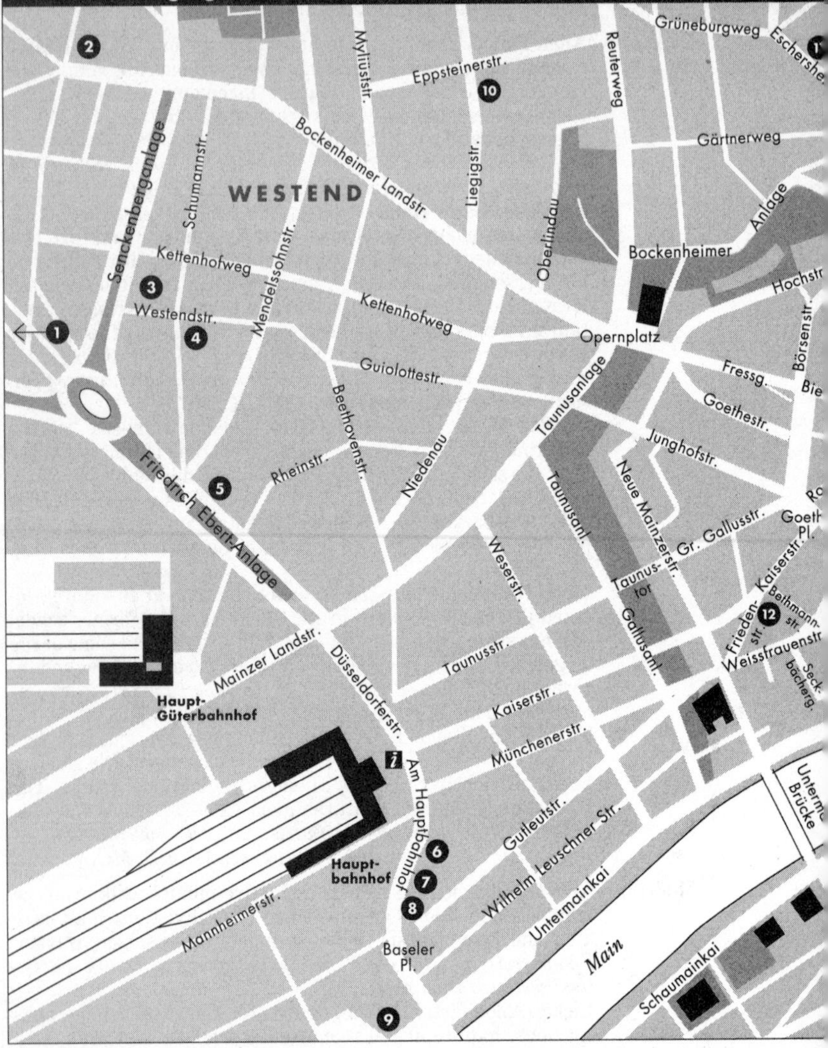

Altea Hotel, **1**
An der Messe, **3**
Arcade, **9**
Diana, **4**
Frankfurt Savoy Hotel, **6**
Hessischer Hof, **5**
Hotel Gravenbruch Kempinski, **16**
Hotel National, **8**
Hotel Pension West, **2**
Liebig, **10**
Maingau, **14**
Mövenpick Parkhotel Frankfurt, **7**
Neue Kräme, **13**
Steigenberger Frankfurter Hof, **12**
Turm Hotel, **11**
Waldhotel Hensels Felsenkeller, **15**

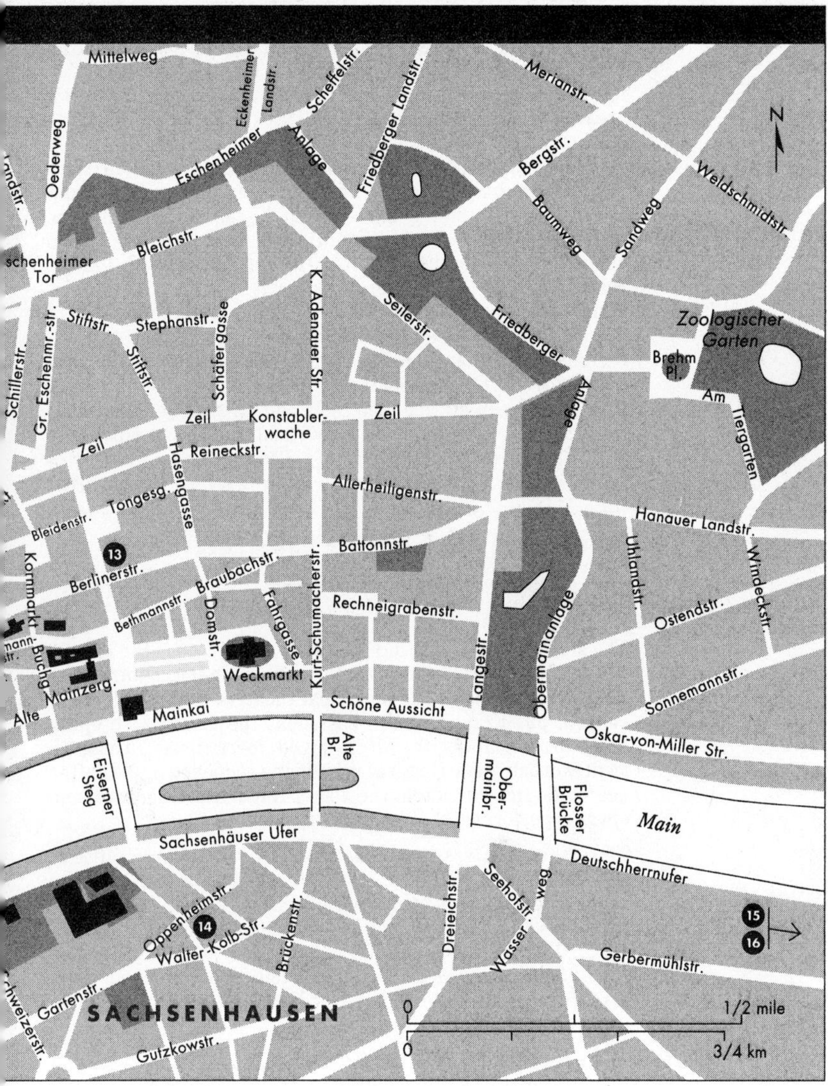
Mittelweg
Eckenheimer Landstr.
Scheffelstr.
Friedberger Landstr.
Merianstr.
Oederweg
Eschenheimer Anlage
Bergstr.
Weldschmidtstr.
Baumweg
Sandweg
Bleichstr.
Eschenheimer Tor
K. Adenauer Str.
Seilerstr.
Friedberger
Zoologischer Garten
Brehm Pl.
Am Tiergarten
Stiftstr.
Stephanstr.
Schäfergasse
Schillerstr.
Gr. Eschenmr.-str.
Anlage
Zeil
Konstablerwache
Reineckstr.
Hasengasse
Allerheiligenstr.
Tongesg.
Bleidenstr.
Hanauer Landstr.
Battonnstr.
Uhlandstr.
Windeckstr.
13
Kornmarkt
Berlinerstr.
Braubachstr.
Kurt-Schumacherstr.
Fahrgasse
Recheneigrabenstr.
Obermainanlage
Ostendstr.
Bethmannstr.
Domstr.
Langestr.
Buchg.
Weckmarkt
Mainzerg.
Sonnemannstr.
Alte
Mainkai
Schöne Aussicht
Oskar-von-Miller Str.
Alte Br.
Eiserner Steg
Obermainbr.
Flosser Brücke
Main
Sachsenhäuser Ufer
Deutschherrnufer
Seehofstr.
Dreieichstr.
Oppenheimstr.
14
Walter-Kolb-Str.
Brückenstr.
Wasserweg
15
16
Gerbermühlstr.
Gartenstr.
SACHSENHAUSEN
0
1/2 mile
0
3/4 km
Gutzkowstr.
Schweizerstr.

Inexpensive ★ **Diana.** For a postwar building, the Diana offers surprising charm, and feels more like a private home than a hotel. The location, just northeast of the trade-fair building, is a plus, too; it's a quiet, residential area, with easy access to the downtown area. Rooms are plain but spotless. *Westendstr. 83, tel. 069/747–007. 27 rooms, 9 with bath. AE, DC, MC, V.*

Hotel Pension West. For home comforts, a handy location (close to the university), and good value, try this family-run pension. It's in an older building and scores highly for old-fashioned appeal. The rooms are hardly luxurious but are more than adequate for a night or two. *Gräfstr. 81, tel. 069/778–011. 18 rooms with bath. MC. Closed Christmas.*

Waldhotel Hensels Felsenkeller. Some may find the location of the Hensels Felsenkeller a drawback; others will value its off-the-beaten track appeal. It's south of the river, in the Oberrad district, a short walk from the Stadtwald and a 10-minute walk from an S-bahn station. The hotel offers terrific value and, though basically furnished, is spotlessly clean and efficiently run. *Buchrainstr. 95, tel. 069/652–086. 21 rooms, most with bath. Facilities: restaurant, café, indoor pool. No credit cards.*

The Arts and Nightlife

The Arts

The arts get top billing in Frankfurt—the city has the largest budget for cultural expenditure of any city in the country. The **Stadtische Bühnen**—the municipal theaters—are the leading venues, but Frankfurt also has about the most lavish opera house in the country, the **Alt Oper** (Old Opera House), a magnificently ornate heap that was rebuilt and reopened in 1981 after near-total destruction in the war; paradoxically, however, no opera is performed there today.

Tickets for theaters can be purchased from the tourist office at the Hauptwache and from all theaters. Alternatively, try the **Ludwig Schäfer** agency in Sachsenhausen (Schweizer-Str. 28a, tel. 069/623–779). For information about concerts, call 069/11517. Pick up a copy of the twice-monthly listings magazine *Frankfurter Wochenschau* from any tourist office. The *Frankfurter Theaterzeitung* is published monthly and is available from all municipal theaters.

Theater The **Kammerspiele Theater** (Hofstr. 2, tel. 069/256–2435) and the municipally owned **Schauspiel Theater** (Theaterpl. tel. 069/256–2435) present highbrow German drama, old and new. Productions at **Die Komödie** theater (Neuer Mainzerstr. 18, tel. 069/284–330) are less earnest but no less impenetrable if your German is poor. For a more zany theatrical experience, try **Die Schmiere** (Seckbächer Gasse 2, tel. 069/281–066), which offers trenchant satire and also disarmingly calls itself "the worst theater in the world." If you're looking for English-language productions, try either the **Café-Theater** (Hamburger Allee, tel. 069/777–466) or the **Playhouse** (Hansaallee 152, tel. 069/151–8326).

Concerts and Opera The most glamorous venue for classical music concerts is the **Alter Oper** (Opernpl. tel. 069/256–2335). The main hall, a restrained, elegant auditorium, seats 2,500. The rear of the auditorium can be sealed off to form a 500-seat theater. Below, there's another auditorium, Hindemuth Hall, with seating for 340. Even if you don't take in a performance, it's worth having a look at the ponderous and ornate lobby, an example of 19th-century classicism at its most self-confident. The city's respected opera company performs at the **Municipal Opera House** (Theaterpl., tel. 069/256–2335).

The **Festhalle** (tel. 069/75750) at the trade-fair building is the scene for many rock concerts and other large-scale spectaculars. Frankfurt's new cultural center, the **Mouson Turm** (Waldschmidtstr. 4, tel. 069/405–8950) hosts a regular series of concerts of all kinds, as well as plays and exhibits.

Nightlife

Frankfurt, for all its unashamed internationalism and sophisticated expense-account living, is unlikely to win many votes as Germany's premier after-hours town. True, there's a red-light district, centered on the tawdry streets around the train station, especially **Kaiserstrasse** and **Münchnerstrasse,** though it's hardly in the same league as Hamburg's Reeperbahn. Most of the larger hotels also have bars, discos, and nightclubs. There's little to distinguish them from thousands of similar haunts the world over, but they're tried and tested.

For more genuinely local nightlife, head over the river to **Sachsenhausen,** Frankfurt's "Left Bank." It's hardly the quaint old Bohemian quarter it likes to sell itself as, but for bars, discos, clubs, and beer and wine restaurants this is about the best place to try. If you're in search of a rowdy night out, check out the **Apfelwein** taverns—they're touristy but fun. A green wreath over the door identifies them. Some visitors complain that the crowds and creeping tawdriness of Sachsenhausen are threatening to take the place over. If the area doesn't agree with you, try the ever-more-fashionable district of **Bornheim,** northeast of downtown. It has an almost equal number of bars, clubs, and the like, but the atmosphere is less forced, more authentic.

Frankfurt does have one trump card, however—**jazz.** Many German cities like to call themselves the jazz capital of the country, but Frankfurt probably has a better claim than most to the title. Fittingly, it's here in the fall that the German Jazz Festival is held. There are hundreds of jazz venues, from smoky back-street cafés to concert halls.

Bars and Nightclubs

Cooky's (Am Salzhaus 4) is probably the number-one nightspot, open till 4 AM Sunday–Thursday and till 6 AM Friday and Saturday. The proceedings take place under the watchful eye of Mahmoud, the doorman, an amateur wrestler from Lebanon. **Henry's Pinte** (Moselstr. 47) is another firm favorite, open till 7 AM and located close by the train station. **Jimmy's Bar** (Friedrich-Ebert-Anlage 40), in the Hessischer Hof Hotel, is distinctly more classy—and expensive. It's a favorite with high-flying executives and other big spenders. **John's Place** (Steinweg 7) is intimate and relaxed, taking its cue from genial owner John Paris. He offers good food and a mellow atmosphere. **St. John's Inn** (Grosser Hirschgraben 20) is the place to unwind after pulling off that big deal; there are more than 300 different whiskeys from which to choose, and the restaurant stays open till 4:30 AM. For an altogether more sedate night on the tiles, try **Stadt Wein** (Weckmarkt 13), an Austrian haunt that brings a touch of Viennese class to high-rise, high-tech Frankfurt.

Discos Bizarre though it may seem, about the best disco in the city is at the airport. It's **Dorian Gray,** easily reached by S-bahn and located in section C, level O. It attracts a surprisingly upscale crowd and has loud music and soft soft lights. **Plastic** (Seilerstr. 34) is more obviously trendy, the sort of place where the Frankfurt beau monde flocks to see and be seen. **Construction Five** (Alte Gasse 5) is a New York–style gay disco for men.

Jazz **Der Frankfurter Jazzkeller** (Kleine Bockenheimer Str. 18a) is the oldest jazz cellar in Germany, founded by legendary trumpeter Carlo Bohländer. It offers a wide range of sounds, from New Orleans to hot, modern jazz. **Jazz Kneipe** (Berlinstr. 70) is a reliable bet for more traditional jazz and is open till late. **Schlachthof** (Deutschhernufer 36) is the place for Dixieland jazz, beer by the barrelfull, and apple wine; the mood is rowdy and fun. **Sinkkasten** (Brönnerstr. 9) features jazz, rock, pop, and African music; it's sometimes hard to get into but worth the effort for serious fans.

Excursions

Frankfurt is so centrally located in Germany that the list of possible excursions—day trips and longer treks—is nearly endless. It is a gateway to the Rhineland in the west, the Neckar Valley in the south, and Franconia in the southeast, and the ideal starting point for journeys into all of these regions. Thus, the list of excursions here is merely a selection of destinations that are not covered in other chapters. For full details of other excursions from Frankfurt, *see* chapters 8, 9, 11, and 13.

Tour 1: Bad Homburg

Just a few miles north of Frankfurt, Bad Homburg lies at the foot of the **Taunus** hills. The Taunus, with their rich forests, medieval castles, and picturesque towns, are regarded by many Frankfurters as their territory. On weekends you can see them enjoying "their" playground; hiking through the hills; climbing the **Grosse Feldberg;** taking the waters at a health-giving mineral spring; or just lazing in the sun. The Bad Homburg spa was first known to the Romans but was rediscovered and made famous in the 19th century. Illustrious visitors included the Prince of Wales, the son of Queen Victoria, and Tsar Nicholas II. And here in 1841, the world's first casino was founded. Today, the sights in Bad Homburg include a 17th-century castle and the picturesque Altstadt (Old Town), but perhaps the most captivating sight is the enchanting Kurpark.

Getting There *By Car* Less than 45 minutes of driving on the A-5 Autobahn (Frankfurt–Dortmund) will take you to Bad Homburg.

By Train or Bus Bad Homburg has its own station. Take the S-bahn from Frankfurt at Konstable Wache (S-5 line). Buses and streetcars can also get you there.

Exploring The first stop you'll want to make in Bad Homburg is at the **tourist bureau** downtown. There you'll find local maps, advice, and assistance in booking accommodations, if necessary. You can also get information about and tickets to various local events. *Verkehrsamt. Louisenstr. 58, tel. 06172/121–310. Open weekdays 8:30–6, Sat. 8–1.*

The most historically noteworthy sight in the city itself is the 17th-century **Schloss.** The 172-foot **Weisser Turm** (White Tower) is all that remains of the medieval castle that once stood here. The Schloss that stands here today was built between 1680 and 1685 by Friedrich II of Hesse-Homburg, and a few alterations were made in the 19th century. The state apartments are exquisitely furnished, and the Spiegelkabinett (Hall of Mirrors) is especially worth a visit. In the surrounding park, look for two venerable trees from Lebanon, now almost 150 years old. *Schlosspl. Admission: DM 2 adults, 50 pf children. Open Mar.–Oct., Tues.–Sun. 10–5; Nov.–Feb., Tues.–Sun. 10–4.*

Also within the town, and certainly its greatest attraction over the centuries, is the **Kurpark,** with its more than 31 fountains. In the park you'll find not only the popular, highly saline Elisabethenbrunnen spring but also a Siamese temple and a Russian chapel, mementos left by two distinguished guests, King Chulalongkorn of Siam and Tsar Nicholas II.

Only 4 miles from Bad Homburg, and accessible by direct bus service, is the **Saalburg Limes** fort, the best-preserved Roman fort in Germany. Built in AD 120, the fort could accommodate a cohort (500 men) and was part of the fortifications along the 342-mile-long Limes Wall. The fort has been rebuilt as the Romans originally left it, with wells, armories, parade grounds, and catapults, as well as shops, houses, baths, and temples.

About a 30-minute walk from the fort is a fine open-air museum at **Hessenpark,** near Neu Anspach. The museum consists of 135 acres of rebuilt villages with houses, schools, and farms typical of the 18th and 19th centuries. A visit here yields a clear, concrete picture of the world in which the 18th- and 19th-century Hessians lived. *Admission: DM 3.50. Open Mar. 21–Oct. 1, Sun.–Tues. 9–6; Oct. 1–mid-Nov., Sun–Tues. 9–5; mid-Nov.–Mar. 20, weekends only 9–5.*

Just a short, convenient bus ride from Bad Homburg is the highest mountain in the Taunus, the 2,850-foot **Feldberg.** After a hike in the mountains, there are easy bus connections to the towns of Königstein and Kronberg. **Königstein** is a health-resort town with the ruins of a 13th-century castle and a noteworthy **Rathaus** (Town Hall). Many painters have chosen the nearby town of **Kronberg** as their setting. This picturesque old town, with its half-timbered houses and winding streets, was the home of the Kronberger School, an important contributor to 19th-century German art. Visit the 15th-century **Johaniskirche** with its late-Gothic murals.

Dining Most of the well-known spas in Bad Homburg have restaurants, but they tend to be very expensive. For an inexpensive and enjoyable meal, try one of the numerous Italian or Greek restaurants located throughout the city.

Casino-Restaurant. Bring your passport with you to this exclusive restaurant in the Kurpark. The cuisine is French and the atmosphere glittering. *Kurpark, tel. 06172/20041. Reservations required. Jacket and tie required. AE, DC, MC, V. Very Expensive.*

Zum Adler. This simple restaurant serves traditional Hessian fare. It's a good break after a tour of the open-air museum at

Hessenpark. *Neu Anspach. Dress: casual. AE, DC, MC, V. Moderate.*

Lodging **Hardtwald Hotel.** Located in a quiet spot in the forest but within easy access of the town center, this modern hotel is quite comfortable and offers pleasantly and intelligently furnished rooms. *Philosophenweg 31, tel. 06172/25016. 39 rooms with bath. Facilities: restaurant, terrace café. AE, DC, MC, V. Moderate.*

Haus Fischer Garni. This family-operated pension is simple and clean. It is located near a park and convenient to the old town. *Landgrafenstr. 12, tel. 06172/24927. 11 rooms with bath. No Credit Cards. Inexpensive.*

Tour 2: Limburg

The imposing seven-spired cathedral at **Limburg** will greet you upon arrival, seeming to grow out of the cliff that holds it. Modern Limburg grew around its old town—a city that developed because it was at the crossroads of the Köln–Frankfurt and Hessen–Koblenz highways in the 9th century. The old town still boasts a number of beautiful patrician and merchant houses, evidence of the city's importance in the Middle Ages.

Getting There
By Car The Frankfurt–Köln Autobahn (A-3) has two Limburg exits. Take either. The drive should take you less than an hour from Frankfurt.

By Train or Bus Limburg has its own railway station as well as regular bus service from Frankfurt, Koblenz, Wiesbaden, and the Frankfurt airport.

Exploring Upon arriving in the center of Limburg, visit the **Verkehrsverein** (tourist office) to receive city maps, help with accommodations if necessary, and other general information. *Hospitalstr. 2, tel. 06431/6166. Open Apr.–Oct., weekdays 8–12:30 and 1:30–5, Sat. 10–noon; Nov.–Mar., closed Fri. afternoons and Sat.*

The first sight to take in is the **Stifts-und Pfarrkirche St. Georg und Nikolaus,** the cathedral that you'll see towering over the Lahn River. Construction of the cathedral began in 1220, and evident in the building is the transition from Romanesque to Gothic style; each side presents a new perspective. Extensive restoration recently uncovered the original medieval coloring and bright frescoes from the 13th century.

Treasures from the cathedral are on display in the **Diozesanmuseum** in the **Schloss,** next door to the cathedral. It houses ecclesiastical art treasures from the bishopric of Limburg. Be sure to see the Byzantine cross reliquary that was stolen from the palace church in Constantinople in 1204 and the Patri-Stab (Peter's Staff), set with precious stones and adorned with gold.

The **Schloss** adjacent to the cathedral dates back to the 7th or 8th century, although the castle's current building only goes back to the 13th century. The group of residences, the chapel, and other buildings added in the 14th to 16th centuries serve as an architectural counterbalance to the cathedral. *Admission to Schloss and museum: DM 2 adults, DM 1 children. Open mid-Mar.–mid-Nov., Tues.–Sat. 9:30–12:30 and 2–5; Sun. 11–5.*

Only 4 miles from Limburg is the small town of **Runkel,** with an impressive 12th-century fortress. The fortress tower provides a panoramic view over the Taunus and the Westerwald.

About 12 miles south of Limburg is the state-recognized spa resort of **Bad Camberg,** a historic town located in the western foothills of the **Hochtaunus** (Taunus highlands). This city offers numerous half-timbered houses, remains of the city's gate and fortifications, and an attractive ensemble of buildings in the center of town, including the **Hohenfeldsche Kapelle** (chapel) of 1650. They stand in striking contrast to the modern **Kurhaus** across the street.

Dining **St. Georgs-Stuben.** In the Stadthalle, only a few minutes' walk from the center of Limburg, this pleasant restaurant serves local and international dishes. Try the house specialty, the St. Georgsteller, a filling pork-steak meal. *Hospitalstr. 4, tel. 06431/26027. Dress: casual. AE, DC, MC, V. Moderate.*

Lodging **Martin Hotel.** Within walking distance of the old town, this hotel has been in the same family for three generations. It was completely renovated in 1981, converting it into a modern, comfortable hotel. *Blumenroderstr. 2, tel. 06431/41001. 35 rooms, most with bath. Facilities: restaurant (closed Wed.). AE, DC, MC. V. Moderate.*

Zimmerman. Recent renovation has left some of the rooms of this pleasant hotel decorated in an elegant "English" style. The service is attentive and the breakfasts hearty. The restaurant is for hotel guests only. *Blumenroderstr. 1, tel. 06431/4611. 27 rooms, most with bath. Facilities: restaurant. AE, DC, MC, V. Moderate.*

Tour 3: Marburg

Built on and around a steep hill overlooking the Lahn river, Marburg, with its many half-timbered houses and small streets winding up to the castle, attracts many visitors. History buffs will especially enjoy Marburg, for it was here in 1256 that the State of Hesse was founded. The nation's oldest Protestant university was also begun here in 1527, and it is still going strong; 20% of the population of Marburg is students. Marburg was also the site of the 1529 **Colloquy of Marburg,** a document intended to bring about the unification of the Protestant and Reformed princes.

Getting There
By Car Take the A-5 Autobahn (Frankfurt–Kassel). The 60-mile trip should take about an hour.

By Train or Bus There are regularly departing direct connections from both Frankfurt and Kassel.

Exploring Once again, you may want to stop in at the **Verkehrsamt** (tourist office) for maps and assistance. *Neue Kasseler Str. 1, tel. 06421/201–248 or 06421/201–262.*

Near the city center is the town's emblem, the **Elisabethkirche,** one of the most important Gothic sacred buildings in Germany. The church, consecrated in 1283, was built over the grave of St. Elisabeth, ancestor of the Hessian nobles and champion of the poor. Details on the altar, six Gothic windows, and choir stall tell about her life. Intended as a pilgrimage church, Elisabethkirche has an extraordinarily well-preserved interior, with beautiful long murals. The finest feature of the church is the shrine of St. Elisabeth, a gold masterpiece from the 13th century, encrusted with jewels and enamels.

The nearby **Schloss** stands on the city's highest elevation. Construction was started by Duchess Sophie of Brabant, St. Elisabeth's daughter, but took centuries to complete; hence the many different shapes and styles the building displays. The church remains—in spite of the different builders—distinctly symmetrical. The Schloss ballroom is also worth seeing. Other noteworthy sites in the town are **St. Michaels Kapelle** and other buildings of the 13th-century Teutonic Order, as well as the 16th-century **Rathaus** (Town Hall), which was originally a meat market.

Dining **Gasthaus zur Sonne.** This quaint tavern for students serves hearty, reasonably priced meals. Inside the half-timbered walls of this 16th-century house you can dine and relax where generations of students have supped. *Markt 14, tel. 06421/26036. Dress: casual. Closed Mon. No credit cards. Moderate.*

Zum Alten Brauhaus. Another typical student hangout, this old brewery restaurant offers inexpensive, filling meals. *Pilgrimstein 34, tel. 06421/22180. Dress: casual. Closed Wed. No credit cards. Inexpensive.*

Lodging **Fasanerie.** This modern hotel is about 4 miles from Marburg's main train station. It offers quiet rooms with a fine view of the city. The service is friendly and competent, and the garden restaurant serves good-quality international specialties. *Zur Fasanerie 15, tel. 06421/7038 or 06421/7039. 36 rooms, 2 apartments, most with bath. Facilities: restaurant. AE, DC, MC, V. Moderate.*

Bahnhofshotel Rump Garni. Centrally located and near the train station, this hotel has functional furnishings and a comfortable atmosphere. *Bahnhofstr. 29, tel. 06421/65400. 20 rooms, most with bath. No credit cards. Inexpensive.*

13 The Rhineland

Introduction

The importance of the Rhine can hardly be overestimated. Throughout recorded history—at least for the past 2,000 years—the Rhine has served as Europe's leading waterway. While by no means the longest river in Europe (the Danube is more than twice its length), it has long been the main river-trade artery between the heart of the Continent and the North Sea.

The Rhine runs for 1,355 kilometers (840 miles), from Lake Constance to Basel in Switzerland, then north through Germany, and then west through the Netherlands to Rotterdam. It forms a natural frontier between Germany and France for part of its length, and was once Europe's major highway between Basel and the Atlantic, before the advent of overland transportation.

Great cities—such as Basel, Strasbourg, Mainz, Cologne, and Düsseldorf—grew up along the Rhine's banks. No wonder Germans refer to their favorite river as *Vater Rhein,* or Father Rhine, the way Americans call the Mississippi Old Man River.

One section of the Rhine became Germany's top tourist site all of 200 years ago. Around 1790, a spearhead of adventurous travelers from various parts of Europe arrived by horse-drawn carriages to explore the sector of the river between Bingen and Koblenz, now known as the Middle Rhine Valley. Needless to say, they were all but overwhelmed by the dramatic and romantic scenery, which exists nowhere else on the Continent. It didn't take long for the word to spread.

Other travelers followed in their coach tracks, and soon thereafter the first sightseeing cruises went into operation.

Poets, painters, and other artists were attracted by this magnet: Goethe, Germany's greatest poet, was enthralled; Heinrich Heine wrote a poem tied to the Lorelei legend that was eventually set to music and made the unofficial theme of the landmark; and William Turner captured misty Rhine sunsets on canvas. In 1834, the first-ever Baedeker guidebook detailed the attractions of this stretch of the river in meticulous detail. At about the same time, the advent of the railroad opened up the region to an early form of mass tourism. By the mid-19th century, the Rhine Valley was known throughout Europe; in 1878, Mark Twain's "A Tramp Abroad" spread the word to potential travelers in the United States.

Today, the passage through the Rhine Valley still makes for one of Europe's most memorable journeys. Ideally, the way to go is by car—up one side and down the other—with time out for a cruise. But even the train route between Wiesbaden and Koblenz offers thrilling views—the landmarks may flash by at top speed, a little like a home movie running out of control, but you still gain exposure to the essential aspects of the Rhine's beauty: hilltop castles silhouetted against the sky, ravishing river sights, and glimpses of pretty-as-a-picture wine villages.

The Mittel Rhein (Middle Rhine) could be considered an obligatory day trip out of Frankfurt—it's quite possibly Germany's number-one, not-to-be-missed excursion. But there's far more to the Rhine as it wends its way north to Cologne and Düsseldorf.

This chapter divides the Rhineland into four tours. The first covers the Middle Rhine, the 129-kilometer (80-mile) stretch from Mainz (40 kilometers; 25 miles, west of Frankfurt, the natural starting point for any visit to the Rhineland) to Koblenz. Of all the many and varied regions of the river, no other has the same array of scenery, history, architecture, and natural beauty as this magical stretch. Mention the Rhineland to most visitors, and this is the area they'll assume you mean. It is a land of steep and thickly wooded hills, of terraced vineyards rising step by step above the river banks, of massive hilltop castles, and of tiny wine villages hugging river shores. It is also a land of legend and myth. For example, the Lorelei, a steep mountain of rock jutting out of the river, was once believed to be the home of a beautiful and bewitching maiden who lured boatmen to a watery end in the swift currents. It was the home, too, of the Nibelungs, a Burgundian race said to have lived on the river banks, who serve as subjects for no less than four of Wagner's epic operas.

The most famous tributary of the Rhine is the Mosel, which flows into the river at Koblenz. The second tour covers its snaking passage through another great wine-producing area, with scenery almost as striking as that found along the Rhine. At its western end, almost on the French border, is Trier, once one of the greatest cities in the Roman Empire.

The third tour covers Bonn, a sleepy university town that unexpectedly became the capital of West Germany, and Köln (Cologne), the greatest of the Rhine cities, a vibrant and bustling metropolis boasting the largest and most dramatic Gothic cathedral in the country.

The fourth tour is a side trip to Aachen, capital of Charlemagne's Holy Roman Empire in the 9th century and site of the most important pre-Romanesque cathedral in Europe. Today, this elegant spa town on the Belgian and Dutch borders has a quiet, civilized charm.

If you plan to make any trip through the Rhineland, remember that this is one of Germany's major tourist areas, drawing visitors from around the world. As a result, prices here in summer are high, often substantially above those found elsewhere in the country. Make reservations well in advance, and don't expect to have the place to yourself.

Essential Information

Important Addresses and Numbers

Tourist Information The Rhineland regional tourist, **Fremdenverkehrsverband Rheinland Pfalz** office (Postfach 1420, 5400 Koblenz, tel. 0261/31079), provides general information on the entire region. There are also local tourist information offices in the following towns and cities:

Aachen: Verkehrsverein Bad Aachen, Haus Löwenstein, Am Markt 39, 5100 Aachen, tel. 0241/33491.
Bernkastel-Kues: Stadt. Verkehrsbüro, Am Gestade 5, 5550 Bernkastel-Kues, tel. 06531/4023.
Bonn: Tourist Information Cassius-Bastei, Münsterstrasse 20, 5300 Bonn, tel. 0228/773466.

Cochem: Verkehrsamt, Enderplatz, 5590 Cochem, tel. 02671/3971.

Köln: Verkehrsamt der Stadt Köln, Untere Fettenhenen 19, 5000 Köln 1, tel. 0221/2213345.

Koblenz: Fremdenverkehrsamt der Stadt Koblenz, Verkehrspavillon, 5400 Koblenz, tel. 0261/31304.

Rüdesheim: Städtisches Verkehrsamt, Rheinstrasse 16, 6200 Rüdesheim, tel. 06722/2962.

St. Goarshausen: Verkehrsamt, Bahnhofstrasse 5422 St. Goarshausen, tel. 06771/427.

Trier: Tourist Information, an der Porta Nigra, Postfach 3830, 5500 Trier, tel. 0651/48071.

Wiesbaden: Verkehrsbüro, Rheinstrasse 15, Ecke Wilhemstrasse, 6200 Wiesbaden, tel. 06121/312847.

Embassies

United States, Deichmanns Aue, 5300 Bonn, tel. 0228/3391.

Great Britain, Friedrich-Ebert-Allee 77, 5300 Bonn, tel. 0228/3440.

Canada, Friedrich-Wilhelmstrasse 18, 5300 Bonn, tel. 0228/2310.

Travel Agencies

American Express: Burgruauer 14, 5000 **Köln,** tel. 0221/235–613; 5 Steinweg, Postfach 100146, 6000 **Frankfurt,** tel. 069/21051; Webergasse 8, Postfach 1245, 6200 **Wiesbaden,** tel. 06121/39144.

Car Rental

Avis: Bahnhofplatz 7, **Aachen,** tel. 0241/24025; Adenauerallee 4–6, **Bonn,** tel. 0228/223–047; Clemensstrasse 29, **Köln,** tel. 0221/384–041; Mainzer Vandstrasse 170, **Frankfurt,** tel. 069/230–101; Moselweisserstrasse 3, **Koblenz,** tel. 0261/44050; Herzogenbuscherstrasse 31, **Trier,** tel. 0651/12722; Wiesbadener Landstrasse 13, **Wiesbaden,** tel. 06121/609–041.

Europcar: Renterstrasse 124, **Bonn,** tel. 0228/221–075; Mainzer Landstrasse, 160, **Frankfurt,** tel. 069/234–002; Köln-Bonn Airport, **Köln,** tel. 02203/402–304; Luisenstrasse 28, **Wiesbaden,** tel. 06121/39391.

Hertz: Juelienerstrasse 250, **Aachen,** tel. 0241/162–686; Adenauerallee 216, **Bonn,** tel. 0228/217–041; Köln-Bonn Airport, **Köln,** tel. 02203/61085; Mainzer Landstrasse 139, **Frankfurt,** tel. 069/233–151; Burgstrasse 3, **Wiesbaden,** tel. 06121/374–073.

Arriving and Departing by Plane

The Rhineland is served by three international airports: Frankfurt, Düsseldorf, and Köln-Bonn. There are direct flights from the United States and Canada to Frankfurt and Düsseldorf. Both airports, together with the one at Köln-Bonn, are part of a comprehensive network of air services throughout Europe. Bus and rail lines connect each airport with its respective downtown area and provide rapid access to the rest of each region.

Getting Around

By Car

The Autobahns and other highways of the Rhineland are busy, so allow plenty of time to complete any trip you make. Frankfurt is 126 kilometers (79 miles) from Koblenz, 175 kilometers (110 miles) from Bonn, and 190 kilometers (119 miles) from Köln. The most spectacular stretch of the Rhineland is along the Middle Rhine, between Mainz and Koblenz. Highways (though not Autobahns) hug the river on each bank, and car ferries crisscross the Rhine at many points. Road conditions throughout the region are excellent.

By Train Intercity and Eurocity expresses connect all the cities and towns of the area. Hourly Intercity routes run between Düsseldorf, Köln, Bonn, and Mainz, with most services extending as far south as Munich and as far north as Hamburg. The Mainz-Bonn route runs beside the Rhine, between the river and the vine-covered heights, offering spectacular views all the way.

By Bus There are two Europabus routes running across the Rhineland: one originates in Britain and terminates in Munich, crossing the Rhineland between Köln and Frankfurt; the other runs between Frankfurt and Trier, stopping at the Frankfurt airport, Wiesbaden, Mainz, Bingen, and several towns along the Mosel River. All Europabuses are comfortable and fast. For details on services and reservations, contact **Deutsche Touring** (am Römerhof 17, Postfach 900244, 6000 Frankfurt/Main 90, tel. 069/79030). Local bus services connect most smaller towns and villages throughout the Rhineland.

By Boat No visit to the Rhineland is complete without at least one river trip. Fortunately, there are many cruise options from which to choose (*see* Guided Tours, below).

Guided Tours

Boat Trips Trips along the Rhine and Mosel range from a few hours to days or even a week or more in length. The major operator, with a fleet of 25 boats, is the **Köln-Düsseldorfer Deutsche Rheinschiffahrt,** (Frankenwerft 15, 5000 Köln 1, tel. 0221/208–8288), known as the K-D line. It offers daily services on the Rhine, Mosel, and Main rivers from April through October, as well as a year-round program of excursions, principally along the Rhine. For the best values, check out the K-D's combined river-rail tickets, which allow you to break your river trip at any place the boats stop and continue on by train. For further sailings along the Rhine, contact the Boppard-Basel **Hebel** line (tel. 06742/2420), which operates from March through December; for trips along the Mosel, contact **Mosel-Personenschiffahrt Bernkastel-Kues** (Goldbachstr. 52, Bernkastel-Kues, tel. 06531/8222).

If you want to combine the Rhine with wine, the K-D line has a series of week-long "floating wine seminars," with ships running between Köln and Basel along the German-Swiss border. The K-D line also organizes three- and four-day cruises along the Mosel that stop at most of the wine villages between Koblenz and Trier.

Two shipping companies in Koblenz organize short "castle cruises" from Easter through September. Two boats, the *Undine* and the *Marksburg*, ply the Rhine between Koblenz and Boppard, passing 10 castles during the 75-minute, one-way voyage. Details and reservations are available from **Personenschiffahrt Merkelbach** (Emserstr. 87, 5400 Koblenz-Pfaffendorf, tel. 0261/76810); and **Personenschiffahrt Wolfgang Vomfell** (Koblenzerstr. 64, 5401 Spay/Rhein, tel. 02628/2431). Another Koblenz operator, **Rhein und Moselschiffahrt Gerhard Collee-Holzenbein** (Rheinzollstr. 4, tel. 0261/37744), runs day cruises as far as Rüdesheim on the Rhine, and Cochem on the Mosel.

From Köln, three shipping companies operate boat tours on the Rhine: The **Köln-Düsseldorfer** line (Frankenwerft 15, tel. 0221/20880) has hourly trips starting at 10:30, daily, April through September; the **Rhein-Mosel Schiffahrt** (Konrad-Adenauer-Ufer, tel. 0221/121600) has daily departures every 45 minutes starting at 10, April through September; and the **Dampfschiffahrt Colonia** (Lintgasse 18, tel. 0221/211325) has daily departures every 45 minutes beginning at 10, May through September. All tours leave from the landing stages near the Hohenzollern Brücke, a short walk from the cathedral.

Bus Tours **Deutsche Touring** (Mannheimerstr. 4, tel. 069/790–3253) has a daily bus trip from Frankfurt along the "Riesling Route" that encompasses the vineyards of the Rhineland between Frankfurt and Rüdesheim. The tour includes a wine tasting (by candlelight) and a trip along the Rhine to the wine village of St. Goar. Cost is DM 72.

Bus trips into the countryside around Köln (to the Eifel Hills, the Ahr Valley, and the Westerwald) are organized by several city travel agencies. Two leading tour operators are: **Globus Reisen** (Hohenzollernring, tel. 0221/120–111); and **Univers-Reisen,** (am Rinkenpfuhl 57, tel. 0221/235–771). The **Küppers-Reiseburo-Etrav** company (Longericher-Strasse 183, tel. 0221/171–173) combines a tour of the Belgian Ardennes with a visit to a spa casino. Buses leave daily from outside the cathedral at 1:15 and 5:30, and return around 10 PM.

City Tours **Bus tours** of Köln leave from outside the tourist office (opposite the main entrance to the cathedral) at 10, 11, 1, 2, and 3, May through October, and at 11 and 2 November through April. The two-hour tour costs DM 17; English-speaking guides are available. **"Köln by Night"** bus tours are offered Fridays and Saturdays in July and August. These trips leave the tourist office at 8 PM and feature a tour of the city, a boat ride on the Rhine, a cold supper, and visits to a wine tavern and the Köln TV tower; cost is DM 40. A two-hour **walking tour** of the city, with an English-speaking guide, is also available. Tours leave from outside the tourist office daily at 4:30, May through September; cost is DM 7. Most central hotels offer a special tourist package, the **"Kölner Knüller,"** which includes a sightseeing tour voucher, a pass for all the city's museums, and other reductions. The package costs DM 22.

Exploring the Rhineland

Highlights for First-time Visitors

Aachen Cathedral
Beethovenhaus, Bonn
Burg Eltz
Köln Cathedral
Porta Nigra, Trier
Römische Palastula, Trier
Trier Cathedral
View from Siebenburgenblick
Wilhelmstrasse, Wiesbaden

The Mittel Rhein

Numbers in the margin correspond with points of interest on the Rhineland map.

1 If you're flying in to Frankfurt, you'll begin your tour of the Rhine 40 kilometers (25 miles) west of the city at the point where the Main River joins the mighty Rhine, at **Wiesbaden.** It's located on the east bank of the Rhine, almost opposite the town of Mainz (*see* Chapter 10), and marks the start of the most famous stretch of the Rhine, the **Rheingau,** home of Germany's finest wines and some of its most enchanting (and crowded) wine villages.

Wiesbaden, one of the oldest cities in Germany, was founded 2,000 years ago by Roman legions attracted by its hot springs. It's elegant 19th-century face, however, is what captures one's attention today. The little city gained prominence in the mid-19th century when Europe's leisure classes rediscovered the hot springs. The English, in particular, had a weakness for Wiesbaden—witness the church of **St. Augustine of Canterbury,** built between 1863 and 1865 for the city's many English visitors—but the Germans, too, were enticed.

By 1900, Wiesbaden boasted the largest number of millionaires of any German city, Berlin included. To get a taste of its 19th-century opulence, wander along **Wilhelmstrasse,** whose mint-condition fin-de-siecle buildings and expensive stores provide eloquent proof of the city's continuing affluence. Wiesbaden hasn't always prospered in this century, however. The outbreak of World War I in 1914 halted the social whirl, and in the war's aftermath, the city was occupied by French and British troops.

The 19th-century residence of the dukes of Nassau, one-time rulers of Wiesbaden, is perhaps symbolic of Wiesbaden's fall from the social heights. Today the classical facade of the former palace houses the mundane offices of the provincial government of Hessen.

Time Out Soak up Wiesbaden's 19th-century charm in the wood-paneled warmth of the centrally located **Café Maldaner** (on Marktstr.). Don't be surprised if you think you're in Vienna—the café was opened in 1859 as a Viennese coffee house catering to the city's Austrian visitors.

Having paid homage to Wiesbaden, you'll want to set off down the Rhine to explore the Rheingau, whose vine-covered slopes rise up from the river between Wiesbaden and Bingen, 25 kilometers (15 miles) to the west. There, the Rhine abruptly turns north. Technically, the Rheingau begins just east of Wiesbaden, at Hochheim (the town that gave its name to Hock wine), but it's the sunny, south stretch you're about to explore that people generally think of when they hear a reference to the Rheingau. For the most scenic route, take the river-hugging B-42.

2 The first town you'll reach on the road west is **Eltville.** It's the geographic heart of the Rheingau, though Rüdesheim, 15 kilometers (9 miles) west, enjoys greater fame. Eltville's half-timbered buildings crowd narrow streets that date back to Roman times. Though the Romans imported wine to Germany,

The Rhineland

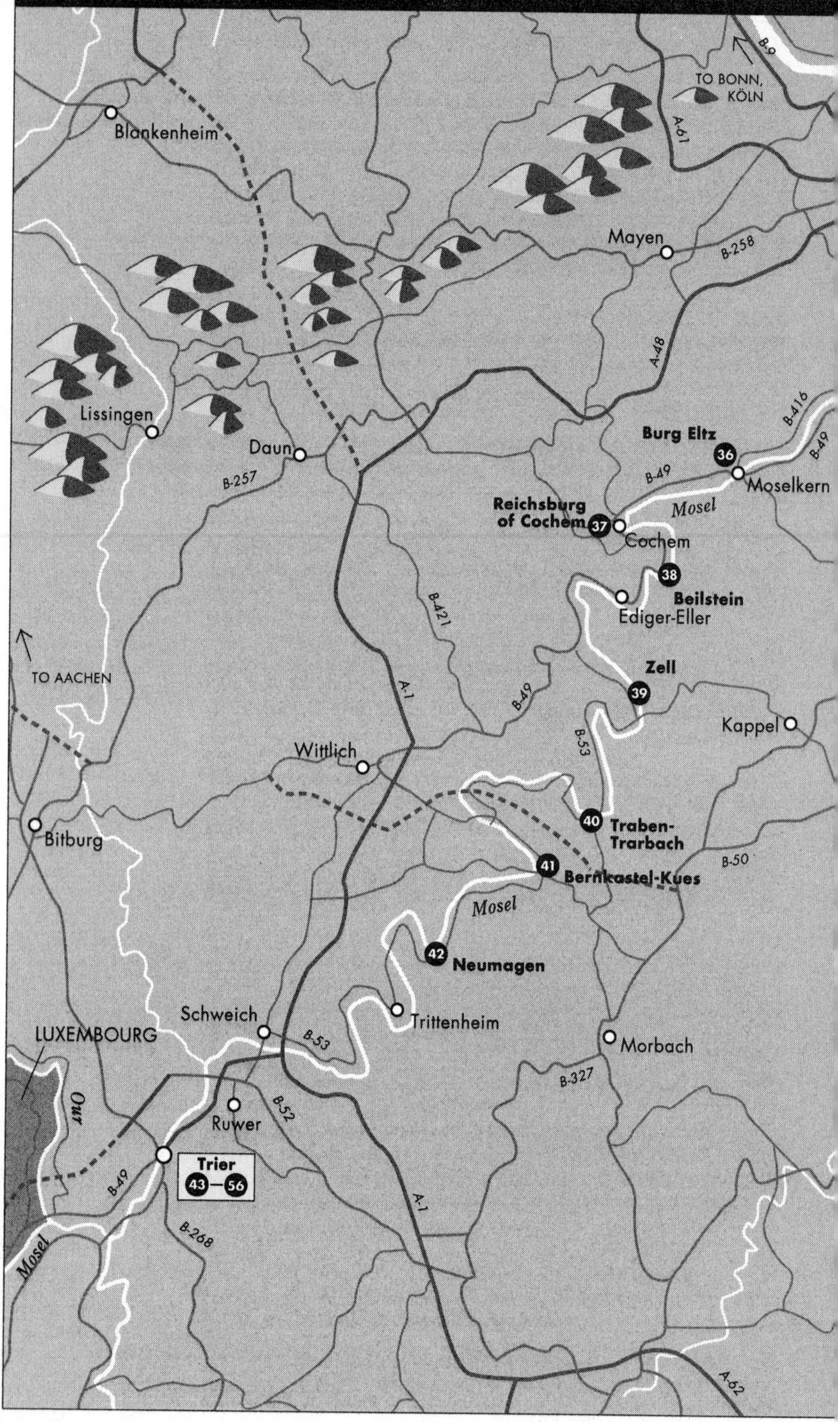

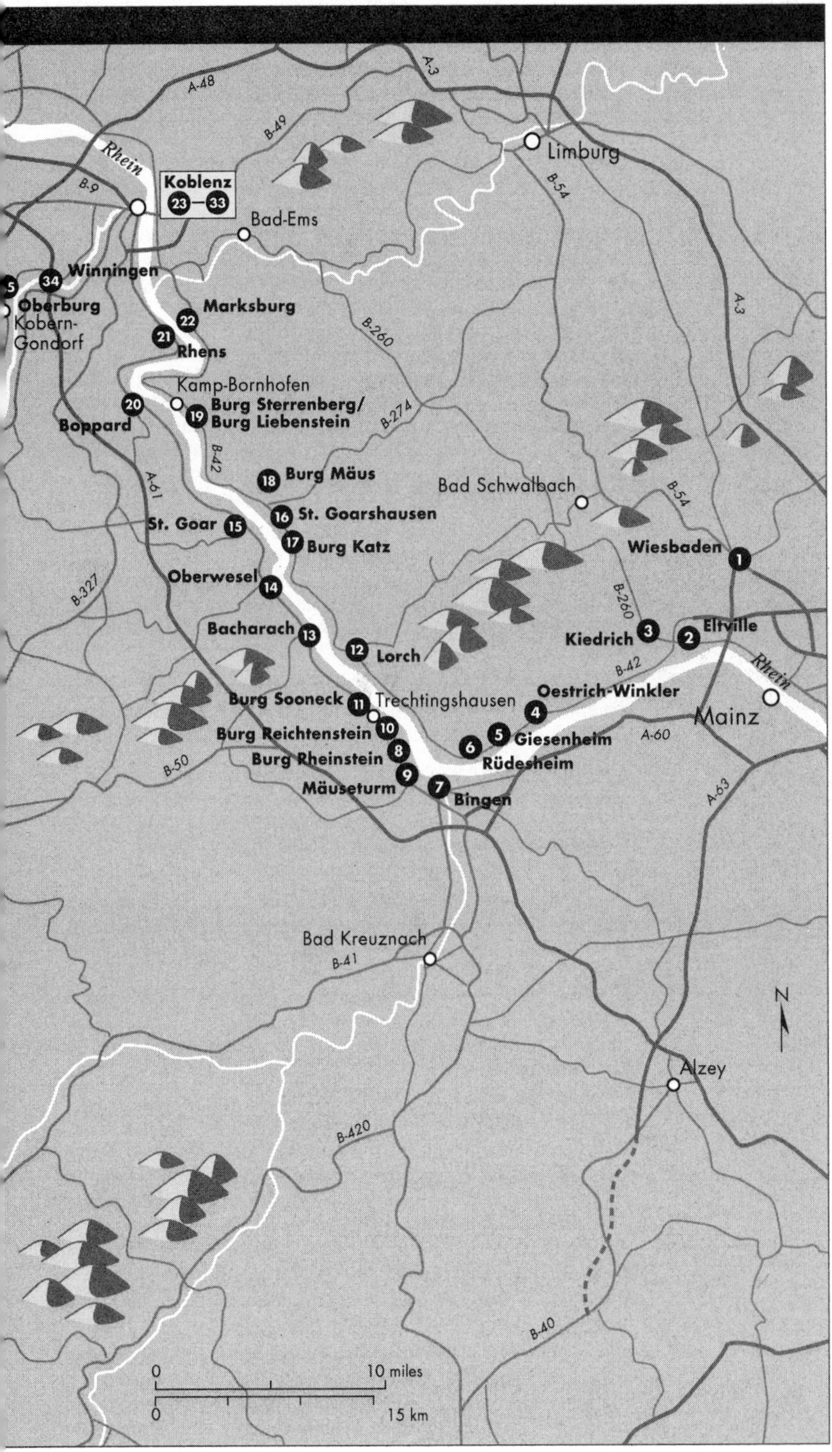
A-48
A-3
B-49
Rhein
Koblenz
23—33
Limburg
B-54
B-9
Bad-Ems
34 Winningen
Oberburg
Kobern-Gondorf
22 Marksburg
21 Rhens
B-260
A-3
Kamp-Bornhofen
20 Boppard
19 Burg Sterrenberg/ Burg Liebenstein
B-274
B-42
18 Burg Mäus
Bad Schwalbach
B-54
A-61
16 St. Goarshausen
St. Goar 15
17 Burg Katz
Wiesbaden 1
B-327
Oberwesel 14
B-260
Bacharach 13
12 Lorch
Kiedrich 3
2 Eltville
B-42
Rhein
Oestrich-Winkler 4
Burg Sooneck 11
Trechtingshausen
Mainz
Burg Reichtenstein 10
5 Giesenheim
A-60
6
Burg Rheinstein 8
Rüdesheim
B-50
Mäuseturm 9
7 Bingen
A-63
Bad Kreuznach
B-41
N
Alzey
B-420
B-40
0
10 miles
0
15 km

they never made it here. It was Charlemagne, so the story goes, who in the 9th century first realized that the sunny slopes of the Rheingau could be used to produce wines. Eltville's vineyards may not go that far back, but some, including **Hanach** and **Rheinberg,** have been in use since the 12th century. Today, the town is best known for the production of Sekt, sparkling German wine (champagne by any other name, though the French ensured that it could not legally be called that by including a stipulation in the Treaty of Versailles in 1919). Sekt cellars rest coolly beneath the town's winding streets. Those of the **Matheus Muller** company are several miles long and hold up to 15 million bottles. While the cellars are not open to the public, you can amble through the courtyards of some formidable old vineyard buildings, including the white-walled, slate-roofed **Eltzerhof,** one of the more beautiful. Eltville also has its own **castle,** commissioned by the Archbishop of Trier in 1330. In it is a museum devoted to **Johannes Gutenberg,** father of the modern printing press. The Prince-Archbishop of Mainz admitted Gutenberg to the court in Eltville, thereby saving the inventor from financial ruin. *Admission: DM 1.50 adults, 50 pf children. Open May–Sept., Sun. only, 2–5.*

In Eltville, the Gothic parish church of **Sts. Peter and Paul** has some fine 14th-century stained glass and ceiling frescoes; its walls are lined with the tombstones and monuments of noble families who rose to prominence on the prestige of the local wine.

To see one of Germany's oldest church organs, dating from around 1500, drive inland for a mile or so to the village of
3 **Kiedrich.** The west entrance to the church is richly carved.

4 The drive from Kiedrich back to the river at **Oestrich-Winkel** takes you past the largest vineyard in the Rheingau. Oestrich-Winkel is the site of the oldest stone dwelling in the country, the **Graues Haus** (Gray House). It dates from the 9th century and is now open as a restaurant.

5 Continue on to **Geisenheim,** a name inextricably linked with Rheingau wines at their finest. "Rhineland is wineland" is a saying in this part of the world, and indeed, you'll see a checkerboard of terraced vineyards stretching from the Rhine's riverside villages all the way back to a protective line of forests at the base of the Taunus mountains. Geisenheim has some of the most renowned vineyards in the area, with grapes that create wines on a par with those from Burgundy's Côte d'Or and the Medoc of the Bordeaux region.

From the vintner's point of view, this part of Germany has the ideal conditions for the cultivation of the noble Riesling grapes: a perfect southern exposure; shelter from cold winds from the north; slopes with the proper pitch for drainage; soil containing slate and quartz to reflect the sun and hold heat through the night and moisture in the morning; and long sunny days from early spring until late fall. (Although the Rheingau is at approximately the same latitude as Newfoundland, you'd never know it from the weather.)

In Geisenheim, visit the 18th-century **Schloss Johannisberg,** built on the site of a 12th-century abbey and still owned by the von Metternich family. Schloss Johannisberg produces what is generally regarded as one of the very best Rheingau wines, along with a renowned Sekt. On the castle terrace you can order the elegant estate-bottled golden wine by the glass. As you savor the cool, rich, clear-as-crystal drink, you can contemplate all that makes this corner of Europe so special. Views down across the vineyards take in the river at its calmest. If you're lucky, the Rhine will be enveloped in a pastel mood worthy of a Turner painting. As you leave the castle, you can buy a bottle or two of the excellent wine at a shop just outside the walls.

Rüdesheim and Bingen beckon now, 8 kilometers (5 miles)
6 north, along the banks of the Rhine. **Rüdesheim** is arguably the Rhine Valley's prettiest and most popular wine town. Set along the river's edge, it is a picturesque place of half-timbered and gabled medieval houses. Everything here is somehow related to either wine or tourists or both. You can visit wine cellars to inspect great casks with elaborate and lovingly carved heads.

Angling up from the river toward the romantic old town is the region's most famous Weingasse (wine alley), the extraordinary Drosselgasse. This narrow, 200-yard-long cobbled lane is lined with cozy wine taverns and rustic restaurants. At night, voices raised in song and brass bands create a cacophony, shattering whatever peace the town may have known by day.

Rüdesheim turns out to be very much of a plus-and-minus affair. You can love it in the morning, before the day's quota of tour buses start disgorging their passengers, and hate it at night, when an aura of exploitation takes over and it gets far too crowded for comfort. It is definitely worth a visit, though—how long of a visit may depend on the circumstances or time of day.

Above Rüdesheim, at an elevation of 1,000 feet, stands the **Niederwald-Denkmal,** a colossal stone statue of Germania, the heroically proportioned woman who symbolizes the unification of the German Empire in 1871. Built between 1876 and 1883 on the orders of Bismarck, this giant figure came within an inch of being blown to smithereens during the dedication ceremonies. At the unveiling, held in the presence of the Kaiser and Bismarck, an anarchist attempted to blow up the statue and the assembled dignitaries. However, in true comic-opera style, a rain shower put out the fuse on the bomb, and all survived.

Niederwald can be reached by car or chair lift, or you can climb to the statute's steep perch. Whichever way you choose, the ascent offers splendid views, including one of the little island in the middle of the Rhine where the Mäuseturm (Mouse Tower) is situated (*see* below). The chair lift station to the monument is located a short walk from the Drosselgasse. It operates continuously every day from late March to early November; round-trip fare is DM 7 adults, DM 3.50 children.

Wine buffs and those who enjoy wandering through old castles won't want to miss Rüdesheim's **Schloss Brömserburg,** one of the oldest castles on the Rhine, built more than 1,000 years ago by the Knights of Rüdesheim on the site of a Roman fortress. Inside its stout walls are wine presses, drinking vessels, and collections related to viticulture from prehistoric times to the present. *Weinmuseum in der Brömserburg, Rheinstr. 2. Admission: DM 2.50 adults, DM 1.50 children. Open Apr.–Oct., daily 9–12:30 and 1:30–6.*

7 The town of **Bingen,** on the opposite riverbank, celebrates the festival of St. Rochus every year in mid-August. In **St. Rochus chapel,** built in 1666 in memory of Bingen's plague victims, you'll see a portrait of Goethe, the 18th-century man of letters and prophet of Romanticism, posing improbably as the saint. To get to Bingen, the short ferry ride from the Adlertrum jetty in Rüdesheim (DM 1.50 adults, 75 pf children).

The number-one excursion from Bingen is the boat ride to the romantic **Castle of Burg Rheinstein.** It was Prince Friedrich von Preussen, a cousin of Emperor Wilhelm I, who acquired the original medieval castle in 1825 and transformed it into the picture-book castle you see high above the Rhine today. The prince is buried in the castle's fanciful Gothic chapel.

8 The ride to **Burg Rheinstein** takes you past one of the most fa-
9 mous sights on the Rhine, the **Mäuseturm** (Mouse Tower), a 13th-century edifice clinging to a rock in the river. According to legend, it was constructed by an avaricious bishop as a customs post to exact taxes from passing river traffic. The story suggests that the greedy bishop grew so unpopular that he was forced to hole up in the tower, where he was eventually devoured by mice.

Beyond the Mäuseturm there are two other medieval castles
10 you can visit: **Burg Reichenstein,** which towers high above the
11 picturesque wine town of **Trechtingshausen;** and **Burg Sooneck,** which in the 12th century was the most feared stronghold in the Rhineland. Reichenstein castle is now a luxurious hotel where you can enjoy lunch in an excellent restaurant with a sensational view. Sooneck, towering above the Rhine on a rocky outcrop, was destroyed several times during its colorful history and rebuilt in its present form in 1840 by the Prussian King Friedrich Wilhelm IV. From the castle you can follow a path through vineyards to one of the most spectacular vantage points of the whole Rhineland: the **Siebenburgenblick** (Seven-Castle View).

Two miles north of Burg Sooneck, at the village of **Nieder-**
heimbach, take the ferry back across the Rhine to the historic
12 little wine town of **Lorch,** whose ancient walls mark the northernmost limit of the Rhinegau. Its parish church of **St. Martin** has a Gothic high altar and 13th-century carved choir stalls.

Northwards from Lorch, both banks of the river offer competing attractions. The only way anyone could get to see them all would be to zigzag back and forth across the river by ferry. Fortunately, at most points between here and Koblenz, crossing the Rhine is easy via small ferries that run frequently.

13 Downstream from Lorch, on the west bank, lies busy **Bacharach,** whose long association with wine is indicated by its name, which comes from the Latin "Bacchi ara," meaning altar of Bacchus, the Roman god of wine. The town was a thriving center of Rhine wine trade in the Middle Ages. Something of its medieval atmosphere can still be found in the narrow streets within its 14th-century defensive walls and towers.

Time Out Stop by the old marketplace and look for the gold painted sign of the **Wein Haus Altes Haus.** Wine has been served in this half-timbered tavern for four centuries. Ask for any Bacharach Riesling and you won't be disappointed. *Marktpl.*

14 **Oberwesel,** 8 kilometers (5 miles) north of Bacharach, also retains its medieval look. Sixteen of the original 21 towers that studded the town walls still stand; one does double duty as the bell tower of the 14th-century church of **St. Martin.** Towering above the town are the remains of the 1,000-year-old **Burg Schönburg,** whose massive walls, nearly 20 feet thick in places, were not strong enough to prevent its destruction by rampaging French troops in 1689. Part of the castle has been restored and today houses a comfortable hotel.

The ruins of another medieval castle, **Burg Rheinfels,** stand at the outskirts of the next stop along the road, the town of **St.**
15 **Goar,** named after an early missionary who became the patron saint of Rhine boatmen and tavern keepers. The Rhine here narrows dramatically, funneling its waters into a treacherous maelstrom of fast-flowing currents and eddies. These rushing torrents are what gave rise to the legend of the Lorelei, a grim, 400-foot-high rock that protrudes from the river just outside
16 **St. Goarshausen.** So many boats were wrecked on it that people began to say a bewitching water nymph with golden tresses inhabited the rock, and lured sailors to watery graves by her beauty and strange songs.

These days, in season, the Lorelei's siren song can serve as a trap for tourists rather than sailors. Excursion boats leave regularly from Koblenz and Bingen on Lorelei cruises, and as these overcrowded vessels pass within sight of the famed cliffs, each and every one plays a taped version of the Lorelei song (a Heinrich Heine poem set to music), blasting the creation above the roar of the river.

You can see a statue of the Lorelei in St. Goarshausen. To get there, take the ferry from St. Goar.

North and south of St. Goarshausen are two castles whose 14th-century owners feuded so unrelentingly that the for-
17 tresses came to be known as Katz (cat) and Maus (mouse). **Burg Katz,** just north of St. Goarshausen, was built in 1371 by Count Wilhelm II von Katzenelnbogen (literally, cat's elbow). It was
18 he who dubbed the rival castle south of St. Goarshausen **Burg Mäus.** The rivalry, however, was a serious matter. There was constant competition between many of the castle-bound nobles of the Rhine to establish who would extract tolls from passing river traffic, a lucrative and vicious business. Napoléon, not one to respect medieval traditions, put an end to the fighting in 1806 when he destroyed Burg Katz. It was later reconstructed using the original medieval plans. Neither castle is open to the public.

If you visit this area in September, stay for the Rhein in Flammen (Rhine in Flames) festival, a pyrotechnic orgy of rockets and flares that light up the towns of St. Goar and St. Goarhausen and their surrounding vineyards.

Rivalry between neighboring castles was common even when
19 the keepers were members of the same family. At **Kamp-Bornhofen,** 12 kilometers (8 miles) north of St. Goar, are **Burg Sterrenberg** and **Burg Liebenstein,** once owned by two brothers. When their relations deteriorated over a river-toll feud, they built a wall between them. Today, the castles keep the rivalry going by running competing wine taverns.

20 Across from Kamp-Bornhofen is the mile-long promenade of elegant **Boppard,** usually lined with excursion and pleasure boats. Luxurious hotels, restaurants, and spa facilities are Boppard's hallmarks. There are also wine taverns of every caliber. The old quarter is part of a walking tour marked by signs from the 14th-century **Carmelite church** on Karlmeliterstrasse. (Inside the church, grotesque carved figures peer from the choir stalls). There are substantial ruins from a 4th-century Roman fort in Boppard. Take the chair lift up **Gedeonseck** to view this stretch of the Rhine from on high.

21 At Boppard, the river swings west and then north to **Rhens,** a town that traces its origins back some 1,300 years. A vital center of the Holy Roman Empire, Rhens was where German kings and emperors were elected and then presented to the people. The monumental site where the ceremonies took place, the **Königstuhl,** is on a hilltop just outside Rhens, on the road to Waldesch. It was here, in 1388, that the rift between the Holy Roman Empire and the papacy (to which the emperor was nominally subject) proved final. The six German prince-electors who nominated the emperor declared that henceforward their decisions were final and need no longer be given papal sanction.

22 **Marksburg,** the final castle on this fortress-studded stretch of the Rhine, is located on the opposite bank of the river, 500 feet above the town of **Braubach.** Marksburg was built in the 12th century to protect silver and lead mines in the area; so successfully were its medieval builders that the castle proved impregnable—it is the only one in the entire Middle Rhine Valley to have survived the centuries intact. Within its massive walls are a collection of weapons and manuscripts, a medieval botanical garden, and a restaurant.

Koblenz

23 The ancient city of **Koblenz** now looms ahead. Located at a geographical nexus known as the **Deutsches Eck** (corner of Germany), Koblenz is the heart of the Middle Rhine region. Rivers and mountains converge here, where the Mosel flows into the Rhine on one side and the Lahn flows in on the other. Three mountain ridges intersect at Koblenz as well.

Koblenz serves as the cultural, administrative, and business center of the Middle Rhine. Its position at the confluence of two rivers bustling with steamers, barges, tugs, and every other kind of river boat makes it one of the most important traffic points on the Rhine.

The heart of historic Koblenz is close to the point where the Rhine and Mosel meet. Koblenz was founded by the Romans in AD 9. Its Roman name, Castrum at Confluentes (the castle at the confluence), was later corrupted to Koblenz. It became a powerful city in the Middle Ages, when it controlled trade on both rivers. The city suffered severe bomb damage from air raids during the last world war (85% of its buildings were destroyed), but some of the most architecturally valuable structures remained at least partially intact, and extensive restoration has done much to recreate the atmosphere of old Koblenz.

Numbers in the margin correspond with points of interest on the Koblenz map.

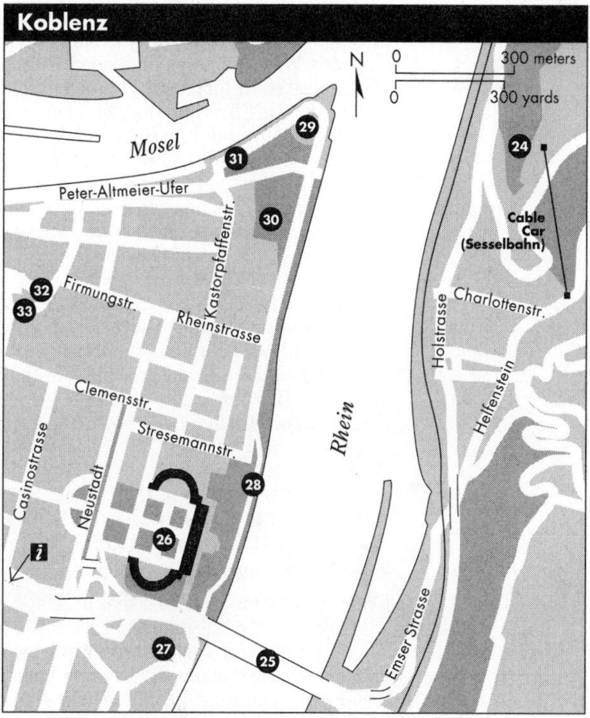

Koblenz is centered on the west bank of the Rhine, but begin **24** your tour on the opposite side, at **Festung Ehrenbreitstein,** Europe's largest fortress. Set 400 feet above the river, it offers a commanding view of the old town (the view alone justifies a visit). Ride the cable car (the Sesselbahn) up if the walk is too daunting. The earliest buildings date from about 1100, but the bulk of the fortress was constructed in the 16th century. In 1801, Napoléon's forces partially destroyed Festung Ehrenbreitstein; the French then occupied Koblenz for 18 years, a fact that some claim accounts for the Gallic joie de vivre of the city. More concrete evidence of the French occupation can be seen in the shape of the fortresses' 16th-century **Vogel Greif cannon.** The French absconded with it after they first penetrated the city in 1794; the Germans took it back in 1940; and the French commandeered it again in 1945. The 15-ton cannon was peaceably returned in 1984 by French President François Mitterand. It is on view at the **Staatliche Sammlung Technischer Kulturdenkmäler Museum,** one of several museums in the fortress. The others include the **Rheinmuseum,** which charts the history of the Rhineland, and the **Museum für Vorgeschichte und Volkskunde,** the museum of pre-history and ethnography. If you can schedule your visit to Koblenz for August, you'll catch one of the most spectacular firework displays in Europe at the fortress on the second Saturday of the month. *Fortress and museum: Admission free. Open Easter–Oct., daily 9–5.*

25 The place to begin a tour of the **old town** is the **Pfaffendorfer** Brücke. Three competing attractions stand at its western end.

26 The most conspicuous is the gracious **Residenzschloss,** the prince-elector's palace. It was built in 1786 by Prince-Elector Clemens Wenzeslaus as an elegant replacement for the grim Ehrenbreitstein fortress. The popular prince, who also built the city's still-thriving theater, cemented his popularity by throwing a three-day party when he moved in. He only lived there for three years, however; in 1791 he was forced to flee to Augsburg when the French stormed the city. Today, the palace is home to the city government. To the left of the palace is the
27 **Weindorf,** a self-contained wine "village," constructed for a mammoth exhibition of German wine in 1925. It is now one of the city's prime tourist attractions.

Time Out If the weather's good, there are few more enjoyable ways to spend time in Koblenz than over a glass of wine at one of the tables covered in checked cloth in the **Weindorf's** leafy gardens. In winter, move into the atmospheric taverns. **Frühschoppen** (brunch) time is enlivened by jazz bands.

The third attraction here is the 6-mile-long riverside prome-
28 nade, the **Rheinanlagen,** the longest in the Rhineland. If you want to cover it all, rent a bike (*see* Sports and Fitness, below). When the weather's good, it can be fun to wile away an hour or so pedaling along the Rhine.

From the bridge, you can either head straight into the old town
29 or stroll along to the **Deutsches Eck.** You'll have seen this curious structure from the fortress; if you have a taste for the more unusual manifestations of Germany's nationalism, it's worth a closer look. The sharply pointed piece of land juts into the river like the prow of some early iron-clad warship. It's an historic site, first settled and named by the German Order of Knights in 1216. In 1887 a statue of Kaiser Wilhelm I, the first emperor of the newly united Germany, was erected on the Deutsches Eck. It was destroyed at the end of World War II, however, and replaced by the ponderous altar-like monument to German unity you see today.

30 Standing just behind the Deutsches Eck is **St. Kastor Kirche,** a sturdy Romanesque basilica erected in 836 and remodeled through the centuries. It was here in 843 that the Treaty of Verdua was signed, formalizing the division of Charlemagne's great empire and leading to the creation of Germany and France as separate states. Inside, compare the squat columns in the nave, typical of the muscular architecture of the Romanesque with the complex and decorative fan vaulting of the Gothic sections. The **St. Kastor fountain** outside the church is an intriguing piece of historical oneupmanship. It was built by the occupying French to mark the beginning of Napoléon's ultimately disastrous Russian campaign of 1812. When the Russians, having inflicted a crushing defeat on Napoléon, reached Koblenz, they added the ironic inscription "Seen and approved" to the base of the fountain.

31 From the Deutsches Eck, head along the **Moselanlangen** (Mosel Promenade) to the old town. The focus is the little square called
32 **Am Plan.** On one side of it is the **Liebfrauenkirche** (Church of Our Lady), which stands on Roman foundations at the old town's highest point. The bulk of the church is of austere and weighty Romanesque design, but its choir is one of the Rhineland's finest and most ornate examples of 15th-century

Gothic architecture. Rising incongruously above the west front are two 17th-century Baroque towers topped by onion domes. Walk around to the rear of the church to reach the 17th-century town hall, a former Jesuit college. You'll be
33 drawn to the little **Schängelbrunnen** (statue of a little boy) in the square—every three minutes he spouts water at unwary passers-by.

Along the Mosel to Trier

Numbers in the margin correspond with points of interest on the Rhineland map.

While a tour along the meandering Mosel River to the historic city of Trier could be considered a side trip from the Rhine, it's actually an excursion endowed with a magic and charm all its own. In fact, Trier could easily qualify as the best-kept secret when it comes to German cities.

You don't have to travel far up the Mosel Valley to be reminded that wine plays every bit as important a role here as it does along the Rhine. The river's zigzag course passes between steep, terraced slopes where grapes have been grown since Roman times.

The Mosel is one of the most hauntingly beautiful river valleys on earth: turreted castles look down from its leafy perches, its hilltops are crowned with bell towers, and throughout its expanse, skinny church spires stand against the sky. For more than 100 miles, the silvery Mosel River meanders past a string of storybook medieval wine villages, each more attractive than
34 the other. The first village you'll reach, **Winningen,** 15 kilometers (10 miles) from Koblenz, is the center of the valley's largest vineyards. Stop off to admire Germany's oldest half-timbered house in **Kirchenstrasse** (no. 1); it was built in 1320. On the slopes above Winningen's narrow medieval streets is a mile-long path reached by driving up Fährstrasse to Am Rosenhang. Once there, high above the Mosel, you'll get a bird's-eye view of the **Uhlen, Röttgen, Bruckstück, Hamm,** and **Domgarten** vineyards.

For an even finer view of the river and its rich valley, follow the road for 8 kilometers (5 miles) to **Kobern-Gondorf,** on the north bank of the river, and turn off into the idyllic little Mühlental Valley. Here you can climb up through the steep vineyards to
35 the remains of **Oberburg** castle, built in the 12th century by the powerful Knights of Leyen. On the way, you'll pass a 13th-century Romanesque chapel, **St. Matthew's.**

The Mosel bristles with almost as many castles as the Rhine. Among them is what many deem the most impressive in the
36 country, **Burg Eltz.** It's located above the village of Moselkern, 15 kilometers (10 miles) from Koben-Gondorf. The only way to reach the castle from Moselkern is to walk 2 miles along a gentle footpath that winds through the wild valley. It's worth the trek to see what may well be the most perfectly proportioned medieval castle in Germany. Perched on the spine of an isolated, rocky outcrop, bristling with towers and pinnacles, it at first looks unreal—like an image suspended in time and space. Upon closer exposure, Burg Eltz turns out to be the apotheosis of all one expects of a medieval castle: it's easily as impressive in its own special way as "Mad" King Ludwig's fantasy creation,

Neuschwanstein. But Burg Eltz is the real thing: an 800-year-old castle, with modifications from the 16th century. It's a mystery why Burg Eltz is not better known, or more visited, particularly since its picture is printed on the DM 500 bill. There are few sites in Germany where the sense of the centuries unfolding is as vivid. The magic continues in the interior, which is decorated with heavy Gothic furnishings. *Admission: DM 5.50 adults, DM 3.50 children. Open Apr.–Oct., Mon.–Sat. 9–5:30, Sun. 10–5:30.*

Destruction was the fate suffered by the next castle along the
37 valley, the famous **Reichsburg** (Imperial Fortress) of **Cochem,** 15 kilometers (10 miles) from Berg Eltz. The 900-year-old castle was rebuilt in the 19th century after Louis XIV stormed it in 1689. Today it stands majestically over Cochem. *Admission: DM 3.50 adults, DM 1.50 children. Open daily 9–6.*

Cochem itself is one of the most attractive towns of the Mosel Valley, with a riverside promenade to rival any along the Rhine. If you're traveling by train, just south of Cochem you'll be plunged into Germany's longest railway tunnel, the Kaiser-Wilhelm, an astonishing two-and-a-half mile-long example of 19th-century engineering that saves travelers from a 21-kilometer (13-mile) detour along one of the Mosel's great loops.

By car, follow the loop of the river for 8 kilometers (5 miles)
38 past Cochem and you'll reach the little town of **Beilstein.** It has a mixture of all the picture pretty features of a German river and wine town in this romantic area of the country. Take a look at the marketplace carved into the rocky slope.

Time Out At the village of **Ediger-Eller,** 10 kilometers (6 miles) from Beilstein, stop by the roadside vineyard of **Freiherr von Landenberg** (Moselstr. 60). Sample a glass of wine from the Baron's vines and visit his private viticulture museum.

39 **Zell,** 12 kilometers (8 miles) up river, on another great loop, is a typical Mosel River town, much like Cochem. Located about mid-way between Koblenz and Trier, this small, historic town is made up of picturesque red-roofed homes and age-old fortifications falling into ruin. A scenic backdrop is provided by the vineyards that produce the famous Schwarze Katz (Black Cat) wine, which is rated as one of Germany's very best whites. Stroll the town's medieval arc along the river. On your way you'll notice a small, twin-towered castle, Schloss Zell, dating from the 14th century. After considerable restoration, the castle evolved into an elegant hotel furnished with exquisite antiques. Its restaurant serves regional cuisine and wine from the owner's own Black Cat vineyards.

Straddling the Mosel 18 kilometers (11 miles) further along is
40 **Traben-Trarbach,** a two-town combination that serves as headquarters of the regional wine trade and offers a popular wine festival in summer. Visit the ruins of **Mount Royal** high above Traben on the east bank. This enormous fortress was built around 1687 by Louis XIV of France, only to be dismantled 10 years later under the terms of the Treaty of Rijswick. Partially restored by the Nazis, the fortress retains some of its original forbidding mass.

41 **Bernkastel-Kues** is 27 kilometers (17 miles) away by road, but if you're in the mood for some exercise, you can reach it on foot

from Traben-Trarbach in about an hour (the road, following the river, practically doubles back on itself as it winds leisurely along). Bernkastel, on the north bank of the river, and Kues, on the south, were officially linked early this century. **Marktplatz,** the heart of Bernkastel, meets all the requirements for the ideal small-town German market square. Most of the buildings are late-Gothic/early Renaissance, with facades covered with intricate carvings and sharp gables stabbing the sky. In the center of the square is **Michaelsbrunnen** (Michael's fountain), a graceful 17th-century work. During the town's wine festival in the first week of September, wine replaces the fountain's water. There's a fortress here, too: **Burg Landshut,** a 13th-century castle glowering above the town. Visit it for some amazing views of the river and to wander around its flower-strewn remains. In summer, a bus makes the trip up to the castle every hour from the parking lot by the river. The town's most famous wine is known as Bernkasteler Doktor. According to a story, the wine got its unusual name when it saved the life of the prince-bishop of Trier, who lay dying in the castle. After all other medicinal treatment had failed to cure him, he was offered a glass of the local wine—which miraculously put him back on his feet. Try a glass of it yourself at the castle (or buy a bottle from the vineyard bordering the street called Hinterm Graben).

The town's remaining attraction owes its existence to Cardinal Nikolaus Cusanus, a 15th-century philosopher and pioneer of German humanist thought. He founded a religious and charitable institution, complete with a vineyard, on the riverbank in Kues. The vineyard is still going strong, and tastings are held daily at 3 in the St. Niklaus-Hospital (Cusanusstr. 2). The buildings here comprise the largest Gothic ensemble on the Mosel. Among them is the Mosel-Weinmuseum. *Admission: DM 2 adults, DM 1 children. Open May–Oct., daily 10–5; Nov.–Apr., daily 2–5.*

From Bernkastel-Kues to Trier is a further 66 kilometers (41 miles) of twisting river road. Endless vineyards and little river towns punctuate the snaking path of the Mosel. Among them is
42 **Neumagen,** settled by the Romans in the 4th century. In its main square, there's a modern copy of the famous carved relief of a Roman wine ship plying a choppy looking Mosel. If you continue on to Trier, you can see the original in the Landesmuseum.

Numbers in the margin correspond with points of interest on the Trier map.

43 **Trier's** claim to fame is not only that it's the oldest town in Germany, but it's also the first settlement in Europe. It dates from 2,000 BC, when Prince Trebeta, son of an Assyrian queen, arrived here and set up residence on the banks of the Mosel; he named the place Treberis, after himself. An inscription along Trier's marketplace states "*Ante Roman Treveris stetit annis mille trecentis*" ("1,300 years before Rome stood Trier").

Eventually, the legions of Julius Caesar set up camp at this strategic point of the river and Augusta Treverorum (the town of Emperor Augustus in the land of the Treveri), was founded in 15 BC. It was described as "*urbs opulentissima*"—as beautiful a city as existed beyond Rome itself, and jewel of the strategic Rhineland.

Amphitheater, **54**
Barbarathermen, **53**
Bischöfliches Museum, **49**
Dom, **48**
Hauptmarkt, **46**
Kaiserthermen, **52**
Karl-Marx-Haus, **55**
Liebfrauenkirche, **47**
Porta Nigra, **44**
Rheinisches Landesmuseum, **51**
Römische Palastula, **50**
Städtisches Museum Simeonstift, **45**
Weininformation Mosel-Saar-Ruwer, **56**

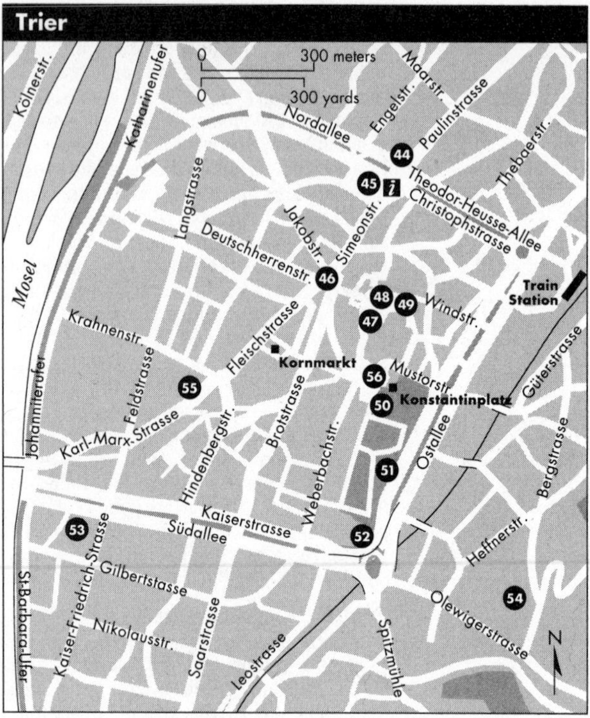

Around AD 275, an Alemannic tribe stormed Augusta Treverorum and reduced it to rubble. But it was rebuilt in even grander style and renamed Treveris. Eventually it evolved into one of the leading cities of the empire and was promoted to *Roma Secunda*, a second Rome north of the Alps. As a powerful administrative capital, it was adorned with all the noble civic buildings of a major Roman settlement, plus public baths, palaces, barracks, an amphitheater, and temples. Roman emperors such as Diocletian (who made it one of the four joint capitals of the empire) and Constantine lived in Trier for years at a time.

Trier survived the collapse of Rome and became an important center of Christianity; it was later one of the most powerful archbishoprics in the Holy Roman Empire. The city thrived throughout the Renaissance and Baroque periods, taking full advantage of its location at the meeting point of major east-west and north-south trade routes, and growing fat on the commerce that passed through. It also became one of Germany's most important wine-exporting centers. A later claim to fame is as the birthplace of Karl Marx. To do justice to the city, consider staying for at least two full days. A ticket good for all the Roman sights in Trier costs DM 6 adults, DM 3 children and senior citizens.

44 Begin your tour at the **Porta Nigra** (the Black Gate), located by the city's tourist office. This is by far the best-preserved Roman structure in Trier and one of the grandest Roman buildings in northern Europe. It's a city gate, built in the 4th century. Its name is misleading, however: The sandstone gate

is not actually black, but dark gray. Those with an interest in Roman construction techniques should look for the holes left by the original iron clamps that held the whole structure together. This city gate also served as part of Trier's defenses and was proof of the sophistication of Roman military might and ruthlessness. Attackers were often lured into the two innocent-looking arches of the Porta Nigra only to find themselves enclosed in a courtyard—and at the mercy of the defending forces. *Admission: DM 2 adults, DM 1 children and senior citizens. Open Apr.–Oct. daily 9–1 and 2–5; Nov. and Jan.–Mar., Tues.–Sun. 9–1 and 2–5; closed Dec.*

To the side are the remains of the Romanesque Simeonskirche,
45 today the **Städtisches Museum Simeonstift** (open the same
hours as the gate). The church was built in the 11th century by
Archbishop Poppo in honor of the early medieval hermit Simeon, who, for seven years, shut himself up in the east tower of the
Porta Nigra. Collections of art and artifacts produced in Trier
from the Middle Ages to the present now commemorate
Simeon's feat. Simeon also has one of Trier's main streets
named after him: Simeonstrasse. It leads directly to
46 **Hauptmarkt,** the main square of old Trier. A 1,000-year-old
market cross and a richly ornate 16th-century fountain stand in
the square.

From Hauptmarkt, turn left (east) down Stirnstrasse to see
Trier's great **Dom** (cathedral). Before you go in, take a look at
47 the adjoining 13th-century **Liebfrauenkirche** (Church of Our
Lady). It's one of the oldest purely Gothic churches in the country. The interior is elegantly attenuated.

48 If you want a condensed history of Trier, visit the **Dom:** There is almost no period of the city's past that is not represented here. It stands on the site of the Palace of Helen of Constantine, mother of the Emperor Constantine, who knocked the palace down in AD 326 and put up a large church in its place. The church burned down in 336 and a second, even larger one was built. Parts of the foundations of this third building can be seen in the east end of the current structure (begun in about 1035). The cathedral you see today is a weighty and sturdy edifice with small, round-headed windows, rough stonework, and asymmetrical towers, as much a fortress as a church. Inside, Gothic styles predominate—the result of remodeling in the 13th century—though there are also many Baroque tombs, altars, and confessionals. This architectural jumble of Romanesque, Gothic, and Baroque styles gives the place the air of a vast antiques shop. Make sure you visit the Baroque **Domschatzmuseum** in the treasury, site of two extraordinary objects. One is the 10th-century **Andreas Trag Altar** (St. Andrews's Altar), made of gold by local craftsmen. Called the "Portable Altar," it is smaller than the Dom's main altar, but it is no lightweight. The other attraction is the **Holy Robe,** the garment supposedly worn by Christ at the time of his trial before Pontius Pilate and gambled for by Roman soldiers. The story goes that it was brought to Trier by Helen of Constantine, a tireless collector of holy relics. It is so delicate and old that it is displayed only every 30 years (you'll have to come back in 2019 if you want to see it); the rest of the time it lies under a faded piece of 9th-century Byzantine silk. *Admission: DM 1 adults, 50 pf children. Open Apr.–Oct., daily 6–6; Nov.–Mar., daily 6–noon and 2–6.*

Excavations around the cathedral have unearthed a series of
49 antiquities, most of which are housed in the **Bischöfliches Museum** (Episcopal Museum) in Windstrasse, just behind the cathedral. The exhibits include a 4th-century ceiling painting believed to have adorned the Emperor Constantine's palace. *Windstr. 6–8. Admission: DM 1 adults, 50 pf children. Open Mon.–Fri. 9–5, Sat., Sun., and holidays 9–1.*

Just south of the cathedral complex—take Konstantinstrasse—is another impressive reminder of Trier's Roman past: the
50 **Römische Palastula** (Roman Palace). Today, this is the major protestant church of Trier. When first built by the Emperor Constantine around AD 300, it was the Imperial Throne Room of the palace. At 239 feet long, 93 feet wide, and 108 feet high, it demonstrates the astounding ambition of its Roman builders and the sophistication of their building techniques. It is the second largest Roman interior in existence—only the Pantheon in Rome is larger. Despite the rough stone walls (which would have been plastered and painted in Roman times), the overwhelming impression is of great lightness and spaciousness. Look up at the deeply coffered ceiling: more than any other part of the building, it conveys the opulence of the original structure. *Konstantinstr. Open Apr.–Oct., Mon.–Sat. 9–1 and 2–6, Sun. 11–1 and 2–6; Nov.–Mar., Tues.–Sat. 11–2 and 3–4, Sun. 11–noon.*

From the Palastula, turn south. To your left, facing the
51 grounds of the prince-elector's palace, is the **Rheinisches Landesmuseum** (Rhineland Archaeological Museum), which houses the largest collection of Roman antiquities in Germany. Pride of place goes to the 3rd-century stone relief of a Roman ship transporting immense barrels of wine up the river. If you stopped off in Neumagen on the way to Trier, you will have seen the copy of it in the town square. *Ostallee 44. Admission free. Open Mon.–Fri. 9:30–4, Sat. 9:30–2, Sun. 9–1.*

52 From the museum, walk down to the ruins of the **Kaiserthermen** (imperial baths), just 200 yards away. Begun by Constantine in the 4th century, these were once the third largest public baths in the Roman empire, exceeded only by Diocletian's baths in Yugoslavia and the baths of Caracalla in Rome. They covered an area 270 yards long and 164 yards wide. Today, only the weed-strewn fragments of the **Calderium** (hot baths), are left, but they are enough to give a fair idea of the original splendor and size of the complex. When the Romans pulled out, the baths were turned into a fortress (one window of the huge complex served as a city gate for much of the Middle Ages), then a church, and then a fortress again. Don't confuse
53 them with the much smaller **Barbarathermen** (open same hours) in Kaiser-Friedrich-Str. *Admission: Open Jan.–Mar. and Nov., Tues.–Sun. 9–1 and 2–5; Apr.–Sept., daily 9–1 and 2–6; Oct., daily 9–1 and 2–5; closed Dec.*

54 Just east of the Kaiserthermen are the remains of the **Amphitheater** built around AD 100, the oldest Roman building in Trier. In its heyday it seated 20,000 people. You can climb down to the cellars beneath the arena to see the machines that were used to change the scenery and the cells where lions and other wild animals were kept before being unleashed to devour maidens and do battle with gladiators. *Olewigerstr. See Porta Nigra for hours and admission.*

After this profusion of antiquities, you may want to shift gears
55 and see the **Karl-Marx-Haus** on Karl-Marx-Strasse, south of Kornmarkt in the old town. It was here that Marx was born in 1818. Serious social historians will feel at home in the little house, which has been converted into a museum charting Marx's life and the development of socialism around the world. A signed first edition of *Das Kapital*, the tome in which Marx sought to prove the inevitable decline of capitalism, may prove a highlight for some. *Admission: DM 2 adults, DM 1 children. Open Apr.–Oct., Tues.–Sun. 10–6, Mon. 1–6; Nov.–Mar., Tues.–Sun. 10–1 and 3–6, Mon. 3–6.*

Trier is, of course, also a city of wine, and beneath its streets are cellars capable of storing nearly 8 million gallons. To get to know the wines of the region, drop in at the tavern run by the
56 **Weininformation Mosel-Saar-Ruwer** (Konstantinpl. 11, tel. 0651/73690). The city also has a wine trail, a picturesque mile-and-a-half walk studded with information plaques that leads to the wine-growing suburb of **Olewig.**

Tour 3: Bonn and Köln

Numbers in the margin correspond with points of interest on the Bonn map.

57 **Bonn** is the incongruously small and undistinguished capital of West Germany. You might wonder how this little university town on the Rhine could possibly hope to rival Berlin, the former capital and one of the great cities of Europe. And why wasn't Frankfurt made the new capital after the war. The choice, in 1949, of Bonn as capital of the newly created Federal Republic was never meant to be permanent. At the time, few Germans thought the division of their country between the capitalist West and the communist East would prove anything other than temporary, and they were certain that Berlin would again become the capital before long. The concern was that Frankfurt might be such a good choice that when the time came to reunite the country, it would be impossible to reinstate Berlin. Thus, insignificant Bonn was propelled to its present status.

Germans tend to deride their capital for its lack of character. Some suggest that Bonn's greatest asset is its surrounding countryside: the legendary **Siebengebirge** (Seven Hills) and the **Kölner Bucht Valley.** In the capital's streets, old markets, stores, pedestrian malls, parks, and the handsome Südstadt residential area, life is unhurried and unsophisticated by larger city standards. In comparison to Frankfurt or Munich, Bonn might even seem provincial.

Bonn's status as a capital may be new but its roots are ancient. The Romans settled this part of the Rhineland 2,000 years ago,
58 calling it Castra Bonnensia. Bonn's cathedral, the **Münster,** stands where two Roman soldiers were executed in AD 253 for Christian beliefs. **Münsterplatz,** site of the cathedral and the tourist office, is the logical place to begin your tour. The 900-year-old cathedral is vintage late Romanesque, with a massive octagonal main tower and a soaring spire. It was chosen by two Holy Roman emperors for their coronations (in 1314 and 1346), and was one of the Rhineland's most important ecclesiastical centers in the Middle Ages. The bronze 17th-century figure of

Alter Friedhof, **62**
Beethovenhaus, **64**
Government Buildings, **65**
Kurfürstliches Schloss, **59**
Münster, **58**
Poppelsdörfer Schloss, **60**
Rathaus, **63**
Rheinisches Landesmuseum, **61**

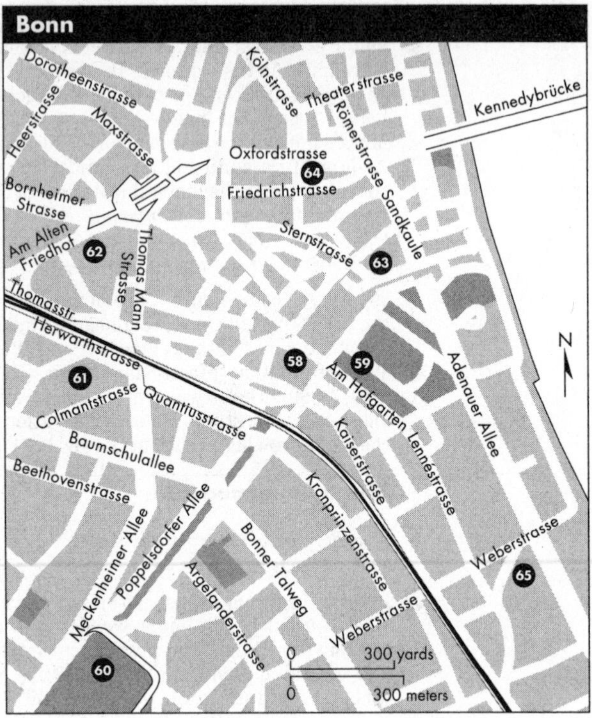

St. Helen and the ornate Rococo pulpit are highlights of the interior. *Open daily 9:30–5:30.*

59 Facing the Münster is the grand **Kurfürstliches Schloss,** built in the 18th century by the prince-electors of Köln; today it houses a university. If it's a fine day, stroll through the Hofgarten (Palace Gardens), or follow the chestnut tree avenue called Poppelsdörfer Allee southwards to another electors' palace,
60 the smaller **Poppelsdörfer Schloss,** built in baroque style between 1715 and 1740. The palace has a beautiful botanical garden with an impressive display of tropical plants. *Meckenheimer Allee. Admission free. Open Apr.–Sept., 8–7, Sun. 9–1; Oct.–Mar., weekdays 8–4:30.*

On your way back to the old town, take Meckenheimer Allee
61 and then Colmanstrasse to see the **Rheinisches Landesmuseum** (the walk is about a quarter-mile long). The museum, one of the largest in the Rhineland, charts the history, art, and culture of the Rhine Valley from Roman times to the present day. The main draw is the skull of a Neanderthal man, regarded by anthropologists as a vital link in the evolutionary chain. The skull was put together from fragments found in the Neander Valley near Düsseldorf in 1856. *Colmanstr. 14–16. Admission: DM 4 adults, DM 2 children. Open Tues., Thurs., and Fri. 9–5, Wed. 9–8, weekends 10–5.*

At the end of Colmanstrasse, take the underpass below the rail-
62 road line and follow Thomastrasse for 300 yards to the **Alter Friedhof** (the Old Cemetery). This ornate graveyard is the resting place of many of the country's most celebrated sons and

daughters. Look for the tomb of composer Robert Schumann and his wife Klara. *Am Alten Friedhof. Open Mar.–Aug., daily 7 AM–8 PM; Sept.–Feb., daily 8–6. Guided tours at 3 on Tues. and Thurs.*

From the Alter Friedhof, follow Sternstrasse into the old town center and proceed to the **Markt** (market), where you'll find an
63 18th-century **Rathaus** (Town Hall) that looks like a pink doll's house.

Just north of the town hall (head up Kölnstrasse) are Bonn-
64 gasse and the **Beethovenhaus.** The latter has been imaginatively converted into a museum celebrating the life of the great composer. Here you'll find scores, paintings, a grand piano (his last, in fact), and an ear trumpet or two. Perhaps the most impressive exhibit is the room in which Beethoven was born—empty save for a bust of the composer. *Bonngasse 20. Admission: DM 5 adults, DM 1.50 children. Open Mon.–Sat. 9–1 and 3–6, Sun. 9–1.*

A tour of Bonn could not be complete without some mention of the government buildings, which are located in a complex about a mile south of downtown. Strung along the Rhine, in spacious, leafy grounds between Adenauerallee and the river, are the of-
65 fices of the **Federal President,** the high-tech **Chancellery,** and the **Federal Parliament;** the '60s high rise you see contains the offices of members of parliament. There's little to divert anyone here unless you have a particular interest in the workings of the German government.

Time Out On your way back to town, turn left off Adenauerallee at its intersection with Weberstrasse, cross the railway line, and make for the **Mierscheid** bar-restaurant. This is the route taken by many Bonn politicians at the end of a hard day in parliament, and chances are you'll find yourself rubbing shoulders with one or two of them.

Numbers in the margin correspond with points of interest on the Köln map.

66 **Köln** (Cologne), 27 kilometers (17 miles) north of Bonn, is the largest city on the Rhine (the fourth largest in Germany) and one of the most interesting. While not as old as Trier, it has been a dominant power in the Rhineland since Roman times. Known throughout the world for its scented toilet water, eau de cologne (first produced here in 1705 from an Italian formula), the city is today a major commercial, intellectual, and ecclesiastical center. Many business travelers are attracted to its numerous trade fairs, held in the two massive convention centers located on the Deutzer side of the Rhine.

Köln is a vibrant, bustling city, with something of the same sparkling spirit that makes Munich so memorable. It claims to have more bars than any other German city and a host of excellent eating places. It also puts on a wild carnival every February, with three days of orgiastic revelry, bands, parades and parties that last all night.

In many ways, Köln could be considered Germany's most diverse city; its host of attractions—cultural and otherwise—can keep a visitor occupied for several days. The city is divided into

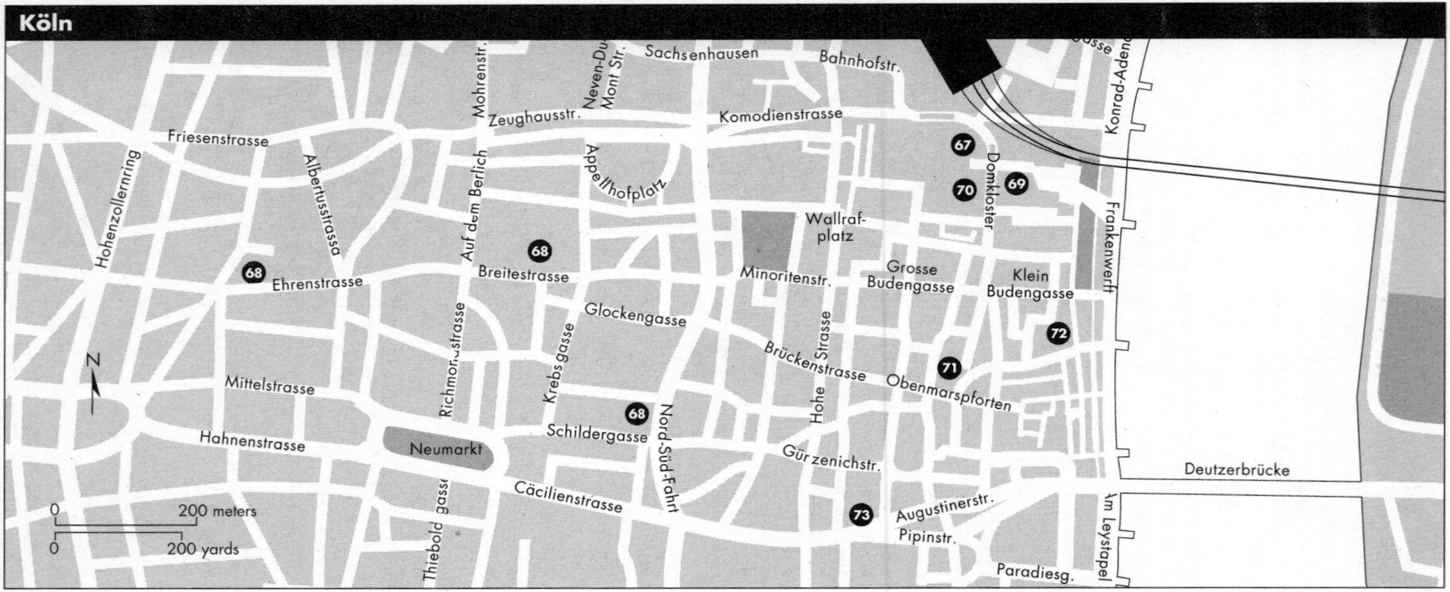

Altes Rathaus, **71**
Gross St. Martin, **72**
Gürzenich, **73**
Kölner Dom, **67**
Römisch-Germanisches Museum, **70**
Shopping District, **68**
Wallraf-Richartz-Museum, **69**

above-ground and underground: pre-war and post-war. On occasion, its past glory seems to overshadow its present.

Köln was first settled by the Romans in 38 BC. For nearly a century it grew slowly, in the shadow of imperial Trier, until a locally born noblewoman, Julia Agrippina, daughter of the Roman general Germanicus, married the Roman Emperor Claudius. Her hometown was elevated to the rank of a Roman city and given the name Colonia Claudia Ara Agrippinensis. For the next 300 years, Colonia (hence Cologne, or Köln) flourished. Proof of the richness of the Roman city is provided today by the **Römisch-Germanisches Museum** (Roman-German Museum)—one place you won't want to miss if you have any interest in Roman heritage. When the Romans left, Köln was ruled first by the Franks, then by the Merovingians. In the 9th century, Charlemagne, the towering figure who united the sprawling German lands (and ruled much of present-day France) and was the first Holy Roman Emperor, restored Köln's fortunes and elevated it to its preeminent role in the Rhineland. Charlemagne also appointed the first archbishop of Köln. The ecclesiastical heritage of Köln forms one of the most striking characteristics of the city, which has no fewer than 12 Romanesque churches. Its Gothic cathedral is the largest and the finest in Germany.

Köln eventually became the largest city north of the Alps and, in time, evolved into a place of pilgrimage second only to Rome. In the Middle Ages, it was a member of the powerful Hanseatic League, occupying a position of greater importance in European commerce than either London or Paris.

Köln entered modern times as the number-one city of the Rhineland. Then, in World War II, bombings destroyed 90% of it. Only the cathedral remained relatively unscathed. Almost everything else had to be rebuilt more or less from the ground up, including all of the glorious Romanesque churches.

Early reconstruction was accomplished in a big rush—and in what might seem something of a slap-dash manner. A good part of the former old town along the Hohe Strasse (old Roman High Road), was turned into a pedestrian shopping mall, the very first in Germany. Though it won accolades in the press when it opened, it is pretty much without charm or grace.

The same could be said for the totally re-created facades of the old-town dwellings facing the river—they emerged looking like Disneyland kitsch, nothing to be taken seriously. Add the fact that six-lane expressways wind their way along the rim of the city center—barely yards from the cathedral—and the heart of Köln turns out to be something of a mishmash of bad and beautiful, a mixed blessing.

On the plus side, much of the Altstadt (Old Town), ringed by streets that follow the line of medieval city walls, is closed to traffic. Most major sights are within this orbit, easily reached on foot. Here, too, you'll find the best shops.

Towering over the old town is the extraordinary Gothic cathe-
67 dral, the **Kölner Dom,** dedicated to Sts. Peter and Mary. It's comparable to the best French cathedrals; a visit to it may prove a highlight of your trip to Germany. What you'll see is one of the purest expressions of the Gothic spirit in Europe. Here, the desire to pay homage to God took the form of building as large and as lavish a church as possible, a tangible expression of

God's kingdom on earth. Its spires soar heavenward and its immense interior is illuminated by light filtering through acres of stained glass. Spend some time admiring the outside of the building (you can walk almost all the way around it). Notice how there are practically no major horizontal lines—all the accents of the building are vertical. It may come as a disappointment to learn that the cathedral, begun in 1248, was not completed until 1880. Console yourself with the knowledge that it was still built to original plans. At 515 feet high, the two west towers of the cathedral were by far the tallest structures in the world when they were finished (they are still the tallest in a church). The length of the building is 470 feet; the width of the nave is 147 feet; and the highest part of the interior is 140 feet.

The cathedral was built to house what was believed to be the relics of the Magi, the three kings or wise men who attended the birth of Jesus (the trade in holy mementos was big business in the Middle Ages, and not always too scrupulous). Since Köln was by then a major commercial and political center, it was felt that someplace special had to be constructed to house the relics. Anxious to surpass the great cathedrals then being built in France, the masons set to work. The size of the building was not simply an example of self-aggrandizement on the part of the people of Köln, however; it was a response to the vast numbers of pilgrims who arrived to see the relics. The ambulatory, the passage that curves around the back of the altar, is unusually large, allowing cathedral authorities to funnel large numbers of visitors up to the crossing (where the nave and transepts meet, and where the relics were originally displayed), around the back of the altar, and out again. Today, the relics are kept just behind the altar, in the same enormous gold-and-silver **reliquary** in which they were originally displayed. The other great treasure of the cathedral is the **Gero Cross,** a monumental oak crucifixion dating from 975. Impressive for its simple grace, it's in the last chapel on the left as you face the altar.

Other highlights to admire are the stained glass windows, some of which date from the 13th century; the 15th-century altar painting; and the early 14th-century high altar with its surrounding arcades of glistening white figures and its intricate choir screens. The choir stalls, carved from oak around 1310, are the largest in Germany, seating 104 people. There are more treasures to be seen in the **Dom Schatzkammer,** the cathedral treasury, including the silver shrine of Archbishop Engelbert, who was stabbed to death in 1225. *Admission: DM 2 adults, DM 1 children. Open Mon.–Sat. 9–5:30, Sun. 12:30–4:30.*

Back down at street level, you have the choice of more culture
68 or commerce. Köln's **shopping district** begins at nearby **Wallrafplatz,** and a recommended shopping tour takes you down Hohe Strasse, Schildergasse, Neumarkt, Mittelstrasse, Hohenzollernring, Ehrenstrasse, Breite Strasse, Tunisstrasse, Minoritenstrasse, and then back to Wallrafplatz.

Grouped around the cathedral is a collection of superb muse-
69 ums. If your priority is painting, try the ultra-modern **Wallraf-Richartz-Museum** and Museum Ludwig complex (which includes the Philharmonic concert hall beneath its vast roof). Together, they form the largest art collection in the Rhineland. The Wallraf-Richartz-Museum contains pictures spanning the years 1300 to 1900, with Dutch and Flemish schools particular-

ly well-represented (Rubens, who spent his youth in Köln, has a place of honor, but there are also outstanding works by Rembrandt, Van Dyck, and Franz Hals). Of the other old masters, Tiepolo, Canaletto, and Boucher are all well-represented. Renoir, Bonnard, Monet, Sisley, Pissarro, and Cézanne number among the more-modern painters. The **Museum Ludwig** is devoted exclusively to 20th-century art; its Picasso collection is outstanding. *Bischofsgartenstr. 1. Admission: DM 3 adults, DM 1.50 children. Open Tues.–Thurs. 10–8, Fri.–Sun. 10–8.*

70 Opposite the cathedral is the **Römisch-Germanisches Museum,** built from 1970 to 1974 around the famous Dionysus mosaic that was uncovered at the site during the construction of an air raid shelter in 1941. The huge mosaic, more than 100 yards square, once covered the dining room floor of a wealthy Roman trader's villa. Its millions of tiny earthenware and glass tiles depict some of the adventures of Dionysus, the Greek god of wine and, to the Romans, the object of a widespread and sinister religious cult. The pillared 1st-century tomb of Lucius Publicius, a prominent Roman officer, some stone Roman coffins, and a series of memorial tablets are among the museum's other exhibits. Bordering the museum on the south is a restored 90-yard stretch of the old Roman harbor road. *Roncallipl. 4. Admission: DM 3 adults, DM 1.50 children. Open Tues.–Fri. and weekends 10–5, Wed. and Thurs. 10–8.*

71 Head south now to the nearby **Alter Markt** and its **Altes Rathaus,** the oldest town hall in Germany (if you don't count the fact that the building was entirely rebuilt after the war). The square has a handsome assembly of buildings—the oldest dating from 1135—in a range of styles. There was a seat of local government here in Roman times, and directly below the current Rathaus are the remains of the Roman city governor's headquarters, the Praetorium. Go inside to see the 14th-century **Hansa Saal,** whose tall Gothic windows and barrel-vaulted wood ceiling are potent expressions of medieval civic pride. The figures of the prophets, standing on pedestals at one end, are all from the early 15th century. Ranging along the south wall are nine additional statues, the so-called *Nine Good Heroes*, carved in 1360. Charlemagne and King Arthur are among them. *Altes Rathaus, Alter Markt. Admission: DM 2 adults, DM 1 children. Open Mon.–Fri. 8:30–4:45, Sat. 10–4. Praetorium. Open Tues.–Sun. 10–5.*

Head now across Unter Käster toward the river and one of the
72 most outstanding of Köln's 12 Romanesque churches, the **Gross St. Martin.** Its massive 13th-century tower, with distinctive corner turrets and an imposing central spire, is another landmark of Köln. The church was built on the riverside site of a Roman granary.

Gross St. Martin is the parish church of Köln's colorful old city, the **Martinsviertel,** an attractive combination of reconstructed, high-gabled medieval buildings, winding alleys, and tastefully designed modern apartments and business quarters. Head here at night—the place comes to vibrant life at sunset.

At the southern end of the district, in Gürzenichstrasse, you'll find one of Germany's most attractive cultural centers, the
73 **Gürzenich.** This Gothic structure, all but demolished in the war but carefully reconstructed, takes its name from a medieval knight (von Gürzenich), from whom the city acquired a quanti-

ty of valuable real estate in 1437. The official reception and festival hall built on the site has played a central role in the city's civic life through the centuries. A concert here can be a memorable experience. Part of the complex consists of the remains of the 10th-century Gothic church of **St. Alban,** left ruined after the war as a memorial to the city's war victims. On what's left of the church's floor (made of slate from the nearby Eifel Hills and Rhine cobblestones) you can see a sculpture of a couple kneeling in prayer. It's an oddly moving work, a fitting memorial to the ravages of war.

Tour 4: Aachen

It's not in the Rhineland proper, but **Aachen,** 70 kilometers (45 miles) from Köln, less than an hour away by car or train, is an essential excursion for anyone staying in Köln. It's an essential excursion, too, if you have any interest in German history, for as the city of Charlemagne, Aachen bears the stamp of this most famous Holy Roman Emperor as no other place in Germany. Aachen is also known by two other names: Bad Aachen, because of the hot springs that give it health-resort status; and Aix-la-Chapelle, because of the eight-sided chapel built by Charlemagne in the late 8th century that now serves as the core of the city's imposing cathedral.

Charlemagne's father, Pippin, had settled in Aachen because of the healthy sulphur springs emanating from the nearby Eifel mountains (Roman legions earlier pitched camp here because of these same healing waters). After his coronation in Rome in 800, Charlemagne spent more and more time in Aachen, building his spectacular palace and ruling his vast empire from within its walls.

The **Dom** (cathedral) remains the single greatest storehouse of Carolingian architecture in Europe. Built over the course of 1,000 years, it features a mixture of styles ranging from the imperial chapel at its heart to its 19th-century bell tower. In the cathedral's cool, august interior, you'll find Charlemagne's sturdy marble throne, a battered but still impressive monument. It's just one of many extraordinary treasures here: The **Domschatzkammer** (cathedral treasury) is about the richest in Europe. Though Charlemagne had to journey all the way to Rome for his coronation, the next 32 Holy Roman Emperors were crowned here in Aachen. The coronations were almost invariably accompanied by the presentation of a lavish gift to the cathedral. In the 12th century, Barbarossa gave the great chandelier you'll find hanging in the center of the imperial chapel; his grandson, Emperor Friedrich II, donated the glistening, richly ornamented golden shrine in which the remains of Charlemagne are kept. Emperor Karl IV, son of the King of Bohemia, journeyed from Prague in the late 14th century with the sole purpose of commissioning a bust of Charlemagne for the cathedral. The bust, on view in the treasury, contains a piece of bone from Charlemagne's skull. The Ottonian Emperor Otto III gave the cathedral its fine 10th-century altar painting, while the 11th-century Emperor Heinrich II donated its fine copper pulpit. *Dom open 7–7. Domschatzkammer admission: DM 3 adults, DM 2 children and senior citizens. Open Apr.–Sept., Mon. 10–2, Tues., Wed., Fri., Sat. 10–6, Thurs. 10–8, Sun. 10:30–5; Oct.–Mar., Tues.–Sat. 10–5, Sun. 10:30–5, Mon. 10–2.*

Opposite the cathedral, across Katschhof Square, is the **Rathaus** (Town Hall). It was built starting in the early 14th century on the site of the Aula, or great hall, of Charlemagne's palace. Its first major official function was the coronation banquet of the Emperor Karl IV in 1349, held in the great Gothic hall you'll find there today. The austere, vaulted hall, with its archways decorated with lightly drawn emblems and its rough stone walls bearing the 20th-century equivalent of medieval torches, was largely rebuilt after the war. On the north wall of the building are statues of 50 Holy Roman Emperors. The greatest of them all, Charlemagne, stands in bronze atop a graceful fountain, the Kaiserbrunnen, in the center of the square. *Rathaus. Admission: DM 1. Open Mon.–Fri. 8–1 and 2–5, Sat.–Sun. 10–1 and 2–5.*

Time Out Opposite the Rathaus on the market square, look for the gleaming sign of the Golden Kette, a café-restaurant that's open late. In summer, sit outside on the terrace.

The hot springs that drew the Romans and Charlemagne's father to Aachen can still be enjoyed by the visitor. Just south of the cathedral is the arcaded, Neoclassical **Elisenbrunnen.** Experts agree that the spa waters here—the hottest north of the Alps—are effective in helping cure a wide range of ailments. Drinking the sulphorous water in the approved manner, however, can be an unpleasant business. Still, if you want to emulate the great and the good who have, through the centuries, dutifully swallowed their medicine—Dürer, Frederick the Great, and Charlemagne himself, among them—hold your nose as you drink it. There are three pools in the city where you can sit in the waters, too. In Dürer's time, the baths were enjoyed for more than their health-giving properties, and there were regular crackdowns on the orgy-like goings-on. Today, modesty reigns in the hot pools of Aachen.

Like all German spas, Aachen also has its **casino** (Spielbank). It's housed in the porticoed former **Kurhaus,** in the park-like grounds fronting Monheimsallee (facing the Kurbad Quellenhof). The casino is open daily from 3 PM.

What to See and Do with Children

There are few parts of Germany that offer more for children than the Rhineland, with its castles, its legends, and its easily accessible rivers. In the wooded hills above the Rhine and Mosel are several **wild animal parks.** The one near the village of **Rheinböllen** (follow the signs from Bacharach) has bears and bison, as well as the usual fallow deer. (Open daily Mar.–Sept.) There's another well-stocked animal park just outside the Mosel wine village of **Klötten.** (Open year-round, daily.) **Königswinter,** near Bonn, has a **crocodile and snake farm,** the only one of its kind in Germany. (Open year-round, daily.)

You'll find **fairy-tale parks** in several parts of the Rhineland—Wiesbaden's **Taunus Wonderland** has an Indian village and a miniature Wild West railway. (Open year-round, daily.) In Dötzheim, just outside Wiesbaden, there's a miniature **Grimm fairy-tale landscape,** with scaled-down hamlets complete with tiny houses and streets. Bonn has a young people's theater, the **Theater der Jugend** (Hermannstr. 50, tel. 0228/463–672), and a fascinating natural history museum, the **Museum Alexander König** (Adenauerallee 150–164).

Köln's **zoo,** founded in 1860, is West Germany's third oldest and one of the most interesting. Local children love it, perhaps because of its large monkey population and newly opened jungle house. *Riehlerstr. 73. Admission: DM 6 adults, DM 2.50 children. Open Apr.–Sept., daily 9–6; Oct.–Mar. 9–5.*

Köln also has a **puppet theater** (Rösratherstr. 133, tel. 02208/2408) and a **children's theater** (Bürgerzentrum Alte Feuerwache, Melchiorstr. 3, tel. 0221/739–1073). For possibly the most popular outing of all in Köln (and perhaps the most expensive), take your kids to the **Gebrüder Grimm** (Brothers Grimm) book and toy shop on Mauritiussteinweg 110.

Shopping

Wine is more or less synonymous with the Rhine. If you haven't room for a bottle or two in your carry-on luggage, settle for one of the next best things: a couple of boxed glasses, or a locally carved corkscrew, or a basketwork wine server. If it's wine you want, bear in mind that there are few bargains to be found in Germany's duty-free airport shops, so buy before you fly.

Every Rhine and Mosel village has several wine shops, as well as cellars where you can sample before you buy. Many cellars offer tours with English-speaking guides. One of the best is the **Weingut Wilhelm Wasum** (Mainzerstr. 20–23, Bacharach). Another reliable Bacharach cellar is the **Weingut Wolfgang Eberhard** (Borbacherstr. 6–7); it's been in the same family for more than 250 years.

For wine glasses and Westerwald ceramics, seek out the **Phil Jost** shop in Bacharach (Blucherstr. 4). It offers some real bargains on "seconds." Along the Mosel, the **J. Köll** company (Ravenestr. 35, Cochem) encourages callers to try the local wines in its cask-lined cellars. For fine Mosel wine glasses in Cochem, head for **Karl Hürter** (Herrenstr. 20). On the same street, **Faber's** and **Die Vitrine** have large selections of locally made handicrafts, as well as fine linens, glassware, and pewter.

In **Wiesbaden,** you'll find one of Germany's most elegant shopping streets: the broad, tree-lined **Wilhelmstrasse.** At the end of June, when the **Wilhelmstrassenfest** is held, it's partytime along Wilhelmstrasse—Rheingau wine and Sekt flow in abundance. Wine corks pop again in mid-August for Wiesbaden's **Rheingauer Weinfest,** Germany's largest wine festival. Wiesbaden is a German **antiques** center, too; you'll find the best selections along **Taunusstrasse.**

The international comings and goings in **Bonn** keep antiques dealers busy there. Two to visit are **Paul Schweitzer** (Löbestr. 1) in the Bad Godesberg suburb, and **Kunsthaus Brucke** (Gangolfstr. 9). Bonn is a city of **markets,** with two open daily: the **Wochenmarkt** on Marktplatz; and the **Blumenmarkt,** a flower market, on Remigiusplatz. There's a **flea market** April through October on the third Saturday of each month at **Rheinaue** (Ludwig-Erhard-Str.). If you're in the Bonn area on the second weekend of September, don't miss the **Pützchens Markt,** a huge country fair.

Koblenz has two flea markets held each Saturday in summer at **Peter-Almeier-Ufer** and at **Florinsmarkt.** For antiques and handicrafts, prowl the old city around the cathedral or make for the **Weindorf** (wine village), where more than just wine is offered.

Trier boasts high-class shops along the pedestrian streets in the **old town:** Simeonstrasse, Fleischstrasse, Nagelstrasse, Palatstrasse, and Hauptmarkt. For local handicrafts, glassware, ceramics, and fabrics, make for **Kunsthandwerkerhof** (Simeonstiftpl.).

The center of **Köln,** south of the cathedral, is one huge pedestrian shopping zone. It'll take you about half an hour to stroll through it all. From the cathedral, head south along Hohe Strasse to Schildergasse, then to Neumarkt, Mittelstrasse, Hohenzollernring, Ehrenstrasse, Breitestrasse, Tunisstrasse, Minoritenstrasse, and back to the starting point, Wallrafplatz. Between Mittelstrasse and Ehrenstrasse is a glass-roofed bazaar where dozens of shops share space. **Mittelstrasse** and **Hohestrasse** are best for German fashions and luxury goods (**Offermann's** on Hohestrasse has a large selection of fine leather items and beautifully finished travel accessories). Hohestrasse is also the best place to look for Köln's most celebrated product: **eau de cologne.** In nearby Glockengasse (No. 4711, of course) you can visit the house where the 18th-century Italian chemist Giovanni-Maria Farina first concocted it. Köln is also known for delicious **Ludwig chocolate.** You'll have no difficulty finding it in any of the delicatessens along the route. **Lintgasse** is the place for antiques; flea markets are held every third Saturday at the **Alter Markt** in the old town, and every fourth Sunday at **Nippes** (Wilhelmpl.). The best department stores are **Kaufhof** (Hohestr.), **Hertie** (Neumarkt), and **Karstadt** (Breitestr.).

Sports and Fitness

Bicycling Most local train stations have bikes to rent for DM 10 a day (half that if you have a valid train ticket). Listings of additional outlets for rental bikes are available from train stations.

Boating Row boats and canoes can be hired at most Rhine and Mosel river resorts. For a motor boat, try the **Lahr Charter Boot** (Grenzerstr. 29, Koblenz, tel. 02603/6541).

Swimming Even though West Germany's environment minister swam the Rhine in 1988 to prove the river was no longer polluted, only the brave and/or foolhardy are likely to follow his example in either the Rhine or the Mosel. The Rhineland has a substantial number of pools, indoor and outdoor, where the swimming is much safer. Trier's **Stadtbad,** with five heated pools, and Wiesbaden's **Opelbad,** located high above the city on the Neroberg, are among the best. Köln has more than 20 outdoors pools; the one at **Müngersdorfer Stadium** (Aachenerstr.) is heated. There are also two lido-type complexes in Köln: **Deutz-Kalker Bad,** on the street of the same name; and **Kornbibad Hohenberg** (Schwarzburgerstr. 91).

Tennis The **Freizheit Park** (tel. 02603/81095) in Koblenz's Industriekreisel has eight indoor tennis courts plus a swimming pool and a sauna for post-match relaxation. Wiesbaden's **Henkell ice stadium** (Höllerbornstr.) becomes a tennis court during the summer months. The **Ferienpark Hochwald** (tel. 06589/1011) at Kell, near Trier, is one of the leading tennis complexes in Germany. In Köln, try **City Sport** (Rhondroferstr. 10, tel. 0221/411-092), or **Squashpark** (Neusserstr. 718a, tel. 0221/740-8866).

Dining and Lodging

Dining

If you come to the Rhine hoping to eat fish, you'll be disappointed: the polluted waters of the river have destroyed all but a few of the fish that once thrived. Practically the only fish dishes in the region feature seafood flown in from France; prices are correspondingly high. However, there are numerous local specialties that are hearty rather than sophisticated: *Himmel und Erde*, a mixture of potatoes, onions, and apples; *Hammchen*, or pork knuckle; *Hunsrücker Festessen*, sauerkraut with potatoes, horseradish, and ham. There are also many small inns and restaurants offering these and other regional dishes. At the other end of the scale, Köln and Wiesbaden boast some of the most sophisticated restaurants in Europe, many offering delectable nouvelle cuisine. The Rhineland is wine country, and every restaurant and café offers a large selection of wines.

Highly recommended restaurants are indicated by a star ★.

Category	Cost*
Very Expensive	over DM 90
Expensive	DM 55–DM 90
Moderate	DM 35–DM 55
Inexpensive	under DM 35

**per person for a three-course meal, including tax but not alcohol*

Lodging

There's a vast selection of places to lay your head. The most romantic are the old, riverside inns and hotels and the castle-hotels, some of which are enormously luxurious. In the cities of the Rhineland, there's a similarly large choice. Some of the most expensive hotels are among the finest in Europe. Modern high rises are common. A great many hotels close for the winter; most are also booked well in advance, especially for the wine festivals in the fall. Whenever possible, make reservations long before you visit.

Highly recommended hotels are indicated by a star ★.

Category	Cost*
Very Expensive	over DM 180
Expensive	DM 120–DM180
Moderate	DM 80–DM 120

Inexpensive	under DM 80

**for two people in a double room, excluding service charges*

Aachen
Dining
★
Gala. For the most elegant dining in Aachen, make for the Gala restaurant, adjoining the casino. The mood is discreetly classy, with dark paneled walls and original oil paintings; the food is regional, with nouvelle touches. *Monheimsallee, 44, tel. 0241/153–013. Reservations required. Jacket and tie required. AE, DC, MC, V. Closed Mon. Very Expensive.*

La Becasse. Sophisticated French nouvelle cuisine is offered in this upscale modern restaurant, located just outside the old town by the Westpark. Try the distinctively light calf's liver. *Hanbrucherstr. 1, tel. 0241/74444. Reservations required. Jacket and tie required. AE, DC, MC, V. Closed Sat. for dinner and Sun. Expensive.*

Os Oche. For simple, filling meals served on long wood tables, beer from the barrel, and informal, friendly service, this is a place that's hard to beat. The Os Oche likes to claim the best stews in Germany. *Alexanderstr. 109, tel. 0241/36670. No reservations. Dress: informal. DC, V. Inexpensive.*

Lodging
★
Steigenberger Hotel Quellenhof. The Quellenhof offers the sort of pampered luxury that often appeals to older guests. Built during World War I as a country home for the Kaiser, it's very much one of Europe's grande dames: spacious, elegant, and formal. The flower-filled Parkrestaurant, one of the best restaurants in north Germany, serves haute cuisine in the grand manner. The hotel is located by the Kurpark and the casino. *Monheimsallee 52, tel. 0241/152–081. 200 rooms with bath. Facilities: pool, thermal treatments, restaurant, parking. AE, DC, MC, V. Very Expensive.*

★ **Romantik Hotel Altes Brauhaus Burgkeller.** Located 15 minutes by car east of Aachen in Stolberg, this one-time brewery stands at the foot of Stolberg castle in the heart of the old town. Try for a room in the main building—the modern Parkhotel annex is imaginatively designed but lacks time-honored charm. The hotel boasts an elegantly rustic restaurant. *Hammerbrg 11, Stolberg, tel. 02402/20031. 32 rooms with bath. Facilities: pool, sauna, tennis courts, restaurant. AE. Expensive.*

Benelux. For low-cost accommodations, the centrally located Benelux offers one of the best deals in town. Small and family run, it has comfortable modern rooms and a smattering of antiques in the public areas. *Franzstr. 21, tel. 0241/22343. 33 rooms with bath. Facilities: parking. AE, DC, MC, V. Moderate.*

Bacharach
Dining and Lodging
Altkölnischer Hof. Tucked in a quiet square in medieval Bacharach, the Altkölnischer is a small, half-timbered hotel built at the turn of the century. Vivid geraniums are planted under the small windows; rooms are simply but attractively furnished in country style; and the rustic restaurant offers typical local dishes and some excellent wines. *Am Marktpl., tel. 06743/1339. 20 rooms with bath. Facilities: restaurant, parking. AE, V. Closed Oct.–Apr. Moderate.*

Bernkastel-Kues
Dining and Lodging
★
Burg Landshut. Built in 1883, this elegantly classical edifice has become one of the Rhineland's leading hotels. All the well-appointed rooms are individually decorated, but try for one with a view of the river. The restaurant, decked out with exposed beams and rough plaster walls, offers nouvelle versions of local specialties. Try the Mosel pike dumplings in Reisling

sauce for a memorable (and unusual) culinary experience. *Gestade 11, tel. 06531/3019. 30 rooms with bath. Facilities: restaurant, bar. AE, DC, V. Closed Dec. 15–27. Expensive.*

Zur Post. Picture-book Germany is alive and well at the appealing, early-19th-century Zur Post. Behind its colorful, flower-laden facade lurk the obligatory exposed wood beams, a dark paneled restaurant (with over 100 wines), and tastefully decorated bedrooms. *Gestade 17, tel. 06531/2022. 39 rooms with bath. Facilities: solarium, sauna, restaurant, parking. AE, DC, MC, V. Closed Jan. Moderate.*

Bingen
Lodging

Rheinhotel Starkenburger Hof. In business since the middle of the 19th century, the Starkenburger Hof, decorated throughout in warm shades of brown and gold, is the number-one choice in Bingen. It overlooks the Rhine, so don't settle for a room without a view. There's no restaurant. *Am Rheinkai, 1, tel. 06721/14341. 30 rooms, 25 with bath. AE, DC. Closed Jan. Moderate.*

Bonn
Dining

★ **Schaarschmidt.** Oysters, lamb, and the best asparagus in Bonn make this atmospheric old restaurant a winner. In summer, sit on the terrace and watch the world go by. When the place is busy, the service can't always cope (take consolation in the extensive wine list). *Brüdergasse 14, tel. 0228/654–407. Reservations recommended. Dress: informal. DC. Closed Sat. dinner and Sun., and Aug. 10–Sept. 1. Expensive.*

Das Haus Daufenbach. The stark white exterior of the Daufenbach, located by the church of St. Remigius, disguises one of the most distinctive restaurants in Bonn. The mood is rustic, with simple wood furniture and antlers on the walls. Specialties include *Spanferkel* (suckling pig) and a range of imaginative salads. Wash them down with wines from the restaurant's own vineyards. *Brüderfasse 6, tel. 0228/637–9944. Reservations recommended. Dress: informal. AE, DC, MC, V. Closed Sun. dinner. Moderate.*

★ **Im Stiefel.** Standing just a few doors from the Beethovenhaus, this is the sort of place those in search of filling food at low prices will appreciate. A great student hangout, it's noisy and nearly always full, but it comes complete with basic wood tables, pewter plates, and dark wood paneling. *Bonngasse 30, tel. 0228/634–806. No reservations. Dress: informal. V. Closed Sun. and holidays. Inexpensive.*

Lodging

★ **Königshof.** The Königshof is modern chic, understated but luxurious, a favorite with visiting politicians and powerbrokers. It's located by the river in leafy and spacious grounds. The restaurant, with a spectacular vaulted wood ceiling, offers about the best view of the Rhine in Bonn. Rooms are plushly comfortable and large. *Adenauerallee 9, tel. 0228/26010. 137 rooms with bath. Facilities: restaurant, parking. AE, DC, MC, V. Very Expensive.*

Bristol. The Bristol could be in Dallas for all the German atmosphere it has, but for modern elegance and a terrific central location, it's an established favorite. *Poppelsdorferallee, tel. 0228/26980. 120 rooms with bath. Facilities: indoor pool, sauna, solarium, bowling alley, restaurant. AE, DC, MC. Expensive.*

Godesburg Hotel. The chief attraction of this otherwise nondescript modern hotel, located five miles south of Bonn in Bad Godesburg, is the adjoining 13th-century castle (now ruined). The views are great. The Rittersaal restaurant—where you can eat outside in summer—offers superior food. *Auf dem Berg 1, Bad Godesburg, tel. 0228/316–071. 12 rooms with bath. Facilities: restaurant, wine bar. AE, DC, V. Expensive.*

Sternhotel. For good value, solid comfort, and a central location, the family-run Stern is tops. Rooms can be small, but all are pleasantly furnished. There's no restaurant. *Markt 8, tel. 0228/654–455. 70 rooms with bath. AE, DC, MC, V. Moderate.*

Boppard
Dining and Lodging

★ **Hotel Klostergut Jakobsberg.** Stay here for the amazing location on the north bank of the Rhine (the hotel's about 12 kilometers, or 8 miles, north of Boppard), the array of sports facilities, the excellent food, and the sumptuous furnishings. The hotel is housed in a castle (make sure you see its gem of a chapel) and boasts a sophisticated baronial atmosphere. The place has an extensive collection of hunting trophies and rifles and a considerable assembly of paintings and prints, not to mention imposing tapestries. This is real Prisoner of Zenda stuff. The hotel raises its own cattle and cultivates Japanese *shiitaki* mushrooms. Both are put to good use in its restaurant. The veal medallions in goose liver sauce are superb. *5407 Boppard–Rhein, tel. 06742/3061. 39 rooms with bath. Facilities: indoor pool, indoor and outdoor tennis courts, sauna, solarium, squash, bowling alley, skeet and trap shooting, horseback riding, heliport, restaurant. AE, DC, V. Very Expensive.*

Cochem
Dining and Lodging

★ **Alte Thorschenke.** There are few more authentic or atmospheric old inns in the Rhineland than this ancient and picturesque spot in the heart of Cochem. Creaking staircases, four-poster beds, river views, and exposed beams combine to produce an effect that's almost too good to be true. The restaurant boasts an extensive selection of local wines. Avoid the modern annex if you want to experience the full charm of this romantic haunt. *Brückenstr. 3, tel. 02671/7059. 51 rooms with bath. Facilities: restaurant. AE, DC, MC, V. Closed Jan.–mid-Mar. Expensive.*

Brixiade. Despite its modern-looking facade, the Brixiade has been welcoming guests—Kaiser Wilhelm II among them—for more than 100 years. Ask for a room with a view over the town and the river. The restaurant offers a fixed-price menu and magnificent local wines. Dine on the terrace in summer. *Uferstr. 13, tel. 02671/3015. 38 rooms with bath. Facilities: restaurant. AE. Closed Dec. 20–27. Moderate.*

★ **Weissmühle.** You'll want to stay—or eat—here as much to see the picture-book village of Endertal, just outside of Cochem, as to lay your head on the hotel's ample pillows. The place is decorated in that inimitable German gingerbread style, with carved beams and lace curtains galore. Try the trout or the spit-roasted kebabs. *Endertal, tel. 02671/7475. 36 rooms with bath. Facilities: restaurant. No credit cards. Moderate.*

Koblenz
Dining

Le Gourmet. For sophisticated international dining, try the restaurant of the Scandic Crown hotel (*see* below). The food is nouvelle chic; the mood upscale and expensive. Eat on the terrace in summer. *Julius-Wegeler-Str. 6, tel. 0261/1360. Reservations required. Jacket and tie required. AE, DC, MC, V. Expensive.*

Weinhaus Hubertus. This is about the most atmospheric restaurant in Koblenz. The flower-laden, half-timbered 17th-century exterior gives a good idea of the country-style mood inside. Antiques and dark wood predominate. The food is ample and cooked with gusto. *Florinsmarkt. 54, tel. 0261/31177. Reserva-*

tions advised. Dress: informal. No credit cards. Closed lunch. Moderate.

Lodging **Scandic Crown.** The elegantly modern Scandic Crown is full of style and class. It may be short on old-German atmosphere, but it's long on polished service, well-upholstered comfort, and terrific views. The rooms are elegantly understated. *Julius-Wegeler-Str. 6, tel. 0261/1360. 170 rooms with bath. Facilities: sauna, Jacuzzi, 2 restaurants, bar. AE, DC, MC, V. Expensive.*

Hohenstaufen. Though short on atmosphere, the modern Hohenstaufen, located near the train station, provides reliable comforts. Rooms are sleek and well designed. There's no restaurant. *Emil-Schüller-Str. 41, tel. 0261/37081. 50 rooms with bath. AE, MC, V. Moderate.*

Kleiner Riesen. The riverside location and simple comforts of the Kleiner Riesen single it out as the sort of well-run, straightforward hotel that's not always easy to find. It's an older hotel, offering basic, no-nonsense value for the money. There's no restaurant. *Kaiserin-Augusta-Anlagen 18, tel. 0261/32077. 27 rooms with bath. Facilities: parking. AE, DC, MC, V. Moderate.*

Köln
Dining

★ **Bado-La Poêle d'Or.** At first glance, the heavy furnishings and hushed atmosphere of the Poêle d'Or make it seem like the last place you'd find light and sophisticated nouvelle cuisine in Germany. But for some years, those in the know have been claiming this as one of the finest dining establishments in Europe. Even such apparently simple dishes as onion soup have been winning plaudits. Order salmon with lemon ginger sauce if you want to sample the full glory of the place. *Komödienstr. 50–52, tel. 0221/134–100. Reservations required. Dress: casual chic. AE, DC. Closed Sun., Mon. for lunch, Christmas, July 18–Aug. 9, and holidays. Very Expensive.*

★ **Chez Alex.** For upscale nouvelle cuisine with a strong French accent, check out the delicate offerings here. The decor is very classy, with antiques, fine paintings, and deep leather chairs. The lamb fillet Provençal with Roquefort sauce is memorable. *Mühlengasse 1–3, tel. 0221/230–560. Reservations required. Jacket and tie required. AE, DC, MC. Closed Sat. dinner and Sun. Expensive.*

★ **Franz Keller's Restaurant.** No prizes for guessing who owns this elegant haunt! Keller provides additional evidence of upscale Köln's love affair with nouvelle cuisine—no surprise since he trained under the man who invented it, the great Paul Bocuse. To eat on the terrace under a warm summer sky can be magical, especially if you've ordered the quail and truffle salad. *Aachenerstr. 21, tel. 0221/219–549. Reservations required. Jacket and tie required. AE, DC. Closed Sat. dinner and Sun. Expensive.*

Gaststätte Früh am Dom. For real down-home German food, there are few places to compare with this time-honored former brewery. Bold frescoes on the vaulted ceilings establish the mood. Dishes such as Hamchen provide an authentically Teutonic experience. The beer garden is delightful for summer dining. *Am Hof 12–14, tel. 0221/236–618. Reservations advised. Dress: informal. No credit cards. Moderate.*

★ **Weinhaus im Waldfisch.** The black-and-white gabled facade of this 400-year-old restaurant signals that here, too, you'll come face to face with no-holds-barred traditional specialties in a time-honored atmosphere. Try Himmel und Erde and any one of the wide range of wines. The restaurant is tucked away between the Heumarkt (Haymarket) and the river. *Salzgasse 13, tel. 0221/219–575. Reservations advised. Dress: informal. DC, MC. Closed weekends and holidays. Moderate.*

Lodging

★ **Dom-Hotel.** The Dom is in a class of its own. Old-fashioned, formal, and gracious, with a stunning location right by the cathedral, it offers the sort of old-world elegance and discreetly efficient service few hotels aspire to these days. The flower-filled public rooms are sumptuously grand; the antique-filled bedrooms are high-ceilinged and spacious; the view of the cathedral is something to treasure. *Domkloster 2A, tel. 0221/20240. 126 rooms with bath. Facilities: restaurant, terrace café, bar, parking. AE, DC, MC, V. Very Expensive.*

Inter-Continental. If you value the reliable comforts of a large, upscale chain hotel, the modern Inter-Continental will provide all you need. It's located in the old town, handy for just about everything, and offers classy, streamlined accommodations and a wide range of facilities. *Helenstr. 14, tel. 0221/2280. 279 rooms and 11 suites, all with bath. Facilities: indoor pool, sauna, solarium, massage, disco, bar, restaurant. AE, DC, MC, V. Very Expensive.*

Haus Lyskirchen. Despite its downtown location, the Lyskirchen offers a taste of the country. Behind its ornate, high-gabled facade are chalet-style rooms (some are aggressively modern; specify which you prefer) and a rustic, paneled restaurant. The breakfast room, by contrast, is starkly modern. *Filzengraben 26, tel. 0221/234–891. 95 rooms with bath. Facilities: restaurant, bar, indoor pool, sauna, solarium. AE, DC, MC, V. Expensive.*

★ **Altstadt.** Located close by the river in the old town, this is the place for charm and low rates. All the rooms are individually decorated, and the service is impeccable—both welcoming and efficient. There's no restaurant. *Salzgasse 7, tel. 0221/234–187. 28 rooms with bath. Facilities: sauna. AE, DC, MC, V. Closed Christmas. Moderate.*

Rüdesheim

Dining and Lodging

Hotel Jagdschloss Niederwald. This is not so much a place to overnight as a luxury resort hotel where you might want to spend your entire vacation. It's set in the hills three miles out of Rüdesheim, with predictably good views over the Rhine and the Rheingau. The former hunting lodge of the dukes of Hesse, it has a lavish, baronial atmosphere. The restaurant can be magnificent. Families will appreciate the wide range of activities offered. *Auf dem Niederwald 1, tel. 06722/1004. 92 rooms with bath. Facilities: restaurant, bar, indoor pool, sauna, gym, tennis courts, horseback riding. AE, DC, MC, V. Restaurant closed Dec.–Mar. Expensive.*

★ **Romantik Hotel Schwan.** This must be one of the most "romantic" of the Romantik chain. A Renaissance half-timbered building with green shutters, tubs of flowers, high gables, and sloping roofs, it sits in the village of Oestrich, about 5 miles east of Rüdesheim, right on the Rhine. The restaurant offers fine local specialties and an extensive wine list; wine tasting sessions are held among the oak casks in the ancient cellars. *Rheinallee 5–7, Oestrich, tel. 06723/3001. 66 rooms with bath. Facilities: restaurant, terrace, parking. AE, DC, MC, V. Closed Nov.–mid-Mar. Expensive.*

Rüdesheimer Hof. For a taste of Rheingau hospitality, try this typical inn. There's a terrace for summer dining on excellent local specialties, which you can enjoy along with any of the many wines offered. *Geisenheimerstr. 1, tel. 06722/2011. 48 rooms with bath. Facilities: restaurant, terrace, parking. AE, MC. Closed mid-Nov.–mid-Mar. Moderate.*

St. Goar/St. Goarshausen
Dining and Lodging

Schlosshotel auf Berg Rheinfels. Located directly opposite Burg Maus, this castle-hotel breathes a regal air. Its ponderously grand interior is furnished with intricate French and Spanish antiques. Ask for a room with a view. The restaurant offers hearty regional specialties. Medieval-style banquets *(Spektalmus)*, complete with minstrels, serving wenches, and oxen on spits, are offered in the summer. *Schlossberg 47, tel. 06741/2071. 46 rooms with bath. Facilities: indoor and outdoor (heated) pools, miniature golf, fishing, restaurant, bar. AE, DC, MC, V. Expensive.*

Herrensmühle. This is an Alpine chalet-style hotel with heavy pine furnishings decorated with floral patterns. It stands just outside town by its own vineyards and offers good value at low prices. *Forstbachstr. 46, tel. 06771/7317. 37 rooms, some with bath. Facilities: restaurant. No credit cards. Inexpensive.*

Trier
Dining

★ **Pfeffermühle.** The stately Pfeffermühle stands alongside the Mosel, by the cable car station. This former fisherman's home is now considered the best restaurant in town. The food is nouvelle French. The rabbit in sherry sauce is outstanding, as is the lobster in champagne gelée with asparagus tips. The wine list features vintage Mosels. *Zurlaubener Ufer 76, tel. 0651/26133. Reservations required. Dress: casual chic. MC. Closed Sun. and July 10–31. Expensive.*

★ **Zum Domstein.** Colorful and crowded, the centrally located and atmospheric Domstein offers simple local specialties and a wide range of wines (stored in the Roman cellar below). In the summer, this is the place to be to watch the bustle outside. *Hauptmarkt 5, tel. 0651/74490. No reservations. Dress: informal. AE, DC, V. Closed Christmas. Moderate.*

Ratskeller zur Steipe. Buried in the vaults beneath the town hall, the Ratskeller offers Teutonic mood and fare. Try *Steipenteller*, the house specialty, a massive tray of mixed meats. In summer, you can move upstairs and eat on the terrace. *Hauptmarkt 14, tel. 0651/75052. Reservations advised. Dress: informal. AE, DC, V. Closed Mon. and Jan.–Easter. Inexpensive.*

Lodging

Dorint Porta Nigra. This stylish modern building stands opposite the Roman city gate whose name it bears. Its interior is boldly decorated, with chic bedrooms and a delightful restaurant done up in convincing rustic style. The café has a terrific view of the Porta Nigra itself. *Porta-Nigra-Pl. 1, tel. 0651/27010. 67 rooms with bath. Facilities: restaurant, bar, café, parking. AE, DC, V. Expensive.*

★ **Petrisberg.** This will be the choice of anyone who values classic modern design and a location away from the downtown area. The building is unimposing externally, but inside features striking antiques and rooms with superb views over vineyards, forests, and park lands. For all that, it's no more than a 10-minute walk from the old town. There's a moody weinstube (wine bar) in the basement, but no restaurant. *Sickingenstr. 11, tel. 0651/41181. 35 rooms with bath. Facilities; bar, weinstube, parking. No credit cards. Moderate.*

Wiesbaden
Dining

★ **Die Ente vom Lehel.** The formal and elegant restaurant of the Nassauer Hof (*see* below) provides one of the most memorable dining experiences in Germany. Nouvelle cuisine is king here.

For a dessert you'll never forget, try *Dialog der Früchte* (dialogue of fruits), a startling combination of vivid pureed fruits that swirls around your plate. *Kaiser-Friedrich-Pl. 3, tel. 06121/133–666. Reservations required. Jacket and tie required. AE, DC, MC, V. Closed Sun., Mon., and July–early Aug. Very Expensive.*

★ **Restaurant de France.** Serious gourmands dispute the relative merits of the restaurant of the Hotel de France, and Die Ente vom Lehel. The food here is not wholeheartedly nouvelle—seafood is the specialty; much of it is flown in daily—but the mood is unmistakably chic. *Taunusstr. 49, tel. 06121/520–061. Reservations required. Jacket and tie required. AE, DC, MC. Closed Christmas and New Year's. Very Expensive.*

Weihenstephan. Bavarian specialties are offered in this Alpine-style restaurant; even Bavarian beer is available, despite this being the most famous wine-producing area of the country. The mood is as hearty as the cooking. *Armenruhstr. 6, tel. 06121/61134. Reservations advised. Dress: informal. AE. Closed Sat. Moderate.*

Lodging

★ **Nassauer Hof.** Located opposite the Kurpark, the Nassauer Hof epitomizes elegance and style. Set in a turn-of-the-century building, it combines the best of old-world graciousness with German efficiency and comfort. Rooms are large and classy; the bar is a chic place for rendezvous. *Kaiser-Friedrich-Pl. 3–4, tel. 06121/1330. 210 rooms with bath. Facilities: indoor pool, sauna, massage, restaurant, bar, parking. AE, DC, V. Expensive.*

★ **Schwarzer Bock.** For period charm, there are few hotels to beat the stylish Schwarzer Bock. The building dates back to 1486, though most of what you see today is from the 19th century. The lavish public rooms are filled with antiques, flowers, and paintings; the opulent bedrooms are individually decorated in styles ranging from baroque to modern. The thermal swimming pool will soothe away the pain of paying the bill. *Kranzpl. 12, tel. 06121/3821. 186 rooms with bath. Facilities: indoor pool, sauna, massage, beauty farm, roof garden, restaurant, bar, parking. AE, DC, V. Expensive.*

The Arts and Nightlife

The Arts

Music

Aachen has a municipal orchestra that gives regular concerts in the **Kongresszentrum Eurogress,** Monheimsallee. **Bonn** means Beethoven, and every three years (the next year is 1992) the city hosts a **Beethoven Festival.** The Bonn **Symphony Orchestra** opens its winter season in grand style every September with a concert on the market square, in front of City Hall. Otherwise, concerts are given in the Beethovenhalle. From May through October, the **Bonner Sommer** festival offers a colorful program of folklore, music, and street theater, much of it outdoors and most of it free. In May and June, concerts are held on Sunday evenings in the **Bad Godesberg Redoute;** admission is free. In July and August, **organ recitals** are given Wednesday evenings at 8 in the **Church of the Holy Cross** (Kaiserpl.).

In **Koblenz,** the **Rheinische Philharmonie** orchestra plays regularly in the **Rhein-Mosel-Halle,** (Julius-Wegeler-Str). **Organ recitals** are frequently given in two fine churches: the

Christuskirche, and the **Florinskirche. Köln's Westdeutsche Rundfunk Orchestra** performs regularly in the city's excellent concert hall, the **Philharmonie** (Bischofsgarten 1, tel. 0221/2040820). The smaller **Gürzenich Orchestra** also gives regular concerts in the Philharmonie, but the natural setting for its music is the restored **Gürzenich,** medieval Köln's official reception mansion. Year-round **organ recitals** in Köln's cathedral are supplemented from June to August with a summer season of organ music. Organ recitals and chamber concerts are also presented in the churches of St. Maria Himmelfahrt (Marzellenstr. 26), St. Aposteln (Neumarkt 30); and Trinitätskirche (Filzengraben 4). For details on all church concerts, tel. 0221/534–856.

Trier's cathedral is the magnificent setting for much of the sacred music to be heard in the city; there are **organ recital festivals** in May, June, August, and September.

Wiesbaden's Symphony Orchestra gives concerts in the **Staatstheater's Grosses Haus** and in the equally impressive **Kurhaus.** Organ recitals are given every Saturday at 11:30 in the Gothic **Marktkirche** (Marktpl.).

Theater **Bonn** is a city of theaters. The **Euro Theater Central Bonn** (Münsterpl. 30, tel. 0228/652–951) includes both German and foreign-language productions in its program.

Koblenz has a theatrical tradition dating back to the 18th-century rule of the Prince-Elector Clemens Wenzeslaus. The gracious Neoclassical theater he built in 1787 is still in regular use; tel. 0261/34629 for program details and tickets. **Köln's** two principal theaters are the **Schauspielhaus** (Offenbachpl. 1), and the smaller **Kammerspiele** (Ubierring 45). Telephone 0221/212–651 for program details and tickets for both. Of the 20 or so private theaters in the city, **Der Keller** (Kleingedankstr. 6, tel. 0221/318–059) is the best-known venue for contemporary drama.

The **Hessisches Staatstheater** is based in Wiesbaden's fine late-19th-century theater on Christian-Zais-Strasse (opposite the Kurhaus and casino). Classical drama, opera, ballet, and musicals are presented in the **Grosses Haus** (tel. 06121/132–325); less-ambitious productions are given in the **Kleines Haus** (tel. 06121/132–327). The Grosses Haus is also the scene in early summer of Wiesbaden's annual **International May Arts Festival,** West Germany's second oldest. **Bonn** hosts a famous dance festival, the **International Dance Workshop,** in July and August. For program details and tickets, tel. 0228/11517. Opera, ballet, and musicals are also staged regularly at the **Oper der Stadt Bonn** (Am Böselagerhof 1, tel. 0228/773–668).

Köln's opera company, the **Oper der Stadt Köln** (Schauspielhaus, Offenbachpl. 1) has a countrywide reputation for exciting classical and contemporary productions. The city's small ballet company, the **Kölner Tanzforum,** hosts an international festival, the **Internationale Sommerakademie des Tanzes,** every July.

Nightlife

Nightlife in Bonn? Locals tell the story of the visitor who asked a cop where he could find some action in Bonn. "She's taken the night off to visit her aunt in Köln," was the reply. Things have obviously changed since then, considering the number of bars and taverns in the Altstadt. Try a Budweiser or Pilsener Urquell in the **Lampe** (Breitestr. 35); after midnight, move on to the **Locke** (Prinz-Albertstr. 20). The **Marktschänke** (Eifelstr. 2) is popular with the dawn chorus of taxi drivers, market traders, and all-nighters. No wonder: It *opens* at 5 AM. Singles could try a bar called **Die Falle** (Belderberg 15). The **Cave Club '77** (Bertha von Süttnerpl. 25); the **CD Nightclub** (Rheingasse 14), and the **Carlton** (Wilhelmstr. 1), have music and some adult spice. The **Jazz Galerie** (Oxfordstr. 24) has live jazz and rock three or four times a week. The **Pinte** (Breitestr. 46) is smaller, smokier, and good fun.

Singles in **Koblanz** make for the **Tanzcafé Besselink** (opposite the main train station)—it's open until 3 AM. Disco fans favor the **Apropos** (Schulgasse 9) and the **Metro Club** in Koblenz-Hochheim (Alte Heerstr. 130). The nightclub scene is dominated by the **Mocambo** (Poststr. 2a) and the **Petit Fleur** (Rheinstr. 30), while the best jazz can reportedly be heard at the **Lampenputzer** (Gemüsegasse 4).

Wiesbaden's nightlife tends to center on the **casino** and **Kurhaus** complex. You'll find a mix of casino winners and losers celebrating or drowning their sorrows in the **Pavillon Bar** of the Kurhaus.

Köln's nightlife is found in three distinct areas: around the **Friesenplatz** S-bahn (suburban railway) station, in **Zulpicherstrasse,** and between the **AlterMarkt** and **Neumarkt** in the old city. While this is not Hamburg, virtually all tastes are catered to. Singles head for any one of three bars in the area of the Friesenplatz S-bahn: **Goldener Spiegel** (Norbertstr. 18), **Madame** (Klapperhof 49), or **Tingel-Tangel** (Maastrichtstr. 6–8). This is disco land, too. **Club 54, Santa Cruz, Show-Boat, Morocco,** and **Zorba the Buddha** (yes, the Buddha) are all "in." For the last word (or final whistle) in disco experience, make for the **Hauptbahnhof** on Friday or Saturday night. The old waiting room has been turned into a concert hall and disco, enabling Köln's boppers do their thing on ancient polished parquet and check their style in original mahogany-framed mirrors. Just across the square is another popular disco that shares space under one roof with 18 pubs and a small theater: the **Bierdorf Colon** (Breitestr. 29). For sheer variety of beers, however, it's overshadowed by the **Deutsches Bierhaus** (Roonstr. 33), a cellar measuring 418 yards square that offers 17 different kinds of brew. Jazz fans make for the **Initiative Kölner Jazz Haus** (Mozartstr. 60) where top overseas performers are featured. **Streckstrump Papa Joe's** (Buttermarkt 37) is the place for traditional and dixie jazz. The **Subway** (Aachenerstr. 82) is not for mainstream and avant-garde jazz.

14 The Fairy-tale Road

Introduction

The majority of holiday visitors to West Germany who arrive via the international airport at Frankfurt head west to the Rhineland or south into the Black Forest or Bavaria. Some may find their way into the Taunus mountains on Frankfurt's doorstep. Relatively few, however, venture north to follow a fascinating trail that leads deep into the heart of Germany, not only into the land itself but into the German character as well.

This is the Fairy-tale Road, or Märchenstrasse. It starts just a 20-minute rail or car journey east of Frankfurt in the town of Hanau and from there wends its way north for some 600 kilometers (about 370 miles) through parts of Germany that shaped the lives and imaginations of the two most famous chroniclers of German folk history and tradition, the brothers Grimm. (Note that though the route is best explored by car, many of the attractions along its meandering path can also be reached by train.)

The Fairy-tale Road is a new addition to Germany's tourist scene. The concept of this route was dreamed up to commemorate the 200th anniversary of the births of the brothers Grimm, Jacob and Wilhelm, in Hanau on January 4, 1785, and February 24, 1786, respectively. It seemed like a neat peg to call attention to parts of Germany usually bypassed by visitors and to open new areas to international tourism, perhaps in the process creating the equivalent of a new Romantic Road.

So, starting early in 1985, with a minor media blitz and publicity barrage, the Fairy-tale Road was launched to great acclaim. In its own way the route can indeed be compared to the Romantic Road, so long as travelers accept the realities of the venture.

To follow this course from stem to stern—in other words, from Frankfurt all the way to Bremen—can make for a fairly long and tiring journey. However, you can pick up the route anywhere along its length to take in the highlights and still come remarkably close to the spirit and essence of fairy-tale Germany as recorded by these two master storytellers.

The zigzag course detailed here follows the spine of the Fairy-tale Road and includes a number of side trips and detours to nearby destinations worthy of a visitor's attention.

No matter how long you follow the Fairy-tale Road, the idea is to take it slow and easy, soak up the atmosphere, and ponder the world of "once upon a time" that originated here.

Fairy tales come to life in forgotten villages where black cats snooze in the windows of half-timbered houses; in ancient forests where wild boar snort at timid deer; in misty valleys where the silence of centuries is broken only by the splash of a ferryman's oar.

If you join the relatively few who tackle this enchanting part of Germany, leave skepticism behind, and be sure to take along a copy of the Grimm stories to add an extra dimension to the passage through this magical realm.

In a way, this could be considered a dual trip, going forward geographically and at the same time back into the reaches of childhood, imagination, and German folk consciousness, to visit

Old World settings steeped in legend and fantasy. The Grimms set it all down for posterity.

From early childhood they were enthralled by tales of enchantment, of kings and queens, of golden-haired princesses saved from disaster by stalwart princes—folk tales, myths, epics, and legends that dealt with magic and wicked witches, predatory stepmothers, along with supporting casts of goblins, and wizards.

However, the Grimms did not invent these tales, which were in the public domain long before they started to collect them. In time the brothers gathered some 200 of their favorite stories to create a book that would become known and loved in every part of the world and in many languages.

The Grimms' devotion to fairy tales could be considered more or less a diversion, merely a sideline to their main careers. Jacob was a grammarian who formulated Grimm's Law, a theory of linguistics relating Greek and Latin to German. Wilhelm was a literary scholar and critic. Together they spent most of their energies compiling a massive dictionary of the German language.

But it is as the authors of *Kinder und Hausmarchen (Children's and Household Tales)*, a work that has been called the best-known book after the Bible, that they are remembered. In 1812, the Grimms introduced the world to a cast of characters that included Cinderella, Hansel and Gretel, Little Red Riding Hood, Rapunzel, Rumpelstiltskin, Sleeping Beauty, Snow White, and other unforgettable stars of the world of make-believe.

The Fairy-tale Road leads through parts of West Germany in which the brothers lived and gathered and situated their tales; through the states of Hesse and Lower Saxony, to follow along the Fulda and Weser rivers via a string of highways and byways that lead through a countryside as beguiling as any in Europe.

Rivers flow past pastoral landscapes. Forests stretch off to infinity. Legendary castles tower against the sky. Here you can wander in forests where Red Riding Hood and Hansel and Gretel had their adventures and spend a night in the enchanted castle where Sleeping Beauty languished for a century before being awakened by a kiss.

Essential Information

Important Addresses and Numbers

Tourist Information Information on the Fairy-tale Road can be obtained from the **Deutsche Märchenstrasse** (Box 120420, Humboldstr. 26, 3500 Kassel, tel. 0561/100–3288). There are local tourist information offices in the following towns:

Bad Karlshafen. Kurverwaltung, 3522 Bad Karlshafen, tel. 05672/1022.

Bad Pyrmont. Kur-und-Verkehrsverein, Arkaden 14, 3280 Bad Pyrmont, tel. 05281/4627.

Bodenwerder. Städtische Verkehrsamt, Bruckenstrasse 7, 3452 Bodenwerder, tel. 05533/2560.

Fulda. Städtische Verkehrsbüro im Stadtschloss, 6400 Fulda, tel. 0661/102–345.
Göttingen. Fremdenverkehrsverein, Altes Rathaus, 3400 Göttingen, tel. 0551/54000.
Hanau. Verkehrsbüro, Altstädter Markt 1, 6450 Hanau, tel. 06181/252–400.
Hameln. Verkehrsverein, Deisterallee (am Bürgergarten), 3250 Hameln, tel. 05151/202–517.
Kassel. Tourist Information, Königsplatz, 3500 Kassel, tel. 0561/17159.
Münden. Verkehrsburo Naturpark Münden, 3510 Hannover Münden, tel. 05541/75313.
Steinau an der Strasse. Verkehrsamt, 6497 Steinau an der Strasse, tel. 06663/6336.

Travel Agencies **American Express,** Am Wall 138, Bremen, tel. 0421/14171.

Car Rental **Avis:** Kirchbachstrasse 200, tel. 0421/211–077, **Bremen;** Mainzer Landstrasse 170, tel. 069/230–101, **Frankfurt;** Drehbahn 15–25, tel. 040/341–651, **Hamburg.**
Europcar: Neuenland Airport, tel. 0421/553–737, **Bremen;** Mainzer Landstrasse 160, tel. 069/234–00204, **Frankfurt;** Spaldingstrasse 77–79, tel. 040/244–455 or 244–457, **Hamburg.**
Herz: Neuenland Airport, tel. 0421/555–350, **Bremen;** Hanauer Landstrasse 106–108, tel. 069/449–090, **Frankfurt;** Kirchenallee 34–36, tel. 040/280–1201, **Hamburg.**

Arriving and Departing by Plane

Frankfurt, Hanover, and Hamburg are the nearest airports to the area. Each is within an hour's drive or rail journey from one or more of the Fairy-tale Road's major centers. Frankfurt, for instance, is less than half an hour from Hanau, the start of the route. Hamburg is less than an hour from Bremen, the end of it.

Arriving and Departing by Bus

Long-distance Europabus services from Scandinavia through Germany to the Balkans call at Bremen, Kassel, and Göttingen. For information, timetables, and reservations, contact **Deutsche Touring GmbH.** (Am Römerhof 17, 6000 Frankfurt/Main 90, tel. 069/79030).

Getting Around

By Car Germany's Autobahn network penetrates deep into the area. Hanau, Fulda, Kassel, Göttingen, and Bremen are all served directly by autobahns. The Fairy-tale Road itself incorporates for part of its length one of Germany's loveliest scenic drives, the Wesertalstrasse, or Weser Valley Road, from Münden in the south to Hameln in the north.

By Train Fulda, Kassel, Göttingen, and Bremen are all on the Intercity network, with hourly connections to and from major German cities. All other centers and most of the smaller towns are connected by rail, supplemented by railroad buses.

By Bus Frankfurt, Kassel, Göttingen, and Bremen all have city bus services that extend into the countryside along the Fairy-tale Road.

By Boat From May through September two companies—**Oberweser-**

Dampfschiffahrt and **Weisse Flotte Warnecke**—operate daily services on the Weser River between Hameln, Bodenwerder, and Bad Karlshafen. On Monday, Wednesday, Friday, and Saturday, the Oberweser-Dampfschiffahrt boats sail as far as Münden, and on Tuesday, Thursday, Saturday, and Sunday, from Münden to Hameln. On the days when there is no service between Bad Karlshafen and Münden, a bus service ferries boat passengers between the two towns. For further information and bookings, contact **Oberweser-Dampfschiffahrt** (Inselstr. 3, 3250 Hameln, tel. 05151/22016) or **Weisse Flotte Wernecke** (Hauptstr. 39, 3250 Hameln, tel. 05151/3975, and on Weserstr., Bodenwerder, tel. 05533/4864).

Guided Tours

By Bus Erwin Radke's bus company in Oldendorf operates regular tours throughout the region. For details, contact **Erwin Radke** (Hesslingen 143, 3253 Hess. Oldendorf 19, tel. 05152/2172). Excursions are also offered by a Hameln company, **Rattenfänger-Reisen** (Bahnhofstr. 18/20, tel. 05151/108–491). Some local authorities—Bad Karlshafen, for example—also organize bus tours. Contact individual tourist offices for details.

By Boat The Oberweser-Dampfschiffahrt company and Warnecke's Weisse Flotte (White Fleet) operate summer services on the Weser River between Hameln and Münden (*see* Getting Around, above). Both companies will give you advice on how to combine a boat trip with a tour by bike, bus, or train. The Oberweser Dampfschiffahrt company also has a daily excursion from Hameln to the nearby Ohrberg Park and pleasure gardens: On Sunday afternoons it offers a 2½-hour "Kaffeereise" (coffee trip) on the river. From April through October, an excursion boat makes a four-hour trip daily up to the Fulda River from Kassel. It leaves the Altmarkt pier at 2 and returns at 6. The trip costs DM 13 adults, DM 8 children.

Exploring the Fairy-tale Road

Numbers in the margin correspond with points of interest on the Fairy-tale Road map.

Highlights for First-time Visitors

Schloss Philippsruhe
Steinau Castle and Amtshaus
Kassel's Stadtische Kunstsammlungen
Münden
The Sababurg
Hameln (Hamlin)

Hanau

The Fairy-tale Road begins in "once upon a time" fashion at a point you can reach only on foot—the brothers Grimm memori-
1 al in the Neustädter Marktplatz of **Hanau,** the little town where the brothers were born, Jacob in 1785, Wilhelm a year later.

The Fairy-tale Road

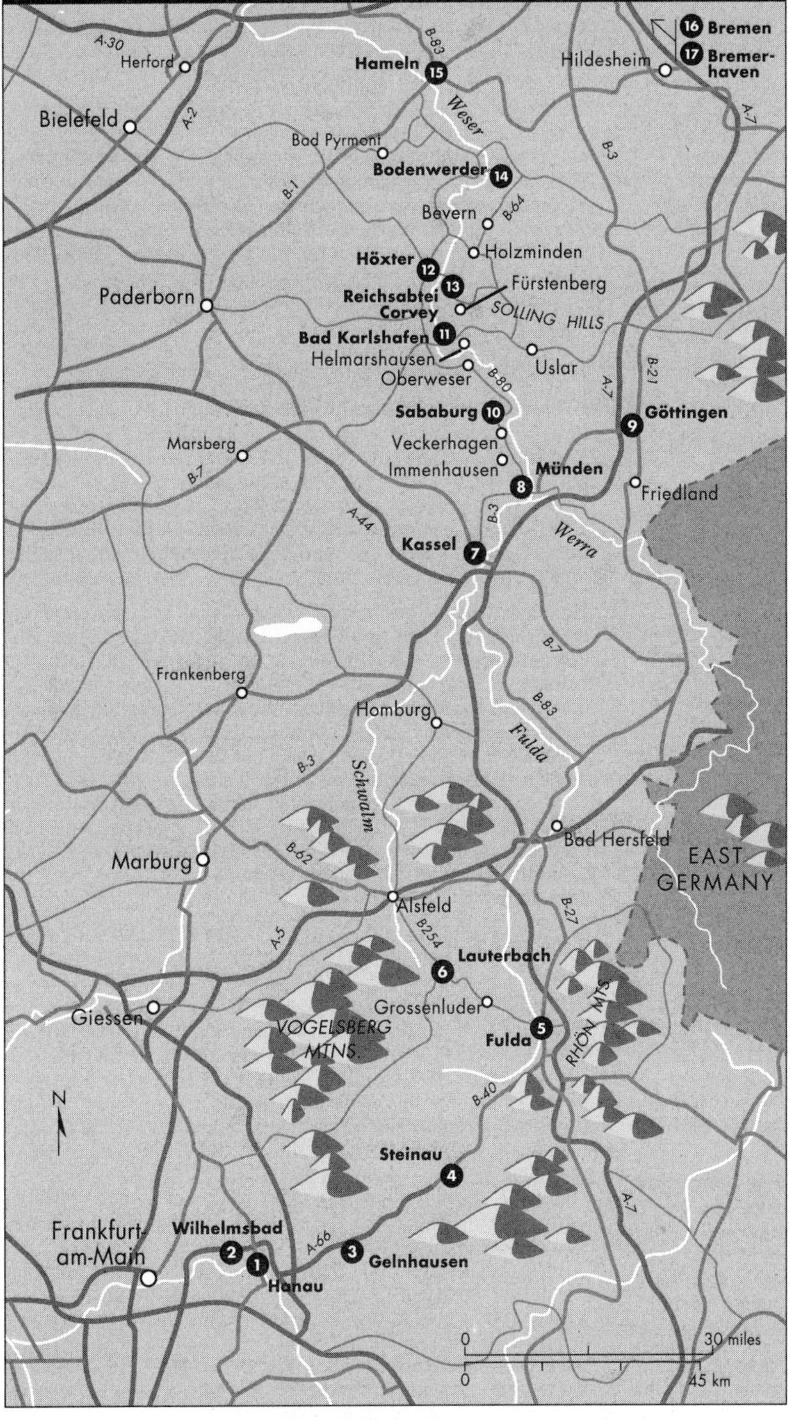

The bronze memorial, erected in 1898, is a larger-than-life-size statue of the brothers, one seated, the other leaning on his chair, the two of them deep in conversation, in a fitting pose for these scholars who unearthed so many medieval myths and legends, earning their reputation as the fathers of the fairy tale.

The degree to which the brothers have influenced the world's concept of fairy tales—those of the 1,001 Arabian Nights excepted—is remarkable. But it would be a mistake to imagine them as kindly, bewhiskered old gents telling stories in their rose-clad cottage for the pleasure of village children. As already mentioned, they were serious and successful academics, with interests ranging far beyond what we may think of as children's light amusements. Their stories probe deep into the German psyche and deal with far more complex emotions than suggested by the occasional "Happily ever after" endings, as witness the Stephen Sondheim–James Lapine musical *Into the Woods* based to a large extent on the Grimm works.

Behind the statue is the solid bulk of Hanau's 18th-century **Rathaus** (Town Hall). Every day at noon its bells play a tribute to another of the city's famous sons, the composer Paul Hindemith (1895–1963), by chiming out one of his canons. At 10 AM the carillon plays a choral composition; at 2 a minuet; and at 4 a piece entitled *Guten Abend* (Good Evening) rings out for the crowds hurrying across the Marktplatz to complete their shopping before returning home.

Hanau was almost completely obliterated by wartime bombing raids, and there's little of the Altstadt (Old Town) that the Grimm brothers would recognize now. Behind the Rathaus, however, is a corner that has been faithfully reconstructed. It's dominated by the **Altes Rathaus** (Old Town Hall), a handsome 16th-century Renaissance building, its two half-timbered upper stories weighted down by a steep slate roof. Today it's the home of the German goldsmiths' craft. Known as the **Deutsches Goldschmiedehaus** (German Goldsmiths' House), it contains a permanent exhibit and regular national and international displays of goldsmiths' and silversmiths' crafts. *Altstädter Markt 6. Admission charge depends on exhibit. Open Tues.–Sun. 10–noon and 2–5.*

You'll find various memorials and museums devoted to the brothers Grimm all along the Fairy-tale Road. For the first memorial, however, you have to head in another direction—to **Schloss Philippsruhe,** a palace on the banks of the Main River in the suburb of Kesselstadt (a 1 or 10 bus will take you there in 10 minutes). Schloss Philippsruhe has much more than Grimm exhibits to offer: It's the oldest French-style Baroque palace east of the Rhine. Philippsruhe may remind you of Versailles, although its French-trained architect, Julius Ludwig Rothweil, planned it along the lines of another palace in the Paris area, the much smaller Clagny palace. Philippsruhe—as its name, "Philipp's Rest," suggests—was built for Count Philipp Reinhard von Hanau. He didn't enjoy its riverside peace for long, however: He died less than three months after moving in. After the French builder Jacques Girard completed work on the palace, creating its very French appearance, the invading French confiscated it in 1803. Later Napoléon gave it as a present to his sister Pauline Borghese, who then put it up for sale. American forces took over Philippsruhe as a military quarters for a time in 1945, and until the postwar reconstruction of

Hanau was complete it served as the town hall. Every year on the first weekend of September, the palace grounds are invaded again—this time by the people of Hanau, for a great party to commemorate the rebuilding of their war-ravaged town. *Schloss Philippsruhe, Kesselstadt. Admission free. Open Tues.–Sun. 10–noon and 2–5.*

In the early 19th century, following the withdrawal of the French from Hanau, the original formal gardens were replanned as an informal, English-style park. You'll find the contrast between formal palace and informal wooded grounds striking. As you leave or enter, pause to study the entrance gate; the 19th-century gilding, made by Parisian masters, is real gold.

Time Out If the weather's fine, seek out a place beneath the white canvas sunshades on the palace terrace, now a café with a view over the Main River that was once enjoyed by Count Philipp Reinhard. In inclement weather head for the palace's bistro, with its open fire and hot, strong coffee.

2 Just north of Philippsruhe and a short bus ride from the center of Hanau is the city spa of **Wilhelmsbad.** It was built at the end of the 18th century by Crown Prince Wilhelm von Hessen-Kassel at the site where two peasant women, out gathering herbs, had discovered mineral springs. For a few decades Wilhelmsbad rivaled Baden-Baden as Germany's premier spa and fashionable playground. Then, about 100 years ago the springs dried up, the casino closed, and Europe's wealthy and titled looked for other amusements. But this is still Grimm fairy-tale land, and Wilhelmsbad, the sleeping-beauty spa, awoke from its slumber in the '60s to become a rejuvenated resort. The fine Baroque buildings and bathhouses were restored, parkland cleared and relaid in informal English style, riding stables opened, and one of Germany's loveliest golf courses laid out where the leisure classes once hunted pheasants.

3 Return to Hanau to rejoin the Grimm Fairy-tale Road, following B-43 about 20 kilometers (12 miles) northeast to **Gelnhausen.** Here on an island in the sleepy little Kinzig River are the remains of a castle that might well have stimulated the imaginations of the Grimm brothers in their travels in this area. Emperor Friedrich I—known as Barbarossa, or Red Beard—built the castle in this idyllic spot during the 12th century; in 1180 it was the scene of the first all-German Imperial Diet. Located on an island, the castle was hardly designed as a defensive bastion and was accordingly sacked in the Thirty Years' War. Today only parts of the russet walls and colonnaded entrance remain. Still, stroll beneath the castle's ruined ramparts on its watery site and you get a tangible impression of the medieval importance of the court of Barbarossa. *Follow the signs to Burg Barbarossa. Admission: DM 1 adults, 50 pf children. Castle open Mar.–Oct., Tues.–Sun. 10–1 and 2–5:30; Nov.–Feb., Tues.–Sun. 10–1 and 1–4:30.*

4 For clear evidence of the formative influence on the brothers Grimm, you need only travel another 20 kilometers (12 miles) along the Fairy-tale Road, to the little town of **Steinau**—full name Steinau an der Strasse (Steinau "on the road," referring to an old trade route between Frankfurt and Leipzig). Here fa-

ther Grimm served as local magistrate and the Grimm brothers spent much of their childhood.

Steinau dates from the 13th century and is typical of villages in the region. Marvelously preserved half-timbered houses are set along cobblestone streets; imposing castles bristle with towers and turrets. In its woodsy surroundings one can well imagine encountering Little Red Riding Hood, Snow White, or Hansel and Gretel.

The main street is named after the brothers; the building where paterfamilias was employed is now known as the "fairy-tale house." At the top of the town stands a castle straight out of a Grimm fairy tale. Originally an early medieval fortress, it was extended in Renaissance style and used by the counts of Hanau as their summer residence. It's not difficult to imagine the young Grimm boys playing in the shadow of its great gray walls, perhaps venturing into the encircling dry moat. They are certainly known to have loved splashing around in the spring-fed trough set into the northern section of the old town wall.

The fine, half-timbered, turreted house where the family resided is only a few hundred yards from the castle. Officially called the **Amthaus,** it now contains the tourist office and a museum of exhibits from the childhood of the brothers Grimm. *Open Mon.–Fri. 8–noon and 1–5. There's another, larger Grimm museum in the castle itself, the Grimm Museum im Schloss. Admission: DM 2 adults, DM 1 children. Open Mar.–Oct., Tues.–Sun. 10–11:30 and 1–4:30; Nov.–Feb., Tues.–Sun. 10–11 and 1–3.*

In front of the castle, in Steinau's ancient market square, Am Kumpen, is the Gothic church of **St. Catherine,** where the Grimm brothers' grandfather, Friedrich, was priest. Across the square, in the former stables of the castle, is a small puppet theater, **Die Holzkuppe,** where presentations of the Grimm fairy tales are staged. *Die Holzkuppe Marionettentheater. Call 06663/245 for program details.*

In the center of the square is a **Grimm memorial fountain.** It was built only in 1985, but its timeless design blends perfectly with the background provided by Steinau's 16th-century **Rathaus** (Town Hall). The six bronze figures you see on the white stucco facade of the Rathaus represent a cross section of 16th-century Steinau's population—from the builder who helped construct the town to the mother and child who continue its traditions.

With the Rhön mountains on your right, head north now on B-40 and leave the Fairy-tale Road for a detour to the ancient
5 episcopal city of **Fulda,** a treasure trove of Baroque architecture. Its grandest example is the immense **bishops' palace,** on Schlossstrasse, crowning the heights of the city. The great collection of buildings began as a Renaissance palace in the early 17th century and was transformed into its present Baroque splendor a century later by Johann Dietzenhofer. Much of the palace is now used as municipal offices but you can visit several of the former public rooms. The Fürstensaal (Princes' Hall) on the second floor provides a breathtaking display of Baroque decorative artistry, with ceiling paintings by the 18th-century Bavarian artist Melchior Steidl. Concerts are regularly held within its fabric-clad walls (contact the city tourist office in the palace for program details; tel. 0661/102–345). The palace also

has permanent displays of the Fayence porcelain for which Fulda was once famous, as well as some fine local glassware. *Schlossstr. Admission: DM 2 adults, DM 1 children. Open Mon.–Thurs. 10–12:30 and 2:30–5, Fri. 2:30–5, Sat.–Sun. 10–12:30.*

Pause at the windows of the great Fürstensaal to take in the view across the palace park to the **Orangery.** If you have time after your palace tour, stroll over for a visit. There's a pleasant café on the first floor.

Across the broad boulevard that borders the park you'll see the tall twin spires of the **Dom,** Fulda's 18th-century cathedral. The Dom was built on the site of an 8th-century basilica, which at the time was the largest church north of the Alps. The basilica had to be big enough to accommodate the ever-growing number of pilgrims from all parts of Europe who converged on Fulda to pray at the grave of the martyred St. Boniface, the "Apostle of the Germans." A black alabaster bas-relief depicting his death marks the martyr's grave in the crypt. The cathedral museum contains a document bearing his writing, along with several other treasures, including a fine 16th-century painting by Lucas Cranach that depicts Christ and the adulteress (who looks very comely in her velvet Renaissance costume). *Dom Museum, Dompl. Admission: DM 2 adults, DM 1.50 children. Open Apr.–Nov., Mon.–Fri. 10–5:30, Sat. 10–2, Sun. and holidays 12:30–5:30; Dec.–Mar., Mon.–Fri. 10–noon and 1:30–4, Sat. 10–2, Sun. and holidays 12:30–4.*

To one side of the cathedral you'll see one of Germany's oldest churches, the **Michaelskirche,** or Church of St. Michael, built in the 9th century along the lines of the Church of the Holy Sepulcher in Jerusalem. It has a harmony and dignity that match the majesty of the Baroque facade of the neighboring Dom.

From the Dom, head into the center of town, passing on your right the former guardhouse of the bishops' palace and on your left the 18th-century city parish church. Your goal is the Rathaus, about the finest Renaissance half-timbered town hall in this part of the country. The half-timbering, separating the arcaded first floor from the steep roof and its incongruous but charming battery of small steeples, is particularly delicate.

Kassel is the next major stop on the road north. If you're in a hurry, the quickest route is via Autobahn 7. But the Fairy-tale Road gives autobahns a wide berth, so take B-254 into the Vogelsberg mountains via Grossenluder to Lauterbach, some
6 25 kilometers (15 miles) northeast of Fulda. **Lauterbach,** a resort town of many medieval half-timbered houses, has not just one castle but two—the Riedesel and the Eisenbach—and a country palace besides—Schloss Hohhaus. The palace is the setting of one of the Grimm fairy tales, the one in which the Little Scallywag loses his sock. But the town's greatest claim to fame is its garden gnomes, turned out here by the thousands and exported all over the world. These ornaments are made in all shapes and sizes, from three inches to three feet tall, by the firm of Heissner Keramik. Several shops in Lauterbach sell the gnomes if you'd like to take one home with you.

The Fairy-tale Road continues north to **Alsfeld,** a medieval gem of a town composed primarily of great half-timbered houses. The four-story, towered town hall (built in 1512) is one of Germany's showpieces. Within its shadow stands a statue of

Little Red Riding Hood, who the town claims is a former resident.

From there the routing follows the little Schwalm River through a picturesque region so inextricably linked with the Grimm fairy tales that it's known as Rotkappchenland (Little Red Riding Hood country). On a side road, **Neustadt** is the home of the 13th-century circular tower from which Rapunzel supposedly let down her golden tresses. About 10 kilometers (6 miles) north is **Schwalmstadt,** the capital of the area. If you happen to be here on one of the town's many festival days, you'll see local people decked out in the traditional folk costumes that are still treasured in these parts.

Of passing interest is the fact that some 40 kilometers (25 miles) southwest, on the route 3 Kassel highway, is **Marburg,** where the Grimm brothers attended the university and began their folktale research.

Time Out At Homberg, 19 kilometers (12 miles) north of Schwalmstadt, stop at the 15th-century **Krone inn,** on the market square; it's the oldest guest house in Germany. Within its half-timbered walls you can eat and drink and dream of centuries past.

Some 40 kilometers (24 miles) north of Homberg you'll arrive at
7 the ancient city of **Kassel.**

Here the brothers Grimm worked as librarians at the court of the King of Westphalia, who was Jerome Bonaparte, Napoléon's youngest brother. The Grimms continued to collect stories and legends. Many French tales were recounted to them by Dorothea Viehmann, "the Fairy-tale Lady," who lived in the neighboring village of Baunatal.

In the center of Kassel, the **Brüder Grimm Museum** occupies five rooms of the Palais Bellevue, where the brothers once lived and worked. Exhibits include furniture, memorabilia, letters, manuscripts, and editions of their books, as well as paintings, aquarelles, etchings, and drawings by Ludwig Emil Grimm, a third brother and a graphic artist of note. *Palais Bellevue, Schöne Aussicht 2. Admission free. Open Tues.–Sun. 10–5.*

Although seldom included on tourist itineraries in the past, Kassel turns out to be one of the unexpectedly delightful cities of West Germany, full of contrasts and surprises. Much of its center was destroyed in World War II, and Kassel subsequently became the first German city to construct a traffic-free pedestrian downtown. The city has an unusually spacious and airy feel, due in large part to the expansive parks and gardens along the banks of the Fulda River. Today it is a major cultural center, with a vibrant theater and an internationally known arts festival.

Kassel's leading art gallery, the **Staatliche Kunstsammlungen** (State Art Collection), is one of Germany's best. It houses 17 Rembrandts, along with outstanding works by Rubens, Hals, Jordaens, Van Dyck, Dürer, Altdorfer, Cranach, and Baldung Grien. *Schloss Wilhelmshöhe. Admission free. Open Tues.–Sun. 10–5.*

The art gallery is located in part of the 18th-century **Wilhelmshöhe Palace,** which served as a royal residence from 1807 to 1813, when Jerome, Napoléon's brother, was king of Westphalia. Later, it became the summer residence of the German Emperor Wilhelm II. The great palace stands at the end of the 3-mile-long Wilhelmshöher Allee, an avenue that runs straight as an arrow from one side of the city to the other. Beyond the palace, the Wilhelmshöhe heights are crowned by an astonishing monument, a red-stone octagon bearing a giant statue of **Hercules,** built at the beginning of the 18th century. You can climb inside the octagon to the base of the Hercules statue. *Admission: DM 2 adults, DM 1 children. Open Tues.–Sun.*

From there, the view of Kassel spreads below you, bisected by the straight line of the Wilhelmshöher Allee. But that's only for starters: On Sundays and Wednesdays from mid-May through September, water gushes from a fountain beneath the Hercules statue, rushes down a series of cascades to the foot of the hill, and ends its precipitous journey on a 175-foot-high jet of water. It's a natural phenomenon, with no pumps. It takes so long to accumulate enough water that the sight can be experienced only on those two special days, on holidays, and, during the summer, on the first Saturday of each month, when the cascades are also floodlit. The no. 1 bus runs from the city to the Wilhelmshöhe. The no. 23 climbs the heights to the octagon and the Hercules statue. A café lies a short walk from the statue, and there are several restaurants in the area.

The Wilhelmshöhe was laid out as a Baroque park, its elegant lawns separating the city from the thick woods of the Habichtswald (Hawk Forest). It comes as something of a surprise to see the turrets of a romantic medieval castle, the **Löwenburg** (Lion Fortress), breaking the harmony. There are more surprises, for this is no true medieval castle but a fanciful mock-up built around the same time as the nearby Wilhelmshöhe Palace. The architect was a Kassel ruler who displayed an early touch of the mania later seen in the castle-building excesses of Bavaria's eccentric Ludwig II. The Löwenburg contains a collection of medieval armor and weapons, tapestries, and furniture. *Admission, including guided tour: DM 2 adults, DM 1 children. Open Mar.–Oct., daily 10–5; Nov.–Feb., daily 10–4.*

One other museum has to be included in this tour of Kassel. It's the **Deutsches Tapeten museum,** the world's most comprehensive museum of tapestry, with more than 600 exhibits tracing the history of the art through the centuries. *Brüder-Grimm-Pl. 5. Admission free. Open Tues.–Fri. 10–5, Sat.–Sun. 10–1.*

Leaving Kassel, follow B-3 16 kilometers (10 miles) north to
8 **Münden;** its official name is Hannoversch-Münden, but it is usually referred to by the contraction. Back in the 18th century the German geographer Alexander von Humbolt included Münden in his short list of the world's most beautiful towns (Passau, in eastern Bavaria, was another choice). You may just agree with him when you get here.

A 650-year-old bridge crosses the Weser River to lead into this old walled settlement that appears untouched by recent history—frozen in the dim and distant past, you might think. You'll have to travel a long way through Germany to find a grouping of half-timbered houses as harmonious as that in this beautiful old town, surrounded by forests and the Fulda and Werra rivers, which join and flow as the Weser River to Bremen and the North Sea.

Take your camera with you on a stroll down Langenstrasse; no. 34 is where the famous Dr. Eisenbarth died, in November 1727. The extraordinary doctor won a place for himself in German folk history as a result of his success both as a physician and as a marketplace orator; a quack who delivered what he promised! A dramatization of his life is presented in the summer in front of the medieval Rathaus. (Contact the Verkehrsbüro Naturpark Münden, 3510 Münden, tel. 05541/75313, for details.)

From Münden, you have the choice of following the Fairy-tale Road northward along the Weser River or making a short detour to another of the cities so closely associated with the
9 brothers Grimm: **Göttingen,** where they served as professors and librarians at the ancient university from 1830 to 1837.

The university appears to dominate every aspect of life in Göttingen, and there's scarcely a house more than a century old that doesn't bear a plaque linking it with a famous person who once studied or taught here. In one of the towers of the city's old defense wall, Otto von Bismarck, the "Iron Chancellor" and founder of the 19th-century German Empire, pored over his books as a 17-year-old law student. It looks like a romantic student's den now (the tower is open to visitors), but Bismarck was a reluctant tenant—he was banned from living within the city center because of "riotous behavior" and his fondness for wine. The taverns where Bismarck and his cronies drank are still there, all of them associated with Göttingen luminaries. Even the defiantly 20th-century Irish Pub has established itself within the half-timbered walls of a historic old house that once belonged to an 18th-century professor.

The strong link between the students and their university city is symbolized by a statue in the central market square. There stands the **Gänseliesel,** the little Goose Girl of German folklore, carrying her geese and smiling shyly into the waters of a fountain. Above her pretty head is a charming wrought-iron *Jugendstil* (German Art Nouveau) bower of entwined vines. The students of Göttingen contributed money toward the erection of the bronze statue and fountain in 1901, and they have given it a central role in a custom that has grown up around the university: Graduates who earn a doctorate traditionally give Gänseliesel a kiss of thanks. Göttingen says she's the most kissed girl in the world. There was a time, however, when the city fathers were none too pleased with this licentious boast, and in 1926 they banned the tradition. A student challenged the ban before a Berlin court but lost the case. Officially the ban still stands, although neither the city council nor the university takes any notice of it.

Directly behind the Gänseliesel is the Rathaus. It was begun in the 13th century but never completely finished. The result is the part-medieval, part-Renaissance building you see today. The bronze lion's-head knocker on the main door dates from early in the 13th century and is the oldest of its type in Germany. Step through the door, and in the lobby striking murals tell the city's story. The medieval council chamber served for centuries as the center of civic life. Within its painted walls and beneath its heavily beamed ceiling, the council met, courts sat in judgment, visiting dignitaries were officially received, receptions and festivities were held, and traveling theater groups performed.

In the streets around the town hall you'll find magnificent examples of Renaissance architecture. Many of these half-timbered, low-gabled buildings house businesses that have been there for centuries. The **Ratsapotheke** (pharmacy) across from the town hall is one; medicines have been doled out there since 1322.

A short stroll up the street on your left, Weenderstrasse, will bring you to the most beautiful shop front you're likely to find in all Germany: the 16th-century Schrödersches Haus. On the way, you'll pass the ancient student tavern Zum Szultenburger. Another tavern, Zum Altdeutschen, is around the corner on Prinzenstrasse (the street is named after three English princes, sons of King George III, who lived in a house here during their studies in Göttingen from 1786 to 1791). Don't be shy about stepping into either of these taverns, or any of the others that catch your eye: The food and drink are inexpensive, and the welcome invariably warm and friendly.

Back in Weenderstrasse, take note of the Sparkasse bank building. It was once the Hotel zur Krone, where King George V of Hannover had his headquarters in June 1866 before setting off for the fateful battle of Langensalza, where he lost his kingdom to Bismarck's warrior state of Prussia, soon to preside aggressively over the newly united Germany.

Behind Weenderstrasse, on Ritterplan, is Göttingen's only noble home, a 16th-century palace that is now the **Städtisches Museum** (City Museum). It has an instructive exhibition charting the architectural styles you'll come across in this part of Germany, as well as a valuable collection of antique toys and a reconstructed apothecary's shop. *Ritterplan. Admission free. Open Tues.–Fri. 10–1 and 3–5, Sat. and Sun. 10–1.*

Not far from the city, near Gleichen, outdoor performances of Grimm fairy tales are presented on a woodland stage at Bremke on certain summer weekends. Check with the local tourist office for dates.

To pick up the Fairy-tale Road where it joins the scenic Weser Valley road, return to Münden and head north on B-64. Ten kilometers (6 miles) north of Münden in the village of
10 Veckerhagen, take a left turn to the signposted **Sababurg.** You're now on the road to Dornröschen's, or Sleeping Beauty's castle. It stands just as the Grimm fairy tale tells us it did, in the depths of the densely wooded Reinhardswald, still inhabited by deer and wild boar. Sababurg was built as a 14th-century fortress by the archbishop of Mainz to protect a nearby pilgrimage chapel. Later, it was destroyed and then rebuilt as a turreted hunting lodge for the counts of Hessen. Today it is a fairly luxurious hotel. Even if you don't stay the night, a drive to the castle (it has an excellent restaurant) will be a highlight of any stay in this region.

From the castle, follow another road back to the Weser Valley riverside village of Oberweser. Turn left and take B-80 north. This is one of Germany's most haunting river roads, where the fast-flowing Weser snakes between green banks that hardly show where land ends and water begins. After some 13 kilometers (8 miles), you'll come to the Weser harbor town and spa of
11 **Bad Karlshafen.** From its inland harbor hundreds of German troops embarked to join the English Hanoverian forces in the

American War of Independence. George III, the English king who presided over the loss of the American colonies, was a Hanoverian—his grandfather, George I, spoke only German when he became king of England in 1715—and it was only natural that the people of Hanover should rally to the English cause in times of crisis. Flat barges took the troops down the Weser to Bremen, where they were shipped across the North Sea for the long voyage west. Many American families can trace their heritage to this small spa and the surrounding countryside.

Viewed from one of the benches overlooking the harbor, there's scarcely a building that's not in the imposing Baroque style. The grand Rathaus behind you is the best example. Bad Karlshafen stands out in solitary splendor amid its neighboring Weser Valley towns, whose half-timbered architecture has given rise to the expression "Weser Renaissance." You'll see examples of that style wherever you travel in this area, from Münden to Hameln (where it reaches a spectacular climax).

12 The Rathaus at **Höxter,** the next stop on the road north, is a picture-postcard-pretty example of the Weser Renaissance style, combining three half-timbered stories with a romantically crooked tower.

13 Across the river from Höxter lies **Reichsabtei Corvey** (the Imperial Abbey of Corvey), optimistically described by some as the "Rome of the North" and idyllically set between the wooded heights of the Solling region and the Weser. The 1,100-year history of the abbey is tightly bound up with the early development of German nationhood. It was chosen as the site of several sessions of the German Imperial Council in the 12th century, and in the 9th-century abbey church you can step into the lodge used by several Holy Roman Emperors. The composer of the German national anthem, Hoffmann von Fallersleben, worked for 14 years in the abbey's vast library, where, in the 16th century, the first six volumes of the annals of the Roman historian Tacitus were discovered. *Admission: DM 3.50 adults, DM 2 children. Open Mon.–Fri. 9–1 and 2–6, Sat. and Sun. 9–6.*

Follow the Weser River north another 33 kilometers (20 miles) and you'll reach a town that plays a central role in German popular literature,
14 **Bodenwerder,** the birthplace of the Lügenbaron ("Lying Baron") von Münchhausen. Münchhausen used to entertain friends with a pipe of rich Bremen tobacco, a glass of good wine, and stories of his exploits as a captain in wars against the Turks and the Russians. They were preposterous, unbelievable stories, which one of his friends, on the run from the German authorities, had published in England. From England they found their way back to Germany, and the baron became a laughingstock—as well as a famous figure in German literary history. The imposing family home in which he grew up is now the Rathaus; one room has been turned into the **Münchhausen Museum,** crammed with mementos of the baron's adventurous life. Included is a cannonball on which the baron claimed to have ridden into orbit during the Russo-Turkish War of 1736, flying around the Earth to reach the moon, or so he insisted. In front of the house you'll see a statue of Münchhausen in a scene from one of his most outlandish stories. He's riding half a horse; the other half, said Münchhausen, was chopped off by a castle portcullis, but he rode on without noticing the accident.

15 It's back to the Grimm trail that we return now, to **Hameln** (or Hamlin, to give the city its English name), the German town of Pied Piper fame. The story of the Pied Piper of Hameln had its origins in an actual event. In the 13th century an inordinate number of young men in Hameln were being conscripted to fight in an unpopular war in Bohemia and Moravia, so that citizens became convinced they were being spirited away by the Devil playing his flute. In later stories the Devil was changed to a gaudily attired rat catcher who rid the town of rodents by playing seductive melodies on his flute so that the rodents followed him willingly, waltzing their way right into the Weser. However, when the town defaulted on its contract with the piper and refused to pay up, the piper settled the score by playing his merry tune to lead Hameln's children on the same route he had taken the rats. As the children reached the river, the Grimms wrote, "they disappeared forever."

This tale is included in the Grimms' other book, *German Legends*. A variation of the story appears on the plaque of a 17th-century house at No. 28 Osterstrasse, fixing the date of the event as June 26, 1284. In more recent times, the Pied Piper tale has been immortalized via an ultramodern sculpture group set above a reflecting pool in a pedestrian area of town. Today, you'll find Hameln tied to its Pied Piper myth every bit as much, say, as the little Bavarian village of Oberammergau is dominated by its Passion Play. There are even rat-shaped pastries in the windows of Hameln's bakeries. The house that bears the Pied Piper plaque—a brilliant example of Weser Renaissance—is known as the Rattenfängerhaus, the rat catcher's house, despite the fact that it was built some time after the sorry story is said to have occurred. To this day, no music is played and no revelry of any kind takes place in the street that runs beside the house, the street along which the children of Hameln are said to have followed the piper.

The Rattenfängerhaus is one of several beautiful half-timbered houses on the central Osterstrasse. At one end is the Hochzeitshaus (Wedding House), now occupied by city government offices and a tourist information center. Every Sunday from mid-May to mid-September the story of the Pied Piper is played out at noon by actors and children of the town on the terrace in front of the building. The half-hour performance is free: Get there early to ensure a good place. The carillon of the Hochzeitshaus plays a "Pied Piper song" every day at 8:35 and 11:05, and mechanical figures enacting the story appear on the west gable of the building at 1:05, 3:35, and 5:35.

Time Out Just up the street is the historic old hostelry **Zur Krone.** If it's a sunny day, take a seat on the terrace in front of the hotel's half-timbered facade. If it's cool, there's a warm welcome inside.

Bremen

Although the influences that shaped the lives and the work of the Grimm brothers weaken north of Hameln, the Fairy-tale
16 Road continues as far as the great seaport of **Bremen,** a city that plays a central role in the delightful fable of the Bremer Stadtmusikanten, or Bremen Town Musicians, a rooster, cat, dog, and donkey quartet that came to Bremen to seek its fortune. You'll find statues of this group in various parts of the

city, the most famous being a handsome bronze of the four, one perched on the back of another, to form a pyramid of sorts. This statue stands alongside the northwest corner of the Rathaus on one of Europe's most impressive market squares, bordered by the Rathaus, an imposing 900-year-old Gothic cathedral, a 16th-century guild hall, and a modern glass and steel parliament building, with a high wall of gabled town houses as backdrop.

On the square stands the famous stone statue of the knight Roland, erected in 1400. Three times larger than life, the statue serves as Bremen's shrine, good-luck piece, and symbol of freedom and independence.

The ancient Rathaus is a structure of great interest, a Gothic building that acquired a Renaissance facade in the early 17th century. The two styles combine harmoniously in the magnificent, beamed banquet hall, where painted scenes from Bremen's 1,200-year history are complemented by model galleons and sailing ships that hang from the ceiling in vivid recollection of the place such vessels have in the story of the seafaring city. Bremen is West Germany's oldest and second-largest port—only Hamburg is bigger—and it has close historical seafaring ties with North America. Forty-eight kilometers
17 (30 miles) upriver, at **Bremerhaven,** is the country's largest and most fascinating maritime museum, the **Deutsches Schiffahrtsmuseum,** with a harbor containing seven genuine old trading ships. *Admission: DM 3 adults, DM 1.50 children. Open Apr.–Sept., Tues.–Sun. 10–6.*

Bremen, together with Lübeck and Hamburg, was an early member of the Hanseatic League, and its rivalry with the larger port on the Elbe is still tangible. Though Hamburg may still claim its historical title as Germany's "door to the world," Bremen likes to boast: "But we have the key."

Charlemagne established a diocese here in the 9th century, and a 15th-century statue of him, together with seven princes, adorns the Rathaus. In its massive vaulted cellars is further evidence of the riches accumulated by Bremen in its busiest years: barrels of fine, 17th-century Rhine wine. Other bounty from farther afield formed the foundation of one of the city's many fascinating museums, the **Übersee Museum,** a unique collection of items tracing the histories and cultures of the many peoples with whom the Bremen traders came into contact. One section is devoted to North America. *Bahnhofspl. 13. Admission: DM 2 adults, 50 pf children. Open Tues.–Sun. 10–6.*

Don't leave Bremen without strolling down Böttcherstrasse, a stretch of houses and shops reconstructed between 1924 and 1931 in historical exactitude at the initiative of a Bremen coffee millionaire, Ludwig Roselius. Walk, too, through the idyllic Schnoorviertel, a jumble of houses and shops once occupied by fishermen and tradespeople.

Shopping

Grimm-related souvenirs are to be found everywhere in this region, ranging from the cheap and vulgar to finely designed porcelain figures. Among the most popular gift ideas are bound editions of the brothers' fairy tales. The incredible tales of Baron Münchhausen make equally popular buys.

Kassel, Fulda, Göttingen, and Hameln all have attractive central pedestrian areas where it's a pleasure to shop for all manner of gift items. In Hannover, the place to shop is Georgstrasse and the streets around the reconstructed city hall, while in Bremen bargain-hunters make for the idyllic Schnoorviertel.

Germany's oldest **porcelain** factory is at Fürstenberg, high above the Weser River, halfway between Kassel and Hameln. The crowned gothic letter *F* that serves as its trademark is world famous. You'll find Fürstenberg porcelain in shops throughout the area, and in some of the towns (Bad Karlshafen and Höxter, for instance); Fürstenberg also has its own sales outlets. By far the most satisfactory way of starting a Fürstenberg collection, or adding to it, is to make the journey up to the 18th-century castle where production first began in 1747 and buy directly from the manufacturer. Fürstenberg and most dealers will take care of shipping arrangements and any tax refunds.

There are some excellent small, privately run **potteries** and **glassworks** in the area. In Bad Karlshafen, you can watch the craftsmen and craftswomen at work in a studio in the Baroque Rathaus and buy goods directly from them. Hans and Jutta Gess's studio at Helmarshausen, just outside Bad Karlshafen, is also well worth visiting. In the village of Immenhausen, just north of Kassel, you can visit a local glass foundry (the **Glashütte Süssmuth**) and watch glassblowers create fine works that are also for sale.

Sports and Fitness

Bicycling Bicycles can be rented from most railway stations for DM 10 a day (half that with a valid ticket) and from many tourist offices. The two Weser River excursion companies (*see* Guided Tours, above) take bikes aboard their boats and recommend routes that combine riverside cycle tours and boat trips.

Golf There are golf courses at Bad Orb, Bad Pyrmont, Fulda, Göttingen, Hanau, Kassel, and Polle-Holzminden; guests are welcome at all. There are also attractive courses at Hanau (on the former hunting grounds at Wilhelmsbad) and Kassel (high above the city on the edge of the Wilhelmshöhe park).

Hiking The hills and forests between Hanau and Hameln are a hiker's paradise. The valleys of the Fulda, Werra, and Weser rivers make enchanting walking country, with ancient waterside inns positioned along the way. Local tourist information offices of the area have established a hiking route from Münden in the south to Porta-Westfalica, where the Weser River breaks through the last range of north German hills and into the lower Saxony plain. Contact **Fremdenverkehrsverband Weserbergland-Mittelweser** (3250 Hameln, tel. 05151/202517) for information.

Riding This part of Germany is horse country, and most resorts have riding stables. There's a large and well-equipped equestrian center at Löwensen, near Bad Pyrmont (call 05281/10606 for information).

Water Sports Great canoeing can be enjoyed on both the Fulda and Weser rivers. For information on Fulda river trips and canoe rental, call

0561/22433. **Busch Bootstouristik** (3525 Oberweser, tel. 05574/818) rents canoes on the Fulda, Weser, and Werra and organizes trips of up to a week on all three rivers. Motorboats can be rented from **Weisse Flotte Warnecke** in Bodenwerder (tel. 05533/4864).

Dining and Lodging

Dining

If you are in the west of the region, try Westphalian ham, famous for more than 2,000 years. The hams can weigh as much as 33 pounds and are considered particularly good for breakfast, when a huge slice is served on a wood board with rich, dark pumpernickel bread baked for some 20 hours. If you're keen to do as the locals do, you'll wash it down with a glass of strong, clear Steinhäger schnapps. A favorite main course is *Pfefferpothast*, a sort of heavily browned goulash with lots of pepper. The "hast" at the end of the name is from the old German word *Harst*, meaning roasting pan. Rivers and streams filled with trout and eels are common around Hameln. Göttinger *Speckkuchen* is a heavy and filling onion tart. In Bremen, *Aalsuppe grün*, eel soup seasoned with dozens of herbs, is a must in summer.

Ratings Highly recommended restaurants in each price category are indicated by a star ★.

Category	Cost*
Very Expensive	over DM 90
Expensive	DM 55–DM 90
Moderate	DM 35–DM 55
Inexpensive	DM 20–DM 35

** per person for a three-course meal, including tax and excluding drinks and service.*

Lodging

Make reservations well in advance if you plan to visit in the summer. Though it's one of the less-traveled tourist routes in Germany, the main points of the Fairy-tale Road are popular. Accommodations cover the spectrum from modern high rises to ancient and crooked half-timbered buildings.

Ratings Highly recommended hotels in each price category are indicated by a star ★.

Category	Cost*
Very Expensive	over DM 180
Expensive	DM 120–DM 180
Moderate	DM 80–DM 120
Inexpensive	under DM 80

** for two people in a double room, excluding service charges.*

Bad Karlshafen
Dining

Gaststätte-Hotel Weserdampfschiff. You can step right from the deck of a Weser pleasure boat into the welcoming garden of this popular riverside hotel-tavern. Fish from the river land right in the tavern's frying pan. *Weserstr. 25, tel. 05672/2425. Dress: informal. No credit cards. Inexpensive.*

Bad Oeynhausen
Lodging
★

Romantik Hotel Hahnenkamp. This attractive, homey, half-timbered country house is known throughout the region for the huge collection of miniature cockerel figures from which it takes its name. *Alte Reichstr. 4 (on the Minden road), tel. 05731/5041. 20 rooms with bath or shower. Facilities: restaurant. AE, DC, MC, V. Closed Dec. 21–24. Expensive.*

Bevern
Dining

Enzianhutte. The Weser river winds lazily below this terraced restaurant. If it's too chilly to sit outside, there's a cozy room with an open fireplace. Some traditional dishes are cooked on the grill over the fire. *Am Ochsenbrink 2, tel. 05535/8710. Reservations advised. Dress: informal. AE, DC, MC. Closed Wed. Moderate.*

Bodenwerder
Dining

Restaurant Goldener Anker. You'll want to work up an appetite before tucking into the vast portions of regional specialties offered by the Golden Anchor. Sit on the terrace in the summer and enjoy the view over the Weser river. There are 12 inexpensive rooms if you fancy staying the night. *Weserstr. 13, tel. 05533/2135. Reservations advised. Dress: informal. No credit cards. Inexpensive.*

Lodging

Hotel Deutsches Haus. The fine half-timbered facade of this solidly comfortable country hotel vies for attention with the nearby former home of Baron Münchhausen, now Bodenwerder's town hall. The town park is outside the front door, and the Weser River is a short walk away. *Münchhausenpl. 4, tel. 05533/3925. 43 rooms with bath. Facilities: restaurant. AE, DC, MC, V. Moderate.*

Bremen
Dining
★

Deutsches Haus. Climb the stairs of this patrician house on the city's central Marktplatz and you'll find a restaurant of charm and culinary delights. Some claim it's Bremen's best fish restaurant, a coveted honor in Germany's oldest seaport. *Am Markt 1, tel. 0421/329–0920. Reservations advised. Dress: informal. AE, DC, V. Moderate.*

★ **Ratskeller.** Said to be Germany's oldest and most renowned Ratskeller restaurant, this one specializes in solid, typical North German fare, including the finest poultry and freshest seafood, prepared in ingenious ways. However, it's no place for beer drinkers. Shortly after the restaurant's foundation in 1408, the city fathers decreed that only wine could be served there, and the ban on beer still exists today. You dine in a cellar lined with wine casks, including an 18th-century barrel that could house a family of wine drinkers. Wine connoisseurs have 600 labels to choose from. *Am Markt, tel. 0421/329–0910. Reservations advised. Dress: informal. AE, DC, MC. Moderate.*

Friesenhof. This is the place if you want to try something local other than fish. Traditional meat dishes dominate the menu; portions are large. *Hinter dem Schütting 12–13, tel. 0421/321–661. Reservations advised. Dress: informal. No credit cards. Inexpensive.*

Lodging

Queen's Hotel Bremen. A recent acquisition of the British Queen's Moat Houses chain, this modern, functional hotel is located in the Neue Vahr district. There are fast, frequent bus links with the downtown. Public rooms were completely renovated in 1988. *August-Bebel-Allee 4, tel. 0421/23870. 141 rooms and 3 suites with bath or shower. Facilities: sauna, solarium. AE, DC, MC, V. Expensive.*

★ **Hotel Landhaus Louisenthal.** American visitors particularly like this family-run country-house hotel on the outskirts of Bremen—30% of its guests are from the United States. The 150-year-old building boasts old-world charm and a caring management. *Leher Heerstr. 105, tel. 0421/232–076. 58 rooms and 2 apartments, most with bath or shower. Facilities: sauna, solarium, restaurant. AE, DC, MC, V. Moderate.*

Fulda
Dining

★ **Dianakeller.** The bishops of Fulda used to keep their wine here, within the vaulted walls of what is now one of Fulda's finest restaurants, located in the Maritim Hotel am Schlossgarten. Candlelight flickers off those same ancient walls, now paneled and hung with historic pictures. *Paulusspromenade 2, tel. 0661/2820. Reservations advised. Jacket and tie required. AE, DC, MC, V. Moderate.*

Lodging

Maritim Hotel am Schlossgarten. This is the luxurious showpiece of the Maritim chain, housed in a spacious building overlooking Fulda palace park. Try for a room with a view of the park. Chandeliers, oil paintings, and antiques establish an elegant air. *Paulusspromenade 2, tel. 0661/2820. 112 rooms with bath. Facilities: restaurant, indoor pool, sauna, solarium, bowling alleys. AE, DC, MC, V. Expensive.*

★ **Romantik Hotel Goldener Karpfen.** Fulda is famous for its Baroque buildings, and this hotel is a short walk away from the finest of them. The hotel, too, dates from the Baroque era, but has a later facade. Inside, it has been renovated to a high standard of comfort. Afternoon coffee in the comfortable, tapestry upholstered chairs of the hotel's lounge is one of Fulda's delights. *Simpliciuspl. 1, tel. 0661/70044. 50 rooms with bath or shower. Facilities: restaurant, sauna, fitness room. AE, DC, MC, V. Expensive.*

Hotel Bachmühle. Once a mill, this comfortable, well-appointed hotel is on the outskirts of Fulda, a 20-minute walk from the town center. *Kunzellerstr. 133, tel. 0661/77800. Facilities: restaurant, 2 taverns. AE, MC, V. Moderate.*

Gelnhausen
Lodging

Hotel Burg Mühle. *Mühle* means mill, and this recently expanded and modernized hotel was once the tithe-mill of the neighboring castle. In the restaurant, the mill wheel churns away as you eat. *Burgmühle, tel. 06051/5005. 26 rooms with shower. Facilities: restaurant. AE, DC, MC, V. Expensive.*

Göttingen
Dining

Ratskeller. You dine here in the vaulted underground chambers of Göttingen's 15th-century city hall, choosing from a traditional menu with the friendly assistance of chef Michael Jansen. *Am Markt 9, tel. 0551/56433. Reservations advised. Dress: informal. AE, DC, MC, V. Moderate.*

★ **Zum Schwarzen Bären.** The "Black Bear" is one of Göttingen's oldest tavern-restaurants, a 16th-century half-timbered house that breathes history and hospitality. Specialty of the house is *Bärenpfanne*, a generous portion of local meats. *Kurzestr. 12, tel. 0551/58284. Reservations advised. Dress: informal. AE, DC, MC. Closed Mon. Inexpensive.*

Gebhards
Lodging

Gebhards Hotel. Though located just across a busy road from the train station, this hotel stands aloof and unflurried on its own grounds, a sensitively modernized fin-de-siècle building that's something of a local landmark. *Goethe-Allee 22–23, tel.*

0551/56133. 61 rooms, most with bath or shower. Facilities: restaurant, indoor pool. AE, DC, MC, V. Expensive.

Hotel Stadt Hannover. This modernized city villa, built around 1800, was the home of the pioneering 19th-century scientist Professor E. E. Berthold. The quiet atmosphere is as much like a private home as a hotel. *Goethe-Allee 21, tel. 0551/45957. 35 rooms, 20 with bath or shower. AE, DC, MC, V. Closed Dec. 20–Jan. 10. Moderate.*

Hotel Beckman Garni. The Beckman family runs this pleasant and homey hotel with friendly efficiency. The family takes particular pride in the hotel garden, a quiet and lush retreat in all seasons. The hotel is 3 miles out of town, with good bus links to downtown. *Ulrideshuser-Str. 44, Gottingen-Nikolausberg, tel. 0551/21055. 26 rooms, 18 with bath or shower. Facilities: neighboring rustic restaurant with bowling alley. DC, MC. Inexpensive.*

Hameln
Dining
★

Rattenfängerhaus. This is Hameln's most famous building, reputedly the place where the Pied Piper stayed during his rat-removing assignment. Rats are all over the menu, from "Rat-remover cocktail" to a "Rat-tail dessert." But don't be put off: The traditional dishes are excellent, and the restaurant is guaranteed to be rodent-free. *Osterstr. 28, tel. 05151/3888. Reservations advised. Dress: informal. AE, DC, MC, V. Inexpensive.*

Lodging
★

Hotel zur Kröne. If you fancy a splurge, ask for the split-level suite. At DM 240 a night, it's an expensive but delightful luxury. The building dates from 1645 and is a half-timbered marvel. Avoid the modern annex, however; it lacks all charm. *Osterstr. 30, tel. 05151/741. 35 rooms, 1 apartment, most with bath or shower. Facilities: restaurant. AE, DC, MC, V. Expensive.*

Dorint Hotel. This new, centrally located hotel is part of the chain of the same name, a guarantee of efficient service and comfort. *164er Ring, tel. 05151/7920. 103 rooms with bath or shower. Facilities: restaurant, indoor pool, sauna, solarium. AE, DC, MC, V. Moderate.*

Hotel zur Börse. Modern and centrally located, this hotel offers comfortable accommodations and friendly service. Its attractive winter garden is a pleasant retreat. *Osterstr. 41 (entrance on Kopmanshof), tel. 05151/7080. 34 rooms with shower. AE, DC, MC. Closed Christmas and New Year's Day. Moderate.*

Hanau
Lodging

Brüder Grimm Hotel. Located a few minutes' walk from the Brüder Grimm memorial in Hanau's central market square, the hotel that carries their name has a fairy-tale restaurant on the top floor. Accommodations are modern and comfortable. Try for the "Eckzimmer"; it's the largest and best-decorated room. *Kurt-Blaum-Pl. 6, tel. 06181/3060. 80 rooms and 15 apartments with bath or shower. Facilities: sauna, whirlpool. AE, DC, MC, V. Moderate.*

Höxter
Dining
★

Schlossrestaurant Corvey. Two miles south of the charming town of Höxter lies Corvey Abbey, whose attractions include an excellent restaurant. You can dine outside under centuries-old trees in summer and before a blazing hearth in winter. The lunchtime menu is a particularly good value. *Reichsabtei Corvey, tel. 05271/8323. Weekend reservations advised. Dress: informal. AE, DC, MC, V. Closed Feb. Moderate.*

Kassel
Dining

Die Pfeffermühle. The "Peppermill" is in Kassel's Gude Hotel, but it's no conventional hotel restaurant. The menu is truly international: Indian and Russian dishes share space with traditional German fare. *Frankfurterstr. 299, tel. 0561/48050. Reservations advised. Dress: informal. AE, DC, MC, V. Closed Sun. evening. Moderate.*

Ratskeller. You eat here within the embracing surroundings of cellar vaults. If you're lucky, you'll call when owner-chef Robert Kuhn is holding one of his "specialty" weeks. *Obere Konigstr. 8, tel. 0561/15928. Reservations advised. Dress: informal. AE, DC, MC, V. Inexpensive.*

Lodging **Moat House Hotel.** Formerly the Holiday Inn, the Moat House (run by a British chain) retains the modern features and comforts of its predecessor. It's located 3 miles from downtown, at the Kassel-east Autobahn exit. Convenience, not charm, is the reason to stay here. *Heiligenröderstr. 61, tel. 0561/52050. 141 rooms with bath. Facilities: restaurant, indoor pool, sauna, solarium. AE, DC, MC, V. Expensive.*

Schlosshotel Wilhelmshöhe. Set in the beautiful Baroque Wilhelmshöhe park, this is no ancient palace but a modern hotel with its own sports center. *Schlosspark 2, tel. 0561/30880. 100 rooms with bath. Facilities: restaurant, indoor pool, whirlpool, sauna, solarium; tennis, golf, and riding stables all in immediate vicinity. DC, MC, V. Moderate.*

Sababurg
Lodging
★

Burghotel Sababurg. A medieval fortress thought to have been the inspiration for the brothers Grimm's tale of The Sleeping Beauty, this is now a small luxury hotel snugly set in the castle walls and surrounded by the oaks of the Reinhardswald. You need a car to reach it, but even the drive is an experience to be remembered. *3520 Hofgeismar, tel. 05678/1052. 15 rooms with bath. Facilities: restaurant. No credit cards. Expensive.*

Steinau an der Strasse
Lodging
★

Burgmannenhaus. If you value atmosphere and history you'll find it hard to dislike this little hotel. It was formerly the home of a city official and comes complete with crooked roofs, sloping floors, leaded windows, and flower-filled window boxes. Be sure to make reservations well in advance. *Brüder-Grimm-Str. 49, tel. 06663/6539. 5 rooms with bath. Facilities: restaurant. No credit cards. Moderate.*

Uslar
Dining
★

Romantik Hotel Menzhausen. The half-timbered exterior of this 16th-century establishment is matched by the cozy interior of its comfortable, well-appointed restaurant. The 400-year-old wine cellar harbors outstanding vintages, served with reverence at excellent prices. The hotel itself has 29 well-appointed rooms, many with antiques. *3418 Uslar, tel. 05571/2051. Weekend reservations advised. Dress: informal. AE, DC, MC. Expensive.*

The Arts and Nightlife

The Arts

Music **Bremen** has a Philharmonic orchestra of national stature. It plays regularly throughout the year at the city's concert hall; call 0421/36361 for program details and tickets. In **Fulda,** chamber-music concerts are given regularly from September through May in the chandelier-hung splendor of the bishops' palace; call 0661/102–326 for program details and tickets. **Göttingen's** symphony orchestra presents about 20 concerts a year. In addition, the city has a nationally known boys' choir and an annual Handel music festival in June. Call 0551/56700 for program details and tickets for all three. In **Kassel,** outdoor concerts are held in Wilhelmshöhe Park on Wednesday, Saturday, and Sunday afternoons from May through September. Classical-music concerts are also given by the city's municipal orchestra in the Stadttheater; call 0561/10940 for program details and tickets.

Theater **Bremen** has three theaters that regularly stage classical and modern dramas, comedies, and musical comedies: the Schauspielhaus; the Concordia; and the Musiktheater. Call 0421/36361 for program details and tickets. In **Fulda,** one wing of the magnificent bishops' palace is now the city's main theater; call 0661/102–326 for program details and tickets. **Göttingen's** two theater companies—the 100-year-old Deutsche Theater and the Junge Theater—are known throughout Germany; call 0551/496–911 for program details and tickets. **Hameln's** main theater, the Weserbergland Festhalle (Rathauspl. tel. 0515/3747), has a regular program of drama, concerts, opera, and ballet from September through June; call for program details and tickets. **Kassel** has no fewer than 35 theater companies. The principal venues are the Schauspielhaus, the Tif-Theater, the Stadthalle, and the Komödie. Call 0561/15853 for program details and tickets for all.

Nightlife

Bremen may be Germany's oldest seaport, but it can't match Hamburg for racy nightlife. Nevertheless, the streets around the central Marktplatz and in the historic Schnoor district are filled with atmospheric taverns and bars of various kinds. In **Göttingen** the ancient student taverns that crowd the downtown area are the focus of local nightlife, but for something more sophisticated try the Flair Club (Reinhauser Landstr.). **Kassel** is disco city. The Jet Set (Untere Königstr.) and Jenseits von Eden (Untere Königstr.) are two to try. New York (Obere Königstr.) is another favorite.

15 Hamburg

Introduction

Until not so very long ago Hamburg could have been considered Germany's best-kept secret, virtually ignored by the streams of foreign visitors to the Federal Republic whose itineraries invariably included the Rhine, the Romantic Road, and Munich.

Of late this has been changing, as repeat visitors to Germany move further afield from the tried and true routings of the past. And yet Hamburg still has something of an image problem. Mention of the city invariably triggers thoughts of the gaudy night world of the Reeperbahn, that sleazy strip of clip joints, sex shows, and wholesale prostitution. With reputedly the Continent's most wicked after-dark diversions, the Reeperbahn has helped make Hamburg Europe's "sin city" supreme. But to those who know Hamburg, the Reeperbahn's presence could be considered an indication of the city's prevailing live-and-let-live attitude, part and parcel of the dramatic diversity and apparently irreconcilable contradictions that make up this fascinating port.

Hamburg is both a city and a state. Its official title—the Free and Hanseatic City of Hamburg—refers to its status as an international trading post dating from the Middle Ages. For hundreds of years Hamburg ranked as Europe's leading port, yet it is situated 100 kilometers (62 miles) from the sea.

Hamburg gained world renown as the kingpin of the Hanseatic League, that medieval mafia of north-German merchant cities that banded together to dominate shipping in the Baltic and the North Sea, with trading satellites set up in Bergen, Visby, Danzig, Riga, Novgorod, and other points of the compass.

Between the 12th and 16th centuries Hamburg and her sister cities held a virtual monopoly on trade in this part of Europe. But it was only after the demise of the Hansa that Hamburg arrived at the crest of its power.

During the 19th century the largest shipping fleets on the seas, with some of the fastest ships afloat, were based here; tentacles of shipping lanes reached to the far corners of the Earth. Ties to New York, Buenos Aires, and Rio de Janeiro were stronger than those to Berlin or Frankfurt. During the four decades leading up to World War I, Hamburg became one of the world's richest cities. Its aura of wealth and power was projected right up to the outbreak of World War II, and even today it shows.

The miracle of present-day Hamburg is that in spite of having been virtually wiped off the map by the 1940–1944 bombing raids it now stands as a remarkably faithful replica of that glittering prewar city. In what surely must rank as the most successful reconstruction of any major German city, Hamburg is once again a place of enormous style, verve, and elegance—what many regard as the only truly cosmopolitan metropolis in the Federal Republic, even though its image might suggest otherwise.

Situated at the mouth of the Elbe, one of Europe's great rivers and the 60-mile-long umbilical cord that ties the harbor to the North Sea, Hamburg is still one of Europe's busiest ports. Each year some 15,000 ships sail up the lower Elbe carrying more than 50 million tons of cargo—from petroleum and locomotives to grain and bananas.

Hamburg, or "Hammaburg," was founded in 810 by Charlemagne. For centuries it was, of course, a walled city, its gigantic outer fortifications making for a tight little world that remained relatively impervious to outside influences. The Thirty Years' War passed it right by. Napoleon's domination of much of the Continent in the early 19th century hardly touched Hamburg. However, the Great Fire of 1842 all but obliterated the original city; a century later World War II bombing raids destroyed port facilities and leveled more than half of the city proper. So what you see today is the "new" Hamburg, with some Old World touches, and a handsome place it turns out to be.

The distinguishing feature of downtown Hamburg is the Alster. Once an insignificant waterway, it was dammed during the 18th century to form an artificial lake. Divided at its southern end, it is known as the Binnenalster (Inner Alster) and the Aussenalster (Outer Alster), the two separated by a pair of graceful bridges, the Lombardsbrucke and the John F. Kennedy Brucke. The Inner Alster is lined with stately hotels, department stores, fine shops, cafés; the Outer Alster is framed by the spacious greenery of parks and gardens against a backdrop of private mansions.

From late spring into fall, sailboats and Windsurfers skim across the surface of the Outer Alster. White passenger steamers zip back and forth. The view from one of these vessels (or from the shore of the Outer Alster) is of the stunning skyline of six spiny spires (five churches and the Rathaus) that is Hamburg's identifying feature. It all makes for one of the most distinctive and appealing downtown areas of any European city.

Sometimes called a "Venice of the North," the city is threaded with countless canals and waterways, spanned by some 2,000 bridges. Swans glide on the canals. Arcaded passageways run along the waterways. In front of the renaissance-style Rathaus is a square that resembles the Piazza San Marco. So the allusion to Venice is not totally frivolous.

But what truly distinguishes Hamburg from most other cities is the extent of greenery at its heart. Almost half its area is devoted to either agriculture or parkland. This fondness for growing things has been a dominant treasure of Hamburg for centuries. In the 16th century anyone caught chopping down a tree was sentenced to death! Even today, conservation remains high on the agenda at the Rathaus (Town Hall). Every new-building proposal must provide for enough green space to ensure the continued ecological balance of the city.

Hamburg is endowed with considerable architectural diversity. Of particular interest are the 14th-century houses of Deichstrasse—the oldest residential area in Hamburg—and the Kontorhausviertel (literally, "Business House Quarter").

The latter contains some unique clinker-brick buildings from the '20s. A variety of turn-of-the-century Jugendstil (German Art Nouveau) buildings can also be found in various parts of the city. Of course, as in most German cities, high rises are much in evidence. A few project a certain grace and style, others are merely functional and undistinguished.

Anyone accustomed to the *Gemütlichkeit* (conviviality) and jolly camaraderie of Munich should be advised that Hamburg on initial exposure presents a more somber face.

Hamburgers are staunchly conservative in dress and demeanor and liberal in politics. Members of the merchant elite are extremely status-conscious, yet not inclined to put on airs. People here are reputed to be notoriously frugal on the one hand, generous hosts on the other, with a penchant for indulging their tastes for the most refined delicacies. The city has an inordinate number of attractive women, as stylishly turned out (in an understated way) as those in Paris or Rome. In a city that vibrates with energy, the people work hard and play hard, and turn out to be friendlier than they may appear at first. You might say they are cool on the outside, warm inside.

Apart from the museums and sights, there is much by way of entertainment: world-famous opera, renowned ballet, operettas, three symphony orchestras, several concert stages, and some 20 theaters, including one of the last of Germany's old-fashioned variety theaters.

The restaurants here offer some of Germany's finest food. For those who can afford the fairly steep prices of the shops therein, there are no fewer than nine attractive glass-roofed shopping malls. Bars and cafés abound. Discos are very big. Hamburg has what may well be the most active live-music scene in Europe, with pop, rock, folk, and Dixieland and modern jazz all competing for your attention. For a time the city was known as "New Orleans on the Elbe," because some 60 resident bands were playing old-time jazz, or a reasonable facsimile thereof. It was in Hamburg that the Beatles had their first major success, propelling them on the road to fame and fortune.

Last but not least, for those who prefer entertainment of a more red-blooded form, there is the infamous Reeperbahn in St. Pauli, near the harbor, with reputedly the raunchiest red-light district in Europe. St. Pauli is an area that caters to all tastes and predilections. Whatever your choice, either as spectator or participant, you can get it here.

While some visitors might consider St. Pauli the real heart and soul of Hamburg, those who live in the city take a different view. For them, the Reeperbahn is simply an extension of the mercantile concept; sex is a commodity with a price tag. Once, all major seaports around the world offered similar services and entertainment to sailors who came off ships after weeks or months at sea. Hamburg is probably the only European port still operating on such a grand scale. While the Reeperbahn is an unusual tourist attraction, you'll find few Hamburg residents there. Caveat emptor!

Essential Information

Important Addresses and Numbers

Tourist Information The main branch of the tourist office is the **Tourismus Zentrale Hamburg** (Burchardstr. 14, tel. 040/300–510). It's open Monday–Friday 7:30 AM–6 PM, Saturday 7:30 AM–3 PM. In addition to its comprehensive hotel guide, the tourist office also publishes a monthly program of events in the city, *Hamburg*

Vorschau, available for DM 2.30, which details upcoming shows, plays, movies, and exhibits. The illustrated magazine *Hamburg Tip* is issued quarterly and details major seasonal events; the cost is 50 pfennigs.

Other tourist offices include **Tourist Information im Bieberhaus** (Hachmannplatz, tel. 040/3005–1245. Open Mon.–Fri. 7:30 AM–6 PM, Sat. 8 AM–3 PM). It's located just outside the main train station. There's also a tourist office in the **station** (tel. 040/300–51230); it's open daily 8 AM–11 PM. The **airport tourist office** (tel. 040/300–51240) is open the same hours. At the harbor, there's an office at the **St. Pauli Landungsbrücken** (boat landings); it's open daily 9–6 (tel. 040/300–51200). There's also an office in the **Hanse Viertel** shopping mall, open weekdays 10–6:30 (Thurs. 10–9), Saturday 10–3 (10–9 on the first Sat. of the month); tel. 040/300–51220.

All offices can help with accommodations. A DM 5 fee is charged for every room reserved; the cost is then deducted when you pay the hotel.

Consulates **U.S. Consulate General,** Neuer Jungfernstieg 6a, tel. 040/411–710. **British Consulate General,** Hervestehuder Weg 8a, tel. 040/446–071.

Emergencies **Police:** tel. 110. **Ambulance** and **Fire Department:** tel. 112. **Medical Emergencies:** tel. 040/228–022. **Dentist:** tel. 040/468–3260.

English-Language Bookstore **Frensche** (Spitalerstrasse 26e, tel. 040/327–585) stocks books and newspapers.

Travel Agencies **American Express,** Rathausmarkt 5, tel. 040/331–141.

Car Rental **Avis,** Drehbahn 15–25, tel. 040/341–651. **Hertz,** Amsinckstrasse. 45, tel. 040/230–045.

Arriving and Departing by Plane

Hamburg's international airport, **Fulsbüttel,** is 11 kilometers (7 miles) northwest of the city. All major U.S. airlines fly to Hamburg; there are also regular flights from Britain. There are frequent flights from other major German cities.

Between the Airport and Downtown An **Airport-City-Bus** runs between the airport and Hamburg's Hauptbahnhof (main train station) daily at 20-minute intervals. Buses stop on the way at the hotels Reichshof, Atlantic, and Hamburg-Plaza and at the fairgrounds. Buses run from 6:30 AM to 10:30 PM. Tickets are DM 3.10 adults, DM 1.10 children. The **Airport-Express** (bus no. 110) runs every 10 minutes between the airport and the Ohlsdorf U- and S-bahn station, a 15-minute ride from the main train station. The fare is the same as above. A taxi from the airport to the downtown area will cost about DM 25. If you're picking up a rental car at the airport, follow the signs to "Stadtmitte" (downtown).

Arriving and Departing by Train, Bus, and Car

By Train Euro-City and Intercity trains connect Hamburg with all German cities and many major European cities. There are two principal stations: the centrally located **Hauptbahnhof** and **Hamburg-Altona,** located west of the downtown area. For information, call 040/19419 for the main station, and 040/39181 for Hamburg-Altona.

By Bus The ZOB, or **Zentral-Omnibus-Bahnhof,** Hamburg's bus station, is located right behind the Hauptbahnhof (Adenauerallee 78). For information call 040/247–575, or contact the **Deutsche Touring-Gesellschaft** in Frankfurt, (Am Römerhof 17, tel. 069/7931).

By Car Hamburg is rather easier to handle by car than many other German cities, and relatively uncongested by traffic. Incoming autobahns connect with Hamburg's three beltways, which then take you easily to the downtown area. Follow the signs for "Stadtmitte."

Getting Around

On Foot The historic center of Hamburg can be explored easily on foot. The downtown area's Binnenalster and Jungfernstieg, many shopping streets and shopping galleries, and harbor are all close enough to make walking easy.

By Public Transportation The HVV, Hamburg's public-transportation system, includes the **U-bahn** (subway), the **S-bahn** (suburban train), and **buses.** A one-way fare is DM 3.10 adults, DM 1.10 children, and tickets are available on all buses and at the automatic machines in all stations and at most bus stops. An **all-day ticket** (Tageskarte) valid from 9 AM to 9 PM costs DM 6 for unlimited rides on the HVV system. A **tourist ticket** runs until 4:30 AM and costs DM 11.20 (DM 7.20 children). If you're traveling with family or friends, a **group or family ticket** (Gruppen- od. Familienkarte) is a good value; a group of up to four adults and three children can travel around for the whole day for only DM 10.50.

In the north of Hamburg, the HVV system connects with the **A-bahn** (Alsternordbahn), a suburban train system that extends into Schleswig-Holstein.

Night buses (nos. 600–640) serve the downtown area all night, leaving the Rathausmarkt and Hauptbahnhof every hour.

Information on the HVV system can be obtained directly from the **Hamburg Passenger Transport Board** by calling 040/322–911 (open daily 7 AM–8 PM).

By Taxi Taxi meters start at DM 3, and the fare is DM 1.60 per kilometer, plus 50 pfennigs for each piece of luggage. To order a taxi, call 040/441–011.

By Bike Most major streets in Hamburg have paths reserved for bicyclists. From May through September, rent bikes at the tourist information office in Bieberhaus, outside the main train station. Prices range from DM 2 per hour to DM 20 for the whole weekend. For information, call 040/300–51245.

Guided Tours

Orientation Tours The tourist office organizes bus tours of the city, all with English-speaking guides. The tours leave from Kirchenallee by the main train station, across from the Hotel Phoenix. May through November, there's a two-hour city tour taking in all the main sights in the downtown area. Departures are at 9, 11, 3, and 4; cost is DM 18 adults, DM 9 children under 14. December through April, tours leave at 2 only. A longer tour (it lasts 2½ hours) also visits parts of the harbor, the new tunnel under the Elbe, and the Elbchaussee. Departures are at 10 and 2 May

Hamburg Underground

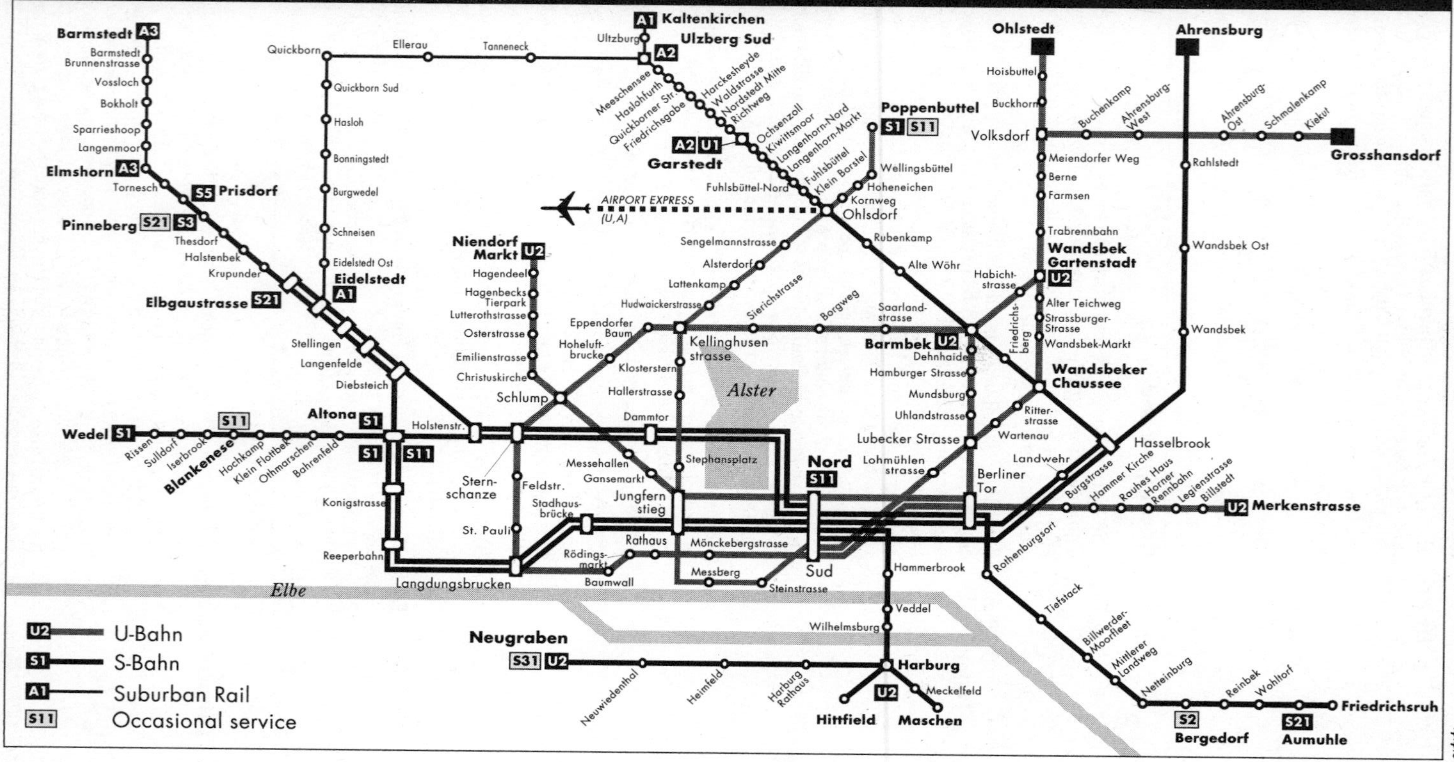

through November, and at 2 only December through April; cost is DM 22 adults, DM 11 children under 14. A combination city tour and boat tour of the harbor departs at 9, 11, 3, and 4 May through November and at 2 December through April; cost is DM 23 adults, DM 12 children under 14.

Walking Tours Tours of the downtown area are organized by the **Museum für Arbeit.** They are held weekends only, May through September. Call 040/298–42364 for information.

Boat Tours Water dominates Hamburg, and there are few better ways to get to know the city than a trip around the massive harbor. Mid-March through November, there are daily one-hour tours, with English-speaking guides, at 11, leaving from pier 1 on the Landungsbrücken. Cost is DM 14 adults, DM 7 children. December through mid-March, tours can be set up in advance only. For information on all harbor tours, call 040/564–523.

The **Alstertouristick** company offers two-hour tours of Hamburg's **canals** every 40 minutes between 9:45 and 5:15. Cost is DM 15 adults, DM 7 children. Call 040/341–14541 for information.

Nighttime cruises around the harbor, with dinner and dancing, are offered Saturdays at 8 PM. The cost is around DM 50, depending on what you eat. Call 040/313–687 for information. A more lavish nighttime cruise around the harbor—it lasts four hours and features a six-course meal, served in 16th-century style—is also offered. Departures for both types of cruise are from pier 6. Call 040/220–2552 for information and reservations.

Hamburg by Night The tourist office offers tours of city hot spots on Fridays and Saturdays at 8 PM. Tours last three hours and include visits to a number of bars, including the Bierhaus Zillertal on the Reeperbahn. Cost is DM 50. A marginally more raunchy offering is the "Hamburg for Adults Only" tour, a four-hour hike around the St. Pauli district that also takes in a sex show. Cost, including three drinks, is DM 80. If you want a taste of Hamburg's no-holds-barred nightlife but don't want to head out on your own, this is a reasonable introduction.

Exploring Hamburg

Numbers in the margin correspond with points of interest on the Hamburg map.

Highlights for First-time Visitors

Alter Botanische Garten (Old Botanical Gardens)
Hauptbahnhof
Michaelis Kirche
Reeperbahn
Fischmarkt (Fish Market)

Downtown Hamburg

1 Your tour begins at **Dammtor** train station, an elevated steel and glass Jugendstil structure built in 1903. Recently renovated, it is one of many Art Nouveau buildings you'll see during your stay in Hamburg. Pick up a detailed city map from the first-floor Booking Hall. Turn left out of the station and head toward the Congress Centrum Hamburg (CCH), a vast, mod-

Hamburg

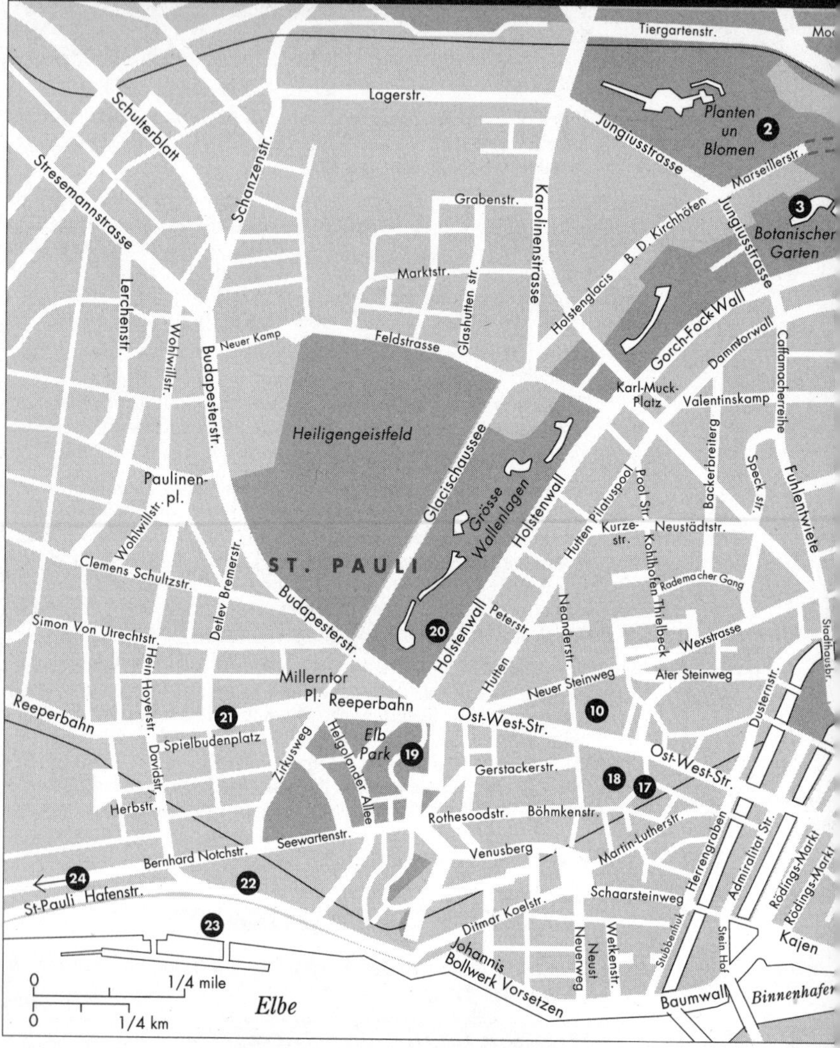

Alter Botanischer Garten, **3**
Bismarckdenkmal, **19**
Blankenese, **24**
Chilehaus, **12**
Dammtor, **1**
Deichstrasse, **15**
Fischmarkt, **22**
Hauptbahnhof, **7**
Jacobikirche, **10**
Jungfernstieg, **4**
Katherinenkirche, **13**
Kontorhausviertal, **11**
Krameramts-wohnungen, **17**
Kunsthalle, **8**
Landungsbrücken, **23**
Michaeliskirche, **18**
Mönckebergstrasse, **6**
Museum für Hamburgische Geschichte, **20**
Museum für Kunst und Gewerbe, **9**
Nikolaikirche, **16**
Planten un Blomen, **2**
Rathaus, **5**
Reeperbahn, **21**
Speicherstadt, **14**

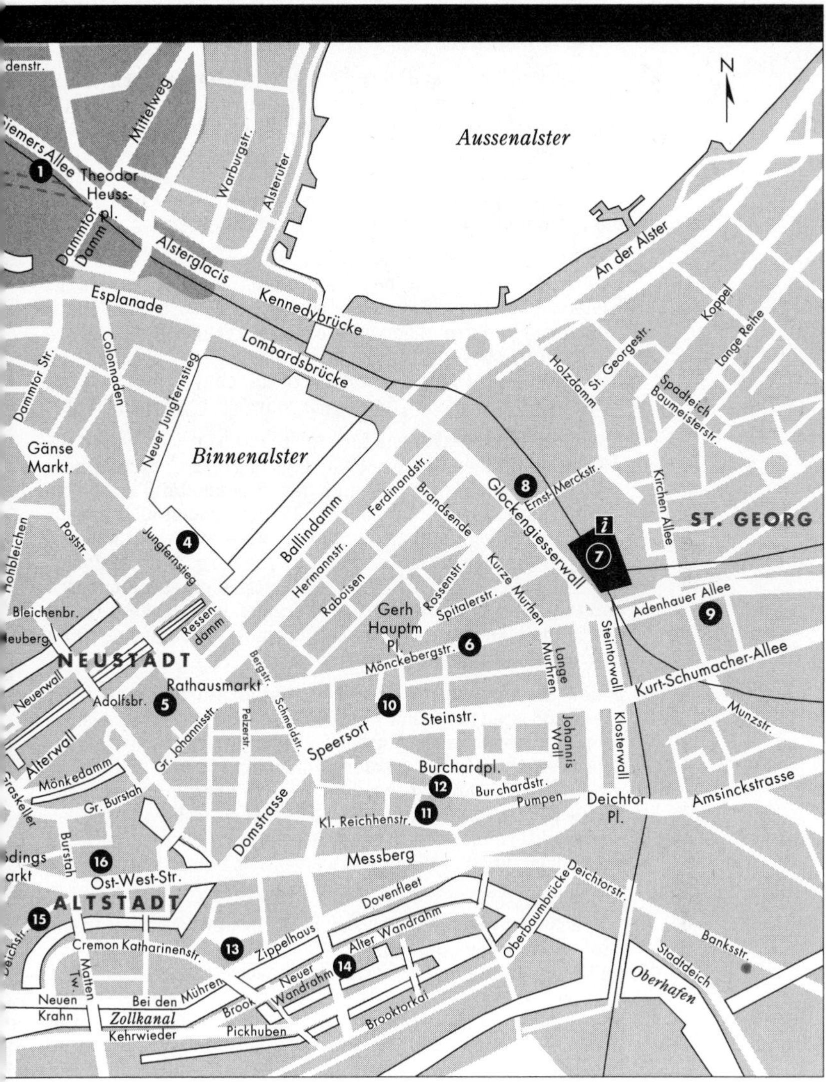

Aussenalster
Binnenalster
ST. GEORG
NEUSTADT
ALTSTADT
Theodor Heuss-pl.
Dammtor Damm
Mittelweg
Warburgstr.
Alsterufer
Alsterglacis
Kennedybrücke
Esplanade
Lombardsbrücke
An der Alster
Colonnaden
Dammtor Str.
Neuer Jungfernstieg
Gänse Markt.
Jungfernstieg
Poststr.
Ballindamm
Ferdinandstr.
Brandsende
Glockengiesserwall
Ernst-Merckstr.
Holzdamm
St. Georgestr.
Koppel
Lange Reihe
Spadteich
Baumeisterstr.
Kirchen Allee
Hermannstr.
Raboisen
Rossenstr.
Spitalerstr.
Kurze Murhen
Gerh Hauptm Pl.
Mönckebergstr.
Lange Murhren
Steintorwall
Adenhauer Allee
Kurt-Schumacher-Allee
Munzstr.
Bleichenbr.
Ressen-damm
Rathausmarkt
Adolfsbr.
Bergstr.
Schmeidstr.
Pelzerstr.
Gr. Johannisstr.
Neuerwall
Alterwall
Mönkedamm
Gr. Burstah
Burstah
Speersort
Steinstr.
Johannis Wall
Klosterwall
Burchardpl.
Burchardstr.
Pumpen
Deichtor Pl.
Amsinckstrasse
Kl. Reichhenstr.
Domstrasse
Messberg
Ost-West-Str.
Dovenfleet
Deichtorstr.
Oberbaumbrücke
Bankstr.
Stadtdeich
Oberhafen
Zippelhaus
Alter Wandrahm
Neuer Wandrahm
Cremon
Katharinenstr.
Matten Tw.
Bei den Mühren
Brook
Brooktorkai
Neuen Krahn
Zollkanal
Kehrwieder
Pickhuben
1
4
5
6
7
8
9
10
11
12
13
14
15
16

ern conference-and-entertainment complex at the northeast
2 corner of **Planten un Blomen** park.

3 Planten un Blomen and the adjoining **Alter Botanischer Garten** (Old Botanical Gardens) lie within the remains of the 17th-century fortified wall that defended the city during the Thirty Years' War, the cataclysmic religious struggle that raged in Germany between 1618 and 1648. Remains of the old fortifications and moats have since been cleverly integrated into a huge, tranquil park on the edge of the city center.

The entire park area is known as **Wallringpark** and includes Planten un Blomen and the Alter Botanischer Garten, plus the Kleine and Grosse Wallanlagen parks to the south. You'll need to cover a lot of ground on foot to see everything Wallringpark has to offer, but a trip on the light railway—which crosses all four parks—will give you a taste of its many aspects. If you take the railway, aim to finish your journey at Stephansplatz.

The walking tour takes you through Planten un Blomen and the Alter Botanischer Garten. Past the Congress Centrum, bear left in a sweeping arc through the ornamental Planten un Blomen park. This park, opened in 1935, is famous all over Germany for its well-kept plant, flower, and water gardens and offers many places to rest and admire the flora. If you visit on a summer's evening, you'll see the **Wasserballet,** an illuminated fountain "dance" in the lake set to organ music. Make sure you get to the lake in good time for the show—it begins at 10 PM each evening during the summer.

Follow the signs to the Alter Botanischer Garten, an equally green and open park that specializes in rare and exotic plants. Tropical and subtropical species are grown under glass in hothouses, with specialty gardens—including herbal and medicinal—clustered around the old moat. The special appeal of the **Kleine** and **Grosse Wallanlagen** parks is their well-equipped leisure facilities, including a children's playground and theater, a model-boat pond, roller- and ice-skating rinks, and outdoor chess.

When you leave, make your way to the eastern entrance to the Alter Botanischer Garten at Stephansplatz. Take the U-bahn
4 south for one stop to **Jungfernstieg,** the most elegant boulevard in downtown Hamburg. You emerge from the U-bahn station onto Jungfernstieg's wide promenade, looking out over one of the city's most memorable vistas—the Alster lakes. It's these twin lakes that give downtown Hamburg its distinctive sense of openness and greenery.

Today's attractive Jungfernstieg promenade, laid out in 1665, used to be part of the muddy millrace that channeled water into the Elbe River. The two lakes meet at the 17th-century defensive wall at Lombardsbrücke, the first bridge visible across the water.

Hamburg's best-known café, the **Alsterpavillon** (Jungfernstieg 54), is an ideal vantage point from which to observe the constant activity on the Inner Alster. It's open daily 10 AM–11 PM. In summer, the boat landing below is the starting point for the *Alsterdamfer*, the flat-bottomed steamships that teem on the lakes. Small sailboats and rowboats hired from yards on the eastern shore of the Alster are very much a part of the summer scene. But in winter conditions can be severe enough to freeze both lakes (only 8 feet deep at their deepest point), and commuters take to their ice skates to get to work. *Alster lake and canal tours, Jungfernstieg, tel. 040/341–141. Fare for lake tour: DM 9 adults, DM 4 children. Operates Apr.–Oct., departing daily every half hour 10–6. Fare for combination lake and canal tour: DM 15 adults, DM 7 children. Operates Apr.–Oct., departing daily every 40 min. 10–6.*

Every Hamburger dreams of living within sight of the Alster, but only the wealthiest can afford it. Hamburg has its fair share of millionaires, some of whom are lucky enough to own one of the magnificent garden properties around the Alster's perimeter (the locals call it "Millionaire's Coast"). But you don't have to own one of these estates to be able to enjoy the waterfront—the Alster shoreline offers 4.6 miles of tree-lined public pathways. Popular among joggers, these trails are a lovely place for a stroll.

It's hardly surprising that the area around Jungfernstieg contains some of Hamburg's most exclusive shops. Even the unpredictable nature of the north-German weather isn't enough to deter Hamburgers from pursuing a favorite pastime: window-shopping. Hidden from view behind the sedate facade of Jungfernstieg is a network of nine covered arcades that together account for almost a mile of shops offering everything from cheap souvenirs to expensive haute couture. Many of the air-conditioned passages have sprung up in the last two decades, but some already existed in the 19th century (the first glass-covered arcade, called Sillem's Bazar, was built in 1845) (*see* Shopping, below).

5 Turn off the Jungfernstieg onto Reesendamm street and make your way to the next stop on your tour—the **Rathaus** (Town Hall). To most Hamburgers this large building is the symbolic heart of the city. As a city-state—an independent city and simultaneously one of the 10 Federal States of West Germany—Hamburg has a city council and a state government, both of which have their administrative headquarters in the Rathaus.

Both the Rathaus and the Rathausmarkt (Town Hall Market) lie on marshy land—a fact that everyone in Hamburg was reminded of in 1962 when the entire area was severely flooded. The large square, with its surrounding arcades, was laid out after Hamburg's Great Fire of 1842. The architects set out to create an Italian-style square, drawing on St. Mark's in Venice for their inspiration. The rounded glass arcade bordered by trees was added in 1982.

Building began on the Nordic Renaissance-style Rathaus in 1866 when 4,000 wooden piles were sunk into the moist soil to provide stability for its mighty bulk. Building was completed in 1892, the year a cholera epidemic claimed the lives of 8,605 people in 71 days. A fountain and monument to that unhappy chapter in Hamburg's life can be found in a courtyard at the rear of the Rathaus.

No one is likely to claim that this immense building, with its 647 rooms and towering central clock tower, is the most graceful structure in the city, but for the sheer opulence of its interior, it's hard to beat. Although you only get to see the state rooms, the tapestries, huge staircases, glittering chandeliers, coffered ceilings, and grand portraits convey forcefully the wealth of the city in the last century and give insight into the bombastic municipal taste. The starting point for tours of the Rathaus interior is the ground-floor Rathausdiele, a vast pillared hall.

Time Out One of Germany's oldest vegetarian restaurants is the **Vegetarische Gaststatte,** on the square. *Neuer Wall 13, tel. 040/344–702. Open weekdays 11:15–7, Sat. 11:15–3:30. Closed Sun. and holidays.*

Leaving the Rathaus square by its east side will bring you to
6 *the start of* **Mönckebergstrasse,** a broad, bustling street of shops that ends at the Hauptbahnhof (main train station). Mönckebergstrasse is a relatively new street—it was laid out in 1908, when this part of the old town was redeveloped. Although the shops here are not quite as exclusive as those of Jungfernstieg, the department stores and shopping precincts on both sides of the street provide a wide selection of goods at more easily affordable prices. One word of warning to shoppers: If you want to go on a shopping spree on a Saturday, you will find that the shops close at 2 PM—unless it is the first Saturday of the month, when the shops are open from 9 to 6:30. This rather quirky rule applies to all of Hamburg's shopping centers and throughout most of Germany.

When you reach the end of Mönckebergstrasse you meet the busy main road of Steintorwall, which was the easternmost link of the former defense wall encircling the old town in the 17th century. Rather than battling to cross against the fast-moving
7 traffic, take the subway to the **Hauptbahnhof.**

The Hauptbahnhof was built at the turn of the century and opened in 1906. Today it caters to a heavy volume of international, national, and suburban rail traffic. Despite the fact that it was badly damaged during the Second World War and has been modernized many times over, its architectural impact remains intact. This enormous 394-foot-long building is accentuated by a 460-foot-wide glazed roof that is supported only by pillars at each end. The largest structure of its kind in West Germany, it is remarkably spacious and light inside. It contains a number of small shops and kiosks, some of which sell international newspapers. A Tourist Information Office (Fremdenverkehrszentrale) is located at the Bieberhaus in the Hauptbahnhof. *Tel. 040/248–700. Open 7:30–6.*

Retrace your steps and leave the Hauptbahnhof by the entrance you came in. Turn right on Steintorwall, which continues as Glockengiesserwall Road, until you come to the
8 **Kunsthalle** (Art Gallery) on the corner of Ernst-Merck Street.

The Kunsthalle houses one of the most important art collections in West Germany. It comprises two linked buildings: The one facing you is known as the Kunsthaus, exhibiting mainly contemporary works; adjoining it on your left is the Renaissance-style Kunsthalle, built in 1868. The entrance to both, which are known collectively as the Kunsthalle, is via the Kunsthaus building.

The Kunsthalle's 3,000 paintings, 400 sculptures, and coin and medal collection present a remarkably diverse picture of European artistic life from the 14th century to the present. Masterpieces in the gallery's possession include the oldest known representation of the murder of Thomas à Becket, the head of the English church in the 14th century. This painting, called *Thomas Altar,* was painted by Meister Francke in 1424 and depicts Becket's death in Canterbury Cathedral.

One room of paintings shows works by local artists since the 16th century. There is also an outstanding collection of German Romantic paintings, including works by Runge, Friedrick, and Spitzweg. An exhibition of European art from such painters as Holbein, Rembrandt, Van Dyck, Tiepolo, and Canaletto is on display, as are examples of the late-19th-century Impressionist movement by artists from Leibl and Lieberman to Manet, Monet, and Renoir. *Glockengeisserwall 1, tel. 040/248-251. Admission: DM 4 adults, DM 1 children. Open Tues.-Sun. 10-5.*

9 A quite different but equally fascinating perspective on art is offered by the nearby **Museum für Kunst und Gewerbe** (Museum of Art and Industry). To reach it, head in the direction from which you came until you see the major crossroads with Kurt-Schumacher-Allee on your left. Turn down this street, and you'll find the museum in the first block on your left.

The Museum für Kunst und Gewerbe was built in 1876 as a museum and school combined. Its founder, Justus Brinckmann, intended it to be a stronghold of the applied arts to counter what he saw as a decline in taste due to industrial mass production. A keen collector, Herr Brinckmann amassed a wealth of unusual objects, including a fine collection of ceramics from all over the world. The museum houses a wide range of exhibits from a collection of 15th-to-18th-century scientific instruments (ground floor) to an Art Nouveau room setting, complete with ornaments and furniture, all either original or faithfully reproduced (first floor). *Steintorpl. 1, tel. 040/248-252630. Admission: DM1. Open Tues.-Sat. 10-5.*

Time Out The museum has a small restaurant called **Destille** on the first floor, offering an extensive buffet that includes salads and desserts. Open Tues.-Sat. 10-5.

10 Return to the city center for a visit to the **Jacobikirche** (St. Jacob's Church), just off the Mönckebergstrasse. Turn right out of the museum onto Kurt-Schumacher-Allee, cross over Steintorwall by the subway and continue west along Steinstrasse to the Jacobikirche on your right—you'll recognize it by its needle spire.

This 13th-century church was almost completely destroyed during the Second World War. Only the furnishings, put into storage until restoration of the building was completed in 1962, survived. The interior is not to be missed—it houses such treasures as the vast Baroque organ on which J. S. Bach played in 1720 and three Gothic altars from the 15th and 16th centuries. *Steinstr. Open weekdays 10-4, Sun. 10-1.*

Upon leaving the Jacobikirche, cross over Steinstrasse and head down Mohlenhofstrasse, bearing left at the end onto Burchardstrasse. This area, south of the Jacobikirche between
11 Steinstrasse and Messberg, is known as the **Kontorhausviertal** (Business-House Quarter). Its fascination lies in a series of imaginative clinker-brick buildings designed in the New Objectivity style of 1920s civic architect Fritz Schumacher.

12 Of particular interest in this quarter is the **Chilehaus** at the corner of Burchardstrasse and Pumpen, a fantastical 10-story

building that at first looks like a vast landlocked ship. The Chilehaus was commissioned by businessman Henry Sloman, who traded in saltpeter from Chile. This building is the most representative example of the north-German clinker-brick architecture of the '20s.

Next, your tour takes you south toward the Freihafen (Free Port) to see the 19th-century warehouse city of **Speicherstadt,**
13 with a visit to the restored **Katherinenkirche** (St. Catherine's Church) en route. From the Messberg end of Pumpen Street cross the busy Ost-West-Strasse by Messberg station and continue down Dovenfleet, which runs alongside the Zoll Kanal (Customs Canal). Continue until Dovenfleet turns into Bei den Mühren, and you'll see the distinctive green copper spire of the Katherinenkirche.

The church is dedicated to St. Catherine, a princess of Alexandria martyred at the beginning of the 4th century. Both the exterior and interior of the church were severely damaged during World War II, but it has since been carefully reconstructed according to the Baroque design. Almost none of the original interior furnishings escaped destruction. Only two 17th-century epitaphs (to Moller and von der Feehte) remain. *Bei den Mühren. Open daily in the summer 10–6, in winter 10–4.*

Continue for about 200 meters along Bei den Mühren with the
14 looming bulk of the **Speicherstadt** warehouses in view across the canal. Cross the first bridge you come to—it leads to the center of the warehouse district in the Free Port.

Hamburg's free-port status has existed since the 12th century, when Emperor Barbarossa, the Holy Roman Emperor Frederick I, granted the city special privileges, which included freedom from customs dues on the Elbe River. The original free port was situated at the point where the Alster meets the Elbe near Deichstrasse, but it was moved farther south as Hamburg's trade increased over the following centuries. The advent of steamships in the middle of the 19th century necessitated a total restructuring of the free port, and the Speicherstadt warehouses came into being.

The warehouses offer another aspect of Hamburg's extraordinary architectural diversity. A Gothic influence is apparent here, with a rich overlay of gables, turrets, and decorative outlines. These massive rust-brown warehouses are still used today to store and process every conceivable commodity, from coffee and spices to raw silks and handwoven Oriental carpets. Although you won't be able to go in, the nonstop comings and goings give you a good sense of a port at work.

As you leave the Free Port over the bridge by which you entered, you pass through a customs control point, at which you may be required to make a customs declaration. Turn left after the bridge, where Bei den Mühren Road becomes Neuen
15 Krahn. Take your second right—onto **Deichstrasse,** which runs alongside Nikolaifleet, a former course of the Alster and one of Hamburg's oldest canals.

You are now in one of the oldest residential areas of the Old Town of Hamburg, which dates back to the 14th century. Many of the original houses on Deichstrasse were destroyed in the Great Fire of 1842, which broke out in No. 42 and left some 20,000 people homeless. The houses you see today date mostly from the 17th to 19th centuries, but a few of the early dwellings escaped the ravages of the fire.

No. 27 Deichstrasse, for example, built in 1780 as a warehouse, is the oldest of its kind in Hamburg. And farther along at No. 39 is the Baroque facade of a house built in 1700. Today, Deichstrasse is a protected area of great historical interest. All the buildings in the area have been painstakingly restored—thanks largely to the efforts of public-spirited individuals. You may wish to make a small detour down one of the narrow alleys between the houses (Fleetgäuge) to see the fronts of the houses facing the Nikolaifleet. After exploring this lovely area, take the Cremon Bridge at the north end of Deichstrasse. This angled pedestrian bridge spans Ost-West-Strasse.

Time Out There are three good basement restaurants in this area if you are ready for a break. The **Alt Hamburger Aalspeicher** serves fresh fish dishes; the **Alt Hamburger Burgerhaus** specializes in traditional Hamburg fare; and the **Nikolaikeller,** an upscale old Hamburg tavern, offers local specialties. All three are on Deichstrasse and Cremon.

The Cremon bridge brings you to Hopfenmarkt square, just a
16 stone's throw from the ruins of the **Nikolaikirche** (St. Nicholas's Church). You won't need precise directions to find the church, with its 476-foot tower—the second-highest in Germany. Only the tower and outside walls of the 19th-century Neogothic church survived World War II. Unlike most of the other war-torn churches in Hamburg, the Nikolai was not rebuilt. Instead, the tower was declared a monument to those killed and persecuted during the war.

The Weinkeller unter St. Nikolai, a wine cellar and small wine museum located beneath the former church, is open for browsing and wine tasting as well as for the purchase of wine. *Ost-West-Str. between Hopfenmarkt and Neue Berg. Open weekdays 1–6, Sat. 9–1.*

Turn right onto Ost-West-Strasse and cross to the other side at the Rödingsmarkt U-bahn station. Continue along Ost-West-Strasse until you reach Krayenkamp, a side street to your left
17 that opens onto the historic **Krameramtswohnungen** (Shopkeepers-Guild Houses). The distance from the Nikolaikirche to Krayenkamp is about half a mile.

This tightly packed group of courtyard houses was built between 1620 and 1626 for the widows of members of the shopkeepers' guild. They were used as homes for the elderly after 1866, when the freedom to practice trades was granted. The half-timbered, two-story dwellings were restored in the 1970s and are now protected buildings. Their unusual twisted chimneys and decorative brick facades have drawn more than curious visitors—an artists' colony has taken firm root here.

One of the houses, marked "C," is open to the public. A visit inside the furnished setting gives one a sense of life in one of these 17th-century dwellings. Some of the houses have been converted to suit modern-day commercial purposes—you'll find a gallery, shops, and a bar-cum-restaurant in the style of Old Hamburg. *Historic House "C," Krayenkamp. Admission free. Open Tues.–Sun. 10–5.*

Time Out The restaurant **Galerie Stuben** (Krayenkamp 10, tel. 040/365-800) in the Krameramtswohnungen quarter is open daily from noon to midnight.

18 The Krameramtswohnungen lie in the shadow of Hamburg's best-loved and most famous landmark, **Michaeliskirche** (St. Michael's Church), on the other side of Krayenkamp Road. Michaeliskirche, or "Michel," as it is called locally, is Hamburg's principal church and Germany's most important surviving Protestant church. Constructed on this site in the 17th century, it was razed when lightning struck almost a century later. It was rebuilt in the late 18th century in the decorative Nordic Baroque style but fell victim in 1906 to a terrible fire, which destroyed much of the church. A replica was erected in 1912, but it suffered yet more bad luck during the Second World War. By 1952 it had once again been restored.

The Michel has a distinctive 433-foot brick and iron tower bearing the largest tower clock in Germany, 26 feet in diameter. Just above the clock is the viewing platform (accessible by an elevator or stairs), which affords a magnificent panaroma of the city, the Elbe River, and the Alster lakes. Twice a day, at 10 AM and 9 PM, a watchman plays a trumpet solo from the tower platform, and during festivals an entire wind ensemble crowds onto the platform to perform. Traffic permitting, the music can be heard at street level. *Michaeliskirche: open daily in the summer 9–5:30, in winter Mon.–Sat. 10–5:30, Sun. 11:30–5:30. St. Michael's Tower: open in the summer Mon.–Sat. 9–5:30, Sun. 11:30–5:30; in winter Mon., Tues., and Thurs.–Sat. 10–4, Sun. 11:30–4. Elevator fee: DM 2.50 adults, DM 1.50 children. Staircase fee (449 steps): DM 1.50.*

Time Out Just opposite the Michel is one of Hamburg's most traditional restaurants, the **Old Commercial Room** (Englische Plank 10, tel. 040/366-319). Try one of the local specialties here, like Labskaus (a traditional sailors' dish) or Aalsuppe (eel soup). Open daily 11–midnight.

19 Return to the Krayenkamp entrance to the Michel and turn right. Stay on this road for about 200 meters, until you reach a park, the enormous **Bismarckdenkmal** (Bismarck Monument) rising high above the greenery. Take the pathway leading to it, and as you climb you'll realize that part of its height is due to the sandy hill on which it stands. The colossal 111-foot granite monument, erected between 1903 and 1906, is a mounted statue of Chancellor Bismarck, the Prussian "Iron Chancellor" who was the force behind the unification of Germany. The plinth features bas-reliefs of various German tribes. Created by the sculptor Hugo Lederer, the statue symbolizes the German Reich's protection of Hamburg's international trade.

20 Leave the monument by the north exit onto Ost-West-Strasse. Cross it and continue straight ahead up Holstenwall Street to the **Museum für Hamburgische Geschichte** (Museum of Hamburg History). Because Holstenwall is a fast-flowing street, you may wish to cross by the St. Pauli U-bahn station on the traffic island.

A visit to this museum is highly recommended—it gives you an excellent overall perspective of the forces that have guided Hamburg's development over the centuries. The museum's vast and comprehensive collection of artifacts charts the history of Hamburg from its origins in the 9th century to the present day. The Hamburg Historical Society began building the collection in 1839—three years before the Great Fire—and salvaged a number of items for display in the museum. More material was acquired in 1883 when several street blocks were torn down to make way for the expansion of the Free Port, and these provide an excellent record of life at the time.

Of particular interest to American visitors is the record of German immigrants to the United States between 1850 and 1914. The Historic Emigration Office's microfilm file lists the names of almost 5 million people who left the Port of Hamburg for the promise of a better life in the New World. The first-floor office will research individual cases for visitors and provide information and documents. Allow an hour for this service, and expect to pay a fee of between $30 and $60.

Among the museum's many attractions are an exhibit that describes, through pictures and models, the development of the port and shipping between 1650 and 1860 and a 16th-century architectural model of Solomon's Temple measuring 11 feet square and made of five different types of wood.

Railway buffs will delight in the railway section and escape into past eras of train travel. The centerpiece of this section is a model layout of the Hamburg-to-Harburg rail link, complete with a puffing miniature steam locomotive. As a modern Intercity train is put through its paces, you may also see a 32:1 scale model of the legendary propeller-driven Reichsbahn *Zeppelin* of 1931 heading past in the opposite direction. Trains from every decade of the 20th century run strictly according to timetable on what is the largest model railway in Europe today. *Holstenwall 24, tel. 040/350–01050. Admission to the museum: DM 2 adults, 70 pf children. Open Tues.–Sun. 10–5. Historic Emigration Office: open Tues.–Sat. 10–1 and 2–5.*

Return along Holstenwall to the St. Pauli U-bahn station—you are now at the start of a long, neon-lit street stretching as far as
21 the eye can see. This is the **Reeperbahn**. The hottest spots in town are concentrated in the St. Pauli harbor area, on the Reeperbahn and on a little side street known as the Grosse Freiheit (or Great Freedom, and that's putting it mildly!). The shows are expensive and explicit, but to walk through this area is an experience in itself, and you can soak up the atmosphere without spending anything. It's *not* advisable, however, to travel through this part of the city alone, especially if you're a woman.

St. Pauli is sometimes described as a "Babel of sin," but that's not entirely fair. It offers a broad menu of entertainment in addition to the striptease and sex shows. Among its other attractions are theaters, clubs, music pubs, discos, a bowling alley, and Panoptikum, the only waxworks museum in West Germany (located between the St. Pauli U-bahn and Davidstrasse). The Theater Schmidt on the Reeperbahn, a newcomer to the local scene, offers a repertoire of live music, vaudeville, chansons, and cabaret, while the St. Pauli Theater in Davidstrasse, a veteran of the age of velvet and plush, serves up a popular brand of lowbrow theater.

It's no understatement to say that while some of the sex clubs may be quite good fun and relatively harmless, a good many others are pornographic in the extreme. None gets going until about 10; all will accommodate you till the early hours. Order your own drinks rather than letting the hostess do it for you, pay for them as soon as they arrive, and be sure to check the price list again before handing over the money. If you order whiskey, for example, you can be sure you will not get an inexpensive brand.

Saturday night finds St. Pauli pulsating with people determined to have as much fun as possible. As the bright lights begin to fade sometime around daybreak, those who are made
22 of stern stuff continue their entertainment at the **Fischmarkt** (Fish Market).

The Altona Fischmarkt swings into action every Sunday morning at 5 in the summer and one hour later in the winter. It is by far the most celebrated of Hamburg's many markets and is worth getting out of bed early for. If you're coming from the Reeperbahn, return to the St. Pauli U-bahn station and travel for one stop south to Laundungsbrücken station. Turn right at the crossroads at the foot of the hill and walk beside the Elbe for about 200 meters, and you'll see the market stalls on the road to your left.

Sunday fish markets became a tradition in the 18th century when fishermen used to sell their catch before church services began. Today freshly caught fish is only one of a compendium of wares on sale at the popular Fischmarkt in Altona. In fact, you can buy almost anything—from live parrots and palm trees to armloads of flowers and bananas, valuable antiques to second-, third- and fourth-hand junk. You'll find plenty of bars and restaurants in the area where you can breakfast on strong coffee or even raw herring. *Fischmarkt: between Grosse Elbstr. and St. Pauli Landungsbrücken. Open Sun. 5–9:30* **AM** *in summer and 6–9:30* **AM** *in winter.*

A visit to the port is not complete without a tour of one of the most modern and efficient harbors in the world. Hamburg is Germany's largest seaport, with 33 individual docks and 500 berths lying within its 30 square miles. Short round-trips by
23 ferry leave from the nearby landings at **Landungsbrücken.** To find the booking hall and departure point, leave the Fischmarkt and return the way you came, but instead of turning left up the hill to the U-bahn station, bear right toward the long limestone building instantly recognizable by its two towers. This is Landungsbrücken, the main passenger terminal for a whole range of ferry and barge rides, both one-way and round-trip, along the waterways in, around, and outside Hamburg. In the first-floor booking hall is the main ticket office and information desk.

There's usually a fresh breeze, so do dress warmly enough for your trip, but don't expect rolling surf and salty air, as Hamburg's port is 56 nautical miles from the North Sea. The HADAG line and other companies organize round-trips in the port lasting about one hour and taking in several docks. *Harbor tours run year-round with frequent starting times. Fare for 1-hour trip: DM 11 adults, DM 5.50 children. From mid-March through November, harbor tours with English-speaking guides start at 11:15 and 3:15 from Pier 1 at Landungsbrücken. In winter, tours with English guides can be arranged in advance by calling 040/564–523.*

You can combine an evening trip around the harbor with dinner and dancing on a "party ship." Book at the HADAG pavilion on Landungsbrücken (tel. 040/313–687). Fare: DM 49. Departures May 3–Dec. 6 at 8 PM.

24 One trip you should try to make is to the waterside village of **Blankenese,** 9 miles west of Hamburg. Take a ferry to get there. But you'll need plenty of energy when you arrive to tackle the 58 flights of steep and narrow lanes crisscrossing the hills and valleys of the village.

Blankenese is another of Hamburg's surprises—a city suburb with the character of a quaint fishing village. Some Germans like to compare it to the French and Italian Rivieras. Many of them consider it the most beautiful part of Hamburg. In the 14th century Blankenese was an important ferry point, but it wasn't until the late 18th and 19th centuries that it became a popular residential area.

Time Out A fine view and good food await you at **Sagebiel's Fahrhaus** (Blankenese Hauptstr. 107, tel. 040/861–514), a former farmhouse where Kaiser Wilhelm once celebrated his birthday. The fish dishes are recommended.

You have a choice of transportation back to the city—by ferry, by S-bahn, or on foot. The celebrated Elbe River walk is long—about 8 miles from Blankenese to Landungsbrücken—but it's one of Hamburg's finest.

Sightseeing Checklists

All sites listed below are discussed in the Exploring Hamburg section, above, unless noted.

Historical Buildings and Sites

Bismarckdenkmal (Bismarck Monument). Monument to Chancellor Bismarck, the "Iron Chancellor," who was the force behind the unification of Germany. *U-bahn: St. Pauli.*

Chilehaus (Chile House). An unconventional office building in the heart of the Kontorhausviertal district, built in the 1920s for a businessman who traded with Chile. *U-bahn: Messberg.*

Dammtorbahnhof (Dammtor Train Station). A fine example of turn-of-the-century Jugendstil (German Art Nouveau) architecture.

Deichstrasse. This is the oldest residential area of the Old Town of Hamburg. *U-bahn: Rödingsmarkt.*

Fischmarkt (Fish Market). This colorful Sunday-morning market starts at 5 AM in summer and 6 AM in winter and closes at 9:30 AM. *U-bahn: Landungsbrücken.*

Hamburger Hafen (Hamburg Harbor). There's a constant bustle around the port, the largest in West Germany. Choose one of the many boat excursions that leave regularly from the boat landings at Landungsbrücken. *U-bahn: Landungsbrücken.*

Hauptbahnhof (Main Train Station).

Krameramtswohnungen (Shopkeepers-Guild Houses). A tightly packed group of courtyard houses built in the late 17th century by the Merchants' Guild for the widows of its late members. *U-bahn: Rödingsmarkt.*

Rathaus (Town Hall). The late-19th-century Nordic Renaissance–style building is home to Hamburg's city council and state government. *U-bahn: Rathaus.*

Reeperbahn. This street cuts through Hamburg's lively St. Pauli entertainment quarter. *S-bahn: Reeperbahn or U-bahn: St. Pauli.*

Speicherstadt. These imposing warehouses in the Free Port offer the world's largest continuous storage facility. *U-bahn: Baumwall, Rödingsmarkt, or Messberg.*

Churches

Jakobikirche (St. Jacob's Church). This 13th-century church was rebuilt after severe damage during World War II, but some of its treasures remained intact, including a unique Baroque organ and three Gothic altars. *U-bahn: Monckebergstr.*

Katherinenkirche (St. Catherine's Church). This restored Baroque church overlooking the harbor was dedicated to the martyred 4th-century Princess Catherine of Alexandria. *U-bahn: Messberg.*

Michaeliskirche (St. Michael's Church). Hamburg's most famous landmark and one of the most important late-Baroque churches in West Germany. The viewing platform, accessible by stairs and an elevator, affords a magnificent panorama of the city, encompassing the Elbe River and Alster lakes. *U-bahn: Rödingsmarkt or St. Pauli.*

Nikolaikirche (St. Nicholas's Church). Only the tower and outside walls remained of this 19th-century neogothic church destroyed in the Second World War II. *U-bahn: Rödingsmarkt or Rathaus.*

Petrikirche (St. Peter's Church). Considered the oldest church in Hamburg, this early 13th-century building fell victim to the Great Fire of 1842 and was rebuilt shortly afterward. It has a tall copper-covered spire and contains a number of attractions, including a Gothic pulpit and various votive panels. *U-bahn: Rathaus.*

Museums and Galleries

Kunsthalle (Art Gallery). Hamburg's principal gallery houses one of the most important art collections in West Germany, with paintings from the Middle Ages to the present day. *U-bahn: Hauptbahnhof.*

Museum fur Hamburgischer Geschichte (Museum of Hamburg History). The museum traces the history of Hamburg from its origins in the 9th century to the present day. *U-bahn: St. Pauli.*

Museum für Kunst und Gewerbe (Museum of Art and Industry). This interesting little museum houses a wide variety of examples of the applied arts. *U-bahn: Hauptbahnhof.*

Museum für Völkerkunde (Museum of Ethnology). One of the largest museums of its kind in West Germany, it has particularly good displays on Africa and South America. *Rothenbaumchausee 64. Open Tues.–Sat. 10–5. U-bahn: Hallerstr.*

Oevelgönne Museumhafen (Oevelgönne Harbor Museum). The aim of this privately owned museum is to maintain and restore ships for occasional outings and public display. Most of the restored ships are seaworthy, and among the collection are steam tugs, wooden cutters, and fire-fighting ships. *Beim Anleger Neumuhlen; take bus no. 183. Open Sat.–Sun. 11–8. Closed Jan. and Feb.*

Open Markets

Blankenese. A lively fruit and vegetable market in the heart of this suburb manages to preserve the charm of a small village. *Bahnhofstr. S-bahn: Blankenese train station. Open Tues. 8–2, Fri. 8–6, Sat. 8–1.*

Isemarkt. This market is considered by many Hamburgers to be the city's best, with more than 300 stalls offering everything from fresh produce to clothing and toys. The stalls are set up on a strip of land beneath the elevated railway between the Reeperbahn and Poppenbüttel. Some of the older houses on Isestrasse have particularly attractive Jugendstil facades. *Between the U-bahn stations of Hoheluftbrücke and Eppendorfer Baum. Tues. and Fri. 8:30–2.*

Fischmarkt (Fish Market). Fish of all shapes and sizes can be bought at this market, as well as a wide range of other goods, including flowers, fruit and vegetables, antiques, and secondhand junk. Its location by the harbor adds a further dimension to the attractiveness of this weekly market. *In summer, Sun. 5–9:30 AM; in winter, 6–9:30 AM. S- or U-bahn: Landungsbrücken.*

Parks and Gardens

Alsterpark. Lying on the northwest bank of the Alster is the 173-acre Alsterpark, a well-kept park of trees and gardens with a magnificent view of the city skyline. It is a popular destination for weekend strollers. *Harvestehuderweg.*

Hagenbecks Tierpark (Zoological Gardens). Opened in 1874, this zoo was the first in the world to use open-air animal enclosures. It has 62 acres of landscaped gardens and parkland, with some 2,500 animals separated from the public by invisible ditches. It also has a large dolphinarium and a well-equipped children's playground. *Hagenbeckallee at Hamburg-Stellingen. Admission: DM 12 adults, DM 6 children. U-bahn: Hagenbecks Tierpark.*

Hirschpark (Deer Park). This is an attractively landscaped park with a game enclosure. Stop by the Hirschparkhaus for tea and homemade whole-grain breads at the nearby Witthüs Teestuben, a charming old thatched-roof cottage. *Main entrance: Mühlenberg. S-bahn: Blankenese.*

Stadtpark. This park, north of the city center, offers 445 acres of parkland and 19 miles of footpaths as well as recreational facilities, including open-air pools, sunbathing areas, and a planetarium. Plays are staged and rock concerts held here in the summer. *In Winterhude. U-bahn: Saarlandstr. or Borgweg.*

Wallringpark. A vast and well-kept park and garden area just to the west of the city center containing four parks: the ornamental Planten un Blomen flower garden; the herbal and specialty gardens of the Alter Botanischer Garten, and the Kleine and Grosse Wallanlagen parks, which offer numerous leisure facilities. A miniature railway crosses all four parks. *Main entrance: Stephansplz. Open Mar.–Oct., daily 7–10; Nov.–Feb., daily 7 AM–8 PM.*

Shopping

Gift Ideas

As a great port, Hamburg offers goods from all over the world. You may find it bizarre, but this is one of the best places in Europe to buy tea, for example. Smoked salmon and caviar are also terrific buys here. But for those with salt in their veins, it's the city's maritime heritage that produces some of the most typical goods. The most famous must be a *Buddelschiffe*, a ship in a bottle. There are few better places to look for one, or for a blue-and-white striped sailor's shirt, a sea captain's hat, ship models, even ship's charts, than the little shops and stalls lining the landing stages at **St. Pauli harbor. Binikowski** (Lokstedter Weg 68) is great for ships in bottles. **Gäth & Peine** (Hermannstr. 46) is the place to look for flags from around the world. **Harry's Hamburger Hafenbasar** (Bernard-Nocht-Str. 63) is the best place of all for any of these specialty goods, a Hamburg institution and an experience not to be missed. The city has the distinction of being home to the largest caviar mail-order business in Europe, **Seifarth and Company** (Robert-Koch-Str. 19, tel. 040/524–0027); it offers lobsters, salmon, and exotic teas, too.

Antiques Check out the **Antik-Center** in the old market hall, close to the main train station at Klosterwall 9–21. It features a wide variety of pieces, large and small, valuable and not so valuable, from all periods. Alternatively, take a look at the shops in the **St. Georg** district, especially those between **Lange Reihe** and **Koppel.** You'll find a mixture of genuine antiques *(Antiquitäten* in German) and junk *(Trödel).* You won't find too many bargains, however. **ABC-Strasse** is another happy hunting ground for antique lovers.

Shopping Districts Hamburg's main shopping districts are among the most elegant in Europe. The leading street is **Jungfernstieg,** just about the most upscale and expensive in the country. It's lined with classy jewelers—**Wempe, Brahmfeld & Guttruf,** and **Hintze** are the top names—and chic clothing boutiques such as **Linette** and **Ursula Aust.** Prices are high, but the quality is tops. The streets called **Grosse-Bleichen** and **Neuer Wall** that lead off Jungfernstieg continue the high-price-tag mood. They also lead to the city's three most important covered or indoor shopping malls: the marble-clad **Galleria; Hanse Viertel;** and **Kaufmannshaus.** The malls all connect, and hardened shoppers may want to spend several hours exploring them. The mood is busily elegant.

Spitalerstrasse, running from the main train station to Gerhard-Hauptmann-Platz, is a pedestrian's-only shopping street that's lined with stores. Prices here are noticeably lower than in Jungfernstieg. Parallel **Mönckebergstrasse** is also a pedestrians-only shopping street and the site of the city's best-known chain stores: **Kaufhof, Karstadt,** and **Hertie.**

Away from the downtown area in fashionable **Pöseldorf,** take a look at **Milchstrasse** and **Mittelweg.** Both are bright and classy, with small boutiques, restaurants, and cafés. The leading name is **Jill Sander** (Milchstr. 8), the city's best-known designer of women's clothing and accessories.

Department Stores Hamburg's most famous department store is the **Alsterhaus** on Jungfernstieg. Large and elegant, it's a favorite with locals and a must for visitors. Even Prince Charles and Princess Diana stopped in here during a visit to Hamburg. Don't miss its amazing food department. Reward yourself for having braved the crowds by ordering a glass of champagne; it's a surprisingly good value. Other leading chain stores are **Kaufhof, Karstadt,** and **Hertie** *(see* above), offering much the same goods at similar prices as in branches in other cities across the country.

Food and Flea Markets There are more than 50 markets in Hamburg each week; check with the tourist office for a full listing. The most famous is the **St. Pauli Fischmarkt,** held on Sundays between 6 AM (7 AM in winter) and 9 AM. Fish is the main offering, some of it sold directly from fishing boats, but you can also find fruits and vegetables and a miscellaneous selection of bric-a-brac. It's a terrific place for early morning browsing. The market's also a traditional setting for a last beer after a night on the town. In the heart of **Blankenese,** there's a lively fruit and vegetable market on Tuesdays (8 AM–2 PM), Fridays (8 AM–6 PM), and Saturdays (8 AM–1 PM) that offers real village charm. Take the S-Bahn to Blankenese to reach it. The **Isemarkt,** near the Hoheluftbrücke, is considered the most beautiful market in the city; it boasts around 300 stalls selling produce, fish, clothing, and toys. The market is held Tuesdays and Fridays 8:30 AM–2 PM.

Sports and Fitness

Bicycling There are bike paths throughout downtown and many outlying areas. You can rent bikes from the tourist office (*see* Important Addresses and Numbers, above) for DM 2 per hour, April through September.

Golf There are two leading clubs: **Hamburger Golf-Club Flakenstein** (In de Bargen 59, tel. 040/812–177); and **Golf-Club auf der Wendelohe** (Oldesloerstr. 251, tel. 040/550–5014).

Jogging The best places for jogging are around the Planten un Blomen and Alt Botanischer Garden parks and along the leafy promenade around the Alster. The latter is about 4 miles long.

Sailing You can rent rowboats and sailboats on the Alster in the summer between 10 AM and 9 PM for around DM 12 an hour, plus DM 3 per additional person. For more advanced sailing, contact the **Yacht-Schule Bambauer** (Schöne Aussicht 20a, tel. 040/220–0030).

Swimming Don't even think about swimming in the Elbe or the Alster. There are pools, indoor and outdoor, throughout the city. A full listing is available from the tourist office. Three to try are: **Alster Schwimmhalle** (Ifflandstr. 21), **Blankenese** (Simrockstr.), and **St. Pauli** (Budapester-Str. 29).

Tennis and Squash The **Hamburger Tennis Verband** (Hallerstr. 89, tel. 040/445–078) has full listings of the many indoor and outdoor courts in the city. Listings are also available from the tourist office. For squash, try **Squash Point Hamburg** (Eimsbüttler Chaussee 63, tel. 040/430–1031).

Dining

The city offers a wide range of dining experiences, from sophisticated nouvelle cuisine in sleekly upscale restaurants to robust local specialties in simple harbor-side taverns. Seafood naturally figures prominently. The most celebrated dish is probably *Aalsuppe*, eel soup, a tangy concoction not entirely unlike Marseilles's famous bouillabaisse. A must in summer is *Aalsuppe grün*, seasoned with dozens of herbs. Smoked eel, *Räucheraal*, is equally good. In fall, try *Bunte oder Gepflückte Finten*, a dish of green and white beans, carrots, and apples. Available any time of year is *Küken ragout*, a concoction of sweetbreads, spring chicken, tiny veal meatballs, asparagus, clams, and fresh peas cooked in a white sauce. Other Hamburg specialties include *Stubenküken* (chicken), *Vierländer Mastente* (duck), *Birnen, Bohnen und Speck* (pears, beans, and bacon), and the sailors' favorite *Labskaus*, a stew made from pickled meat, potatoes, and (sometimes) herring and garnished with a fried egg, sour pickles, and lots of beetroot.

Highly recommended restaurants in each price category are indicated by a star ★.

Category	Cost*
Very Expensive	over DM 95
Expensive	DM 65–DM 95
Moderate	DM 45–DM 65
Inexpensive	DM 25–DM 65

**per person for a three-course meal, excluding drinks*

Very Expensive

★ **L'Auberge Française.** Monsieur Lemercier, proprietor of Hamburg's most successful French restaurant, offers resolutely traditional dishes. Seafood is his specialty. Try the warm scampi salad in garlic butter or the goose liver in truffle sauce with apples. The restaurant is located north of the Planten un Blomen park. *Rutschbahn 34, tel. 040/410–2532. Reservations required. Jacket and tie required. AE, DC, MC, V. Closed Sat. lunch, weekends in summer, and Dec. 20–Jan. 5.*

Le Canard. It's worth making the 15-minute ride north of the downtown area to the Eppendorf suburb to dine in one of the finest restaurants in Hamburg. The setting is unobtrusively modern, with fresh flowers much in evidence; the food is subtly nouvelle. Try the salmon and avocado gratin or the calves'-brain soufflé with mushrooms in champagne sauce. *Martinistr. 11, tel. 040/460–4830. Reservations required. Jacket and tie required. AE, DC, MC, V. Closed Sun. and July.*

★ **Landhaus Dill.** Located in a former coach inn on the road to Blankenese, this restaurant offers a varied and imaginative menu, with nouvelle specialties predominating. In summer, try the lobster salad—it will be prepared right at your table. In fall, try the wild duck with port-wine sauce. Vegetarian meals are also available. *Elbchaussee 404, tel. 040/828–443. Reservations required. Jacket and tie required. AE, DC, MC, V. Closed Tues.–Fri. lunch, Sat. and Sun. dinner, and all day Mon.*

★ **Landhaus Scherrer.** Though this establishment is located only minutes from the downtown area in Altona, its parklike setting—the building was originally a brewery—seems worlds away from the high-rise bustle of the city. The mood is elegantly low-key, with wood-paneled walls and soft lighting. The food fuses sophisticated nouvelle specialties with more down-to-earth local dishes. Try the pickled calves' brains with lentils in a sherry sauce. The wine list is exceptional. *Elbchaussee 130, tel. 040/880–1325. Reservations required. Jacket and tie required. AE, DC, MC, V. Closed Sun. and holidays.*

Expensive

★ **Fischereihafen-Restaurant Hamburg.** For the best fish in Hamburg, make for this discreetly upscale restaurant in Altona, just west of the downtown area and located right on the Elbe. The menu changes daily, according to what's available in the fish market that morning. It's a favorite with the city's beau monde. *Grosse Elbstr. 143, tel. 040/381–816. Reservations required. Jacket and tie required. AE, DC, MC.*

La Mer. This is just about the best hotel restaurant in the city, the elegant dining room of the Hotel Prem, memorably located on the Aussenalster, a 10-minute ride from downtown. A host of subtle specialties is featured in the gold-and-white restaurant, including marinated *inoki* mushrooms with imperial oysters and salmon roe, and spring venison with elderberry sauce. *An der Alster 9, tel. 040/241–1726. Reservations advised. Jacket and tie required. AE, DC, MC, V. Closed Sat. and Sun. lunch.*

★ **Peter Lembcke.** The best of traditional north German cuisine is featured in this simply decorated and long-established restaurant, located just north of the train station. There's no better place to eat eel soup or Labskaus. The restaurant is nearly always crowded; the service, though warm, can be uncertain. *Holzdamm 49, tel. 040/243–290. Jacket and tie required. Reservations advised. AE, DC, MC. Closed Sun.*

Moderate

Ahrberg. This restaurant on the river in Blankenese has a pleasant terrace for summer dining and a cozy, wood-paneled dining room for colder days. The menu features a range of traditional German dishes and seafood specialties. Try the shrimp and potato soup or, in season, the fresh carp. *Strandweg 33, tel. 040/860–438. Reservations advised. Dress: informal. AE, DC, MC.*

★ **Le Château.** The elegant surroundings of a modernized 19th-century mansion in fashionable Pöseldorf are the scene of some of the classiest eating in the city. The food has a distinct French bias, with nouvelle specialties well to the fore. Fish "potpourri" with champagne and saffron is a longtime favorite. *Milchstr. 19, tel. 040/444–200. Reservations advised. Jacket and tie required. AE, DC, MC, V. Closed Sat. and Sun. lunch.*

Il Giardino. The attractive courtyard garden here makes a delightful setting for low-key summer dining. The menu offers Italian and nouvelle specialties. The wine list is extensive. *Ulmlinstr. 17–19, tel. 040/470–147. Reservations advised. Dress: informal. AE, MC, V. Closed lunch.*

★ **Ratsweinkeller.** For atmosphere and robust local specialties, there are few more compelling restaurants in Germany than this cavernous, late-19th-century haunt under the town hall. High stone and brick arches, with ship models suspended from them, and simple wood tables set the mood. You can order a surprisingly fancy or no-nonsense meal; the fixed-price menus at lunch are a bargain. Fish specialties predominate, but there's a wide choice of other dishes, too. *Grosse-Johannisstr. 2, tel. 040/364–153. Reservations advised. Dress: informal. AE, DC, MC, V. Closed Sun. and holidays.*

Inexpensive

At Nali. This is one of Hamburg's oldest and most popular Turkish restaurants; it has the added advantage of staying open till 2 AM, handy for those hankering after a late-night kebab. Prices are low and the service is reliable and friendly. *Rutschbahn 11, tel. 040/410–3810. Reservations advised. Dress: informal. AE, DC, MC, V.*

★ **Fischerhaus.** Always busy (expect to share a table) and plainly decorated, this establishment offers time-honored Hamburg fish specialties. It's hardly haute cuisine, but the standards, like the service, are ultrareliable. This is a great place to try eel soup. The clientele matches the food. *Fischmarkt 14, tel. 040/314–053. No reservations. Dress: informal. No credit cards. Closed Sun.*

Sagres. Portuguese and Spanish restaurants are part of the city's seafaring tradition, and this is one of the best. Fight your way through the Portuguese dockworkers to find a place at the bar, where you'll probably have to wait for a table. The mood is busy and cheerful, the decor simple. Try swordfish for an ad-

Hamburg Dining

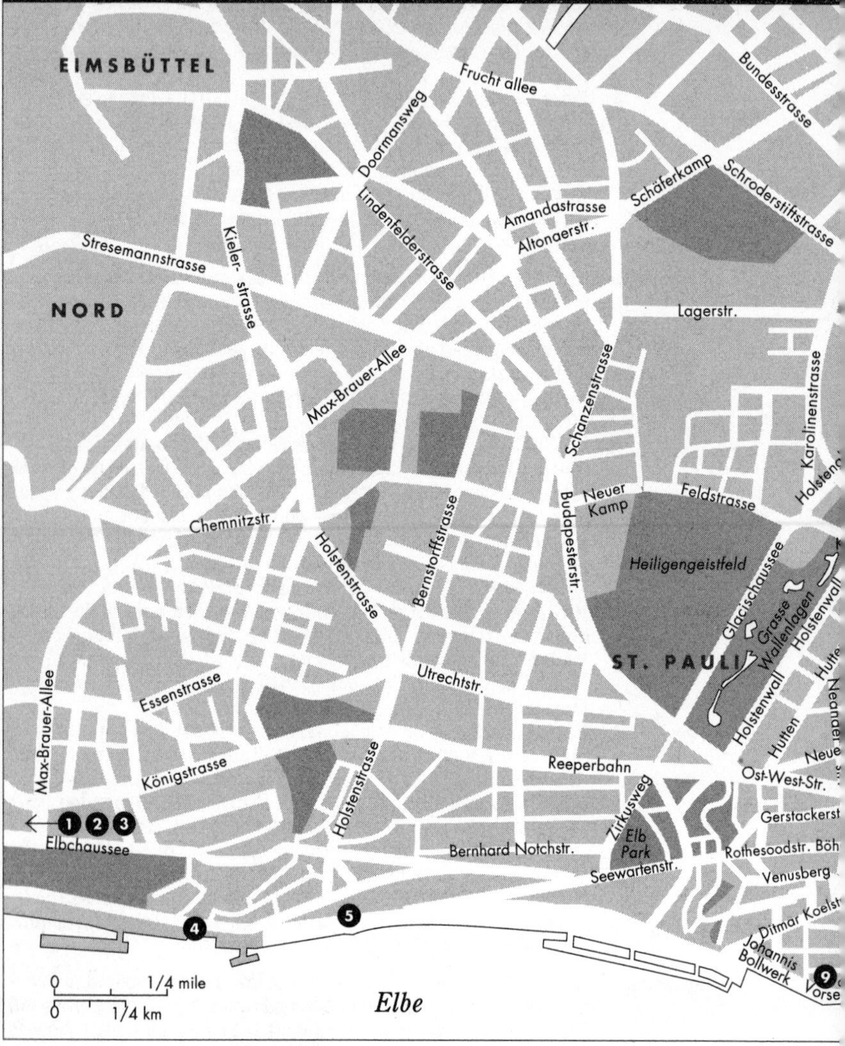

Ahrberg, **3**
At Nali, **7**
L'Auberge Française, **8**
Le Canard, **6**
Le Château, **11**
Fischereihafen-Restaurant Hamburg, **4**
Fischerhaus, **5**
Il Giardino, **10**
Landhaus Dill, **1**
Landhaus Scherrer, **2**
La Mer, **14**
Peter Lembcke, **13**
Ratsweinkeller, **12**
Sagres, **9**

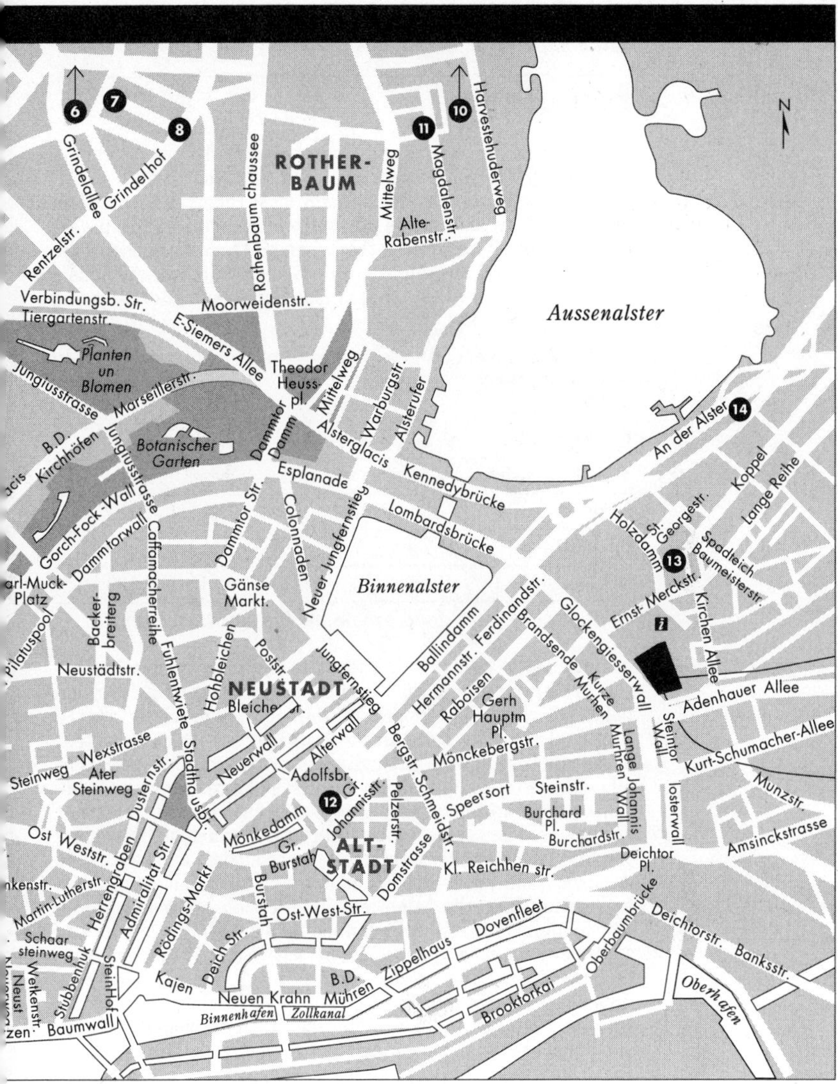
ROTHER-BAUM
Aussenalster
Binnenalster
NEUSTADT
ALT-STADT
Planten un Blomen
Botanischer Garten
Grindelallee
Grindelhof
Rentzelstr.
Rothenbaum chaussee
Mittelweg
Magdalenstr.
Harvestehuderweg
Alte-Rabenstr.
Verbindungsb. Str.
Tiergartenstr.
Moorweidenstr.
E-Siemers Allee
Theodor Heuss-pl.
Warburgstr.
Alsterufer
Jungiusstrasse
Marseillerstr.
B.D. Kirchhöfen
Dammtor Damm
Alsterglacis
Esplanade
Kennedybrücke
Lombardsbrücke
An der Alster
Koppel
Lange Reihe
St. Georgestr.
Holzdamm
Spadteich
Baumeisterstr.
Gorch-Fock-Wall
Dammtorwall
Dammtor Str.
Colonnaden
Neuer Jungfernstieg
Gänse Markt.
Caffamacherreihe
Backerbreiteg
Pilatuspool
Neustädtstr.
Hohbleichen
Poststr.
Jungfernstieg
Ballindamm
Ferdinandstr.
Brandsende
Glockengiesserwall
Ernst-Merckstr.
Kirchen Allee
Adenhauer Allee
Kurt-Schumacher-Allee
Steintor Wall
Hermannstr.
Raboisen
Gerh Hauptm Pl.
Kurze Muhren
Lange Muhren
Johannis Wall
Fuhlentwiete
Bleichenstr.
Neuerwall
Alterwall
Bergstr.
Mönckebergstr.
Wexstrasse
Steinweg
Ater Steinweg
Stadthausbr.
Adolfsbr.
Gr. Johannisstr.
Pelzerstr.
Schmeidstr.
Speersort
Steinstr.
Burchard Pl.
Burchardstr.
Iosterwall
Munzstr.
Amsinckstrasse
Dusternstr.
Mönkedamm
Gr. Burstah
Domstrasse
Kl. Reichhen str.
Deichtor Pl.
Ost Weststr.
Herrengraben
Admiralität Str.
Rödings-Markt
Burstah
Ost-West-Str.
Dovenfleet
Oberbaumbrücke
Deichtorstr.
Banksstr.
Martin-Luthersrtr.
Schaar steinweg
Stubbenhuk
SteinHof
Wetkenstr.
Kajen
Deich Str.
Neuen Krahn
B.D. Mühren
Zippelhaus
Brooktorkai
Oberhafen
Binnenhafen
Zollkanal
Baumwall
Neust
N

venturous meal. *Vorsetzen 46, tel. 040/371–201. No reservations. Dress: informal. AE.*

Lodging

Hamburg has a full range of hotels, from five-star, grande-dame luxury to simple pensions. The near year-round conference and convention business keeps most rooms booked well in advance. But it also means that many of the more expensive hotels offer lower weekend rates, when all those businesspeople have gone home. The tourist office can help with reservations if you arrive with nowhere to stay (*see* Important Addresses and Numbers, above).

Highly recommended hotels in each price category are indicated by a star ★.

Category	**Cost***
Very Expensive	over DM 250
Expensive	DM 180–DM 250
Moderate	DM 120–DM 180
Inexpensive	under DM 120

**for two people in a double room, including tax and service*

Very Expensive

★ **Atlantic Hotel Kempinski.** There are few more sumptuous hotels in Germany than this expansive and gracious Edwardian palace, located just north of the old town, close by the Aussenalster. The mood throughout is one of thick-carpeted, dark-paneled panache (though regular renovations have kept all facilities thoroughly up-to-date). The lobby is positively baronial, with an imposingly grand staircase and deep leather armchairs. The rooms are appropriately luxurious, the suites are little short of palatial, the service is hushed and swift. The Atlantic Rendezvous Bar is a chic city watering hole, while the main restaurant, the Atlantic Grill, offers elegant nouvelle cuisine in high-ceilinged surroundings. *An der Alster 72, tel. 040/28880. 282 rooms and 13 suites, all with bath. Facilities: 2 restaurants, bar, nightclub, rooftop pool, sauna, masseur, airport check-in desk. AE, DC, MC, V.*

★ **Hamburg Plaza.** If you value stylishly sleek modernity over old-world charm, this striking black high rise on the edge of the Planten un Blomen will be your choice. The views are good; the service, polished. Many rooms are swankily decorated, with dark paneling; public rooms are elegant and large. *Marseillerstr. 2, tel. 040/35020. 570 rooms and suites, all with bath. Facilities: 2 restaurants, bar, sauna, indoor pool, masseur. AE, DC, MC, V.*

Ramada Renaissance. Behind an imposing 19th-century facade in the heart of town—the hotel is next door to the best shopping malls—lurks this classic modern hotel. The mood throughout is understated and luxurious, with subtle lighting, gleaming brass, and rich wood. Rooms are spacious and tasteful. *Grosse Bleichen, tel. 040/349–180. 211 rooms and 5 suites, all with bath. Facilities: restaurant, bar, sauna, masseur. AE, DC, MC, V.*

★ **Vier Jahreszeiten.** Some claim this handsome 19th-century town house on the edge of the Binnenalster is the best hotel in

Germany, combining the very best of old-world elegance with impeccable service and luxury. If they're right, it's probably because it's still a family-owned concern. The hotel opened in 1897, and it's still owned and run by the Haerlin family. Antiques—the hotel has a set of near-priceless Gobelins tapestries—line the public rooms and stud the stylish bedrooms; forests of flowers stand in massive vases; rare oil paintings hang from the walls; and, of course, all the rooms are individually decorated. Of the four restaurants, the Haerlin is the most formal and features superb nouvelle and classic specialties. If you want a room with a view of the lake, make reservations well in advance. *Neuer Jungfernstieg 9–14, tel. 040/34941. 175 rooms and 12 suites, all with bath. Facilities: 4 restaurants, 2 bars, tearoom, pastry shop, wine shop. AE, DC, MC, V.*

Expensive

Aussen Alster. Only minutes from the train station and overlooking the lake, this small, discreet hotel is set in a gracious 19th-century town house. Try for a balcony room with a view of the lake. Bikes and sailboats are available for sports-minded guests; joggers can even borrow tracksuits. There's no restaurant. *Schmilinskystr. 1, tel. 040/241–1557. 27 rooms with bath. Facilities: sauna, solarium. AE, DC, MC, V.*

Hotel Abtei. Located on a quiet, tree-lined street a mile north of the downtown area in Hervestehude, this elegant period hotel offers understated comfort and reliable levels of service. Try for a room with a view of the garden. There's no restaurant. *Abteistr. 14, tel. 040/442–2905. 14 rooms with bath. AE, DC, MC, V.*

★ **Garden Hotel Pöseldorf.** The location in chic Pöseldorf, a mile from the downtown area, may discourage those who want to be in the thick of things, but this is one of the most appealing hotels in Hamburg, in business since the 18th century and offering classy and chic accommodations. It's very much the insider's choice. There's no restaurant, however. *Magdalenenstr. 60, tel. 040/449–958. 70 rooms with bath. Facilities: garden. AE, DC, MC, V.*

Moderate

Baseler Hospiz. Centrally located near the Binnen Alster and the opera house, this hotel offers friendly and efficient service. Rooms are neatly if functionally furnished. *Esplanade 11, tel. 040/341–921. 160 rooms, most with bath. Facilities: restaurant. AE, DC, MC, V.*

Mellingburger Schleuse. If you want off-the-beaten-track lodgings, this hotel is the place for you. Only a 20-minute drive from the downtown area, it is idyllically located in a forest—the Alsterwanderweg hiking trail passes right by the doorstep. The hotel itself is 250 years old, with a thatched roof, peasant-style furnishings, and a restaurant that serves traditional north German dishes. *Mellingburgredder 1, tel. 040/602–4001. 28 rooms, most with bath. Facilities: restaurant, terrace café, indoor pool. AE, DC, MC.*

Metro Merkur. The main reason for staying here is the convenient central location, close to the train station; though the service is good, rooms are functional and offer little that's special. There's no restaurant, but the bar has snacks in the evening. *Bremer Reihe 12–14, tel. 040/247–266. 109 rooms, most with bath. Facilities: bar. AE, DC, MC, V.*

Steens Hotel. Small and intimate, this hotel is decorated in light and airy Scandinavian style, with pale wood and modern furnishings. It's conveniently located close to the train station.

Hamburg Lodging

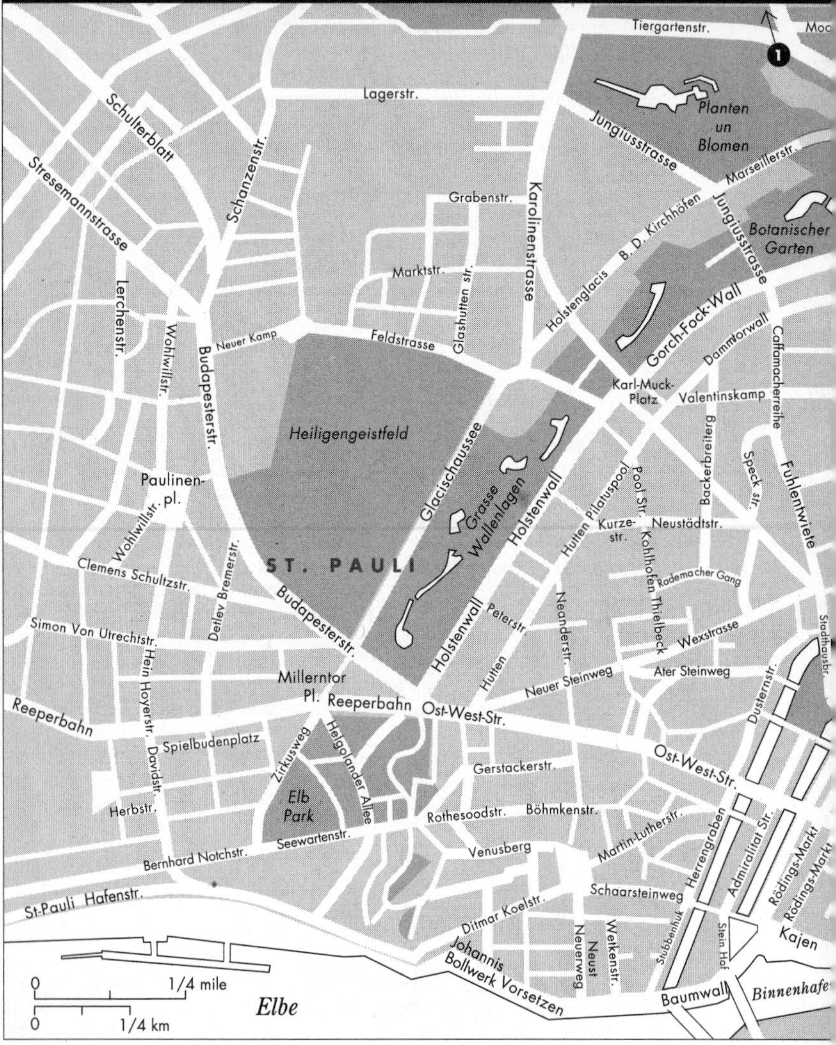

Alameda, **4**
Atlantic Hotel Kempinksi, **10**
Aussen Alster, **12**
Baseler Hospitz, **7**
Garden Hotel Pöseldorf, **9**
Hamburg Plaza, **2**
Hotel Abtei, **6**
Hotel-Pension am Nonnensteig, **1**
Hotel-Pension bei der Esplanade, **4**
Mellingburger Schleuse, **3**
Metro Markur, **4**
Ramada Renaissance, **5**
Steens Hotel, **11**
Vier Jahreszeiten, **8**
Wedina, **13**

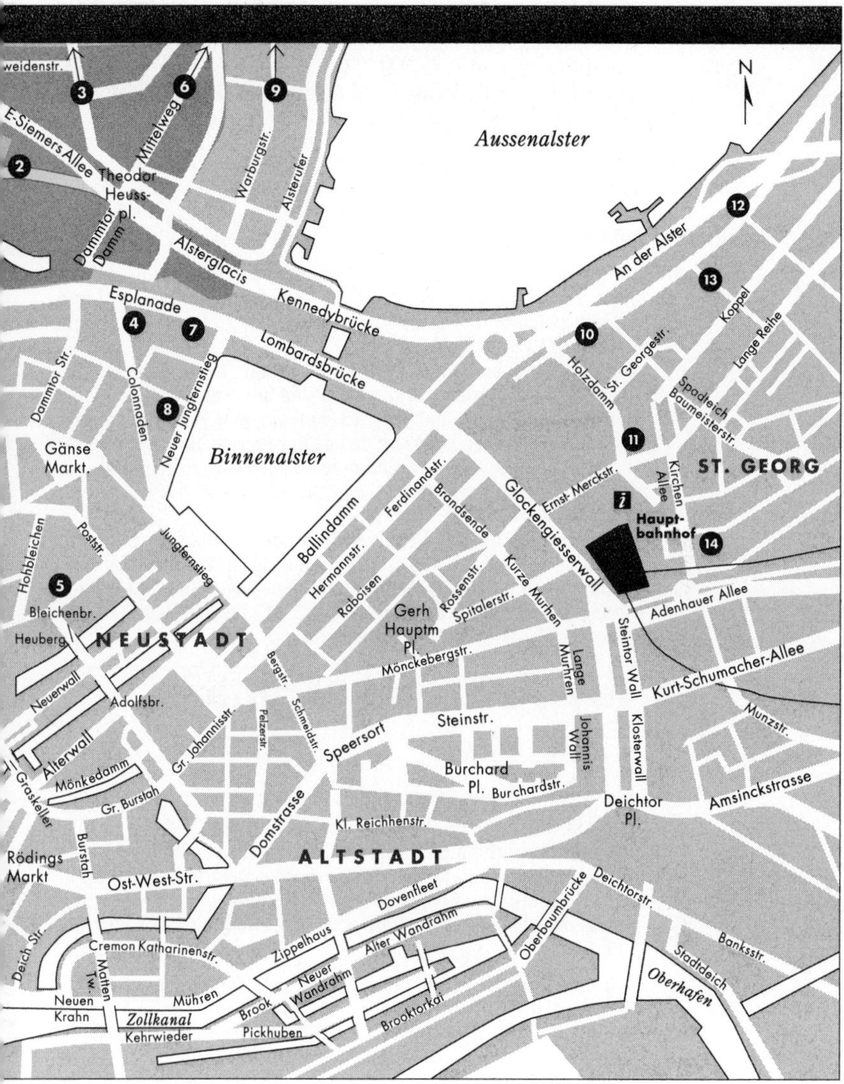
Aussenalster
Binnenalster
N
NEUSTADT
ALTSTADT
ST. GEORG
Hauptbahnhof
E-Siemers Allee
Theodor Heuss-pl.
Mittelweg
Warburgstr.
Alsterufer
Dammtor Damm
Alsterglacis
Esplanade
Kennedybrücke
Lombardsbrücke
An der Alster
Dammtor Str.
Colonnaden
Neuer Jungfernstieg
Gänse Markt.
Hohbleichen
Poststr.
Jungfernstieg
Ballindamm
Hermannstr.
Ferdinandstr.
Brandsende
Raboisen
Rossenstr.
Spitalerstr.
Gerh Hauptm Pl.
Kurze Murhen
Glockengiesserwall
Holzdamm
St. Georgestr.
Koppel
Lange Reihe
Spadreich
Baumeisterstr.
Ernst-Merckstr.
Kirchen Allee
Adenhauer Allee
Steintor Wall
Lange Murhren
Kurt-Schumacher-Allee
Munzstr.
Bleichenbr.
Heuberg
Neuerwall
Adolfsbr.
Bergstr.
Mönckebergstr.
Alterwall
Gr. Johannisstr.
Pelzerstr.
Schmeidstr.
Speersort
Steinstr.
Johannis Wall
Klosterwall
Burchard Pl.
Burchardstr.
Amsinckstrasse
Deichtor Pl.
Mönkedamm
Graskeller
Gr. Burstah
Domstrasse
Kl. Reichhenstr.
Burstah
Rödings Markt
Ost-West-Str.
Dovenfleet
Deichtorstr.
Oberbaumbrücke
Zippelhaus
Alter Wandrahm
Neuer Wandrahm
Brooktorkai
Cremon
Katharinenstr.
Matten Tw.
Deich Str.
Neuen Krahn
Mühren
Zollkanal
Kehrwieder
Brook
Pickhuben
Banksstr.
Stadtdeich
Oberhafen
2
3
4
5
6
7
8
9
10
11
12
13
14

Have breakfast in the garden when the weather's good. *Holzdamm 43, tel. 040/244–642. 11 rooms, most with bath. Facilities: garden. AE, DC, MC, V.*

Wedina. Centrally located and family run, this establishment offers simple and reliable comforts that are more than adequate for overnighting. The little garden provides a leafy retreat; try for a room opening onto it. There's no restaurant. *Gurlittstr. 23, tel. 040/243–011. 23 rooms, most with bath. Facilities: pool, sauna, bar. AE, DC, MC, V. Closed mid-Dec.–mid-Feb.*

Inexpensive

Alameda. For no-frills lodging, this is a good bet. Small and basic, the hotel occupies the first two floors of a downtown building. *Colonnaden 45, tel. 040/344–290. 18 rooms, some with bath. AE, DC, MC, V.*

Hotel-Pension am Nonnenstieg. The owner, Frau Hedermann, is friendly and helpful and makes this unassuming little hotel homey. Ask for a room with a kitchen alcove if you want to cook for yourself. Extra beds can be put in rooms at no extra charge to accommodate a family, and prices are lower for longer stays. *Nonnenstieg 11, tel. 040/473–869. 30 rooms with bath. No credit cards.*

Hotel-Pension bei der Esplanade. Bei der Esplanade takes up the third and fourth floors of the building that houses the Alameda (there's no elevator). The rooms are basic but quiet, clean, and comfortable. *Colonnaden 45, tel. 040/342–961. 14 rooms, some with bath. No credit cards.*

The Arts and Nightlife

The Arts

The arts flourish in this elegant metropolis. The Hamburg city ballet is one of the finest in Europe—the Ballet Festival in July is a cultural high point. Full information on upcoming events is available in the magazine *Hamburger Vorschau*—pick it up in tourist offices and most hotels for DM 2.30—and the magazine *Szene Hamburg*, sold at newsstands throughout the city for DM 4.

A number of travel agencies sell tickets for plays, concerts, and the ballet. Alternatively, try any of the following ticket agencies in the downtown area: **Theaterkasse im Alsterhaus** (Jungfernstieg 16, tel. 040/359–01323); **Theaterkasse Central** (Gerhart-Hauptmann-Pl., tel. 040/324–312); and **Theaterkasse Wickers** (at the tourist office in the Bieberhaus, tel. 040/342–742).

Theater

The city has a full program of theater year-round, though you'll need to understand German well to get the most of the productions. Leading theaters include: **Deutsches Schauspielhaus** (Kirchenallee 39, tel. 040/248–710), probably the most beautiful theater in the city, lavishly restored to its full 19th-century opulence in the early 1980s and now the most important venue in Hamburg for classical and modern theater; **Thalia-Theater** (Alstertor, tel. 040/32266), presenting a varied program of plays old and new; and **Ohnsorg-Theater** (Grosse Bleichen 23, tel. 040/350–80321), presenting works in the local dialect, which even those who know German are likely to find largely incomprehensible. The **English Theater** (Lerchenfeld 14, tel.

040/22554) may provide the antidote: As the name suggests, all productions are in English.

Concerts The **Musikhalle** (Karl-Muck-Pl., tel. 040/346–920) is Hamburg's most important concert hall; both the Hamburg Philharmonic and the Hamburg Symphony Orchestra appear regularly. Visiting orchestras from overseas are also showcased here. The **Norddeutscher Rundfunk Studio 10** (Oberstr., tel. 040/413–2504) has regular concerts by the symphony orchestra and guest appearances by visiting musicians.

Opera and Ballet The **Hamburgische Staatsoper** (Dammtorstr. 28, tel. 040/351–555) is one of the most beautiful theaters in the country and the leading north-German venue for top-class opera and ballet. The **Operettenhaus** (Spielbudenpl. 1, tel. 040/270–75270) puts on light opera and musicals (the German production of *Cats* was rapturously received here).

Film The **British Film Club** (Rothenbaumchaussee 34, tel. 040/448–057) shows films in English.

Nightlife

The Reeperbahn Whether you think it sordid or sexy, the Reeperbahn in the St. Pauli district is as central to the Hamburg scene as the classy shops along Jungfernstieg. A walk down the street leading off it called Grosse Freiheit (an appropriate name: It means "Great Freedom"), lined with windows behind which sit prostitutes can be quite an eye-opener. (Women on their own shouldn't head down here unless they happen to have a black belt in karate.) **Colibri** at no. 34; **Safari** at no. 24; and **Salambo** at no. 11 are the best known clubs and cater to the package-tour trade as much as to those on the prowl by themselves. Prices are high. If you order anything to drink, ask to see the price list first (legally, it has to be on display), and pay as soon as you're served. Don't expect much to happen here before 10 PM.

Jazz Clubs The jazz scene in Hamburg is thriving as never before. There are more than 100 venues and few nights when you won't have a wide selection from which to choose. Among the leading clubs are: **Birdland** (Gärtnerstr. 122, tel. 040/405–277), featuring everything from traditional New Orleans sounds to avant-garde electronic noises; **Fabrik** (Bamerstr. 36, tel. 040/391–565), which offers Sunday-morning *Früschoppen* (brunch) concerts at 11 (they're always packed, so get here early); and **Pö'dingsmarkt/Riverkasematten** (Rödingsmarkt/Ost-West-Str., tel. 040/367–963), one of the oldest and biggest jazz cellars in Germany, presenting a wide range of concerts.

Discos **Alsterufer 35** (Alsterufer 35, tel. 040/418–155) is one of the biggest night spots in Hamburg, a disco and a restaurant in one. Prices can be high, but it's always chic. **Offline** (Eimbütteler Chaussee 5, tel. 040/439–8094) has an amazing laser show at midnight. **Skyy** (Spielbudenpl.) is tiny and plays African music.

Excursions

Tour 1: Ahrensburg

One of Schleswig-Holstein's major attractions is the romantic 16th-century **Schloss Ahrensburg** (Ahrensburg Castle), in the town of Ahrensburg, about 16 miles northwest of Hamburg. Ahrensburg itself is mainly a commuter town, home to about 27,000 people. The magnificent castle and nearby **Bredenbecker Teich** lake make it worth a visit—it's an ideal day's excursion.

Getting There
By Car Take the A-1 Autobahn for 25 kilometers (15 miles), and get off at the Ahrensburg exit. Alternatively, you can take Bundestrasse B-75.

By Train Take the S-bahn line S-4 to Ahrensburg or the U-bahn line U-1 to Ahrensburg-Ost.

Exploring Surrounded by lush parkland on the banks of the Hunnau, Schloss Ahrensburg, a whitewashed-brick, moated Renaissance castle, stands much as it did when it was constructed at the end of the 16th century. Originally built by Count Peter Rantzau in honor of "family and country," it changed hands in 1759 and was remodeled inside by its new owner, Heinrich Carl Schimmelmann. The interior was once again altered in the mid-19th century and recently underwent renovation.

Inside you'll find an extensive inventory of period furniture and paintings, fine porcelain, and exquisite crystal. On the grounds stands a simple 16th-century Baroque church erected at the same time as the castle, although the west tower was not completed until later. The church is nestled between two rows of 12 almshouses, or *Gottesbuden* (God's cottages). *Admission: DM 3. Open Tues.–Sun. 10–12:30 and 1:30–5.*

Tour 2: Altes Land

The marshy **Altes Land** extends 19 miles west from Hamburg along the south bank of the river Elbe to the town of Stade. This traditional fruit-growing region is dotted with huge half-timbered farmhouses and crisscrossed by canals. The fertile land is a popular hiking spot, especially in spring, when the apple and cherry trees are in blossom. Some of the prettiest walks take you along the dikes running next to the rivers Este and Lühe. Much of the territory is best covered on foot, so wear your walking shoes. You may want to bring a picnic lunch as well.

Getting There By Car: Take B-73 west from Harburg.

By Ferry Ferries depart from the Landungsbrücken boat landing in the St. Pauli district of Hamburg every hour between 9 and 5 from May to September. Take the ferry to Cranz or Lühe.

Exploring From the dock at **Cranz** walk south into the suburb of **Neunfelde** and visit the Baroque St. Pancras Church, with its unusual painted barrel roof. The altar inside was built in 1688, and the organ, dating from the same period, was designed by Arp Schnitger, an organ builder and local farmer.

The village of **Jork** in Lower Saxony lies some 5 miles on foot to the west of Neunfelde, just beyond the confluence of the Este and Elbe rivers. Stroll through Jork and take in the early 18th-century church and highly decorative farmhouses. The old windmill in the nearby parish of **Borstel** is worth a short detour.

Lühe is the ferry docking point that's closest to the town of Stade, but be prepared to walk about 8 miles to reach it. Stade lies on the western edge of the Altes Land on the river Schwinge and was once a member of the Hanseatic League of trading towns. Four times the size of Jork, with a population of 45,000, Stade is notable for the ruins of a rampart wall around the Altstadt (Old Town); it also contains the obligatory half-timbered houses.

Tour 3: Buxtehude

Buxtehude is a quaint old town about 20 miles southwest of Hamburg on the Este River, a tributary of the Elbe. Despite the unquestionable charm of its ornate, half-timbered town houses, Buxtehude is best known for the fairy tale about the hare and the hedgehog that is believed to have originated here. The story goes like this: The two animals held a race in the town, and the hedgehog won—not because he was faster, but because he cleverly took turns with his wife, who was his spitting image. Thus, one or the other of them was at the finish line when the hare arrived, breathless.

Getting There

By Car From Harburg take the B-73 towards Cuxhaven, or head south on the A-7 through the Elbe Tunnel, exiting at Heimfeld.

By Train Take the S-bahn to Neugraben and change for Buxtehude.

By Ferry From May to August on Wednesday, Saturday, and Sunday, the MS *Forelle* departs from Landungsbrücken and makes a three-hour voyage through the Altes Land to Buxtehude. A return trip by bus is included in the tour.

Exploring The well-kept city of Buxtehude is a delightful place to spend an afternoon. Its origins go back to 959, when it began to emerge as an important trading post. Buxtehude joined the Hanseatic League in 1363 and was the main intermediate stop for grain en route from Lübeck to the Netherlands and cattle en route from Jutland.

A section of the old wall that protected the city is still standing, and a sturdy tower, the **Zwinger,** overlooks the massive wooden locks of the former harbor.

16 Berlin

Introduction

West Berlin is a world of its own. No other city quite like it exists anywhere else. For once the term *unique* is no exaggeration. One need only consider Berlin's location (and status) to realize why this should be so.

Situated deep inside the Soviet-dominated German Democratic Republic, 177 kilometers (110 miles) from the nearest border with West Germany, the city has remained isolated and insulated from the rest of Western Europe for four and a half decades.

Right after World War II, when Germany was divided into East and West, Berlin was partitioned into four geographic sectors, each administered by the armed forces of one of the four powers on the winning side: the United States, Great Britain, France, and the Soviet Union. Then, in 1948, in an attempt to force the Western Allies to relinquish their stake in the city, Russia split with the others and set up a blockade to close off all overland supply routes from the West, the idea being to starve out and freeze out the people of Berlin so they would be forced to depend on the Soviets for survival.

The Russians had not figured on the Berlin Airlift mounted by the West, with some 750,000 flights delivering 2 million tons of goods to keep Berlin alive for most of a fateful year, until the Soviets finally gave up and lifted the blockade.

But from then on, Berlin would be a divided city, to serve as storm center of the Cold War, eye of the hurricane. And the Russians didn't give up.

In 1961, to stem the tide of East Berliners escaping into West Berlin, they put up their infamous Wall to make the dividing line physical as well as political, and to emphasize the sealed-off nature of life in what was to become the spy capital of the Western World, and serve as favored setting for espionage thrillers.

Since then the beleaguered city's image has been indelibly tied to the wall that cuts Berlin in two. While not exactly what we think of as a tourist attraction, the fortifications of concrete and barbed wire, studded with watchtowers and gun emplacements, rimmed by tank traps and mine fields, are what most visitors head for soon after arrival. The Wall is the city's number-one sight but should be regarded as no more than a single aspect in the overall scheme of this fascinating city, which has far more to offer than its notorious Cold War symbol.

What makes Berlin so special is a matter of intangibles. There's an extra dimension—a kind of chemistry, really—beyond the city's physical aspects. The *spirit* and *bounce* of Berlin makes the difference. Berliners are survivors one and all. Here we are exposed to life in a pressure-cooker; life on the edge, close to the cusp. Berliners of whatever age have lived with adversity all their lives, and have managed to do so with a mordant wit and cynical acceptance of life as it is rather than the way one hopes it might be.

Berliners are brash, outspoken, no-nonsense types endowed with a high-voltage supercharged energy invariably attributed to the bracing Berlin air, the renowned *Berliner Luft.* They speak a racy dialect instantly recognizable in any part of the Federal Republic as emanating from this island of freedom in the East. Crisis has been a way of life here for as long as anyone can remember. "To survive with a measure of style and humor" could serve as the city's theme.

Like so many of today's great cities, Berlin owes its modest beginnings in the 13th century to its location at the crossroads of important trade routes. Although already a royal residence in the 15th century, Berlin came into its own three centuries later, under the rule of King Friedrich II—Frederick the Great. His enlightened reforms and liberal acceptance of outside artistic influences dictated the leading role Berlin was to play in the political, social, and cultural life of Europe.

Berlin served as capital of the newly established German Empire from 1871 to 1918, the Weimar Republic from 1919 to 1933, and the Third Reich (under Hitler) from 1933 to 1945. Today, of course, West Berlin is the capital of absolutely nothing, and is situated in the middle of nowhere that matters to anyone. Technically, it is not even part of the German Federal Republic, although it is tied in to the West German legal and economic system.

Any reference to Berlin invariably calls up its heyday in the 1920's and early '30s, when it served as what is frequently described as Europe's social and cultural capital.

For a first-time visitor the appeal of Berlin may not be that apparent. Some consider this the continent's most exciting city. Others may well ask, "What's all the excitement about?"

To begin with, West Berlin could by no means be considered a beautiful city. During the war, as capital of Nazi Germany, and headquarters of Hitler's general staff, it was, of course, bombed to smithereens.

At the end of hostilities, after the Russian army had taken over the city, there was more rubble in Berlin than in all other German cities combined. Most of what you see today has been built, or rebuilt, since 1945. And yet it is suggested that even before the war Berlin was lacking in noteworthy architecture, in spite of the fact that Mies van der Rohe, Walter Gropius, and other members of the Bauhaus school were associated with Berlin.

Its particular charm lay in its spaciousness, its trees and greenery, its racy atmosphere, and the ease with which you could reach the surrounding forests and lakes within its perimeter. It still is like that. You might say Berlin is a phenomenon of sorts, greater than the sum total of its parts. It is a city of paradoxes and surprises. One that strikes almost every visitor is the sheer size of the place. It is a vast city, laid out on a heroic scale. West Berlin alone is four times the size of Paris. Whole towns and villages are inlaid into the countryside beyond the downtown area. And West Berlin contains only a small portion of historic Berlin. The really stunning parts of Germany's prewar capital are all in the Soviet sector, the grand boulevards and monumental buildings, reminders of the Berlin of high style and opulence that existed beyond the Brandenburg Gate, along the stately, tree-lined avenue of Unter den Linden; the area is not nearly as grandiose today as it once was but is still worth seeing if you want to know the special world of the two Berlins.

We suggested that the following tour be broken up into segments, starting with the Kurfürstendamm, Brandenburg Gate, and the Wall one day, and visiting the major museums on another day.

Essential Information

Important Addresses and Numbers

Tourist Information The **Verkehrsamt Berlin** (main tourist office) is located in the heart of the city in the Europa Center (tel. 030/262–6031). If you want materials on the city before your trip, write **Verkehrsamt Berlin Europa Center** (D-1000 Berlin 30). For information on the spot, the office is open daily 7:30 AM–10:30 PM. There are also offices at **Tegel Airport** (tel. 030/410-1314; open daily 8 AM–11 PM); **Bahnhof Zoo** train station (tel. 030/313-9063; open daily 8 AM–11 PM); and at the **Dreilinden** border crossing (tel. 030/803–9057; open daily 8 AM–11 PM). Berlin has an information center especially for women, offering help with accommodations and information on upcoming events. Contact **Fraueninfothek Berlin** (Leibizstr. 57, tel. 030/324–5078; open Tues.–Sat. 9–9, Sun. and public holidays 9–3).

For information on all aspects of the city, pick up a copy of *Berlin Turns On*, free from any tourist office.

Consulates **United States Consulate** (Clayallee 170, tel. 030/823–4087). **British Consulate** (Uhlanderstr. 7–8, tel. 030/309–5292).

Emergencies **Police** (tel. 030/110). **Ambulance and emergency medical attention** (tel. 030/310–031). **Dentist** (tel. 030/1141). **Pharmacies:** For emergency pharmaceutical assistance, call tel. 030/1141.

English-Language Bookstores **Marga Schoeller** (Knesebeckstr. 33, tel. 030/881–1112). **Buchhandlung Kiepert** (Hardenbergstr. 4–5, tel. 030/331–0090).

Travel Agencies **American Express Reisebüro** (Kurfürstendamm 11, tel. 030/882–7575). **American Lloyd** (Kurfürstendamm 36, tel. 030/883–7081).

Car Rental **Avis** (Tegel Airport, tel. 030/410–13148; Budapesterstr. 43, Am Europa Center, tel. 030/261–1881).
Europcar (Kurfurstenstr. 101, tel. 030/213–7097).
Hertz (Tegel Airport, tel. 030/410–13315; Budapesterstr. 39, tel. 030/261–1053).

Arriving and Departing by Plane

Airlines flying to West Berlin from major U.S. and European cities include Pan Am, TWA, Air France, British Airways, some charter specialists, and EuroBerlin, a Lufthansa subsidiary (Lufthansa itself is not permitted to fly to the city). There are also a number of domestic carriers linking West Berlin to the other major German cities. Despite substantial government subsidies, domestic fares are high. Tegel Airport is only 6 kilometers (4 miles) from the downtown area.

Between the Airport and Downtown Blue airport bus 9 runs at 10-minute intervals between Tegel and downtown via Kurfürstendamm (the main avenue), Bahnhof Zoologischer (the main train station), and Budapester Strasse. The total trip is 30 minutes; fare is DM 2.70. Expect to pay about DM 20 for the same trip by taxi. If you rent a car at the airport, take the Stadtautobahn (there are signs), the highway into Berlin. The Halensee exit leads to Kurfürstendamm (Ku'damm for short).

Arriving and Departing by Train, Bus, and Car

By Train There are five major rail corridors across East Germany into West Berlin. Transit visas are issued free of charge on trains but you must have your passport. The trains are jointly run by the East German Deutsche Reichsbahn (DR) and West Germany's Deutsche Bundesbahn (DB), and reduced-price DB tickets are accepted. Check out the 10-day "Berlin Saver Ticket," sold at West German stations; it offers reductions of 33%. Trains from West Germany arrive at Berlin's main terminus, Bahnhof Zoologischer Garten (Bahnhof Zoo). The U-bahn (subway) and S-bahn (suburban railroad) stop here, too. For details, call **Deutsche Bundesbahn Information** (West, tel. 030/ 19419) or **Deutsche Reichsbahn** (tel. 030/31102116); **reservations** (tel. 030/311022112).

By Bus Buses are slightly cheaper than trains; Berlin is linked by bus to 170 European cities. The main station is at the corner of Masurenallee and Messedam. Reserve through DER (state), commercial travel agencies, or the station itself. For information, call 030/301–8028.

By Car There are eight major routes into Berlin; the shortest journey through East Germany is 170 kilometers (105 miles), the longest 330 kilometers (208 miles). Transit visas are issued at the border for DM 5 (free for West German citizens), but you must show your passport, driver's license, car registration, and insurance documents to get one. Tolls are payable in western currency only. The speed limit is 100 kilometers (62 miles) an hour and seat belts are mandatory. You must stay on official transit roads in East Germany and stop only at designated parking areas and service stations (clearly marked). Traffic is closely monitored by radar. Speeding and drunk-driving offenders are charged hefty fines on the spot.

Getting Around

By Public Transportation West Berlin is too large to be explored on foot. To compensate, the city has one of the most efficient public transportation systems in Europe, a smoothly integrated network of U-bahn and S-bahn lines, buses, and even a ferry (across the Wannsee Lake), making every part of the city easily accessible. There's also an all-night bus service, indicated by the letter "N" next to route numbers. In summer, there are excursion buses linking the downtown area with the most popular recreation areas.

A DM 2.70 ticket (DM 1.70 for children) covers the entire system for two hours and allows you to make an unlimited number of changes between trains and buses. A multiple ticket, valid for five trips, costs DM 11.50 (DM 7 for children). The best deal for visitors who plan to travel extensively around the city is the **Berlin Ticket,** valid for 24 hours and good for all trains and buses; it costs DM 9 (DM 5 for children). If you plan to visit the Wannsee Lake, buy the **combined day ticket,** good for the entire network and the excursion boats of the Stern- und Kreisschiffahrt line; it costs DM 15 (DM 7.50 for children). If you are

Berlin Underground

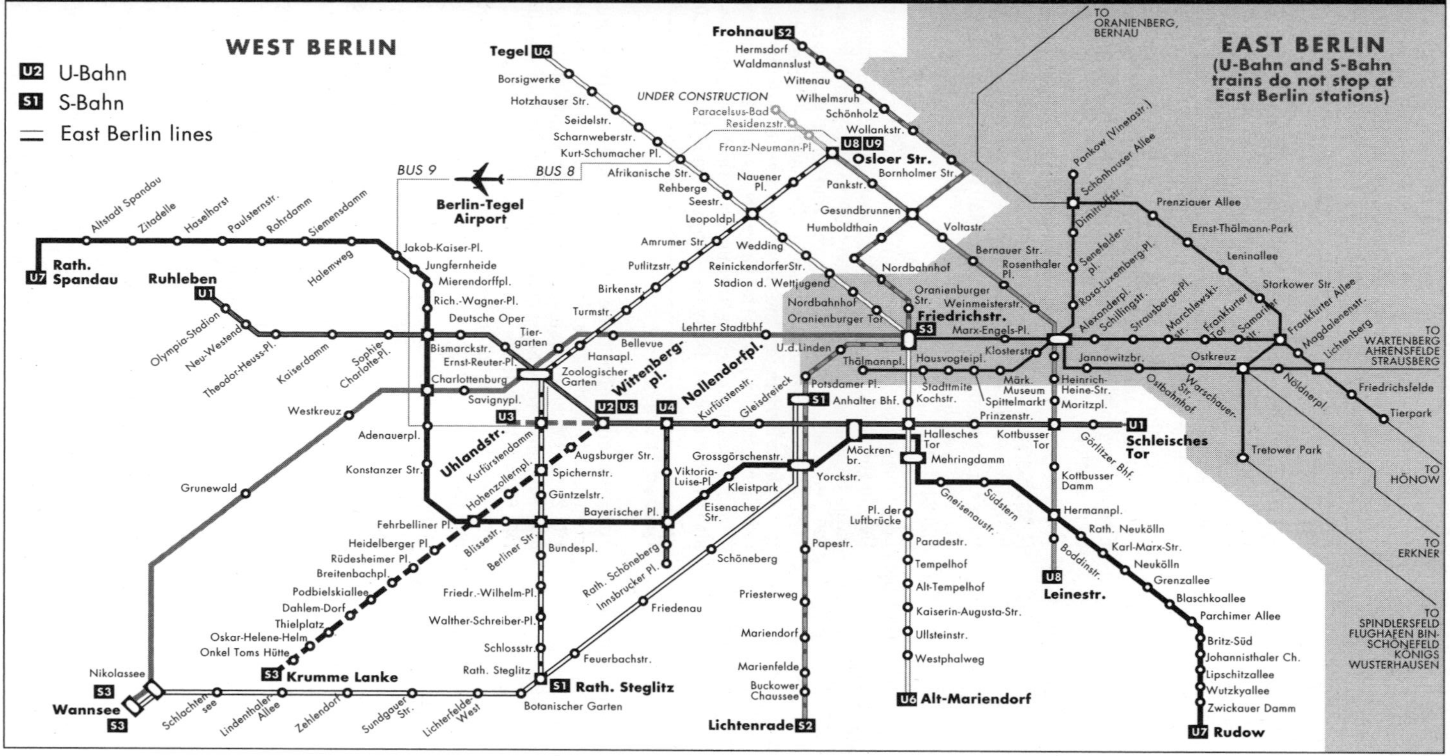

just making a short trip, buy a **Kurzstreckentarif.** It allows you to ride six bus stops or three U-bahn or S-bahn stops for DM 1.70 (DM 1.20 for children). Buy it in packs of five for the best value (DM 7 adults, DM 5 children). Finally, there's a ticket good only for rides along the Ku'damm on buses 19 and 29; it costs DM 1.

All regular tickets are available from vending machines at U-bahn and S-bahn stations. Punch your ticket into the red machine on the platform. The Berlin Ticket and the combined day ticket can only be bought from the main BVG ticket offices at the Bahnhof Zoo station and at the Kleistpark U-bahn station. For information, either call the **BVG** (Berliner Verkehrsbetriebe, tel. 030/216–5088) or go to the information office on Hardenbergplatz, directly in front of the Bahnhof Zoo train station.

By Taxi Fares start at DM 3.40 and increase by DM 1.50 per kilometer (DM 1.69 after midnight). There's an additional charge of 50 pfennigs per piece of luggage. Figure on paying around DM 10 for a ride the length of Ku'damm. Hail cabs in the street or order one by calling tel. 030/6902, 030/216–060, 030/261–026, or 030/240–202.

By Bike Bicycling is popular in Berlin. While it's not recommended in the downtown area, it's ideal in outlying areas. Some bike paths have been set up and many stores that rent bikes carry the Berlin biker's atlas to help you find them. Outfits renting bicycles are **Fahrradbüro** Berlin (Crellestr. 6 Schöneberg), the **Faarradverleih** at the Krumme Lanke U-bahn station (Fischerhuttenstr.), and the **Faarradverleih** at the Grunewald U-bahn station or Schmetterlingsplatz (bicycles-built-for-two also available here). Daily fees range from DM 10 to DM 20.

Guided Tours

Orientation Tours Four companies offer more or less identical tours (in English), covering all major sights. Tours last two to three hours and cost DM 20 to DM 30. Combined tours of West and East Berlin are also available; they last between four and five hours and cost DM 65 to DM 70. If the prospect of visiting both halves of the city in one day is daunting, see one half on one day and the other half the following day.

Tour Operators **Berliner Bären Stadtrundfahrten** (BBS, Rankestr. 35, tel. 030/213–4077). Groups depart from the corner of Rankestrasse and Kurfürstdendamm.

Berolina Stadtrundfahrten (Kurfürstendamm 220, tel. 030/883–3131). Groups depart from the corner of Kurfürstendamm and Meinekestrasse.

Bus Verkehr Berlin (BVB, Kurfürstendamm 225, tel. 030/882–6847). Tours leave from Kurfürstendamm 225.

Severin & Kühn (Kurfürstendamm 216, tel. 030/883–1015). Groups leave from the corner of Kurfürstendamm and Fasanenstrasse.

Special-Interest Tours Sightseeing tours with a cultural/historical bias are offered by **Kultur Kontor** (Savignypl. 9–10, tel. 030/310–888). Tours include "Berlin Becoming Berlin," "Berlin 1933–45," and "The Roaring '20s." Departures are from the corner of Savignyplatz and Kantstrasse.

Boat Trips A tour of the **Havel lakes** is the thing to do in summer. Trips begin at Wannsee (S-bahn: Wannsee) and at the Greenwich Promenade in Tegel (U-bahn: Tegel). You'll sail on either the whale-shaped vessel *Moby Dick* or the *Havel Queen*, a Mississippi-style boat, and cruise 17 miles through the lakes and past forests. Tours last 4½ hours and cost between DM 10 and DM 15. See below for operators.

Tours of downtown Berlin's **canals** take in sights such as the Charlottenburg Palace and the Congress Hall. Tours depart from Kottbusser Bridge in Kreuzberg and cost around DM 10.

Tour Operators **Stern- und Kreisschiffahrt** (Scahtlebenstr. 60, tel. 030/803–8750).
Reederei Bruno Winkler (Levetzowstr. 12a, tel. 030/391–7010).
Reederei Heinz Winkler (Planufer 78, tel. 030/691–3782).

Exploring Berlin

Numbers in the margin correspond with points of interest on the Berlin map.

Highlights for First-time Visitors

Kaiser Wilhelm Gedächtniskirche (Memorial Church)
Kaufhaus des Westen (Department Store of the West)
Zoologischer Garten (Zoological Gardens)
Checkpoint Charlie
Schloss Charlottenburg (Charlottenburg Palace)
Ägyptisches Museum (Egyptian Museum)

West Berlin

Your tour of West Berlin begins on its best-known street, the
1 **Kurfürstendamm.** Berliners (and most visitors as well) refer to it affectionately as the Ku'damm. It serves as West Berlin's main street, as close to a grand boulevard as you'll find on this side of the Wall. It is the city's busiest artery and best-known shopping street and promenade. Its two-mile length is lined with shops, department stores, art galleries, theaters, movie houses, hotels, and some 100 restaurants, bars, clubs, and sidewalk cafés. It bustles with shoppers and strollers most of the day and fairly far into the night. Traffic can remain heavy into the wee hours of the morning.

This busy thoroughfare was first laid out in the 16th century as the path by which Elector Joachim II traveled from his palace on the Spree River to his hunting lodge in the Grunewald. The Kurfürstendamm (Elector's Causeway) was developed into a major route in the late 19th century on the initiative of Chancellor Bismarck, the "Iron Chancellor," who was the force behind the unification of Germany.

In prewar Berlin the Ku'damm occupied not nearly the importance it does today in West Berlin. It was a busy shopping street, but by no means the city's most elegant one, being fairly far removed from the heart of the city, which was on the opposite side of the Brandenburg Gate in what is East Berlin today. The Ku'damm's prewar fame was tied mainly to the rowdy bars and dance halls that studded much of its length and its side streets. Some of these were really low-down dives, scenes of erotic circuses, where kinky sex was the norm.

Berlin

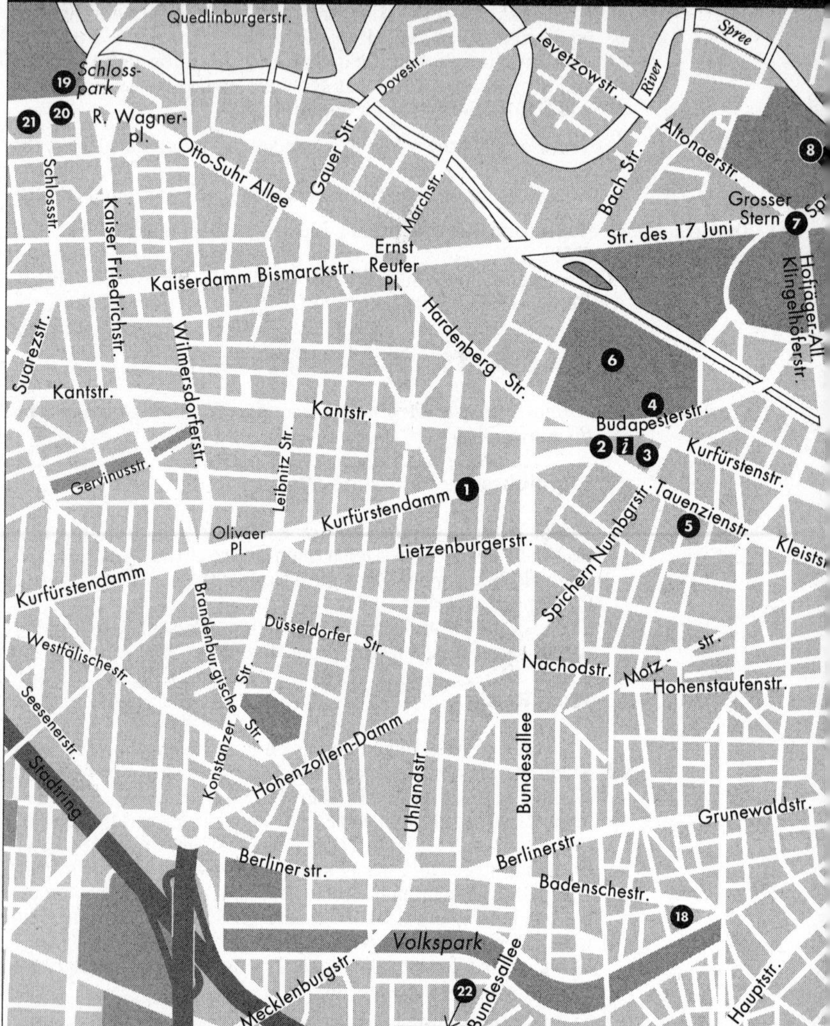

Ägyptisches Museum, **20**
Alte Kammergericht, **14**
Antikenmuseum, **21**
Brandenburger Tor, **11**
Checkpoint Charlie, **16**
Dahlem Museum Complex, **22**
Elefantor, **4**
Europe-Centre, **3**
Kaiser Wilhelm Gedächtniskirche, **2**
Kaufhaus des Westen, **5**
Kongresshalle, **9**
Kreuzberg, **17**
Kulturforum, **15**
Kurfürstendamm, **1**
Potsdamerplatz, **13**
Rathaus Schöneberg, **18**
Reichstag, **10**
Schloss Bellevue, **8**
Schloss Charlottenburg, **19**
Siegessäule, **7**
Soviet Victory Memorial, **12**
Zoologischer Garten, **6**

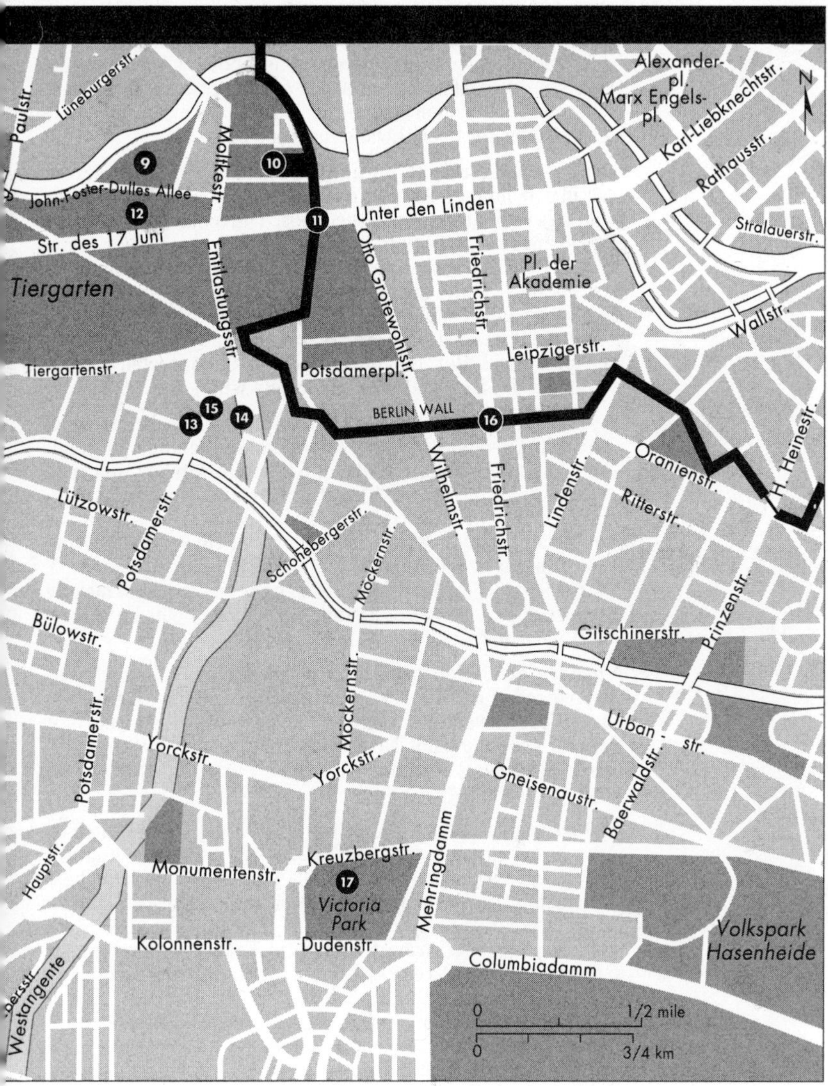
Alexander-
pl.
Marx Engels-
pl.
Karl-Liebknechtstr.
Rathausstr.
Stralauerstr.
Lüneburgerstr.
Paulstr.
Moltkestr.
John-Foster-Dulles Allee
Unter den Linden
Str. des 17 Juni
Entlastungsstr.
Otto Grotewohlstr.
Friedrichstr.
Pl. der
Akademie
Tiergarten
Wallstr.
Leipzigerstr.
Tiergartenstr.
Potsdamerpl.
BERLIN WALL
Oranienstr.
H. Heinestr.
Ritterstr.
Lindenstr.
Wilhelmstr.
Lützowstr.
Potsdamerstr.
Schöneberger str.
Möckernstr.
Bülowstr.
Gitschinerstr.
Prinzenstr.
Urban
str.
Yorckstr.
Gneisenaustr.
Baerwaldstr.
Mehringdamm
Kreuzbergstr.
Monumentenstr.
Victoria
Park
Hauptstr.
Kolonnenstr.
Dudenstr.
Columbiadamm
Volkspark
Hasenheide
Westangente
0
1/2 mile
0
3/4 km
N
9
10
11
12
13
14
15
16
17

Similar clubs, along with cabarets and avant-garde theaters, were set on and along side streets of the Friedrichstrasse, now in the Soviet sector just beyond Checkpoint Charlie. While there's no nighttime action at all on the now dreary Friedrichstrasse, Ku'damm certainly has its share of *Kneipen*, the German term for friendly neighborhood bars.

Along with the rest of Berlin, the Ku'damm suffered severe wartime bombing. Almost half of its 245 late 19th-century buildings were destroyed in the 1940s. The remaining buildings were damaged in varying degrees. What you see today (as in most of Berlin) is either restored, or was constructed over the past decades. While the street is frequently described as "glittering" and/or "sophisticated," there are those who are convinced it has lost whatever real charm and flair it may once have possessed. But it is certainly the liveliest stretch of roadway in Berlin, East and West, definitely where the action is.

The Ku'damm starts at the western end of the Breitscheidplatz, a large square on which several notable landmarks stand. 2 The ruins of the **Kaiser Wilhelm Gedächtniskirche** (Memorial Church), built between 1891 and 1895, stand as a dramatic reminder of the war's destruction. The bell tower, now known as the "hollow tooth," is all that remains of this once-imposing church that was dedicated to the Emperor, Kaiser Wilhelm I. On the hour, you'll hear the chimes in the tower play a melody composed by the emperor's grandson, Prince Louis Ferdinand von Hohenzollern.

A historic exhibition inside the tower features a religious cross constructed of nails that were recovered from the ashes of the burned-out Coventry Cathedral in England, destroyed in a German bombing raid, November 1940. *Kaiser Wilhelm Memorial Church. Admission free. Open Tues.–Sat. 10–6, Sun. 11–6.*

In stark contrast to the old bell tower is the adjoining Memorial Church and tower built in 1961. This ultramodern octagonal church, with its myriad honeycomb windows, is perhaps best described by its nickname: the lipstick and powder box. The interior is dominated by the brilliant blue of its stained glass windows, imported from Chartres in France. Church music and organ concerts are presented in the church regularly.

Time Out Set some time aside for a coffee at the Einstein Stadtcafe where you can have your pick among a variety of exotic coffees. You'll also find an art gallery on the first floor of this fine 19th-century mansion.

3 Mere steps away from the new Memorial Church is the **Europa-Centre,** a vast shopping and business complex on the east side of the Briedscheidplatz. This 1960's 22-story tower block—dubbed "Pepper's Manhattan" after its architect, K. H. Pepper—houses more than 100 shops, restaurants and cafés, an ice rink, two cinemas, a casino, and the Verkehrsamt (Tourist Information Center). The Europa-Centre caters to the visitor's every whim. You can even find thermal baths above the car park at the very top.

For a spectacular view of the city, take the lift to the i-Punkt restaurant and observation platform on the 22nd floor.

Across from the entrance to the Tourist Information Center is
4 Budapesterstrasse and the **Elefantor** (Elephant Gate), which is the main entrance to Berlin's aquarium, part of the adjoining zoo complex. Before visiting the zoo, take a stroll along Tauenzienstrasse, the boulevard that runs southeast away from the corner of the Europa-Centre. Tauenzienstrasse leads you straight to West Germany's largest department store, the
5 **Kaufhaus des Westen** (Department Store of the West), known to Berliners as KadeWe. A wide selection of goods can be found on its six floors, but it is most renowned for its food and delicatessen counters, restaurants, champagne bars, and beer bars covering the entire top floor.

Go into the U-bahn station near KadeWe on Wittenbergplatz. This subway station, Berlin's first, was built in 1913 and has recently been painstakingly restored. Take the train for one stop to the Zoologischer Garten. This station, also known as Bahnhof Zoo (Zoo Station), also serves as West Berlin's main railway station and the point of arrival for trains coming from West Germany.

6 Opposite the station is the entrance to the **Zoologischer Garten** (Zoological Gardens). Dating from 1844, it is the oldest zoo in Germany and is set in the southwestern corner of the 630-acre park called the Tiergarten (Animal Garden). The northern edge of the park is bounded by the Spree River, which flows from East Berlin. Even if you're not a zoo enthusiast, both the park and the very modern zoo offer much of interest.

After being destroyed during the Second World War, the zoo was carefully redesigned to create surroundings as close to the animals' natural environment as possible. The zoo houses more than 11,000 animals, and has been successful at breeding rare species. The zoo boasts the most modern birdhouse in Europe, a terrarium renowned for its crocodiles, and an aquarium with over 10,000 fish, reptiles, and amphibians. *Zoologischer Garten. Hardenbergpl. 8. Admission to zoo only: DM 7 adults, DM 3.50 children. Combined tickets to zoo and aquarium: DM 11 adults, DM 5.50 children. Open daily 9–7, and 9–dusk in winter.*

From the zoo, you can set off diagonally through the Tiergarten, which in the 17th century served as the hunting grounds of the Great Elector. The park suffered severe damage from World War II bombing raids. Later, Berliners, desperate for fuel during the freezing winter of 1945–46, cut down much of its ancient forest for firewood. Replanting began in 1949, and today's visitor will see a beautifully laid-out park with some 14 miles of footpaths and 6½ acres of lakes and ponds.

At the center of the park you approach the traffic intersection known as the Grosser Stern (Big Star), so-called because five roads meet here. This is the park's highest point, and the site of
7 the **Siegessäule** (Triumphal Column). This 210-foot-high granite, sandstone, and bronze column was originally erected in 1873 to commemorate Prussia's victory in the Franco-Prussian War. However, it was not placed in its present location. Rather, it was set up on the Königsplatz (King's Square)—today's Platz der Republik (Square of the Republic).

The column came close to being finished off by anarchists in 1921, after the collapse of the empire. Six kilos of explosives were placed in its stairwell. The fuse was already sizzling when the bomb was discovered. In 1939, as Hitler was having Berlin redesigned according to his megalomaniacal plans, the column was moved to its present site. World War II bombs missed the column. What you see today is the original structure.

A climb of 285 steps up through the column to the observation platform affords splendid views across much of Berlin, West and East. *Siegessäule at Grosse Stern. Admission: DM 1.20 adults, 70 pf children. Open Mon. 1–7, Tues.–Sun. 9–7.*

8 Follow the Spreeweg Road from the Grosser Stern to **Schloss Bellevue** (Bellevue Palace). Built on the Spree River in 1775 for Frederick the Great's youngest brother Prince Augustus-Ferdinand, it has served as the West German president's official residence in West Berlin since 1959. The 50-acre palace grounds have been transformed into a park with an English garden on its western edge. This park-within-a-park was originally dedicated by an English statesman, Anthony Eden, who later became one of Nazi Germany's staunchest political opponents. Berliners often refer to it jokingly as the Garden of Eden. *Schloss Bellevue Park. Open daily 8–dusk. Closed when the president is in residence.*

Leave the Schloss Bellevue and head east along the John-Foster-Dulles Allee, keeping the Spree River in sight on your
9 left. You'll soon arrive at the **Kongresshalle** (Congress Hall), a meeting and conference center. The hall was built in 1957 as the American contribution to the International Building Exhibition, Interbau. Its resemblance to an open oyster shell earned it the title "pregnant oyster." A daring construction at the time, the roof collapsed in 1980 but has since been rebuilt.

Rejoin John-Foster-Dulles Allee again and continue east to the
10 **Reichstag** (Parliament Building), which stands in the shadow of the Berlin Wall. The building was erected in the late 19th century to house the Prussian parliament and later performed a similar function for the ill-fated Weimar Republic.

The Reichstag was burned to a shell under mysterious circumstances on the night of February 28, 1933, an event that provided the Nazis with a convenient pretext for outlawing all opposition parties. After rebuilding, the Reichstag was again badly damaged in 1945 in the last Allied offensive of the war. Today the west wing houses a popular exhibition of German history since 1800. *Reichstag Exhibition: Questions of German History in the Reichstag. Pl. der Republik. Admission free. Open Tues.–Sun. 10–5.*

Next to the Reichstag is one of a number of viewing platforms enabling you to look across the Wall into East Berlin. To the north, a number of crucifixes along the banks of the Spree River indicate points where East Germans died trying to escape. Construction of the Wall started on August 13th, 1961; it is now 102 miles long and snakes through Berlin for 28 miles. Here, it is at its thickest—more than three feet of tank-proof concrete—and the strip on the far side is equipped with sophisticated alarm systems. Just across the way you can see heavily armed guards in their watchtowers, in all likelihood studying you through high-powered field glasses.

Most West Berliners have long since grown accustomed to this concrete boundary around their world, but to the firsttime visitor it's a chilling spectacle; graffiti on the West side of the Wall provides the only relief from the stark power of this massive structure.

11 From the platform you'll get a good view of the **Brandenburger Tor** (Brandenburg Gate), and you can get better, relatively close-up, views from the square directly in front of this imposing monument.

The Brandenburg Gate stands in East Berlin and is inaccessible to both East and West Berliners alike because it is placed in the no-man's-land on the East Berlin side of the Wall.

Once the city's proud emblem, it has become a symbol of Germany's division. The gate, built in 1789 for King Frederick William II as a triumphal arch, was inspired by the Proplyaea of the Parthenon. Troops paraded before it after successful campaigns. The last time the gate was witness to a triumphant army was in 1945 when units of the Red Army stormed through its portal.

The Victory Quadriga—a two-wheeled chariot driven by the Goddess of Peace and drawn by four stallions—which sits atop the gate, was added in 1793. Originally naked, the goddess was later modestly clothed in sheet copper after a wave of protests. It was smashed to pieces during World War II and not replaced until 1957, when the original molds were discovered in West Berlin and a new Quadriga was cast in copper. It was presented as a gift to the people of East Berlin, who hoisted it to the top of the newly refurbished gate. The story is still remembered as a remarkable instance of East-West cooperation.

A short way back along the wide boulevard that is the east-
west axis on a direct line between the Siesgessaule and Bran-
12 denburg Gate you will reach the **Soviet Victory Memorial,** a
Russian enclave in the West. Built directly after the end of hostilities, before power plays between opposing sides had been set in motion, it was located in the western rather than the eastern sector. Through an East-West arrangement it has been allowed to remain there, and now serves as a major attraction. It is on Strasse des 17 Juni (June 17th Street), a name that commemorates the unsuccessful uprising of East Berlin workers against the Soviets in 1953.

The semicircular monument, built in 1946, shows a bronze statue of a soldier. It rests on a marble plinth taken from Hitler's former Berlin headquarters. Flanked by what are said to be the first two tanks to have fought their way into Berlin in 1945, the monument is permanently guarded by Soviet soldiers who are in turn guarded by British soldiers and West German police. The guard is changed every hour, a ceremony you are permitted to watch from a discreet distance.

Turn south from the memorial and cross the tip of the
13 Tiergarten to **Potsdamerplatz,** a somewhat dull-looking square
that was once among the busiest squares in prewar Berlin. Potsdamerplatz is the point where the British, American, and Russian sectors meet and is often referred to as the three-sector corner. The Wall cuts through the center of the square. Not far from the square, part of the leveled wasteland on the other side of the wall (seen from the viewing platforms), lie the remains of Hitler's reinforced concrete bunker where he spent his last days.

14 On nearby Potsdamerstrasse is the former **Alte Kammergericht** (Prussian Court Building) in which many Nazi show trials were held before the infamous Judge Roland Freisler. The building was taken over by the Allies in 1945 and is still used by the Allied forces. It was here that the four-power agreement, which set the rules governing communication between the two halves of the city, was signed in 1971.

15 Just a block north, in nearby Kemperplatz, lies the **Kulturforum** (Cultural Forum), a large square where you'll find a series of fascinating museums and galleries. The roof that resembles a great wave belongs to the **Philharmonie** (Philharmonic Hall). Built in 1963, it is home to the renowned Berlin Philharmonic Orchestra. The functional design of the concert hall allows an audience of 2,000 to sit on all sides of the orchestra. The brilliant accoustics more than make up for those who face the backs of the orchestra. *The Philharmonie Ticket Office. Mattäikirchst. 1. Open weekdays 3:30–6 and weekends 11–2.*

The Philharmonie added the **Musikinstrumenten-Museum** (Musical Instruments Museum) to its attractions in 1984. It is well worth a visit for its fascinating collection of keyboard, string, wind, and percussion instruments. *Tiergartenstr. 1, tel. 030/254–810. Admission free. Open Tues.–Sat. 9–5, Sun. 10–5. Guided tours on Saturdays at 11 with a noon presentation of the Wurlitzer organ. Tour admission: DM 3.*

Opposite the Philharmonie is the **Kunstgewerbemuseum** (Museum of Decorative Arts). Inside this three-story building you'll find a display of the development of the arts and crafts in Europe from the Middle Ages to the present day. Among its treasures is the Welfenschatz (Guelph Treasure), a collection of 16th-century gold and silver plate from Nürnburg. The most impressive single piece is a reliquary in the form of a domed Byzantine church. Made in Köln in 1175, it is believed to have held the head of St. Gregory when it was brought back from Constantinople in 1773. Other displays of particular interest are the ceramics and porcelains. *Tiergartenstr. 6, tel. 030/266–92911. Admission free. Open Tues.–Sun. 9–5.*

Leave the museum and walk south past the mid-19th-century church of St. Matthaeus to the **Nationalgalerie** (New National Gallery), a modern glass and steel building designed by Mies van der Rohe and built in the mid-1960's.

The gallery's collection comprises paintings, sculptures, and drawings from the 19th and 20th centuries with an accent on works by such Impressionists as Manet, Monet, Renoir, and Pissarro. Other schools represented are German Romantics, Realists, Expressionists, Surrealists, and the Bauhaus. The gallery also has a growing collection of contemporary art from Europe and America. *Potsdamerstr. 50, tel. 030/2666. Admission free to downstairs gallery. Open Tues.–Sun. 9–5.*

The last stop on the tour of West Berlin's Cultural Forum is the **Staatsbibliothek** (National Library), opposite the Nationalgalerie. This modern building housing one of the largest libraries in Europe, was designed by Hans Scharoun, the architect of the Philharmonie. *Potsdamerstr. 33. Admission free. Open Mon.–Fri. 9–5, Sat. 9–1. The reading room, catalogues, and bibliographies are open weekdays 9–9, Sat. 9–5.*

Since it's a fairly long walk along the Wall to the next point on the tour—20 minutes or more—it is suggested you take one of a number of buses that will get you to Friedrichstrasse and
16 **Checkpoint Charlie,** the Allied checkpoint through which foreign motorists must pass to enter and leave East Berlin, and one of two points where you, as a pedestrian, can cross into and out of East Berlin on your own. (For excursions into East Berlin, see Chapter 17.) At Checkpoint Charlie you can visit the (Wall Museum), **Haus am Checkpoint Charlie,** located to the right of the Allied control booth. The museum contains a history of the tragic events leading up to the erection of the Wall as well as records and photographs documenting methods used by individuals to cross over into the West. One of the more ingenious instruments of escape is a miniature submarine. Also displayed are paintings and drawings and historical exhibits of Berlin history since the erection of the Wall. *Friedrichstr. 44. Admission free. Open daily 9 AM–10 PM.*

From here, move away from the oppressiveness of the Wall and into the open air of West Berlin's highest natural hill, the
17 **Kreuzberg** (Hill of the Cross) in Victoriapark. Take the U-bahn at Kochstrasse, across from Checkpoint Charlie, and travel two stops on the U-6 line to Mehringdamm station. Leave by the Kreuzbergstrasse exit.

The Kreuzberg is on your left, crowned by an iron cross. The monument was erected in 1821 to commemorate the 1813–15 Wars of Liberation. The view from the top embraces the center of East Berlin to the north and Tempelhof military airfield to the south. A vineyard on the sheltered southern slope of the Kreuzberg produces Germany's rarest wine, the Kreuznerberger. It is produced in such small quantities that it is only served at official Berlin functions.

Leave the park by the western exit on Monumentenstrasse and continue until you reach the intersection with Potsdamerstrasse on the right. Turn left into Hauptstrasse and continue south until you reach Dominicus-Strasse. Turn right here and take the first turning on your left, Elsas-Strasse. It will lead
18 you straight to the **Rathaus Schöneberg** (Schöneberg Town Hall).

Since the division of the two Berlins in 1948, the Rathaus Schöneberg has been home to the West Berlin Chamber of Deputies and their Senate. The Rathaus is of special interest to Americans, for it was here, on June 26, 1963, that John F. Kennedy made his memorable "Ich bin ein Berliner" speech just months before his assassination.

In German the term "Berliner" refers both to a native of Berlin and to a popular type of jelly doughnut (without the hole). Kennedy's remark is remembered today as much for this unfortunate gaffe of referring to himself as *a* Berliner (a doughnut?) as for its intended meaning. (If he had said "Ich bin Berliner," all would have been well.)

Completed in 1914, the Rathaus has a 237-foot-high tower from which a replica of the Liberty Bell is rung each day at noon. The bell was given by the American people as a symbol of their support for the West Berliners' struggle to preserve freedom. A document bears the signatures of 17 million Americans who pledged their solidarity with the people of West Berlin. *Rat-*

haus Schöneberg Bell Tower. Innsbrücke Str. Open Wed. and Sun. 10–4.

After the Kreuzberg and Rathaus, you will undoubtedly have had more than enough touring for one day. This makes for the perfect place to break the tour, and pick up with Schloss Charlottenburg and the most important museums on another day.

However, should you want to continue, then leave the Rathaus and head north up the Innsbrücke strasse to the U-bahn station at Bayerischer Platz. Take the U-7 line toward Rathaus Spandau eight stops and get off at Mierendorffplatz. Head
19 south along Mierendorffstrasse to the **Schloss Charlottenburg** (Charlottenburg Palace).

The Charlottenburg Palace complex can be considered the showplace of West Berlin, the most monumental memento of imperial days in the western sector. (Since it's a considerable distance from city center, get there on bus number 74 leaving from near Memorial Church.) This sumptuous palace served as a city residence for the Prussian rulers. It has on occasion been referred to as Berlin's very own Versailles. Indeed, some claim that it was Napoléon, when he invaded Berlin in 1806, who first made the comparison to the Sun King's spectacular château near Paris. The comparison hardly seems appropriate. Charlottenburg is on a smaller, more intimate scale than Versailles. Its proportions are restrained; formal gardens are not nearly as vast. Nor are you likely to encounter the kind of crowds that flock to Versailles. But you are sure to be suitably impressed.

A full day is not too much time to devote to Charlottenburg. In addition to the apartments of the Prussian nobility, there are the landscaped gardens to be visited, and three excellent museums are set within the grounds.

This gorgeous palace started as a modest royal summer residence in 1695, built on the orders of King Frederick I for his wife, Queen Sophie-Charlotte. Later, in the 18th century, Frederick the Great made a number of additions, such as the dome and several wings in the Rococo style. In time the complex evolved into the massive Teutonic royal domain you see today.

The palace was severely damaged during World War II but has been painstakingly restored. Many of the original furnishings and works of art survived the war and are on display today.

Behind heavy iron gates, the Court of Honor—the courtyard in front of the palace—is dominated by a fine Baroque statue, the Reiterstandbild des Grossen Kurfursten (the equestrian statue of the Great Elector). A 156-foot-high domed tower capped by a gilded statue of Fortune rises above the main entrance to the palace.

Inside, in the main building, the suites of Frederick I and his wife Sophie-Charlotte are furnished in the prevailing style of the era. Paintings include royal portraits by Antoine Pesne, a noted court painter of the 18th century. On the first floor you can visit the Oak Gallery, the early 18th-century Palace Chapel, and the suites of Frederick Wilhelm II and Frederick Wilhelm III, furnished in the Biedermeier style.

Visits to the royal apartments are by guided tour only; tours leave every hour on the hour from 9 to 4. Parks and gardens can be visited for free and offer a pleasant respite from sightseeing.

A gracious staircase leads up to the sumptuous State Dining Room and the 138-foot-long Golden Gallery. West of the staircase are the rooms of Frederick the Great, in which the king's extravagant collection of works by Watteau, Chardin and Pesne are displayed. In one glass cupboard you'll see the coronation crown, stripped of its jewels by the king, who gave the most valuable gemstones to his wife. Also in the new wing is the National Gallery's collection of masterpieces from 19th-century German painters such as Caspar David Friedrich, the leading member of the German Romantic school. *Schloss Charlottenburg. Luisenpl. Admission DM 6. Open: Tues.–Sun. 9–5.*

The park surrounding the palace was first laid out in 1697. Destroyed during the war, it has since been restored to its original Baroque design. An avenue of cypress trees leads to the lake.

There are several buildings in the park that deserve particular attention, among which are the Belvedere, a teahouse overlooking the lake and Spree River, and the Shinkel Pavilion behind the palace near the river. The pavilion, modeled on a villa in Naples where the king stayed in 1822, was built in 1824–25 by Karl Friedrich Schinkel, one of 19th-century Berlin's favorite architects. It houses paintings by Caspar David Friedrich and late 18th-century furniture. Also of interest in the park is the mausoleum, which contains the tombs of King Friedrich Wilhelm II and Queen Louise.

Just to the south of the palace are three small, distinguished
20 museums. The first, across from the palace, is the **Ägyptisches Museum** (Egyptian Museum). The building, once the east guardhouse and residence of the king's bodyguard, is now home to the famous bust of the exquisite Queen Nefertiti. The 3,300-year old Egyptian queen is the centerpiece of a collection of works that spans Egypt's history from 4,000 BC and includes one of the best preserved mummies outside Cairo. *Östlicher Stülerbau, Schlosstr. 1, tel. 030/320–911. Admission free. Open Sun.–Thurs. 9–5.*

Opposite the Ägyptisches Museum in the former west guard-
21 house is the **Antikenmuseum** (Antique Museum). The collection comprises ceramics and bronzes as well as everyday utensils from ancient Greece and Rome and a number of Greek vases from the 6th to 4th century BC. Also on display is a collection of Scythian gold and silver ware and jewelry found in the Mediterranean basin. *Weslicher Stuelerbau, Schlosstr. 1, tel. 030/320–911. Admission free. Open Sat.–Thurs. 9–5.*

The final museum, the **Museum für Vor- und Frügeschichte** (Museum of Pre- and Proto-history), is located in the western extension of the palace opposite Klausener Platz. The museum depicts the stages of the evolution of man from 1,000,000 BC to the Bronze Age. *Admission free. Open Sat.–Thurs. 9–5.*

Another stop on your tour of West Berlin is also a cluster of mu-
22 seums, the **Dahlem Museum complex.** The best way to get there is by the U-2 subway line, to Dahlem-Dorf station.

The Dahlem complex includes the **Gemäldegalerie** (Picture Gallery), the **Kupferstichkabinett** (Drawings and Prints Collection), the **Museum fur Völkerkunde** (Ethnographic Museum) and the **Skulpturengalerie** (Sculpture Gallery).

Begin with the **Gemäaldegalerie.** One of Germany's finest art galleries, it houses a broad selection of European paintings from the 13th to 18th century. Rembrandt devotees will be particularly pleased to find the world's second largest Rembrandt collection located on the second floor.

Several rooms on the first floor are reserved for paintings by German masters, among them Dürer, Cranach, and Holbein. An adjoining gallery houses the works of the Italian masters—Botticelli, Titian, Giotto, Filippo Lippi, and Raphael—and another gallery on the first floor is devoted to paintings by Dutch masters of the 15th and 16th centuries: van Eyck, Bosch, Brueghel, van Dyck, and van der Weyden.

Flemish and Dutch paintings from the 17th century are displayed on the floor above. In the Rembrandt section, where there are 21 paintings by the master, you can see "The Man with the Golden Helmet," a painting formerly attributed to Rembrandt that has since proved by radioactive testing to have been the work of another artist of the same era. *Arnimallee 23–27, tel. 030/83011. Admission free. Open Tues.–Sun. 9–5.*

The **Kupferstichkabinett** (Drawings and Prints Collection) includes European woodcuts and engravings from the 15th to 18th century, several pen-and-ink drawings by Dürer, and 150 drawings by Rembrandt. There is also a photographic archive. *Entrance: Arnimallee. Admission free. Open Tues.–Fri. 9–4, Sat.–Sun. 9–5.*

The **Museum für Völkerkunde** (Ethnographic Museum) is internationally famous for its arts and artifacts from Africa, Asia, the South Seas, and ancient America. American visitors, homesick for a taste of their own history, should look out for the North American Indian wigwams and the feather cape that once belonged to Hawaii's 18th-century King Kamehameha I. Also of interest is the display of native huts from New Guinea and New Zealand. *Museum für Völkerkunde. Open Tues.–Fri. 9–5. Admission free. Entrance: Lansstr.*

The **Skulpturengalerie** (Sculpture Gallery) houses Byzantine and European sculpture from the 3rd to 18th century. Included in its collection is Donatello's "Madonna and Child," sculpted in 1422. *Entrance: Lansstr. Admission free. Open Tues.–Sun. 9–5.*

Beyond the tour of monuments, museums, and aspects relating to the Wall and the divided city, no visit to West Berlin would be complete without seeing the vast world of lakes and greenery along its western extremities. In no other city has such an expanse of uninterrupted natural surroundings been preserved within city limits.

Here, along West Berlin's fringe, are some 60 lakes, connected by rivers, streams, and canals, in a verdant setting of meadows, woods, and forests. Excursion steamers ply the water wonderland of the Wannsee and Havel. (*See* Boat Trips, above, for details.) You can tramp for hours through the green belt of the Grünewald. On weekends in spring and fall and daily in summer the Berliners are out in force, swimming, sailing their boats, tramping through the woods, riding horseback. To the north, practically within sight of the barbed-wire barriers, there are still a few working farms. Time and progress seem to have passed right by the rustic village of Lubars.

You can reach Grünewald and the Wannsee on the S-3 suburban line from Zoo Station. To reach Lubars, take the U-6 subway to Tegel, then bus no. 20 to Lubars.

Finally—last but hardly least—there is East Berlin. Excursions into the city on the other side of the Wall are discussed in detail in Chapter 17. You can arrange a guided bus tour (*see* Guided Tours, above) from West Berlin, or cross over on foot at that Cold-War icon, Checkpoint Charlie at Friedreichstrasse. It is also possible to cross the border by subway, on the U-6 line, after making a stop at Friedrichstrasse where you pass through a customs and passport control (*see* Chapter 17 for more information).

Shopping

Gift Ideas Berlin is a city of alluring stores and boutiques. Despite its cosmopolitan gloss, prices are generally lower than in cities like Munich and Hamburg.

Fine **porcelain** is still produced at the former Royal Prussian Porcelain Factory, now called **Staatliche Porzellan Manufactur,** or KPM. This delicate, handmade, hand-painted china is sold at KPM's store at Kurfürstendamm 264, but it may be more fun to visit the factory salesroom at Wegelystrasse 1. It also sells seconds at reduced prices. If you long to have the Egyptian Museum's Queen Nefertiti on your mantelpiece at home, try the **Gipsformerei der Staatlichen Museen Preussischer Kulturbesitz** (Sophie-Charlotte-Str. 17). It sells plaster casts of this and other treasures from the city's museums.

Take home a regiment of **tin figures,** painted or to paint yourself, from the **Berliner Zinnfigurenkabinett** (Knesebeckstr. 88).

Antiques On Saturdays and Sundays from 8 to 4, the colorful and lively **antiques flea market** on Strasse des 17 Juni swings into action. Don't expect to pick up many bargains—or to have the place to yourself. Not far from Wittenbergplatz is **Keithstrasse,** a street given over to antiques stores. There are also several small antiques stores in the converted subway cars of the **Nollendorf Flohmarkt.** Eisenacherstrasse, Fuggerstrasse, Kalckreuthstrasse, Motzstrasse, and Nollendorfstrasse—all close to Nollendorfplatz—have many antiques stores of varying quality. Another good street for antiques is **Suarezstrasse,** between Kantstrasse and Bismarckstrasse.

Shopping Districts The liveliest and most famous shopping area in West Berlin is the **Kurfürstendamm** and its side streets, especially between **Breitscheidplatz** and **Olivaer Platz.** The **Europa-Centre** at Breitscheidplatz encompasses nearly 100 stores, cafés, and restaurants—this is not a place to bargain-hunt, though! Running east from Breitscheidplatz is **Tauenzienstrasse,** another shopping street. At the end of it is Berlin's most celebrated department store, **KadeWe.** New and elegant malls include the **Gloria Galerie** (opposite the Wertheim department store on Ku'damm) and the **Uhland-Passage** (connecting Uhlandstrasse and Fasanenstrasse). In both, you'll find leading name stores as well as cafés and restaurants.

For trendier clothes, try the boutiques along **Bleibtreustrasse.** One of the more avant-garde fashion boutiques is **Durchbruch** (Schlutterstr. 54), around the corner. The name means "breakthrough," and the store lives up to its name by selling six different designers' outrageous styles. Less trendy and much less expensive is the mall, **Wilmersdorferstrasse** where price-conscious Berliners do their shopping. It's packed on weekends.

Department Stores The classiest department store in Berlin is **KadeWe,** the Kaufhaus des Westen (Department Store of the West, as it's modestly known in English), at Wittenbergplatz. The biggest department store in Europe, the KadeWe is a grand-scale emporium in modern guise. Be sure to check out the food department, which occupies the whole sixth floor. The other main department store downtown is **Wertheim** on Ku'damm. Neither as big nor as attractive as the KadeWe, Wertheim nonetheless offers a large selection of fine wares.

Specialty Stores
Men's Clothing **Mientus** (Wilmersdorferstr. 73), a large, exclusive men's store, caters to expensive tastes. It offers both conventional businesswear as well as sporty and modern looks, and carries many top designer labels. Slightly less expensive and exclusive but still up there is **Erdmann,** (in the Europa-Centre facing Tauenzienstr.). For men's shoes, try **Budapester Schuhe** (Ku'damm 199).

Women's Clothing For German designer wear, try **Zenker** (Ku'damm 45). It's not cheap, but the styling is classic. If you're looking for international labels, drop by **Kramberg** (Ku'damm 56), and then go next door to **Granny's Step** where you'll find eveningwear styled along the lines of bygone times. For modern, Berlin-designed chic, check out **Filato** (Nürnbergstr. 24A). If you're feeling daring, browse through the extraordinary lingerie store **Nouvelle** (Bleibtreustr. 24). Elegant '20s intimate-wear made of fine, old-fashioned materials is its specialty.

Jewelry Fine hand-crafted jewelry can be found at **Wurzbarcher** (Ku'damm 36). **Axel Sedlatzek** (Ku'damm 45) also offers a good selection, but with a twist: He'll custom design body jewelry for men and women.

Sports and Fitness

Bicycling There are bike paths throughout the downtown area and the rest of the city. *See* Getting Around, above, for details of renting bikes.

Golf Berlin's leading club is the **Golf- und Landclub Wannsee** (Stölpchenweg, Wannsee, tel. 030/805–5075).

Jogging The **Tiergarten** is the best place for jogging in the downtown area. Run its length to the Wall and back and you'll cover five miles. Joggers can also take advantage of the grounds of **Charlottenburg** castle, two miles around. For longer runs, anything up to 20 miles, make for **Grunewald.**

Riding Horses are rented out by the **Reitschule Onkel Toms Hütte** (Onkel-Toms-Str. 172, tel. 030/813–2081). Children's ponies are stabled at **Ponyhof Lange** (Buckower Chaussee 82, Marienfelde, tel. 030/721–6008) and the **Ponyhof Wittenau** (Wittenauerstr. 80, tel. 030/402–8535).

Sailing and Windsurfing Boats and boards of all kinds are rented by **Jürgen Schöne** (tel. 030/381–5037) and **Scharfe Lanke** (tel. 030/361–5066).

Swimming The **Wannsee** and **Plötzensee** both have beaches; they get crowded summer weekends, however. There are pools throughout the city; there's bound to be at least one near where you're staying. For full listings, ask at the tourist office. The most impressive pool is the **Olympia-Schwimmstadion** at Olympischer Platz (U-bahn: Olympiastadion).

Tennis and Squash There are tennis courts and squash centers throughout the city; ask your hotel to direct you to the nearest. **Tennis & Squash City** (Brandenburgischestr. 31, Wilmersdorf, tel. 030/879–097) has seven tennis courts and 11 squash courts.

Dining

Dining in Berlin can mean sophisticated nouvelle specialties in upscale restaurants with linen tablecloths and hand-painted porcelain plates or hearty local specialties in atmospheric and inexpensive inns: The range is as vast as the city. Specialties to try include *Bockwurst*, a chubby frankfurter that's served in a variety of ways and sold in restaurants and at Bockwurst stands all over the city. *Schlesisches Himmelreich* is roast goose or pork served with potato dumplings in rich gravy. *Königsberger Klopse* consists of meatballs, herring, and capers —it tastes much better than it sounds. *Eisbein* (knuckle of pork) is a favorite throughout Prussia. It's served with sauerkraut and comes in portions that would make a caveman happy.

Highly recommended restaurants are indicated by a star ★.

Category	Cost*
Very Expensive	over DM 95
Expensive	DM 65–DM 95
Moderate	DM 45–DM 65
Inexpensive	DM 25–DM 45

* *per person for a three-course meal, excluding drinks.*

Very Expensive

★ **Bamberger Reiter.** Often proclaimed the city's best restaurant, Bamberger Reiter is the pride of its chef, Franz Raneburger. He relies on fresh market produce for his *Neue Deutsche Küche* (new German cuisine), so the menu changes daily. Fresh flowers set off this attractive oak-beamed restaurant. *Regensburgerstr. 7, tel. 030/24482. Reservations essential. Jacket and tie required. No credit cards. Closed lunch, Sun., Mon., and Aug. 1–20.*

Frühsammer's Restaurant an der Rehwiese. Here you can watch chef Peter Frühsammer at work in his open kitchen. His choice of daily menu is never remiss; the salmon is always a treat. The restaurant is in the annex of a turn-of-the-century villa in the Zehlendorf district (U-bahn to Krumme Lanke and then bus 53 to Rehweise). *Matterhornstr. 101, tel. 030/803–2720. Reservations essential. Jacket and tie required. AE, DC, MC, V. Closed lunch, Sun., and Mon.*

Rockendorfs. Only fixed-price menus, some up to nine courses, are offered in this elegant restaurant in the north of the city. Exquisitely presented on fine porcelain, the mainly nouvelle

Berlin Dining

Alt-Berliner Weissbierstube, **14**
Alt-Luxembourg, **2**
Alt-Nürnberg, **9**
Bamberger Reiter, **11**
Blockhaus Nikolskoe, **4**
Conti Fischstuben, **10**
Forsthaus Paulsborn, **5**
Frühsammer's Restaurant an der Rehwiese, **3**
Hardtke, **7**
Hecker's Deele, **6**
Mundart Restaurant, **13**
Ponte Vecchio, **1**
Ratskeller Schöneberg, **12**
Rockendorfs, **8**

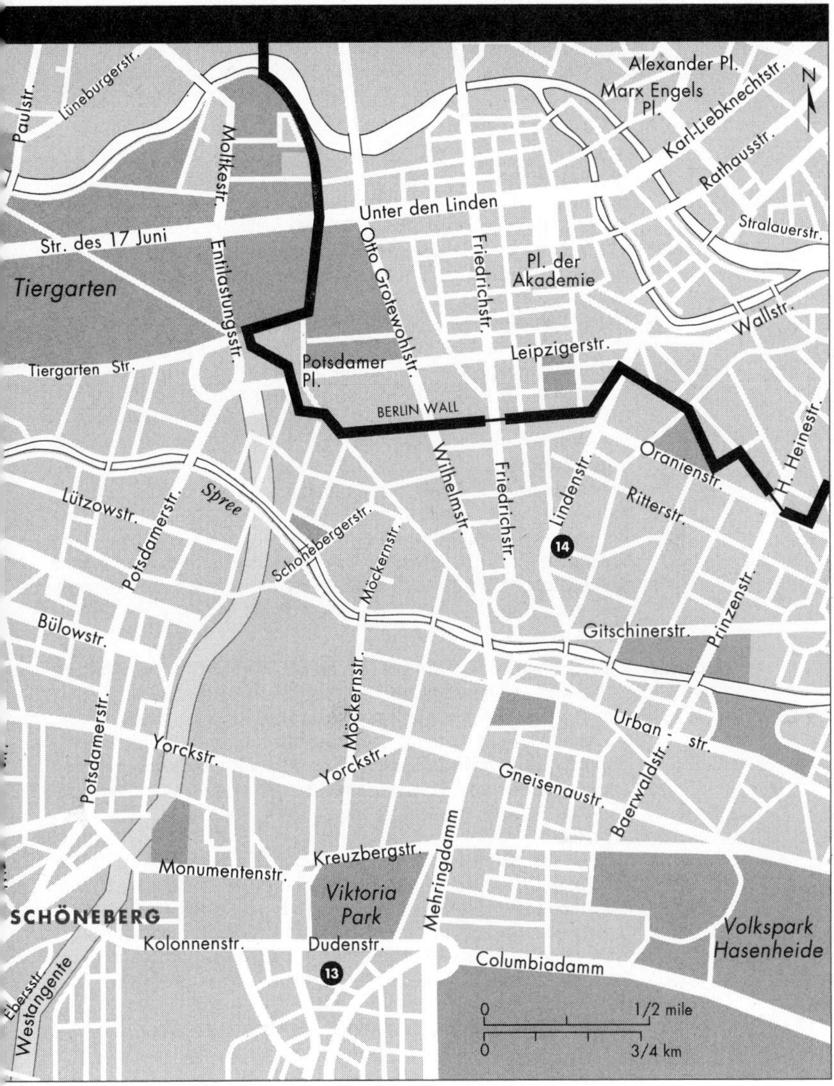
Alexander Pl.
Marx Engels Pl.
Karl-Liebknechtstr.
Rathausstr.
Stralauerstr.
Wallstr.
N
Paulstr.
Lüneburgerstr.
Moltkestr.
Unter den Linden
Str. des 17 Juni
Tiergarten
Entlastungsstr.
Otto Grotewohlstr.
Friedrichstr.
Pl. der Akademie
Leipzigerstr.
Tiergarten Str.
Potsdamer Pl.
BERLIN WALL
Wilhelmstr.
Friedrichstr.
Lindenstr.
Oranienstr.
Ritterstr.
H. Heinestr.
Lützowstr.
Spree
Potsdamerstr.
Schoneberger str.
Möckernstr.
Bülowstr.
Gitschinerstr.
Prinzenstr.
Möckernstr.
Potsdamerstr.
Yorckstr.
Yorckstr.
Urban str.
Gneisenaustr.
Baerwaldstr.
Mehringdamm
Monumentenstr.
Kreuzbergstr.
Viktoria Park
SCHÖNEBERG
Kolonnenstr.
Dudenstr.
Volkspark Hasenheide
Columbiadamm
Eberstr.
Westangente
0 1/2 mile
0 3/4 km

specialties are sometimes fused with classic German cuisine. The furnishings are intentionally spare. *Dusterhauptstr. 1, tel. 030/402–3099. Reservations essential. Jacket and tie required. AE, DC, MC. Closed Sun., Mon., 3 weeks in summer, Christmas, and New Year's.*

Expensive

★ **Alt-Luxembourg.** There are only nine tables at this popular restaurant in the Charlottenburg district, with attentive service enhancing the intimate setting. Chef Kurt Wannebacher produces a divine lobster lasagna. *Pestalozzistr. 70, tel. 030/323–8730. Reservations essential. Jacket and tie required. No credit cards. Closed Sun., Mon., 2 weeks in Jan., and 3 weeks in July.*

★ **Conti Fischstuben.** Located in the Hotel Ambassador, this is the best fish restaurant in Berlin. Watery light from the fish tank in the center of the dining room reflects from the dark-paneled walls to create a sophisticated and different atmosphere. *Bayreuthstr. 42, tel. 030/219–020. Reservations essential. Jacket and tie required. AE, DC, MC, V. Closed Sat. lunch and Sun.*

★ **Ponte Vecchio.** The best Italian food in Berlin is served here in a handsome, light-wood dining room. Ask the friendly waiters for their recommendations—the food is excellent and simply presented. Try the delicate *Vitello tonnato*, veal with a tuna sauce. *Spielhagenstr. 3, tel. 030/342–1999. Reservations essential. Jacket and tie required. DC. Closed lunch, Tues., and 4 weeks in summer.*

Moderate

Alt-Nürnberg. Step into the tavernlike interior and you could be in Füssen or Garmisch in Bavaria: The waitresses even wear dirndls. The Bavarian colors of blue and white are everywhere, and that region's culinary delights, like *Schweinshaxe* (knuckle of pork), dominate the menu. If you prefer to eat Prussian-style, order calves' liver *Berliner Art. Europa-Centre, tel. 030/261–4397. Reservations advised. Dress: informal. AE, DC, MC, V.*

Blockhaus Nikolskoe. Prussian King Wilhelm III built this Russian-style wooden lodge for his daughter Charlotte, wife of Russian Czar Nicholas I. Located south of the city on Glienecker Park, it offers open-air riverside dining in the summer. Game dishes are prominently featured. *Nikolskoer Weg, tel. 030/805–2914. Reservations advised. Dress: informal. AE, DC, MC, V.*

★ **Forsthaus Paulsborn.** Dine in a onetime woodsman's home, deep in the Grunewald. Sturdy oak tables and hunting trophies on the walls create an authentically rustic mood. Game is the specialty, but there is a choice of other, less intimidatingly nice dishes, too. *Am Grunewaldsee, tel. 030/813–8010. Reservations advised. Dress: informal. AE, DC, MC, V. Closed Mon., and for dinner Oct.–Mar.*

Hecker's Deele. Antique church pews complement the oak-beamed interior of this restaurant that specializes in Westphalian dishes. The *Westfälische Schlachtplatte* (a selection of meats) will set you up for a whole day's sightseeing—the Ku'damm is right outside. *Grolmannstr. 35, tel. 030/88901. Reservations advised. Dress: informal. AE, DC, MC, V.*

Mundart Restaurant. Five chefs work the kitchen of this popular restaurant in the Kreuzberg district. You can't go wrong with the fish soup or any of the daily specials. *Muskauerstr. 33–34, tel. 030/612–2061. Dress: informal. Reservations advised. No credit cards. Closed lunch, Mon., and Tues.*

Inexpensive **Alt-Berliner Wiessbierstube.** A visit to the Berlin Museum must include a stop at the museum's pub-style restaurant. There's a buffet packed with Berlin specialties, and you can take in live jazz here on Sunday mornings. *Berlin Museum, Lindenstr. 14, tel. 030/251–0121. No reservations. Dress: informal. No credit cards. Closed Mon.*

★ **Hardtke.** This is about the most authentic old Berlin restaurant in the city. The decor is simple, with parellel walls and wood floor. The food is similary traditional and hearty. It's a great place to try *Eisbein*. Wash it down with a large stein of beer. *Meinekestr. 27, tel. 030/881–9827. Reservations advised. Dress: informal. No credit cards.*

★ **Ratskeller Schöneberg.** If you're visiting the Liberty Bell at the Rathaus Schöneberg, be sure to drop into the Ratskeller. Fixed-price menus keep costs low, but there's an à la carte menu, too. The food is resolutely traditional. *John-F.-Kennedy-Pl., tel. 030/783–2127. Reservations not required. Dress: informal. AE, DC, MC, V. Closed 3–6 PM and Thurs.*

Lodging

Berlin lost all its grand old luxury hotels in the war. Though some were rebuilt, most of the best hotels are modern. They lack little in service and comfort, but you may find some short on atmosphere. At the lower end of the scale, there are large numbers of good-value pensions and small hotels, many of them in older buildings and correspondingly atmospheric. Business conventions year-round and the influx of summer tourists mean that you should make reservations well in advance. If you arrive without reservations, consult the board at Tegel Airport that shows hotels with vacancies or go to the tourist office at the airport. The main tourist office in the Europa-Centre can also help with reservations (*see* Important Addresses and Numbers, above).

Highly recommended hotels are indicated by a star ★.

Category	Cost*
Very Expensive	over DM 250
Expensive	DM 180–DM 250
Moderate	DM 120–DM 180
Inexpensive	under DM 120

**for two people in a double room, including tax and service*

Very Expensive ★ **Bristol Hotel Kempinski.** Destroyed in the war, rebuilt in 1952, and renovated in 1980, the "Kempi" is a renowned Berlin classic. Located on the Ku'damm in the heart of the city, it has the best shopping at its doorstep plus some fine boutiques of its own within. Rooms and suites are luxuriously decorated, English-style, and with all amenities. *Ku'damm 27, tel. 030/884–340. 325 rooms with bath. Facilities: 3 restaurants, indoor pool, sauna, solarium, masseur, hairdresser, limousine service. AE, DC, MC, V.*

Grand Hotel Esplanade. Opened in 1988, the Grand Hotel Esplanade exudes luxury. Uncompromisingly modern architecture, chicly styled rooms, and works of art by some of Berlin's most acclaimed artists are its outstanding visual aspects.

Berlin Lodging

Atrium Hotel, **9**
Berlin Excelsior Hotel, **5**
Berlin Penta Hotel, **12**
Bristol Hotel Kempinski, **6**
Casino Hotel, **2**
Econotel, **1**
Grand Hotel Esplanade, **15**
Hospiz Friedenau, **14**
Inter-Continental Berlin, **13**
Landhaus Schlachtensee, **4**
Palace, **10**
Ravenna, **7**
Riehmers Hofgarten, **16**
Schweizerhof Berlin, **11**
Seehof, **3**
Steinberger Berlin, **8**

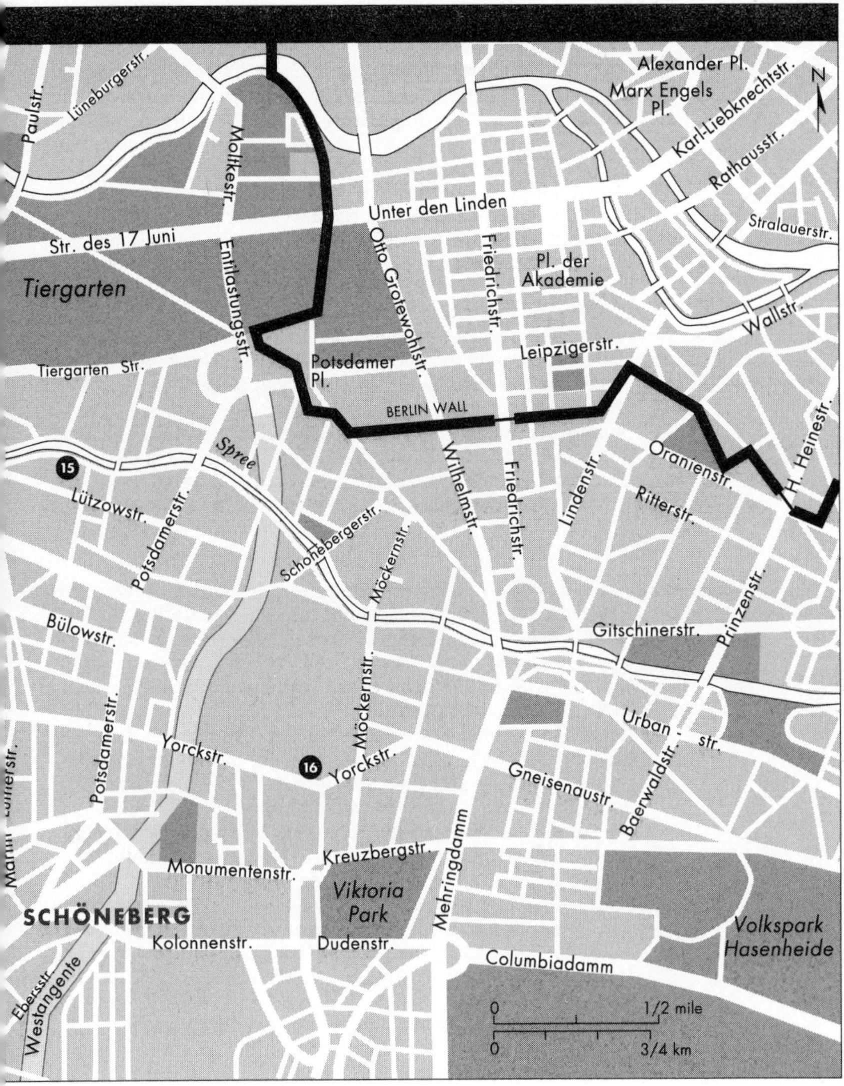
Alexander Pl.
Marx Engels Pl.
Karl-Liebknechtstr.
Rathausstr.
Stralauerstr.
Lüneburgerstr.
Paulstr.
Moltkestr.
Unter den Linden
Str. des 17 Juni
Tiergarten
Entlastungsstr.
Otto Grotewohlstr.
Friedrichstr.
Pl. der Akademie
Wallstr.
Leipzigerstr.
Tiergarten Str.
Potsdamer Pl.
BERLIN WALL
Spree
Oranienstr.
H. Heinestr.
Lützowstr.
Potsdamerstr.
Schönebergerstr.
Möckernstr.
Wilhelmstr.
Friedrichstr.
Lindenstr.
Ritterstr.
Prinzenstr.
Gitschinerstr.
Bülowstr.
Möckernstr.
Urban str.
Potsdamerstr.
Yorckstr.
Yorckstr.
Gneisenaustr.
Baerwaldstr.
Mehringdamm
Kreuzbergstr.
Monumentenstr.
Viktoria Park
SCHÖNEBERG
Kolonnenstr.
Dudenstr.
Columbiadamm
Volkspark Hasenheide
Ebersstr.
Westangente
0
1/2 mile
0
3/4 km
N
15
16

Then there are the superb facilities and impeccable service. The enormous grand suite comes complete with sauna, whirlpool, and a grand piano for (DM 1,200 bill per night). *Lützowufer 15, tel. 030/261–011. 369 rooms, 33 suites. Facilities: 2 restaurants, pub, poolside bar, pool, sauna, whirlpool, steam bath, solarium, masseur, hairdresser, boutique, medical station, library. AE, DC, MC, V.*

★ **Inter-Continental Berlin.** The top-billed "Diplomaten Suite" is in a class of its own: It's as large as a suburban house and furnished in exotic Oriental style. Other rooms and suites may not be so opulently furnished but still show individuality and taste. The lobby is worth a visit even if you're not staying here. It's a quarter the size of a football field and lavishly decorated; stop by for afternoon tea and pastries. *Budapesterstr. 2, tel. 030/26020. 600 rooms with bath. Facilities: 3 restaurants, indoor pool, sauna, boutiques, Pan Am check-in service. AE, DC, MC, V.*

Steinberger Berlin. Part of a modern deluxe hotel chain, the Steinberger offers the best in contemporary accommodations. The hotel has a casino and is centrally located near the Ku'damm. *Los-Angeles-Pl. 1, tel. 030/21080. 337 rooms with bath. Facilities: 3 restaurants, 2 bars, indoor pool, solarium. AE, DC, MC, V.*

Expensive

Berlin Excelsior Hotel Five minutes from the Ku'damm, the Excelsior has comfortable rooms furnished in dark teak. The helpful front-office staff will arrange sightseeing tours and help with hard-to-get theater and concert tickets. *Hardenbergerstr. 14, tel. 030/31991. 320 rooms with bath. Facilities: garden terrace, winter garden. AE, DC, MC, V.*

Berlin Penta Hotel. Its central location (five minutes from the Ku'damm, KadeWe, and the Berlin Zoo) plus an accommodating atmosphere attract many repeat visitors. This modern hotel (opened 1981) has 425 well-equipped rooms, 75 of which are reserved for nonsmokers. Service is attentively friendly. The Globetrotter restaurant features changing art exhibitions. Try for a table in the winter garden. *Nürnbergerstr. 65, tel. 030/240–011. 425 rooms with bath. Facilities: restaurant, pub, bar, poolside bar, indoor pool, sauna, solarium, masseur, boutique, hairdresser. AE, DC, MC, V. Call toll-free from the United States for reservations, tel. 800/225–3456 or 800/238–9877.*

★ **Palace.** While the rooms here are commodious and well furnished, they can't quite match the grandeur of the palatial lobby. Ask for a room overlooking the Budapesterstrasse: The view is grand. If you want to splash out, take a suite with a Jacuzzi. The Palace is part of Berlin's Europa-Centre, and guests have free use of the center's pool and sauna. *Europa-Centre, tel. 030/269–111. 160 rooms with bath. Facilities: restaurant. AE, DC, MC, V.*

Schweizerhof Berlin. There's a rustic, Swiss look to most of the rooms in this centrally located hotel, but the extras, like room video players and mini-bars, are up-to-the-minute. Ask for a room in the west wing, where rooms are larger. Standards are high throughout. The indoor pool is the largest hotel pool in Berlin. *Budapesterstr. 21–31, tel. 030/26960. 430 rooms with bath. Facilities: sauna, solarium, pool, fitness room, hairdresser, beauty salon. AE, DC, MC, V.*

★ **Seehof.** This handsome lakeside hotel is close to the Berlin fairgrounds and within easy reach of downtown. Most rooms overlook Lietzensee lake; ask for a balcony room on the second floor. The indoor pool overlooks the lake, too, and has access to a bar. Dine in the Au Lac restaurant, with its frescoed ceilings and Gobelin tapestries; it specializes in French cuisine and serves a fine six-course gourmet menu. *Lietzensee-Ufer 11, tel. 030/320–020. 77 rooms with bath. Facilities: restaurant, outdoor bar, indoor pool, sauna. AE, DC, MC, V.*

Moderate

★ **Casino Hotel.** What was once a barracks has been skillfully converted into an appealing hotel with large, comfortable rooms, all tastefully furnished and well equipped—the Prussian soldiers never had it so good! You'll detect the Bavarian owner's influence in the south-German cuisine at the restaurant. The Casino is in the Charlottenburg district. *Königen-Elisabeth-Str. 47a, tel. 030/303–090. 24 rooms with bath. Facilities: restaurant. AE, DC, MC, V.*

★ **Landhaus Schlachtensee.** Opened in 1987, this former villa (built in 1905) is now a fine small hotel. Cozy and yet elegant, the Landhaus Schlachtensee offers personal and efficient service, well-equipped rooms, and a quiet location in the Zehlendorf district. The nearby Schlachtensee and Krumme Lanke lakes beckon you to swim, boat, or walk along their shores. *Bogotastr. 9, tel. 030/816–0060. 19 rooms with bath. Facilities: breakfast buffet. AE, DC, MC, V.*

Riehmers Hofgarten. A few minutes' walk from the Kreuzberg hill in the heart of the colorful Kreuzberg district, the Riehmers Hofgarten is a small hotel housed in a late 19th-century building. The high-ceilinged rooms are comfortable, with crisp linens and firm beds. *Yorckstr. 83, tel. 030/781–011. 21 rooms with bath. AE, DC, MC, V.*

Inexpensive

Atrium Hotel. This little privately run hotel is located within reasonable reach of downtown. The modest rooms are comfortably furnished and clean, the staff efficient and helpful. The only drawback is that there's no restaurant. *Motzstr. 87, tel. 030/244–057. 22 rooms with bath. MC.*

Econotel. This family-oriented hotel is within walking distance of Charlottenburg Palace. Rooms have a homey feel and are spotlessly clean. *Sommeringstr. 24, tel. 030/344–001. 205 rooms with bath. Facilities: snack bar. MC.*

Hospiz Friedenau. This quiet, out-of-the-way hotel in the Friedenau district is linked to the downtown area by U-bahn. The clean, comfortable rooms are—surprisingly—plushly furnished. *Fregestr. 68, tel. 030/851–9017. 12 rooms with bath. No credit cards.*

★ **Ravenna.** A small, friendly hotel in the Steglitz district, Ravenna is near the Botanical Garden and Dahlem museums. All the rooms are well-equipped. Suite 111B is a bargain: It includes a large living room and kitchen for only DM 200. *Grunewaldstr. 8–9, tel. 030/792–8031. 45 rooms with bath. AE, DC, MC, V.*

The Arts and Nightlife

The Arts

Today's Berlin has a tough task living up to the reputation it gained from the film *Cabaret*, but if nightlife is a little toned down since the '30s, the arts still flourish. In addition to the many hotels that book seats, there are three main ticket agencies: **Theaterkasse** (Ku'damm 24), **Theater-kasse im Europa-**

Centre, and **Theaterkasse Centrum** (Mienekestr. 25). Detailed information about what's going on in Berlin can be found in *Berlin Programm*, a monthly guide to Berlin arts (DM 2.50), and the magazines *Tip* and *Zitty*, which appear every two weeks and provide full arts listings.

Theater Theater in Berlin is outstanding, but performances are usually in German. The exceptions are operettas and the (nonliterary) cabarets. Of the city's 18 theaters, the most renowned for both its modern and classical productions is the **Schaubühne am Lehniner Platz.** Also important are the **Schiller-Theater** (Bismarchstr. 110, tel. 030/319–5236), which has an excellent workshop—the **Werkstatt,** which specializes in experimental and avant-garde theater; **the Schlosspark-Theater** (Schlossstr. 48, tel. 030/791–1213); **the Renaissance-Theater** (Hardenbergstr. 6, tel. 030/312–4202); the **Freie Volksbühne** (Schaperstr. 24, tel. 030/881–3742). For *Boulevard* plays (fashionable social comedies), there is the **Komödie** (Kurfurstendamm 206, tel. 030/8827893), and at the same address the **Theater am Kurfürstendamm** (tel. 030/882–3789), and the **Hansa Theater** (Alt Moabit 47, tel. 030/391–4460). Among the smaller, more experimental theaters is the **Tribune** (Otto-Suhr-Allee 18–20, tel. 030/341–2600), a youthful enterprise. Berlin's savage and debunking idiom is particularly suited to social and political satire, a long tradition in cabaret-theaters here. The **Stachelschweine** (Europa-Centre, tel. 030/261–7047) and **Die Wühlmäuse** (1/30 Nümbergerstr. 33, tel. 030/213–7047) carry on that tradition with biting wit and style. For children's theater, try **Klecks** (Schinkestr. 8/9, tel. 030/693–7731) or the **Literarisches Figurentheater** (Kleiststr. 13–14, Schöneberg). (*See* What to See and Do with Children, above.)

Concerts Berlin is the home of one of the world's leading orchestras, the **Berliner Philharmonisches Orchester** (Berlin Philharmonic), in addition to a number of other major symphony orchestras and orchestral ensembles. The **Berlin Festival Weeks,** held annually from August to October, combine a wide range of concerts, operas, ballet, theater, and art exhibitions; 1990 marks the 40th Festival. For information and reservations, write **Festspiele GmbH** (Kartenbüro, Budapesterstr. 50, 1000 Berlin 30).

Other concert halls in Berlin include:

Grosser Sendesaal des SFB (Haus des Rundfunks, Masurenallee 8–14, tel. 030/30310). Part of the Sender Freies Berlin, one of Berlin's broadcasting stations, the Grosser Sendesaal is the home of the Radio Symphonic Orchestra.

Konzertsaal der Hochschule der Künste (Hardenbergstr., tel. 030/318–52374). The concert hall of the Academy of Fine Arts is Berlin's second biggest—also known as the "symphony garage."

Philharmonie (Matthaikircherstr. 1, tel. 030/261–4383). The Berlin Philharmonic is based here. The hall also houses the new Kammermusik-Saal, dedicated to chamber music.

Waldbühne (Am Glockenturm, close to the Olympic Stadium). Modeled along the lines of an ancient Roman theater, this open-air site accommodates nearly 20,000 people. Tickets are available through ticket agencies.

Opera The **Deutsche Oper Berlin** (Bismarckstr. 35, tel. 030/341–4449) is one of Germany's leading opera houses and presents outstanding productions year-round. The ballet also performs here. Tickets for both are expensive and sell out quickly. At the **Neuköllner Oper** (Karl-Marx-Str. 131–133, tel. 030/687–6061) you'll find showy, fun performances of long-forgotten operas and humorous musical productions. The skillfully restored **Theater des Westens** (Kantstr. 12, tel. 030/312–1022) is the ideal setting for comic operas and musicals like *West Side Story*, *A Chorus Line*, and *Cabaret*. Experimental ballet and modern dance are presented at the **Tanzfabrik** in Kreuzberg (Möckernstr. 66, tel. 030/786–5861).

Film Berlin has more than 70 movie theaters, showing about 100 movies a day. International and German movies are shown in the big theaters around the Ku'damm; the "Off-Ku-damm" theaters show less commercial movies. For (un-dubbed) movies in English, go to the **Odeon** (Hauptstr. 116, tel. 030/781–5667).

Nightlife

Berlin's nightlife has always been notorious. There are scads of places to seek your nighttime entertainment, and the quality ranges widely from tacky to spectacular. All Berlin tour operators offer either **Illumination Tours** (DM 75) or **Night Club Tours** (DM 100, including entrance fees to three shows, and three drinks). Most places stay open late; some have all-night liquor licenses.

Clubs **Chez Nous** (Marburgerstr. 14, tel. 030/213–1810) lives up to Berlin's reputation as the drag-show center of Germany. Empire-style plush is the backdrop for two nightly shows (reservations recommended).

You'll find three more conventional stage shows at no less than **Dollywood** (Welserstr. 24, tel. 030/248–950) each night, plus a disco. **La Vie en Rose** (Europa-Centre, tel. 030/323–6006) is a revue theater with spectacular light shows that also showcases international stars (book ahead). If the strip show at the **New Eden** (Ku'damm 71, tel. 030/323–5849) doesn't grab you, maybe the dance music will (two bands nightly). The **New York Bar** (Olivaer Pl. 15, tel. 030/883–6258) is a mellow drinking haven compared to its rowdier neighbors. Despite Mississippi-inspired decor, the **Riverboat** (Hohenzollerndamm 177, tel. 030/878–476) has great Berlin atmosphere. You have a choice at **Zeleste** (Marburgerstr. 2): Sit back and listen to jazz or dance the night away in its disco.

Jazz Clubs Berlin's lively music scene is dominated by jazz and rock. For jazz enthusiasts, *the* events of the year are the summer's **Jazz in the Garden** festival and the international autumn **Jazz Fest Berlin.** For information call the **Berlin Tourist Information Center** (tel. 030/262–6031).

Traditionally, the best **live jazz** can be found at:

Eierschale (Podbielskialle 50, tel. 030/832–7097). A variety of jazz groups appear here at the "egg shell"; seating is outside in the garden for summertime performances.
Flöz (Nassauischestr. 37, tel. 030/861–1000). The sizzling jazz at this club is sometimes incorporated into theater presentations.
Joe am Ku'damm (Ku'damm 225, tel. 030/883–6373). A predominantly over-30 crowd frequents this lively jazz club on the Ku'damm. Live music nights are Wednesday, Thursday, and Sunday.

Quartier Latin (Potsdamerstr. 99, tel. 030/261–1721). The Quartier Latin is one of the leaders in Berlin's jazz scene. Jazz and rock are both presented.

Discos **Blue Note** (Courbierestr. 13, tel. 030/247–248). For an escape from the usual disco sounds, try the Blue Note; you'll find a tasty mixture of jazz, bebop, and Latin American rhythms. Open until 6 AM.

Dschungel (Nürnbergerstr. 53, tel. 030/246–698). Their funky disco, "Jungle," is a current "in" spot. Dance until you drop, or at least until 4 AM. Closed Tuesdays.

Metropol (Nollendorfpl. 5, tel. 030/216–4122). Berlin's largest disco, which stages occasional concerts, is a hot spot for the younger tourist. The black dance floor upstairs is the scene for a magnificent light and lazer show. The DM 10 cover includes your first drink.

Kneipen Berlin has roughly 5,000 bars and pubs; this includes the dives, too. All come under the heading of *Kneipen*—the place round the corner where you stop in for a beer, a snack, a conversation, and, sometimes, to dance.

Bogen 597 (Savignypl., S-bahn passage). Sound effects are provided by the S-bahn—you'll hear and feel the trains passing on the tracks overhead. This is a cozy place that serves a fine selection of wines in addition to the inevitable beer.

Ku'dorf (Joachimstaler-Str. 15). The Ku'dorf makes it easy to go from one Kneipe to another—there are 18 located under one roof here, underground, just off the Ku'damm. Open Monday–Saturday from 7 PM.

Leydicke (Mansteinstr. 4). This historic spot is a must for out-of-towners. The proprietors operate their own distillery and have a superb selection of wines and liqueurs; definitely the right atmosphere in which to enjoy a few glasses.

Nolle (Nollendorfpl.). You can sit in an old subway car in this converted (above ground) subway station and enjoy live Dixieland music. Berlin specialties are served from the buffet. Check it out on a Sunday morning as you stroll around the local flea market.

Sperlingsgasse (Lietzenburgerstr. 82–84). Look for the replica of the Brandenburg Gate on the sidewalk. It'll point you in the direction of the 13 different Kneipen here. All open at 7 PM.

Wilhelm Hoeck (Wilmersdorferstr. 159). Berlin's oldest Kneipe is also its most beautiful. Its superb interior dates back to 1892—all original. Frequented by a colorful cross section of the public, this is a place that's definitely worth a visit.

Wirthaus Wuppke (Schlüterstr. 21). Come here if you're seeking a mellower, quieter atmosphere. It gets as crowded as the others, but it's not so hectic. The food is good and inexpensive.

Yorckschlösschen (Yorckstr. 15). In the summer you can sit in the garden and enjoy a beer and a snack or a hearty meal. If you're lucky, there may be live music.

Zwiebelfisch (Savignypl. 7). Literally translated as the "onion fish," this Kneipe has become the meeting place of literary Bohemians of all ages. It has a good atmosphere for getting to know people. The beer is good, the menu small.

17 Excursions to East Germany

Introduction

East Germany, or, to give the country its proper name, the German Democratic Republic, or G.D.R., conjures up images of dour landscapes and grim, industrial cities, the whole presided over by a repressive and anonymous communist government. Its reputation as the Soviet Union's most loyal client state seems well deserved. Moreover, the old adage that only the East Germans could make a success of communism—economically at any rate—seems hard to refute. There is—or so it appears to the casual visitor—a slightly deadening quality to the country, something born of a singled-minded but blinkered commitment to communism, and a marked absence of the drive for personal enrichment, if not exactly *joie de vivre*, that is so conspicuous a feature of West Germany.

Yet East Germany has much to recommend it. What other country of comparable size—East Germany is about the same size as Missouri—could so reliably produce so many world-caliber athletes? What other Eastern European state, Romania excepted, would react so coolly to the reforming promise of *glasnost* and *perestroika?* It's not just because the government is so peculiarly inclined toward a pre-Gorbachev form of government, you feel; more that the people themselves seem quite uninterested in swapping their ordered lifestyles for the promise of Western-style freedoms. The fast cars, foreign vacations, and chic fashions of West Germany are as hard to imagine in East Germany as a Wartburg—East Germany's only production car and a less-than-desirable piece of engineering—tearing down the Autobahn to Munich, its headlights flashing as it jams its brakes on only inches from a Porsche. In fact, the contrast between Wartburg and Porsche is as apt a symbol of the division between West and East Germany as any. East Germany is of course no more or less "German" than its western neighbor, yet in many ways it seems an alien land, superficially quite different from West Germany.

Scratch the surface, however, and you'll find another side of the country that will tell you much more about its German past than its communist present. For all the obvious signs that this is the Eastern bloc—the drab public housing, the brutal high rises, the decaying industrial plant, the acrid smell of coal smoke, the banners and slogans exhorting the people to do their best for the greater glories of socialism—the communist influence here is in some ways not as deep as the American influence on West Germany. There's a quiet conservatism and identification with traditions in many small East German towns and cities that tells you much more about an older Germany than do the frenetic lifestyles of Frankfurt or Hamburg, Stuttgart or Köln. Time has not stood still on this side of the border, but it has taken much less of a toll than it has in the West. The rampant overdevelopment that has blighted much of the West German landscape is practically unknown in this people's republic.

Culturally, too, East Germany proclaims its German spirit; the nation's monumental heritage is never far from view. Luther, Bach, Goethe, Schiller, Liszt, and Wagner are just a few of the heroic figures who sprang from what is now East Germany. Meissen porcelain, Frederick the Great's palace at Potsdam, and the astounding collections of the Pergamon and Bode museums in East Berlin are further testimony to the cultural richness of this land, and of its European nature.

At heart, perhaps, it's this German heritage that explains not only the relative success of communism here but the rather austere nature of the government, too. It's a Prussian inheritance first and foremost. The same efficiency that made 18th-century Prussia so formidable, that underpinned the rise of the Prussian-dominated German Reich (empire) under Bismarck in the 19th century, and that made the Nazi war machine so potent in this century, is easily recognizable in both the economic strength of the government and in the long-standing commitment to a style of communism that is looking less and less viable today. True, the senior members of the government have much to do with the anti-reformist stance of the state. These were young men in the late '40s when the communists came to power, and they have grown old with the system; change is not something that comes easily to them. Nonetheless, it's hard to imagine this rigid adherence to the party line in the heady atmosphere of volatile Poland, say, or in Hungary, a land that has never embraced communism with enthusiasm. But, unlike other Eastern bloc countries, the East German government can point to the fact that Marxist central planning has largely worked in this country, and that the need for reform is accordingly less pronounced. Quite what impact the withdrawal, announced by Mikhail Gorbachev in 1988, of perhaps 3 of the 19 Soviet military divisions currently stationed in East Germany will have remains to be seen.

Essential Information

Important Addresses and Numbers

Passports and Visas All visitors to East Germany require a passport and a visa. If you're planning just a day trip to East Berlin, buy your visa as you cross the border; it costs DM 5. These visas can be extended for stays up to one week at any Interhotel or Reisebüro der DDR (*see* Tourist Information, below). If you're planning a longer visit, get your visa in advance from any officially accredited travel agent in the United States (*see* Tour Groups, below). A fee of about $20 is charged for all visas issued in this way; apply six to eight weeks in advance. An "express service" is also offered; the fee is about $30. As you enter East Germany, you'll be given a small form to fill out that will be stamped with the entry date. The form must be surrendered when you leave, so be careful not to lose it. Bear in mind, too, that all foreign visitors are required to change DM 25 a day, or its equivalent in other Western currencies. Once converted into East German marks, this money can't be taken out of the country. Note, too, that though you can bring in as much foreign currency as you like, it must be declared; otherwise, you won't be allowed to take it with you when you leave.

Tourist Information Information on travel and tours to and around East Germany is available from any accredited travel agent. For full lists, write **Consulate of the GDR** (1717 Massachusetts Ave., NW, Washington, DC 20036). Leading agents include:

Koch (157 East 86th St., New York, NY 10028, tel. 212/369-3800).
Orbis (500 Fifth Ave., New York, NY 10110, tel. 212/391–0844).
Lindblad Travel (Box 912, Westport, CT 06881, tel. 800/243-5657).
Security Travel (1631 Washington Plaza, Reston, VA 22090, tel. 703/471–1900).
Pecum Tours (2002 Colfax Ave. So., Minneapolis, MN 55405, tel. 612/871–6399).
Travcoa (875 North Michigan Ave., Suite 3732, Chicago, IL 60611, tel. 800/992–2003).
Maupintours (1515 St. Andrews Dr., Lawrence, KS 66046, tel. 800/255–4266).
Hemphill Harris (16000 Ventura Blvd., Encino, CA 91436, tel. 818/906–8086).
Love Tours (15315 Magnolia Blvd., Suite 110, Sherman Oaks, CA 91403, tel. 818/501–6868).

In the **United Kingdom,** GDR tourist affairs including visa assistance are handled by **Berolina Travel** (20 Conduit St., London W1R 9TD, tel. 01/629–1664).

The main office of the **Reisbüro der DDR** (State Tourist Office) in East Berlin is Alexanderplatz 2, tel. 02/215–4328. There's another branch at Schönefeld airport (tel. 02/678–8248).

Embassies **United States** (Neustädtische Kirchstr. 4–5, tel. 02/220–2741). **British** (Unter den Linden 32–34, tel. 02/220–2431). There is no Canadian Embassy in East Berlin at present; if circumstances demand, call the Canadian Embassy in Warsaw (from East Berlin, tel. 064–822–0298–051; address: Ulica Matejika 1–5, PL–00481 Warsaw, Poland). Alternatively, try the Canadian Military Mission in West Berlin (tel. 849/261–1161). If that fails, the British Embassy will help, provided they know you have made an effort to contact the other two.

Emergencies **Police** (tel. 110). **Ambulance** (tel. 115). **Doctor, Dentist** (tel. 1259, or call the United States or British Embassies). **Pharmacies** (tel. 160). **Driver assistance** (tel. 02/524–3565, 6 AM to 10 PM).

Tour Groups

Package tours of East Germany can be booked through any officially accredited travel agency (*see* above). Tours cover a variety of interests, such as Bertolt Brecht and Berlin; the towns of the south (Weimar, Leipzig, Meissen, and Dresden); railways, including a number of the country's remaining steam trains around the Harz and Erzgeberge mountains; and Martin Luther. On most tours you'll spend some time in East Berlin. Tours of East Berlin can be arranged through your hotel or the Reisebüro der DDR. Rates range from M 3 to M 12. Taxi sightseeing tours of the city cover six fixed routes, all beginning and ending at Alexanderplatz. Rates range from M 16.50 to M 55 for up to four people. Call tel. 02/246–2255 for details.

Getting Around

By Car Nearly 1,000 miles of Autobahn and 7,000 miles of secondary roads crisscross the country. Drive on the right, as in Western Europe. Signs follow the European standard, giving distances in kilometers. Traffic regulations are strictly enforced, from parking rules to speed limits. A copy of the rules in English may help avoid problems, but the police levy fines (in West German currency, for foreigners) for the slightest offense. Drinking and driving is strictly forbidden and fines are heavy for violators. If not otherwise indicated, cars coming from the right have the right-of-way. Speed limits on the Autobahns are 100 kph (63 mph), on main roads 80 kph (50 mph), and in towns 50 kph (30 mph). Gasoline is available at either **Minol** or **Intertank** filling stations. Minol filling stations are found at most of the **Mitropa** rest houses along expressways. Both chains sell regular and premium grades by the liter. Diesel fuel is not available at all stations, and distribution of unleaded fuel is limited to expressways and main towns. Minol stations supply gasoline for either East German marks (you may be asked to show your currency exchange receipt) or coupons, which may be bought at a discount at the border. Otherwise, the Intertank stations sell gasoline at reduced prices for West German marks. Foreign drivers pay a tongue-twisting *Strassenbengsgebühr*—road toll or user's tax—at up to DM 5 for 200 kilometers (120 miles); DM 15 for up to 300 kilometers (180 miles); DM 20 for up to 400 kilometers (240 miles); or DM 25 for up to 500 kilometers (300 miles). The tax can be paid in other foreign currencies, too.

Car Rental Cars can be rented at all Interhotels. Rental cars can be driven into West Germany and Czechoslovakia, though an additional fee is charged if the car is not returned to East Germany. Rates are quoted in West German marks and are payable in any Western currency. Rentals are not expensive but the cars tend to be neither luxurious nor brand new. The most expensive model, a Volvo 264, costs DM 510 per week; the least expensive, a Lada 1300, costs DM 200 per week for basic rental, plus mileage ranging from DM 1 (for the Volvo) to DM 0.35 per kilometer. The widest choice of models is to be found in Berlin, but reserve in advance, particularly if you want a more comfortable car. Cars may be unavailable at Leipzig Fair time, even in Berlin. Car rentals may be charged to all major Western credit cards.

By Train East Germany has three types of trains—Express, the fastest, shown as "IEx" or "Ex" in timetables; fast, shown as "D"; and regular/local services indicated with an "E." The fast categories have varying supplementary fares; local trains do not. Most long- and medium-distance trains have both first- and second-class cars and many have either dining or buffet cars, although these may be joined to the train only from and to specific destinations. Meals are not expensive but choices may be limited. First- and second-class sleeping cars and couchettes are available. As rail travel is popular and space is limited, trains are usually full and reservations—make them either via the Reisebüro der DDR or at any major train station—are recommended.

Railway buffs are increasingly welcome, particularly around the narrow-gauge lines in the mountainous south, but, in general, photographers ought to avoid taking pictures of rail installations.

By Boat "White Fleets" of inland boats, including paddle sidewheelers, ply the inland lakes around Berlin and the Elbe River with their starting point at Dresden, going downstream and on into Czechoslovakia.

By Bicycle Sadly, visitors are not allowed to enter East Germany by, or with, a bicycle; the northern part of the country would be ideal for cycling. Bicycles are theoretically available for rent at the Interhotels along the Baltic coast, but, while spare parts can be found, the complete article is much harder to locate.

East Berlin

In defiance of the Four Power Agreement in 1949, East Germany established its capital in Berlin—formerly the capital of all Germany—and officially dubbed it "Berlin, Capital of the GDR." (Only foreigners call it East Berlin.) The appeal of East Berlin for the visitor goes beyond its historic relics, and beyond the contrast it provides with its more frenetic Western half. In fact, its main appeal is a quality it *shares* with West Berlin: of doom and damage, and of a glorious, gilded past. The eastern half of the city, having suffered the excommunication imposed on it by the Wall, conveys vividly the feeling that the ghost of a war-torn Europe still stalks its streets.

Berlin actually began as two cities over 750 years ago. Museum Island, on the Spree River, was once called Cöllin, while the mainland city seems always to have been known as Berlin. As early as the 1300s, Berlin was a prospering city filled with merchants and artisans of every description. The Thirty Years' War, which began with Bohemia's declaration of independence (within what is now the modern state of Czechoslovakia) in 1618 and which subsequently tore central Europe asunder, took an enormous toll on Berlin. But the Brandenburg Dynasty rose up soon after, and Berlin, made the seat of Brandenburg power, rose with it. Two hundred years later, the Brandenburgian and Prussian realms united under the Hohenzollerns, with Berlin again the chosen capital. With the crowning of Friedrich III there in 1701, Berlin underwent a renaissance of new building. The establishment of several academic institutes, the Academy of Arts and the Academy of Sciences among them, was to endow the city with enduring symbols of some of Germany's proudest academic achievements.

The next three centuries saw the gradual growth of the Prussian empire, which was to be the dominant force in German unification. Unification meant the conglomeration of many previously independent principalities, and was engineered by Count Bismarck in the late 19th century. Berlin stood firm as the principal city, meaning that, from Germany's very beginnings up until World War I, it garnered the riches of German heritage. It is then no wonder that East Berlin, though a fragment of the historic capital, reveals so much about German culture.

The city today is of a more eclectic nature—a true study in contrasts. Much has been cleaned up, carefully scrubbed and restored, the idea being that when you cross from West Berlin, you should see a modern, fresh, and, above all, orderly city. This is indeed the immediate impression: The lower end of the Friedrichstrasse has been rebuilt and much of the rest of the center of the city—the "Berlin Mitte" district, which is only 11 kilometers square—has been given a thorough facelift. But when you wander off the beaten path, you will find the drabness and communist sameness for which the eastern zone of the city is better known. Some of the massive showcase housing and other communal projects hastily built in the '50s and '60s are now more than showing their age and their shoddy construction. Newer housing projects are being planned on a more human scale with greater effort to incorporate them into their surroundings.

Exploring East Berlin

Numbers in the margin correspond with points of interest on the Berlin map.

If you're visiting East Berlin from the West, cross the border at
1 **Checkpoint Charlie,** which turns out to be not nearly as difficult or scary as it might seem. While it is possible to get into East Berlin by taking the U-6 subway line to Friedrichstrasse (where you can pass through passport and customs control), a preferred route is on foot and above ground through Checkpoint Charlie. Those who have passed through this border-control station in the past may have found it a grim experience, straight out of a novel by John le Carré, or perhaps George Orwell. Today they will be in for a pleasant surprise. While the East Berliners have not exactly initiated a friendly open-door policy, they have certainly toned down their harassment and trimmed the seemingly interminable waits while they go through your passport with the proverbial fine-tooth comb.

You'll still have to purchase a one-day tourist permit for DM 5 and exchange DM 25 into East German currency (DM 15 for seniors), which you can use to pay for lunch. You'll also have to fill out a currency declaration form, meaning exactly how much you are carrying with you in various currencies. This, too, turns out to be a mere formality, but the less you have with you the easier it will be. The form has to be returned at the end of your visit, and in theory what you start with and what you spend should balance out to what you have on the way out. Rows of busy stores and shops line the street. Turn right onto Johann-Dieckmann-Strasse and you come to the large square called **Platz der Akadamie.** It's the site of the beautifully recon-
2 structed **Schauspielhaus,** built in 1818 and now the city's main
3 concert hall, and the rebuilt **German** and **French cathedrals.**
4 The French cathedral contains the **Huguenot Museum,** with exhibits charting the history and the art of the Protestant refugees from France—the Huguenots—expelled at the end of the 17th century by Louis XIV. Their energy and commercial expertise did much to help boost Berlin in the 18th century. *Admission M 3. Open Mon.–Fri. 10–5.*

Time Out The **Arkade Café** at the northwest corner of the square is the right spot for light snacks, a cup of coffee, and a beer. The pastries are excellent, too. *Französischerstr. 25.*

5 Head down Französischerstrasse to **St. Hedwig's Cathedral,** a substantial, circular building that's similar to the Pantheon in Rome. Note the tiny street called Hinter der Katholische Kirche; it means "Behind the Catholic Church." When the cathedral was built in 1747 it was the first Catholic church built in resolutely Protestant Berlin since the Reformation in the 16th century.

East Berlin

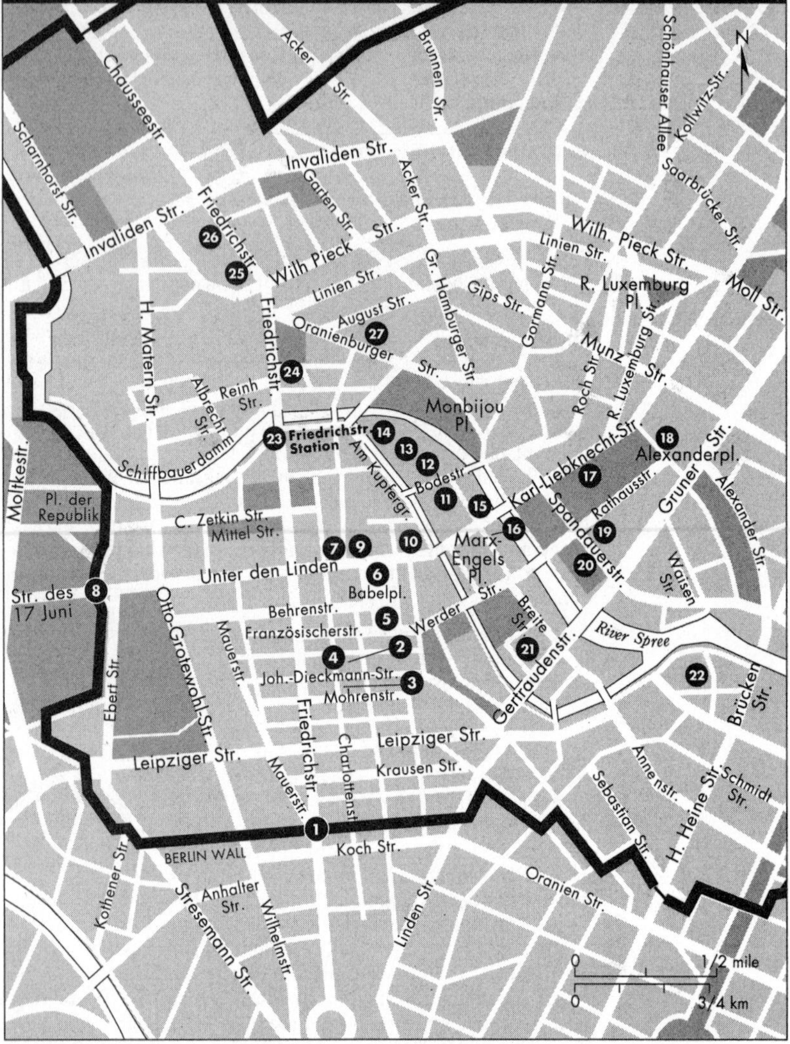

Alexanderplatz, **18**
Altes Museum, **11**
Berlin Cathedral, **15**
Bertolt Brecht House and Museum, **25**
Bodemuseum, **14**
Brandenburger Tor, **8**
Checkpoint Charlie, **1**
Deutsche Staatsoper, **6**
Dorotheer Cemetery, **26**
Fischerinsel, **21**
French Cathedral/Huguenot Museum, **4**
Friedrich-stadtpalast, **24**
German Cathedral, **3**
Humboldt University, **9**
International Trade Center, **23**
Marienkirche, **17**
Märkisches Museum, **22**
Museum für Deutsche Geschichte, **10**
Nationalgalerie, **12**
Nikolaikirche, **20**
Palais Unter den Linden, **7**
Palast der Republik, **16**
Pergamon Museum, **13**
Rathaus, **19**
St. Hedwig's Cathedral, **5**
Schauspielhaus, **2**
Synagogue, **27**

6 Head north and you reach the **Deutsche Staatsoper** (State Opera House), lavishly restored in the late '80s. A performance here can be memorable. *The box office is open weekdays, noon–5:45.*

You are now on **Unter den Linden,** the central thoroughfare of old Berlin; its name means, simply, "Under the Linden Trees." Something of its former cosmopolitan elegance is left, though it can hardly claim these days to rival the Champs Elysées. The
7 **Palais Unter den Linden** is here; it's the former crown prince's palace, today used as a government guest house. Look west (left) down the avenue. At its far end, just inside the East
8 German border, is monumental **Brandenburger Tor** (Brandenburg Gate), topped by a giant quadriga—a chariot drawn by four horses—that's driven by the Goddess of Peace. Perched so near the wall, with all *its* ramifications of war and division, the irony of the statue's presence is doubled by the fact that it was turned to face east once Germany was split. The Brandenburg is the only remaining gate of an original group of 14 and was built by Carl Langhans in the late 18th century, in virile classical style, as a triumphal arch. It was once as potent and evocative a symbol of Berlin as the Statue of Liberty is of New York or as the Eiffel Tower is of Paris. These days its symbolism is rather different, a tragic reminder of the sundered state of the city.

9 Cross Unter den Linden and look into the courtyard of **Humboldt University,** originally built in 1766 as a palace for the brother of Friedrich II of Prussia. It became a university in 1810, and Karl Marx and Friedrich Engels were once among its students.

Next door, housed in the onetime arsenal (Zeughaus), is the
10 **Museum für Deutsche Geschichte** (Museum of German History), constructed from 1695 to 1705. This magnificent Baroque building was later used as a hall of fame glorifying Prusso-German militarism. Today, it provides a compendium of German history from 1789 to the present, with a Marxist bias that may surprise Western visitors. Displays focus on a range of relics, from the hat Napoléon wore at the Battle of Waterloo to relief portrayals of faces of soldiers through the ages. *Unter den Linden 2. Admission: M 3. Open Mon.–Thurs. 9–7, weekends 10–5.*

Turn left and follow the Spree Canal and you come to East Berlin's Museum Island, or **Museuminsel,** on the site of one of Berlin's two original settlements, Cöllin, dating back to 1237. Today, you'll find a complex of four remarkable museums here. *Admission: Varies from free to M 3 (M 1 extra if you want to take photographs). All museums open Wed.–Thurs. and weekends 9–6, Fri. 10–6; check hours before visiting as they can occasionally change.*

11 The **Altes Museum** (Old Museum; entrance Lustgarten) is an austere Neoclassical building just north of Marx-Engels-Platz that features postwar East German art; its large etching and drawing collection, from the Old Masters to the present, is a
12 treasure trove. The **Nationalgalerie** (National Gallery, entrance on Bodestrasse) houses an outstanding collection of 19th- and 20th-century paintings and sculptures and often hosts special temporary exhibits. Works by Cézanne, Rodin,

Degas, and one of Germany's most famous portrait artists, Max Liebermann, are part of the permanent exhibition.

Even if you aren't generally inclined toward the ancient world,
13 make an exception for the **Pergamon Museum** (entrance on Am Kupfergraben). It is not only the standout in this complex; it is one of Europe's greatest museums. The museum's name is derived from its principal and best-loved display, the Pergamon altar, a monumental Greek temple found in what's now Turkey and dating from 180 BC. Adorning it are finely carved figures of gods locked in battle against giants. As much as anything, perhaps, this vast structure illustrates the zeal of Germany's 19th-century archaeologists, who had it shipped piece by piece to Berlin. Equally impressive is the Babylonian Processional Way in the Asia Minor department. As you walk through the museum, you cannot help but wonder how the Germans ever got away with dismantling and exporting these vast treasures.

14 Last in the complex is the **Bodemuseum** (entrance on Monbijoubrücke), with its superb Egyptian, Byzantine, and early Christian relics, sculpture collections, and coin gallery. The Sphinx of Hatshepsut, from around 1500 BC, is stunning, as are the Burial Cult Room and Papyrus Collection. There is also a representative collection of Italian Renaissance paintings.

From the museum complex, follow the Spree Canal back to Unter
15 den Linden and the enormous, impressive **Berlin Cathedral.** A small museum in it (entrance on Unter den Linden) records the postwar reconstruction of the building—which was paid for by West Germany!

The stupendously hideous modern building across Unter den
16 Linden is the **Palast der Republik** (Palace of the Republic), a ponderous, postwar monument to socialist progress. It houses a theater, a dance hall, and several restaurants.

Time Out The self-service **Quick** restaurant in the nearby Palast Hotel, although packed at noon, serves up unexpectedly good fastfood. *Karl-Liebknecht-Str.*

Cross the street (at the intersection: the police here are very
17 particular) for a closer look at the 13th-century **Marienkirche** and its late Gothic fresco *Den Totentanz* ("Dance of Death"). Obscured for many years, refurbishment in 1950 revealed it in all its macabre allure. Like something out of an Ingmar Bergman movie, Death dances with everyone, from peasant to king. The fresco and the tower were both 15th-century additions.

The remarkable Marienkirche, the second oldest church in
18 Nilolaikirche, *see* below) is at the lower end of **Alexanderplatz,** the square that forms the hub of Berlin city life. It's a bleak sort of place, open and windswept, surrounded by grimly ugly modern buildings, with not so much as a hint of its prewar elegance, a reminder not just of the Allied bombing of Berlin but of the ruthlessness with which what remained of the old buildings was demolished by the East Germans. Finding Alexanderplatz from any other part of the city is no problem; just head toward the **Funktum,** the unmissable TV tower (completed in 1969 and 1,170 feet high) that stands at its center.

In the base of the TV Tower is the Berlin Information Office. Here, you'll be able to get an excellent brochure, listing (in English) every worthwhile sight in the city, along with the clearest of maps and a diagram of the public transportation system, infinitely better than anything that's available from the West Berlin Tourist Office, which can't even supply visitors with a decent map.

For a few marks you can take the elevator to the viewing platform halfway up the tower. On a clear day, you will see Berlin East and West extend in all directions. The revolving café is ideal for a coffee break with a view, though the food is not worth the time you'll have waited in line to get up here. The area around the tower offers ample shopping opportunities, including the chance to buy goods from other socialist countries. The focal point for shopping is the **Centrum Warenhaus** (department store), next to the Hotel Stadt Berlin at the very top of the plaza.

19 Walk across the lower end of the square past the **Rathaus** (Town Hall, also known as the *Rates Rathaus* or Red Town Hall), a marvel of red brick and friezes depicting the city's history. The complex of buildings next to the town hall has been handsomely rebuilt, centering around the remains of the twin-spired, 12th-
20 century **Nikolaikirche** (St. Nicholas's Church), which now houses a small auditorium. The quarter that has grown around it, the **Nikolai quarter,** is filled with stores, cafés, and restaurants.

Wander back down Mühlendamm into the area around the Breite Strasse—there's an array of fine old buildings here, some rebuilt, some actually moved to this location from else-
21 where in Berlin)—and on over to the **Fischerinsel** area. This was the heart of Berlin 750 years ago, and today retains some of its medieval character. It provides a refreshing change, too, from some of the heavy and uninspired postwar architecture, which you may by now feel the need to get away from.

Time Out The **Alt-Cöllner Schankstuben,** right on the Spree Canal, is charming and friendly, with tables outside for you to enjoy the waterside view on pleasant days. West along the canal is the Jungfernbrücke, the oldest bridge in the city. *Friedrichsgracht 50.*

Cross over the Gertraudenstrasse and wander up the south
22 bank of the canal to the red-brick **Märkisches Museum,** the museum of city history. It includes a special section on the city's theatrical past and a fascinating collection of mechanical musical instruments. These are displayed only Wednesday 11–noon and Sunday 4–5. *Am Köllnischen Park 5. Admission: M 3. Open Wed. and Sun. 9–6, Thurs. and Sat. 9–5, Fri. 9–4.*

The upper Friedrichstrasse is undergoing reconstruction.
23 Among its landmarks are the tall **International Trade Center,** next to the Friedrichstrasse rail station, and, farther up, the
24 **Friedrichstadtpalast,** featuring a nightclub, dancing, and occasional musical shows. Despite the rebuilding, the street still houses a number of small shops, bookstores, and neighborhood establishments. Walk up beyond the bend where the street
25 turns into the Chauseestrasse to find the **Bertolt Brecht House and Museum** and a library for Brecht scholars (Chauseestr. 125. Admission: M 3. Open Tues. and Fri. 10–noon, Thurs. 5–7, Sat. 9:30–noon and 12:30–2).

Brecht is actually buried next door, along with his wife Helene
26 Weigel, in the **Dorotheer Cemetery.** The Neoclassical architects Schinkel and Schadow are buried here, too, as is the Berlin printer Litfass, the man who invented the kiosk, those stumpy cylindrical columns you'll find across Europe carrying advertisements and theater schedules.

Head back toward the center and turn left down Oranienburger
27 Strasse to the ruins of the massive city **synagogue,** now being restored. It's an exotic amalgam of styles, the whole faintly Middle Eastern, built between 1894 and 1905. It was largely ruined on the night of November 11, 1938, the infamous "crystal night," when Nazi looters and soldiers rampaged across Germany and Austria, burning synagogues and smashing the few Jewish shops and homes left in the country. It was further ruined during the bombing of the city toward the end of the war.

Shopping

Gift Ideas East Germany produces appealing dolls, wood toys, and Christmas ornaments, plus beautiful lace, pewter, ceramics, glass, crystal ware, and, of course, Meissen porcelain (known as "Dresden" china). Sheet music is a real bargain, either in the shops on Unter den Linden or opposite the Thomaskirche in Leipzig. Books, too, are inexpensive, although books in English are relatively scarce.

Antiques Look for antiques in Berlin at the state-run stores in the Metropol and Palast hotels and at the main store at Friedrichstrasse 180/184. Some private stores along the stretch of Friedrichstrasse north of the Spree Bridge offer old books and prints.

Boutiques A host of smaller stores have sprung up around the Nikolai quarter. Basically all are supplied from the same central sources, but nevertheless may be fun places to shop for trinkets. Jewlery from **Galerie Skarabäus** (Frankfurter Allee 80) and **Galerie "re"** (Finowstr. 2) is good value.

Shopping Districts The best stores in Berlin are along the Friedrichstrasse, Unter den Linden, and in the area around Alexanderplatz. Stores run by other socialist countries along the north side of Alexanderplatz may have some interesting offerings. The Palast and Grand hotels have small shopping malls.

Department Stores For a wider range of items, including souvenirs, head for the **Centrum** department store at the north end of Alexanderplatz. The (subsidized) prices for some goods make them ridiculously cheap, if style is not a major factor. Wooden toys are dependable gifts that take little luggage space and aren't breakable.

Dining

Possibilities for the hungry range from the street stands which offer mainly frankfurters and various types of (very good) sausages; the "quick lunch" stops, called *Imbiss-stube*, often specializing in a local favorite such as knuckle of pork; cafés, most of which have at least a limited offering at noon if not a full fixed "menu"; Bierkellers, which usually offer hearty local fare; and restaurants, which can be divided between "SB" (meaning *Selbstbedienung*, or self-service, cafeteria-style) and the more traditional restaurants in all price ranges. If not provided by a hotel, breakfast is a café affair; restaurants generally do not open until about 10 AM. East Germany's ties to the East Bloc are reflected in the frequency of national restaurants featuring the cuisines of other socialist states, although such exotica as Japanese, Chinese, Indonesian, and French food is now appearing.

Translations in English of the menu are often available; sometimes there will be a separate English menu. In general, the smaller the establishment, the more limited the choice. Unfortunately the traditional European custom of posting a menu outside of a restaurant seems to be disappearing, at least in Berlin, but headwaiters comply when would-be diners ask to see a menu before being seated.

Tipping may have long since been officially abolished, but it's still very much the norm in all restaurants. A fully booked restaurant will often turn out to have an extra table for between DM 2 and DM 5 (though certainly not for the same amount in East German marks). A tip of about 10% in most restaurants (again, West German currency is appreciated) suffices; in smaller establishments, just add two or three marks (East German). If you're paying by credit card, tip in cash.

National favorites include *Eisbein mit Sauerkraut*, knuckle of pork with pickled cabbage; *Rouladen*, rolled stuffed beef; *Spanferkel*, suckling pig; *Berliner Schüsselsülze*, potted meat in aspic; *Schlachteplatte*, mixed grill; *Hackepeter*, ground beef; and *Kartoffelpuffer*, fried potato cakes. Regional cuisine is finding wider acceptance; some restaurants now feature dishes of the Thuringia and Harz areas. Typical would be *Thüringer Sauerbraten mit Klössen*, roast corned meat with dumplings; *Bärenschinken*, cured ham; and *Harzer Köhlerteller mit Röstkartoffeln*, charcoal-grilled meat with roast potatoes. Freshwater fish is found in the many restaurants in the lake area outside of Berlin or those along the river in the Dresden/Meissen region. In cities, the "Gastmahl des Meeres" restaurants feature fish dishes.

Wines and spirits are nearly all imported, although there are a few local wines. Most of the imports are from other East European countries; and many are quite good, particularly Hungarian, Yugoslav, and Bulgarian wines (the whites are lighter), and Polish and Russian vodkas. Some varieties of East German *Schnapps* (liquors) can be devastating. The East Germans themselves often take beer with a meal. If you prefer to avoid alcohol, ask for a cola (curiously, called *Limonade*, although there is no lemon involved), or *Sodawasser* or *Mineralwasser* (carbonated or noncarbonated waters); if you want just a glass of plain water, specify *Trinkwasser* (normal tap water). Coffee is usually ordered at the end of the meal.

Highly recommended restaurants are indicated by a star ★.

Category	**Cost**
Very Expensive	over M 40
Expensive	M 25–M 30
Moderate	M 15–M 25
Inexpensive	under M 12

**per person for three courses (in the top two categories; one in the lower categories) and a beer or glass of wine.*

Very Expensive

★ **Ermelerhaus.** The Rococo grandeur of this wine restaurant located in a series of upstairs rooms, reflects the elegance of the restored patrician house—which dates from at least 1567—in which it's housed. The atmosphere is subdued and formal, the wines are imported, and the service and German cuisine are excellent. There's dancing every Saturday evening. *Märkisches Ufer 10–12, tel. 02/279–4036. Reservations advised. Jacket and tie required. AE, DC, MC, V.*

★ **Ganymed.** The atmosphere here is keyed by velvet drapes, oil paintings, and brass chandeliers—as well as by the piano music at night in the front room; it was a favorite of the Bertolt Brechts! The menu offers a wide range of choices, including cold plates, *cordon bleu* dishes, mixed grills, and even Indonesian cuisine. *Schiffbauerdamm 5, tel. 02/282–9540. Reservations essential. Dress: informal at lunch, jacket and tie required at dinner. No credit cards. Closed Mon.*

Expensive

★ **Schwalbennest.** On the edge of the Nikolai quarter, overlooking the Marx-Engels-Forum, this is a fairly new establishment yet is already known for its outstanding food and service. The choice is wide for main dishes and wines. The grilled selections are excellent, but note that the flambéed dishes cost extra, although no additional price is indicated on the menu. *Am Marstall (upstairs), Rathauss-str. at Marx-Engels-Forum, tel. 02/212–4569. Reservations essential. Dress: informal at lunch, jacket and tie required at dinner. AE, DC, MC, V.*

Zur Goldenen Gans. Regional specialties are featured here, particularly game and venison dishes prepared Thuringer Forest–style. *Friedrichstr. 158–162, in the Grand Hotel, tel. 02/20920. Reservations advised. Dress: informal. AE, DC, MC, V.*

Moderate

★ **Berlin Esprit.** For authentic Berlin specialties you'll probably do no better; the atmosphere is also thoroughly relaxing. *Alexanderpl., in the Hotel Stadt Berlin, tel. 02/2190. Reservations advised. Dress: informal. AE, DC, MC, V.*

★ **Cafe Flair.** This new café is immensely popular despite its somewhat limited menu—more intended for snackers than diners—but what there is is good, and no complaints about the service, either. There are tables outside for warm-weather sidewalk dining. *Am Marstall (ground floor), Marx-Engels-Forum, tel. 02/212–4569. Reservations advised. Dress: informal. AE, DC, MC, V.*

Moskau. The strong Russian influence shows itself here in its food and drink offerings—superb chicken Kiev and real Russian vodka—but you'll also find a good range of Berlin-style fare to choose from. Some find the restaurant overpriced, but the Moskau has been a favorite among Berliners for years. It is, however, less central and offers less atmosphere than many other restaurants listed here. *Karl-Marx-Allee 34, tel. 02/279–4052 and 02/279–2158. Reservations advised. Dress: informal. No credit cards.*

Ratskeller. This is actually two restaurants in one, composed of a wine and a beer cellar, each highly popular, and each with great atmosphere (entrances at opposite corners of the building). Menus are somewhat limited, but include good solid Berlin fare. The brick-walled beer cellar is guaranteed to be packed during main dining hours, at which time reservations sometimes get ignored; Berliners simply line up to get in. The wine cellar is less crowded, in part because it is slightly more expensive. Among the menu selections are Hungarian goulash soup, chicken, and steaks. *Rathausstr. 14 (in the basement of the Rotes Rathaus, or Red Town Hall), tel. 02/212–4464 and 02/212–5301. Reservations advised. Dress: informal. No credit cards.*

Inexpensive **Alex Grill.** This cafeteria-style restaurant pulls in the crowds because of its range of offerings and the good value it gives for money—it is truly a feat to get in at lunchtime. *Alexanderpl., in the Hotel Berlin, tel. 02/2190. Dress: informal. No credit cards.*

★ **Alt-Cöllner Schankstuben.** Four tiny restaurants are contained within this charming, historic Berlin house. The section to the side of the canal on the Kleine Gertraudenstrasse, where there are tables set outside, serves as a café. The menu is relatively limited, but quality, like the service, is good. *Friederichsgracht 50, tel. 02/212–5972. No reservations. Dress: informal. No credit cards.*

★ **Arkade.** The art-deco style interior is a refreshing change from other East Berlin restaurants, though in good weather you may choose to dine outside. Inside, the front section is more of a café, while the grill counter at the back offers a greater variety. This is a convenient place to grab a snack after a performance at the nearby Komische Oper (Comic Opera). *Französische Str. 25, tel. 02/208–0273. No reservations. Dress: informal. No credit cards.*

★ **Quick.** Low prices and tip-top quality have long made this self-service cafeteria popular. It's mobbed at noon; go slightly earlier or later if possible. Note that it closes at 8 PM. *Karl-Liebknecht-Str. 5, in the Palast Hotel, tel. 02/2410. No reservations. Dress: informal. No credit cards.*

★ **Raabe Diele.** The location of this restaurant is the basement of the 16th-century Ermelerhaus. It was largely rebuilt in 1969, meaning that the pine-paneled cellar is new—with canned music piped in—and offers considerably less elegance and atmosphere than the handsome rooms upstairs. On the other hand, the prices are far lower and the menu consists of good Berlin-style cuisine. The service down here is just as attentive as it is upstairs. *Märkisches Ufer 10–12, in Ermelerhaus, tel. 02/279–4036. Dress: informal. Reservations not required. AE, DC, MC, V.*

★ **Zur letzen Instanz.** Unquestionably Berlin's oldest restaurant, established in 1525, this place is imbued with an old-world charm rarely found these days in the modern city. The choice of food is, as usual, limited, but it is prepared in the genuine Berlin tradition and is truly hearty—you'll find beer in the cooking as well as in your mug. Being on the standard tourist route hasn't spoiled the place, either. *Waisenstr. 14–16 (U-bahn Klosterstr.), tel. 02/212–5528. Reservations essential. Dress: informal. No credit cards.*

Lodging

Most Western visitors to East Germany are effectively obliged to stay in hotels belonging to the state-run Interhotel chain. These include the major hotels in all cities and other tourist centers. The Interhotels such as the Grand, Palast, and

Metropol in Berlin, Merkur in Leipzig, and Bellevue in Dresden are fully up to best international standards, prices included. Tourists seeking more moderate accommodations may try the "H-O" chain or the hostels run by the Evangelical Church. The few private hotels are real bargains but are almost impossible to book for Western visitors. Travel officials will try to steer you to one of the best hotels; if you want more moderately priced accommodations, stick to your guns.

Highly recommended hotels are indicated by a star ★.

Category	**Cost***
Very Expensive	M 230–M 350
Expensive	M 190–M 230
Moderate	M 130–M 170
Inexpensive	under M 100

**Prices are for two people in a double room. A single room will cost a little more than half the double rate. Breakfast is included in room rates.*

Very Expensive

Grand Hotel. East Berlin's newest hotel, opened in 1987, is also by a considerable margin its most expensive, and no wonder: It's clearly intended for Western guests. Despite the central location, you'll feel you've left the streets of East Berlin far behind the moment you step into the air-conditioned lobby. From there on in, all is couched in luxury, and really, you could be in any modern, commodious hotel in the world. *Friedrichstr. 158–164, corner Behrenstr., tel. 02/20–920. 350 rooms or suites, all with bath. Facilities: 4 restaurants, winter garden, Bierstube (beer room), bars, concert café, pool, sauna, squash courts, shopping arcade, hairdresser, theater ticket office; car and yacht rental. AE, DC, MC, V.*

★ **Metropol.** This is the choice of businessmen, not just for its excellent location across from the Friedrichstrasse train station and the International Trade Center; the service is outstanding. The best rooms are on the front side, facing north. All rooms are well-equipped (but note that only public areas are air-conditioned); the hotel's antiques gallery is small but interesting, and the nightclub is an unusually good one, while the restaurants are only fair (except in price!). *Friedrichstr. 150–153, tel. 02/22–040. 320 rooms with bath. Facilities: 3 restaurants, nightclub, bars, garage, pool, sauna, fitness room, solarium, antiques gallery, shopping mall, car, horse-drawn carriage, and yacht rental available. AE, DC, MC, V.*

★ **Palast.** This is a favorite with tour groups because of its proximity to East Berlin's museums—and because it's another of the city's mega-facility hotels. The best rooms overlook the Spree River; those on the Alexanderplatz side can be noisy. The shopping mall includes a travel agency, an antiques gallery, and the most convenient theater ticket office in the downtown area. The restaurants are recommended. *Karl-Liebknecht-Str. 5, tel. 02/2410. 600 rooms with bath. Facilities: 6 restaurants, 4 bars, garage, Bierstube, nightclub, pool, sauna, fitness room, solarium, bowling, travel office, theater ticket office, antiques gallery, shopping mall; car and yacht rental. AE, DC, MC, V.*

Expensive **Berolina.** If being a little way from the city's main tourist attractions is no deterrent, this is a pleasant place to stay near Alexanderplatz. Its roof-garden restaurant (Restaurant Krögel, on the 11th floor) will give you a fine view out over Berlin. *Karl-Marx-Allee 31, tel. 02/210–9541. 350 rooms with bath. Facilities: 3 restaurants, roof garden, souvenir shop, café, bar, garage. AE, DC, MC, V.*

Stadt Berlin. With its 40 stories, the Stadt Berlin at the top end of Alexanderplatz competes with the nearby TV tower for the title of premier downtown landmark. The roof dining room features good food and service and stunning views (reservations are essential). As the city's largest hotel, it is understandably less personal. The bar on the 37th floor is open until 5 AM. *Alexanderpl., tel. 02/2190 (02/210–9211 for reservations). 975 rooms with bath or shower. Facilities: 4 restaurants (including roof dining room), 3 bars, garage, shopping, beer garden, Bierstube, sauna. AE, DC, MC, V.*

★ **Unter den Linden.** The international quality of the gigantic, newer hotels may be missing here, but the location couldn't be better. The restaurant is known for the best food on Unterden Linden. *Unter den Linden 14, corner Friedrichstr., tel. 02/220–0311 (02/210–9211 for reservations) 307 rooms with bath or shower. Facilities: restaurant. AE, DC, MC, V.*

Moderate ★ **Adria.** Because it's in a lower price range and in a decent location, this is a hotel that fills up fairly far in advance. Its restaurant is also quite popular and inexpensive. Try for one of the quieter rooms at the back. *Friedrichstr. 134, tel. 02/282–5451. 70 rooms with bath or shower. Facilities: restaurant. No credit cards.*

Newa. This older hotel, popular because of its affordability, is just a 10-minute streetcar-ride away from the downtown area. Request a room with its own bathroom; not all have them. Rooms in the back are quieter. *Invalidenstr. 115, tel. 02/282–5461. 57 rooms, most with bath. No credit cards.*

Inexpensive ★ **Hospiz am Bahnhof Friedrichstrasse.** This evangelical, church-run hostel, both because of price and a convenient location, gets booked up months in advance. It is enormously popular with families, so the public areas are not always particularly restful. The restaurant is cheap and usually busy. Not all rooms have their own bathrooms. *Albrechtstr. 8, tel. 02/282–5396. 110 rooms, most with bath. Facilities: restaurant. No credit cards.*

Hospiz Augustrasse. Comfortable rooms and friendly staff make this very low-priced hotel—also run by the evangelical church—appealing. It is roughly a 10-minute streetcar ride into downtown Berlin. Breakfast is the only meal served here. *Augustr. 82, tel. 02/282–5321. 70 rooms, some with bath. No credit cards.*

The Arts and Nightlife

The Arts Opera and concerts are of the highest caliber. Theater and cabaret can also be good—if you can handle German. Tickets for most arts events can be obtained at the individual theater box offices in advance or an hour before performance. Tickets are also available from the central tourist office at Alexanderplatz 5, the special ticket offices in the Palast and Grand hotels, or from your hotel service desk. To find out what's currently being performed, pick up a copy of the monthly publication *Wohin in*

Berlin? or check the newspapers. The daily newspaper listings show if events are sold out.

Concerts take place mainly either in the rebuilt **Schauspielhaus** (Pl. der Akadamie, tel. 02/227–2156) or in the **Palast der Republik** (Marx-Engels-Pl., tel. 02/238–2354).

Opera, operetta, ballet, and **musicals** are performed at the **Deutsche Staatsoper** (Unter den Linden 7, tel. 02/20–540); the **Komische Oper** (Behrenstr. 55–57, tel. 02/220–2761); the **Metropol Theater** (Friedrichstr. 101, tel. 02/200–0651); and in the **Palast der Republik.**

Films from the state archives are shown on Tuesday and Friday at 5:30 and 8 PM at Filmtheater Babylon (Rosa-Luxemburg-Str. 30, tel. 02/212–5076).

Leading **theaters** include:

Berliner Ensemble, dedicated to Brecht and works of other international playwrights (Bertolt-Brecht-Pl., tel. 02/28880).
Deutsches Theater, the center for outstanding classical and contemporary German drama (Schumannstr. 13–14, tel. 02/287–1225).
Distel, cabaret with satire as prickly as the regime allows; plays at various locations (Friedrichstr. 100, tel. 02/287–1226).
Friedrichstadtpalais, a glossy showcase for variety, revue, and historic old Berlin theater pieces (Friedrichstr. 107, tel. 02/28360).
Kammerspiele, a studio theater offering the works of contemporary and classical authors, as well as jazz concerts (Schumannstr. 13–14, tel. 02/287–1226).
Maxim-Gorki-Theater, featuring plays by local authors plus some contemporary classics and sharp humor (Am Festungsgraben, tel. 02/207–1843).
Puppentheater, the puppet theater, is nominally for children but can be good entertainment for adults as well (Griefswalder Str. 81–84, tel. 02/436–1343).
Theater im Palast, a studio-style theater offering readings, literary programs, and musical events (in Palast der Republik, Marx-Engels-Pl., tel. 02/238–2354).
Volksbühne, featuring classical and contemporary drama (Rosa-Luxemburg-Pl., tel. 02/282–9607).

Nightlife

With a few exceptions, nightlife here is not on a par with that of West Berlin, but then neither are the prices. An evening of dancing, entertainment, and wine at the Stadt Berlin hotel can cost as little as DM 25 (payable with Western currency or credit card). The other larger hotels offer dinner-dancing as well. For nightclubs with music and atmosphere, try one of the following, bearing in mind that music in the hotels is generally live, while the clubs have disk jockeys:

Cabaret

Shows vary, but the **Friedrichstadtpalais** (*see* The Arts, above) is a good bet.

Dancing

Club Metropol in the Metropol Hotel has a cabaret, as does the **Panorama Bar** on the 37th floor of the Hotel Stadt Berlin.
For disco dancing, try the **Hafenbar** (Chauseestr. 20) **Haifishbar** (Unter den Linden 5, in the Opern Café complex), and **Sinusbar,** in the Palast Hotel.

Excursions from East Berlin

Dresden

Splendidly situated on the banks of the Elbe River, Dresden was the capital of Saxony as early as the 15th century. Its architectural masterpieces are newer; most date from the 18th century and were heavily damaged during the war. These, along with much of the rest of the old city, have been lovingly restored and rebuilt almost piece-by-piece into the showcase that is Dresden today. Italianate influences are everywhere, most pronounced in some of the most glorious Rococo architecture in Europe. The outstanding buildings are the Zwinger Palace, the opera house, the cathedral—with its fine Silbermann organ—and the National Gallery, which once again houses a unique collection of paintings. The magnificent Semper Oper, the opera house named for the architect who designed it, has been rebuilt. Reopened in 1985, the house quickly regained its reputation as one of Europe's leading operas. Most of Richard Strauss's operatic works were first performed here, and the Strauss tradition is being nurtured.

The picture gallery in the Semper wing of the Zwinger Palace complex is among the most magnificent in the world. In addition to its most famous masterpiece, the *Sistine Madonna* of Raphael, the collection boasts 12 Rembrandts, 16 Reubens, and five Tintorettos, to name but a few of the masters represented. For Italian and Dutch paintings of the 16th and 17th centuries, few museums can match this collection. But this is not the only reason for heading toward Dresden: there are over 20 other museums as well.

Tourist Information **Reisebüro der DDR** (Prager-Str. 11, tel. 051/495–5025. Open Mon.–Wed. 9–6, Thurs. 9–6:30, Fri. 9–7, Sat., Sun., and holidays 9–2).

Getting Around There are regular trains from East Berlin to Dresden. Local public transport, in the form of buses and streetcars, is cheap and efficient. Taxis are also inexpensive, but the city is not large and exploration on foot is one of the best ways to discover Dresden's hidden surprises. Boats from the Brühl Terrace at riverside go upstream to Meissen, downstream to and into Czechoslovakia.

Guided Tours Tours are organized by the tourist office (*see* above). City sightseeing trips on foot take place daily. Streetcar tours run from Postplatz Tuesday to Sunday at 9, 11, and 1:30. By bus, tours run from Dr.-Kulz-Ring on Tuesday, Wednesday, and Thursday at 11.

Exploring Aside from the remaining ruins and the gloriously restored buildings, you will search in vain for evidence of Dresden's former architectural glory, victim of a British bombing raid, as tour guides will incessantly remind you. But do wander through the "new" as well as the old city; Dresden's location, straddling the Elbe River, is stunning. From the main rail station, wander down the Prager Strasse to the **Old Market.** The rebuilt Rathaus (Town Hall) is on your right, as is the **Museum für Geschichte der Stadt Dresden** (City Historical Museum).

Excursions from East Berlin

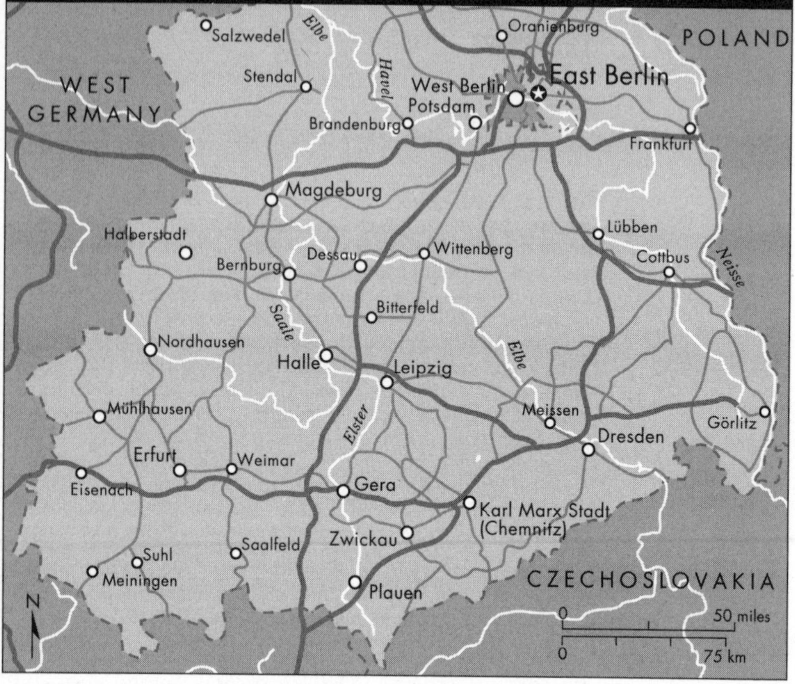

Ernst-Thälmann-Pl. 2. Admission: M3. Open Mon.–Thurs. and Sat. 10–6, Sun. 10–4.

Around the end of the square to the left is the Postplatz and just beyond, the **Zwinger Palace** complex. Be sure to look at the buildings from all sides, inside and out, particularly for the view of the gardens in the middle. The picture gallery is located in the wing on the river side. *Admission: M 3. Art gallery open Tues.–Sun. 10–5; porcelain collection open Mon.–Thurs. 9:30–4, Sat. and Sun. 9–4; gallery of new masters open Fri.–Wed. 10–5, Tues. 10–6, closed Thurs.*

The **Semper Oper** is next door to the right. Opposite the opera you will find the **Hofkirche,** with its ornate bastions and spire. Follow the river upstream past the church and turn right to find the **Albertinum** and **Johanneum,** now housing the **Verkehrsmuseum** (Transportation Museum). *Johanneum am Neumarkt. Admission: M 3. Open Apr.–Sept., Tues.–Sun. 9–5.*

Walk across the Elbe, over the Georgi-Dimitroff-Bridge past the blockhouse on the other side. Up to your left in back of the Hotel Bellevue complex is the Japanese Palace.

Other less central curiosities in Dresden include the **Armeemuseum** (Military Museum of the GDR), which includes military history predating the GDR (Dr.-Karl-Fischer-Pl. Admission: M 3. Open Tues.–Sun. 9–5). **Buchmuseum** (Book Museum), which traces the history of books from the Middle Ages to the present. *(Marienallee 12. Admission free. Open Mon.–Sat. 9–4:30); The* **Deutsches Hygene-Museum** (German

Museum of Health), with a history of medical equipment and a unique glass anatomical figure (*Lingnerpl. 1. Admission: M 3. Open Sat.–Thurs. 9–6.*

Dining **Canaletto** (French restaurant), **Elbterrasse, Wackerbarth's Keller** (wine restaurant), and **Buri Buri** (Polynesian restaurant à la Trader Vic's). All are excellent and are located in the Hotel Bellevue. *Köpckestr., tel. 051/56620. Reservations recommended for all but Elbterasse. Dress: generally tie and jacket, except Elbterrasse, informal. AE, DC, MC, V. Expensive.*

★ **Café Pöppelmann.** The café offers a very comfortable pseudo-elegant atmosphere, overstuffed furniture and all, in a restored old city house cleverly incorporated into the Hotel Bellevue. This is the place to take tea. *Grosse Meissner-Gasse 15, tel. 051/56620. Reservations advisable for dinner. Dress: studied casual. AE, DC, MC, V. Moderate.*

★ **Sekundogenitur.** This is one of the city's more famous wine restaurants, situated on the riverbanks with a view of the river. Dining is outside as well, weather permitting. *Brühlsche Terrasse, tel. 051/495–1435. Dress: informal. No credit cards. Closed Mon. Moderate.*

★ **Kügeln Haus.** The complex includes a grill, coffee bar, restaurant, and historic beer cellar. The place is justifiably popular, so go early or book ahead. *Strasse der Befreiung 14, tel. 051/52791. Reservations advised. Dress: informal. No credit cards. Inexpensive.*

Lodging ★ **Hotel Bellevue.** Across the river from the Zwinger, opera, and main museums, this is Dresden's best and newest hotel, opened in 1985. The design cleverly incorporates an old restored town house. *Köpckestr., tel. 051/56620. 328 rooms with bath. Facilities: 4 restaurants, wine cellar, café, bars, nightclub, swimming pool, sauna, solarium, bowling, jogging course, souvenir shop, jeweler, antique shop, Intershop, car rental, parking. AE, DC, MC, V. Very Expensive.*

★ **Hotel Newa.** This modern hotel offers less charm but is close to the main train station. The restaurant has a good reputation (it accepts Western currency or credit cards only). *Leningrader-Str. 34, tel. 051/496–7112. 314 rooms with bath or shower. Facilities: café, 2 bars, sauna, souvenir shop, Intershop, garage. AE, DC, MC, V. Expensive.*

Interhotel Prager Strasse. This is a modern complex consisting of two hotels in tandem, the **Königstein** and **Lilienstein,** located between the train station and the old city. Back rooms are quieter. *Prager-Str., tel. 051/48460, and 051/48560. 300 rooms each, all with bath. Facilities: restaurants, sauna, souvenir shop, garage. AE, DC, MC, V. Moderate.*

Parkhotel Weisser Hirsch. This hotel is a considerable distance from city center (if driving, take the Bautzner Str. from Pl. der Einheit) in pleasant country surroundings. Facilities are simple, but the setting makes up for the lack of luxury. Parking is no problem. *Bautzner-Landstr. 7, tel. 051/36851. 54 rooms, none with bath. Facilities: restaurant, café (dancing in evenings). No credit cards. Inexpensive.*

Leipzig

The city of Leipzig has long been a center of printing and book selling. Astride major trade routes, it was an important market town in the Middle Ages, and it is a trading center to this day. The twice-yearly trade fairs in March and September bring together buyers and sellers from East and West; Leipzig is subsequently the single most important meeting place for East European and Western commerce and trade.

Those who know music and German literature will associate Leipzig with Johann Sebastian Bach, who was organist and choir director at the St. Thomas Church; with Handel; and with Richard Wagner, who was born here; and with German poets Goethe and Schiller.

But trade and the arts are only two aspects of the city's fame: One of the greatest battles of the Napoléonic Wars—the Battle of Nations—was fought here in 1813, and was instrumental in leading to the French general's defeat. That battle is commemorated today by several monuments in Leipzig.

Following wartime devastation, little is left of old Leipzig, although considerable restoration in the old city has been undertaken. Nevertheless, the city retains touches of its medieval and Renaissance character, which somehow even today penetrates the heart of the city center.

Tourist Information Because of the semiannual influx of fair visitors, Leipzig is well able to cater to tourist needs. You can get information on local events as well as on tours and excursions from the **Reisebüro der DDR** (Katharinenstr. 1, tel. 041/79210) or **Leipzig Information** (Sachsenpl. 1, tel. 041/79590). Both are open weekdays 9–7 (theater tickets until 6), Saturday 9:30–2.

Getting Around Frequent trains run between Berlin and Leipzig. At fair time, there are flights from most West European cities to Schkeuditz Airport, but only a few days before and after the events. The airport is about 20 minutes from the downtown area, with regular bus connections. Rental cars are available at the airport.

Leipzig itself tends to sprawl, but most tourist attractions are within walking distance. Otherwise, ride buses, streetcars, and the S-bahn. Tickets for both must be obtained in advance. Get S-bahn tickets at the main train station. For ticket and other information on public transport, call tel. 041/795–9331. Taxis are more abundant than in other East German cities because of the number needed to cope with peak traffic at fair time; call tel. 041/7160 or 041/70171. Nearby communities can be reached by train or S-bahn.

Guided Tours City sightseeing bus tours run daily at 10 and 1:30; from March to mid-October, there's an extra tour at 4. Tours leave from the Information Building downtown (tel. 041/795–9329).

Exploring Railroad buffs may want to start their tour of Leipzig at the **Hauptbahnhof,** the main train station. With its 26 platforms, it is the largest in Europe. From there, cross Platz der Republik to enter the pedestrian area. This leads to Sachsenplatz and on to the **Markt,** the old city market square. Here you will find the **Altes Rathaus,** the Renaissance town hall, now housing the city museum. *Markt 1. Admission: M 3. Open Tues.–Sun. 9–5.*

Wander through the passageways and windowshop in the building complex ahead. Tucked away here is the **Auerbachs Keller** restaurant (1530), made famous in Goethe's *Faust.* Backtrack to the square and turn right into the Thomasgasse to come to the **Thomaskirche,** with its Bach Memorial and the statue alongside the church where Bach worked and is buried. *Thomaskirchhof 16. Admission free. Open Tues.–Sun. 9–noon, Mon. 2–4.*

From this point, Leipzig's other attractions are scattered. It is a bit of a stroll, but you can walk out across the Martin-Luther-Ring and head up the Harkortstrasse to the **Georgi Dimitrov Museum,** the city's outstanding fine arts museum. *Georgi-Dimitrov-Pl. 1. Admission: M 3. Open Tues.–Sat. 9–noon and 1–5; picture gallery open Tues.–Fri. 9–6, Sat. 9–5, Sun. 9–1.*

Head toward the enormous tower that marks Karl-Marx-University, and you come to a large square, Karl-Marx-Platz. The **Opera House** and the **Neues Gewandhaus,** both centers of Leipzig's musical life face the square.

Head across the Ring up the short Grimmaisch Steinweg to reach the **Grassimuseum** complex (Johannespl. 5–11. Admission: M 3). It includes the **Museum of Arts and Crafts** (open Tues.–Fri. 9:30–6, Sat. 10–4, Sun. 9–1); the **Geographical Museum** (open Tues.–Fri. 10–3, Sun. 9–1); and the **Musical Instruments Museum** (enter from Täubchenweg 2; open Tues.–Thurs. 3–6, Fri. and Sun. 10–1, Sat. 10–3).

The **Botanischer Garten** (Botanical Garden) is a set of splendid gardens and greenhouses. *Linnestr. 1. Admission: M 2. Open Mon.–Fri. 9–4, Sun. 10–4; greenhouses Sun. 10–12:30 and 2–4.*

Outside of the center of Leipzig but reachable by public transportation (streetcar 20, 24, then walk left up Poetenweg or take streetcar 6 to Menckestrasse) are the delightfully rococo **Gohliser Schlösschen** (Gohliser House), which contains the Bach archive. (Menckestr. 23. Open Mon. and Fri. 1–5, Tues., Thurs., and Sat. 9–1, Wed. 1–8) and, beyond that, **Schiller's House,** for a time the home of the German poet and dramatist Friedrich Schiller (Menckestr. 21. Open Tues., Wed., Fri., and Sat. 11–5).

Schloss Dölitz (streetcar line 22, 24, walk up Helenstrasse) contains an exhibition of *Zinnfiguren,* historical tin soldiers. *Torhaus, Schloss Dölitz, Helenstr. 24. Admission: M 3. Open Sun. 9–1.*

Dining

★ **Altes Kloster.** Game is featured in a fascinating, old-world environment, once part of a cloister. *Klostergasse 5, tel. 041/282–252. Reservations advised. Jacket and tie required. No credit cards. Moderate.*

★ **Auerbachs Keller.** The historic restaurant (built 1530) in city center is immortalized in Goethe's *Faust.* Both a visit and a prior reservation are musts. *Grimmaische-Str. 2–4, tel. 041/209–131. Jacket and tie required. AE, DC, MC, V. Moderate.*

★ **Paulaner.** Intimate, attractive, and quiet, this small place offers good local food. *Klostergasse 3, tel. 041/28–1985. Reservations advised. Dress: informal. No credit cards. Moderate.*

Kaffeebaum. Allegedly the country's oldest café (established 1694!), this Burgerhaus has a limited menu but the atmosphere and the "regulars" make a visit worthwhile. *Fleischergasse 4. Dress: informal. No credit cards. Inexpensive.*

Regina. A cozy wine restaurant with pleasant ambiance. *Hainstr. 14, tel. 282052. Reservations essential. Dress: informal. No credit cards. Inexpensive.*

Lodging Note that during fair time, all hotels increase their prices.

★ **Hotel Astoria.** An older hotel, many value its solid comfort and atmosphere and the central location by the main train station. Traffic in the area is considerable, so rooms at the rear are quieter. *Pl. der Republik 2, tel. 041/71710. 309 rooms with bath. Facilities: 2 restaurants, bar, dance café, nightclub, sauna, car rental, garage. AE, DC, MC, V. Very Expensive.*

Hotel Merkur. The city's newest and by far most luxurious hotel, imposing as well for its high-rise profile, is central, close to the main train station, and fully air-conditioned. *Gerberstr., tel. 041/7990. 440 rooms with bath. Facilities: 4 restaurants (one Japanese, one Italian), 2 bars, coffee bar, nightclub, swimming pool, sauna, solarium, bowling, jogging course, Japanese garden, shops, car rental, parking. AE, DC, MC, V. Very Expensive.*

Hotel Stadt Leipzig. Set back from the Ring, the hotel is surprisingly quiet, considering its central location close by the main train station. The style is postwar modern. *Richard-Wagner-Str. 1, tel. 041/288–814. 340 rooms with bath. Facilities: 3 restaurants, café, bar, nightclub, sauna, souvenir shop, and Intershop, car rental, garage. AE, DC, MC, V. Expensive.*

★ **International.** This older hotel offers appropriate charm and friendly personnel. The central location is not far from the train station. *Tröndlinring 8, tel. 041/71880. 104 rooms, most with bath. Facilities: restaurant, BierStube, bar, sidewalk café, shops with souvenirs and Intershop wares, car rentals, garage. AE, DC, MC, V. Moderate.*

★ **Hotel zum Löwen.** This is another of the postwar modern hotels built to handle fair traffic, but in this case, the house is personable and cheerful, if not opulent. It is around the corner from the Astoria, close to the train station. Offerings include a restaurant, souvenir shop, and Intershop, plus car rental and garage. *Rudolf-Breitscheid-Str., tel. 041/7751. 108 rooms with bath. AE, DC, MC, V. Moderate.*

Parkhotel. The location directly across from the train station could hardly be better, but with virtually no rooms with baths, the accommodations are simple if not downright spartan. *Richard-Wagner-Str. 7, tel. 041/7821. 174 rooms, few with bath. Facilities: restaurant, gift shop, parking. No credit cards. Inexpensive.*

German Vocabulary

Words and Phrases

Basics

English	*German*	*Pronunciation*
Yes/no	Ja/nein	yah/nine
Please	Bitte	**bit**-uh
Thank you (very much)	Danke (vielen Dank)	**dahn**-kuh (**fee**-lun dahnk)
Excuse me	Entschuldigen Sie	ent-**shool**-de-gen zee
I'm sorry	Es tut mir leid.	es toot meer lite
Good day	Guten Tag	**goo**-ten tahk
Good bye	Auf Wiedersehen	auf **vee**-der-zane
Mr./Mrs.	Herr/Frau	hair/frau
Miss	Fräulein	**froy**-line
Pleased to meet you.	Sehr erfreut.	zair air-**froit**
How are you?	Wie geht es Ihnen?	vee **gate** es **ee**-nen?
Very well, thanks.	Sehr gut, danke.	zair goot **dahn**-kuh
And you?	Und Ihnen?	oont **ee**-nen

Numbers

1 eins	eints	6 sechs	zex
2 zwei	tsvai	7 sieben	**zee**-ben
3 drei	dry	8 acht	ahkt
4 vier	fear	9 neun	noyn
5 fünf	fumph	10 zehn	tsane

Days of the Week

Sunday	Sonntag	**zone**-tahk
Monday	Montag	**moan**-tahk
Tuesday	Dienstag	**deens**-tahk
Wednesday	Mittwoch	**mit**-voah
Thursday	Donnerstag	**doe**-ners-tahk
Friday	Freitag	**fry**-tahk
Saturday	Samstag	**zahm**-stahk

Useful Phrases

Do you speak English?	Sprechen Sie Englisch?	**shprek**-hun zee **eng**-glish?
I don't speak German.	Ich spreche kein Deutsch.	ich **shprek**-uh kine doych
Please speak slowly.	Bitte sprechen Sie langsam.	**bit**-uh **shprek**-en zee **lahng**-zahm
I am American/British	Ich bin Amerikaner(in)/ Engländer(in)	ich bin a-mer-i-**kahn**-er(in) **eng**-glan-der(in)
My name is . . .	Ich heiße . . .	ich **hi**-suh
Yes please/No, thank you	Ja bitte/Nein danke	yah **bi**-tuh/**nine** dahng-kuh
Where are the restrooms?	Wo ist die Toilette?	vo ist dee twah-**let**-uh
Left/right	Links/rechts	links/rechts
Open/closed	Offen/geschlossen	O-fen/geh-**shloss**-en

Where is . . .	Wo ist . . .	**vo** ist
the train station?	der Bahnhof?	dare **bahn**-hof
the bus stop?	die Bushaltestelle?	dee **booss**-hahlt-uh-**shtel**-uh
the subway station?	die U-Bahn-Station?	dee OO-bahn-**staht**-sion
the airport?	der Flugplatz?	dare **floog**-plats
the post office?	die Post?	dee **post**
the bank?	die Bank?	dee **banhk**
the police station?	die Polizeistation?	dee po-lee-**tsai**-staht-sion
the American/ British consulate?	das amerikanische/ britische Konsulat?	dahs a-mare-i-**kahn**-ishuh/**brit**-ish-uh cone-tso-**laht**
the Hospital?	das Krankenhaus?	dahs **krahnk**-en-house
the telephone	das Telefon	dahs te-le-**fone**
I'd like to have . . .	Ich hätte gerne . . .	ich **het**-uh gairn
a room	ein Zimmer	I-nuh **tsim**-er
the key	den Schlüssel	den **shluh**-sul
a map	eine Karte	I-nuh **cart**-uh
How much is it?	Wieviel kostet das?	**vee**-feel **cost**-et dahs?
I am ill/sick	Ich bin krank	ich bin krahnk
I need . . .	Ich brauche . . .	ich **brow**-khuh
a doctor	einen Arzt	I-nen artst
the police	die Polizei	dee po-li-**tsai**
help	Hilfe	**hilf**-uh
Stop!	Halt!	hahlt
Fire!	Feuer!	**foy**-er
Caution/Look out!	Achtung!/Vorsicht!	**ahk**-tung/**for**-zicht

Dining Out

A bottle of . . .	eine Flasche . . .	I-nuh **flash**-uh
A cup of . . .	eine Tasse . . .	I-nuh **tahs**-uh
A glass of . . .	ein Glas . . .	ein glahss
Ashtray	der Aschenbecher	dare Ahsh-en-bekh-er
Bill/check	die Rechnung	dee **rekh**-nung
Do you have . . . ?	Haben Sie . . . ?	**hah**-ben zee
Food	Essen	**es**-en

I am a diabetic.	Ich bin Diabetiker.	ich bin dee-ah-**bet**-ik-er
I am on a diet.	Ich halte Diät.	ich **hahl**-tuh dee-**et**
I am a vegetarian.	Ich bin Vegetarier.	ich bin ve-guh-**tah**-re-er
I cannot eat . . .	Ich kann . . . nicht essen	ich kan . . . nicht **es**-en
I'd like to order	Ich möchte bestellen . . .	ich **mohr**-shtuh buh-shtel-en
Is the service included?	Ist die Bedienung inbegriffen?	ist dee beh-**dee**-nung **in**-beh-grig-en
Menu	die Speisekarte	dee **shpie**-zeh-car-tuh
Napkin	die Serviette	dee zair-vee-**eh**-tuh
Separate/all together	Getrennt/alles zusammen	ge-**trent/ah**-les tsu-**zah**-men

Menu Guide

English	*German*
Made to order	Auf Bestellung
Side dishes	Beilagen
Extra charge	Extraaufschlag
When available	Falls verfügbar
Entrees	Hauptspeisen
Home made	Hausgemacht
. . . (not) included	. . . (nicht) inbegriffen
Depending on the season	je nach Saison
Local specialties	Lokalspezialitäten
Set menu	Menü
Lunch menu	Mittagskarte
Desserts	Nachspeisen
. . . style	. . . nach . . . Art
. . . at your choice	. . . nach Wahl
. . . at your request	. . . nach Wunsch
Prices are . . .	Preise sind . . .
Service included	*inklusive Bedienung*
Value added tax included	*inklusive Mehrwertsteuer(Mwst.)*
Specialty of the house	Spezialität des Hauses
Soup of the day	Tagessuppe
Appetizers	Vorspeisen
Is served from . . . to . . .	Wird von . . . bis . . . serviert

Breakfast

Bread	Brot
Roll(s)	Brötchen
Butter	Butter
Eggs	Eier
Hot	heiß
Cold	kalt
Decaffeinated	koffeinfrei
Jam	Konfitüre
Milk	Milch
Orange juice	Orangensaft
Scrambled eggs	Rühreier
Bacon	Speck
Fried eggs	Spiegeleier
White bread	Weißbrot
Lemon	Zitrone
Sugar	Zucker

Appetizers

Oysters	Austern
Frog legs	Froschschenkel
Goose liver paté	Gänseleberpastete
Lobster	Hummer
Shrimp	Krabben
Crawfish	Krebs
Salmon	Lachs
Mussels	Muscheln
Prosciutto with melon	Parmaschinken mit Melone
Mushrooms	Pilze
Smoked . . .	Räucher . . .
Ham	Schinken

Snails	Schnecken
Asparagus	Spargel

Soups

Stew	Eintopf
Semolina dumpling soup	Grießnockerlsuppe
Goulash soup	Gulaschsuppe
Chicken soup	Hühnersuppe
Potato soup	Kartoffelsuppe
Liver dumpling soup	Leberknödelsuppe
Oxtail soup	Ochsenschwanzsuppe
Tomato soup	Tomatensuppe
Onion soup	Zwiebelsuppe

Methods of Preparation

Blue (boiled in salt and vinegar)	Blau
Baked	Gebacken
Fried	Gebraten
Steamed	Gedämpft
Grilled (broiled)	Gegrillt
Boiled	Gekocht
Sauteed	In Butter geschwenkt
Breaded	Paniert
Raw	Roh

When ordering steak, the English words "rare, medium, (well) done" are used and understood in German.

Fish and Seafood

Eel	Aal
Oysters	Austern
Trout	Forelle
Flounder	Flunder
Prawns	Garnelen
Halibut	Heilbutt
Lobster	Hummer
Scallops	Jakobsmuscheln
Cod	Kabeljau
Crawfish	Krebs
Salmon	Lachs
Spiny lobster	Languste
Mackerel	Makrele
Herring	Matjes
Mussels	Muscheln
Red sea bass	Rotbarsch
Sole	Seezunge
Squid	Tintenfisch
Tuna	Thunfisch

Meats

Mutton	Hammel
Veal	Kalb(s)
Lamb	Lamm
Beef	Rind(er)
Pork	Schwein(e)

Cuts of Meat

Example: For "Lammkeule" see "Lamm" (above) + ". . . keule" (below)

breast	. . . brust
scallopini	. . . geschnetzeltes
knuckle	. . . haxe
leg	. . . keule
liver	. . . leber
tenderloin	. . . lende
kidney	. . . niere
rib	. . . rippe
Meat patty	Frikadelle
Meat loaf	Hackbraten
Cured pork ribs	Kasseler Rippchen
Liver meatloaf	Leberkäse
Ham	Schinken
Sausage and cold cut platter	Schlachtplatte
Brawn	Sülze
Cooked beef with horseradish and cream sauce	Tafelspitz

Game and Poultry

Duck	Ente
Pheasant	Fasan
Goose	Gans
Chicken	Hähnchen (Huhn)
Hare	Hase
Deer	Hirsch
Rabbit	Kaninchen
Capon	Kapaun
Venison	Reh
Pigeon	Taube
Turkey	Truthahn
Quail	Wachtel

Vegetables

Eggplant	Aubergine
Red cabbage	Blaukraut
Cauliflower	Blumenkohl
Beans	Bohnen
green	*grüne*
white	*weiße*
Button mushrooms	Champignons
Peas	Erbsen
Cucumber	Gurke
Cabbage	Kohl
Lettuce	Kopfsalat
Leek	Lauch
Asparagus, peas and carrots	Leipziger Allerlei
Corn	Mais
Carrots	Mohrrüben
Peppers	Paprika
Chanterelle mushrooms	Pfifferlinge
Mushrooms	Pilze
Brussels sprouts	Rosenkohl
Red beets	Rote Beete
Red cabbage	Rotkohl(kraut)

Celery	Sellerie
Asparagus (tips)	Spargel(spitzen)
Tomatoes	Tomaten
Cabbage	Weißkohl
Onions	Zwiebeln

Side dishes

Potato(s)	Kartoffel(n)
fried	*Brat . . .*
boiled in their jackets	*Pell . . .*
with parsley	*Petersilien . . .*
fried	*Röst . . .*
boiled in saltwater	*Salz . . .*
mashed	*. . . brei*
dumplings	*. . . klöße (knödel)*
pancakes	*. . . puffer*
salad	*. . . salat*
Pasta	Nudeln
French fries	Pommes Frittes
Rice	Reis
buttered	*Butter . . .*
steamed	*gedämpfter . . .*

Condiments

Basil	Basilikum
Vinegar	Essig
Spice	Gewürz
Garlic	Knoblauch
Herbs	Kräuter
Caraway	Kümmel
Bay leaf	Lorbeer
Horseradish	Meerettich
Nutmeg	Muskatnuß
Oil	Öl
Parsley	Petersilie
Saffron	Safran
Sage	Salbei
Chives	Schnittlauch
Mustard	Senf
Artificial sweetener	Süßstoff
Cinnamon	Zimt
Sugar	Zucker

Cheese

Mild:	Allgäuer Käse, Altenburger (goat cheese), Appenzeller, Greyerzer, Hüttenkäse (cottage cheese), Kümmelkäse (with carraway seeds), Quark, Räucherkäse (smoked cheese), Sahnekäse (creamy), Tilsiter.
Sharp:	Handkäse, Harzer Käse, Limburger.
curd	frisch
hard	hart
mild	mild
ripe	reif

sharp	scharf
soft	weich

Fruits

Apple	Apfel
Orange	Apfelsine
Apricot	Aprikose
Blueberry	Blaubeere
Blackberry	Brombeere
Strawberry	Erdbeere
Raspberry	Himbeere
Cherry	Kirsche
Grapefruit	Pampelmuse
Cranberry	Preiselbeere
Raisin	Rosine
Grape	Weintraube

Nuts

Peanuts	Erdnüsse
Hazelnuts	Haselnüsse
Coconut	Kokosnuß
Almonds	Mandeln
Chestnuts	Maronen

Desserts

. . . soufflé	. . . auflauf
. . . ice cream	. . . eis
. . . cake	. . . kuchen
Honey-almond cake	Bienenstich
Fruit cocktail	Obstsalat
Whipped cream	(Schlag)sahne
Black Forest cake	Schwarzwälder Kirschtorte

Drinks

chilled	eiskalt
with/without ice	mit/ohne Eis
with/without water	mit/ohne Wasser
straight	pur
room temperature	Zimmertemperatur
. . . brandy	. . . geist
. . . distilled liquor	. . . korn
. . . liqueur	. . . likör
. . . schnapps	. . . schnaps
Egg liquor	Eierlikör
Mulled claret	Glühwein
Caraway flavored liquor	Kümmel
Fruit brandy	Obstler
Vermouth	Wermut

When ordering a Martini, you have to specify "gin (vodka) and vermouth", otherwise you will be given a vermouth (Martini & Rossi).

Beers

non-alcoholic	Alkoholfrei
A dark beer	Ein Dunkles

A light beer	Ein Helles
A mug (one quart)	Eine Maß
Draught	Vom Faß
Dark, bitter, high hops content	Altbier
Strong, high alcohol content	Bockbier (Doppelbock, Märzen)
Wheat beer with yeast	Hefeweizen
Light beer, strong hops aroma	Pils(ener)
Wheat beer	Weizen(bier)
Light beer and lemonade	Radlermaß
Wines	Wein
Red wine	Rotwein
White wine and mineral water	Schorle
Sparkling wine	Sekt
White wine	Weißwein
dry	herb
light	leicht
sweet	süß
dry	trocken
full-bodied	vollmundig

Non-alcoholic Drinks

Coffee	Kaffee
decaffeinated	*koffeinfrei*
with cream/sugar	*mit Milch/Zucker*
with artificial sweetener	*mit Süßstoff*
black	*schwarz*
Lemonade	Limonade
orange	*Orangen . . .*
lemon	*Zitronen . . .*
Milk	Milch
Mineral water	Mineralwasser
carbonated/non-carbonated	*mit/ohne Kohlensäure*
. . . juice (see fruit)	. . . saft
(hot) Chocolate	(heiße) Schokolade
Tea	Tee
iced tea	*Eistee*
herb tea	*Kräutertee*
with cream/lemon	*mit Milch/Zitrone*

Index

Personal Itinerary

Departure *Date*

Time

Transportation

Arrival *Date* *Time*

Departure *Date* *Time*

Transportation

Accommodations

Arrival *Date* *Time*

Departure *Date* *Time*

Transportation

Accommodations

Arrival *Date* *Time*

Departure *Date* *Time*

Transportation

Accommodations

Personal Itinerary

Arrival *Date* *Time*

Departure *Date* *Time*

Transportation

Accommodations

Arrival *Date* *Time*

Departure *Date* *Time*

Transportation

Accommodations

Arrival *Date* *Time*

Departure *Date* *Time*

Transportation

Accommodations

Arrival *Date* *Time*

Departure *Date* *Time*

Transportation

Accommodations

Addresses

Name

Address

Telephone

Name

Address

Telephone

Name

Address

Telephone

Name

Address

Telephone

Name

Address

Telephone

Name

Address

Telephone

Name

Address

Telephone

Name

Address

Telephone

Name

Address

Telephone

Name

Address

Telephone

Name

Address

Telephone

Name

Address

Telephone

Name

Address

Telephone

Name

Address

Telephone

Name

Address

Telephone

Name

Address

Telephone

Fodor's Travel Guides

U.S. Guides

Alaska
Arizona
Atlantic City & the New Jersey Shore
Boston
California
Cape Cod
Carolinas & the Georgia Coast
The Chesapeake Region
Chicago
Colorado
Dallas & Fort Worth
Disney World & the Orlando Area
Florida
Hawaii
Houston & Galveston
Las Vegas
Los Angeles, Orange County, Palm Springs
Maui
Miami, Fort Lauderdale, Palm Beach
Michigan, Wisconsin, Minnesota
New England
New Mexico
New Orleans
New Orleans (Pocket Guide)
New York City
New York City (Pocket Guide)
New York State
Pacific North Coast
Philadelphia
The Rockies
San Diego
San Francisco
San Francisco (Pocket Guide)
The South
Texas
USA
Virgin Islands
Virginia
Waikiki
Washington, DC
Williamsburg

Foreign Guides

Acapulco
Amsterdam
Australia, New Zealand, The South Pacific
Austria
Bahamas
Bahamas (Pocket Guide)
Baja & the Pacific Coast Resorts
Barbados
Beijing, Guangzhou & Shanghai
Belgium & Luxembourg
Bermuda
Brazil
Britain (Great Travel Values)
Budget Europe
Canada
Canada (Great Travel Values)
Canada's Atlantic Provinces
Cancun, Cozumel, Yucatan Peninsula
Caribbean
Caribbean (Great Travel Values)
Central America
Eastern Europe
Egypt
Europe
Europe's Great Cities
Florence & Venice
France
France (Great Travel Values)
Germany
Germany (Great Travel Values)
Great Britain
Greece
The Himalayan Countries
Holland
Hong Kong
Hungary
India, including Nepal
Ireland
Israel
Italy
Italy (Great Travel Values)
Jamaica
Japan
Japan (Great Travel Values)
Jordan & the Holy Land
Kenya, Tanzania, the Seychelles
Korea
Lisbon
Loire Valley
London
London (Great Travel Values)
London (Pocket Guide)
Madrid & Barcelona
Mexico
Mexico City
Montreal & Quebec City
Munich
New Zealand
North Africa
Paris
Paris (Pocket Guide)
People's Republic of China
Portugal
Rio de Janeiro
The Riviera (Fun on)
Rome
Saint Martin & Sint Maarten
Scandinavia
Scandinavian Cities
Scotland
Singapore
South America
South Pacific
Southeast Asia
Soviet Union
Spain
Spain (Great Travel Values)
Sweden
Switzerland
Sydney
Tokyo
Toronto
Turkey
Vienna
Yugoslavia

Special-Interest Guides

Health & Fitness Vacations
Royalty Watching
Selected Hotels of Europe
Selected Resorts and Hotels of the U.S.
Shopping in Europe
Skiing in North America
Sunday in New York